W9-CUJ-679

Heuristics and the Law

Goals for this Dahlem Workshop:

To explore the power of fast and frugal heuristics in the
creation and implementaion of law.

Report of the 94th Dahlem Workshop on
Heuristics and the Law
Berlin, June 6–11, 2004

Held and published on behalf of the
President, Freie Universität Berlin

Funded by:
VolkswagenStiftung

Heuristics and the Law

Edited by
G. Gigerenzer and C. Engel

Program Advisory Committee:

C. Engel and G. Gigerenzer, Chairpersons
R. Hastie and J. Rachlinski

The MIT Press

Cambridge, Massachusetts
London, U.K.

in cooperation with Dahlem University Press

MIT Press books may be purchased at special quantity discounts for business or sales promotional use. For information, please email special_sales@mitpress.mit.edu or write to Special Sales Department, The MIT Press, 55 Hayward Street, Cambridge, MA 02142.

This book was set in TimesNewRoman.
Printed and bound in the United States of America.

Library of Congress Cataloging-in-Publication Data

Heuristics and the law / edited by G. Gigerenzer and C. Engel
    p.   cm.—(Dahlem workshop reports)
"Report of the 94th Dahlem Workshop on Heuristics and the Law, Berlin, June 6–11, 2004"—P. ii.
Includes bibliographical references and index.
ISBN-13: 978-0-262-07275-5 (alk. paper)
ISBN-10: 0-262-07275-0 (alk. paper)
1. Law—Methodology. 2. Heuristic. I. Gigerenzer, Gerd, 1947– II. Engel, Christoph, 1956– III. Dahlem Workshop on Heuristics and the Law (2004 : Berlin, Germany) IV. Series.

K212.H48 2006
340'.1—dc22

2006045005

Contents

Dahlem Workshops

History

During the last half of the twentieth century, specialization in science greatly increased in response to advances achieved in technology and methodology. This trend, although positive in many respects, created barriers between disciplines, which could have inhibited progress if left unchecked. Understanding the concepts and methodologies of related disciplines became a necessity. Reuniting the disciplines to obtain a broader view of an issue became imperative, for problems rarely fall conveniently into the purview of a single scientific area. Interdisciplinary communication and innovative problem-solving within a conducive environment were perceived as integral yet lacking to this process.

In 1971, an initiative to create such an environment began within Germany's scientific community. In discussions between the *Deutsche Forschungsgemeinschaft* (German Science Foundation) and the *Stifterverband für die Deutsche Wissenschaft* (Association for the Promotion of Science Research in Germany), researchers were consulted to compare the needs of the scientific community with existing approaches. It became apparent that something new was required: an approach that began with state-of-the-art knowledge and proceeded onward to challenge the boundaries of current understanding; a form truly interdisciplinary in its problem-solving approach.

As a result, the *Stifterverband* established *Dahlem Konferenzen* (the Dahlem Workshops) in cooperation with the *Deutsche Forschungsgemeinschaft* in 1974. Silke Bernhard, formerly associated with the Schering Symposia, was

Figure adapted from *L'Atmosphère: Météorologie Populaire*, Camille Flammarion. Paris: Librairie Hachette et Cie., 1888.

engaged to lead the conference team and was instrumental in implementing this unique approach.

The Dahlem Workshops are named after a district of Berlin known for its strong historic connections to science. In the early 1900s, Dahlem was the seat of the Kaiser Wilhelm Institutes where, for example, Albert Einstein, Lise Meitner, Fritz Haber, and Otto Hahn conducted research. Today the district is home to several Max Planck Institutes, the *Freie Universität Berlin*, the *Wissenschaftskolleg*, and the Konrad Zuse Center.

In its formative years, the Dahlem Workshops evolved in response to the needs of science. They soon became firmly embedded within the international scientific community and were recognized as an indispensable tool for advancement in research. To secure its long-term institutional stability, *Dahlem Konferenzen* was integrated into the *Freie Universität Berlin* in 1990.

Aim

The aim of the Dahlem Workshops is to promote an international, interdisciplinary exchange of scientific information and ideas, to stimulate international cooperation in research, and to develop and test new models conducive to more effective communication between scientists.

Concept

The Dahlem Workshops were conceived to be more than just another a conference venue. Anchored within the philosophy of scientific enquiry, the Dahlem Workshops represent an independently driven quest for knowledge: one created, nurtured, and carefully guided by representatives of the scientific community itself. Each Dahlem Workshop is an interdisciplinary communication process aimed at expanding the boundaries of current knowledge. This dynamic process, which spans more than two years, gives researchers the opportunity to address problems that are of high-priority interest, in an effort to identify gaps in knowledge, to pose questions aimed at directing future inquiry, and to suggest innovative ways of approaching controversial issues. The overall goal is not necessarily to exact consensus but to search for new perspectives, for these will help direct the international research agenda.

Governance

The Dahlem Workshops are guided by a Scientific Advisory Board, composed of representatives from the international scientific community. The board is responsible for the scientific content and future directions of the Dahlem Workshops and meets biannually to review and approve all workshop proposals.

Workshop Topics

Workshop topics are problem-oriented, interdisciplinary by nature, of high-priority interest to the disciplines involved, and timely to the advancement of science. Scientists who submit workshop proposals, and chair the workshops, are internationally recognized experts active in the field.

Program Advisory Committee

Once a proposal has been approved, a Program Advisory Committee is formed for each workshop. Composed of 6–7 scientists representing the various scientific disciplines involved, the committee meets approximately one year before the Dahlem Workshop to develop the scientific program of the meeting. The committee selects the invitees, determines the topics that will be covered by the pre-workshop papers, and assigns each participant a specific role. Participants are invited on the basis of their international scientific reputation alone. The integration of young German scientists is promoted through special invitations.

Dahlem Workshop Model

A Dahlem Workshop can best be envisioned as a week-long intellectual retreat. Participation is strictly limited to forty participants to optimize the interaction and communication process.

Participants work in four interdisciplinary discussion groups, each organized around one of four key questions. There are no lectures or formal presentations at a Dahlem Workshop. Instead, concentrated discussion—within and between groups—is the means by which maximum communication is achieved.

To enable such an exchange, participants must come prepared to the workshop. This is facilitated through a carefully coordinated pre-workshop dialog: Discussion themes are presented through "background papers," which review a particular aspect of the group's topic and introduce controversies as well as unresolved problem areas for discussion. These papers are circulated in advance, and everyone is requested to submit comments and questions, which are then compiled and distributed. By the time everyone arrives in Berlin, issues have been presented, questions have been raised, and the Dahlem Workshop is ready to begin.

The discussion unfolds in moderated sessions as well as during informal times of interaction. Cross-fertilization between groups is both stressed and encouraged. By the end of the week, through a collective effort directed that is directed by a rapporteur, each group has prepared a draft report of the ideas, opinions, and contentious issues raised by the group. Directions for future research are highlighted, as are problem areas still in need of resolution. The results of the draft reports are discussed in a plenary session on the final day and colleagues from the Berlin–Brandenburg area are invited to participate.

Dahlem Workshop Reports

After the workshop, attention is directed toward the necessity of communicating the perspectives and ideas gained to a wider audience. A two-tier review process guides the revision of the background papers, and discussion continues to finalize the group reports. The chapters are carefully edited to highlight the perspectives, controversies, gaps in knowledge, and future research directions.

The publication of the workshop results in book form completes the process of a Dahlem Workshop, as it turns over the insights gained to the broad scientific community for consideration and implementation. Each volume in the Dahlem Workshop Report series contains the revised background papers and group reports as well as an introduction to the workshop themes. The series is published in partnership with The MIT Press.

Julia Lupp, Program Director and Series Editor
Dahlem Konferenzen der Freien Universität Berlin
Thielallee 50, 14195 Berlin, Germany

List of Participants

Ronald J. Allen   School of Law, Northwestern University, 357 East Chicago Avenue, Chicago, IL 60611, U.S.A.

Legal theory, constitutional law, evidence, procedure, epistemology

Hal R. Arkes   Dept. of Psychology, Ohio State University, 240 N. Lazenby Hall, Columbus, OH 43210–1222, U.S.A.

Medical, legal, and economic decision making; holistic versus disaggregated rating procedures; determinants of malpractice verdicts; behavioral finance; cooperation in nonpoint source pollution abatement

Peter Ayton   Dept. of Psychology, City University, Northampton Square, London ECIV OHB, U.K.

Judgmental forecasting, human decision making

Susanne Baer   Juristische Fakultät der Humboldt Universität zu Berlin, Unter den Linden 6, 10099 Berlin, Germany

Legal theory, comparative constitutionalism, administrative law and change, gender studies/theory

Martin Beckenkamp   Max Planck Institute for Research on Collective Goods, Kurt-Schumacher-Str. 10, 53113 Bonn, Germany

Social dilemmas, decision making, decision theory, game theory

Robert Cooter   Law School, University of California, Berkeley, 2240 Piedmont Ave., 792 Simon, Berkeley, CA 94720–7200, U.S.A.

Law and economics, social norms and psychology in law and economics

Leda Cosmides   Center for Evolutionary Psychology, 1332 Psychology, University of California, Santa Barbara, Santa Barbara, CA 93106–9660, U.S.A.

Evolutionary psychology, cognitive science, coalitional psychology, cooperation

Mandeep K. Dhami   Institute of Criminology, University of Cambridge, Sidgwick Avenue, Cambridge CB3 9DT, England, U.K.

Legal decision making, restorative justice, prison psychology, decision science

Robert C. Ellickson   Yale Law School, Yale University, 127 Wall St., New Haven, CT 06520–8215, U.S.A.

Property law, social norms, tort law, land use

Christoph Engel   Max Planck Institute for Research on Collective Goods, Kurt-Schumacher-Str. 10, 53113 Bonn, Germany

Institutional analysis and institutional design; law and economics; law and psychology

Richard A. Epstein   The University of Chicago Law School, 1111 East 60th Street, Chicago, IL 60637, U.S.A., and The Hoover Institution, Stanford, CA 94305, U.S.A.

Behavioral economics, complexity theory, definitions of rationality and expert evidence

Wolfgang Fikentscher   Chair, Commission for Studies in Cultural Anthropology, Bavarian Academy of Sciences, Philosophical–Historical Class, Alfons-Goppel-Str. 11, 80539 Munich, Germany

Anthropology of law, economics, and religion; international competition law; international intellectual property protection

Axel Flessner   Juristische Fakultät, Humboldt Universität zu Berlin, Bertramstr. 65, 60320 Frankfurt am Main, Germany

Developing European private law; contracts, insolvency law, conflict of laws; jurisprudence, legal theory, language

Robert H. Frank   327 Sage Hall, Cornell University, Ithaca, NY 14853, U.S.A.

Consumption externalities, income inequality, emotions and behavior

Bruno S. Frey   Institute for Empirical Research in Economics, University of Zurich, Bluemlisalpstr. 10, 8006 Zurich, Switzerland

Political economy, economics and psychology, law and economics, happiness research

Gerd Gigerenzer   Center for Adaptive Behavior and Cognition, Max Planck Institute for Human Development, Lentzeallee 94, 14195 Berlin, Germany

Fast and frugal heuristics, decision making with little information and time, risk, bounded rationality, social rationality

Paul W. Glimcher   Center for Neural Science, New York University, 4 Washington Place, Rm. 809, New York, NY 10013, U.S.A.

Neurobiology and economics of human and animal decision making; psychology of decision making

Daniel G. Goldstein   London Business School, Regent's Park, Sussex Place, London NW1 4SA, U.K.

Behavioral economics, marketing, judgment and decision making

Chris Guthrie   Vanderbilt University Law School, 131 21st Ave. South, Nashville, TN 37203–1181, U.S.A.

Behavioral law and economics, alternative dispute resolution, negotiation, judicial decision making

Jonathan Haidt   Dept. of Psychology, University of Virginia, P.O. Box 400400, Charlottesville, VA 22904–4400, U.S.A.

Moral judgment, moral emotions, cultural psychology

Reid Hastie   Center for Decision Research, Graduate School of Business, University of Chicago, 1101 E. 58th Street, Chicago, IL 60637, U.S.A.

Judgment and decision making, human reasoning, law and psychology, cognitive neuroscience

Ralph Hertwig   Dept. of Psychology, University of Basel, Missionsstrasse 60/62, 4055 Basel, Switzerland

Bounded rationality, judgment and decision making, experimental economics

Eric J. Johnson   Columbia Business School, Uris Hall 514, Columbia University, 3022 Broadway, New York, NY 10027, U.S.A.

Constructed preference; consumer and managerial decision making; electronic commerce

Jonathan J. Koehler   McCombs School of Business, The University of Texas at Austin, CBA 5.202, Austin, TX 78712–1175, U.S.A.

Probabilistic reasoning in the law, behavioral decision making, psychology of chance

Russell Korobkin   UCLA School of Law, University of California, Los Angeles, 405 Hilgard Ave., Los Angeles, CA 90095–1476, U.S.A.

Law and behavioral science, negotiation, health care law, contracts

Stephanie Kurzenhäuser   Applied Cognitive Science, Psychologische Fakultät, Universität Basel, Missionsstr. 60/62, 4055 Basel, Switzerland

Risk communication, legal implications of bounded rationality, the impact of external representations of information on statistical thinking and risk perception

Douglas A. Kysar   Cornell Law School, 218 Myron Taylor Hall, Ithaca, NY 14853, U.S.A.

Environmental law, products liability, risk regulation, law and psychology, behavioral law and economics

Donald C. Langevoort   Georgetown University Law Center, 600 New Jersey Avenue, N.W., Washington, D.C. 20001, U.S.A.

Corporate and securities law, behavioral law and economics

Richard Lempert   National Science Foundation, Room 995, 4201 Wilson Boulevard, Arlington, VA 22230, U.S.A.

Evidence law, social science and evidence, scientific evidence, sociology of law, juries

Stefan Magen   Max Planck Institute for Research on Collective Goods, Kurt-Schumacher-Str. 10, 53113 Bonn, Germany

Public law, state and church law, behavioral law and economics, empirical theories of justice

Callia Piperides   Max Planck Institute for Human Development, Lentzeallee 94, 14195 Berlin, Germany

Psychology and law: legal decision-making; eye-witness testimony

Jeffrey J. Rachlinski   Cornell Law School, Myron Taylor Hall, Ithaca, NY 14853–4901, U.S.A.

Psychology and law

Clara Sattler de Sousa e Brito   Max Planck Institute for Intellectual Property, Competition and Tax Law, Marstallplatz 1, 80539 Munich, Germany

Intellectual property law, philosophy of law, law and psychology, biotechnology

Joachim Schulz   Fachbereich Rechtswissenschaften, Universität Osnabrück, Heger-Tor-Wall 14, 49069 Osnabrück, Germany

History of procedural law, theory of evidence, European business law (criminal law)

Indra Spiecker genannt Döhmann   Max Planck Project Group Common Goods Law, Kurt-Schumacher-Str. 10, 53113 Bonn, Germany

Public and administrative law; behavioral law and economics; decision making (especially under uncertainty); risk research; information law; information and data presentation and proceedings

Gerhard Wagner   Institut für Zivilprozeßrecht, Rheinische Friedrich-Wilhelms-Universität, Adenauerallee 24–42, Bonn 53113, Germany

International commercial arbitration, harmonization of European private law, European civil practice, torts

Elke U. Weber   Graduate School of Business, Columbia University, 3022 Broadway, 716 Uris Hall, New York, NY 10027, U.S.A.

Risk perception and risky decision making; cross-cultural and cross-species differences in decision making; memory processes in decision making; analysis, affect, and recognition risks in complementary decision rules

Preface

As true believers in fast and frugal heuristics, we relied on the services of a coin to make a fast and frugal decision regarding the order of the editors for this book. We not only contributed equally, but our ideas and contributions, in the course of this process, became more and more indistinguishable and took on a life of their own.

When we originally approached the Scientific Advisory Board with this project, we did not conceal our anxiety about its high-risk nature. The Board was not daunted by this. Much to our comfort, even before we left the building, the Board had already approved this project.

Thus we had to face up to the task. There was no backing down.

Had it been our job to organize an ordinary conference, failure would have been almost certain. But the underlying philosophy of Dahlem provided an environment where risk taking is possible. Let us describe this briefly:

The beauty of a five-day Dahlem Workshop is that there are no presentations. Instead, this unique communication process begins well in advance: invited papers are submitted and are commented on by all participants before everyone arrives in Berlin. Thus, the entire time is spent together in discussion and collective writing, and an environment of trust evolves. With this trust, people are more willing to expose their own ignorance—a precondition for any interdisciplinary exchange.

At ordinary conferences, people fly in, perform on the stage, respond to a few comments, and fly out. At Dahlem, however, competitive athletes are converted into enthusiastic team players—at least most, if not all, of them.

None of this would have been possible if we had not been in the experienced hands of the Dahlem spirit personified: Julia Lupp, Caroline Rued-Engel, Gloria Custance, and Angela Daberkow.

If we could be granted one wish, we would invite our readers from different areas to begin experimenting with meeting formats. The current monopoly of all-too-sterile conference routines could be trans-substantiated into an open market of spirited encounters.

The Editors

We dedicate this volume to our late colleague and friend,
Joachim Schulz.

1

Law and Heuristics

An Interdisciplinary Venture

Christoph Engel[1] and Gerd Gigerenzer[2]

[1]Max Planck Institute for Research on Collective Goods, 53113 Bonn, Germany
[2]Max Planck Institute for Human Development, 14195 Berlin, Germany

In 1908, the director of the Harvard psychology laboratory, Hugo Münsterberg, complained that the "lawyer and the judge and the juryman are sure that they do not need the experimental psychologist.…They go on thinking that their legal instinct and their common sense supplies them with all that is needed and somewhat more" (pp. 10–11). For much of history, laws were passed and cases decided with little more than intuitive knowledge about how the mind works. A judicial attitude of suspicion verging on hostility toward psychology—just as toward statistics—can still be found. Yet a territorial instinct to maintain disciplinary seclusion conflicts with the natural attraction of ideas. Three centuries ago, statistics and probability were shaped by legal questions and vice versa: early probabilists were more concerned about equity than about chances, and statistics in turn modified legal concepts such as negligence, liability, and intent (Daston 1988). Three decades ago, a dose of economics reformed American law. Legal scholars were introduced to a new way of thinking: people are rational maximizers of expected utility. Seller and buyer, saint and sinner, miser and spendthrift—they all hold and act on a consistent set of preferences, revise probabilities according to Bayes's rule, and walk through their lives with a relentless forward-looking perspective. Among interdisciplinary marriages, the *law and economics* movement is one of the more happy ones on record. It covers areas where the law is explicitly engaged in regulating economic activity, such as taxation and antitrust, but has been also extended to include tort, contract, criminal, family, and antidiscrimination law, among others.

The present book explores a new union of ideas not unconnected to the previous two, this time between law and psychology. This engagement has a long past, but a short history. Psychological intuitions were present at the dawn of law, but the interdisciplinary venture is in its teens. Our focus is on heuristics, that is, simple strategies that professionals and laypeople use when making decisions with limited time and information. Many lawyers would posit "heuristics and the law" to be a nonissue. Similarly, most psychologists would not think of the law when they think of heuristics. Upon closer inspection, however, one finds courts cutting through complex cases by relying on rules of thumb, administrators making decisions based on one good reason, and legislators responding to scandal. Should that be seen as irrational and irresponsible? Or can simplicity, transparency, limited search, aspiration levels, and the other tools of heuristic decision making actually help? After all, social scientists report that ordinary people can achieve "better than rational" results by using heuristics that build on reciprocal altruism, recognition, reputation, and trust (e.g., Gigerenzer et al. 1999; Ostrom 1998). Are these results, however, relevant for legal decisions? The purpose of this book is to elucidate the power and limits of fast and frugal heuristics in the creation and implementation of law.

WHY HEURISTICS?

What is a heuristic? Why would anyone rely on heuristics? The term *heuristic* is of Greek origin and means "serving to find out or discover." In the title of his Nobel Prize–winning paper of 1905, Einstein used the term *heuristic* to indicate an idea that he considered incomplete, due to the limits of our knowledge, but useful. For the Stanford mathematician Polya (1954), heuristic thinking was as indispensable as analytical thinking for problems that cannot be solved by the calculus or probability theory—for instance, how to find a mathematical proof. The advent of computer programming gave heuristics a new prominence. It became clear that most problems of importance are computationally intractable; that is, we do not know the optimal (best) solution, nor do we know a method for how to find it.

The Gestalt psychology of the first half of the twentieth century used the term *heuristic* in the original Greek meaning to describe exploratory behavior, such as looking around and searching for information. Herbert A. Simon and Allen Newell conceptualized and partly formalized this approach in terms of search heuristics that find a reasonable solution in a huge search space, such as in chess. Heuristics were introduced in chess and artificial intelligence to make computers as smart as humans. In the analysis of experimental games, a simple heuristic called *Tit-for-Tat* won two computer tournaments against sophisticated competitors (Axelrod 1984). In the 1970s, however, the term *heuristic* became negatively tainted in other fields. Heuristics were introduced to explain why humans are not smart, and the term *heuristics and biases* came into use (Tversky and Kahneman 1974). Economists and lawyers were first exposed to the latter, rather than to the heuristics of artificial intelligence or of the adaptive decision maker (Payne et al. 1993).

Why do people rely on heuristics instead of logic, maximization of utility, or some other optimization technique? Open a textbook and the answer is likely that people have limited cognitive capacities, such as memory. This answer provides the red thread through many of the chapters in the *Behavioral Law and Economics* reader assembled by Sunstein (2000). Here, the case for heuristics is made by pointing to constraints located inside our minds. The account is consistent with the internalist bias of much of cognitive psychology, where explanations for behavior are sought exclusively inside the mind.

A different answer is provided by Simon (1956, 1990) and Gigerenzer and Selten (2001). Heuristics are needed in situations where the world does not permit optimization. For many real-world problems (as opposed to optimization-tuned textbook problems), optimal solutions are unknown because the problems are computationally intractable or poorly defined. Important issues such as what to do with the rest of your life, whom to trust, and whom to marry are typically ill-defined; that is, there is uncertainty about the goals, about what counts as an alternative and how many alternatives there are, and what the consequences might be and how to estimate their probabilities and utilities reliably. This uncertainty is not stressed by scholars who routinely take optimization or maximization as a feasible option, "edit" real-world problems into a form that allows for optimization, and conclude that people's limited cognitive capacities prevent them from optimizing. Moreover, even well-defined problems may be computationally intractable, such as chess, the classic computer game Tetris, and the traveling salesman problem (Michalewicz and Fogel 2000). Such problems are characterized by combinatorial explosion. Yet when optimal solutions are out of reach, people are not paralyzed to inaction or doomed to failure. We act by habit, imitation of others, and trust in institutions, on reputation or a good name.

In this alternative view, heuristics are needed because of the complexity of the outside world, and rationality concerns the question whether a heuristic is adapted to the environmental structure. Rationality is ecological rather than logical, as in some versions of rational choice. Internal cognitive constraints, such as limited memory and forgetting, can actually enhance rather than constrain performance (Schooler and Hertwig 2005). The study of *ecological rationality* investigates in which environment (social or physical) a given heuristic works and in which it fails (Gigerenzer et al. 1999; see also Smith 2003). A heuristic is defined as a simple rule that exploits both evolved abilities to act fast and structures of the environment to act accurately and frugally. The complexity and uncertainty of an environment cannot be determined independently of the actor. What matters is the degree of complexity and uncertainty encountered by the decision maker.

This brief sketch indicates that there are different definitions and uses of the term *heuristics* in the social sciences, and these uses are intimately linked to differing notions of rationality. At a minimum, it is useful to distinguish between views of heuristics based on logical rationality and on ecological rationality. Logical rationality is defined by syntax alone—such as the laws of logic or probability—whereas semantics (contents) and pragmatics (goals) are external to the norms. In this view, when judgment deviates from a logical structure, it is considered a bias or error—as in endowment effects, conjunction fallacies, and framing effects. As a consequence, a heuristic is by definition always second-best to logical thinking, at least when information is free. From an ecological (and evolutionary) point of view, this implication does not follow. The double grounding of a heuristic in the human brain and in the environment enables simple heuristics to be highly robust in an uncertain world, whereas complex strategies tend to *overfit*, that is, not generalize well to new and changing situations. Less can be more.

TWO DIMENSIONS OF THE HEURISTICS PROGRAM AND WHAT THEY MEAN FOR THE LAW

Traditionally, and for good reason, the law is not content with just seeing effects. It aims at what any scientist will consider futile from the outset: understanding all the relevant features of the problem at hand. This is, after all, what justice requires. Given this definition of the legal task, the concept of heuristics is particularly appropriate. It is tailored for decisions under circumstances of unmanageable complexity or uncertainty.

The heuristics program in psychology asks two distinct questions: Why and under which conditions does ignoring information work? When do people actually rely on simple heuristics for decision making? In the interaction between psychology and law, this generates two overlapping topics: heuristics as law, and heuristics as facts to be taken into account of by the law. Can the law as it stands, or the practice of generating and applying law, be interpreted in terms of heuristics? Would the law be better off if it (further) opened itself up to the idea of heuristics? These are the questions to be asked under the heading of heuristics as law.

Heuristics as facts matter for the law in multiple respects. Heuristics impact on the behavior of two classes of actors: those who make and apply the law as well as the general public to whom the law applies. Rule generation and rule application can react to heuristics used by the public, and both can themselves be the result of heuristics at work. Understanding these heuristics is relevant for the law in two respects. First, the law must properly reconstruct the governance problem to which it responds. If people rely on heuristics rather than on optimization, this may diminish or increase the social problem. Second, designing a good rule is not enough. The legislator must also ensure that the rule has the intended effect. The law must therefore anticipate how people are likely to react to its intervention. Again, this assessment will vary, subject to the heuristics upon which people rely.

Heuristics may be of help in making new laws. In civil law countries, the ordinary mechanism for this is legislation. Consequently, understanding the design of new law is best done by understanding political process. A standard model from political science, the policy cycle, helps do that. It structures an often messy chain of events into five steps: agenda setting, problem definition, policy choice, implementation, and evaluation (May and Wildavsky 1978). Each step is heavily influenced by the heuristics of those contributing to legislation. Finally, the process of rule application can capitalize on heuristics. Yet the heuristics of judges and administrators can also be seen as a problem by the legislator, or by the scientific observers of the legal order.

ILLUSTRATIONS

1. At the Medical Center of the University of California, San Diego, when a heart attack patient was admitted, 19 medical symptoms were measured to decide whether he or she should be treated as low or high risk. By contrast, Breiman et al. (1984) designed a simple heuristic that asked three yes–no questions at most. Is the minimum systolic blood pressure below a critical level? If so, the patient is immediately treated as high risk. All other symptoms are ignored. If not, is the patient's age less than or equal to 62.5 years? If so, the person is classified as low risk. No further information is sought. If not, a third question is asked that finally determines the treatment. Common sense asserts that this diagnosis, with at most three variables, must be less accurate than one with 19 variables (which included the three). Yet the simple heuristic made more accurate classifications than did decisions based on intricate combinations of all symptoms. Ignoring information can save lives.

2. National governments seek autonomous measures to combat climate change, facing an uncertain success of the Kyoto Protocol. A majority of climatologists contend that climate change is to be expected, with anthropogenic CO_2 emissions as a major source of the problem. Most of them originate from three kinds of activities: industry with high-energy consumption, heating, and fuel combustion in cars. As long as other countries do not follow suit, targeting the first is difficult. Industry would likely threaten government with relocation. Heating systems would be a likelier target, but are only replaced in very long cycles. Cars, by contrast, are replaced much more quickly, and inducing individuals to drive less would be instrumental. Most importantly, only a very small number of private households is likely to ever leave the country just because of driving restrictions, which makes globalization almost irrelevant for this regulatory option. However, the price elasticity of household demand for mobility is low; that is, even considerable increases in gas prices do not substantially reduce the amount of driving. One explanation for this fact is behavior. In their decisions about the amount of mobility and the means of transportation, households usually do not

carefully weigh pros and cons. Instead, they follow habits and simple routines. If the law wants to change driving behavior, it must therefore directly
target routines. Put differently, it must impose the unlearning of previous
routines, and the learning of new, socially more beneficial ones (Engel
2004).

3. Campaigns to change public attitudes toward organ donation are widespread. Why are only 12% of Germans but a striking 99.9% of French citizens donors? One might speculate about different national characters, German egoism and perfectionism versus French altruism and generosity. Still,
why are 17% of the British and 28% of Americans donors, compared to
99.9% of Austrians and Hungarians? That fact alone may prevent us from
speculating with stereotypes. According to a classical rational choice view,
people have stable preferences, and the Germans and British might simply
find too little value in donation. Yet if people act by heuristics rather than
preferences, the national differences can be understood. In explicit-consent
countries such as Germany, Great Britain, and the U.S., the law states that
nobody can be a donor without prior registration. In presumed-consent
countries such as France, Austria, and Hungary, everyone is a donor unless
they stipulate otherwise. Thus, in the latter group of countries the default is
to be a donor, whereas in the first group, the default is not to be a donor. Most
people's heuristic seems to be "don't change the status quo," reflecting the
belief that the existing laws generally make sense, or might even be recommendations by the policy maker. From a rational choice perspective, legal
defaults should have little effect because people will override a default if it is
not consistent with their preference. However, the empirical evidence suggests that heuristics matter more. The far majority of citizens in all countries
seem to employ the same heuristic, rather than having strikingly divergent
preferences. A legal system that understands the heuristics that drive the majority of citizens can make the desired option the default and therewith find
simple solutions for what looks like a complex problem (Johnson and
Goldstein 2003; Sunstein and Thaler 2003).

ISSUES

How do heuristics relate to law and economics? In a narrow reading of rational
choice theory, heuristics play virtually no role. People either maximize their expected utilities, or they behave *as if* they did so. In the first of these two readings
of rational choice theory, the process of decision making is consciously or unconsciously assumed to be optimization. In the second, *as-if* version, no statement is made about the process, only about the resulting behavior. In neither version do heuristics play a part. Law and economic scholars such as Posner (2002)
represent a broader conception of rational choice, which has abandoned a

hyperrational, emotionless, unsocial, and utterly selfish model of man and woman. Here, psychology enters the law, although psychologists might respond that it does so mainly intuitively or ad hoc. Posner tries to assimilate notions such as the *availability heuristic* as consistent with rational choice once the efforts or costs of deliberative thinking are factored in: "For example, the argument for allowing the prosecution in a capital case to place 'victim impact' statements before the jury is that without them jurors would have to exert extra effort to imagine the victim's suffering in order to counterbalance the impact of the immediate perception of the suffering defendant, pleading for his life" (Posner 2002, p. 3).

What would psychologists say to this? Psychologists might have two criticisms, not about Posner's attempt at assimilation but rather its object: the notion of *availability*. First, the term is a commonsense label, neither clearly defined nor formalized as psychological theories usually are. Second, as a consequence of this ambiguity, one cannot deduce in what situations this heuristic will be irrational, as proponents of the heuristics-and-biases program emphasize, or rational, as Posner wants to argue (Posner 2002, Chap. 2). The danger is that legal scholars "explain" every irrationality and human disaster by proclaiming their "availability." What the emerging science of heuristics needs first of all is theoretical precision, that is, models of the heuristic process and the environments or institutions in which they work and fail. Precise and testable models of heuristics exist in psychology. This research agenda is still little known in the law, even though it is exemplified by the work of two Nobel laureates, Herbert Simon (1986, 1990) and Reinhard Selten (2001) on satisficing; Tversky's (1972) elimination-by-aspect; the heuristics for preferential choice studied by Payne et al. (1993); and the study of the adaptive toolbox by Gigerenzer et al. (1999) and Gigerenzer and Selten (2001).

THEORY

A theory can fail on two counts: It can be empirically wrong or indeterminate. Rational choice theory has been criticized as being indeterminate because it provides no theoretical basis for specifying the content and shape of the utility function. As an illustration, consider Becker's (1981, Chaps. 6 and 7) analysis of the opportunities of children, which he uses to question whether public compensatory education programs will achieve their goal in that parents will simply reallocate resources they would have otherwise invested in these children. As Arthur Goldberger argued, this conclusion follows from specific assumptions about the utility functions, such as that the child's income is an additive function of parent's investment and child's luck (see Simon 1986). If the latter function is multiplicative instead of additive, however, Becker's conclusion does not follow. No empirical support is provided for the auxiliary assumption that makes all the difference. This case illustrates the general critique that rational choice theory is indeterminate without additional assumptions about the utility functions that are external to the theory. Yet critics of rational choice theory and proponents of heuristics need to be aware of the same problem. Unless the heuristics in "heuristics and the law" are clearly specified, including their ecological rationality, the critics will fall prey to repeating the flaw they criticize: to be able to account, *post hoc*, for everything.

Lack of theory is a major critique of the emerging field of law and psychology: Experimental phenomena are presented en masse, but left unexplained. Psychologists would respond that economists and legal scholars have so far encountered a biased sample of psychology, one that indeed favors collecting effects (biases) above developing theory. They would also point out that for several of those effects, formal explanations exist in other parts of psychology. For instance, prospect theory proposes a nonlinear probability weighting function, consistent with existing data, but without providing an independent rationale for its shape. Critics argue that the weighting function is only a redescription of the empirical data and is obtained by tinkering with the curves of expected utility theory. Kahneman and Tversky (1979) actually said something similar, although in a more positive way. Yet the precise form of the curves can be deduced from Parducci's (1965, 1995) range-frequency theory, an independently motivated theory of psychophysical judgments. Moreover, this formal theory predicts the degree of over/underweighting of high and low probabilities, depending on the properties of the probability distributions (Stewart et al. 2006). For example, people often base decisions on name recognition alone, such as when they choose a supermarket brand they have heard of over one they have not, predict that the tennis player whom they are not familiar with will lose the match, or believe that colleges whose names they recognize are better. Moreover, they may ignore other cues. This phenomenon might be labeled as another case of "availability." Yet there exist precise models of heuristics, such as the recognition heuristic and the fluency heuristic (Schooler and Hertwig 2005), that allow deduction of strong and counterintuitive predictions, which labeling cannot. Research on the recognition heuristic specifies the situations in which people with *less* knowledge make *more* correct judgments (Goldstein and Gigerenzer 2002) or when a jury does best by following its least knowledgeable member (Reimer and Katsikopoulos 2004). Formal models enable predictions of when people behave in apparently strange ways, and also why they do so; that is, they distinguish between situations in which a behavior is beneficial or disadvantageous.

NORMS

A common strategy for attacking rational choice theory is to inundate it with cognitive biases. For instance, according to Conlisk (1996, pp. 669–670):

People display intransitivity; misunderstand statistical independence; mistake random data for patterned data and vice versa; fail to appreciate law of large number effects; fail to recognize statistical dominance; make errors in updating probabilities on the basis of new information; understate the significance of given sample sizes; fail to understand covariation for even the simplest 2×2 contingency tables; make false inferences about causality; ignore relevant information; use irrelevant information (as in sunk cost fallacies); exaggerate the importance of vivid over pallid evidence; exaggerate the importance of fallible predictors; exaggerate the *ex ante* probability of a random event which has already occurred; display overconfidence in judgment relative to evidence; exaggerate confirming over disconfirming evidence relative to initial beliefs; give answers that are highly sensitive to logically irrelevant changes in questions; do redundant and ambiguous tests to confirm an hypothesis at the expense of decisive tests to disconfirm; make frequent errors in deductive reasoning tasks such as syllogisms; place higher value on an opportunity if an experimenter rigs it to be the "status quo" opportunity; fail to discount the future consistently; fail to adjust repeated choices to accommodate intertemporal connections; and more.

What should legal scholars make of this litany of apparent sins against reason? Ask for more paternalism in legislation? Demand more government regulation to protect people from using their minds? Or start teaching law students statistics and experimental methods? The latter would not hurt, but statistical literacy is a different point (see Hertwig, this volume). Let us take a close look at the notion of rationality implicit in this list of sins. Note that almost all of the behaviors are evaluated from the perspective of logical rationality or probability theory. In other words, the norms are syntactical, unconditional to the semantics (the content) and the pragmatics (the intentions). By definition, logical rationality is content and purpose blind. In this view people are rational when disregarding everything that matters except logic or probability; otherwise their judgments rank in the above list.

Chicago-style economists defend human rationality against lists of cognitive illusions by arguing that these might be the product of artificial experimental settings or of the lack of sufficient monetary incentives, or that the biases might be real but the market will eliminate individual cognitive quirks eventually, or that all of this holds. Such arguments dispute the phenomenon. Psychologists, interestingly, tend to dispute the logical norms against which the phenomenon is evaluated as a fallacy (e.g., Gigerenzer 1996, 2000; Hertwig and Todd 2003; Lopes 1991). Note that clarifying norms does not assume that people never err; at issue is what erring means in the first place. Almost every item in Conlisk's list has been challenged, and—more fruitfully—in some cases, situations have been distinguished where the reported behavior is beneficial or detrimental. Consider the first three items in the list.

First, Sen (2002) has argued that purely syntactical definitions of consistency are meaningless for deciding between rational and irrational behavior; one must take a person's motives or objectives into account. Since consistency is necessary for transitivity, the same holds for transitivity. Moreover, heuristics that occasionally lead to intransitive judgments can be faster and more accurate than "rational" strategies that never "sin" (Gigerenzer and Goldstein 1996). Second, heuristics that ignore the statistical dependence between cues tend to be more robust and accurate than complex strategies that do not (Czerlinski et al. 1999). This is true in environments that are moderately or highly unpredictable, such as judging the guilt of defendants. Finally, is mistaking randomness for patterns and vice versa an error? Again it depends on people's objectives and motives. If a miss is more dangerous than a false alarm, signal detection theory advises one to increase the chance of mistaking random data for patterned data, that is, of false alarms, in order to decrease the chance of misses. If the false alarm is more costly, the opposite recommendation follows (Green and Swets 1966). For example, if a legal system takes a conservative view emphasizing societal security over individual rights, then the probability of a miss (not convicting the culprit) should be decreased at the cost of an increase in false alarms (convicting an innocent). In this world, a good judge is one who tends to see patterns (guilt) where there are none. If a legal system, by contrast, takes a libertarian view emphasizing the reduction of false alarms at the cost of increasing misses, then the judge should make the opposite error more often of not convicting the culprit so that fewer innocents will end up convicted, which corresponds to increasing the error of not seeing a pattern of guilt when there actually is one. The general point is again that there is no way to decide whether a behavior is an error unless the semantics and pragmatics of the situation are factored in. This point is not new; it was discussed in the eighteenth-century encounter of statistics and the law, among others by Laplace, who took a conservative view, and Condorcet, who endorsed liberal reforms (Daston 1981).

The alternative to logical rationality is ecological rationality. Simon (1956, 1990) promoted this view when he emphasized that rationality is about the adaptation of cognition to its environment (not to the laws of logic), as illustrated by his analogy of a pair of scissors, with the mind and the environment as the two blades. A similar view is expressed when Posner (2002) critiques the puzzling refusal of behavioral law and economics to seek theoretical grounding in evolutionary biology. An evolutionary perspective emphasizes that heuristics are anchored in the evolved abilities of the brain (e.g., the ability for pattern recognition and reciprocal altruism) and in the structure of the environment, and exploits both to obtain good results. Rational choice theory, in its narrow form, does not have these evolved tools. This evolutionary perspective can help us understand how heuristics can be "better than rational," such as when decisions based on only one reason result in higher predictive accuracy than those based on regression models of many reasons (Czerlinski et al. 1999) or sophisticated statistical models designed to promote the robustness of prediction (Chater et al. 2003; Martignon and Laskey 1999). Epstein (this volume) makes a related point for the benefit of simple rules in legislation.

ONE OR MANY

The term *health* is in the singular, but *diseases* come in the plural. The question of one or many, and its association with good and bad, provides an instructive analogy for understanding rational behavior. Rational choice theorists tend to treat rationality in the singular, and behavior, too—at least as long as people follow the theory. This double singular is consistent with the health/disease analogy, since there is only one state of health (although no chronic mental disease) in the model. The heuristics-and-biases outlook follows the health/disease pattern more directly. Cognitive processes (or judgments) are in the plural, as are many forms of biases, but rationality is still in the singular: Rational choice is challenged only descriptively, not as a norm. The adaptive toolbox paradigm, by contrast, overthrows the health/disease analogy. It treats both norms and cognitive processes in the plural. Normative statements involve the adaptation of a given heuristic to a given environment, of which there are several methods, and similarly, there are many heuristics in the adaptive toolbox.

This discussion makes one point obvious: The various positions on heuristics and the law are developing and incomplete, each can learn from the other, and there are signs of convergence. It is with this perspective in mind that we asked proponents of all positions, those in-between, and impartial minds to come together for five days to discuss the issues. Our goal was to utilize the present healthy tension between various approaches to help promote the emerging field of law and psychology. We have centered the discussion on four broad questions.

Are Heuristics a Problem or a Solution?

Heuristics have been presented both as the cause of problems and the means for their solutions. After an overemphasis on the dark side of heuristics in the early behavioral law and economics movement, few scholars would claim today that heuristics are always bad or always good. Once one moves beyond the formula "heuristics = good; optimization = always better," some interesting questions emerge: Can the use of heuristics be normative? As a consequence, can ignoring information be normative, and if so, in what situations? Can the attempt to optimize be detrimental? What is the role of simplicity and transparency in the law?

What Is the Role of Heuristics in Making Law?

The German parliament passed a law, effective in 2005, that women between 50 and 69 have access to free screening mammograms. The members of parliament were apparently unaware of the medical research. Randomized clinical trials with some 280,000 women provided no evidence that women who participate in screening will live longer but only that two less women out of 1,000 will die of breast cancer (Nyström et al. 1996), although even this benefit has since been disputed (Olsen and Gotzsche 2001). The annual costs, including follow-up treatments of false positives, amount to hundreds of millions of euros every year. How did such a law get passed in a time of government cuts to health care provisions? The case illustrates that laws do not always reflect scientific evidence or reason, but can arise from an emotional climate fueled by public anxiety, lobbyism, and misinformation. What turns an issue into a public issue, and then into a law? What is the role of heuristics in the process of agenda setting and political decision making?

What Is the Role of Heuristics in the Court?

In high-energy physics, experimenters decide when a fact is a fact, and when to end an experiment, by a process of collective discussion in group meetings (Galison 1987). In experimental psychology, this decision is made individually by computing an effect size or simply looking at the level of significance. How do judges, jurors, and other legal fact finders decide whether a witness is trustworthy or a defendant is guilty? What uncertain cues does a judge attend to, which are most important, and which are ignored? What is the process of searching for information, stopping search, and decision making? Many legal orders have explicitly prescribed the circumstances under which a court may hold a particular fact to have been proven. Some of these rules of thumb appear ghastly to modern minds: If a woman survives cruel treatment, she is a witch; otherwise she is not. Other rules of thumb may have a grain of wisdom in them: You may not convict a person for a serious crime based on the testimony of a single witness, as common law holds. But what if, as in some Arab countries, you need four eyewitnesses to convict a man of rape? More is not always better.

How Do Heuristics Mediate the Impact of Law on Behavior?

According to some traditional teaching, the law has an impact on behavior through its moral, spiritual, or religious authority. In a rational choice perspective, the law has an impact on behavior because it changes the opportunity structure. Still, how can the law change behavior when many citizens have only faint ideas about the text of the law? Hardly anyone consults a statute or a casebook before taking actions. Economists adhering to the Austrian school stress rule following as a key element in their evolutionary picture of the world. Rule following, in turn, seems to imply that there are not too many rules, and moral and legal systems may increase the impact of the law on citizens if the law is simple. The Ten Commandments embody a simplicity that respects the limits of human memory. The U.S. and the German tax system do not. They create complexity, loopholes, and a feeling of helplessness, whereas simplicity can create trust and increase compliance.

CONTROVERSIES

This Dahlem Workshop was not without passionate controversies, in some groups more than in others, and the individual chapters and group reports reflect these issues. The chapters definitely do not speak with one voice. What did not take place, however, was a conflict between legal scholars trained in the heuristics-and-biases view and psychologists studying how fast and frugal heuristics are adapted to institutions and other form of environments. This does not mean that all differences of opinions simply evaporated. A constant source of debate was the issue whether and under what conditions heuristics can be normative. Considerable argument emerged from diverging standards for evidence in the law and in the social sciences. Some legal scholars asked for a degree of certainty and consistency of empirical evidence that the social sciences cannot deliver, specifically when social scientists analyzed the heuristics upon which the legal professionals based their decisions. What are exceptionally clear results by social standards did not always meet the standards of legal scholars with little hands-on experience in research.

Controversy transcended group boundaries. One central issue came up in all groups: Heuristics ignore information. Is this acceptable for the law? Specifically, is it sufficient to demonstrate the good performance of a heuristic, or of decision making by heuristics generally? A similar question has a long tradition in the discussion about clinical judgment and evidence-based medicine. On average, clinical decisions improve if doctors rely on statistical evidence, rather than on mere intuition (Meehl 1954; Meadow and Sunstein 2001). Yet implicitly, statistics also ignore information, for they only consider what has been observed in sampling. The best statistic may have ignored what is irrelevant on average, but highly relevant for this specific patient. In the jargon of this literature, the problem is referred to as the "broken-leg cue" (Astebro and Chen 2004; Dawes et al. 1989). If a patient with a problem in his throat sees a doctor, no statistical expert system will notice if the patient had a broken leg that day. However, a doctor should take account of this fact when deciding on treatment. Yet not every contextual factor is as important as a broken leg. The theoretical possibility of an unusual feature is no excuse for lightly setting statistical evidence aside. In a way, an often-heard criticism of lawyers against the use of heuristics makes the same point: The law must be open to factors ignored by a given heuristic procedure. However, the theoretical possibility that there might be such factors is not sufficient to disparage heuristics from the outset. The controversial insight seems to be that good decision making under uncertainty must always ignore part of the information available. The art is to find a good strategy that captures the right part and ignores the rest.

Uncertainty demands normative choices that certainty does not. The users of evidence-based medicine must choose between two kinds of errors. Which looms larger: false positives or false negatives? Since overlooking cases that would have called for intervention is legally and socially more problematic in medicine, expert systems typically generate many false positives. Doctors aware of this problem can carefully check other evidence before taking action. Once they use an expert system, however, they systematically seem to underestimate the opposite risk of false negatives, compared to doctors relying on mere intuition (Alberdi et al. 2004). There is no similar evidence for the performance of lawyers relying on heuristics in court as yet, but it is likely that there would be a similar phenomenon. Given that uncertainty cannot be totally eliminated, each institutional policy for reducing false negatives, such as the number of culprits who are mistakenly not convicted, will automatically increase the rate of false positives, such as the number of convictions of innocents, and vice versa. Understanding heuristics can thus help the law make better choices—but they will remain choices, and hence open to argument.

PROSPECTS

What psychology can learn from the law is the relevance of institutions for understanding adaptive behavior. The role of institutions still constitutes a blind spot in cognitive psychology. Heuristics do not exist solely because of the mind's limited capacities. Heuristics develop and adapt to their changing environments, past and present, including institutional structures. What legal scholars can learn from psychology is the relevance of the mind for understanding the design and impact of institutions.

REFERENCES

Alberdi, E., A.A. Povyakalo, L. Strigini, and P. Ayton. 2004. Effects of incorrect CAD output on human decision making in mammography. *Acad. Radiol.* **11**:909–918.

Astebro, T., and G. Chen. 2004. Decision-making models and treatment effects. http://ssrn.com/abstract=578525

Axelrod, R. 1984. The Evolution of Cooperation. New York: Basic.

Becker, G.S. 1981. A Treatise on the Family. Cambridge, MA: Harvard Univ. Press.

Breiman, L., J.H. Friedman, R.A. Olshen, and C.J. Stone. 1984. Classification and Regression Trees. Belmont, CA: Wadsworth.

Chater, N., M. Oaksford, R. Nakisa, and M. Redington. 2003. Fast, frugal, and rational: How rational norms explain behavior. *Org. Behav. Hum. Dec. Proc.* **90**:63–86.

Conlisk, J. 1996. Why bounded rationality? *J. Econ. Lit.* **34**:669–700.

Czerlinski, J., G. Gigerenzer, and D.G. Goldstein. 1999. How good are simple heuristics? In: Simple Heuristics That Make Us Smart, G. Gigerenzer, P.M. Todd, and the ABC Research Group, pp. 97–118. New York: Oxford Univ. Press.

Daston, L.J. 1981. Mathematics and the moral sciences: The rise and fall of the probability of judgments, 1785–1840. In: Epistemological and Social Problems of the Sciences in the Early Nineteenth Century, ed. H.N. Jahnke and M. Otte, pp. 287–309. Dordrecht: Reidel.

Daston, L.J. 1988. Classical Probability in the Enlightenment. Princeton, NJ: Princeton Univ. Press.

Dawes, R.M., D. Faust, and P. Meehl. 1989. Clinical versus actuarial judgment. *Science* **243**:1668–1674.

Engel, C. 2004. Learning the law. Preprints of the Max Planck Institute for Research on Collective Goods Bonn 2004/5. http://www.mpp-rdg.mpg.de/pdf_dat/2004_5 online.pdf

Galison, P. 1987. How Experiments End. Chicago: Univ. of Chicago Press.

Gigerenzer, G. 1996. On narrow norms and vague heuristics: A reply to Kahneman and Tversky (1996). *Psychol. Rev.* **103**:592–596.

Gigerenzer, G. 2000. Adaptive Thinking: Rationality in the Real World. New York: Oxford Univ. Press.

Gigerenzer, G., and D.G. Goldstein. 1996. Reasoning the fast and frugal way: Models of bounded rationality. *Psychol. Rev.* **103**:650–669.

Gigerenzer, G., and R. Selten, eds. 2001. Bounded Rationality: The Adaptive Toolbox. Dahlem Workshop Report 84. Cambridge, MA: MIT Press.

Gigerenzer, G., P.M. Todd, and the ABC Research Group. 1999. Simple Heuristics That Make Us Smart. New York: Oxford Univ. Press.

Goldstein, D.G., and G. Gigerenzer. 2002. Models of ecological rationality: The recognition heuristic. *Psychol. Rev.* **109**:75–90.

Green, D.M., and J.A. Swets. 1966. Signal Detection Theory and Psychophysics. New York: Wiley.

Hertwig, R., and P.M. Todd. 2003. More is not always better: The benefits of cognitive limits. In: The Psychology of Reasoning and Decision Making: A Handbook, ed. D. Hardman and L. Macchi, pp. 213–231. Chichester: Wiley.

Johnson, E.J., and D.G. Goldstein. 2003. Do defaults save lives? *Science* **302**:1338–1339.

Kahneman, D., and A. Tversky. 1979. Prospect theory: An analysis of decision under risk. *Econometrica* **47**:263–291.

Lopes, L.L. 1991. The rhetoric of irrationality. *Theor. Psychol.* **1**:65–82.

Martignon, L., and K.B. Laskey. 1999. Bayesian benchmarks for fast and frugal heuristics. In: Simple Heuristics That Make Us Smart, G. Gigerenzer, P.M. Todd, and the ABC Research Group, pp. 169–188. New York: Oxford Univ. Press.

May, J.V., and A.B. Wildavsky. 1978. The Policy Cycle. Beverly Hills, CA: Sage.

Meadow, W., and C.R. Sunstein. 2001. Statistics, not experts. *Duke Law J.* **51**:629–646.

Meehl, P.E. 1954. Clinical versus Statistical Prediction: A Theoretical Analysis and a Review of the Evidence. Minneapolis: Univ. of Minnesota Press.

Michalewicz, Z., and D. Fogel. 2000. How to Solve It: Modern Heuristics. New York: Springer.

Münsterberg, H. 1908. On the Witness Stand: Essays on Psychology and Crime. New York: Doubleday.

Nyström, L., L.-G. Larsson, S. Wall et al. 1996. An overview of the Swedish randomised mammography trials: Total mortality pattern and the representativity of the study cohorts. *J. Med. Screening* **3**:85–87.

Olsen, O., and P.C. Gotzsche. 2001. Cochrane review on screening for breast cancer with mammography. *Lancet* **358**:1340–1342.

Ostrom, E. 1998. A behavioral approach to the rational choice theory of collective action. *Am. Pol. Sci. Rev.* **92**:1–22.

Parducci, A. 1965. Category judgment: A range-frequency model. *Psychol. Rev.* **72**: 407–418.

Parducci, A. 1995. Happiness, Pleasure, and Judgment: The Contextual Theory and Its Applications. Mahwah, NJ: Erlbaum.

Payne, J.W., J.R. Bettman, and E.J. Johnson. 1993. The Adaptive Decision Maker. Cambridge: Cambridge Univ. Press.

Polya, G. 1954. Mathematics and Plausible Reasoning. Vol. 1: Induction and Analogy in Mathematics. Princeton, NJ: Princeton Univ. Press.

Posner, R.A. 2002. Behavioral law and economics: A critique. *Econ. Educ. Bull.*, American Institute for Economic Research, August 2002.

Reimer, T., and K. Katsikopoulos. 2004. The use of recognition in group decision-making. *Cog. Sci.* **28**:1009–1029.

Schooler, L.J., and R. Hertwig. 2005. How forgetting aids heuristic inference. *Psychol. Rev.* **112**:610–628.

Selten, R. 2001. What is bounded rationality? In: Bounded Rationality: The Adaptive Toolbox, ed. G. Gigerenzer and R. Selten, pp. 13–36. Dahlem Workshop Report 84. Cambridge, MA: MIT Press.

Sen, A. 2002. Rationality and Freedom. Cambridge, MA: Harvard Univ. Press.

Simon, H.A. 1956. Rational choice and the structure of environments. *Psychol. Rev.* **63**:129–138.

Simon, H.A. 1986. Rationality in psychology and economics. *J. Business* **59**:209–224.

Simon, H.A. 1990. Invariants of human behavior. *Ann. Rev. Psychol.* **41**:1–19.

Smith, V.L. 2003. Constructivist and ecological rationality in economics. *Am. Econ. Rev.* **93**:465–508.

Stewart, N., N. Chater, and G.D.A. Brown. 2006. Decision by sampling. *Cog. Sci.*, in press.

Sunstein, C.R. 2000. Behavioral Law and Economics. Cambridge, MA: Univ. of Cambridge Press.

Sunstein, C.R., and R.H. Thaler. 2003. Libertarian paternalism is not an oxymoron. *Univ. Chicago Law Rev.* **70**:1159–1202.

Tversky, A. 1972. Elimination by aspects: A theory of choice. *Psychol. Rev.* **79**:281–299.

Tversky, A., and D. Kahneman. 1974. Judgment under uncertainty: Heuristics and biases. *Science* **185**:1124–1131.

2

Heuristics

Gerd Gigerenzer

Max Planck Institute for Human Development, 14195 Berlin, Germany

ABSTRACT

For many legal problems, finding the absolutely best solution to a problem (i.e., optimization) is out of reach. The problem is too complex, information is scarce and contradictory, too many players are involved with dissimilar goals, or time is pressing and the world uncertain. Yet experts and laypeople are not paralyzed in such circumstances; they find solutions by using what is often called intuition, habit, or rules of thumb. The science of heuristics explicates the processes underlying intuition and habit. These heuristics are often unconscious, and their systematic study can help to improve decision making. Heuristics are not good or bad per se. Instead, their rationality is ecological; that is, they are successful in the environments (institutions) to which they are adapted. The study of the structure of environments, and their systematic change, is thus a necessary part of efforts to improve decision making under uncertainty.

INTRODUCTION

There are two views on the nature of heuristics. In the first, heuristics are seen as the solution to a problem. This view is common in mathematics, where heuristic methods are indispensable for problems that analysis cannot solve. Finding a proof, as opposed to checking its steps, is one example. Here, a heuristic is not a mental shortcut or a second-best solution: It is *the* way to find a solution. Similarly, in artificial intelligence and machine learning, heuristics provide solutions when optimization is out of reach. Optimization—as opposed to the use of heuristics—means finding the absolutely best strategy for a given problem. An example of this is calculating the maximum of a function. However, we do not know the optimal strategy for the majority of interesting problems, including well-defined problems such as chess, ill-defined problems with ambiguous pay-off structures or multiple goals, and social interactions whose present rules may change in the future. Heuristics are essential when the optimal strategy cannot be computed by mind or machine (as in chess), or when optimization is too costly, slow, and dangerous (as in intensive care unit decisions). According to this first view, heuristics are indispensable, because optimization can only solve a small class of problems in the real world.

In the second view, heuristics are the problem itself. This approach assumes that we can find the optimal strategy for a given problem and considers heuristics to be second-best strategies. The use of heuristics is attributed to people's cognitive limitations rather than to the nature of the problem. These limitations are, in turn, seen as the source of various cognitive illusions or biases. The terms *heuristics* and *biases* are often used interchangeably, since both are seen as creating the problem, even though the one term describes a process and the other an outcome. This second view is widespread in social psychology and behavioral economics and has, accordingly, shaped behavioral law and economics.

If the first view is true, heuristics are indispensable for lawyers, lawmakers, judges, legal institutions, and their clients; the only question that remains is which heuristics should be used in which situations. If the second view is true, these legal agents fare better without heuristics by relying on logic, probability theory, or optimization. In this chapter, I will sketch the foundations of a science of heuristics that resolves the tension between these two views. I begin with some widespread misconceptions about the nature of heuristics.

SIX MISCONCEPTIONS

1. *People use heuristics only because they have limited cognitive capacities.* This much-repeated phrase incorrectly locates the reason for heuristics exclusively inside the human mind, which is seen as an impoverished instrument.[1] However, as mentioned before, external reasons (e.g., that a problem is computationally intractable, the future is uncertain, and the goals are ambiguous) are sufficient for minds and computers to rely on heuristics. For instance, when former chess world champion Kasparov played against the IBM chess program Deep Blue, both had to rely on heuristics. The reason is not simply because people or computers have limited cognitive capacities, but because the problem is computationally intractable. Its solution is not computable for even the most brilliant minds and the fastest machines. Limits of attention, memory, and reasoning can, of course, contribute to the use of simple heuristics, but external reasons are sufficient.

2. *Limited cognitive capacities are always bad.* This phrase is often implied but rarely stated, perhaps because it seems so obvious. Yet limited capacities can in fact enable cognitive functions, not only constrain them (Hertwig and Todd 2003). For instance, large memory capacities can prevent language acquisition in children as well as in neural networks, whereas starting small (limited capacity) and with simple sentences (baby talk) enables learning (Elman 1993). Luria's (1968) famous mnemonist with almost unlimited

---

[1]   For example, "Employing simplifying heuristics is a rational approach to decision making only *because* of our cognitive limitations" (Korobkin 2003, pp. 1292–1293).

memory could perfectly recite pages of text, but his memory was flooded by detail, so that he had problems summarizing the gist of the text and thinking on an abstract level. The short-term memory capacity limit of "seven plus/minus two" seems to enable us to detect covariation of events better than with higher (or lower) capacities (Kareev 2000). Zero-intelligence traders make as much profit as intelligent people do in experimental markets (Gode and Sunder 1993). Last but not least, satisficers are reported to be more optimistic and have higher self-esteem and life satisfaction, whereas maximizers excel in depression, perfectionism, regret, and self-blame (Schwartz et al. 2002). Limited capacities can have a function.

3. *Heuristics lead to second-best outcomes whereas optimizing leads to best outcomes.* If the optimal strategy is not known, or too slow, heuristics cannot be the second-best solution. They may be the only one. For this reason, the science of heuristics is both *positive* (what heuristics do people use?) and *normative* (what heuristics should be used in what situations?). Moreover, every optimization model is optimal only relative to a set of mathematically convenient assumptions. To the degree that these assumptions do not hold in the real world, the outcome of optimization can be disappointing. In these cases, optimizing theories are second best (Bookstaber and Langsam 1985). Thus, it is important to separate the terms *optimization* and *heuristics*, which refer to the internal process of decision making, from external evaluations such as *optimal, good,* and *bad results,* which refer to the outcome of decision making.

4. *Labels such as availability and representativeness "explain" behavior.* To explain and predict behavior, we need models of heuristics, not mere labels. A model of a heuristic is a rule that specifies a *process* anchored in mind and environment. For instance, *Tit-for-Tat* specifies the process "cooperate in the first move, keep a memory of size one, and then imitate the other player's move." This process exploits evolved abilities such as reciprocal altruism—the ability to cooperate with genetically unrelated members of the same species, which is almost uniquely human (as a consequence, there is little evidence that animals use Tit-for-Tat; see Hammerstein 2003). It also exploits structures of environments such as the rules of the prisoner's dilemma; when this environment changes, its seminal performance can deteriorate. The task of the science of heuristics is to understand and modify behavior based on the triad of heuristics, evolved abilities, and environmental structures. In contrast, commonsense labels such as availability neither specify a process rule nor the situations where a heuristic succeeds or fails. Labeling allows almost every phenomenon to be accounted for *post hoc,* inviting just-so story telling.[2] Explanations of behavior such as "actor A uses Tit-

---

[2] The seductive plausibility of labeling is a problem both in psychological studies and legal applications. For instance, a frequently cited study reported that people estimated that there are more

for-Tat in a class S of social situations" can be falsified, as they have been (Hammerstein 2003), whereas mere labels cannot be disproved, proved, or improved. Without precise models, one is left with the vague phrase that "heuristics are sometimes good and sometimes bad." To make this phrase informative, one needs to specify what the "sometimes"refers to, that is, to study the *ecological rationality* of a heuristic (see below). This task, however, cannot be accomplished until there are precise models rather than mere labels.

5. *Everything except optimization and logic is a heuristic.* Not every proposed explanation of behavior is a heuristic. A heuristic is a process model, that is, a type of strategy rather than a state. Long-term states, such as traits and attitudes, and short-term states, such as moods and affects, are possible explanations of behavior, but not heuristics. Strategies exist that are not fast and frugal, nor do they involve optimizing; endless committee meetings are one example. A fast and frugal heuristic is a strategy that ignores part of the information and enables fast decisions.

---

words beginning with the letter "r" in English than words having "r" as their third letter. In fact, words beginning with "r" are far less numerous. The proposed explanation for this bias was that people judge "frequency by availability, that is, by an assessment of the ease with which instances could be brought to mind" (Tversky and Kahneman 1982, p. 166). This sounds plausible, but note that there was no definition or independent measure of "ease" in that study (or elsewhere; no replication seems to exist). When Sedlmeier et al. (1998) measured "availability" independently as the time it takes a person to recall the first word ("ease"), or alternatively as the number of words that a person can produce within a fixed time ("number"), it was found that neither of these two measures actually predicted people's frequency judgments of words with "r" or other letters. Thus, there was in fact no evidence for "availability," defined as "ease" or as "number." One could conjecture that there might be different ways to define availability, which might actually predict frequency judgments, but this possibility is the very problem. Vague labels such as availability and representativeness explain at once too little and too much. Too little, because we do not know when and how these heuristics work; too much because, *post hoc*, one of them seems to "explain" almost any experimental result (Gigerenzer 2000).

The same problem arises in legal writings, where the term *availability* has been used to "explain" many phenomena, from residents worrying about the health effects of Love Canal to their fear of nuclear accidents. However, the meaning of the term is constantly being changed; here are some illustrations. People judge the frequency of events, we are told, (a) by the *actual ease of retrieval* ("people tend to think that risks are more serious when an incident is readily called to mind or 'available' "; Sunstein 2000, p. 5); (b) by its *imagined ease* ("the frequency of some event is estimated by judging how easy it is to recall other instances of this type [how 'available' such instances are]"; Jolls et al. 1998, p. 1477), (c) by the *number of instances that come to mind* ("a person may overestimate the incidence of AIDS simply because many of his acquaintances have the disease and he can easily think of AIDS cases"; Kuran and Sunstein 2000, p. 381), (d) by the *recency of witnessing one instance* ("People tend to conclude, for example, that the probability of an event [such as a car accident] is greater if they have recently witnessed an occurrence of that event than if they have not"; Jolls et al. 1998, p. 1477), and (e) by the *salience of instances* (" 'availability,' after all, is in many respects just another name for the 'salience' of standard political theory"; Noll and Krier 2000, p. 353). Ease, imagined ease, number, recency, and salience are, however, not the same thing and may not even be correlated (Sedlmeier et al. 1998).

6. *More information is always better.* In most models of rationality, it is taken for granted that the quality of the decision (or prediction) always improves—or at least cannot diminish—with increasing amounts of information. However, this assumption is incorrect; the relation between amount of information and quality of prediction is often an inversely U-shaped curve (Gigerenzer et al. 1999). One reason for this is that part of the information we have today does not generalize to tomorrow; by ignoring information, heuristics can lead to better predictions than can strategies that use all relevant information. Specifically, when uncertainty is high, one needs to ignore part of the information to make *robust* predictions (see below). The important distinction here is between *data fitting* and *prediction*. To fit the parameters of a model to a body of data that is already known is called data fitting; here and in other situations where one simply explains what has already happened, more information (and more free parameters) is almost always better. To test whether a model with fixed parameters can predict future or unknown events is called prediction. In an uncertain world that is not perfectly predictable, the belief that more information is always better is no longer true. For instance, based on the limited knowledge of semi-ignorant people, the recognition heuristic (Goldstein and Gigerenzer 2002) predicted the outcomes of the Wimbledon tennis matches more accurately than the "official"predictions based on the ATP world rank lists and the seedings of the Wimbledon experts did (Frings and Serwe, submitted). The Tit-for-Tat heuristic, which only keeps a memory of length one, has repeatedly made more money than have strategies using more information and computation. As for every strategy, its success depends on the structure of the environment (the rules of the institution and the strategies of the other players). Experts base judgments on surprisingly few pieces of information (Shanteau 1992), and professional golfers and handball players tend to make better decisions when they have less time (Beilock et al. 2002; Johnson and Raab 2003). Less information, time, and knowledge can be more.

Why are these misunderstandings entrenched in the literature? For one, heuristics are evaluated against divine ideals, which makes them appear to be all-too-human failures. I refer to three ideals: *omniscience, optimization,* and *universality*. Omniscience is the ideal of full knowledge, which is often (at least approximately) assumed in theories of human rationality; its modest sister is the ideal that more information is always better, or cannot hurt. Optimization is the ideal that a best solution for each problem exists and that we know how to find it. Universality is the ideal that this best strategy, such as maximizing expected utility, is universally the same for all problems. Heuristics run counter to these ideals, in that they assume limited knowledge rather than omniscience. Their goal is to find a good solution without the fiction of an optimal one. There is no universal heuristic, but an *adaptive toolbox* with many building blocks from which new heuristics can be constructed.

WHAT IS BOUNDED RATIONALITY?

Paradoxically, three distinct and partially contradicting interpretations of bounded rationality exist. Proponents of law and economics tend to think of bounded rationality as *optimization under constraints*, such as information costs. Here, the omniscience of unbounded rationality is no longer assumed, but the assumption is made that people stop search when the marginal benefits of search equal its costs. The result is "a research program to build models populated by agents who behave like working economists or econometricians" (Sargent 1993, p. 22). In personal conversation, Herbert Simon once remarked with a mixture of humor and anger that he had considered suing those authors who misuse this term of bounded rationality to construct ever more psychologically unrealistic theories (Gigerenzer 2004). Optimization under constraints is silent about the heuristics people use. Proponents of behavioral law and economics tend instead to think of bounded rationality as the study of *cognitive illusions*. These two interpretations are like fire and water: the first emphasizes rationality, the second irrationality. Jolls et al. (1998, p. 1477) wrote, "Bounded rationality, an idea first introduced by Herbert Simon, refers to the obvious fact that human cognitive abilities are not infinite. We have limited computational skills and seriously flawed memories." This second interpretation provides a role for heuristics, but mainly as a problem. Simon's bounded rationality is neither the study of optimization under constraints nor a supplement of mental biases added to rational choice theory. Although the cognitive illusions program seems to be the very opposite of the optimization program, both essentially share the same norms. These (mostly logical norms) are used to define human judgment as an error.

There is a third view of bounded rationality—one that Simon actually put forward (Simon 1956, 1990) upon which others have elaborated (e.g., Gigerenzer et al. 1999; Gigerenzer and Selten 2001; Payne et al. 1993). This interactive view concerns the adaptation of mind and environment. Simon's (1990) ecological conception is best illustrated by his analogy between bounded rationality and a pair of scissors: "Human rational behavior is shaped by a scissors whose blades are the structure of task environments and the computational capabilities of the actor" (p. 7). Just as one cannot understand how scissors cut by looking only at one blade, one cannot understand human behavior by studying cognition or the environment alone. As a consequence, what looks like irrational behavior from a logical point of view can often be understood as intelligent behavior from an ecological point of view (e.g., as a response to a social environment or a legal institution).[3] Furthermore, many remaining true errors can be eliminated by

---

[3] For instance, the argument for paternalism (or for anti-anti-paternalism, in Sunstein's terms) is based, in part, on pointing out logical errors in ordinary people's reasoning. The problem with this argument is that any discrepancy between human judgment and the laws of logic is taken as indicating human irrationality, rather than the limits of logic, or an inappropriate normative use

improving the environment rather than people's minds. Consider, for instance, the well-documented problem: many judges, jurors, and law students are confused when they hear the conditional probabilities in a murder trial with DNA evidence (Koehler 1997). Classical decision theory would advise these legal actors to take a course in Bayesian statistics—the problem and its solution are assumed to be internal; that is, people's cognitive virtues need to be improved. There is, however, a much faster and more efficient external solution: to present the evidence in natural frequencies rather than conditional probabilities. For instance, only 10% of professional lawyers understood the implications of DNA evidence when it was presented in the form of conditional probabilities. This number increased to about 70% with natural frequencies, and guilty verdicts decreased (Hoffrage et al. 2000; Lindsey et al. 2003).

I refer to this third interpretation of bounded rationality as the *science of heuristics.* It has three goals:

1. *Adaptive toolbox.* What are the heuristics and their building blocks in the adaptive toolbox?
2. *Ecological rationality.* In which environments (institutions) will a given heuristic succeed or fail; that is, when is it ecologically rational?
3. *Design.* How can heuristics be designed for given problems (environments), and how can environments be designed to improve human problem solving?

The first question is descriptive, the second normative, and the third concerns human engineering. In my view, the rationality of a heuristic is external or "ecological" (i.e., how well a heuristic performs in a real-world environment) and not internal. External criteria include predictive accuracy, frugality, speed, and transparency. For instance, bail decisions aim to predict the trustworthiness of defendants accurately; frugality is at issue when one asks whether a court should admit all of the 112 defense witnesses, or whether 12 jurors are better than 0; speed is reflected in the doctrine that "only swift justice is good justice" (Dittrich et al. 1998); and transparency is a goal for those who aim at fewer and simpler tax laws, with the hope of increasing public trust and compliance (Epstein 1995). The internal criteria of rational choice theory, such as transitivity,

---

of logic. Sunstein (2005), for illustration, presents Tversky and Kahneman's (1983) Linda problem and calls people's modal response "an obvious mistake, a conjunction error." The issue, however, is far from obvious; there is disagreement whether the fallacy is in people's minds or rather in the researchers' logical norm. Logicians and philosophers such as Hintikka (2004) argue that the problem is in the proposed norm rather than in the human mind, as do linguists and psychologists (e.g., Hilton 1995; Moldoveanu and Langer 2002; Sweetser 1990). Hertwig and Gigerenzer (1999) argue that the majority response arises from social intelligence (which helps to infer what the English terms *probable* and *and* mean in a given pragmatic context) and show how to make the "conjunction fallacy" largely or completely disappear. Apparent "logical errors" that most likely reflect social intelligence (unnoticed by social scientists) are not good arguments for paternalism.

consistency, and additivity of probabilities, are important insofar as they contribute to improving the external criteria.

The science of heuristics has its origins in the work of Nobel laureates Herbert Simon and Reinhard Selten. Early work on heuristics in decision making focused on preferences, not inferences, that is, on problems where no external criterion of success exists (Payne et al. 1993; Tversky 1972). Therefore, the ecological rationality of a heuristic—the conditions in which a heuristic does and does not work—could not be systematically studied. Rather, internal criteria such as dominance or a linear weighting and adding strategy were used as an a priori gold standard and, compared to these standards, heuristics were by definition always second best. Only after studying real-world situations with external criteria for accuracy was it discovered that heuristics were in fact often more accurate than the "normative" weighting and adding strategy (e.g., Czerlinski et al. 1999; Dawes 1979). An introduction to specific models of heuristics and their ecological rationality can be found in Gigerenzer et al. (1999) and Gigerenzer and Selten (2001). Explicit reference to bounded rationality is relatively new in the law. For instance, Engel (1994) reported that he did not know of any German administrative lawyer who had ever referred to bounded rationality. I will now introduce heuristic problem solving with three situations where optimal strategies are unknown.

IF OPTIMIZATION IS IMPOSSIBLE, HOW DO PEOPLE MAKE DECISIONS?

Coronary Care Unit Decisions

A patient with severe chest pains is rushed to the emergency department in a hospital. The physicians need to make a decision, and quickly: Should the patient be assigned to the coronary care unit or to a regular nursing bed with ECG telemetry? In two Michigan hospitals, emergency physicians sent 90% of all patients to the care unit. This "defensive" decision making led to overcrowding, decrease in quality of care, and greater health risks for the patient. Researchers from the University of Michigan were called in to teach the physicians how to use the Heart Disease Predictive Instrument, an expert system (Green and Mehr 1997). This consists of a chart with some 50 probabilities and a logistic formula with which the physician, aided by a pocket calculator, can compute the probability of requiring the coronary care unit for each patient. If the probability is higher than a certain value, then the patient is sent to the care unit, otherwise not. A quick glance at the chart makes it clear why the physicians are not happy using this and similar systems. To them, the calculations are nontransparent; they do not understand the system, as it does not conform to their intuitive thinking, and hence they avoid using it.

The researchers tried a third procedure: a heuristic that has the structure of physicians' intuitions, but is based on empirical evidence. This *fast and frugal*

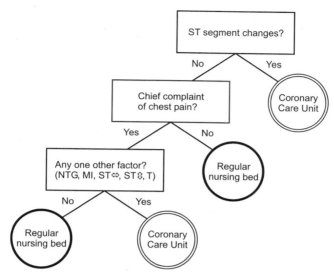

Figure 2.1 A fast and frugal decision tree for coronary care unit allocation (adapted from Green and Mehr 1997).

tree (Figure 2.1) poses only a few yes/no questions. If a patient has a certain anomaly in his electrocardiogram (the so-called ST segment), he is immediately admitted to the coronary care unit; no other information is required. If this is not the case, a second cue is considered: whether the patient's primary complaint was chest pain. If this is not the case, he is immediately assigned to a regular nursing bed. No further information is sought. If the answer is yes, then a third question is asked to classify the patient.

This heuristic violates the ideal of omniscience: It ignores all 50 probabilities, uses only one or a few predictors, and ignores the rest. It also does not combine (i.e., weight and add) the predictors. For instance, an anomaly in the ST segment cannot be compensated for by any of the other predictors. This noncompensatory heuristic allows the physician to stop search for information and make a decision after each question. It is quick, frugal, transparent, and easy to understand, so that physicians are willing to use it. But how accurate is it? Note that every diagnostic technique can make two kinds of errors, which are called *false alarms* (or Type-I errors) and *misses* (or Type-II errors)—a distinction courts rarely make when they talk about *the* rate of error (Faigman and Monahan 2005). Figure 2.2 shows the results of the study, with the false alarm rate on the abscissa and the complement of the miss rate on the ordinate. An ideal diagnostic procedure allocates all of those to the coronary care unit who should be there (who suffer an heart attack) and none of those who should not be there (who do not suffer an heart attack). Thus, the ideal strategy has a miss rate and a false alarm rate of zero, and is located in the upper left corner of Figure 2.2. Still, no perfect strategy is known; the problem of predicting infarctions is too difficult.

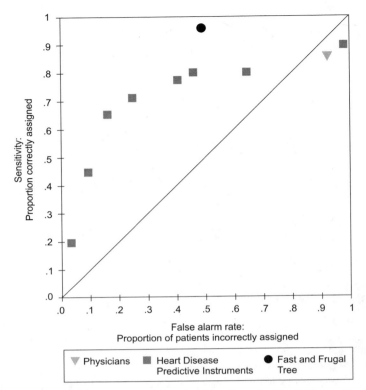

Figure 2.2 Coronary care unit decisions by physicians, the Heart Disease Predictive Instrument (a logistic regression), and the fast and frugal tree (adapted from Green and Mehr 1997). Accuracy is measured by the proportion of patients correctly assigned to the coronary care unit ("sensitivity" = "1 – miss rate"), and the proportion of patients incorrectly sent to the unit ("false alarm rate"). Correct assignment is measured by the occurrence of myocardial infarction. The diagonal represents chance performance.

How do the three methods used to make the coronary care unit decision compare in terms of accuracy? The average accuracy of physicians' intuitive decisions was slightly below (!) chance level (the diagonal). The Heart Disease Predictive Instrument is represented by a series of points; its accuracy was substantially better than chance. The reason why there is more than one point is that one can adjust the criteria, which represent various trade-offs between the two possible errors. The fast and frugal tree was more accurate in classifying actual heart attack patients than were the expert system and physicians. Note that the expert system contained all of the information that the heuristic had, as well as more. Simplicity can pay off.

Yet how can less information be better than more? The study of the ecological rationality of the heuristic specifies the conditions in which this is the case, and in which it is not. Several conditions are known and have been formalized

(Martignon and Hoffrage 1999, 2002; Katsikopoulos and Martignon 2006). Here I summarize two of these. In data fitting, a fast and frugal tree that ignores information will be as accurate as a logistic regression that uses all available information if the weights of the cues are heavily skewed (e.g., regression weights such as 1, 1/2, 1/4, 1/8, ...). If there is substantial unpredictability involved (and heart attacks are highly unpredictable, as Figure 2.2 illustrates), the heuristic is likely to be more accurate than the logistic regression because its simplicity tends to make it more robust. In other words, to make good decisions under high uncertainty, one needs to ignore part of the relevant information.

Do physicians who rely on the heuristic and ignore information run the danger of being sued for malpractice? For illustration purposes, consider a patient who showed no ST segment change and whose primary complaint was not chest pain. Relying on the coronary care heuristic, he was sent to a regular bed. Two days later, he died from heart disease. His relatives sued the hospital for malpractice after they found out that the doctors only checked two variables and ignored all others. Does the hospital have a chance of winning? Time pressure, coronary care unit space, and cost-benefit calculations might count. The answer depends, however, on the standard court practice, which varies across countries. Still, two elements are commonly found: reliance on formal rules of consent and on the state-of-the-art treatment (Engel 2000). Note, however, that the state-of-the-art treatment, at least in the two Michigan hospitals, was the intuitive, holistic decision making by physicians. Its accuracy, which does not seem to have been tested before, was only at chance level (Figure 2.2). Intuitive decisions, whose rationale is not made transparent to the public, and which physicians themselves may not be aware of, seem to protect primarily the physician, not the patient.

Medical malpractice suits are often assumed to increase the costs of negligence and therewith the amount of care that physicians take. However, as the present case illustrates, the threat of malpractice can also backfire and lead to defensive decision making, which decreases the quality of care. In addition, it seems to produce a medical "split brain." In personal conversation, many physicians have told me that they use only a few cues to make a diagnosis or treatment allocation, and are unsure about the accuracy of this procedure. In public, however, they claim to have processed all information and found the optimal treatment (Gigerenzer 2002). The physicians at the two Michigan hospitals, for instance, seem to have relied on the wrong ("pseudodiagnostic") cues, according to the dismal quality of their intuitive decisions (Green and Yates 1995). Once physicians' intuitive heuristics are made public and tested, one can progress to the next step of improving these by better, empirically informed heuristics.

The potentials of fast and frugal heuristics are currently being discussed in medicine. According to Naylor (2001, p. 523), they can lead to "understanding the cognitive processes of those master clinicians who consistently make superb decisions without obvious recourse to the canon of evidence-based medicine." Good experts ignore more information than do novices, but the defensive character of much of present-day health care is an institutional straightjacket that hinders young physicians from learning the art of heuristics.

Due Process

One of the initial decisions of the legal system is whether to bail the defendant unconditionally or to react punitively by bailing with conditions such as curfew or imprisonment. In the English system, magistrates are responsible for making this decision. About 99.9% of English magistrates are members of the local community without legal training. The system is based on the ideal that local justice be served by local people. In England and Wales, magistrates make decisions on some two million defendants every year. They sit in court for half a day every one or two weeks and make bail decisions as a bench of two or three. The law says that magistrates should heed the nature and seriousness of the offense; the character, community ties, and bail record of the defendant; as well as the strength of the prosecution case; the likely sentence if convicted; and any other factor that appears to be relevant.[4] Yet the law is silent on how magistrates should weigh and integrate these pieces of information, and the legal institutions do not provide feedback as to whether their decisions were in fact appropriate or not. The magistrates are left to their own intuitions.

How do magistrates actually make these millions of decisions? To answer this question, several hundreds of trials were observed in two London courts over a 4-month period (Dhami 2003). The average time a bench spent with each case was between 6 and 10 minutes. The analysis of the actual bail decisions revealed a fast and frugal heuristic that fitted 95% of all bail decisions in Court A (predictive accuracy = 92%; Figure 2.3, left). When the prosecution requested conditional bail, the magistrates also made a punitive decision. If not, or if no information was available, a second reason then came into play. If a previous court had already imposed conditions or remand in custody, then the magistrates also made a punitive decision. If not, or if no information was available, they followed the action of the police.

The magistrates in Court B used a heuristic with the same structure, except that one of the reasons differed (Figure 2.3, right). The first two reasons had the same "pass-the-buck" rationale as those in Court A. Both heuristics had the same structure as the coronary care unit heuristic: a *fast and frugal tree* (see below).

The self-presentation of the magistrates in interviews or questionnaires, however, was strikingly different. When magistrates were asked how they made bail decisions, they generally responded that they thoroughly examined all the evidence in order to treat individuals fairly and without bias. For instance, one explained that the situation "depends on an enormous weight of balancing information, together with our experience and training" (Dhami and Ayton 2001,

---

4 The Bail Act 1976 and its subsequent revisions; see Dhami and Ayton (2001).

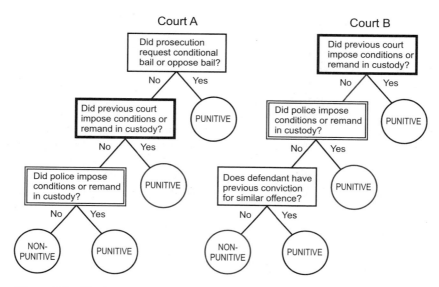

Figure 2.3 The heuristics underlying magistrates' bail decisions in two London courts. The heuristics predict about 92% of 342 actual bail decisions. Adapted from Dhami (2003).

p. 163). Another said that "the decisions of magistrates are indeed complex, each case is an 'individual case' " (Dhami 2001, p. 255). Contrary to the magistrates' self-perception, their heuristic seemed to involve no complex weighing and balancing of pros and cons.

These heuristics raise two issues: *due process* and *defensive decision making*. Both bail heuristics violate the ideal of due process, according to which the number of innocent defendants who are treated punitively—the false alarm rate—should be minimized. However, each bench based a punitive decision on just one reason, such as whether the police had imposed conditions or imprisonment. One could argue that relying on the police or a previous court might be a "short-cut" toward due process and, as we know from the coronary care study, a fast and frugal process need not be less accurate than a due process. However, in the present case, these "short-cut" reasons were not even correlated with the nature and seriousness of the offense. Moreover, nobody knows the accuracy of the bail decisions, because the British institutions seem to collect no information about their quality. Note that like physicians, magistrates can make two kinds of errors: *misses* and *false alarms*: They can bail a person who subsequently does not appear in court, threatens a witness, or commits another crime (a miss), or imprison a person who would not have committed a crime if he or she had been bailed (a false alarm). Even if statistics were kept about the number of misses, no information about false alarms would be available. One cannot find out whether an imprisoned person would have committed a crime if he or she had been bailed. That is, the magistrates operate in an institution in which only one of the two possible errors can be determined (unlike in the clinical institution of the care unit, where both can be measured; see Figure 2.2), but no data for errors is collected. In such an institution, it is difficult to learn how to solve the problem of protecting defendants. But magistrates can solve a different problem, namely of protecting themselves by "passing the buck."

The magistrates' situation shows that the design of institutions can transform the problem that the agents try to solve. Institutions that foster the self-protection of their professionals over the protection of their clients are prone to support forms of self-deception. If magistrates were fully aware of their heuristics, they would come into conflict with the ideal of due process. Thus, the bail heuristics are a solution, but not necessarily to the problem the magistrates are supposed to solve.

Discrimination

In 1985, the Equal Employment Opportunity Commission brought suit against a small Chicago company that offered cleaning and janitorial services. The firm, whose annual sales were only $400,000, went through seven years of federal litigation at outrageous expense for a company of that size.[5] The owner was a Korean immigrant, as were most of its employees. The suit charged that the firm discriminated in favor of persons of Korean origin. For instance, in the first quarter of 1987, 73% of applicants and 81% of those hired were Korean, whereas less than 1% of the national work force and at most 3% of the janitorial and cleaner work force were Korean. This statistical disparity provided the evidence against the firm.

The company owner had previously advertised in Chicago newspapers to hire workers, but these attempts were unsuccessful. The owner then switched to a more frugal method of recruitment, *word of mouth*: *Hire persons whom your employees recommend*.

This heuristic is the cheapest one and seems ecologically rational in the environment of the Korean immigrant community. Employees can inform an applicant more openly and accurately about the job than a newspaper advertisement or an employment agency can, which results in a higher probability of a good match. Furthermore, an employee who recommends someone may get into trouble if the new employee is a dud, so the employer can assume that employees screen new applicants conscientiously. Applying this heuristic in an environment of Korean immigrants provides these benefits without spending a cent, but has the consequence that those hired are mostly Korean. Members of these communities tend to socialize and work with each other rather than with people in

---

5   *Equal Employment Opportunity Commission v. Consolidated Service Systems.* United States Court of Appeals for the Seventh Circuit; 989 F.2d 233; 1993 U.S. App. LEXIS 4102; 61 Fair Empl. Prac. Cas. (BNA) 327; 61 Empl. Prac. Dec. (CCH) P42, 086.

the larger community. Note that this heuristic, like every heuristic, would not work equally well in any environment.

The Seventh United States Court of Appeals affirmed an earlier decision of a district judge that this word of mouth policy was not discrimination, or certainly not intentional discrimination. It was the cheapest and most effective way to recruit.

THE SCIENCE OF HEURISTICS

If people cannot optimize—as in treatment allocation, bail decisions, hiring, and many other real-world situations—how do they make decisions? We say that people rely on routines, habits, intuition, and rules of thumb. The science of heuristics explicates these routines and intuitions, and the resulting models of heuristics provide answers to the normative question as to in what environment a heuristic is successful and where it fails. Consider the decision between coronary care unit and a nursing bed. The optimal solution to this treatment allocation problem is not known, because there are more than 50 valid predictors, and a complete decision tree would have more than 2^{50} branches if the predictors were binary. The exponential increase makes optimization computationally intractable; moreover, there is never sufficient data for all branches. This is why nonoptimizing, yet sophisticated methods, such as logistic regression (the Heart Disease Predictive Instrument), were used. Assume that the instrument was very good (recall that we cannot know whether it was optimal) for the six New England hospitals where it was developed. This alone, however, does not tell us how well it performed in the Michigan hospitals. The patient sample in the Michigan hospitals differs in unknown ways from that in New England, and we have no reason to believe that both samples are random samples from the same population. Even if they were, one has to face the problem of robustness, that is, the limited robustness (generalizability) of a strategy validated in one random sample to another one. The method to improve robustness is to simplify the strategy. In the world of hospitals and patients, where samples come from different populations rather than the same ones, the problem of robustness is further amplified. The solution is the same: to simplify even more. This is exactly what the coronary care unit heuristic does.

The British magistrates' task is similar to that of the emergency physician: There are numerous predictors for the trustworthiness of a defendant, and the optimal solution is unknown. However, it is also more difficult because, as mentioned, the legal institutions do not provide feedback whether or not the magistrates' decisions were correct, and there seems to be no feedback possible for false alarms. Unlike physicians, who could collect data for both error rates (although this is typically not done), the magistrates have no systematic opportunity to learn.

Note the similarity between the care unit heuristic and the bail heuristics. This kind of heuristic is called a *fast and frugal tree* (Katsikopoulos and

Martignon 2006). For n cues (predictors), a complete tree has 2^n branches, whereas a fast and frugal tree has only $n + 1$ branches. This simple decision tree enables a decision to be made after each cue. The cue value that allows for an immediate decision is called a positive value. For three cues, the general structure of a fast and frugal tree consists of three building blocks:

- *Search rule:* Look up top cue.
- *Stopping rule:* Stop search if cue value is positive. Otherwise go back to search rule and look up next cue.
- *Decision rule:* Choose the action that the positive cue value specifies.

The structural properties of the simple trees reflect the motivation of their users. For instance, a tree that promotes professional self-defense (as opposed to diagnostic accuracy) has the same action associated with each cue. For instance, Court A's bail heuristic allows for a punitive action after each cue was looked up, but for bail only after the last cue; that is, after one is sure that none of the three relevant institutions has suggested otherwise. Similarly, a fast and frugal tree for physicians whose primary motivation is self-defense would have "care unit" at all branches, which would minimize the number of cases where physicians can expect to be sued, such as when a patient dies after being sent to a nursing bed. Thus, the same heuristic can be used in different types of problems, and its structural properties can tell us about the underlying motivation.

The Adaptive Toolbox

The contents of the adaptive toolbox are threefold: heuristics, building blocks, and abilities. The coronary care heuristic and the bail heuristics illustrate sequential search heuristics with three building blocks: a search rule (in what order to search cues), a stopping rule (when to stop search), and a decision rule (where to send the client). The two bail heuristics illustrate how slightly different heuristics can be built by changing one building block, in their case the search rule.

Heuristics can be very specific, but the building blocks are more general. I now illustrate how the same building blocks can apply to quite different problems, namely violations of expected utility (EU) theory. Consider Allais's paradox, where one has a choice between alternatives A and B:

A: 100 Million for sure. [*]
B: 500 Million with probability .98, otherwise nothing.

Most people choose A, which is indicated by the star in brackets. Now consider a second choice:

C: 100 Million with probability .01.
D: 500 Million with probability .0098. [*]

Because alternatives C and D are the same as A and B except that the probabilities were multiplied by a common factor of 1/100, EU theory implies that if A is chosen from {A, B} then C is chosen from {C, D}. However, most people now prefer D, which has been called a "paradox." The common reaction to this and other violations has been to retain the EU framework and to add repairs such as nonlinear functions for probabilities, as in prospect theory (there have also been other reactions, such as disregard, or the hope that markets will take care of these violations). In his Nobel acceptance speech, Reinhard Selten called this common reaction the "repair program." The science of heuristics offers a fresh alternative to the EU framework, not another repair. Consider the *priority heuristic*, which has the same sequential process as the coronary care heuristic and the bail heuristics. For positive prospects (all outcomes positive or zero), the heuristic consists of the following steps:

- *Priority rule*: Go through reasons in the order: minimum gain, probability of minimum gain, maximum gain.
- *Stopping rule*: Stop examination if the minimum gains differ by 1/10 (or more) of the maximum gain; otherwise, stop examination if probabilities differ by 1/10 (or more) of the probability scale.
- *Decision rule*: Choose the gamble with the more attractive gain (probability).

The term *attractive* refers to the gamble with the higher (minimum or maximum) gain and the lower probability of the minimum gain. This process is called the *priority heuristic* because it is motivated by first priorities, such as to avoid ending up with the worst of the two minimum outcomes (Brandstätter et al. 2006). EU theory makes conditional predictions of the type "if *A* is chosen over *B*, then it follows that *C* is chosen over *D*." The priority heuristic, in contrast, makes stronger predictions: It predicts whether *A* or *B* is chosen, and whether *C* or *D* is chosen. Consider the choice between *A* and *B*. The maximum payoff is 500 million, and therefore the aspiration level is 50 million; 100 million and 0 represent the minimum gains of the choice problem. Because the difference (100 million) exceeds the aspiration level of 50 million, the minimum gain of 100 million is considered good enough and people are predicted to select gamble *A*. In fact, the heuristic predicts the majority choice correctly.

In the second choice problem, the minimum gains (0 and 0) do not differ. Hence, the probabilities of the minimum gains are attended to, $p = .01$ and .0098, a difference that does not reach the aspiration level. Thus, the higher maximum gain (500 million vs. 100 million) decides choice, and the prediction is that people will select gamble *D*. Again, this prediction is consistent with the choice of the majority. Together, the two predictions amount to Allais's paradox.

The priority heuristic captures the Allais paradox by assuming the principles of order, a stopping rule with a 1/10 aspiration level, and one-reason decision making. For negative prospects, the heuristic is identical except that "gain" is replaced by "loss." The priority heuristic is based on the sequential structure of the Take The Best heuristic (Gigerenzer and Goldstein 1996) combined with aspiration levels (Simon 1990). The aspiration level is not arbitrary; it reflects one order of magnitude in our cultural base-10 system. Unlike cumulative prospect theory, the heuristic does not introduce five adjustable parameters for decision weights and utilities to improve its fit. Yet despite its simplicity, the priority heuristic predicts many deviations of human judgment from EU theory. Consider Rachlinski's (1996) copyright litigation problem:

- *The plaintiff can either accept a $200,000 settlement [*] or face a trial with a 0.5 probability of winning $400,000, otherwise nothing.*
- *The defendant can either pay a $200,000 settlement to the plaintiff, or face a trial with a 0.5 probability of losing $400,000, otherwise nothing [*].*

The stars in brackets indicate which alternative the majority of law students chose, depending on whether they were in the role of the plaintiff or the defendant. Note that the choices of the two groups were diametrical, creating conflict. What does the priority heuristic predict? Plaintiffs who use the priority heuristic first consider the minimum gains, which are $200,000 and $0. This difference is larger than the aspiration level (1/10 of the maximum gain); therefore search is stopped, and all other pieces of information are ignored. The decision is to take the more attractive minimum gain, that is, the settlement. Defendants who use the priority heuristic consider first the minimum losses, which are $200,000 and $0, the difference of which again is larger than the aspiration level. Search is stopped, and the alternative with the more attractive minimum loss is chosen, that is, to opt for trial. In both cases, the heuristic predicts what the majority of participants in Rachlinski's (1996) study chose.

Now consider Guthrie's (2003) frivolous litigation case, where the probabilities of winning are low:

- *The plaintiff can either accept a $50 settlement or face a trial with a .01 probability of winning $5,000, otherwise nothing [*].*
- *The defendant can either pay a $50 settlement to the plaintiff [*], or face a trial with a .01 probability of paying $5,000, otherwise nothing.*

Plaintiffs who use the priority heuristic consider first the minimum gains, which are $50 and $0, a difference that does not exceed the aspiration level ($500). They then turn to the probabilities of the minimum gains, which are 1.0 and 0.99, a difference that again does not exceed the aspiration level (1/10). Thus, the maximum gain decides, and the plaintiff goes for the trial. In the same way, one can deduce that the defendant will not opt for the trial but rather for the settlement. In both cases, the heuristic predicts the response of the majority of the law students as reported by Guthrie (2003). Note that the response of the students in the copyright litigation problem is consistent with the idea that people are risk averse with gains but risk seeking with losses, whereas in the frivolous litigation case, this pattern reverses.

This simple heuristic predicts a wide range of behavior inconsistent with EU theory, including (a) risk aversion for gains if probabilities are high, (b) risk seeking for gains if probabilities are low (e.g., lottery tickets), (c) risk aversion for losses if probabilities are low (e.g., buying insurance), (d) risk seeking for losses if probabilities are high, (e) the certainty effect, (f) the possibility effect, and (g) intransitivities in choice. Thus, sequential search heuristics can predict phenomena that cumulative prospect theory can also predict, as well as many others that prospect theory cannot, such as conditions in which hindsight bias does and does not occur (Hoffrage et al. 2000); how long people search for information; when they ignore information; and how classifications of objects, estimations of quantities, and other inferences with limited time and knowledge are made (Gigerenzer et al. 1999; Gigerenzer and Selten 2001). On the other hand, prospect theory is likely to predict phenomena that fast and frugal heuristics cannot; the overlap and the differences between these two frameworks have not yet been sufficiently analyzed.

Does the simple priority heuristic or the computationally complex modifications of EU theory better predict people's actual choices? Or do they all perform similarly well? The first direct contest (Brandstätter et al. 2006) involved the predictions of the empirical results in 260 choice tasks (four sets, taken from Kahneman and Tversky 1979; Tversky and Kahneman 1992; Lopes and Oden 1999; I. Erev et al., unpublished). Note that three of the four test sets were constructed by proponents of EU modification theories; the fourth was a random sample. The heuristic used only about half of the information that the EU modifications used (Brandstätter et al. 2006). The priority heuristic predicted people's choices most accurately (87%), compared to Tversky and Kahneman's (1992) cumulative prospect theory (77%), Lopes and Oden's (1999) security-potential/aspiration theory (79%), and Birnbaum and Chavez's (1997) transfer of attention exchange model (67%).

Thus, models of fast and frugal heuristics can predict not only people's inferences, but also their preferences. These models are simple and transparent. One can see the conditions in which they fail to predict people's choices, which is difficult for highly parameterized modifications of EU theory. For instance, the priority heuristic has its limits when the expected values of two gambles are highly discrepant, which is when the choice becomes trivial.

Environmental Structures and Institutions

Heuristics do not simply develop in the mind but are equally the product of its past and present environments. Human institutions, not geological or meteorological conditions, are the most important environmental structures for the law. These environmental structures include the signal-to-noise ratio, that is, what proportion of the information transmission in an institution is reliable rather than irrelevant; the framing of information, that is, whether information is transmitted in a confusing form (e.g., expert witnesses often present DNA evidence in "random match probabilities," which tend to confuse jurors and judges) or in a transparent form (such as natural frequencies; see Gigerenzer 2002); the goals of other agents; and the rules of the institution.

For instance, consider the coronary care unit decisions. Emergency physicians make these life-and-death decisions in institutions that tend to punish misses (not sending a patient into the care unit who should be there) substantially more heavily than false alarms (sending patients to the care unit who should not be there). If the patient dies as a consequence of a miss, the physician is likely to be sued for malpractice; if the patient dies as a consequence of being sent to the care unit (because he picked up one of the dangerous viruses that circulate in care units, or the unit was overcrowded because the physicians sent too many patients there), the physician is unlikely to be sued. Such an institution invites defensive decision making; physicians first protect themselves rather than their patients. Not all institutions are designed in that way. One counterexample is commercial aviation, where if the passenger dies in a crash, the pilot will usually die as well. In the patient–physician relationship, however, the risks are decoupled. Furthermore, aviation keeps records of "near misses" whereas in medical institutions, there is no system of reporting errors without punishing the individual physician, and little systematic feedback about the quality of physicians' decisions in the first place. These are some of the environmental structures responsible for the disturbing fact that in U.S. hospitals, an estimated 44,000 to 98,000 patients die every year from (recorded) preventable medical errors, whereas in 2004, only about 500 people died in commercial aviation worldwide. The study of the environmental structure is essential for understanding what heuristics people use: heuristics are "selected" by institutions.

Ecological Rationality

Consider the dots on the left-hand side of Figure 2.4. They appear concave, that is, they recede into the surface, away from the observer. The dots on the right side, however, appear convex—they project up from the surface, extending toward the observer. When you turn the page upside down, the concave dots will turn into convex dots, and vice versa. Why do we see the dots this way or the other?

The answer is that our brain does not have sufficient information to know for certain what is out there, but it is not paralyzed by uncertainty. It makes a good bet, based on the structure of its environment, or what it assumes is its structure. The brain assumes a three-dimensional world and uses the shaded parts of the dots to guess in what direction of the third dimension they extend. The relevant environmental regularity is that light comes from above. This was true in human

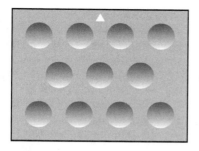 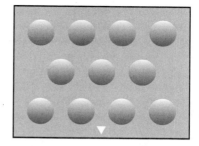

Figure 2.4 Unconscious inferences. The mind infers that the dots in the left picture are curved inward, that is, away from the observer, and those on the right picture are curved outwards, that is, toward the observer. If you turn the book around, the inward dots will pop out and vice versa. The right picture is identical to the left rotated by 180 degrees.

history where sun and moon were the major sources of light, and still holds true for most artificial light that is typically placed above us, such as streetlamps (although there are exceptions, such as car lights). The perceptual heuristic adapted to this regularity is:

> *If the shade is in the upper part, then the dots are concave; if the shade is in the lower part, then the dots are convex.*

For instance, the dots in the right-hand picture are shaded in the lower part. Thus, the brain's unconscious inference is that the dots extend toward the observer because then the light would hit the upper part, which looks bright, and less light would hit the lower part. The heuristic process is not conscious and has been called an unconscious inference (Helmholtz 1856–1866/1962). The heuristic is ecologically rational in three-dimensional environments where light comes from above, but not in other environments such as the two-dimensional pictures in Figure 2.4.

Heuristics for decision making "bet" on environments in a similar way to perceptual heuristics, but are more flexible and can be modified by feedback. The study of the ecological rationality of a heuristic answers the question as to in which environments the heuristic will be successful. It examines the institutions that make heuristic bets correct.

Consider now a fast and frugal tree, as in the coronary care heuristic or in the bail heuristic. These trees base their decision on one reason alone, although they may search through a few. When is one reason as good as many reasons? We know of several structures, including the following condition for data fitting (Martignon and Hoffrage 1999, 2002): Consider a situation with five binary cues, as in Figure 2.5, where the weights correspond to the order of the cues in a fast and frugal tree.

Figure 2.5 (left) shows an environmental structure in which one reason is as good as five (or more). Here, a fast and frugal tree is as accurate as any linear

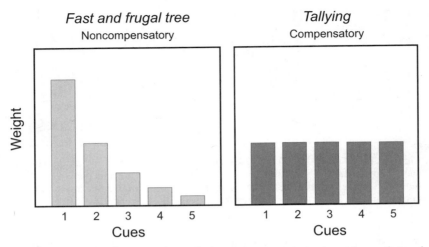

Figure 2.5 Ecological rationality. Left: An environmental structure where a fast and frugal tree (as in the coronary care heuristic or in the bail heuristic) is as accurate as any linear (weighting and adding) combination of all cues. The weights of the cues are 1, 1/2, 1/4, and so on. In other words, one reason is as good as many. Right: An environmental structure where a tallying heuristic (which discards information about weights and treats all cues equal) is as accurate as any linear weighted strategy. Here, cues have equal weights.

(weighting and adding) combination of all cues, including a logistic regression. One can see this result intuitively: The sum of all cue weights to the right of a cue can never be larger than this cue's weight—they cannot compensate for the cues with higher weights. This type of environment is structured by *noncompensatory information*. Here, relying on one reason and ignoring the rest is as accurate as integrating all reasons by any linear strategy. If there is also uncertainty, as is typical in the real world, the heuristic will likely be more *robust* and will have higher predictive accuracy. One example was shown in Figure 2.2, where one-reason decision making led to more accurate predictions (for more demonstrations, see Czerlinski et al. 1999). The term *robustness* refers to the predictive accuracy of a strategy in new situations. In general, the greater the uncertainty is, the more robust simple strategies are compared to ones with a higher greed for information.

Figure 2.5 (right) shows an environmental structure in which cues have equal weights. Here, a fast and frugal tree will not be as accurate. Yet a simple tallying heuristic (which discards information about weights and simply counts positive cues) can be shown to be as accurate as any linear weighted strategy (Martignon and Hoffrage 2002). In summary, a heuristic exploits evolved and learned abilities, which make it simple, and structures of environments, which make it ecologically rational.

INSTITUTIONS SHAPE HEURISTICS

Let us call an institution an *intelligent institution* if it makes all heuristics (that apply to a given problem) ecologically rational. Do such institutions exist? They do. One example is the double auction. Major stock, commodity, currency, and many other markets are organized as double auctions. Here, buyers and sellers can freely enter limit orders (bids or asks) and accept bid requests entered by others. The crucial feature of this institution imposes a budget constraint on the trader: generating a bid (buying) above the redemption value or offering (selling) below their cost is not allowed. This protects the trader from buying or selling at a loss and not being able to settle their accounts. The market discipline imposed by its rules allows "zero intelligence" machine traders, who make random bids or offers, to perform as well as human traders do (Gode and Sunder 1993). In such a market, the choice of heuristic is no problem. In general, lawmakers are among those who decide how much intelligence is in the institution and how much in individuals. For instance, one can decrease fatal traffic accidents in two ways. One is to create safe environments or institutions—more traffic signs, enforced rules, and future car technology such as automatic safety distance control, which reduces the drivers' decisions to a minimum and enables relatively bad drivers to drive safely. The other way is to improve drivers' skills and morals. In the first case, the task-specific intelligence is shifted toward the institution, whereas in the second it is directed toward the individual.

Institutions enable and constrain heuristics, including the extreme case of the double auction described above, where institutions generate a "flat maximum" in which most or all heuristics can flourish. Typically, institutions are not "intelligent enough" to substitute for the intelligence of people, that is, to allow totally ignorant people to succeed equally well as informed ones, but they do pose some constraints. For instance, when the information structure is (approximately) noncompensatory, as shown in Figure 2.5, these institutions support basing a decision on one reason only and ignoring the rest.

A second type of institution supports what I call *split-brain agents*. These agents use a fast and frugal heuristic for decision making yet believe, or want to believe, that they make decisions following the ideals of complete information and optimization. The English bail system and the magistrates are a case in point. The magistrates seem to be largely unaware of the heuristic processes they follow. As mentioned before, when interviewed on what cues they use, they reported the cues explicitly referred to in the Bail Act 1976 (Dhami 2001). None of the magistrates in the two London courts referred to the cues on which their heuristics were actually based. Moreover, in a study with hypothetical cases, magistrates requested additional information about the case and consistently asked for information that was not part of the heuristic process, but compatible with the Bail Act. I have no reason to assume that the magistrates would knowingly waste time discussing information that will have no effect on their decisions, or deceive the interviewers. Rather, the institution of the English bail system seems to support split-brain bail decisions. The Bail Act demands attention to certain cues, so the magistrates tend to ask for these cues, spend considerable time discussing them with the other members of a bench, and believe that they have incorporated them into their decisions. In the end, however, they base their decisions on cues that protect themselves, by passing the buck.

When an institution separates the professional's risk from that of the client, and thus supports the emergence of split-brain agents, heuristic procedures are likely to emerge that protect the professional first, and the client only second. Sending 90% of the clients into the coronary care room is an example. The result is a form of protective malpractice that is tolerated by legal practice.

HEURISTICS SHAPE INSTITUTIONS

Institutions shape heuristics, but the causal arrow also points in the other direction. The heuristics in the adaptive toolbox can shape institutions. Heuristics that build on the capacities of trust and cooperation—such as word-of-mouth and Tit-for-Tat—enable institutions to be designed that do not permanently check its members, but can operate more efficiently by assuming loyalty. Heuristics can constrain the effects of legislation, and knowing the heuristics can give clues as to whether a new legislation will be effective or not. Consider the debate on bail information schemes, which gather and provide information on a defendant's community ties to the court (Dhami 2002). The argument in favor of these schemes assumes that magistrates attend to information concerning community ties. However, the magistrates' heuristics (Figure 2.3) reveal that this information plays no role in their bail decisions. Hence, if magistrates use these or similar heuristics, one can expect that legislating new bail information schemes will have no effect. Consistent with that prediction, an experiment with magistrates showed that introducing the schemes indeed had no effect on the bail decisions (Dhami 2002). The general point is that being aware of the heuristics used can help to design appropriate modifications of institutions and to avoid those that will not produce the desired consequences.

HEURISTICS AND THE LAW

Jurors, judges, and John Q. Public have to make decisions with limited time and knowledge, and under degrees of uncertainty where optimization is typically out of reach. Most politicians do not have the time to read the full text of the law they are going to vote on—many go by word of mouth, party line, or what their peers vote. Many lawyers and law professors appear to not always read the form contracts they sign (Prentice 2003). Physicians simply cannot know the side effects of some 100,000 medications on the market, nor can medical research ever hope to determine the interactions of each pair of medications. A common solution is to reduce the complexity and uncertainty to a minimum that allows optimization, and then assume that the solution in the ideal world also holds in the complex and messy world. But there is no guarantee. As the statistician John Tukey (1966) pointed out, what is optimal under ideal conditions is often dismal in a world that is less than perfect, and heuristics that fare badly in the utopian world can be highly efficient in the real world. The solution is, in my view, to start with the messy one and aim for realistic and good solutions.

The goal of the science of heuristics is to improve our understanding of the heuristics that people use, when these work, and how to improve them. These heuristics operate at different levels, in laypeople and lawyers, offenders and police officers, and in the making as well as execution of the law. Simple heuristics' attributes include transparency and predictability, two potentially important criteria by which people subject to the legal system determine the fairness of a decision. This heuristics program can inform and enrich behavioral law and economics, which began with a negative view of human rationality. The result will be a more balanced view, in which heuristics are seen both as solutions and as problems. Most important, the theoretical framework helps to organize a patchwork of experimental effects, and we are able to go beyond the phrase "heuristics are sometimes good and sometimes bad" by specifying the structures of environments, including the institutions in which heuristics are ecologically rational or not. The science of heuristics can provide the foundations of an integrative theory that explains how human behavior depends on its institutions.

REFERENCES

Beilock, S.L., T.H. Carr, C. MacMahon, and J.L. Starkes. 2002. When paying attention becomes counterproductive: Impact of divided versus skill-focused attention on novice and experienced performance of sensorimotor skills. *J. Exp. Psychol. Appl.* **8**: 6–16.

Birnbaum, M., and A. Chavez. 1997. Tests of theories of decision making: Violations of branch independence and distribution independence. *Org. Behav. Hum. Dec. Proc.* **71**:161–194.

Bookstaber, R., and J. Langsam. 1985. On the optimality of coarse behavior rules. *J. Theor. Biol.* **116**:161–193.

Brandstätter, E., G. Gigerenzer, and R. Hertwig. 2006. The priority heuristic: Making choices without trade-offs. *Psychol. Rev.*, in press.

Czerlinski, J., G. Gigerenzer, and D.G. Goldstein. 1999. How good are simple heuristics? In: Simple Heuristics That Make Us Smart, G. Gigerenzer, P.M. Todd, and the ABC Research Group, pp. 97–118. New York: Oxford Univ. Press.

Dawes, R.M. 1979. The robust beauty of improper linear models in decision making. *Am. Psychol.* **34**:571–582.

Dhami, M.K. 2001. Bailing and Jailing the Fast and Frugal Way: An Application of Social Judgment Theory and Simple Heuristics to English Magistrates' Remand Decisions. Ph.D. diss., City University, London.

Dhami, M.K. 2002. Do bail information schemes really affect bail decisions? *Howard J.* **41**:245–262.

Dhami, M.K. 2003. Psychological models of professional decision making. *Psychol. Sci.* **14**:175–180.

Dhami, M.K., and P. Ayton. 2001. Bailing and jailing the fast and frugal way. *J. Behav. Dec. Mak.* **14**:141–168.

Dittrich, J., J. Gruhl, and R. Hepp. 1998. Ermittlungsverfahren wegen Insolvenzdelikten: Möglichkeiten der Beschleunigung von Ermittlungen [Preliminary inquiries into bankruptcy offences: Means of speeding up inquiries]. *Kriminalistik* **11**:713–716.

Elman, J. 1993. Learning and development in neural networks: The importance of starting small. *Cognition* **48**:71–99.

Engel, C. 1994. Legal responses to bounded rationality in German administration. *J. Instit. Theor. Econ.* **150**:145–162.

Engel, C. 2000. Psychological research on heuristics meets the law [Review of the book Simple Heuristics That Make Us Smart by G. Gigerenzer et al.]. *Behav. Brain Sci.* **23**:747.

Epstein, R.A. 1995. Simple Rules for a Complex World. Cambridge, MA: Harvard Univ. Press.

Faigman, D.L., and J. Monahan. 2005. Psychological evidence at the dawn of the law's scientific age. *Ann. Rev. Psychol.* **56**:631–659.

Gigerenzer, G. 2000. Adaptive Thinking: Rationality in the Real World. New York: Oxford Univ. Press.

Gigerenzer, G. 2002. Calculated Risks: How to Know When Numbers Deceive You. New York: Simon and Schuster. (U.K. edition: Reckoning with Risk, Penguin).

Gigerenzer, G. 2004. Striking a blow for sanity in theories of rationality. In: Models of a Man: Essays in Memory of Herbert A. Simon, ed. M. Augier and J.G. March, pp. 389–409. Cambridge, MA: MIT Press.

Gigerenzer, G., and D.G. Goldstein. 1996. Reasoning the fast and frugal way: Models of bounded rationality. *Psychol. Rev.* **103**:650–669.

Gigerenzer, G., and R. Selten, eds. 2001. Bounded Rationality: The Adaptive Toolbox. Dahlem Workshop Report 84. Cambridge, MA: MIT Press.

Gigerenzer, G., P.M. Todd, and the ABC Research Group. 1999. Simple Heuristics That Make Us Smart. New York: Oxford Univ. Press.

Gode, D.K., and S. Sunder. 1993. Allocative efficiency of markets with zero-intelligence traders: Market as a partial substitute for individual rationality. *J. Pol. Econ.* **101**:119–137.

Goldstein, D.G., and G. Gigerenzer. 2002. Models of ecological rationality: The recognition heuristic. *Psychol. Rev.* **109**:75–90.

Green, L.A., and D.R. Mehr. 1997. What alters physicians' decisions to admit to the coronary care unit? *J. Fam. Pract.* **45**:219–226.

Green, L.A., and J.F. Yates. 1995. Influence of pseudodiagnostic information on the evaluation of ischemic heart disease. *Ann. Emerg. Med.* **25**:451–457.

Guthrie, C. 2003. Prospect theory, risk preferences, and the law. *Northwestern Univ. Law Rev.* **97**:1115–1163.

Hammerstein, P. 2003. Why is reciprocity so rare in social animals? A protestant appeal. In: Genetic and Cultural Evolution of Cooperation, ed. P. Hammerstein, pp. 83–93. Dahlem Workshop Report 90. Cambridge, MA: MIT Press.

Helmholtz, H. von. 1962. Treatise on Psychological Optics, trans. J.P.C. Southall. New York: Dover. (orig. publ. 1856/1866).

Hertwig, R., and G. Gigerenzer. 1999. The "conjunction fallacy" revisited: How intelligent inferences look like reasoning errors. *J. Behav. Dec. Mak.* **12**:275–305.

Hertwig, R., and P.M. Todd. 2003. More is not always better: The benefits of cognitive limits. In: Reasoning and Decision Making: A Handbook, ed. D. Hardman and L. Macchi, pp. 213–231. Chichester: Wiley.

Hilton, D.J. 1995. The social context of reasoning: Conversational inference and rational judgment. *Psychol. Bull.* **118**:248–271.

Hintikka, J. 2004. A fallacious fallacy? *Synthese* **140**:25–35.

Hoffrage, U., R. Hertwig, and G. Gigerenzer. 2000. Hindsight bias: A by-product of knowledge updating? *J. Exp. Psychol.: Learn. Mem. Cog.* **26**:566–581.

Johnson, J.G., and M. Raab. 2003. Take the first: Option generation and resulting choices. *Org. Behav. Hum. Dec. Proc.* **91**:215–229.

Jolls, C., C.R. Sunstein, and R. Thaler. 1998. A behavioral approach to law and economics. *Stanford Law Rev.* **50**:1471–1550.

Kahneman, D., and A. Tversky. 1979. Prospect theory: An analysis of decision under risk. *Econometrica* **47**:263–291.

Kareev, Y. 2000. Seven (indeed, plus or minus two) and the detection of correlations. *Psychol. Rev.* **107**:397–402.

Katsikopoulos, K., and L. Martignon. 2006. Naive heuristics for paired comparisons: Some results on their relative accuracy. *J. Math. Psychol.*, in press.

Koehler, J.J. 1997. One in millions, billions, and trillions: Lessons from *People vs. Collins* (1968) for *People vs. Simpson* (1995). *J. Legal Educ.* **47**:214–223.

Korobkin, R. 2003. Bounded rationality, standard form contracts, and unconscionability. *Univ. Chicago Law Rev.* **70**:1203–1295.

Kuran, T., and C.R. Sunstein. 2000. Controlling availability cascades. In: Behavioral Law and Economics, ed. C.R. Sunstein, pp. 374–397. New York: Cambridge Univ. Press.

Lindsey, S., R. Hertwig, and G. Gigerenzer. 2003. Communicating statistical DNA evidence. *Jurimetrics* **43**:147–163.

Lopes, L.L., and G.C. Oden. 1999. The role of aspiration level in risky choice: A comparison of cumulative prospect theory and SP/A Theory. *J. Math. Psychol.* **43**:286–313.

Luria, A.R. 1968. The Mind of a Mnemonist. Cambridge, MA: Harvard Univ. Press.

Martignon, L., and U. Hoffrage. 1999. Why does one-reason decision making work? A case study in ecological rationality. In: Simple Heuristics That Make Us Smart, G. Gigerenzer, P.M. Todd, and the ABC Research Group, pp. 119–140. New York: Oxford Univ. Press.

Martignon, L., and U. Hoffrage. 2002. Fast, frugal and fit: Lexicographic heuristics for paired comparison. *Theor. Dec.* **52**:29–71.

Moldoveanu, M., and E. Langer. 2002. False memories of the future: A critique of the applications of probabilistic reasoning to the study of cognitive processes. *Psychol. Rev.* **109**:358–375.

Naylor, C.D. 2001. Clinical decision: From art to science and back again. *Lancet* **358**:523–524.

Noll, R.G., and J.E. Krier. 2000. Some implications of cognitive psychology for risk regulation. In: Behavioral Law and Economics, ed. C.R. Sunstein, pp. 325–354. Cambridge: Cambridge Univ. Press.

Payne, J.W., J.R. Bettman, and E.J. Johnson. 1993. The Adaptive Decision Maker. Cambridge: Cambridge Univ. Press.

Prentice, R. 2003. Contract-based defenses in securities fraud litigation: A behavioral analysis. *Univ. of Illinois Law Rev.* **2003**:337–422.

Rachlinski, J.J. 1996. Gains, losses, and the psychology of litigation. *S. Calif. Law Rev.* **70**:113–185.

Sargent, T.J. 1993. Bounded Rationality in Macroeconomics. New York: Oxford Univ. Press.

Schwartz, B., A. Ward, J. Monterosso et al. 2002. Maximizing versus satisficing: Happiness is a matter of choice. *J. Pers. Soc. Psychol.* **83**:1178–1197.

Sedlmeier, P., R. Hertwig, and G. Gigerenzer. 1998. Are judgments of the positional frequencies of letters systematical biased due to availability? *J. Exp. Psychol.: Learn. Mem. Cog.* **24**:754–770.

Shanteau, J. 1992. How much information does an expert use? Is it relevant? *Acta Psychologica* **81**:75–86.

Simon, H.A. 1956. Rational choice and the structure of environments. *Psychol. Rev.* **63**:129–138.

Simon, H.A. 1990. Invariants of human behavior. *Ann. Rev. Psychol.* **41**:1–19.

Sunstein, C.R., ed. 2000. Behavioral Law and Economics. Cambridge: Cambridge Univ. Press.

Sunstein, C.R. 2005. Moral heuristics. *Behav. Brain Sci.* **28**:531–542.

Sweetser, E.E. 1990. From Etymology to Pragmatics: Metaphorical and Cultural Aspects of Semantic Structure. Cambridge: Cambridge Univ. Press.

Tukey, J.W. 1966. A practicing statistician looks at the transactions. *IEEE Trans. Inf. Th.* **12**:87–91.

Tversky, A. 1972. Elimination by aspects: A theory of choice. *Psychol. Rev.* **79**:281–299.

Tversky, A., and D. Kahneman. 1982. Availability. In: Judgment under Uncertainty: Heuristics and Biases, ed. D. Kahneman, P. Slovic, and A. Tversky, pp. 163–178. Cambridge: Cambridge Univ. Press.

Tversky, A., and D. Kahneman. 1983. Extensional versus intuitive reasoning: The conjunction fallacy in probability judgment. *Psychol. Rev.* **90**:293–315.

Tversky, A., and D. Kahneman. 1992. Advances in prospect theory: Cumulative representation of uncertainty. *J. Risk Uncert.* **5**:297–323.

3

The Problems with Heuristics for Law

Russell Korobkin

UCLA School of Law, University of California,
Los Angeles, CA 90095–1476, U.S.A.

ABSTRACT

A large body of evidence, now familiar to the legal community, demonstrates that individual judgment and choice is often driven by heuristic-based reasoning as opposed to the pure optimization approach presumed by rational choice theory. This evidence presents several challenges for consequentialist legal scholars who wish to make normative public policy recommendations. First, the fact that actors subject to the legal system often rely on heuristics suggests that their behavior will not always maximize their subjective expected utility, undermining the traditional assumptions of law and economics scholarship that private contracts are necessarily Pareto efficient and that legal "taxes" and "subsidies" can cause actors to behave in a way that maximizes social efficiency. Second, the fact that the decision makers who create law also rely on heuristics suggests that law will not necessarily maximize either the collective good or the utility of favored groups, and that law that attempts to create incentives for certain behaviors might not be properly calibrated to its goal.

This chapter describes these two problems that heuristics cause for law and recommends four approaches that lawmakers should consider to mitigate the problems: developing context-specific legal rules when possible; creating "heuristic-savvy" legal institutions; manipulating heuristics; and implementing a context-sensitive "cautious paternalism."

INTRODUCTION

Most consequentialist legal theory, exemplified by but not limited to scholarship self-consciously in the law and economics tradition, rests on a positive prediction and a normative commitment. The positive prediction is that legal rules provide a nontrivial behavioral incentive for those subject to them. The normative commitment is that providing behavioral incentives is law's most important (although not necessarily its only) function.

From a consequentialist perspective, a legal rule might have one of three substantive goals: (a) to facilitate private ordering such that actors may maximize their utility subject to external constraints (such as the distribution of initial resources); (b) to provide private incentives for behavior that will maximize social welfare or the welfare of a particular targeted group (by encouraging or discouraging certain actions); or (c) to improve social welfare or the welfare of a targeted group directly (such as by allocating regulatory or budgetary resources or through direct wealth transfers). Consider the following simple examples of legal rules that further each of these goals: Contract law's commitment to enforce private agreements that are not tainted by fraud or duress encourages private parties to enter into Pareto efficient transactions. The tort law of negligence encourages actors to take the efficient amount of care when conducting business and engaging in personal activities, and regulatory limits on pollution attempt to protect citizens' health. Regulations that ban the production of certain pollutants are intended to improve environmental quality, based on either a determination that these benefits outweigh any negative consequences to economic growth or a preference for the victims of pollution over the industries that create it.

Consequentialist approaches to lawmaking require, at least implicitly, assumptions about how actors subject to law will respond to the incentives that the law creates. Traditionally, most legal scholars have relied on one of several versions of rational choice theory (RCT). All versions of RCT assume that actors will process information, make choices, and execute behaviors in a way calculated to maximize their expected utility; that is, to maximize the differential between expected benefits and expected costs.[1] "Thick" versions of RCT assume that actors will act to maximize specified ends, such as their narrow self-interest or material well-being, while "thin" versions of RCT are agnostic about the substantive content of actors' ends (Korobkin and Ulen 2000).

The assumptions of RCT hardly reduce lawmaking to a trivial task, but they do simplify it to some degree. RCT enables legal decision makers to pursue the above-mentioned normative goals of consequentialist legal theory with a quasi-laissez-faire approach. To be sure, the state has a broad, regulatory role: to guarantee property rights, address market failures, force the internalization of negative externalities, and solve collective action problems. Importantly, however, lawmakers can act secure in the "knowledge" that actors' marginal choices will always advance the cause of utility maximization.

It is now widely acknowledged that research in the field of judgment and decision making has severely undermined this assumption. The RCT assumption requires actors to infer facts about the world by applying principles of deductive logic to all known, relevant information. When those actors make decisions and take actions, they must conduct a thorough cost-benefit analysis that makes use of all relevant factual information and a complete ordering of preferences. In reality, individuals more often rely on simpler, heuristic reasoning to make both

---

[1] Scholars differ in the extent to which they assume that acquiring relevant information is itself a costly activity that must be factored into the equation. Most legal scholars implicitly assume that evaluating and processing available information is not costly.

judgments about the world and decisions of how to act within that world. People deal with difficult questions (i.e., which tactic is most dangerous?) by substituting answers to easier questions (i.e., which tactic most easily brings to mind an example of a harmful outcome?), and they resolve difficult decisions (i.e., which tactic will maximize benefits minus costs?) by making easier choices (i.e., which option has the greatest positive affective valence?).

Heuristic reasoning is clearly adaptive, because it makes normal life possible. If all judgments and decisions were made only after considering all relevant data, attaching subjective preference weights to all possible outcomes, and creating probability predictions of each outcome, none of us could complete the myriad cognitive tasks we face each day. Counterintuitively, in an environment where the most accurate judgment or best choice depends on some unknown factors, a heuristic that is particularly well suited to that environment has the potential to yield judgments or choices that are as accurate as *or even more accurate than* approaches that analyze all available information according to principles of deductive logic. This is because regression models can suffer from the problem of "overfitting" when they use existing information to make judgments about new issues if, as is often the case, the new issues are not identical to the old (Gigerenzer et al. 1999).

Notwithstanding its global rationality and its potential to yield optimal results in certain circumstances, heuristic reasoning is extremely problematic for law for two related reasons. First, heuristic reasoning often will cause actors subject to the legal system to make suboptimal judgments and choices because the actors over- or underweight information concerning facts in the world or their subjective preferences relative to that information's probative value. Reliance on a heuristic implies neglect of at least some potentially relevant information, and if the heuristic is not precisely suited to the relevant problem, the decision-making process will yield suboptimal outcomes.[2] An individual assessing the likelihood of various consequences, should he choose course of action A, B, or C, who renders his estimates based on what possible consequences associated with each choice are more mentally accessible (the availability heuristic) or seem most stereotypical (the representativeness heuristic), or whose estimations are skewed because available "anchor" values or excessive confidence affect the potential outcomes that are mentally accessed, often will fail to maximize his expected utility. The same is true of an individual who has clear understanding of each option's expected consequences but chooses between the options without factoring into the decision equation all of that information.

---

[2] Although evolutionary theory suggests that heuristic-based reasoning must be adaptive (although not necessarily optimal), there is no reason to assume a priori that the heuristic mechanisms that developed in the era of evolutionary adaptation are necessarily particularly well suited to the different and more complex problems humans face in modern economic, social, and political life.

These observations render suspect the normative underpinnings of liberal legal regimes that assume private contracting will facilitate a near-Pareto optimal allocation of resources and entitlements. The possible failure of actors to maximize their individual utility also raises concerns that lawmakers' efforts to use law to provide incentives for individuals to take particular actions (e.g., exercise due care, refrain from stealing) will either fail to achieve their desired purpose or will accomplish their purpose with less than optimal efficiency.

Second, just as actors subject to the legal system rely on heuristics, so to do lawmakers. This creates a first-order problem when lawmakers attempt to make decisions for the collective that maximize social utility (or the utility of a particular protected class), because lawmakers' decisions might not be optimal given available information. It creates a second-order problem when lawmakers try to establish or apply legal rules in a way that will create optimal incentives for the citizenry given the lawmakers' policy goals.

In this chapter I describe and illustrate these problems for law that result from heuristic reasoning and then consider how law might best attempt to manage these problems. A general familiarity with the social science research in the "heuristics-and-biases" tradition (Kahneman et al. 1982) is assumed, as space does not permit a detailed summary of that literature here.

HEURISTICS AND THE GOVERNED

Relying on the premise of the Coase theorem that private trade efficiently allocates legal entitlements (given the constraint of the preexisting distribution of resources) in the absence of transaction costs, consequentialist legal theorists believe that private law's predominate goal should be to minimize barriers to private contracting and then rely on the market's "invisible hand." Heuristic reasoning undermines this policy prescription because individual market choices often fail to maximize individual utility. Actors often fail to anticipate correctly the factual consequences of market choices or to account accurately for those consequences when making market decisions. The problem will often be particularly severe because other market participants have profit incentives to exploit actors' reliance on heuristic reasoning.

Inefficiencies in Private Contracting

Law and economics scholars infer from the fact that private contracts are voluntary that any exchange is Pareto efficient: trade increases the welfare of each party. By extension, trade increases social welfare, assuming no negative third-party externalities. To support such welfare-enhancing transactions, the law need only to provide remedies for breach of contract that encourage contractual reliance (such as enforcing liquidated damages provisions or, in their absence, requiring breaching parties to pay "expectation damages") and, in some cases reduce information asymmetries that can serve as a barrier to trade (such as requiring sellers of potentially dangerous products to provide warning information).

Heuristic reasoning requires a reevaluation of this conventional wisdom. If goods usually perform as advertised, use of the availability heuristic could cause purchasers to underestimate the risk of product failure or bodily harm. Egocentric biases could cause even those purchasers who accurately estimate the risk of product failure to underestimate the likelihood that they, as opposed to someone else, will suffer as a result. Related confirmatory biases could lead purchasers initially attracted to a product to overestimate its benefits while underestimating its drawbacks (Rachlinski 2003). Of course, these potential risks exist in all markets, not just those for the sale of goods. Employees who must contract concerning the level of job protection they will receive might misestimate their risk of being fired or the risk of their employer becoming insolvent relative to the true *ex ante* probability of these events occurring. Borrowers might misestimate the likelihood that they will default on their loans or the likelihood of success of their investment projects. Couples entering into marriage, with its associated legal rights and responsibilities, might misestimate their likelihood of getting divorced. Litigants might misestimate their chances of prevailing through adjudication if they refuse to settle out of court. Potential contracting parties might misestimate the likelihood that they or their partner will breach. These examples suggest that the law should not be so sanguine in its assumption that an exchange is Pareto efficient merely because it is voluntary.

Even if private actors accurately estimate the risks of contracting behavior, they still might enter into suboptimal contracts if they use selective or noncompensatory strategies for making market decisions. For example, a buyer who chooses which of several cars to purchase either by using a one-reason decision-making approach, such as "choose the car with the best gas mileage," or by comparing the affective valence of the options, might find that he has purchased a car with suboptimal financing terms and inefficient restrictions on legal remedies should a dispute arise. Depending on the cumulative significance of these inefficient product features, the transaction as a whole might fail the test of Pareto efficiency, or it might create a Pareto improvement for the two parties but produce less utility for both than an alternative agreement could have.

The risk that heuristic reasoning will lead to nonoptimal private transactions is rendered substantial, rather than merely possible, by the fact that market pressures will often force market participants to attempt to exploit others' use of heuristics for their benefit. Hanson and Kysar (1999) have argued that buyers are likely to underestimate the risks of bodily harm caused by dangerous products because the manufacturers of those products have a profit incentive to exploit heuristics that would have this effect. Those authors contend, for example, that sellers attempt to provide a favorable initial impression of the safety of their product, exploit confirmatory biases by presenting further evidence that does not unambiguously contradict the initial impression, exploit self-serving biases by emphasizing the ability of buyers to prevent harmful accidents, and exploit the power of availability and insufficiency of adjustments made to initial anchors by packaging the product attractively and depicting it as safe repeatedly through advertising. Sellers that fail to manipulate buyers' judgments in these ways will find themselves and/or their products displaced by sellers that do.

I have argued elsewhere that market pressures, combined with a population of buyers who rely on heuristic-based reasoning when making purchase decisions, create the conditions for inefficiently low quality product attributes (Korobkin 2003a). Consider, for example, the trend in the United States for sellers of goods and services to include mandatory arbitration clauses in their standard form contracts. Under standard rational choice assumptions, such clauses are unobjectionable to consequentialists because they can survive only if their benefit to sellers outweighs their cost to buyers; otherwise, buyers would demand contracts without such clauses, and competition would guarantee that sellers that continued to require them would lose customers. To conserve cognitive effort, however, most buyers choose between competing products by selectively comparing a limited number of product attributes (Payne et al. 1993). If the contract's dispute resolution provision is not one of the few salient product attributes for many buyers, there will be no market pressure on sellers to include an efficient term. More perniciously, if price is a salient product attribute, sellers will include dispute resolution terms that reduce their costs of doing business, and thereby allow them to compete more effectively on price; this is true even if the value lost to buyers is considerably greater than the value gained by sellers. The consequence is that increasing ubiquity of arbitration provisions in private contracts does not suggest that arbitration agreements necessarily increase overall social welfare or result in transactions that create more net utility for buyers as a class *ex ante*, the conclusions that are implied by the assumptions of RCT.

Heuristic reasoning means not only that some private transactions will be suboptimal, but also that individuals will often fail to enter into Pareto-efficient exchanges, even when transaction costs (as the term is traditionally understood) are low. Substantial evidence suggests that individuals place greater value on entitlements if they possess them than if they do not and, more broadly, that they tend to prefer a state of affairs more if it they identify it as the status quo than if they identify it as an alternative to the status quo (Korobkin 2003b). Arguably, the "endowment effect" or the "status quo bias" reflects a felt preference for the status quo over change, all other things being equal. Even so, this marginal preference almost certainly translates into a heuristic of avoiding change that causes actors to decline proposed transactions that would, in fact, increase their expected utility. When heuristic reasoning results in private actors declining profitable exchange opportunities, lawmakers who desire to maximize either social welfare or the welfare of particular groups arguably need to pay close attention to initial resource allocation decisions, whereas if private contracting behavior conformed to RCT such lawmakers would need concern themselves only with facilitating private transactions. Lawmakers must also consider the fact that "default" (as opposed to mandatory) legal rules (which, as opposed to mandatory rules, parties may contract around) have potential substantive effects on the allocation of legal entitlements, rather than merely effects on transaction costs, because actors might give them weight in excess of what their utility functions suggests that they should (Korobkin 1998).

Incentives to Socially Desirable Behavior

Even assuming, in accordance with RCT, that individuals consider all available information and process it with a demonic degree of deductive logic, encouraging Pareto-efficient private transactions obviously would not be lawmakers' sole objective. In addition to facilitating commerce in a content-neutral way, the law often attempts to incent private individuals to act in a particular substantive way, usually because such behavior is socially desirable but would not necessarily maximize the utility of the individual actor in the absence of such incentives. Heuristic reasoning is problematic for this class of laws as well, because the set of incentives that would be effective and/or cost-effective if individuals followed the precepts of RCT might be ineffective or inefficient when judgments and decisions are driven by heuristics.

Consider two types of problems, represented in turn by the tort law of negligence and the criminal law of murder. In the first situation, the law encourages individuals to conduct a social cost-benefit analysis of their potential actions in order to internalize risks their behavior creates for others. In the second situation, the law seeks to create an incentive significant enough to dissuade actors from the activity altogether.

In American tort law, an action is negligent and the actor liable to pay damages, as described by the well-known "Learned Hand formula," when the risk of resulting harm multiplied by the cost of harm to others exceeds the benefit of the action to the actor (*United States v. Carroll Towing* 1947). If the risk multiplied by the cost is less than the expected benefit, the action is not negligent and the actor is not liable for damages, even if the risk comes to pass. If all actors were to follow the dictates of RCT, this formula would maximize social welfare because individuals would always act when net social benefits were expected to exceed net social costs and would never act when the reverse were true. If actors reason heuristically, however, their cost-benefit estimates will often be skewed, and their resulting choices will often fail to satisfy the law's normative goals, either by leading them to engage in too many risky endeavors or too few.

Criminal law (or, at least, law concerning violent crimes for which lawmakers assume social costs will always or nearly always exceed social benefits[3]),

---

3   Economic theory suggests that when a crime can sometimes have greater social benefit than social cost, deterring every crime would be undesirable, even if this could be done cost-free. For most "traditional," violent crimes, however, the optimal amount of crime is zero, so the state can safely be assumed to desire 100% deterrence (Dana 2001). Even when complete deterrence is economically suboptimal, lawmakers might still desire it.

seeks to convince the actor to never engage in enumerated actions, such as murder. In a RCT world, actors would refrain from committing murder if the expected benefits of committing the crime were less than the expected cost of the punishment multiplied by the probability of being caught and convicted (Becker 1968). In this world, the law could most efficiently deter crime by taking steps to increase either the probability of catching and convicting murderers (e.g., by employing more police and prosecutors) or the severity of punishment (e.g., by lengthening criminal sentences), depending on whether police officers or jails are marginally cheaper. In a world in which actors rely on heuristics, however, the law must take more variables into account because it is not clear that increasing the probability of punishment and increasing the severity of punishment will have the same deterrent effect. Depending on whether arrest rates are low or high, well publicized or not, would-be criminals relying on the availability heuristic might overestimate or underestimate the probability of being arrested; if light sentences are common but executions and life sentences receive significant media attention, the same heuristic could cause the same would-be criminals to over- or underestimate the average penalty.

HEURISTICS AND THE GOVERNORS

Above, I contended that citizens' reliance on heuristics in judgment and decision-making tasks is problematic because this makes it more difficult to use law as a tool to promote welfare. In this section, I argue that lawmakers' reliance on heuristics is also problematic, for two reasons.

Collective Choices

While law attempts to facilitate and incent private choices, it also serves as a vehicle by which the citizenry makes collective choices. These choices can be reflected in both regulatory and budgetary decisions: expansive pollution regulation implicitly favors environmental protection over economic growth; substantial military spending implicitly favors national defense over other collective goods, such as public schools.

Consequentialist legal theory is normatively committed to the proposition that these choices should be made based on a comparison of costs and benefits—either to society as a whole (i.e., is economic growth more or less important than environmental preservation) or to a particular protected group (i.e., will looser control on pollution result in the creation of more jobs for the unemployed). It becomes quite difficult to fulfill these normative requirements, however, if legislators or regulators rely on heuristics that cause them to misestimate costs and benefits when evaluating the likely effects of options or to downplay or ignore certain of those costs and benefits when choosing between them.

Although largely a matter of conjecture, there is some cause for optimism that lawmakers might be less susceptible to judgment biases that result from heuristic-based reasoning than laypeople, both because evidence suggests that intelligence is negatively correlated with judgment biases and that training in statistics can reduce susceptibility to some judgment biases (Mitchell 2002). Normatively desirable collective choice can be undermined in a democratic society if citizens rely on heuristics, however, even if lawmakers do not. Legislators might choose to devote limited resources to risks and problems that receive the most publicity (availability) or seem the most gruesome (affect), if these risks seem most pressing to their heuristic-reliant constituents, even if the legislators themselves do not think that a dispassionate cost-benefit analysis indicates these risks are the most deserving of resources and would maximize actual social utility. After all, it is the citizens that ultimately judge the lawmakers' performance and decide whether or not to retain their services in the future.

Like the problem of individual behavior that fails to maximize expected utility, collective choices made by lawmakers that fail to maximize social utility are made more likely by the fact that groups that can profit from certain heuristics have an incentive to attempt to manipulate the judgments of lawmakers themselves or of the lay public that elects the lawmakers. Interested parties can and do conduct what Kuran and Sunstein (1999) call "availability campaigns" designed to publicize costs and risks that encourage the regulation of others and expenditures that inure to their benefit.

(In)efficient Incentives

Reliance on heuristics is problematic for law when lawmakers are called upon to make collective choices, just as when individuals must make individual choices under the shadow of the law. Both of these can be termed "first-order" problems caused by the fact that decision makers rely on heuristics. Heuristics can cause "second-order" problems for law as well when they impede the ability of lawmakers to create the legal rules that would provide the optimal incentives for individuals if the individuals behaved in strict accordance with RCT. In other words, not only might individuals fail to respond normatively to the incentives that the law provides, lawmakers might fail to provide the normatively optimal incentives.

Where the purpose of law is to create incentives for individuals to behave in a way that will maximize social welfare or the welfare of a group favored by lawmakers, heuristic reasoning can cause lawmakers to make suboptimal rules *ex ante* or apply standards *ex post* in a manner that creates suboptimal incentives. For example, the negligence standard, discussed earlier, can induce actors to avoid taking socially efficient actions if heuristic reasoning causes jurors to suffer from hindsight bias; that is, overestimate the *ex ante* risk associated with a particular action because the actual occurrence of that result makes it highly available (Kamin and Rachlinski 1995). Similarly, the inclination of actors to over-attribute unfortunate circumstances to dispositional rather than situational characteristics (i.e., the fundamental attribution error, Ross 1977) could result in the law providing incentives for actors to be overly cautious whenever an individual's liability depends on a jury's finding of a causal relationship between that individual's action and harm suffered by another (i.e., whenever liability turns on contested issues of "causation").

Recent evidence documents that judges, like laypeople, often rely on heuristic reasoning rather than deductive logic when reaching probability judgments (Guthrie et al. 2001). Heuristic reasoning can impair judges' ability to resolve cases such that the created body of precedent generates optimal *ex ante* incentives for the governed. Moreover, the process of legal reasoning taught to lawyers and employed regularly by common-law judges might promote use of the anchoring heuristic and its associated errors. Judges approach a dispute by (a) looking to how courts in their jurisdiction have resolved similar cases (precedent) and then (b) resolving the present case on the basis of how closely it resembles the precedential cases. To the extent that anchors activate arguments for why the current situation resembles the anchor, or that adjustments made from the basis of an anchor tend to understate the difference between the current situation and the anchor, judicial reasoning could lead to suboptimal case outcomes relative to the ideal.

COPING WITH HEURISTICS

I have discussed how the prevalence of heuristic-based reasoning creates significant problems for the creation and implementation of law, as compared to a world that operates in accordance with the strict deductive logic requirements of RCT. Now let us consider approaches that the law can take to minimize these problems and even, in some instances, harness heuristic reasoning to further the goals of consequentialist legal theory.

Context-specific Legal Rules

There is an enormous body of research demonstrating that outcomes of individual judgment and decision-making tasks often deviate from the assumptions of RCT, but that results vary depending on the content of cognitive tasks, the context of task presentation, and the identity of the subjects. Not all individuals rely on heuristics to the same degree; certain heuristics are more likely to be invoked in some contexts than in others, and some contexts suggest the use of more than one heuristic. This means that if law is to respond to the challenges that heuristic reasoning presents, lawmakers must tailor legal rules to nuanced contextual differences within markets, social life, and political life. Some restrictions on freedom of contract might be appropriate in certain situations but not others. Some methods of government decision making (legislative, administrative, or judicial) might be appropriate with regard to certain problems but not others. In some situations, increased substantive regulation might be called for, whereas information disclosure requirements might be sufficient in others—the parameters of which, of course, will depend on context.

This broad observation does not translate easily into a simple set of rules for lawmakers to follow. To date, social scientists have been unable to provide a detailed understanding of the mechanics of heuristic reasoning (Gigerenzer 1996) sufficient for lawmakers to predict, with a high degree of confidence, the specific contexts in which heuristic reasoning will deviate from the predictions of RCT in ways that will hinder the fulfillment of the law's substantive goals. The available research concerning *which* heuristics are employed *when*, remains a set of disparate empirical results, with each study serving as a small piece to a large puzzle with gaping holes.

Our limited understanding of heuristic reasoning suggests that lawmakers, with the help of scholars interested in legal policy, should, whenever possible, devise experimental and quasi-experimental studies of behavior, in particular contexts in which the law is interested. The results of such targeted studies can then serve as the basis for policy recommendations. Consider, for example, recent studies showing that similarly situated employees are far more likely to invest in an employer-sponsored tax-deferred 401K savings plan if they are required to opt out than if they are required to opt in (Madrian and Shea 2001). If lawmakers wish to encourage more private retirement savings, this study suggests they should require employers to make 401K programs the default rule for their employees.

In the absence of studies that replicate decision-making situations of interest to the law (which are often conceptually impossible or logistically impractical), tailoring legal rules to the reality of heuristic reasoning requires lawmakers and scholars to analogize from research results to law-relevant contexts. For example, lawmakers might analogize between studies that show individuals are relatively more likely to rely on simple heuristics when required to make decisions under time pressure and real-world situations in which merchants present consumers with detailed contract terms at the point of purchase. This analogy suggests that legal restrictions of the substance of contract terms are appropriate in this situation, although they might not be in different contracting situations.

Policy prescriptions rooted in such analogies will always be open to a range of criticisms. The external validity of the underlying studies can be questioned. The appropriateness of the analogy between the context studied and the real-world context to which the studies are compared can be challenged, especially on the ground that the laboratory can demonstrate the effect of one heuristic in a vacuum; in the real world, however, its impact might be undermined by a counteroperation of the heuristic in question or swamped by the operation of a different heuristic. Laboratory studies, by their very nature, require researchers to determine what information to provide subjects, whereas individuals who make judgments and choices in the real world have access to an enormous number of information sources and social influences. For example, individuals who tend to be overconfident concerning probabilistic judgments might take less than the efficient level of care under negligence law, because they underestimate the risk that their actions will cause harm, or more than the efficient level of care, because they overestimate the reduction in risk that their precautions will create (Posner 2005). An experiment might reveal both effects when subjects are prompted to consider explicitly both the risks of their actions and the benefits of possible precautions; however, such results would not address the critical issue of which of the two probability questions would command their attention in a particular real-world context. Finally, there is always the possibility that proposed policies might cause unanticipated second-order consequences that undermine the utility of the proposal.

As imperfect as it may be, consequentialist lawmakers have little choice but to employ this approach until our understanding of heuristic reasoning becomes more precise. The only plausible option is to assume individuals act in accordance with RCT—an approach resembling a drunk looking for his lost keys under a lamp post because that is where the light is best.

Heuristic-savvy Institutions

Many social scientists now subscribe to the theory that individuals have two parallel approaches to judgment and decision-making tasks: one automatically uses intuitive, heuristic reasoning to make judgments quickly and effortlessly; the other employs a more cumbersome, thorough, rule-oriented analysis rooted in deductive logic (Kahneman and Frederick 2002). While "System 1" reasoning is always at work, it is sometimes overruled by the more thorough (but also more effort-intensive) "System 2" reasoning (Stanovich and West 2000).

The normative goals of law might be served by creating institutions that promote System 2 reasoning by the governors and by the governed, at least in situations in which the expected marginal benefits of conducting a more thorough analysis exceed the expected marginal costs of doing so in terms of time and effort. For lawmakers, rules of administrative law that require regulators to conduct an explicit cost-benefit analysis of proposals and authorize judicial review of agency actions to ensure that they are based on rational deliberation might dampen the systematic biases that can result from heuristic reasoning. The rule of evidence prohibiting the introduction of "character evidence" in court might steer jurors away from reliance on the representativeness heuristic rather than charge-specific evidence when determining guilt in a criminal trial (Korobkin and Ulen 2000). Withholding information concerning the outcome of a defendant's action from jurors could prevent them from relying on hindsight in making negligence determinations (Arkes and Schipani 1995).

For individuals subject to the law, research suggests that actors can better evaluate the likelihood of events in some circumstances (the evidence is particularly compelling in the case of conditional probabilities) when statistical information is presented in terms of frequencies rather than probabilities (Gigerenzer 2002). This suggests that mandates requiring product warnings might be more effective in encouraging System 2 reasoning if they require presentation of data on potential harms in that format. "Waiting periods" that require a time lag between individual decisions and substantive actions and "cooling off" periods that permit the rescission of contracts for a reasonable period of time after their formation might increase the likelihood that individuals exercise System 2 reasoning rather than basing behavior on faster System 1 judgments (Camerer et al. 2003). Mandatory mediation might force litigants and their lawyers to confront weaknesses in their legal cases, reducing the force of self-serving biases in judgment tasks. When legal incentives designed to encourage System 2 reasoning seem like they would be either unlikely to succeed or not cost-justified, the government could encourage or subsidize independent consumer or trade organizations to make reasoned decision recommendations to individual actors.

Heuristic Manipulation

Just as market participants can use their knowledge of heuristic-based reasoning to increase their profits, lawmakers should consider how they can harness the power of heuristics to suit the law's ends. When the law attempts to encourage or discourage a particular behavior, lawmakers might attempt to manipulate behavior affirmatively by taking advantage of heuristic-based reasoning. Legal scholars routinely suggest that the government provide—or require private actors to provide—behavior-relevant information. The goal of this suggestion, however, is usually to facilitate comprehensive, deductive reasoning rather than heuristic reasoning. If the law seeks to discourage crime, the government might publicize the volume of petty criminals who are arrested (while downplaying the number who are not) and the lengthiest prison sentences that they receive (rather than the modal or average sentences), in an effort to maximize public perceptions of the probability of arrest and severity of sentences. When lawmakers believe that a particular policy choice will be socially beneficial, they might (and, of course, they routinely do) tout the proposal in a way calculated to harness heuristic reasoning, for example, by framing the policy as maintaining rather than changing the status quo ("this missile system will *keep* our military the finest in the world") (see Frey and Eichenberger 1994, p. 221), or by creating narratives with positive affective valence ("the legislation will ensure that our grandchildren will be able to enjoy pristine mountain lakes").

    Individuals can be manipulated through legal regulations that change the context of judgments and choices that they face, thus activating certain heuristics, as well as through the provision of information. For example, a regime might exploit the status quo bias to ensure greater compliance with the tax laws by withholding expected taxes from earnings and requiring citizens to apply for refunds, rather than by requiring citizens to pay their taxes at year's end. If lawmakers believe that a certain individual choice will have a mild negative externality that is not severe enough to justify prohibiting it, they can set the default rule against that choice to retard but not eliminate its election.

If affirmative attempts to manipulate seem inappropriate for government in democratic societies, a more palatable half-measure might be to ensure that law does not promote the use of heuristics in a way that creates undesirable social consequences. Local newscasts are replete with images that portray African-Americans as criminals, potentially skewing viewers' judgments about minorities in a way that increases unconscious racism (Kang 2005). The U.S. government essentially subsidizes those newscasts by counting local news as satisfying the public service requirements that broadcasters must meet to retain their rights to the airwaves. Perhaps eliminating what is effectively a public subsidy for such broadcasts would be a legal intervention that protects against the power of heuristic-based reasoning without exploiting it.

Cautious Paternalism

Heuristics, and the incentive created by markets to exploit them, suggest a more assertive role for law in directing or limiting the latitude of private behavior than does a consequentialist legal philosophy based on the behavioral assumptions of RCT. Because individuals have heterogeneous preferences and paternalistic regulations will allow some individuals to maximize their utility, while preventing others from doing so, heuristic reasoning suggests a cautious brand of paternalism that is wielded only in situations in which (a) heuristic-savvy institutions cannot effectively be employed to minimize the negative consequences of heuristic reasoning and (b) the large majority of individuals are likely to be led astray by heuristic reasoning. For example, heuristic reasoning might justify that the law mandate product features that are particularly likely to be misjudged (such as safety and reliability) by or be nonsalient (such as form contract terms) to most market participants, but not more functional product features that are likely to be misjudged by or nonsalient to some market participants but not others.

CONCLUSION

Like the economist stranded on a desert island who confronts the challenge posed by canned goods that wash ashore by "assuming" the existence of a can opener, consequentialist legal theorists often approach the complicated challenge of designing maximally beneficial laws by assuming that individuals behave in accordance with strict RCT assumptions. In both cases, the assumption made certainly renders the problem at hand more tractable, but the end result is unlikely to be very satisfying.

One alternative approach is to decide that because optimality in lawmaking is usually impossible lawmakers should not even embark upon its quest. The General Theory of Second Best teaches that we cannot be certain that an approach to lawmaking that aims for optimality but cannot fully achieve it will increase rather than decrease utility (Markovits 1998). Unfortunately, this disheartening observation provides lawmakers with no plausible alternative to pursuing consequentialist goals, however imperfectly, hoping that using the law to reduce barriers to utility maximization to the extent possible moves us closer to, rather than further from, that goal.

Heuristic reasoning is problematic for law because at best it makes policy analysis more complicated; at worst it raises questions for which social science does not (yet) have answers. These are problems that lawmakers have little choice but to confront as best they can with the information available to them.

ACKNOWLEDGMENTS

Helpful comments from Hal Arkes, Christoph Engel, Bruno Frey, Gerd Gigerenzer, Chris Guthrie, Eric Johnson, Rick Lempert, Stephan Magen, Heather Richardson, Tom Ulen, Elke Weber, Jane Yakowitz, and several anonymous participants in the Dahlem Workshop on *Heuristics and the Law* are gratefully acknowledged.

REFERENCES

Arkes, H.R., and C.A. Schipani. 1995. Medical malpractice v. the business judgment rule: Differences in hindsight bias. *Oregon Law Rev.* **73**:587–638.

Becker, G.S. 1968. Crime and punishment: An economic approach. *J. Pol. Econ.* **76**:169–217.

Camerer, C., S. Issacharoff, G. Loewenstein, T. O'Donoghue, and M. Rabin. 2003. Regulation for conservatives: Behavioral economics and the case for asymmetric paternalism. *Univ. Pennsyl. Law Rev.* **151**:1211, 1238–1247.

Dana, D.A. 2001. Rethinking the puzzle of escalating penalties for repeat offenders. *Yale Law J.* **110**:733–783.

Frey, B.S., and R. Eichenberger. 1994. Economic incentives transform psychological anomalies. *J. Econ. Behav. Org.* **23**:215–234.

Gigerenzer, G. 1996. On narrow norms and vague heuristics: A reply to Kahneman and Tversky (1996). *Psychol. Rev.* **103**:592–596.

Gigerenzer, G. 2002. Calculated Risks: How to Know When Numbers Deceive You. New York: Simon and Schuster. (U.K. edition: Reckoning with Risk, Penguin).

Gigerenzer, G., P. Todd, and the ABC Research Group. 1999. Simple Heuristics That Make Us Smart. New York: Oxford Univ. Press, chaps. 4–6.

Guthrie, C., J.J. Rachlinski, and A.J. Wistrich. 2001. Inside the judicial mind. *Cornell Law Rev.* **86**:777–830.

Hanson, J.D., and D.A. Kysar. 1999. Taking behavioralism seriously: The problem of market manipulation.*New York Univ. Law Rev.* **74**:630, 724–733.

Kahneman, D., and S. Frederick. 2002. Representativeness revisited: Attribute substitution in intuitive judgment. In: Heuristics and Biases: The Psychology of Intuitive Judgment, ed. T. Gilovich, D. Griffin, and D. Kahneman, pp. 49–81. Cambridge: Cambridge Univ. Press.

Kahneman, D., P. Slovic, and A. Tversky, eds. 1982. Judgment under Uncertainty: Heuristics and Biases. Cambridge: Cambridge Univ. Press.

Kamin, K., and J. Rachlinski. 1995. *Ex post = ex ante*: Determining liability in hindsight. *Law Hum. Behav.* **19**:89–104.

Kang, J. 2005. Trojan horses of race. *Harvard Law Rev.* **118**:1489–1593.

Korobkin, R. 1998. The status quo bias and contract default rules. *Cornell Law Rev.* **83**:608–687.

Korobkin, R. 2003a. Bounded rationality, standard form contracts, and unconscionability. *Univ. Chicago Law Rev.* **70**:1203, 1216–1244.

Korobkin, R. 2003b. The endowment effect and legal analysis. *Northwestern Univ. Law Rev.* **97**:1227, 1231–1242.

Korobkin, R., and T.S. Ulen. 2000. Law and behavioral science: Removing the rationality assumption from law and economics. *Calif. Law Rev.* **88**:1051, 1060–1070, 1086–1087.

Kuran, T., and C.R. Sunstein. 1999. Availability cascades and risk regulation. *Stanford Law Rev.* **51**:683, 712–768.

Madrian, B.C., and D.F. Shea. 2001. The power of suggestion: Inertia in 401(k) participation and savings behavior. *Qtly. J. Econ.* **116**:1149–1187.

Markovits, R. 1998. Second-best theory and law and economics: An introduction. *Chicago-Kent Law Rev.* **73**:3, 7.

Mitchell, G. 2002.Why law and economics' perfect rationality should not be traded for behavioral law and economics' equal incompetence. *Georgetown Law J.* **91**:67, 87–98.

Payne, J.W., J.R. Bettman, and E.J. Johnson. 1993. The Adaptive Decision Maker. Cambridge: Cambridge Univ. Press.

Posner, E. 2005. Probability errors: Some positive and normative implications for tort and contract law. In: The Law and Economics of Irrational Behavior, ed. F. Parisi and V. Smith, chap. 18. Palo Alto: Stanford Univ. Press.

Rachlinski, J. 2003. The uncertain psychological case for paternalism. *Northwestern Univ. Law Rev.* **97**:1165, 1178–1187.

Ross, L. 1977. The intuitive psychologist and his shortcomings: Distortions in the attribution process. *Adv. Exp. Soc. Psychol.* **10**:173–220.

Stanovich, K.E., and R.F. West. 2000. Individual differences in reasoning: Implications for the rationality debate? *Behav. Brain Sci.* **23**:645–665.

United States v. Carroll Towing, 159 F.2d 169 (2d Cir. 1947).

4

Social Dilemmas Revisited from a Heuristics Perspective

Christoph Engel

Max Planck Institute for Research on Collective Goods, 53113 Bonn, Germany[1]

ABSTRACT

The standard tool for analyzing social dilemmas is game theory. They are reconstructed as prisoner's dilemma games, which aids understanding of the incentive structure. Such analysis, however, is based on the classic *homo oeconomicus* assumptions. In many real-world dilemma situations, these assumptions are misleading. A case in point is the contribution of households to climate change. Decisions about using cars instead of public transport, or about extensive air-conditioning, are typically not based on ad hoc calculation. Rather, individuals rely on situational heuristics for the purpose. This chapter offers a model of heuristics, in the interest of making behavior that is guided by heuristics comparable to behavior based on rational reasoning. Based on this model, the chapter determines the implications for the definition of social dilemmas. In some contexts, the social dilemma vanishes. In others, it must be understood, and hence solved, in substantially different ways.

INTRODUCTION

When God expelled Adam and Eve from paradise, he created rationality. Not only would humans have to cope with scarcity, and hence have to trade some desired goods for others; they would even be pitted against each other. Individually rational behavior would lead to social dilemmas.

This is how economists describe the human condition. Not wrongly, of course. But psychological work on heuristics demonstrates that God was more inventive than economists envisioned. He endowed humans with an entire toolbox for decision making. Most of these tools are heuristics. They are ready-

---

[1] German legal scholars, unlike social scientists, utilize page numbers when citing sources of inspiration, even when there are no direct quotes. After a prolonged struggle about scholarly precision, the editors agreed to sacrifice this convention throughout this volume for the benefit of readability. Just to make sure that the page numbers can be found, however, an electronic version of this chapter can be obtained at: http://ssrn.com/abstract=539442

made and context-specific. Does this cast a more benign light on human destiny? Or does it make their fate even more miserable? It depends. Does this allow us to understand better perceived social dilemmas, and to advise institutional designers more effectively? Yes. This chapter thus serves a prognostic and an explanatory purpose. It does so by modeling, with the rational choice model serving as a contrast.[2]

Social Dilemmas in a Rational Choice World

Climate change presents a standard example. Scientists say it is generated by an increase in CO_2 emissions. The relevant factor is total emissions worldwide on a long-term scale. Only part of the problem is anthropogenic. Most of the natural sources of CO_2, like volcanoes, are beyond human control (National Research Council 2001). They are irrelevant for policy making, and hence for the definition of the social problem. Specifically, if policy makers concentrate on these sources, policy options are narrowed down to adaptation from the start. Mitigation is no longer considered.

From a mitigation perspective, economists use public goods theory for modeling climate change (Cornes and Sandler 1996). The analysis comes in three steps:

1. Individual and social rationality are seen to be in opposition. The utility of generating CO_2 by energy consumption is private; the negative effects on climate are social. Therefore, individuals do not have an incentive to save energy or to switch to more costly primary sources of energy.
2. Individual willingness to solve the problem is hindered. Benevolent actors anticipate that others will free-ride on their efforts.
3. Agreement *ex ante* is futile. Sovereign intervention notwithstanding, nobody has an incentive to keep his word (Ostrom 1998).

Consequently, rational choice analysts call for changing incentives such that individual and social rationality become realigned. Political practice has zoomed in on one tool: tradable permits. Currently, for practical reasons, only those industries that are high in energy consumption, like the producers of concrete, are

---

[2] To make the contrast visible, the rational choice model is presented in a very textbook-like manner. This is not to say that economists were not much more sophisticated, and could integrate many of the points made here into their models. An obvious example is optimizing under the condition that information generation is possible, but costly and uncertain. Also, economics has opened up to the omnipresence of institutions and to evolutionary thinking. However, the fundamental points of the chapter do indeed transcend the economic model, however sophisticated its version. The rational choice model can handle cognition only if translated into motivation—as in information asymmetries. Here, the exact opposite is center stage: the translation of motivation into cognition.

targeted. Such industries can, however, credibly threaten to relocate to foreign countries. Consequently, in practice, thresholds are so high that the environmental effect of the permit scheme remains close to zero. As long as large countries, such as the United States, ignore the policy problem, it will be attractive for policy makers to target consumers. They are captive targets. Their consumption of fossil fuels in heating, air-conditioning, and automobile driving is far from negligible. If one wants to understand how CO_2 emissions from these sources could be reduced, one must understand what drives behavior in the first place.

The rational choice analysis of social dilemmas starts from a number of explicit and implicit assumptions about behavior and context: Actors are modeled as *homines oeconomici* (Becker 1976). They have a well-defined utility function. Before taking action, they thoroughly analyze the situation, taking all available information into account. They calculate the expected value of inactivity and compare it to the expected value of any potential action. They choose the course of action that maximizes utility. Whenever there is a change in the environment, i.e., in the opportunity structure, they reoptimize. They do so instantaneously. Actors solve all decision-making problems the same way. The mental tool thus has zero domain specificity. Actors never make mistakes. They are unboundedly sophisticated. They do not face cognitive limitations (cf. Gigerenzer et al. 1999). All this is known to all other actors. Actors anticipate the behavior of their counterparts and, in particular, their counterparts' reactions to their own action.

Rational choice analysis assumes away context (Granovetter 1985). Specifically, all context is modeled as part of the opportunity structure. Social problems are analyzed in an institution-free state of nature (Hodgson 1988). Implicitly, the world is assumed to be fairly certain and to be cognitively accessible (Thompson et al. 1990). Consequently, task construal is a mechanical exercise. It consists of exploiting the available information.

The Different World of Heuristics

Some of these assumptions are patently unrealistic. Much of the rhetoric in behavioral economics and in psychological decision theory, therefore, reads like a realism crusade. Yet, such a crusade is epistemologically naïve. No one who engages in explanation or even prognosis can avoid modeling. Assuming some elements of reality away is the price one has to pay for gaining insight into the mechanisms that hold the world together. The following is thus deliberately an exercise in modeling. However, instead of just modeling rational, or, better, deliberate reasoning, it models actors who use simple heuristics for decision making most of the time.

Like the rational choice model, the following model makes several assumptions. It allows for two types of decision-making tools only: deliberate reasoning and decision heuristics. It ignores any other decision modes (Goldstein and Weber 1997; Payne et al. 1997). For simplicity, deliberate reasoning is modeled the same way as in rational choice analysis. Actually, even when people reason consciously, they do not follow the norms of rational choice theory. They either engage in narrative reasoning (Pennington and Hastie 1997; Dawes 1999) or in reason-based choice (Pennington and Hastie 1993; Goldstein and Weber 1997; Shafir et al. 2000).

Moreover, individuals use heuristics for much more than just decision making. Heuristics guide attention (Hogarth et al. 1997), perception (Levinson 1995), and judgment (Nisbett and Ross 1980). Heuristics thus contribute to a process of otherwise conscious reasoning. This is ignored here since my goal is to make the contrast between rational reasoning and decision making by heuristics as stark as possible. This also explains why the conscious and deliberate use of heuristics is not considered here (e.g., Gigerenzer et al. 1999).

This is one difference between my research agenda and that of the Gigerenzer group. The researchers of the latter group pursue two overlapping, but nonidentical goals. They want to demonstrate why simple decision rules can perform conspicuously well. This ultimately is an exercise in mapping decision rules to features of the problem space (M. Beckenkamp, pers. comm). Put differently, this line of research has a normative goal. It defines the conditions under which rational reasoning yields poor results. This chapter does not share this interest. Secondly, the Gigerenzer group aims to show how individuals actually deal with decision-making problems. This chapter is only interested in this second, descriptive question. The richer model of decision modes is meant to draw a more appropriate picture of social dilemmas, where appropriateness is assessed from the perspective of potential institutional interventions aiming at social betterment. People often use simple heuristics. In the area where both goals of the Gigerenzer group overlap, they do so in response to features of the problem space. Empirically, however, the use of heuristics is not confined to such problems. People often also rely on them if the characteristics of the problem space allow for variants of rational reasoning.

In this chapter, I focus exclusively on decision making by isolated individuals. This excludes collective and corporate actors (Coleman 1990, chaps. 9, 13, 16) as well as individuals who consult others before taking action.

In addition, I assess rational choice analysis for problem description and revisit social dilemmas, as defined in rational choice terms, but make different assumptions about behavior. Welfare maximization is taken as the norm. None of this is natural from a heuristics perspective. It is done in the interest of making the differences between both approaches as visible as possible.

By way of division of labor, this chapter is confined to problem definition. A natural complement would consist of drawing out the implications for institutional design. This is, however, done by a different working party. Consequently, the institutional designer is assumed to be a standard rational actor. For him, the richer behavioral model only affects the analysis of the social problem, not his own activity.

Criticizing rational choice theory for its behavioral assumptions is nothing new. Analysts from that school typically respond by pointing to the predictive power of their model. Conceptually, this implies that humans behave "as if" they were rational. Individualism is said to be methodological, not ontological (Friedman 1953; Blaug 1980). This claim is intellectually akin to behaviorism in psychology. Regardless of the mental mechanisms employed in action, people are expected to respond in a foreseeable manner to the presence of reinforcers in the environment (Skinner 1938). The cognitive revolution in psychology has demonstrated why this is often not true (Chomsky 1959). The choice between modeling behavior and modeling behavioral dispositions matters.

This chapter is not exclusively cognitive. It aims to demonstrate that introducing heuristics into the behavioral assumptions matters for understanding and predicting social dilemmas. This is not to say that heuristics cannot offer mental shortcuts for behavior in line with rational choice norms. But this does not hold for all heuristics. Modeling heuristics makes a difference even if the social dilemma, like the climate change problem, only results from aggregate behavior, and not from individual behavior. As will be shown, many politically relevant effects of heuristics are not eradicated in the aggregate.

MODELING HEURISTICS

For the sake of simplicity, the model described here allows for no more than two decision modes: rational reasoning and heuristics. Heuristics are the default mode. Rational reasoning is only employed in exceptional cases. This model also explains these exceptions. Rational reasoning is modeled in accord with the standard in economics. The heuristics model has very few mandatory components; instead, it has further optional components, as outlined in Figure 4.1.

Not all of these steps need be taken to initiate behavior. In the simplest case, the individual receives some sensory input. This input seemingly fits to the domain of a heuristic stored in the memory. This initial hypothesis is corroborated by matching. The cue is present. The heuristic fires. This then makes for the core model, as sketched in Figure 4.2.

Decision making by heuristics can, however, be more complex. If the initial hypothesis is refuted, other heuristics may be retrieved from memory. If the original sensory input is inconclusive, the individual may search for more facts. If matching with any of the heuristics originally retrieved fails, the individual may solve the problem by adopting or generating a new heuristic. If using heuristics to make decisions does not work, or does not seem appropriate, the individual may switch to rational reasoning. Moreover, the individual perpetually improves the stock of heuristics by way of a feedback mechanism. A richer model can allow for a separate mechanism for task construal.

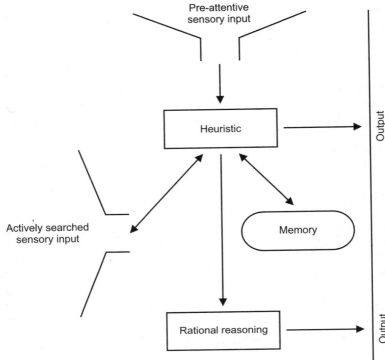

Figure 4.1 Heuristics in perspective.

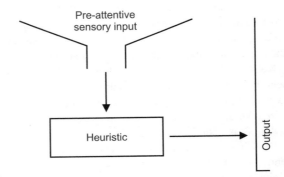

Figure 4.2 Base model.

The Architecture of Individual Heuristics

Heuristics have two characteristic properties. They are radically simple tools for decision making. Although their decision algorithm ignores most information about the environment, they perform conspicuously well. This is due to their second property. Heuristics are ecological. They are not all-purpose tools; they

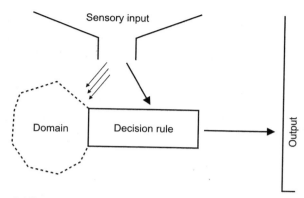

Figure 4.3   Adding the essential: the distinction between the decision rule and the domain.

are context-specific (Gigerenzer et al. 1999). These two properties are modeled in Figure 4.3.

Heuristics have a dual architecture. The actual tool for decision making is labeled the decision rule. For simplicity, it is assumed that the rule combines exactly one input with the output. If this one cue is present, the heuristic fires. The model is, however, open to more complex decision rules, like the one presented by Gigerenzer et al. (1999). The only restriction concerns the relationship between the cue material and the output. This relationship must be fully specified *ex ante*.

This is different for the second element of a heuristic, which is labeled the domain. This second element is assumed to be associational. It is the ecological component. Here, the criterion is not the presence or the absence of a cue, but the perceived goodness of fit. The decision rule is thus precisely defined, whereas the domain is only described. The decision rule is strict, while the domain is open to matching. Information about the cue defines when the heuristic is to fire, whereas information about the domain is used in an associational way.

The decision rule is purely mechanical. It has no judgmental component. There is no weighing of pros and cons. The mechanism is digital. If the cue is present, the heuristic fires. If the cue is absent, the heuristic remains inactive. Note that no decision is being taken. There is no motivational component.

There are several options available for modeling the domain. In the simplest design, the domain would consist of a rather large number of equally weighted criteria. The mind would check for the presence of these features in the environment. Goodness of fit would be defined by an aspiration level—much as satisficing is in the motivational camp (Simon 1955, 1979). In this model, a conceptual tool traditionally used for understanding the decision rule would thus be transposed to the matching process. If, say, 80% of these features were perceived, the heuristic would be deemed applicable (cf. Goldstein and Hogarth 1997; Anderson et al. 2004). Physiologically speaking, this is conceivable. The brain is an extraordinarily powerful tool for information processing, with some 10^{11} nerve cells and some 10^{14} synaptic links (Singer 2003). Much of the performance of the brain can be traced back to the fact that it consists of a well-organized, vast knowledge base (Anderson 2000; Glimcher 2003).

There is, however, compelling evidence of a more intelligent mechanism. Sensory input usually is not processed piece by piece. Down to the physiological level, the brain is permanently striving to generate an ever increasing number of aggregate assemblies (Hebb 1949). It works by associative clusters that are activated jointly (Strack and Deutsch 2004). At the symbolic level they condense in natural categories (Rakison and Oakes 2003), which can take one of two forms: a schema or an exemplar (Anderson 2000). Exemplars remain fully contextualized (Anderson 2000), while schemata abstract from some aspects of the context (Head 1920; Bartlett 1932; Goldstein and Weber 1997; Anderson 2000). They single out more and less characteristic features, and give the former greater weight in matching. Put differently, whenever possible, the brain does not solve problems of categorization merely by deploying brute computational force. It economizes resources by attempting to make sense out of its environment (cf. Turner 2001). Although the mechanism is thus typically more complicated, it retains the idea of partial matching. To apply a heuristic, the perceived features of the environment need not fully coincide with the situation that has helped the individual forge the exemplar. Likewise, not all the features of a schema, not even all highly characteristic ones, must be present in the environment for the heuristic to be applied. The perceived goodness of fit must be satisfactory, not maximal.

The task of categorizing by way of schemata remotely resembles the task of doctrinal lawyers. The similarity is most pronounced in reference to common law. Its prime source is precedent. It is more abstract than an exemplar. Later judges do not just look for similarities across cases, as in Islamic law. Yet it is not as abstract as continental law either, which strives for as much decontextualization as possible. In common law, later judges distill the *ratio iuris* from precedent. Whenever there is doubt about the actual confines of the rule, they go back to the original case. The parallel to the law is helpful since it demonstrates a further possibility for the architecture of the heuristic. Legal rules, at least in their simple form, have an if–then structure. If the features of a case match those spelled out in the rule, the rule applies. In principle, practicing lawyers might turn this into a two-step exercise: first they can try to match the case to the rule; then they can apply it. In actuality, when lawyers are engaged in matching, they always keep the potential outcome in mind (Engisch 1983). The same possibility exists for heuristics. Matching need not be confined to the domain. It might include the cue right from the beginning. This can serve to preclude potentially useless matching. If the cue is not present, the heuristic is discarded without further ado. This can, however, only be stated here as a possibility. As yet, there does not seem to be empirical evidence.

Initial Selection of Heuristics

The contextual character of heuristics implies that individuals have a whole array of heuristics at their disposal. Since the domain is matched associationally, there is at least a possibility that one and the same situation will fall into the domain of several heuristics. There are two reasons that this matters for the behavioral output. One and the same cue may feature in more than one theoretically applicable heuristic (Mantzavinos 2001). In that case, there is competition between several heuristics (Anderson et al. 2004). Moreover, the individual may only test heuristics that are applicable, but that do not have an observable cue in their decision rule. If such heuristics are tested, the individual may engage in more complex forms of decision making, although he would have an applicable heuristic with a pertinent cue at his disposal.

The key to understanding how heuristics are selected lies in understanding how they are stored. When it comes to decision making, they must be retrieved from memory. Consequently, the model for resolving competition among decision-making tools must rely on what is known about how items are retrieved from memory. There are four components: the recency and frequency of usage; an associative component; the degree to which the heuristic matches current retrieval specifications; and a noise component, which introduces an element of stochasticity (Anderson and Lebiere 2003).

The first component is purely statistical. A heuristic is more likely to be retrieved, the more often it has been used in the past. This general base rate of activation is, however, corrected with respect to recency. The latter effect underlies priming. If a cue has been activated recently, it becomes more likely that a heuristic will be retrieved that has that cue in its domain (Lashley 1951).

The associative component is basically the same one that has been described when discussing how matching works (Bartlett 1932; Anderson 2000). It relies on mental representation by way of schemata and exemplars (Bartlett 1932; Anderson 2000). The more sense a heuristic seems to make in the context at hand, the more likely retrieval is. Memory thus exploits meaning (Bartlett 1932; Anderson 2000).

The retrieval and use of heuristics are assumed here to be subconscious. This does not, however, rule out central control. In principle, there are three mechanisms involved in retrieval: attention, attitudes, and instinct. They wield their effects over different time spans. Attention generates short-term selectivity in central action. Attitudes have a midterm effect. Instinct is innate and, hence, has a long-term effect (Hebb 1949).

More Complex Decision Making

Thus far, only the simplest mechanism has been considered. There is some sensory input. It triggers the retrieval of one heuristic from memory. The brain tries to match the observed features of the environment to the domain of the heuristic.

If the aspiration level is met, the brain checks to see whether the cue is present. If it is, the heuristic fires.

What does the brain do if this first attempt fails? The easiest reaction is to repeat the same steps until a pertinent heuristic is found. But the brain has three more options: (a) It may actively search for more facts. If it does this, it goes beyond pre-attentive sensory input (cf. Lewis 2005); (b) it may acquire or generate a new heuristic; and (c) it may switch to rational reasoning (i.e., it may change the decision mode). All of these options are costly. Correctly anticipating the cost of each of these four options leads to the rationalistic nightmare of subjective expected utility theory (Savage 1954). Engaging in this would be anti-parsimonious to the extreme. To avoid doing this, the mechanisms underlying retrieval from memory must be extended to these meta-decisions.

The first solution of the meta-choice problem is a simple probabilistic mechanism. It can be analyzed in parallel to the decision rule of heuristics. There, the mechanism has been dubbed a stopping rule (Simon 1972; Gigerenzer et al. 1999). Theoretically, this mechanism could be extended to guide the meta-choice among the three options for introducing greater complexity into decision making by heuristics. If this were to be done, the mind would set a limit to each type of additional decision-making effort, and specify *ex ante* the order in which it would use each of them. It might, for instance, determine to try out ten alternative heuristics. If this failed to bring positive results, it might engage in a search for facts for five minutes. If this search did not work out either, it might try to generate one new heuristic. If this were not successful, it might switch to conscious reasoning.

This is conceivable, but it would be very rigorous and potentially also unduly costly. For such an *ex ante* specification could not possibly be appropriate across the board. Some contexts are information rich, and it is relatively easy to uncover more information in them. Here, active searches are promising. In other contexts, the perceived degree of uncertainty is high. Here, observing how others with greater experience handle decisions is potentially more promising. Within the model, this would mean acquiring a new heuristic. In yet other contexts, sophisticated tools for rational reasoning are easily available, and they have a good record. Here, quickly switching to rational reasoning seems the best policy if initial attempts at deciding with heuristics do not work.[3]

These meta-decisions may use the same four mechanisms that memory offers for retrieval. The general base rate of activation and the recent rate of activation offer a first approximation. The mind decides how to decide the same way as it usually has in this domain. In appropriate cases, this meta-rule may be overridden by associative impulses. One feature from the environment triggers a switch to a meta-decision that is unusual for the domain. The meta-decision may also be guided by central impulses, like a personal decision-making style. For instance, some people are more inclined to rational reasoning, others rely more on

---

[3]   In this latter respect, image theory makes similar predictions (see Beach 1990, 1998).

experience. Such personality traits can be introduced into the model as attitudes toward more complex decision making, once the initial attempt at using a heuristic has failed. Finally, there is a noise component, i.e., a certain degree of unpredictability with respect to the meta-decisions.

Acquiring New Heuristics

Alternative heuristics are retrieved from memory the same way as the initial heuristic. Both an active search for facts and a switch to rational reasoning are also straightforward activities. But how does the mind acquire new heuristics? This is still very much uncharted territory. The following component of the model must therefore remain fairly sketchy.

In principle, two options exist. The mind can take a new heuristic from the environment, or it can generate it by central activity. The former is learning. In principle, any learning mechanism might be used, ranging from classic conditioning to formal instruction (Anderson 2000). One learning mechanism, however, seems particularly likely: observational learning (Bandura 1986). It allows for the cultural transmission of heuristics (Gigerenzer et al. 1999). Individuals need not have experiences of their own. They may observe how others fare in a context unknown to them. From this, they generate a hypothesis about mechanism—a model, as learning theorists put it (Bandura 1986).

There are two ways of centrally generating new heuristics: one incremental and one fundamental. Heuristics are particularly well-suited for incremental change. The domain is delineated by way of schemata or exemplars. Both lend themselves to the integration of new elements. Likewise, some elements may be dropped. In both cases, one heuristic may be extended to a new domain by analogy (cf. Bartlett 1932).

Central activity is, however, not confined to incremental change. Fundamental change has been dubbed insight (Hebb 1949), accommodation (Piaget and Gabain 1932), and blending. The latter concept offers a particularly plausible mechanism for the generation of new heuristics. Individuals unpack previously stored heuristics and compose elements in new and unprecedented ways (Turner 2001).

Motivation

In psychological terms, rational choice is a theory of motivation. The individual wants to maximize utility, given the current state of the environment. Heuristics, as modeled here, do not have a motivational component at all. There is no choice between alternatives. The decision rule is strict: if the cue is present, the heuristic fires. Matching the perceived environment with the domain is an exercise in goodness of fit, not in the maximization of any goal. Also the selection of heuristics, the active search for facts, and the acquisition of new heuristics are driven by matching, not by a goal. Only rational reasoning has an independent goal-component (modeled here as in rational choice analysis). Is this to say that decision making by heuristics ignores utility?

The answer comes in two parts. The motivational part is not in the architecture of the individual heuristic, but in the mapping of heuristics to domains. Also, the individual is endowed with a feedback mechanism to ensure that decision making by heuristics is consistent with the individual's (or species') goals.

Despite their parsimony, heuristics perform well since they are adaptive (Gigerenzer et al. 1999). At face value, this is exclusively a statement about mechanism. The individual is freed up from calculating the pros and cons of a decision in the concrete situation. He can rely on a ready-made decision-making tool for the purpose. The calculations have been done earlier. It is enough for the individual to check to see whether the new situation comes sufficiently close to the situation for which the decision-making tool has been generated in the first place. Consequently, in decision making that uses heuristics, judgment and the actual decision making are two separate entitites. The judgmental component is confined to the generation of new heuristics, and it is removed from the actual decision making.

This statement about mechanism has an important implication. There is no longer a need for the individual to make any judgment on his own. It suffices for the individual to pick ready-made decision-making tools from trusted sources. Specifically, the individual can choose between centrally generating new heuristics and learning by observation how others solve similar problems. From a social perspective, this has two advantages: individuals can economize on judgmental effort, and they can exploit costly experiences that others have had. They do not even need to observe these experiences directly. It is enough if they adopt the foreign decision-making rules that have resulted from these experiences.

Constructivists like to show that entire populations can survive for a long time in more or less fictitious environments (Berger and Luckmann 1967). Even rational choice theorists admit that there are situations where it is individually rational to ignore base data and to anticipate how others wrongly see the world instead. This is how they explain herding, evident, for example, in a speculative bubble on the stock market (Bru and Vives 2002). The greater the complexity and uncertainty, the more difficult it is to get at a reliable understanding of "the reality" (Engel et al. 2002). This has two implications. In decision making, small mistakes are hard to avoid; individuals are thus well-advised to aim at avoiding big mistakes. This can be done simultaneously and sequentially. The simultaneous mechanisms have already been outlined. If it becomes dubious that the heuristic actually matches the domain, the individual may try out different heuristics stored in memory. He may engage in an explicit search for additional facts. He may adopt or generate new heuristics, or he may switch to rational reasoning. However, there is also a sequential option. It uses the effect of actual decisions on the environment as input for fine-tuning the domain of heuristics. This is done via feedback, as outlined in Figure 4.4.

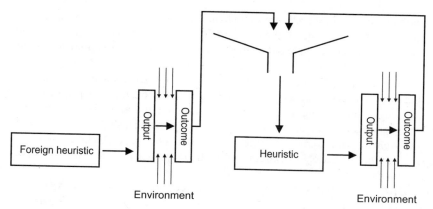

Figure 4.4 Adding a feedback mechanism.

There is evidence of this kind of feedback even for the most basic functions of the brain (Glimcher 2003). It therefore does not seem far-fetched to expect the same at the more aggregate level of heuristics. In principle, the individual has two options. He may use the performance of his own behavior as feedback, or he may observe how his peers do in the same environment.

A distinction familiar in political science helps us to understand a further implication. Political scientists refer to political action, say, a new statute, as output. They distinguish the outcome from this, namely the effect of the new rules on the behavior of addressees. Likewise, using a heuristic generates behavior as an output. For feedback, however, the relevant information is the outcome, that is, the effect of behavior in the environment. It results from the interaction between the output and other environmental factors.

Furthermore, feedback only makes sense if there is a benchmark. In principle, this could be utility, as used in rational choice analysis. In the fundamentally uncertain world for which heuristics are made, this would however be surprising. It is more likely that the benchmark itself is flexible, and that it is developed in interaction with the environment. Aspiration adaptation theory is a way of formalizing the idea (Selten 1998). In principle, the observing individual might infer a changing benchmark from changes in observed behavior. However, the richer the set of potentially relevant criteria, the more it will help the observing individual if others do not just behave, but visibly endow their action with meaning.

Task Construal

There is one final surprise in the basic model: it has no separate component for defining the problem. Pre-attentive sensory input alone sets the mental machinery in motion. It is possible to enrich the model by adding a problem definition component. It is, however, important to understand that such a component is not a necessary ingredient, for the problem definition can be embedded in the domain of the heuristic, no less than the motivational part. Two examples illustrate the possibilities.

In the first, an individual perceives a snake in the environment. This information alone triggers the decision rule: freeze. In the second, the subject is in a cheap bar (the domain). In one corner, guests start shouting (the cue). The heuristic fires: flee. Apparently this individual has learned that a row in a cheap bar can quickly turn violent. The difference between the two cases lies in the thickness of the domain. In the first case, it is extremely thin: no more than the cue is needed. In the second case, the domain is thicker and hence separable from the cue.

Different examples are conceivable. The individual may not always want to flee when there is a risk of a violent row in a bar. He may want to come to the rescue of a friend, or he may prefer watching a good match when enough alcohol makes him feel invincible. One may conceptualize such situations by adding a further component to the model. This would then make for the architecture shown in Figure 4.5. Although the situation can be matched with the domain of the heuristic, and although the individual observes the cue, he nonetheless does not rely on the heuristic.

In Figure 4.5, an additional arrow has deliberately been depicted, pointing from sensory input to the additional component of the heuristic. This is because individuals rarely possess goals they want to see fulfilled regardless of the context. Typically, problems are not out there. Individuals construe tasks in response to information from the environment. If this is the case, adding a separate component for task construal violates the goal of parsimonious modeling, for one may just as well model the difference by postulating two or more heuristics with more specialized domains. The separate component is only necessary if one expects problem definition to be generated solely within the mind.

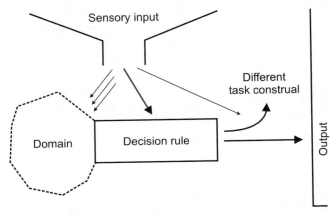

Figure 4.5   Adding a subsidiary mechanism for task construal.

Seemingly, the second example fits here: Under the influence of alcohol, the individual's mood changes. One may just as well model the intervention of mood as impacting on matching, or on the initial retrieval of a heuristic from memory.

SOCIAL DILEMMAS IN A HEURISTICS PERSPECTIVE

Models of behavior can help students of social dilemmas in two ways: they can allow them to explain perceived social dilemmas, and they can help them predict dilemma situations. Differences in modeling behavior matter in two cases. First, a model that takes heuristics into account predicts the absence of a social dilemma where rational choice analysis predicts the presence of one. Conversely, rational choice sees no dilemma in cases in which a dilemma is predicted under the assumption that people can rely on heuristics.

In an epistemologically informed perspective, the difference between explanation and prediction is not categorical. Due to the overwhelming complexity of reality, explanation must rely on the same theoretical constructs that can also be used for prediction. But the field of observation is different. Explanation is backward-looking, whereas prediction is forward-looking. By way of constructing counterfactuals, backward-looking analysis can even chose to explain the absence of a social problem. Such studies are, however, not very frequent. Typically, understanding why a problem predicted by one model is absent in the world of another model is therefore more important for forward-looking policy advice.

Predicting the Absence of a Social Dilemma

Rational choice analysis reconstructs behavior as a reaction to perceived or anticipated changes in the opportunity structure. A whole industry makes a living by showing when the predictions generated by this model are systematically false (Ostrom 1990; Fehr 2000; Kahneman 2000; Ostrom et al. 2002). In quite a number of respects, a behaviorally informed model is more optimistic than rational choice analysis. This also holds for the model offered here, that is, for the model that takes decision making by heuristics into account.

In a first class of situations, the outcome of using one specific heuristic is more socially beneficial than the outcome achievable with rational reasoning. When this is the case, using this heuristic in decision making is, socially speaking, a good thing. The "social performance" of the heuristic is better than that of rational reasoning. One proviso is, however, in place: For society, outcome matters, not output. Doing the right thing in the wrong situation is as socially detrimental as doing the wrong thing in the first place. Consequently, a heuristic can only be said to be socially beneficial in the abstract if the social benefit is independent of context. This is not very frequent (B. Fasolo, pers. comm).

The widespread willingness of most people to keep their promises, however, provides one example of this (Schlicht 1998). It removes what rational choice theorists call the second-order prisoner's dilemma: If the original social problem can be reconstructed as a social dilemma, agreeing on a joint solution is irrelevant, for rational actors have no incentive to implement the agreement (Ostrom 1998). More practical examples are the absence of littering or of killing strangers in the street at night, in most Western countries. There are, of course, laws prohibiting both. Yet hardly anybody calculates whether his long-term utility goes down when he engages in this kind of activity. Rather, the large majority has adopted the socially beneficial heuristic to abstain from both.

Even more important are features of heuristics that reduce problem pressure from social dilemmas, even if the analyst cannot predict the precise confines of the heuristic actually employed. Note, however, that one could not possibly claim that decision making by heuristics outperforms rational reasoning, regardless of the contents of the heuristic, for the performance of heuristics categorically rests on their contextuality. This implies that one can never preclude, in the abstract, that individuals will apply heuristics out of area, with socially detrimental effects.

One advantage seems straightforward: Heuristics are simple. Hence, using heuristics to make decisions saves mental effort (Gigerenzer et al. 1999). Scarce mental resources are freed up for more socially beneficial uses. At closer sight, however, only the decision rule is simple. Even if this were a purely probabilistic process, matching information from the environment to the domain of a heuristic would be a demanding endeavor. This holds even more if sense making is implied. Couched differently, the scarcity argument is warranted. Although mental resources for rational reasoning are fairly limited, the brain is an extremely powerful tool for the parallel processing of sensory input at the subconscious level (Singer 1991; Glimcher 2003). Using heuristics to make decisions transfers most of the mental activity to mental mechanisms that exhibit considerably less scarcity than rational reasoning.

Moreover, due to the makeup of the domain, heuristics are able to exploit much more information from the context than ordinary people can manipulate in conscious reasoning. This explains why switching to rational reasoning makes subjects work harder, but often not smarter (Payne et al. 1997).

When making decisions with heuristics, motivation is only indirectly present: in the description of the domain as well as in feedback. Arguably, even the benchmark is relative, not absolute, and it is generated by observing one's peers. Ultimately, important changes in the opportunity structure will nonetheless have an impact on behavior. But the hyper-reactivity crucial for most of the rational choice predictions is absent. If they use heuristics when deciding, people are likely to ignore small changes altogether. There is no anticipation of strategic interaction. People only react if, due to actual strategic interaction, they have suffered significantly. Consequently, it is less likely that an original set of socially beneficial heuristics will be eradicated because of competition. As long as detrimental experiences remain marginal, it is likely that the population will predominantly stick to the original heuristic. Vice versa, socially detrimental behavior does not instantaneously spread throughout the population. It does not affect the behavior of single individuals as long as nobody whom they consider to be their peer engages in it.

Matching the domain of a heuristic is a demanding cognitive activity. Individuals have to exploit subtle nuances and engage in sense making. No logical calculation, however, is conducted. The predictions of rational choice theory for social dilemmas are based on this activity. If people use heuristics, they do not anticipate others' behavior. They are even less apt to solve complex problems by backward induction. They do not calculate the expected value of entire strategies, that is, of chains of action (more from Fudenberg and Tirole 1991). Consequently, they are much more likely to choose what is locally appropriate, even if careful calculation would have demonstrated that it is individually less than optimal in the long run.

In rational choice analysis, conflict is pervasive. This is a direct result of methodological individualism. Rational choice is a theory about actors striving for their individually best outcome, no matter what that means for the well-being of their interaction partners. There are heuristics for situations of perceived conflict. Some of them are highly socially detrimental, like those driving vendetta. But if people rely on heuristics, conflict is a matter of domain, not of principle. If individuals do not see a context as conflictual, conflict heuristics will not apply, even if the situation can be reconstructed as a conflict in rational choice terms.

Conflictuality is only one possible feature of the domain. If the perception of social dilemmas is not erroneous, there must be more heuristics that can have socially detrimental effects. Yet because of the fundamental contextuality of heuristics, this effect is likely to be confined to the domain of origin (cf. Goldstein and Weber 1997). Social problems are compartmentalized. They do not automatically spread across domains.

Explaining Perceived Social Dilemmas

If one takes heuristics into account, some predictions from rational choice theory become dubious. If so, the need for political intervention vanishes, but social dilemmas do not disappear altogether. There must therefore be a way of explaining the remaining social dilemmas from a heuristics perspective. One cannot even preclude that new social dilemmas, not visible from a rational choice perspective, will be uncovered.

Socially Detrimental Heuristics

Socially beneficial heuristics can eradicate social dilemmas that are predicted by rational choice. Turning this idea upside down, social dilemmas can result from the fact that people rely on socially detrimental heuristics. Illustrations from the area of climate change are not difficult to find. People, for example, routinely drive to work, instead of using public transportation. Even the basic ideas underlying the rational choice analysis of social dilemmas could be mirrored in socially detrimental heuristics. If nobody can be excluded from a common good, the social detriment can be caused by the heuristic: "This is no one's property, you can take it." The fact that there is no rivalry in consumption could translate to the heuristics level the following way. The socially beneficial heuristic might be mute: "Do not take something away if its owner wants to use it." Note, however, that the same proviso holds as for socially beneficial heuristics. Socially, outcome matters, not output. Typically, social detriment will therefore result from the interaction between a heuristic and context, not from the heuristic alone, irrespective of context.

Architecture of Heuristics

Again, socially detrimental effects are even more important if they result from the very architecture of heuristics. At first sight, regulatory attention should focus on the decision rule, for here is the action. The cue and the behavioral output are linked in a socially detrimental way. But, as demonstrated earlier, heuristics are context-specific. There is hardly any combination of a cue and an output that is detrimental in every context. Typically, the description of the domain is therefore more socially relevant.

An overly rigid description of the domain is one primary source of social dilemmas (cf. Schlicht 1998). A typical scenario is the following: initially, applying a given decision rule to the situation characterized by the domain was as beneficial individually as it was socially. Later, however, the situation changed in socially important ways. In such situations, if the description of the domain is not sufficiently flexible, behavior becomes sticky. Evolutionary theorists call this overfitting (Weigend 1994). This seems likely to pose a major problem for climate change. Over the last decades, the populations of industrialized countries have learned that emissions can be toxic, or otherwise cause locally visible environmental damage. However, they have not been taught that CO_2 is a problematic substance. Consequently, they have had no reason to acquire heuristics that help minimize the emissions of CO_2 gases.

A related effect is compartmentalization. Here, a socially beneficial heuristic is confined to too narrow of a domain. For instance, people have learned that they should, in the interest of clean air, drive cars with catalyzers. Used cars without a catalyzer are hard to sell. This is not, however, to say that people have also learned to drive less in the interest of cutting CO_2 emissions.

A third effect is more abstract. In some domains, change is too fast for heuristics to adapt quickly enough. Alternatively, learning by feedback is too costly, such that even the first mistake has to be avoided whenever possible (e.g., Weick and Roberts 1993). In such contexts, regulation can be interpreted as a way of dividing labor. Adopting or generating a new set of heuristics is aided by measures that make the need for change salient. In appropriate cases, the regulator might even offer alternative, socially more beneficial heuristics. This too can be demonstrated in reference to climate change. If scientists are right, waiting until the effects of climate change are patent would be disastrous. Once the process has gained momentum, it becomes extremely difficult, if not impossible, to stop it. In such situations, without intervention, socially less harmful heuristics will only be adopted by coincidence.

In a second set of cases, the social dilemma results from poor matching (cf. Anderson et al. 2004). The individual heuristic is applied outside of the area it was adopted for. This is not unlikely, given the make-up of the domain. The mind does not expect full matching between the schema or the exemplar and sensory input from the environment. Consequently, a heuristic can sometimes be applied, although the case at hand exhibits important features that do not match the normal context in which it is used. This is particularly likely if the case in most respects resembles a standard situation from the environment of the actor, but differs in one important dimension.

Initial Choice of Heuristics

In many situations, there is initially more than one heuristic that the individual might apply. In such situations, choosing a socially inadequate heuristic can be detrimental. This can result from the fact that a socially less beneficial heuristic outperforms the socially more attractive one in initial choice.

Initial choice is heavily reliant upon memory. Consequently, social problems can result from the properties of retrieval. The recency effect explains priming. We are much more likely to use a heuristic in a new context if we have recently employed it in other contexts (Anderson 2000). The associational component of retrieval explains the power of mental models. If individuals reconstruct reality in a socially harmful manner, they are likely to rely on socially detrimental heuristics. This explains how ideology can interact with heuristics. The normative component, however, can be much weaker. In the case of climate change, the social problem can largely be explained by the fact that most individuals reconstruct environmental problems as qualitative, not as quantitative problems. Consequently, they are prepared to switch from one technology or from one substance to another. They are not likely to extend heuristics for economizing into the areas that are relevant for cutting CO_2 emissions.

Since socially beneficial heuristics must be retrieved from memory, a social dilemma can also result from forgetting. In such cases, although the individuals once learned the right heuristic, it is highly unlikely that they will retrieve it when this would be socially beneficial. At the abstract level, forgetting can result from one of three effects: decay, interference, and lost access to the cue necessary for retrieval (Anderson 2000).

By contrast, from a heuristics perspective, social dilemmas can be latent. Within the memory of a sufficiently large part of the population, there is a socially detrimental heuristic. It is currently rarely used. But as a result of a change in the environment, many people retrieve this old heuristic. A mere shift in how a situation is presented to the population may also result in retrieving a previously used heuristic. The presence of such socially detrimental heuristics in memory is particularly likely in periods after fundamental changes. For instance, if a population has recently been freed from dictatorship, for quite some time old behavioral programs will still be mentally available. Likewise, immigrants come with mental histories. Some of them may bring heuristics that cause harm in their new environment.

Search for Facts

In principle, social dilemmas can also result from too many searches for facts. Regulatory addressees who actively search for ways to circumvent the new rule demonstrate how this can happen (Wegner 1996). In accord with a heuristics perspective, however, the opposite situation can cause a problem as well. People are too attentive to vivid evidence and not attentive enough to pallid evidence. They do not engage in any active searches for facts, or they stop their searches too early. Again, this can be illustrated in reference to the climate change issue. As long as the message has not spread that CO_2 emissions are a social problem, people are unlikely to switch to heuristics that are socially less problematic. They might, for example, replace fossil fuels with other forms of primary energy, or different heuristics might allow them to generate the same final utility with less energy input. Detrimental heuristics might even result in deliberately ignoring information that would lead to socially less harmful activity (cf. Baron and Kerr 2003). A classic illustration is behavior misled by stereotypes (Bargh et al. 1996).

Acquisition of New Heuristics

A social dilemma cannot just result from neglecting to search for facts. One can also result if the spread of socially more beneficial heuristics is inhibited. There are cases in which forerunners long ago adopted a type of behavior that would lead to the disappearance of some social dilemma. However, the large majority is simply unaware of this behavioral alternative. Note that the effect can be purely cognitive. If the majority knew about the alternative, it is arguable that they would be willing to switch to it. Or perhaps individuals are just indifferent about both alternatives. They could be convinced that it is necessary to fix the social problem.

The opposite situation also exists. A social dilemma sometimes results from the fact that too many are lured into bad habits. For example, when buying a car, they choose fashionable "sport utility vehicles," although their energy consumption is much higher.

Happily, for most social dilemmas, only aggregate effects matter. When this is the case, the individual generation of a socially detrimental heuristic due to blending is of little concern, socially speaking. Regulators only need to see to it that the bad heuristic does not spread throughout society. This explains why, in accord with a heuristics perspective, biased feedback is often not a strong concern.

Switch to Rational Reasoning

Behavior guided by heuristics is not necessarily more beneficial than behavior resulting from rational reasoning. It can even be more detrimental. This is the case, for instance, if a socially detrimental heuristic is not rational from the individualist perspective. The opposite possibility also exists: as long as a sufficiently large portion of the population relies on heuristics, the social dilemma is absent, or it is at least less harmful. Actually, this is the case whenever rational choice analysis would predict a social dilemma that is not present from a heuristics perspective. In this case, the social dilemma can also be said to result from the fact that too many individuals have switched to rational reasoning.

PROSPECTS

As should be apparent, this chapter is an exercise in partial analysis. It invites the following complements: in a heuristics perspective, context matters. Consequently, social dilemmas are not only caused by behavior. They can also result from socially unfavorable contexts; hence changing context is a serious policy alternative. One element of the status quo ante is particularly relevant for policy makers. In a heuristics perspective, the analysis cannot start from a hypothetical, institution-free state of nature. Today's social dilemmas can result from yesterday's institutional interventions. Practically speaking, it can be much harder to cure the true institutional cause of a problem. It can be more promising to use a further institutional act of intervention to target heuristics that were shaped by earlier institutions.

Using heuristics to make decisions increases behavioral variance. Consequently, even if the individual uses a heuristic that cannot be said to be socially detrimental, agent heterogeneity can still generate a social dilemma (cf. Stanovich and West 2000). This is not an unlikely event since agents have been demonstrated to choose heuristics that are beneficial to them. There is thus a self-serving bias present (Bazerman and Neale 1995; Wade-Benzoni et al. 1996). Even without the self-serving element, the social dilemma can result from the fact that people whose cooperation would be needed for the provision of a common good use incompatible heuristics. For an uninformed interaction partner, this variance could create an almost insurmountable problem of predictability if he tried to anticipate rationally all potential effects (Engel 2005). The same would hold for government if it wanted to design rationally its forms of intervention. Of course, in reality neither government nor interaction partners assume behavior to be random. Only rational choice analysts do, as subjective utility theory requires. Precisely because behavior is contextual, it often is possible to venture a good guess—but no more than that.

Finally, and most importantly, this analysis is confined to problem definition. In a further step, it would have to translate these results into behaviorally informed institutional design. How can purposeful design exploit the generic knowledge about decision making using heuristics? Would such an approach be acceptable from the perspective of the rule of law and the principle of democracy? How can institutional design take into account that not only addressees are likely to rely on heuristics, but also those who operate the institutions, be they judges or administrators? These questions remain to be addressed.

ACKNOWLEDGMENTS

Helpful comments by Hal Arkes, Bruno Frey, Gerd Gigerenzer, Werner Güth, Eric Johnson, Rick Lempert, and Elke Weber are gratefully acknowledged. Thanks also go to the participants of the Dahlem Workshop, the Ringberg Workshop on Behavioural Analysis in the Area of Common Goods, and to the Institutional Design Unit of the Bonn Institute for comments during presentations of earlier versions.

REFERENCES

Anderson, J.R. 2000. Learning and Memory: An Integrated Approach. New York: Wiley.
Anderson, J.R., D. Bothell, M.D. Byrne et al. 2004. An integrated theory of the mind. *Psychol. Rev.* **111**:1036–1060.
Anderson, J.R., and C. Lebiere. 2003. The Newell Test for a theory of cognition. *Behav. Brain Sci.* **26**:587–640.
Bandura, A. 1986. Social Foundations of Thought and Action: A Social Cognitive Theory. Englewood Cliffs, NJ: Prentice Hall.
Bargh, J.A., M. Chen, and L. Burrows. 1996. Automaticity of social behavior: Direct effects of trait construct and stereotype activation on action. *J. Pers. Soc. Psychol.* **71**:230–244.
Baron, R.S., and N.L. Kerr. 2003. Group Process, Group Decisions, Group Action. Philadelphia: Open Univ. Press.
Bartlett, F.C. 1932. Remembering: A Study in Experimental and Social Psychology. Cambridge: Cambridge Univ. Press.
Bazerman, M.H., and M.A. Neale. 1995. The role of fairness considerations and relationships in a judgmental perspective of negotiation. In: Barriers to Conflict Resolution, ed. K.J. Arrow, R.H. Mnookin, L. Ross, A. Tversky, and R.B. Wilson, pp. 86–107. New York: Norton.
Beach, L.R. 1990. Image Theory: Decision Making in Personal and Organizational Contexts. Chichester: Wiley.

Beach, L.R. 1998. Image Theory: Theoretical and Empirical Foundations. Mahwah, NJ: Erlbaum.

Becker, G.S. 1976. The Economic Approach to Human Behavior. Chicago: Univ. of Chicago Press.

Berger, P.L., and T. Luckmann. 1967. The Social Construction of Reality: A Treatise in the Sociology of Knowledge. Garden City, NY: Doubleday.

Blaug, M. 1980. The Methodology of Economics: Or, How Economists Explain. Cambridge: Cambridge Univ. Press.

Bru, L., and X. Vives. 2002. Informational externalities, herding, and incentives. *J. Instit. Theor. Econ.* **158**:91–105.

Chomsky, N. 1959. A review of B.F. Skinner's verbal behavior. *Language* **35**:26–58.

Coleman, J.S. 1990. Foundations of Social Theory. Cambridge, MA: Belknap.

Cornes, R., and T. Sandler. 1996. The Theory of Externalities, Public Goods and Club Goods. Cambridge: Cambridge Univ. Press.

Dawes, R.M. 1999. A message from psychologists to economists: Mere predictability doesn't matter like it should (without a good story appended to it). *J. Econ. Behav. Org.* **39**:29–40.

Engel, C. 2005. Generating Predictability: A Neglected Topic in Institutional Analysis and Institutional Design. Cambridge: Cambridge Univ. Press.

Engel, C., J. Halfmann, and M. Schulte, eds. 2002. Wissen, Nichtwissen, Unsicheres Wissen. Common Goods: Law, Politics and Economics 8. Baden-Baden: Nomos.

Engisch, K. 1983. Einführung in das juristische Denken. Stuttgart: Kohlhammer.

Fehr, E. 2000. Cooperation and punishment in public goods experiments. *Am. Econ. Rev.* **90**:980–994.

Friedman, M. 1953. Essays in Positive Economics. Chicago: Univ. of Chicago Press.

Fudenberg, D., and J. Tirole. 1991. Game Theory. Cambridge, MA: MIT Press.

Gigerenzer, G., P.M. Todd, and the ABC Research Group. 1999. Simple Heuristics That Make Us Smart. New York: Oxford Univ. Press.

Glimcher, P.W. 2003. Decisions, Uncertainty, and the Brain: The Science of Neuroeconomics. Cambridge, MA: MIT Press.

Goldstein, W.M., and R.M. Hogarth. 1997. Judgment and decision research: Some historical context. In: Research on Judgment and Decision Making, ed. W.M. Goldstein and R.M. Hogarth, pp. 3–65. Cambridge: Cambridge Univ. Press.

Goldstein, W.M., and E.U. Weber. 1997. Content and discontent: Indications and implications of domain specificity in preferential decision making. In: Research on Judgment and Decision Making, ed. W.M. Goldstein und R.M. Hogarth, pp. 566–617. Cambridge: Cambridge Univ. Press.

Granovetter, M. 1985. Economic action and social structure: The problem of embeddedness. *Am. J. Sociol.* **91**:481–510.

Head, H. 1920. Studies in Neurology. Oxford: Oxford Univ. Press.

Hebb, D.O. 1949. The Organization of Behavior: A Neuropsychological Theory. New York: Wiley.

Hodgson, G.M. 1988. Economics and Institutions: A Manifesto for a Modern Institutional Economics. Philadelphia: Univ. of Pennsylvania Press.

Hogarth, R.M., B.J. Gibbs, C.R.M. McKenzie, and M.A. Marquis. 1997. Learning from feedback: Exactingness and incentives. In: Research on Judgment and Decision Making, ed. W.M. Goldstein and R.M. Hogarth, pp. 244–284. Cambridge: Cambridge Univ. Press.

Kahneman, D. 2000. Experienced utility and objective happiness: A moment-based approach. In: Choices, Values, and Frames, ed. D. Kahneman and A. Tversky, pp. 673–692. Cambridge: Cambridge Univ. Press.

Lashley, K.S. 1951. The problem of serial order in behaviour. In: Cerebral Mechanisms in Behaviour, ed. L.A. Jeffress, pp. 112–146. New York: Wiley.

Levinson, S.C. 1995. Interactional biases in human thinking. In: Social Intelligence and Interaction, ed. E. Goody, pp. 221–260. Cambridge: Cambridge Univ. Press.

Lewis, M.D. 2005. Bridging emotion theory and neurobiology through dynamic systems modeling. *Behav. Brain Sci.* **28**:169–194.

Mantzavinos, C. 2001. Individuals, Institutions, and Markets. Cambridge: Cambridge Univ. Press.

National Research Council. 2001. Climate Change Science: An Analysis of Some Key Questions. Washington, D.C.: Natl. Acad. Press.

Nisbett, R.E., and L. Ross. 1980. Human Inference: Strategies and Shortcomings of Social Judgment. Englewood Cliffs, NJ: Prentice Hall.

Ostrom, E. 1990. Governing the Commons: The Evolution of Institutions for Collective Action. Cambridge: Cambridge Univ. Press.

Ostrom, E. 1998. A behavioral approach to the rational choice theory of collective action. *Am. Pol. Sci. Rev.* **92**:1–22.

Ostrom, E., T. Dietz, N. Dolsak et al., eds. 2002. The Drama of the Commons. Washington, D.C.: Natl. Acad. Press.

Payne, J.W., J.R. Bettman, and E.J. Johnson. 1997. The adaptive decision maker: Effort and accuracy in choice. In: Research on Judgment and Decision Making: Currents, Connections, and Controversies, ed. W.M. Goldstein and R.M. Hogarth, pp. 181–204. Cambridge: Cambridge Univ. Press.

Pennington, N., and R. Hastie. 1993. Reasoning in explanation-based decision-making. *Cognition* **49**:123–163.

Pennington, N., and R. Hastie. 1997. Explanation-based decision making: Effects of memory structure on judgment. In: Research in Judgment and Decision Making, ed. W.M. Goldstein and R.M. Hogarth, pp. 454–481. Cambridge: Cambridge Univ. Press.

Piaget, J., and M. Gabain. 1932. The Moral Judgment of the Child. London: Trubner.

Rakison, D.H., and L.M. Oakes. 2003. Early Category and Concept Development: Making Sense of the Blooming, Buzzing Confusion. Oxford: Oxford Univ. Press.

Savage, L.J. 1954. The Foundations of Statistics. New York: Wiley.

Schlicht, E. 1998. On Custom in the Economy. Oxford: Clarendon.

Selten, R. 1998. Aspiration adaptation theory. *J. Math. Psychol.* **42**:191–214.

Shafir, E., I. Simonson, and A. Tversky. 2000. Reason-based choice. In: Choices, Values, and Frames, ed. D. Kahneman and A. Tversky, pp. 597–619. Cambridge: Cambridge Univ. Press.

Simon, H.A. 1955. A behavioural model of rational choice. *Qtly. J. Econ.* **69**:99–118.

Simon, H.A. 1972. Theories of bounded rationality. In: Decision and Organisation: A Volume in Honour of Jacob Marschak, ed. C.B. McGuire und R. Radner, chap. 8. Amsterdam: North Holland.

Simon, H.A. 1979. Rational decision making in business organisations. *Am. Econ. Rev.* **69**:493–513.

Singer, W. 1991. Die Entwicklung kognitiver Strukturen: Ein selbstreferentieller Lernprozess. In: Gedächtnis: Probleme und Perspektiven der interdisziplinären Gedächtnisforschung, ed. S.J. Schmidt, pp. 96–126. Frankfurt: Suhrkamp.

Singer, W. 2003. Hirnentwicklung—neuronale Plastizität—Lernen. In: Lehrbuch der Physiologie, ed. R. Klinke and S. Silbernagl, pp. 743–756. Stuttgart: Thieme.

Skinner, B.F. 1938. The Behavior of Organisms: An Experimental Analysis. New York: Appleton Century.

Stanovich, K.E., and R.F. West. 2000. Individual differences in reasoning: Implications for the rationality debate? *Behav. Brain Sci.* **23**:645–665.

Strack, F., and R. Deutsch. 2004. Reflective and impulsive determinants of social behavior. *Pers. Soc. Psychol. Rev.* **8**:220–247.

Thompson, M., R. Ellis, and A. Wildavsky. 1990. Cultural Theory. Boulder, CO: Westview Press.

Turner, M. 2001. Cognitive Dimensions of Social Science. New York: Oxford Univ. Press.

Wade-Benzoni, K.A., A.E. Tenbrunsel, and M.H. Bazerman. 1996. Egocentric interpretations of fairness in asymmetric, environmental social dilemmas: Explaining harvesting behavior and the role of communication. *Org. Behav. Hum. Dec. Proc.* **67**:111–126.

Wegner, G. 1996. Wirtschaftspolitik zwischen Selbst- und Fremdsteuerung: Ein neuer Ansatz. Baden-Baden: Nomos.

Weick, K.E., and K.H. Roberts. 1993. Collective mind in organizations: Heedful interrelating on flight decks. *Admin. Sci. Qtly.* **38**:357–381.

Weigend, A. 1994. On overfitting and the effective number of hidden units. In: Proc. 1993 Connectionist Models Summer School, ed. M.C. Mozer, pp. 335–342. Hillsdale, NJ: Erlbaum.

5

Heuristics inside the Firm

Perspectives from Behavioral Law and Economics

Donald C. Langevoort

Georgetown University Law Center, Washington, D.C. 20001, U.S.A.

ABSTRACT

The learning about cognitive heuristics translates awkwardly when applied to judgment and decision making within firms, for a variety of reasons. These difficulties notwithstanding, there are also reasons to suspect that a fruitful collaboration between studies of heuristics and structures of organizational behavior can produce insights of interest and importance to legal scholars. This chapter speculates on two such possibilities: (a) the resemblance between individual cognitive heuristics and what organizational researchers call the "architecture of simplicity" in the cognitive structure of the firm and (b) the question of whether some kinds of cognitive traits (apart from orthodox economic rationality) can be favored in firm promotion tournaments, leading to a disproportionate representation of such people in senior executive teams. Overconfidence is explored as such a possibility. The chapter concludes with an examination of the socio-legal implications of a more cognitive perspective on human behavior within firms.

INTRODUCTION

Behavioral theories of judgment and decision making translate awkwardly when used to predict decisions by firms. Firm-level decisions—even if necessarily the product of judgments by human actors—typically have a collective character, so that what we know about individual decisions does not neatly apply. Even what we have learned about the cognitive features of small group behavior often fails to capture the layered complexity of organizational choice.

Then there is the rich institutional context in which firms operate. In competitive markets, at least, there are ample incentives to correct for decision-making flaws and opportunities to learn from experience. Because the labor market offers up a mix of potential employees with varying skills and traits, firms can choose to hire and promote only those who demonstrate comparative deliberative fitness. Firms are often well aware of the risks of cognitive bias and engage in wide-ranging organizational correctives. Banks, for example, often separate the lending and work-out functions so as to avoid the "sunk cost" problem (Heath et al. 1998). For these reasons, behavioral law and economics might seem to have little that is compelling to say about organizational decisions (Arlen et al. 2002).

In this chapter, however, I present arguments to the contrary: cognitive heuristics (and perhaps even "biases") play a significant role inside the firm that deserves serious scholarly attention. My starting point is the main insight of the "fast and frugal" research program—that in settings with ill-defined tasks but good feedback mechanisms, heuristics evolve and adapt to the local ecology so as to produce efficient decisions with minimal cognitive effort (e.g., Gigerenzer, this volume). For a variety of reasons, business firms create an ideal environment for these kinds of heuristics to flourish. The adaptive toolkit will support many kinds of business decisions precisely because fast and frugal heuristics are necessary to coordinate multi-party behavior in a high-velocity setting.

My next claim is more aggressive. The ecology of the firm is filled with rewards and penalties, structured in large part by creating a "tournament" in which agents compete for promotions, power, and perquisites. In this competition, cognitive traits are rewarded or punished based on how fit they make the person possessing them. Under these circumstances, we may find that the traits that lead to tournament success inside the firm differ from those that we might discover in more general populations. In other words, traits may be found inside the executive suite as a result of this ecology that we might not find as robustly in other places.

Both points about heuristics inside the firm lead to important normative questions. Are these heuristics good for the firms' agents but suboptimal for the firm itself, so as to be a form of subconscious moral hazard? And even if adaptive at the level of the firm, do the heuristics adapted either to simplicity or survivorship create a risk that decisions inside the firm will unintentionally downplay factors that society values? These questions create a natural bridge connecting the interests of psychologists, economists, and lawyers and point to an important research agenda that is only now starting to take shape.

FAST AND FRUGAL HEURISTICS AND THE ARCHITECTURE OF SIMPLICITY

On an individual level, cognitive heuristics have the virtue of facilitating both thought and action, simplifying decisions in a way that makes them manageable. They pay off in terms of more accurate judgment and decision making. This is a standard reason why rational choice-oriented scholars have chafed at the association of heuristics with error or irrationality. There may be a departure from the

Bayesian model of optimal choice, but that may be an adaptive response to the informational complexity and ambiguity of the world we inhabit.

How does this translate inside the firm? One level is simple: the individuals who populate the firm may be engaged in heuristic judgment, and if that does in fact make them smarter, we can expect such thinking to flourish in an efficient organization. But there is a more subtle perspective that I want to pursue. What is striking about the fast and frugal heuristics concept is its similarity to a line of thought about organizational behavior that has achieved some currency in the literature.

The ultimate problem of organizational behavior is one of coordination: a large group of persons has to be organized so that they act consistently in pursuit of the firm's goals rather than at odds with each other. The hierarchical organization is the typical form, though hardly inevitable. Even putting aside the daunting agency cost problems associated with coordination, getting everyone "on the same page" is a difficult task, especially if different people or groups have varying information about the firm's risks and prospects. If we assume that firms operate in highly ambiguous informational environments, the internal clash of construals and argument about appropriate courses of action is potentially disabling. Successful firms must overcome this problem.

The economists' standard metaphor in the theory of the firm is the "nexus of contracts." While the metaphor is perfectly useful as contract is generally understood in that literature, the organizational behavior perspective suggests that this rhetoric misses something important. What is constantly happening within firms is a set of negotiations among the firm's agents and stakeholders—negotiations not only of power and authority but of inference. How do people define their situation? What is the right direction to proceed? The on-going cognitive dimension to this process leads me to suggest that the firm is more a nexus of negotiations than a nexus of contracts. The adaptive firm is the one where the negotiations are fruitful enough to lead to consistency in productive action. And for this to happen, much of the coordination has to be implicit: agents have to be able to predict the perceptions and judgments of fellow agents without communication.

One way of generating consistent inferences within the firm is through a common culture—an accepted and compelling definition of "who we are and what we're about." The more there is consensus on these kinds of questions, the easier the internal negotiations are to resolve. I will return to culture later. But culture is just one coordinating device among many. More broadly, firms seek coordination in what Miller calls "the architecture of simplicity" (Miller 1993; see also Henderson and Clark 1990). Coordination is possible in the absence of communication only if the behavior of others is readily predictable—and predictability conjoins with efficiency when decisions are made in a fast and frugal fashion. In other words, only when the firm insists on fast and frugal reasoning will the behavior of the group become consistent.

The architecture of the firm extends to its norms, routines, allocations of authority, and day-to-day procedures. What is notable about many firms is the way these norms, routines, and procedures are also simplifying. They reduce the scope of what needs to be paid attention—taking "off the table" thoughts or ideas inconsistent with the processes that have (apparently) been successful in the immediate past. In other words, the message is tacitly communicated that the accepted routines are not easily open to renegotiation. Culture does come into play here as a way of legitimating the "official" construals: one can reasonably call these the firm's internal myths.

The important thing here is that this architectural simplicity makes the firm "smarter" in much the same way as cognitive heuristics do for individuals. Disabling doubts and distractions are removed, and the actors inside the firm concentrate on the information most closely relevant to the task at hand as defined by the firm's previous experience. It is ecologically efficient in that it responds well to the current incentive structure. As with individual heuristics, however, the adaptive character of the simplicity is "on average." What architectural simplification does is focus and concentrate the firm's efforts on the task at hand; what it can deprive the firm of is the ability to react and change in the face of subtle, unpredicted shifts in the firm's external environment. It is highly efficient in the short term. However, sometimes "off the table" ideas deserve attention, and the failure to give them attention is harmful. Indeed, a strain of evolutionary thought in organizational dynamics is that success sows the seeds of a firm's eventual destruction (Hannan and Freeman 1984). Kenneth Arrow describes the process as one where "the very pursuit of efficiency may lead to rigidity and unresponsiveness to further change" (Arrow 1974, p. 49). What worked is built into the firm's simple architecture and sustains the firm well, until those routines lose their competitive fitness.

The obvious question is whether firms anticipate this and build greater cognitive openness into their architecture. Certainly most try, and some succeed. What seems clear, however, is that such flexibility is costly in terms of near-term productivity, that is, the loss of the virtues of simplification by letting in conflicting and contestable information and inferences. (There is also an agency cost problem here, to be sure, because the threat of change disrupts established distributions of rents among agents of the firm.) "Managing change" is recognized as profoundly difficult in organizational behavior studies (e.g., Repenning and Sterman 2002).

ADAPTIVE HEURISTICS: TOURNAMENTS AND INTERNAL COMPETITION

The preceding discussion invoked heuristics simply by analogy inside the organization. Architectural simplicity may operate with similar benefits on a large-scale level as fast and frugal heuristics do for individuals. But we can come closer than that to the relevance of heuristics to organizational behavior, albeit at the risk of tapping into one of the on-going debates in the organizational behavior literature: is it worthwhile to focus on individual decision making, or do social dynamics so dominate the determination of organizational activity that the "macro" approach is the only interesting level of inquiry (Staw and Sutton 1993)?

The argument for the former is straightforward and intuitive. Although some forms of activity by the firm are surely bureaucratic in nature, many decisions of significant consequence are made either by a single individual or small group. Board of directors' decisions would be an example, as would decisions made with relative autonomy by the chief executive officer (CEO) or the senior management team. The characteristic of significant individual or small-group decisions is that they tend to be made by persons who have achieved a high level of power and authority in the firm. Application of our understanding of "ordinary" heuristics to decisions by high-level managers is problematic for a number of reasons noted earlier. A standard one is that persons who rise in the organization to achieve that kind of power are not ordinary, but rather the survivors in a tournament that presumably weeds out those with inferior cognitive traits. The orthodox economist's objection to the sustained presence of cognitive biases in market settings is that markets penalize weak thinking and thus lead to the triumph of the intelligent. The internal labor markets of firms would seem to be a perfect example.

This is a fascinating challenge to the behavioralists, raising a point that work in behavioral law and economics has not yet taken sufficiently seriously. That body of scholarship has, by and large, focused on predictable psychological tendencies found in peoples' judgment and decision making. The search is for statistically significant behavioral commonalities among large normal populations. Upon identifying a common cognitive trait, its presence in actors in interesting legal or economic situations is assumed, leading to predictions about the likely behavioral outcomes and assessments of how effective the law is in addressing that behavior. The road less traveled by legal behaviorists is one that focuses on cognitive differences among people, rather than similarities. Yet this has to be important, for we know not only that many aspects of judgment and decision making are highly situational (and hence not always invoked by the same person, depending on the task and how it is framed) but also that decision-making traits are unevenly distributed among the population. A next-stage project for behavioral economics is how people with different psychological make-ups are likely to fare in economic settings—like employment tournaments—where they interact and compete.

Two profoundly interesting questions are these: is there a kind of person, in terms of cognitive make-up, who is more likely (on average) to win the successive rounds of a promotion tournament inside a firm so that the winner's circle—the executive suite—is disproportionately populated by them? If so, are there peculiar traits of judgment that they bring to the job as a result of this competitive fitness that help us understand decision making at the top in terms of either internal firm efficiency or outward social or legal responsibility?

In order for a trait to be favored in the successive rounds of a labor tournament, it has to be economically adaptive. Unless some story can be told about why the trait makes success more likely, its survivorship is implausible. Hence, the search must be for some reason why a particular heuristic would result in competitive success. We could, of course, posit that fast and frugal modes of thinking are themselves favored because they lead to more ecologically valid decisions in an environment that requires fast-paced judgment (Todd and Gigerenzer 2003). Tournament survivors would be those with well-developed habits about how to make accurate choices with a minimum of deliberation or information search. This is simply a variation on the standard rationality account—fast and frugal heuristics lead to superior results.

Could Overconfidence Be a Corporate Survival Trait?

To illustrate my point that the tournament structure inside the firm create an ecology that may reward cognitive traits different from those found in more general populations, let me turn to a more controversial question: whether overconfidence is a common heuristic or bias. Psychologists debate whether the empirical evidence adequately demonstrates that overconfidence—which I define broadly to include egocentric traits such as overoptimism, inflated self-efficacy, and the illusion of control—exists in real settings or is just a laboratory artifact. As a lawyer, I have no hope of judging this empirical dispute.[1] I simply want to show how the ecology of the firm *could* plausibly reward those who happen to be overconfident in such a way that such a disposition would flourish there even if it is not common generally.

Any application of heuristics to the workings of the firm should not generalize excessively: firms differ markedly in the ecologies in which they operate and those their agents face. To avoid overgeneralization, I want to focus on a specific (but important) type of firm, one that operates in a highly competitive marketplace and—in response to those competitive pressures—imposes strong pressures on its key employees to meet "stretch"-type goals as a condition for promotion up the corporate ladder (e.g., high-tech firms). These kinds of firms are

---

[1] On the debate, see Gigerenzer (2000), Griffin and Tversky (1992), and Juslin et al. (2000). Legal scholars are ill-positioned to choose among competing empirical or descriptive claims, and my chapter makes no effort to judge the psychological research. But legal inquiry cannot wait for scholarly consensus either because legal analysis works inevitably from simplifying models of behavior. For lawyers, the best utilization of the research takes the form of a rough expected value calculation: if the insight has a reasonable likelihood of traction based on laboratory evidence, field observation, or theory-based prediction, legal scholars ought to factor the possibility into their cost-benefit assessment of how fairly or efficiently the law responds to a particular situation or problem.

the ones where I think overconfidence is most likely to be rewarded, causing an interesting form of adaptation.[2]

Some psychologists have argued that a cluster of traits associated with overconfidence has positive payoffs for individuals so long as they do not become excessive. The reasons are fairly straightforward. High levels of self-esteem or self-confidence lead to a greater willingness to take risks and greater persistence in the face of adversity than more realistic assessments, which are rewarded. True, increased risk taking means that some people who fall into this category will suffer dramatically. But the luckier risk takers will outperform more risk-averse realists, and the positive feedback will simply enhance their sense of self-efficacy. This "motivation value," for example, is the heart of Benabou and Tirole's (2002) economic model of why rational agents would prefer to induce through self-deception an inflated sense of confidence in their own abilities. It is a valuable asset for persons with imperfect willpower, even though it imposes costs as well.

A tournament model of the internal labor market as the road to power and authority at the top of the hierarchy suggests one reason why overconfidence could be associated with survivorship. Imagine a large number of people placed in a tournament, selected with some reason to believe that they have the basic technical skills necessary to perform well. If innate talent and skill are imperfectly observable, then outcomes will provide the evidence on which higher-ups decide who wins in the various rounds. Here, risk-preferring agents will be the more extreme winners (and losers), with the more risk averse falling in the middle of the probability distribution. If it is the extreme winners who are favored and chosen to move on to the next round—or are given advantages vis-à-vis others in successive rounds based on their past success—the finalists will be those risk takers lucky enough to have avoided the predictable failures.[3] In a large firm, we can expect that there will be enough contestants so that over many iterations there will be a few who ride a lucky streak to the top once they are willing to bear enough risk. Moderate blindness to the consequences (i.e., overconfidence) encourages such risk taking and prompts the persistence and effort to sustain the gamble. From this alone, we might predict that CEOs of highly entrepreneurial firms exhibit significant egocentric bias, which is consistent with some

---

[2] I would predict that we would see little evidence of overconfidence and greater risk aversion among CEOs of firms that are not subject to strong competitive pressures in either its product or capital markets (e.g., utilities). The older the firm, on average, the less likely it is to reward overoptimism.

[3] A complementary explanation here focuses on the internal budgeting decisions of firms. In firms that put proposed projects in competition with each other for funding, a "winner's curse" emerges—the winner will be the project founded on the greatest optimism, which provides an incentive to managers to adopt such a bias (Kahneman and Lovallo 1993, p. 29). Kahneman and Lovallo also note that a bias toward overconfidence is natural "inside" the firm because managers anchor on salient information (e.g., past success or other unique information) and do not generalize in a way that induces caution.

observations in the business literature (e.g., Bernardo and Welch 2001). Not only do they gain from overconfidence from the beginning, but the fact of their success—even if really more luck than they think—leads to further inflation of that self-perception.

Standing alone, however, the tournament model simply predicts that the lucky risk takers will be the survivors. It does not explain why—unless a bias toward overconfidence at the top enhances *the firm's* efficiency—those who control the firm would allow this to happen. To this, there are many responses. One possibility, of course, is that the disciplining functions of corporate governance are relatively limited. Observations of who "won" each round of the tournament by reference to observed outcomes are themselves fast and frugal. More detailed evaluations are costly and imprecise, inviting substantial influence tactics by the competitors. Once this method of evaluation is invoked, it allocates power to those who possess the relevant traits, which they can be expected to fight to retain. As is well understood in the corporate governance literature, the board may lack the incentive to fight against this distribution of executive power even if it were in the firm's interest to do so.

In fact, there are reasons to suspect that the firm may actually prefer overconfident senior managers. The reasons fall into two basic categories. The first taps into the points made earlier about the positive benefits of overconfidence. If this trait leads to harder work, more persistence, and more willingness to bear risk, these outcomes benefit the firm. Another point is that confidence is contagious and may be an important driver of internal firm culture. As noted, the central task of the organization is to simplify the process of internal negotiation. Disagreement about the firm's situation is disabling, and if that disagreement is coupled with pessimism, the disability produces defensive and self-serving actions by employees. By contrast, confidence inspires, and it may take some degree of overconfidence to generate that kind of leadership in an environment fraught—realistically—with doubt and ambiguity. Benabou and Tirole observe that these kinds of pay-offs explain "why people typically prefer self-confident co-workers, managers, employees, teammates, soldiers, etc., to self-doubting ones, and why they spend substantial time and effort supporting the morale of those with whom they end up being matched" (Benabou and Tirole 2002, p. 878).

The other main reason why firms might prefer overconfident managers connects to the economics of corporate finance. The tournament aside, managers who are heavily invested in firm-specific capital (and have a job to protect) are otherwise risk averse. Diversified shareholders do not share this aversion. Thus, shareholders may want firms to select for overconfident managers, whose risk preferences might well come closer to their own (Heaton 2002; Gervais et al. 2003; Goel and Thakor 2000). In this sense, self-efficacy biases may help neutralize others that incline managers toward maintenance of the status quo. Goel and Thakor also claim that there is another benefit from this: overconfident senior managers select a portfolio of higher-risk projects for subordinates to carry out, permitting a better evaluation of which candidates for promotion are truly skilled as opposed to merely competent (Goel and Thakor 2000).

Finally, we should note that decisions that are the product of small group processes are as likely, if not more so, to demonstrate an optimism bias (Heath and Jourden 1997). The tendency of small groups to become risk preferring suggests that if that group is initially populated by overconfident individuals, the resulting dynamic will strengthen the effect, not be a moderating influence.

Again, none of this proves that overconfidence will dominate in the promotion tournament of any given firm—the matter remains an open empirical question, difficult to resolve scientifically. The point is that one can see why the ecology of a highly competitive firm could be such that executive-level heuristics evolve in that direction. In that sense, it is a good illustration of the fit between the fast and frugal heuristics research program and the study of organizational behavior.

Optimistic Cultures

We can combine certain of the insights in the previous two parts to say something about the "heuristics" likely to be embedded in the cultures of successful, entrepreneurial firms. Firms require a set of simplifying norms, routines, and perceptions to reduce the transaction costs associated with coordinating large numbers of individuals in order to undertake a given task. Perception is the key here, because the norms and routines must be legitimated in the eyes of the firm's agents. They have to be motivated to accept the common script, given the selfish reasons to defect that so often arise. The principal task of executive leadership is to motivate and persuade subordinates of the accuracy and utility of the chosen "vision" (Van den Steen 2001).

Optimism is a more powerful motivator than realism, especially if realism involves the acknowledgment of doubt or, far worse, pessimism. Optimism promises future joint gains that can be distributed liberally among the players, providing a strong incentive to trust and cooperate (Langevoort 1997). By contrast, pessimism provokes "last period" kinds of behaviors that are internally destructive. One can expect that, just like individuals, firms that embrace an optimistic, "can do" culture would take more risks and be more focused and persistent in the face of adversity. In the tournament among competing firms, the same survivorship bias emerges; it is an ecologically robust organizational heuristic.

SOCIO-LEGAL IMPLICATIONS AND THE PRINCIPAL-AGENT PROBLEM

The foregoing points were simply meant to show how the ecology of any given firm might elicit a set of heuristics different from what we might observe in different environments—something the fast and frugal heuristics program should readily embrace. Assessing whether these heuristics really exist inside the firm, and if so, whether they are good or bad, is a different matter.

Many empirical studies of organizational behavior identify persistent departures from firm-level optimality, even in competitive markets, that are consistent with biases (e.g., Zajac and Bazerman 1991). Studies of over-entry into new product markets or ill-advised plant expansion, for example, treat such forms of bureaucratic judgment as commonplace. However, this evidence may just point to a principal-agent problem. Decisions by firms may not be in the firm's long-term best interests because agency cost problems interfere: what influential managers perceive as their self-interest is often different from what is best for the firm, so that managers will engage in influence activities to skew firm-level decisions in their favor (Milgrom and Roberts 1992). If constraints (governance, contracts, markets, and so on) are imperfect, such rent-seeking behavior by managers will dominate. That we should observe overexpansion in plant, equipment, or product lines is not surprising given the tangible rewards that such steps may create and the lax discipline on managerial opportunism found in many firms.

This is an important area for research. The fast and frugal research paradigm simply posits that heuristics will adapt to the incentives in the local environment. Are there particular kinds of heuristics inside the firm that are likely to reflect self-serving rather than firm-oriented goals? One possibility might be those that lead to more myopic forms of perception or judgment because the relevant time horizon for most agents (especially in a given round of the promotion tournament) is shorter than that of the firm. In a well-known study of ethical decision making by corporate managers, Messick and Bazerman describe how decision simplification puts "off the table" second and third level effects in favor of immediate costs and benefits (Messick and Bazerman 1996; see also Loewenstein 1996).

As noted, however, other kinds of internal heuristics may be efficient for the firm so as not to raise an obvious agency cost problem. The more troubling possibility is that what may be internally efficient creates suboptimal decisions from a broader social perspective. This is quite relevant to the problem of compliance with legal rules. A rule of product liability in tort law, for example, might impose on the firm a duty to act "reasonably" in assessing risks and taking appropriate precautions. The reasonableness standard involves a balancing of the likelihood of harm against the costs of intervention. Any systematic bias that causes the firm to disregard or underestimate risk (or overestimate the ability to control the risk) will skew this calculation. The difficulties for law become more severe in a heuristics-driven environment when the law uses constructs such as intent or knowledge as standards for liability. Efficient heuristics may limit the deliberative process so that there is no contemporaneous awareness of what is being disregarded—which may include factors that society values. For example, it may be adaptive for a firm to search for new employees using familiarity tests (see Gigerenzer, this volume). But the effect may be to exclude groups that lack prior connections to the local social network, which may lead to persistent patterns of discrimination.

An example of how heuristics can evolve into a troubling pattern in the face of a poorly designed environment is described by Levy (2001) in a study of behavior by a team of workers in a harbor sewage treatment plant. For a variety of reasons, some of which were purely political, the group felt pressure to keep the system running without inviting intervention from superiors. In this setting, decisions evolved in a highly heuristic form, so that extraordinary efforts were made to make patchwork corrections and keep the system within the prescribed guidelines—even though the effect was to invite disaster by deferring needed structural maintenance. Prior to the predictable breakdown, the group was highly protective of its simplified decision making precisely because of the near-term efficiencies it produced.

Heuristics that are adaptive internally but troublesome socially will arise if we believe that overoptimism is a survivor trait leading to an excess of it in the executive suite, especially when coupled with other biases documented in the behavioral literature, such as those related to commitment. Managers who undertake some risky activity will begin with an inflated sense of their ability to manage the risk, if they perceive it at all. Positive feedback in the early stages of the activity (e.g., no appearance of potential harms) will reinforce the illusion. If in the middle stages evidence of risk surfaces, the managers will be disinclined to acknowledge it or will deny its significance. They are committed to the activity, and acknowledgment of the risk in hindsight calls into question the reasonableness of the decision in the first place (Darley 1996). This "optimism-commitment whipsaw" (Langevoort 1997, p. 167) will gradually lead the firm much deeper into trouble.

Corporate governance is a particularly fertile field in which to explore the impact of these kinds of heuristics. The recent financial scandals in the U.S. may well illustrate some of these dangers. Enron Corporation transformed itself from "hard asset" company into a market maker (or market creator) of largely synthetic financial interests in a variety of natural and technological resources. Early efforts in this transition were remarkably successful, and the company became the acknowledged leader in the transition of energy markets, with a fast rising market capitalization. By all accounts, its leaders and culture were infused with optimism and a rapidly growing sense of control over its environment. Gradually—as its market capitalization grew to make it the seventh largest U.S. firm—the aggressiveness of its bets grew. Soon, it was structuring deals to bring in new capital and move old assets off its balance sheet that were pegged to its own stock price. So long as the stock price stayed high, the source of funding grew. But anything that would bring down the stock price would trigger layers of new debt, which would (and did) ultimately destroy the company's credit rating and hence access to further funding. One cannot read the accounts of Enron's demise without sensing that it was a company—and set of senior managers—with a highly "focused" culture that suppressed thoughtful risk analysis from the beginning, which grew increasingly more aggressive as positive feedback became the only internally legitimate focal point. While there was what seems to be deliberate fraud in the company's disclosures, evidence of real fraud (as opposed to aggressive accounting techniques) appears fairly late in the story, after the company's executives were locked-in to public representations that were increasingly difficult to sustain in the face of unexpected adversity.

The question that has been debated is why those a step removed from the internal culture—outside directors, auditors, lawyers—did not confront the potential for bias effectively. The most likely answers have to do with conflicts of interest and other agency cost problems. However, the evidence is also consistent with the possibility that those in authority are loathe to interfere with an optimistic corporate culture that is on a hot streak of success, for fear of disabling the very motivational forces that make the firm competitive. As Kahneman and Lovallo (1993, p. 30) put it, "a successful effort to improve the realism of assessments could do more harm than good in an organization that relies on unfounded optimism to ward off paralysis." It may be difficult to implement the strategy of allowing managerial overconfidence to have relatively free reign but for the board or investors to step in nimbly when that confidence threatens to take the company out of bounds (Malmendier and Tate 2002). Moreover, the board can itself become subject to bias, for it can mistake tangible evidence of success as reason not to intervene and then resist evidence that it acted imprudently in allowing the managerial aggressiveness to go on as long as it did.

Again, the law can always seek to overcome this, by increasing the severity of the threat for misconduct (and making sure that the label used to impose liability is elastic enough to capture heuristics-driven decisions). Presumably, at some level the threat will be great enough that it becomes worthwhile to make changes in the local ecology, even if they are costly. The important point here is not that the law is impotent in the face of managerial overconfidence, but rather that the legal response will be more costly than we might think, in terms of enforcement resources, the externalities associated with harsh enforcement,[4] and the immeasurable impact on firm motivation.

CONCLUSION

The value added by a behavioral approach comes largely in emphasizing the uncertainty and ambiguity associated with organizational decision making (e.g., Levitt and March 1988)—ambiguity that must be resolved efficiently if the task of intra-firm coordination is to succeed. If the firm is indeed a nexus of

---

[4] For example, the willingness to seek a criminal indictment against the accounting firm of Arthur Andersen—resulting in the firm's destruction—produced severe job loss and a reduction in the competitiveness of the worldwide accounting marketplace.

negotiations, successful coordination begins with agreement about the prevailing state of affairs. The cognitive dimension to the tasks of decision making and coordination offers a useful lens for analyzing and making predictions about the behavior of the firm.

In sum, there is no reason for behavioral legal economists to shy away from the internal workings of the firm as a subject of inquiry. There is ample reason to suspect that heuristics of various sorts are likely to thrive in highly competitive environments, delivering positive pay-offs for both agents and organizations. Whether society benefits or suffers from this is a harder question deserving serious attention.

ACKNOWLEDGMENTS

Thanks to Gerd Gigerenzer, Christoph Engel, and others at the Dahlem Workshop for helpful comments. For a topic this large to be addressed in so few pages, many implications, qualifications, and points of contention—many of which they were kind enough to point out to me—have to be slighted. This chapter is meant to begin a conversation, not fully articulate or justify my claims (much less resolve any of the underlying issues).

REFERENCES

Arlen, J., M. Spitzer, and E. Talley. 2002. Endowment effects within corporate agency relationships. *J. Legal Stud.* **31**:1–37.

Arrow, K. 1974. The Limits of Organization. New York: Norton.

Benabou, R., and J. Tirole. 2002. Self-confidence and personal motivation. *Qtly. J. Econ.* **117**:871–915.

Bernardo, A., and I. Welch. 2001. On the evolution of overconfidence and entrepreneurs. *J. Econ. Manag. Strat.* **10**:301–330.

Darley, J. 1996. How organizations socialize individuals into evildoing. In: Codes of Conduct, ed. D. Messick and A. Tenbrunsel, pp. 13–43. New York: Russell Sage.

Gervais, S., J.B. Heaton, and T. Odean. 2003. Overconfidence, investment policy and executive stock options. Rodney L. White Center for Financial Research Working Paper 15–02. http://ssrn.com/abstract=361200

Gigerenzer, G. 2000. Adaptive Thinking: Rationality in the Real World. New York: Oxford Univ. Press.

Goel, A., and A. Thakor. 2000. Rationality, overconfidence and leadership. Univ. of Michigan Business School Working Paper. http://ssrn.com/abstract=244999

Griffin, D.W., and A. Tversky. 1992. The weighing of evidence and the determinants of confidence. *Cog. Psych.* **24**:411–435.

Hannan, M., and J. Freeman. 1984. Structural inertia and organizational change. *Am. Sociol. Rev.* **49**:149–164.

Heath, C., and F. Jourden. 1997. Illusions, disillusions and the buffering effects of groups. *Org. Behav. Hum. Dec. Proc.* **69**:103–116.

Heath, C., R.P. Larrick, and J. Klayman. 1998. Cognitive repairs: How organizational practices can compensate for individual shortcomings. *Res. Org. Behav.* **20**:1–37.

Heaton, J.B. 2002. Managerial optimism and corporate finance. *Finan. Manag.* **31**: 33–45.

Henderson, R., and K. Clark. 1990. Architectural innovation: The reconfiguration of existing product technologies and the failure of established firms. *Admin. Sci. Qtly.* **35**:9–30.

Juslin, P., A. Winman, and H. Olsson. 2000. Naive empiricism and dogmatism in confidence research: A critical examination of the hard-easy effect. *Psychol. Rev.* **107**:384–396.

Kahneman, D., and D. Lovallo. 1993. Timid choices and bold forecasts: A cognitive perspective on risk taking. *Manag. Sci.* **39**:17–31.

Langevoort, D. 1997. Organized illusions: A behavioral theory of why corporations mislead stock market investors (and cause other social harms). *Univ. of Pennsyl. Law Rev.* **146**:101–172.

Levitt, B., and J. March. 1988. Organizational learning. *Ann. Rev. Sociol.* **14**:319–340.

Levy, P. 2001. The Nut Island effect: When good teams go wrong. *Harvard Bus. Rev.* **79**:51–59.

Loewenstein, G. 1996. Behavioral decision theory and business ethics: Skewed trade-offs between self and others. In: Codes of Conduct, ed. D. Messick and A. Tenbrunsel, pp. 214–227. New York: Russell Sage.

Malmendier, U., and G. Tate. 2002. CEO overconfidence and corporate investment. *J. Finance* **60**:2261–2700.

Messick, D., and M. Bazerman. 1996. Ethical leadership and the psychology of decision making. *Sloan Manag. Rev.* **37**:9–22.

Milgrom, P., and J. Roberts. 1992. Economics, Organization and Management. Englewood Cliffs, NJ: Prentice Hall.

Miller, D. 1993. The architecture of simplicity. *Acad. Manag. Rev.* **18**:116–138.

Repenning, N., and J. Sterman. 2002. Capability traps and self-confirming attribution errors in the dynamics of process improvement. *Admin. Sci. Qtly.* **47**:265–295.

Staw, B., and R. Sutton. 1993. Macro organizational psychology. In: Social Psychology in Organizations, ed. J.K. Murnighan, pp. 350–384. Englewood Cliffs, NJ: Prentice Hall.

Todd, P., and G. Gigerenzer. 2003. Bounding rationality to the world. *J. Econ. Psychol.* **24**:143–165.

Van den Steen, E. 2001. Organizational beliefs and managerial vision. *J. Law Econ. Org.* **21**: 256–283.

Zajac, E., and M. Bazerman. 1991. Blind spots in industry and competitor analysis: Implications of interfirm (mis)perceptions for strategic decisions. *Acad. Manag. Rev.* **16**:37–56.

Left to right: Russell Korobkin, Doug Kysar, Bob Frank, Paul Glimcher, Gerd Gigerenzer, Don Langevoort, Peter Ayton, Stefan Magen, and Bruno Frey

6

Group Report: Are Heuristics a Problem or a Solution?

Douglas A. Kysar, Rapporteur

Peter Ayton, Robert H. Frank, Bruno S. Frey,
Gerd Gigerenzer, Paul W. Glimcher, Russell Korobkin,
Donald C. Langevoort, and Stefan Magen

ABSTRACT

This chapter surveys a range of methodological, descriptive, and prescriptive issues concerning the implications of cognitive psychology for law. Included are (a) a general introduction to the subject of heuristics in decision theory, with particular attention to the distinction between optimality-based and heuristic-based decision making models within psychology; (b) an attempt to synthesize these two psychological research paradigms into a single conceptual framework that helps to identify important areas in which further research and understanding are needed; (c) an overview of scholarship to date on heuristics and the law, including an observation that this scholarship has ignored certain significant lessons of the heuristics research tradition in psychology; and (d) a compilation of suggestions for future interdisciplinary research concerning both the use of heuristics by legal subjects whose behavior the law is attempting to influence and the use of heuristics by policy makers as a model for the substantive design of legal rules.

INTRODUCTION

Between 1889 and 1908, famed Catalan architect Antoni Gaudi designed the *Colonia Güell* chapel, a remarkable structure that one expert described as a "[t]echnologically brilliant" combination of "the magic of traditional religious architecture with the originality of an isolated genius" (Sharp 2002, p. 54). At a time when contemporary designers were committed to the rationalist tools of two-dimensional drawing and mathematical calculation, Gaudi struck upon an innovative design method that was both startling in its simplicity and revolutionary in the possibilities that it unveiled. He began by drawing a scale outline of the church's foundation on a wooden panel, which he then hung upside-down from the ceiling of a small house near the work site. Beneath the inverted wooden panel, Gaudi suspended an elaborate system of ropes and weights, which, when viewed through a mirror, revealed the shape, dimensions, and load-bearing capacities of a massively complex, yet aesthetically beautiful design for the proposed structure. Photographs of the upside-down model also were taken which, when turned right side up, provided Gaudi with the perfect template for painting various architectural details to adorn the church's ingeniously derived form. Between the painted photographs and the inverted rope-and-weights model, Gaudi obtained an unorthodox, but architecturally flawless set of plans for his famous chapel, one that no engineer of his time could have derived using traditional methods.[1]

The real genius in this example rested in Gaudi's willingness to allow the form of the church to be chosen in part by nature, through gravity, rather than by the conventional give-and-take between an artist's vision and an engineer's computational abilities. At other times, however, the choices of nature are less felicitous. Health researcher Michael Tordoff, for instance, has uncovered evidence that a simple—and ordinarily reliable—behavioral heuristic found in rats can become lethal when experimenters alter the animal's environment such that the heuristic no longer provides a good "fit" with surrounding circumstances (Tordoff 2002). In Tordoff's experiment, rats provided with equal amounts of solid carbohydrate, fat, and protein automatically selected a healthy mix of nutrients, reflecting the "nutritional wisdom" that researchers long have believed exists as an innate physiological ability in animals. However, rats provided with "extra" servings of fat shifted the composition of their diet to such a degree that life-threatening protein malnutrition resulted, despite the ready availability of protein in their cages. In another experiment, when sucrose solution was made available to groups of rats in addition to water, the exposed rats gained significantly more weight than control group rats that were provided only with water as a source of liquid. Those rats with sucrose solution available decreased their intake of other nutrients compared to the control group, yet actually gained more weight as a result of their increased sugar intake. As Tordoff dryly concluded, these results provide evidence for the existence of consumption heuristics that may have implications beyond the world of rodents: "The finding that laboratory animals choose to eat what is abundant has obvious relevance for husbandry and for animals in the wild, including humans confronted with many products in the supermarket" (Tordoff 2002, p. 539).

Gaudi's model provided a heuristic device that was both cognitively frugal and well-adapted to his environment, enabling him to exploit the natural laws of physics in an inductively brilliant fashion. Tordoff's rats, on the other hand, employed a behavioral heuristic that no longer matched their altered environments,

---

[1] As physicist Gorit Aharonov observed, "Since the plan of the church was so complicated—towers and arcs emerging from unexpected places, leaning on other arcs and towers—it is practically impossible to solve the set of equations which corresponds to the requirement of equilibrium in this complex. [But through Gaudi's model] all the computation was instantaneously done by gravity! The set of arcs arranged itself such that the whole complex is in equilibrium, but upside down" (Aharonov 1998).

demonstrating the potentially deadly consequences of an "eat fat or sugar when they are available" decision rule in an environment where such nutrients can be found in super-sized portions. Although emerging from quite different fields and utilizing distinct notions of "heuristic" (which, as will be seen, is not uncommon), these two examples nevertheless suggest the answer to our assigned question of whether heuristics are a problem or a solution: They are both, obviously. The real challenge for scholars working at the intersection of law and heuristics research is to determine when heuristics might be thought especially likely to act as problems and when as solutions. As this chapter will detail, resolution of that challenge in turn requires specifying what is meant by the concepts of "problem" and "solution." Although neither of these tasks admits of tidy resolution, as a general principle one might say that the value of a heuristic depends on the degree of its adaptive suitability to the relevant decision-making environment and the social appropriateness of the aim to which it is adapted. The first criterion, adaptive suitability, reminds analysts that the usefulness of heuristics must be evaluated in relation to the particular environment or institution within which they are being employed (Gigerenzer et al. 1999). The second criterion, social appropriateness, reflects the fact that legal theory is often concerned not only with asking whether particular behaviors achieve their goals, but also with evaluating the social desirability of the goals themselves.

This chapter expands on these themes in the following manner. The next section (HEURISTICS IN DECISION THEORY) provides a general introduction to the subject of heuristics in decision theory, with particular attention to the role of heuristics in two major research paradigms within psychology. As will be seen, one program, which will be called the heuristics-and-biases program, has sought to identify cognitive heuristic processes by observing ways in which experimental subjects fail to conform to expected utility maximization or other rational choice theory ideals in their judgment and decision making. Within this program, departures from rational choice theory are thought to provide an evidentiary fingerprint of the operation of particular cognitive heuristics by individuals. A second program, which will be called the heuristics program, has focused on real decision-making environments or more elaborately specified experimental environments and has compared the use of heuristics within these environments to other realistically available decision-making techniques. From this perspective, researchers have uncovered evidence that heuristic decision making—whether understood as evolved cognitive processes or as deliberately adopted decision-making tools—is often well-adapted to the actual tasks faced by actors in concrete settings. After introducing these two research programs and related theoretical points, the section concludes by organizing them within a single conceptual framework in order to identify important areas in which further research and understanding are strongly needed.

The following section (HEURISTICS IN LEGAL THEORY) then turns to the role of heuristics within legal theory. It will be shown that legal theory to date has been heavily influenced by the heuristics-and-biases research program, primarily because legal theory more generally has been dominated by the neo-classical economic tradition which takes expected utility maximization as its prescriptive ideal. Because the heuristics-and-biases program focuses on exper-imentally observed behavior that contrasts with rational choice ideals, the pro-gram offered a natural springboard for legal scholars interested in improving the behavioral models that underwrite legal policy prescriptions within the law and economics tradition. As this section also observes, however, this focus has handicapped legal scholars in their efforts to learn from researchers working in the heuristics program, whose independent lessons and observations have much to offer legal theory. The next two sections point the way toward some of that fruitful unexplored territory by focusing, respectively, on the use of heuristics by legal subjects whose behavior the law is attempting to influence and on the use of heuristics by policy makers as a model for the design of legal rules. In both of these broad contexts, the heuristics program offers opportunities to progress toward deeper understandings of how the law should be constructed in order to best achieve its social aims.

HEURISTICS IN DECISION THEORY

The term *heuristic* invites multiple interpretations. Its Greek origin meant sim-ply, "serving to find out or discover." In most modern English uses, it has signi-fied "useful, even indispensable cognitive processes for solving problems that *cannot* be handled by logic and probability theory." Consistent with that mean-ing, the heuristics program led by Gigerenzer and others views a decision- mak-ing heuristic as "an approach to a problem that is necessarily incomplete given the knowledge available, and hence unavoidably false, but which is useful none-theless for guiding thinking in appropriate directions" (Gigerenzer et al. 1999, pp. 25–26). Within cognitive psychology, the term *heuristic* also has been strongly associated with the heuristics-and-biases research program pioneered by Kahneman and Tversky (1974, p. 1124), in which heuristic processes are un-derstood to be "principles which reduce the complex tasks of assessing proba-bilities and predicting values to simpler judgmental operations" and which "are quite useful, but sometimes … lead to severe and systematic errors." Hence, heuristics have been viewed as a solution, as a problem, and, sometimes, as both. Unraveling these overlapping and contested meanings requires some basic re-marks about modeling conventions within decision theory.

Optimality-based and Heuristic-based Decision Making

Two important categories of decision-making models include optimality-based and heuristic-based models. The former constitute fully specified analytic sys-tems in which the processes of decision making are given by formal rules of logic and computation that can be described with mathematical precision, replicated over multiple trials, and extended across diverse tasks. Optimality-based approaches derive generally from rational choice theory and seek to identify the solution or solutions to a problem that are singularly optimal according to a desired criterion, such as expected utility maximization. Optimization models can be prescriptive, in the sense that they aim to identify the solution that individuals or other decision makers *should* adopt for a given problem, or they can be simply descriptive, in the sense that they aim to predict the choices that decision makers *will* adopt for a given problem. Descriptive models may be further subdivided according to whether they purport to describe the actual processes that decision makers utilize to solve problems, or whether instead they merely aim to predict the outcomes of decisions, while remaining agnostic on the particular cognitive processes that individuals employ in order to produce such outcomes. The latter form of descriptive model is often referred to as an "as-if" model. For instance, individuals may be thought to behave "as-if" they are seeking to maximize expected utility, whether or not they actually undergo the calculative processes modeled by Bayesian decision theory.

Heuristics researchers in contrast seek to model and understand directly the cognitive processes that individuals use to make decisions, although such researchers differ in the extent to which they believe that heuristic models supplement, as opposed to supplant, optimization models. The heuristics-and-biases research program, for instance, has used experimentally observed departures from rational choice theory to glean insights about the mental processes that individuals utilize when evaluating options and making decisions. Thus, many view the heuristics-and-biases program as constituting a "repair model" research agenda, in which heuristics are thought to offer exceptions or additions to the basic theoretical engine of decision making which remains premised fundamentally on expected utility maximization. The heuristics program, on the other hand, seeks to understand decision making from the "bottom up," by identifying and modeling the actual cognitive processes that individuals are believed to use for a given decision-making task and without regard to any basic underlying model of rational choice. Obviously, this level of ambition in the heuristics research agenda carries the risk that the program may for some time appear incomplete to theorists who are accustomed to the parsimonious scalability of rational choice theory. The tradeoff, as usual, is between descriptive attractiveness and theoretical tractability.

Ill-posed and Computationally Intractable Problems

One important reason that researchers in the heuristics program seek to build a new comprehensive decision-making model from the bottom up stems from their belief that optimization models offer limited applicability to many real-world problems. Specifically, in two different manners, decision-making problems may be intractable in the sense that no optimal solution can be identified by any presently available optimization model. First, many goals when specified mathematically take the form of "ill-posed" problems; that is, problems that cannot in principle be solved. In this category fall those problems with unknown, vague, or incalculable criteria, and those problems for which an adequate weighting function among criteria cannot be specified. Second, many of the remaining problems that are well-posed are nevertheless computationally intractable since their complexity exceeds the available computational capacity of not only humans but also machines. In this category fall those problems that are formally NP-hard, by which one means that they are intrinsically harder than those problems that can be solved in nondeterministic polynomial time, and those problems that are otherwise practically insoluble given the limits of currently available technology.

The fact that many problems cannot be solved with traditional optimization-based approaches has both descriptive and prescriptive implications. Descriptively, it raises a further challenge to the notion that individual behavior and decision making can best be predicted by a model of expected utility maximization. Indeed, the fact that humans face many problems that do not admit of optimal solutions has made it adaptively desirable over time that humans *not* replicate optimization-based systems in their cognition, at least not universally. (Similarly, in competitive environments, it is often desirable for human subjects to exhibit some degree of "irreducible uncertainty" in their behavior in order to avoid precise prediction by opponents [Glimcher 2003].) Thus, it is not surprising that rational choice theory has proven unable to accommodate a wide range of stable individual behaviors. To be sure, "as-if" optimization models provide strong predictive utility in many domains, particularly with respect to the identification of equilibrium outcomes that involve interactions among multiple actors and conditions. To admit these strengths of optimization models is not, however, to suggest that process models have no role to play. Process models may be particularly helpful for describing and predicting the way in which individuals respond to ill-posed or computationally intractable problems. Moreover, even in cases where some outer limit of optimal behavior can be identified, an "as-if" rational choice model typically will be consistent with numerous different processes by which people might approach that limit. In contrast, by providing more specific accounts of the cognitive processes that lead to observed behaviors, process models offer the prospect of predicting and explaining the gap between the optimal frontier of the rational choice model and the actual performance of observed behavior. Importantly, in many circumstances, it is precisely this gap between an accepted optimum and an observed behavior that will be of great interest, particularly to a prescriptive field such as law. Thus, psychology's effort to model heuristic decision making at the process level constitutes an important, complementary exercise to the optimization modeling that otherwise seems to dominate legal, economic, and political theory.

Prescriptively, the existence of ill-posed and computationally intractable problems also disrupts the claim of optimization-based regimes to comprehensive application. In many cases the limit of the solution frontier for a decision-making problem will not be given by rational choice theory or any other available optimization systems. Thus, unless one arbitrarily excludes relevant variables or otherwise edits the problem to yield an optimum solution, assessing the usefulness of a heuristic for these types of problems will require specification of some other benchmark for comparison than conventional rational choice ideals. One commendable approach in such a situation is to proceed by systematically examining available decision-making techniques—heuristic or otherwise—and comparing the ease and effectiveness of their results, understanding that as technology and analytic systems evolve, the best practicably available solution may improve as well. Along these lines, researchers from the heuristics program argue that decision-making heuristics generally perform quite well if evaluated according to the criterion of "ecological rationality"; that is, fitness of the heuristics for the environment in which they are being deployed, as judged by their relative success at achieving intended aims compared to other realistically possible decision-making strategies (including, where appropriate, optimization models that are tailored to the specific problem at issue). Indeed, heuristics researchers argue that a variety of cognitive processes identified in the literature as biases or illusions appear well-adapted when viewed within the richer ecological context that shaped their development, rather than against a rational choice benchmark that is divorced from many of the constraints that characterize real-world decision making (Gigerenzer 2004, Table 4.1).

Heuristic and Optimization-based Cognition: The Dual-processing System Concept

Over the last several years, growing numbers of psychologists and other decision theorists have supported a dual-processing system conception of cognition that tracks, perhaps not accidentally, the distinction between heuristic-based and optimality-based theoretical models of decision making. In this dual-processing system conception, individuals are thought to employ both intuitive and analytical reasoning as more or less parallel mental apparatuses (Sloman 1996). The former, dubbed "System 1," provides quick, cognitively effortless, associational or holistic judgments, while the latter, "System 2," provides more deliberate, rule-based, or logical judgments. The processes associated with System 1 on this account are thought to include several "general-purpose heuristics," such as representativeness, availability, and anchoring and adjustment, that are not merely shorthand versions of the more calculative judgments associated with System 2, but rather are categorically different mental processes (Gilovich and Griffin 2002). Indeed, although the heuristics-and-biases research program was not originally devised with the System 1–2 dichotomy in mind, many have come to regard its methodology and findings as mapping nicely onto the two-system conception. From the heuristics-and-biases studies, therefore, has emerged the somewhat caricatured view among legal academics and other secondary audiences that cognitive heuristics are automatic, persistent, and unreliable System 1 phenomena revealed through predictable instances in which they contradict the more sensible deliberations and conclusions that System 2 would prescribe.

This dual-system dichotomy accords well with everyday self-understanding and, for many purposes, may be conceptually helpful. On the other hand, it also may abstract at too general of a level for a host of theoretical and empirical tasks (Gigerenzer and Regier 1996), including legal policy making which must remain keenly attuned to specific features of decision-making environments that the System 1–2 dichotomy largely ignores. A more dynamic model would take the form of a single, continuous device, in which processes that now are associated with System 1 would not be viewed as fixed and immutable, but rather as subject to the same evolutionary forces that influence all of human cognition, including a range of environmental feedback mechanisms and, indeed, the cognitions of System 2. By rejecting the image of mental processes removed from context, such a conception might better remind legal theorists of the degree of environmental specificity needed to generate strong predictions about the operation of heuristics in novel or unfamiliar circumstances. This sensitivity to environmental context and cognitive adaptation has been a hallmark feature of the heuristics research program. Broadly speaking, where the heuristics-and-biases program utilizes failures of optimization in experimental settings to provide evidence of relatively general cognitive processes, the heuristics research program examines more narrowly delineated decision-making processes to inspect the degree of their adaptive fitness to the specific decision-making task for which the process is being utilized. The importance of this sensitivity is recognized now even by proponents of the dual-processing system view, who have begun to investigate the possibility that there may be "special-purpose heuristics" that are triggered only in certain environmental contexts (Gilovich and Griffin 2002; see also, Kahneman and Frederick 2002; Frederick 2002).

A second risk of the dual-system view is that it is often interpreted in a value-laden fashion, in which the "general-purpose heuristics" associated with System 1 are regarded as comparatively primitive and highly likely to lead to systematic error, while the more deliberative analytical and computational processes associated with System 2 are thought to perform the real heavy lifting in cognition. Taken to its extreme, this view of System 2 finds expression in neoclassical economics and other applied versions of rational choice theory, where the results of expected utility maximization equations acquire a prescriptive cast—not merely "optimal" in the statistical sense, but also in the sense of providing an individually or socially desirable outcome. For legal scholars, moreover, the System 1 and 2 typology invites an interpretation that there are two relevant sets of heuristics: those used by individual actors outside of the legal process that are likely to lead to biases and are resistant to learning or debiasing (System 1), and those that are deliberately and flawlessly constructed by legal policy makers to correct for the biases of others (System 2). These are dangerous oversimplifications. There is no doubt that cognitions can be characterized as requiring more or less effort, in the sense presumed by the dual-system conception, but the direct association sometimes drawn between computational effort and efficacy is unwarranted. In this respect, results of the heuristics research program have somewhat unsettled conventional views by identifying heuristic decision-making processes that are remarkably well-adapted to their respective decision-making environments, despite the fact that they are "primitive" in the sense that they both ignore readily available information and eschew processes that deliberately seek to calculate and attain optimum results in the classical sense.

The Next Stage: Selection Models

The contrast between the heuristics-and-biases and heuristics research programs has sparked great debate in the psychological literature (Gigerenzer 1996; Kahneman and Tversky 1996; Gigerenzer 1991), yet some important common ground can be identified. In essence, two successful research paradigms have approached the task of studying cognitive processes from opposite ends of a spectrum: one uses novel, constructed decision-making environments to elicit evidence of heuristic reasoning through predictable errors, and the other uses real or more richly described decision-making environments to infer the heuristics actually being used to solve problems. It was entirely predictable that these different methodologies would uncover evidence of a different valence. What was perhaps not foreseeable was the extent to which secondary users of the psychological research would oversimplify and generalize from the findings of the heuristics-and-biases program. Those who characterize this research as uncovering widespread, systematic cognitive failures neglect the fact that Kahneman and Tversky's original intent in studying heuristic "errors" was to devise a methodology for studying cognition that was akin to the use of optical illusions, forgetfulness, or tongue twisters in order to understand sight, memory, and language. Reflecting on this overlooked aspect of their research, Kahneman and Tversky wrote as early as 1982: "Although errors of judgment are but a method by which some cognitive processes are studied, the method has become a significant part of the message" (Kahneman and Tversky 1982, p. 494). As will be explained below, for reasons having to do with the history of law and economics and rational choice theory in the law, legal scholars in particular seem to have over-learned this part of the message.

   Rather than rehashing the "Great Rationality Debate" (Tetlock and Mellers 2002), we think that more fruitful lines of inquiry will lie in examining the questions of ecological fitness and heuristic selection that have been raised and highlighted by the findings of the respective programs. The next stage of research will require mapping the range of available heuristics, creating a set of useful decision-making environment prototypes, and, finally, devising some model of how heuristics are selected or are triggered for use in the presence of given environmental characteristics. These research needs can be conceptualized as Figure 6.1, in which the class of known and possible cognitive heuristics (e.g., A, B, C) and environment prototypes (e.g., X, Y, Z) reveals a universe of potential matches between them. One may consider the heuristics research to have unearthed a series of heuristic–environment pairings that are well-suited for each other, producing an appearance of ecological rationality on the part of the heuristic (cells labeled "ER"). In other cells, one may consider the heuristics-and-biases research program to have discovered poorly matched heuristic–environment pairings, revealing the appearance of a heuristic process that leads to cognitive bias or illusion (cells labeled "bias").

As one can see, many heuristic–environment combinations remain unexplored and, thus, even as presently formulated the two research programs still offer great promise for future insight. Perhaps of even more importance now, though, is the generation of real understanding of the mechanisms that select among heuristics in the presence of given environmental features. In other words, when and why do individuals utilize a certain heuristic in a certain environment? Is there a selection process on the individual level that responds to identifiable environmental features in ways that afford predictions about heuristic selection? When is such a selection mechanism likely to produce desirable and undesirable results? How is it likely to interact with other forces, such as markets or government policies, that operate on the societal level to influence the use of certain heuristics? Understanding of that nature likely will require developing new research techniques that move beyond both the heuristics-and-biases paradigm, which seeks general mental principles to the detriment of environmental specificity, and the heuristics paradigm, which emphasizes the particularities of decision-making tasks and environments to the detriment of heuristic generalizability.

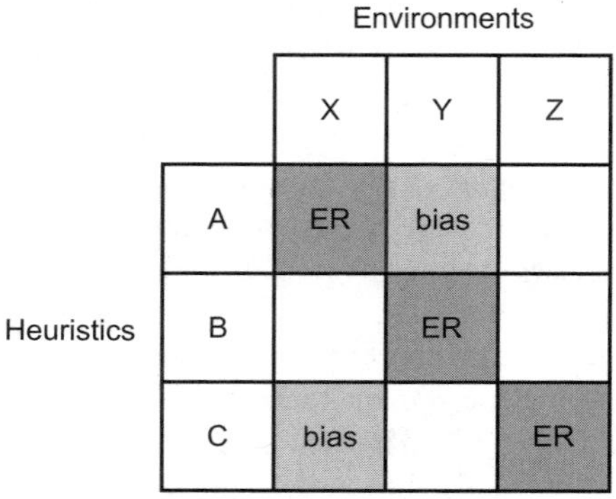

Figure 6.1   Conceptualization of the classes of known and possible cognitive heuristics (A, B, C) and environment prototypes (X, Y, Z).

An Illustrative Example

Research along these lines may be well-illustrated by Ayton and Fischer's recent investigation of the hot-hand fallacy in basketball and the gambler's fallacy, two well-known findings from the heuristics-and-biases literature (Ayton and Fischer 2004). Individuals exhibiting the hot-hand fallacy believe that basketball shooting performance is "streaky" in the sense of being sequentially correlated, yet extensive data analysis of actual shooting performance suggests instead that basketball shots are probabilistically independent events (Gilovich et al. 1985). Individuals exhibiting the gambler's fallacy, on the other hand, believe that probabilistic events such as coin tosses "self-correct" by showing a higher probability of landing heads after a series of tails, when, of course, fair coins possess no such powers of memory and adjustment. Both of these behaviors have been explained in the literature as manifestations of the same heuristic process of representativeness, in which judgments of the likelihood of an event are thought to be based on assessments of how well the event represents or matches particular prototypes (Kahneman and Tversky 1974). Indeed, one recent review introduces the hot-hand fallacy as the "flip side" of the gambler's fallacy (Camerer and Loewenstein 2004).

This conventional account of the two phenomena demonstrates the shortcomings of identifying a cognitive heuristic such as representativeness at too general of a level of abstraction. The representativeness heuristic simultaneously has been proposed to drive both the gambler's fallacy and the hot-hand fallacy, yet the heuristic is unable to predict or explain the fact that subjects' revealed expectations in the two different contexts are mutually contradictory. That is, the two behaviors being "explained" by the representativeness heuristic consist of predictions by individuals that a probabilistic streak will both continue unabated—in the case of the hot-hand fallacy—and reverse direction—in the case of the gambler's fallacy. Policy makers and others interested in extrapolating from the heuristics-and-biases research therefore face difficulty predicting the effect of the representativeness heuristic in other decision-making contexts that are not perfectly symmetric with either of the previously studied environments. Clearly, this is a case in which the type of next generation research called for in this chapter might be of great use.

Ayton and Fischer begin such a project by hypothesizing that the hot-hand fallacy and the gambler's fallacy are better explained as overgeneralizations of, on the one hand, a belief that skill performance is often sequentially correlated such that it demonstrates positive recency and, on the other hand, a belief that natural or inanimate processes such as weather patterns are often characterized by negative recency. Both of these beliefs may prove accurate and useful in a variety of contexts, but appear "fallacious" when applied in an inappropriate setting. For instance, given the nature of the basketball environment, individuals may not receive adequate feedback from their performance in order to learn that, unlike many other skill tasks such as golf putting and throwing darts, basketball seems not to be characterized by performance streaks. In the casino, on the other hand, players do receive feedback, but they also must contend with the fact that casinos offer chance games that resemble very few life tasks for which humans have been selected. In such an environment, the use of ordinary heuristics associated with inanimate processes seems to generate a mismatch between the cognitive heuristic and the decision-making environment, thereby causing individuals to predict erroneously that chance games will demonstrate negative recency. Ayton and Fischer ingeniously support their hypotheses through an experiment in which subjects *simultaneously* exhibit negative recency in their predictions for the results of random binary outcomes from a roulette wheel (which the researchers hypothesized would be perceived as inanimate by subjects) and positive recency in their expectations about the accuracy of their predictions (which they hypothesized would be perceived as a skill performance).

This experiment demonstrates the great care with which legal analysts must treat psychological evidence. Taking the message that representativeness is a "general-purpose heuristic" far too literally, legal scholars have invoked the concept in well over one hundred law review articles across an ambitious range of subject matter contexts. Yet this study suggests that the heuristic may be more profitably decomposed into constituent heuristics that are much more environmentally contingent. Specifically, in Ayton and Fischer's study, the hot-hand fallacy and the gambler's fallacy are revealed to be artifacts of certain underlying expectations about the likely patterns that will be demonstrated by processes that are perceived as inanimate or as involving human skill. This improved understanding has not eliminated the "fallacy" aspect of earlier observed behavior on the basketball court or in the casino, but it has provided a much richer understanding of the heuristics that might be at work in those examples and the environmental features that might be likely to trigger both their operation and their potential for mismatching with new environments. Importantly, Ayton and Fischer's results also form the basis of a more refined and testable pairing of decision-making heuristics: If a pattern appears to be of inanimate origin, expect negative recency; if a pattern appears to involve human skill, expect positive recency. By formulating heuristics with this level of specificity, a host of further research opportunities are created, including opportunities to confirm, deny, or amend the heuristic model, as well as to examine the important question of how individuals come to associate an observed pattern with a particular type of origin. It is precisely this level of sophistication and progress in the experimental research that will be necessary as disciplines like economics and law come to seek deeper inspiration from the psychological literature.

HEURISTICS IN LEGAL THEORY

Law is prescriptive in a way that psychology need not be. The question of whether heuristics provide a "problem" or a "solution" in a given context therefore has different, more significant stakes for law. In a real sense, law must make a judgment on the question in any given policy-making context, even if the judgment is simply to await further evidence before acting. In making these judgments, law must depend on *some* prescriptive theory about the desirable aims toward which social, economic, and political institutions should strive. In addition, to craft responses to perceived problems, law also must depend on *some* implicit or explicit psychological assumptions about human behavior. Particularly for those who evaluate law consequentially, according to the influence that it has on human behavior and well-being, some descriptive model of choice and decision making is necessary to generate conclusions about the effect of legal rules. Thus, law can learn much from decision theory, both prescriptively in terms of identifying the best outcome that, given a set of constraints, society could hope in principle to achieve, and descriptively in terms of developing a predictive model of individual and group decision making that will help to estimate how a given legal response will influence human behavior.

Law and Economics

During the 1970s and 1980s, legal theory underwent a dramatic revolution as the law and economics movement provided compelling methodological assumptions for both of these tasks: in overly simplified terms, the law and economics movement offered rational choice theory as a descriptive account of human behavior and social or aggregate utility maximization as a prescriptive goal for the design of legal rules (Posner 1972). This simultaneous endorsement of utility maximization as both a predictive and prescriptive model did not render law irrelevant, because the law and economics paradigm carried with it important market failure concepts from welfare economics, in which even perfectly rational individual actors were thought to fail to maximize collective utility. Thus, legal theorists influenced by the law and economics movement came to focus on situations of incomplete or asymmetric information, negative externalities, public goods, collective action problems, monopolies, and other circumstances in which individually rational behavior was thought especially likely to lead to suboptimal outcomes, as measured against a standard of collective utility maximization. In those contexts, the prescribed goal for legal rules was to provide incentives or other policy mechanisms that would alter the decision-making environment of the operative individuals, such that overall utility would be improved.

Behavioral Law and Economics

Operating within the law and economics tradition, an exploding number of legal scholars in the late 1980s and throughout the 1990s began to turn to the empirical work of psychologists and experimental economists to enrich the behavioral model of the neoclassical economic framework. To these scholars, a primary theoretical defect of conventional law and economics had been its "sliding scale" approach to defining utility, in which theorists seemed forced to choose between "thin" notions of utility (e.g., revealed preference) that risk tautology by essentially defining an "ought" as an "is," and "thick" notions of utility (e.g., wealth maximization) that provide more rigorous, testable behavioral predictions, but that mounting experimental evidence suggested were demonstrably inaccurate (Korobkin and Ulen 2000). Especially with respect to the models of individual wealth maximization that had tended to dominate law and economics, the heuristics-and-biases research offered a natural advance in that its experimental methodology was designed to identify deviations from the behavioral assumptions of classical rational choice models. Thus, from cognitive psychology and experimental economics, legal scholars hoped to assemble a model of individual behavior and decision making that was more descriptively accurate than rational choice theory, thereby increasing the confidence that one might place in the policy recommendations that emerged from legal economic analysis.

In addition, many scholars in the law and economics tradition were dissatisfied with the generally anemic role that "thin" notions of utility implied for law with respect to individual behaviors that seemed problematic, but that had no "spillover" effects or other collective welfare consequences sufficient to justify legal intervention. By providing a standard of individual utility maximization that sometimes ran dangerously close to being non-falsifiable, the neoclassical approach placed a heavy burden of proof on those who regarded law as a potential solution to perceived problems of individual choice. For instance, actually demonstrating that aggregate levels of smoking or obesity are undesirable can be surprisingly difficult within the confines of a theoretical framework that uses revealed preference as its value criterion. For that reason, the findings of researchers who attempted to uncover individual decision-making anomalies within the framework of rational choice theory became especially attractive to some legal scholars. By altering the behavioral model to become more descriptively accurate, one also might alter the burden of proof on important policy issues by showing that individuals sometimes behave systematically in a suboptimal fashion even in the absence of third party consequences.[2] This had particular salience in areas such as smoking or obesity, where large portions of the policy community simply refused to accept the idea that individual choices were *not* amounting to a problem, even for the individual choosers themselves.

---

[2]   This view was an oversimplification in that it tended both to overgeneralize from existing psychological research and to ignore the administrative burdens, unintended consequences, and other costs of legal intervention that exist even when heuristics are thought to lead to harmful error (Rachlinski 2003).

The Next Stage: Incorporating the Heuristics Research Program into Legal Theory

Thus, into the descriptive void of neoclassical economic approaches to law stepped the new project of behavioral law and economics. To date, behavioral law and economics has been heavily influenced by the conceptual framework of the heuristics-and-biases program. This has been enormously fruitful research (for helpful overviews, see Langevoort 1998; Rachlinski 2003; Guthrie 2003). However, by neglecting the findings of the heuristics research, the behavioral law and economics program has tended to share the same glass-half-empty perspective displayed by the judgment and decision-making literature more generally. To some extent, legal theorists can be more forgiven for this overemphasis than psychologists. After all, law focuses on crimes, resource conflicts, social disputes, accidents, and other events which, although certainly not all driven by cognitive "mistakes," nevertheless are likely to contain circumstances in which overall utility has not been maximized. Thus, the tendency of legal scholars to fixate on moments of mismatch between heuristic and environment in the psychological literature was driven largely by the nature of their enterprise, particularly as it had been influenced by the expected utility maximization tradition of law and economics. In their haste to apply the findings of cognitive psychology to legal problems, however, behavioral law and economics scholars have tended to extrapolate from the heuristics-and-biases research without appreciating the way in which that research's aim of identifying "general-purpose heuristics" might not be well-suited for the purpose of making domain-specific policy recommendations.

In addition, although the heuristics-and-biases research unsettled dramatically the descriptive consensus among legal academics on rational choice theory, it has, perhaps unwittingly, reinforced the primacy of expected utility maximization as the appropriate prescriptive benchmark. By accepting the overall theoretical framework of law and economics, the new movement has focused attention naturally on those instances in which heuristics lead to decision making that fails to comport with rationalist ideals. This focus risks creating a theoretical blind spot, in which legal scholars fail to attend to the variety of ways in which heuristics—whether in the form of evolved cognitive processes or heuristic procedures deliberately contrived for a given task—perform quite well in the context for which they were adapted or devised. Moreover, the focus of behavioral law and economics on cognitive biases has prevented scholars from challenging more fundamentally the prescriptive claims of economics regarding the ideal of expected utility maximization. Instead, behavioral law and economics has become somewhat of a "repair model" itself, in which law is marshaled to refashion the world in the image of the utility maximizing ideal. In so marshalling, scholars overlook the fact that many legal problems in the real world do not admit of an analytically best solution, either because the problem is not well-posed, because the problem is computationally intractable, or because the problem cannot be solved optimally in light of time, resource, or other constraints imposed on the actual decision-making environment in which the problem must be confronted. One important lesson of the heuristics research is that, in such situations, encouraging the pursuit of an analytically derived optimum through the "repair model" of legal intervention may cause more problems than it solves.

In short, legal scholars have much to learn from the heuristics research program, both on the descriptive and prescriptive levels. To be sure, the heuristics research program does seek to create highly specific environmental models and, thus, it may be difficult for legal scholars to extrapolate from the results of particular experiments to different decision-making environments by force of logic alone. This is in contrast to the heuristics-and-biases research which expressly seeks to identify cognitive heuristics at a high level of abstraction and which, consequently, lends itself to ready (mis)application by legal scholars. Weaned on such "general purpose heuristics," legal scholars may be tempted to dismiss the findings of the heuristics research as too narrow and environmentally contingent for purposes of making policy prescriptions. This would be an unfortunate inversion of the earlier mistakes of the behavioral law and economics movement. In its most ambitious formulation, the heuristics research program offers the prospect of accumulating experimental results into a well-specified matrix of decision-making heuristics, environmental conditions, and ecological rationality assessments. Such a matrix would provide legal scholars and policy makers with the ability to create descriptive models of decision making tailored to particular law-relevant settings, ultimately enabling scholars to offer better defined, clearer, and more specific policy recommendations than they are able to generate from the less specific findings of the heuristics-and-biases program.

At present, neither the findings of the heuristics program nor the heuristics-and-biases program accumulate into a matrix of this sort. Thus, for present purposes, interdisciplinary collaboration between those scholars interested in legal policy and those scholars creating and testing process theories of how individuals use heuristics should focus on identifying the types of decision tasks in the types of environments that legal policy makers would benefit most from understanding in greater detail. In that manner, heuristics researchers can focus on investigating decision making in law-relevant environments, such that research results can inform legal policy recommendations directly. In the remainder of this chapter, we seek to further that type of collaborative research by identifying areas and environments in which we expect heuristic processes to be of special relevance to the design and implementation of law. We emphasize that our statements will be highly speculative in nature and should not be thought to make strong claims about what is happening or will happen or should happen in these various contexts. Instead, we seek to offer suggestions, based on theoretical models and informed by existing empirical work, for areas in which further research might be especially fruitful.

HEURISTICS IN THE BEHAVIOR OF LEGAL SUBJECTS

Determining whether the use of heuristics by legal subjects constitutes a "problem" or a "solution" can only be answered in relation to specified goals and realistically available alternatives. This is a complicated task for law because a heuristic must be assessed simultaneously on several different levels, including the adaptive suitability of the heuristic for the environment in question, the social desirability of the goal toward which it is oriented, and the degree to which it is subject to influence by legal rules and other social forces. Comprehending the numerous permutations presented by these variables is an important theoretical task for researchers interested in heuristics and the law. This section offers some preliminary thoughts in furtherance of that task.

Evaluating the Adaptive Suitability of Heuristics

Although legal scholars have tended to overemphasize the biases side of the heuristics-and-biases equation, it would be equally wrong to assume that ecologically evolved heuristics are invariably superior to alternative decision-making approaches. Such an assumption would embrace observed heuristic processes as both the best descriptive account of human decision making and the best prescriptive account, inviting in turn charges of tautology similar to those that have plagued rational choice theory. By process of selection, heuristic reasoning should be expected to move toward greater success at a given task, but it still should be possible to compare the performance of available decision-making techniques against each other and to identify ways in which existing behaviors can be improved upon. Gigerenzer, for instance, evaluates the diagnostic accuracy of three different decision-making techniques for assigning patients who present with chest pains to coronary care units (Gigerenzer, this volume). In this example, a deliberately constructed fast and frugal decision tree outperforms both a conventional holistic expert assessment and, when one considers the cost and time constraints of the actual decision-making environment, an elaborately crafted computational aid. Detailed and ecologically grounded comparison therefore suggests that decision-making strategy performance is highly contingent, and that the best results are provided sometimes by optimization-based models, sometimes by deliberately constructed heuristic devices, and sometimes by the heuristic processes that individuals already employ.

The question then becomes how law can support or encourage the use of heuristic decision making in appropriate circumstances and in an ecologically rational fashion. Scholars should begin by developing a typology of "heuristic failures" akin to the market failure concepts of welfare economics. Just as neoclassical economics depends on theoretical predictions of the circumstances in which markets can be expected to fail to achieve aggregate utility maximization, heuristics research needs some predictions regarding the circumstances in which heuristic decision-making processes can be expected to be ill-adapted to their environments. Presently, one can point to certain general features of decision-making environments—such as abundant information and low uncertainty in the relevant criterion (Gigerenzer et al. 1999, Chaps. 5–6)—in which heuristics might be thought especially likely to provide unreliable or undesirable results. However, much more specific theoretical predictions are necessary to operationalize effectively heuristics research for law. Such a project will parallel, in many respects, the efforts of psychologists and other decision theory researchers to examine the cognitive mechanism that selects and deploys heuristics within particular environments.

Consider, for instance, a long-standing debate in products liability law over whether individual consumers possess adequate awareness and understanding of product injury risks to make utility maximizing purchases. Within the conventional law and economics framework, which assumes that consumers acquire, process, and act upon risk information in accordance with rational choice procedures, debate has focused on information costs, contracting costs, principal-agent problems, and other structural aspects of product markets that might be expected to lead to suboptimal decision making by consumers (e.g., Landes and Posner 1987). Within behavioral law and economics, on the other hand, scholars have assumed that individuals do not process risk information in the manner of rational choice models, but rather utilize heuristic processes to both discern and evaluate cues about product dangerousness. Debate within this framework has focused on whether cognitive heuristics are more likely to cause individuals to accurately estimate, over-estimate, or under-estimate the safety hazards posed by consumer products. As a theoretical matter, if consumers systematically under-estimate the risks of products, then safety levels given by unregulated market equilibriums cannot be trusted to reflect desired levels of investment in risk reduction.

The problem with the behavioral law and economics approach thus far has been its inability to determine through theoretical analysis alone whether and in what direction the psychological research suggests consumers will err when they perceive and evaluate product risks (Hanson and Kysar 1999a). Reflecting the dangers of extrapolating too readily from the heuristics-and-biases research, products liability theorists have offered sometimes sharply conflicting accounts of how the same cognitive heuristic might impact consumer decision making. Scholars have disagreed, for instance, over the implications of the representativeness heuristic for risk perceptions. Schwartz and Wilde (1983) have argued that the representativeness heuristic will lead consumers who experience a series of safe encounters with products to expect an unsafe encounter, just as the gambler's fallacy seems to prompt individuals to expect a heads coin toss after a long series of tosses that land on tails. Latin (1994, p. 1231), on the other hand, notes that most ordinary product risks are very low frequency events, such that "[p]eople who generalize from their own experiences may treat this limited sample as 'representative' of overall product risks and therefore anticipate continued safety."

These contrary predictions parallel the two inconsistent senses of representativeness investigated by Ayton and Fischer. Recall that under the gambler's fallacy, individuals expect a local probability sample to "self-correct" to resemble better the individuals' expectations about the characteristics of the overall distribution. Under the hot-hand fallacy, on the other hand, individuals construct their expectations about the overall distribution from the pattern that is exhibited by the local sample. Ayton and Fischer's study suggests that predicting which of these procedures will be utilized by individuals to estimate a given sequence of events depends in large part on whether the events are perceived to be driven by inanimate processes or by processes involving human skill. For products liability law, therefore, the pertinent question for further empirical research is whether consumer product safety risks are perceived by individuals to be more like the former or the latter. The answer to that question in turn will help to determine whether consumers are more likely to over- or under-estimate products risks. In short, Ayton and Fischer's study points the way both toward a more refined, empirical understanding of an important question that long has plagued products liability law and, more generally, toward the type of next generation research that should be extended across a spectrum of law-relevant questions in order to develop a typology of "heuristic failures."

Evaluating the Social Desirability of Heuristic Goals

In circumstances where individuals have been shown to operate in a stable decision-making environment using heuristics with high ecological rationality, one might be tempted to advise the law to leave well enough alone. However, even well-adapted heuristics may become candidates for legal intervention if they are employed in service of a goal that society regards as illicit, wrongful, or otherwise undesirable. As noted in the section on HEURISTICS IN LEGAL THEORY, legal scholars, in particular those scholars influenced by economics, often take the aggregate maximization of utility to provide the goal of legal rules, coupled with some mechanism for tax and transfer of resources to satisfy any distributive justice concerns that remain after society has progressed toward greater efficiency (Kaplow and Shavell 2001). On this account, legal theorists reserve government policy interventions primarily for those cases in which the individual pursuit of utility maximization is likely to lead to undesirable results, either because the individual lacks sufficient information or ability to maximize her own utility, or because her individual behavior leads to adverse consequences when viewed from an aggregate or collective perspective. With respect to the former category of individual decision failures, the previous section has identified a number of ways in which the heuristics research can improve the ability to diagnose such cases. With respect to the latter category of social problems, the heuristics research again has much to contribute.

An important preliminary research task, for instance, will be to consider how traditional market failure concepts such as monopolies or public goods problems should be adjusted to account for the fact that legal subjects utilize cognitive heuristics in their decision making, rather than purely self-interested optimization procedures. Even the corporate firm, which often is taken to be the actor most likely to approach wealth-maximizing behavior in light of its structure and the competitive environment within which it operates, nevertheless depends on heuristic procedures for much of its decision making (Langevoort, this volume). A primary challenge that all firms face is coordinating the behavior of multiple employees such that those employees act in concert toward the same set of goals, rather than in conflict with each other. Given inherent limitations on the ability of employees to communicate simultaneously along all relevant dimensions of a firm's activities, employees must operate under some shared understanding of how decisions will be made so that the behavior of others easily can be anticipated. As Langevoort argues, only fast and frugal heuristics meet the test of simplicity and predictability necessary to serve this coordinating function well. We therefore should expect heuristics to flourish within the firm because the local ecology makes them not only rational, but essential.

Despite the ecological rationality of these organizational heuristics, however, they will not necessarily serve societal interests for two distinct reasons. First, as is common to many settings, the decision making by employees, officers, and other agents that is facilitated through the use of heuristics may reflect the self-interest of the agents, rather than the interests of the firm itself. When monitoring and incentive mechanisms are imperfect, the principals of the firm become vulnerable to exploitation at the hands of the firm's agents. One important goal for research in law and psychology is therefore to identify heuristics that generate positive returns for agents at the expense of principals, particularly when those heuristics operate in ways that might be either unexpected within the framework of rational choice theory or resistant to the conventional monitoring and incentive mechanisms prescribed as corrective devices by rational choice theory. Conflict of interest disclosure rules, for instance, are often proposed as legal responses to principal–agent problems, yet some experimental evidence suggests that disclosure of conflicts of interest actually can cause principals to become *more* vulnerable to exploitation, primarily because agents who have disclosed their conflicts feel greater "moral license" to engage in behavior at odds with the interests of the principal (Cain et al. 2003). Designing conflict of interest regulations to inform principals without at the same time licensing agents in this manner will require better understanding of the cognitive processes at work in the agents' decision to exploit.

Second, even if organizational decision-making heuristics are adaptive for principals as well as for agents, the price of such adaptation may be the exclusion of important societal interests from consideration. A good example of this exclusion may be found in the area of   employment discrimination. Many common patterns of behavior (e.g., word of mouth communications, the adoption of norms and language that conform to the preferences of incumbent groups) are highly adaptive in simplifying hiring and promotion tasks for employers (Gigerenzer, this volume). Those behaviors, however, frequently have the effect of biasing hiring and promotion decisions against individual members of groups that were not well represented within the local ecology of the firm as its behavioral patterns evolved. The conventional legal approach to correcting such a situation, which largely depends on changing financial incentive structures so as to upset the comfortable equilibrium that has developed within the firm, can be both difficult and costly. Alternative approaches that are designed to minimize heuristic processes such as race encoding may offer "soft solutions" that are both less costly and less likely to be perceived as coercive by regulated actors (Cosmides and Tooby 2004). As discussed below, legal interventions in general should be offered with great sensitivity to the use of decision-making heuristics by those subjects that the law is intending to influence.

It also is important to note that we are not compelled to adopt the optimization standard of utility maximization in order to consider the implications of heuristics for law. Instead, in many cases, we simply can take the social appropriateness or inappropriateness of a heuristic's aim as exogenously given, and describe the implications that might follow for the use of heuristics by legal and nonlegal actors. Peering behind this curtain, one can imagine that the conventional welfare economic analysis of behavior might determine the desirability of ends and, thus, that socially inappropriate aims will be tied to conventional market failure concepts. However, one just as easily can imagine that social ends are prescribed according to deontological principles (Sagoff 1988), objective list criteria of welfare (Nussbaum 2000), well-formulated political procedures (Nozick 1974), happiness and reported well-being studies (Frey and Stutzer 2002b), or a range of other measures or approaches. In some cases, in fact, these other prescriptive criteria may be necessary given limitations of the conventional revealed preference approach to defining utility. How else, for instance, can one evaluate the fact that individuals are willing to pay more for a food item labeled 75% fat-free than one labeled 25% fat (Hanson and Kysar 1999b)? What is the appropriate policy response to the finding that individuals report overwhelming willingness to repeat a prostate surgery procedure that has impaired their urinary and sexual function (Stanford et al. 2000), when the procedure may, in some instances, be medically unadvisable (Gigerenzer 2002)? Or that individuals seem in retrospect to prefer colonoscopy procedures with a certain distribution of pain intensity, even if the aggregate amount of pain is higher than under alternative procedure profiles (Redelmeier and Kahneman 1996)? As one can see, in some contexts, the notion of utility maximization raises more questions than it answers. Heuristics research, which replaces the coherence criteria of formal systems such as utility maximization with more pragmatic correspondence criteria relating to real-world decision-making performance (Gigerenzer et al. 1999), may have much to offer in such situations.

Situating Heuristics within Dynamic, Overlapping Models

The two foregoing parameters—the adaptive suitability of the heuristic for the environment in question, and the social desirability of the goal toward which it is oriented—become multiplied into a host of theoretical and empirical questions when one considers the fact that heuristic users typically operate in environments of enormous social, economic, and political complexity, with multiple sources of feedback exerting parallel and potentially conflicting influences over behavior. Such dynamic, polycentric environments require careful analysis, to say the least. Ideally, theorists should contrive multiple models and identify points of mutual interaction between them, acknowledging not only that the ecological rationality of heuristics depends on the fit between mind and environment, but also that mind and environment both are subject to a variety of influences, some of which are manipulable by law and others of which lie beyond its purview. Instead, to date, behavioral law and economics scholars have tended to view heuristic cognitions as relatively fixed and immutable, perhaps reflecting the influence of the oversimplified System 1–2 dichotomy. By taking heuristics as exogenously given in this manner, scholars have felt comfortable proposing legally based alterations to the decision-making environment of heuristic users, such as information disclosure rules or incentive-based liability rules, that are designed to improve the fit between heuristic and environment in light of identified social goals. A more rigorous modeling exercise, however, would acknowledge that both mind and environment are in flux, and that legal institutions hardly exhaust the class of powerful influences over behavior and cognition.

As a thought experiment to illustrate these various complexities, consider the possibility that economically motivated actors might exploit the use of cognitive heuristics by individuals in ways that lead to undesirable decision making, a possibility that has been observed by many commentators in the literature (Korobkin, this volume; Gigerenzer, this volume; Gigerenzer et al. 1999; Hanson and Kysar 1999a, b; Langevoort 1996, 1997; Frey and Eichenberger 1994). The very notion of a heuristic device assumes that not all information is being utilized by the decision maker, an omission that potentially creates an opportunity for exploitation by actors with the incentive and means to profit from an individual's cognitive habits. Moreover, one lesson of the heuristics-and-biases research seems to be that heuristic users can be "led astray" by experimental researchers who are in a position to carefully control and manipulate the informational environment of research subjects. To the extent that market actors are in a similar position to alter important features of the individual's decision-making environment, the opportunity for exploitation of cognitive heuristics may be even greater. It is important to note in this regard that firms and other potential manipulators need not seek to exploit heuristic decision-making processes consciously or explicitly. Instead, the powerful feedback process of the market might discipline economic actors to behave "as-if" they are exploiting cognitive heuristics of customers, whether or not they appreciate that they are doing so. Indeed, especially powerful market forces might lead economic actors to exploit certain vulnerable heuristics even if they only represent a small fraction of an otherwise highly ecologically rational class of heuristics (Hanson and Kysar 1999a).

To understand better the significance of market manipulation, theorists must evaluate multiple actors and multiple evolutionary processes, including: the firm, acting under the incentives of the market to exploit heuristics; the individual, receiving feedback information from unwise decisions or purchases; the firm's competitors and other informational intermediaries, witnessing the firm's exploitation of customers and recognizing a potential arbitrage opportunity; and the state, playing some more or less active role in trying to police the market. Despite important early theoretical work on the incentives that strengthen and deter psychological anomalies in economic settings (Frey and Eichenberger 1994), much remains unclear about the relative strength of these forces. For instance, what kind and quality of feedback do ordinary consumer purchases generate and how rapidly do consumers adjust heuristics in light of their experiences? Are informational intermediaries such as *Consumer Reports Magazine* serving an adequate educational function for consumers, or do some manipulative traits or practices elude even professional arbitragers? How do the incentives for firms to devise (or stumble upon) manipulative practices compare in strength to the incentives for government regulators to monitor and counteract such practices?[3]

Even assuming the existence of some residually significant amount of harmful deception after these various processes reach an equilibrium point, it remains unclear what the most appropriate policy response should be. Some have argued that with respect to product safety risks, the government should prescribe a uniform risk vocabulary and presentation format, such that consumers will be able to access full actuarial risk information and situate it within their decision making as a rational actor would (Viscusi 1991). Others contend that the bulk of manipulative conduct occurs through means more varied and slippery than could be counteracted by simple informational remedies of regulators. For these theorists, the only policy tool with a chance to keep pace with market manipulation is a market-based regulatory device, such as a strict torts products liability system, which forces manufacturers to bear the full costs of product-caused injuries (Hanson and Kysar 1999b). Such a system seeks to improve consumer product safety by forcing the internalization of product-caused accident costs to market actors who, in turn, obtain strong economic incentives to devise (or stumble

---

[3]   A related empirical question that is worth investigating is whether heuristics might in some instances leave individuals less vulnerable to manipulation than decision-making strategies that seek to replicate expected utility maximization. There is evidence that certain types of decision-making tasks are performed worse by individuals who are asked to give and consider explicit reasons for their judgments (Arkes and Shaffer, this volume). Presumably, therefore, the use of heuristics in some instances might make individuals less vulnerable to exploitation than deliberate optimization strategies.

upon) safer products and more effective hazard warnings. Because a strict liability system attaches financial responsibility only to product-caused health or safety costs, such a system would not address those forms of consumer exploitation that do not involve personal injury. As an indirect dampening force for those kinds of harms, policy makers might consider Frank's proposal to reduce the dead weight loss of competitive arms race advertising through a revenue neutral advertising tax (Frank 1999).

We offer one final prescriptive caveat on this important, but empirically indeterminate issue. One risk of evaluating the danger and extent of market manipulation exclusively through a lens that takes individual utility maximization as its ideal is that policy makers might miss larger questions about the effect that legal and economic structures have on the development of citizens more systemically (Hirsch 1976; Bell 1976). For instance, in the 1970s, the U.S. Federal Trade Commission (FTC) abandoned the practice of regulating comparative price advertising (e.g., 10% off list price), reasoning that "as long as consumers are accurately informed of the [final] offering price," they still can engage in utility maximizing consumption choices (Pitofsky 1977). The heuristics research might be read by legal theorists to support the FTC's assessment, though it would offer a different descriptive account of how consumers adapt to new pricing practices than the rational choice account. A separate question remains, however, regarding the macro-level desirability of a market decision-making environment in which consumers are forced to exert a large amount of cognitive effort to avoid being swindled. By virtue of bearing the burden of scrutinizing illusory price claims, whether through heuristics or otherwise, consumers under the revised FTC rule become forced into a defensive, distrustful market role (Ramsay 1996). Ferreting out "bargains" from among a deluge of fictitious price claims may be cognitively *possible* for consumers, but whether it is desirable remains a separate question altogether.

Offering Legal Responses with Sensitivity to Heuristic Use

Assuming that a particular heuristic decision-making process has been identified as a candidate for legal intervention, the next important task for scholars is to prescribe an appropriate legal response. As an initial matter, the heuristics research calls into doubt some conventional forms of legal policy that seem to have been devised with rational choice actors in mind. For instance, as Guthrie has noted (this volume), the Anglo-American legal tradition frequently attempts to further individual autonomy through the mandatory provision of information to individual decision makers. Although disclosure rules are undoubtedly an important policy tool even in a world where actors are thought to utilize heuristics in order to make decisions, the implicit "more is more" presumption that underlies many modern disclosure regimes should be reexamined in light of the lessons of the heuristics research. In medical contexts, for instance, risk disclosure in furtherance of patient autonomy has been the object of common-law tort liability, legislative directives, and agency rule-making for decades, to the point that individuals are now typically forced to confront a daunting seriatim list of adverse health risks before taking a prescription drug or undergoing a surgical procedure. The tort law doctrine of failure-to-warn liability similarly has encouraged consumer product manufacturers to provide hazard warnings that stretch across several pages of text in product user manuals, listing nearly every conceivable way in which a seemingly innocuous consumer product can become an instrument of death and dismemberment for the unwary user.

We do not intend to make light of the health and safety hazards presented by prescription drugs, surgical procedures, or consumer products, or to cast doubt on the motivation of policy makers who have advanced information disclosure rules as a means for improving individual autonomy and reducing risk. We do question, however, the wisdom of disclosure regimes that are insensitive to the manner in which individuals actually perceive and process risk information. When product safety warnings become ubiquitous across and within product categories, their efficacy may be undermined both because warning proliferation confounds the individual's ability to evaluate information in a consistent, contextual manner (Viscusi 1991), and because it encourages individuals to view warnings merely as tools of pettifoggery that are designed by manufacturers only to avoid liability, rather than to provide useful risk information to consumers (Hanson and Kysar 1999b). Similarly, when prescription drug manufacturers are required to list all clinically observed side effects above a certain minimal threshold, the resulting laundry list of observations may be interpreted by readers in a manner that is insensitive to the actual frequency with which particular side effects appear. A hallmark feature of many decision-making heuristics is their deliberate ignorance of frequency or weighting information in the evaluation of cues. Such a strategy is often ecologically rational in the sense that generally reliable estimates can be obtained at significantly reduced cognitive load. However, these heuristics might provide a poor fit for the evaluation of drug risk disclosure statements that have been designed with readers in mind who process risk identification and frequency data in a textbook Bayesian fashion. Ultimately, this mismatch between heuristics and information presentation may lead to significantly different levels of individuals taking prescription drugs than would be the case if risk information were offered using more ecologically appropriate presentation formats.

In the foregoing examples, the law seems to presume as a descriptive matter that individuals employ rational optimization processes in their decision making. In other contexts, the law may attempt to promote such decision making as a prescriptive matter by holding actors liable for failing to make decisions in a legally required manner. The law of medicine again provides an instructive example, as the standard of liability for medical decision making in the United States has undergone dramatic changes in the past century that might be said to reflect a shift away from locally evolved physician practices to objectively specified "best" practices. Traditionally, the common-law liability rule in the U.S. avoided prescribing specific decision-making processes such as cost-benefit analysis or some other optimization technique, deferring instead to whatever customary standards of care prevailed among medical practitioners in the local community. Eventually, the law began a transition toward national standard requirements, in which medical decisions were evaluated in comparison to the practices prevailing on a national, rather than a local level. This shift created the risk of a mismatch between the incentives provided by the liability rule and the actual environmental conditions facing doctors. Clearly, the best diagnostic heuristic will differ depending on the equipment, facilities, cost structure, and other features that characterize the local environment. In sensitivity to this concern, most jurisdictions made an effort to tailor the national practice standard in light of major impediments or restrictions presented by the local situation.

According to Peters (2000), however, a dramatic development has occurred more recently in nearly half of U.S. jurisdictions, as courts have shifted away from customary medical standards altogether. The argument in favor of such a shift centers on the perceived "lock-in" effect caused by hinging liability on existing customs. In customary medical standard jurisdictions, with minor exceptions the *only* way that plaintiffs can challenge a medical decision as negligent is by arguing that the decision departed from prevailing practices. Importantly, defendants remain free in customary medical standard jurisdictions to argue that their departure from a conventional practice represented an improvement on the possibilities frontier. However, out of fear that this argument would not be understood or accepted, or out of fear simply of the costs of offering and defending such an argument, doctors might face strong disincentives to depart from existing customs, even when heuristics of higher ecological rationality have been identified. Thus, the incorporation of customary standards into tort law, which initially appears to support the ecological rationality of heuristics, may in fact impede the adoption of behavioral improvements over time that would otherwise result from improved technology or advances in knowledge. The extent to which heuristic adaptation is impaired by legal incentives in this manner is an important question for further investigation.

In place of custom, the shifting jurisdictions identified by Peters now typically offer a more general reasonableness standard as the determinative benchmark for liability in medical malpractice cases. The critical difference between these approaches and previous standards is that plaintiffs can now challenge the actual substance of the physician's decision, rather than simply the decision's conformity to an exogenously given custom or practice. Like the "reasonableness" standards of tort law more generally, however, the reasonable medical care standard lacks specific, process-level content. That is, jurors are not told *how* a reasonable medical professional decides and, thus, they are given wide latitude to provide their own understanding of "reasonableness" in the cases before them. An additional area of investigation therefore might be to examine the reaction of mock jurors to various attempts to give specific content to the notion of "reasonableness" in the medical context. For instance, presented with Gigerenzer's analysis of the three available decision-making techniques for coronary care assignment, would subjects agree that the fast and frugal heuristic outperformed competing options, or would they fail to appreciate the beguiling power of the "less is more" thesis? Indeed, one of the potential areas of great interest in law and heuristics may be the extent to which the current legal vocabulary is appropriate for a world in which heuristics aptly describe, and often prescribe, effective human and group decision making. If, for instance, the reasonable medical standard is interpreted by jurors in a manner that requires doctors to demonstrate that they considered as many factors as were available, then the law in practice might discourage the adoption of heuristic processes that are more globally sensible than a comprehensive factor analysis when viewed within the full ecological context of the medical decision.

HEURISTICS AS A MODEL FOR THE DESIGN OF LEGAL RULES

Law typically deals with decision-making tasks involving multiple criteria, imperfect information, unclear additive weights, and a host of other problem features that strongly resemble the areas in which heuristics have been shown to offer great promise. Thus, in addition to examining the implications of heuristic decision making by legal subjects, one should also consider the possibility that heuristics research may help to inform the content and design of legal rules themselves. Like judgment and decision making more generally, legal decision making may benefit from a "less is more" strategy in the face of certain problems or certain environmental conditions. Such a possibility was not lost on Judge Learned Hand, the esteemed U.S. jurist who provided tort law's most famous formal expression of cost-benefit optimization,[4] but who also held the view that "all such attempts [to quantify the determinants of liability] are illusory; and, if serviceable at all, are so only to center attention upon which one of the factors may be determinative in any given situation" (*Moisan v. Loftus* 1949). In other words, Judge Hand, who is often proudly claimed by the law and economics movement as an early proponent of their optimizing prescriptions (Posner 1972), actually seems to have favored a one-reason decision-making heuristic (Gigerenzer et al. 1999). This section considers a variety of implications and questions that follow from Judge Hand's more considered judgment (for a more thorough discussion, see Haidt et al., this volume).

---

[4] Hand opined that negligence may be determined by reference to the following formula: "[I]f the probability [of an accident occurring] be called P; the injury, L; and the burden [of avoiding the accident], B; liability depends upon whether B is less than L multiplied by P: i.e., whether B is less than PL" (*United States v. Carroll Towing* 1947).

Legal Heuristics in the Common Law

Epstein has argued that in many contexts, the traditional and functionally simpler rules of the Anglo-American common law provided superior outcomes to either the complex regulatory schemes devised by modern administrative experts or the multi-part balancing tests favored by more recent (and more ambitious) judicial actors (Epstein, this volume; Epstein 1995). His arguments highlight an important area of research that legal scholars interested in heuristics in the law should address. Specifically, if policy makers are to use heuristics as a model for legal decision making, then they should consider the possibility that, just as decision-making heuristics sometimes adapt poorly to changing environments, legal heuristics may sometimes lag social or economic changes that render previously acceptable maxims harmful to aggregate welfare.

Two widely cited examples from the common law are the fellow servant rule and interspousal immunity, both of which provided a simple (and perhaps well-adapted at the time of their development) on-off liability test by rendering employers and spouses immune from tort liability under specified conditions. With respect to the fellow servant rule, the doctrine's effects became socially undesirable when the process of industrialization dramatically changed the size, structure, and risk level of the workplace. In other words, a well-adapted rule no longer fit its changed environment. With respect to interspousal tort immunity, the doctrine—which had worked systematically to shield male spouses from liability for domestic physical or sexual violence—became socially undesirable when beliefs about family privacy, violence, and gender relations shifted. Thus, a well-adapted rule continued to serve value judgments that no longer reflected the sentiments and beliefs of the community. In both cases, the common law seemed to adapt clumsily (or not at all) to the changed environment.

A similar story can be told from the opposite extreme. Consider the modern development of products liability, in which common-law judges self-consciously set out to change legal rules that they believed were outmoded in light of observed changes in the environment. Offering confident assertions about the degree of information that consumers held regarding product risks, the amount of bargaining influence that manufacturers exerted over consumers, the likelihood that consumers would be positioned to avoid product harms, and the availability and desirability of mandatory product accident insurance, these American judges crafted the products liability revolution as a deliberate effort to update pertinent legal heuristics, such as the common-law privity barrier that previously had rendered product manufacturers relatively immune from tort suits (Hanson and Logue 1993). Although a handful of scholars have attempted to defend this revolution through theoretical and empirical argumentation, the consensus in legal economic scholarship generally has been that the early products liability judges were wrong on each observation that they had used to advance their dramatic changes (Stewart 1987).

What seems needed, plainly, is some analysis of how the law selects, monitors, and modifies its own heuristics, much the way that psychologists must begin to examine more closely the heuristic learning and selection process on the individual decision-making level. Common-law judges applying decision-making heuristics, such as the fellow servant rule or the privity barrier, might not be well positioned to learn from their decisions, given the limited and not necessarily representative selection of cases and facts that they are presented with in order to gain feedback from earlier decisions. In the case of the fellow servant rule, for instance, judges learned too late that conditions had changed dramatically and, as a result, legislatures ultimately encroached on the courts' conventional territory by instituting workers compensation schemes and other statutory displacements of the common-law rule. In the case of the privity barrier, many observers would argue that judges acted prematurely, cutting off adaptive efforts of the market that would have reached a superior solution to the judicially crafted response of modern products liability law. As can be gleaned from these examples, an important research task for scholars interested in heuristics and the law is to undertake comparative analyses of the barriers facing institutional learning for courts, legislatures, and administrative agencies (Rachlinski, this volume).

Legal Heuristics in the Administrative State

One may regard the common-law heuristics devised by judges as being analogous to the process-level cognitive heuristics that are observed in individual decision making and that researchers believe have evolved over time into quick, non-taxing mental procedures for resolving complex decisions. Like these individual heuristics, common-law legal heuristics conserve on deliberation costs by drawing from a storehouse of accumulated wisdom and experience. Also like individual heuristics, however, legal heuristics sometimes fail to adapt in a timely or appropriate fashion to changing conditions. Thus, we should be careful to avoid the mistake of holding up common-law heuristics as both our descriptive account of what legal actors are doing and our prescriptive account of what they should be doing. Such a conflation would risk the same "is/ought" fallacy that heuristics research more generally must seek to avoid. Instead, we should consider the possibility that in some contexts, legislatively or administratively devised legal rules will offer desirable improvements over the background or default rules that have been established by the common-law system. In contrast to the slowly evolving rules of the common law, legislatively or administratively devised legal rules may offer improvements similar to those of expert decision-making aids that are deliberately constructed and prescribed for use in particular contexts (Arkes and Shaffer, this volume).

Like decision-making procedures more generally, the forms that such legal rules might take range from full-blown optimality-based prescriptive models to simple one-factor decision rules. The choice of form in any given context will depend on the type of problem faced and other relevant characteristics of the decision-making environment. Of particular interest to scholars working at the intersection of heuristics and the law will be legal problems that do not admit of optimal solutions, for those areas might be thought especially appropriate for the use of decision-making heuristics of the sort championed by heuristics researchers. Within the law and economics tradition, it has been accepted as commonplace that any particular legal goal, such as eliminating murder, can be addressed through the use of rational choice models that "solve" legal problems by identifying the level of societal resource commitment necessary to generate a desired reduction in the incidence of the targeted activity. However, strong conclusions can be obtained from such models only if they are premised on empirically valid models of behavior and, more fundamentally, only if they specify fully and accurately all possible costs and benefits of social action, as well as a weighting rule for combining those costs and benefits into a single solution or solution frontier. In practice, it is not always possible to specify these costs, benefits, and weighting functions in tractable forms. In such cases, heuristic procedures may provide the most ecologically rational model for the construction of legal rules.

As a concrete example from environmental law, consider the 1990 Clean Air Act Amendments in the U.S., which created a market for sulfur dioxide emissions by issuing a given number of pollution permits and allowing recipient firms to trade the permits after their issuance. In this case, the U.S. Congress devoted almost none of its attention to the question of how many tons of emissions to permit in the aggregate—the efficiency question that, from the societal standpoint, might be considered the most important aspect of designing a pollution market, given that it determines the desired tradeoff between economic costs and human health and the environment. Instead, as one observer has noted, Congress seemed much more preoccupied with the distributive aspect of designing the permit scheme—that is, the question of which favored industries would receive the newly created and economically valuable permits (Heinzerling 1995). In addition to the usual political preoccupation with graft, Congress's single-minded focus on this latter question also could have been caused by the daunting degree of intractability that characterized the former question. Congress was advised to engage in a cost-benefit optimization exercise by proponents of the tradable permit policy instrument, but such an effort in the sulfur dioxide context would have required the generation of enormous amounts of scientific and economic information, as well as the resolution of theoretically indeterminate judgments about such questions as the monetary value of human and nonhuman lives and the appropriate distribution of scarce natural resources between generations (Kysar 2003). Thus, although numerous scholars predicted that adoption of a tradable permit scheme would have the deliberative benefit of ensuring open, democratic discussion concerning the "right" amount of pollution for society to endure (Ackerman and Stewart 1985; Sunstein 1991), in this instance, the U.S. Congress was unwilling to take the bait.

Experience from administrative law suggests that Congress may have been wise to avoid explicit cost-benefit calculation in devising the sulfur dioxide trading program. Within administrative agencies, where cost-benefit analysis of environmental, health, and safety standards is more routinely practiced, one observer has argued that the regulatory rule-making process has become afflicted with a form of "paralysis by analysis" (McGarity 1998). Assuming this diagnosis is accurate, one wonders whether heuristic approaches to such intractable problems as pollution regulation might, in the balance, be preferable. In many environmental contexts, for instance, the U.S. and other nations have followed a simple practice of requiring installation of the best available pollution abatement technology, with opt-out procedures available for firms that are able to demonstrate achievement of equal abatement levels using an alternative technology. This simple heuristic—in essence, "do the best you can"—implies great collective commitment to the preservation of human life and the environment without requiring satisfaction of Herculean informational demands by regulators. Moreover, in actual practice, the approach becomes similar to a "knee of the cost curve" decision-making heuristic, in which pollution abatement is required up to the point that marginal returns from further abatement begin to steeply decline (McGarity 1991). Thus, the legal heuristic approaches cost-benefit optimization without requiring a costly and potentially counterproductive exercise of computation and, importantly, without adopting a decision-making framework that may be politically unpalatable to citizens and other constituents. Indeed, even regulated industries might prefer such "command and control" standards, given the high degree of predictability that they afford.

Legal Heuristics and Process Values

Unlike methods of assessment that evaluate solely according to outcomes, extensive evidence suggests that individuals evaluate decisions according to both the content of the decision outcome itself and certain perceived characteristics of the process that led to the outcome (Frey and Benz 2002; Benz and Stutzer 2002; Frey and Stutzer 2002a, b; Lind and Tyler 1988; Thibault and Walker 1975). Thus, in addition to the instrumental interests that are assessed when we compare the accuracy of decision-making techniques, scholars interested in heuristics and the law must also consider the impact that use of particular legal heuristics might have for the "process values" that are served by law (Summers 1974). For instance, when extolling the virtues of simple common-law maxims, we should be careful not to overlook arguments that might weigh in favor of more elaborately specified legal rules for reasons that do not bear on outcome reliability. Courts must often project the appearance that certain interests have been considered before rendering a decision, irrespective of whether those interests are given significant weight in the court's implicit additive function and, indeed, irrespective of whether a fast and frugal decision rule could achieve the same results with considerably less deliberative load. In that sense, the modern proliferation of balancing tests in the law may further important expressive values by requiring at least nominal consideration of a variety of interests that are of concern to parties and other audiences. Indeed, in light of such process values, we may be forced as a practical matter to keep legal tests that employ cumbersome amalgams of factors, while relying on the heuristics research methodology to "excavate" the real factors and weights that end up being used by judicial actors within the seemingly unpredictable balancing tests (Dhami 2002; Dhami and Ayton 2001).

It is important to note that this argument in favor of multi-factored judicial balancing tests may not extend to formulations of balancing tests that are analytically or computationally formalized. Indeed, in many sensitive areas of law, the specification of a weighted additive function for decision making might do violence to traditional notions of due process, separate and apart from consideration of the reliability of outcomes generated by the prescribed algorithm. In the U.S., for instance, a uniform system of federal criminal sentencing was established in 1988 to produce greater consistency in the punishments that similarly situated defendants would receive from different sentencing judges. The guidelines require an elaborate computational exercise in which a defendant's sentence is determined by various weighted factors relating to the seriousness of the basic offense, the manner in which the crime was committed, the circumstances of the victim, the defendant's degree of acceptance of responsibility for the crime, and the defendant's criminal history. In addition to raising doubts about the guidelines' actual success at bringing consistency to federal sentencing, numerous courts and commentators have also criticized the guidelines for constraining the ability of judicial actors to mete out *individualized* justice according to factors and nuances that inevitably escape the formalized system. To these critics, despite the laudable goal embraced by the drafters of the guidelines, too little attention was devoted to the various process values that would be disserved by a system in which a defendant's penal fate can be modeled and predicted by a computer software program.[5]

In a related fashion, proponents of cost-benefit optimization in the areas of environmental, health, and safety regulation may overlook the desire that individuals seem to have for certain factors *not* to be considered as part of an instrumentalist weighting and balancing of interests. Specifically, individuals have been shown to be especially reluctant to make explicit tradeoffs between

---

[5]   Analogously, the U.S. Supreme Court's requirement of individualized university admissions determinations that include race as a factor seems driven by a desire that university officers project the semblance of nuanced and particularized fairness judgments, even if such decisions ultimately differ little from the explicit weighted-factor systems that they replace (*Gratz v. Bollinger* 2003).

"sacred" categories, such as human life, and "secular" categories, such as monetary profit (Tetlock et al. 2000), an aversion that has also been demonstrated in areas of legal decision making. For instance, mock jurors appear to award higher punitive damages in fact settings in which corporate actors perform explicit, monetized cost-benefit balancing of human safety and products cost (Viscusi 2000). Indeed, as Hastie and Viscusi have concluded, experimental jurors seem to have an "ingrained hostility towards rational, mathematical analyses of benefits and costs in the domain of risk" (Hastie and Viscusi 1998, p. 913). More generally, mock jurors have been shown to impose punitive damages based on their sense of appropriate punishment rather than the level calculated to achieve "optimal deterrence" according to the economic model of punitive damages (Viscusi 2001). Such evidence has led prominent researchers to conclude that "the public will be skeptical of an effort" to adopt the economist's model of optimal deterrence for setting punitive damages because it "could be widely perceived as unfair and wrong" (Sunstein et al. 2000, p. 250).

These various findings suggest that there may be some domains of choice and decision making in which individuals would prefer the use of legal heuristics to avoid explicit calculation and trading off of the "sacred" and the "secular." Of course, such tradeoffs must and do occur at least implicitly on a daily basis; however, as Tetlock explains, nominal adherence to the proposition that life has infinite value serves important social purposes: "[O]ur commitments to other people require us to deny that we can compare certain things quantitatively. To transgress this normative boundary, to attach a monetary value to one's friendships or to one's children or to loyalty to one's country, is to disqualify oneself from certain social roles, to demonstrate that one does not have the faintest idea of what it means to be a true friend or parent or scholar" (Tetlock 2002, p. 596). In this regard, the choice by legal decision makers to adopt a heuristic device that refuses to calculate and compare life-saving interventions explicitly against economic cost may reflect a subtle kind of ecologically rationality—an awareness that, although it is nonsense to say that human life is priceless, it is socially "useful nonsense" (Will 1990). Judge Hand seems to have recognized as much, noting in one of his opinions that the effort to provide a cost-benefit formula for injury law must fail because the negligence determination "always involves some preference, or choice between incommensurables, and it is consigned to a jury because their decision is thought most likely to accord with commonly accepted standards, real or fancied" (*Conway v. O'Brien* 1940).

CONCLUSION

Antoni Gaudi's most famous work, *La Sagrada Familia* cathedral in Barcelona, was designed by the architect using his ingenious inverted rope-and-weights model. Following Gaudi's untimely death in 1926, however, the masterpiece lay dormant for several years and appeared destined to remain unfinished after a fire destroyed most of the existing plans and models of the cathedral during the Spanish Civil War. Later, during the Franco era, fellow architect Francesc Quintana managed to reconstruct several plaster models of Gaudi's intended design for the structure, enabling some limited construction on the project to commence once again. Work has continued on and off for the past several decades, with carefully selected architectural masters standing in as stewards for the original creative vision of Gaudi. Presently, construction of the cathedral is supervised by New Zealand architect Mark Burry, who furthers the strange, intricate beauty of Gaudi's original design through an unlikely tool. Recognizing that Gaudi's complex geometric forms continued to surpass the capabilities of even modern computer-aided design techniques, Burry instead decided to adapt a type of software used in aeronautical engineering for the special purpose of transforming Quintana's plaster models into realizable architectural plans. The result has been a revolutionary advance in architectural modeling software, the influence of which is evident in *La Sagrada Familia* and in the work of Burry's frequent collaborator and world-renowned contemporary designer, Frank O. Gehry.

Gaudi's ingenious architectural design method, which was ecologically rational for its time and for several decades thereafter, finally now can be replicated through high-end digital modeling techniques that are both faster and less labor-intensive than Gaudi's physical exercise. In other words, the formal analytic system underlying Burry's modified computer software now outperforms Gaudi's modeling heuristic. Similarly, one might expect to find many cases in which optimization models outperform simple decision-making heuristics, whether as descriptive models to predict behavior, as prescriptive models to identify optimal solutions toward which individuals or legal policy makers should strive, or as analytical models to guide the design and content of legal rules. Much of law and policy has been premised on this very expectation, particularly as it has been influenced by the law and economics movement. Thus, several of the examples described in this chapter—including the movements toward *caveat emptor* models of consumer protection, toward cost-benefit optimization in medical malpractice and environmental law, and toward elaborately devised criminal sentencing schemes—reflect strong confidence in the suitability of optimality-based decision models for the social, economic, and political environments in which they are being advanced.

We do not object in principle to such efforts to obtain better, or even optimal, results. On the other hand, scholars would do well to recall the remarkable durability of Gaudi's simple gravitational insight and the heuristic solution that it provided. Technological advances such as the development of aeronautical engineering software may mean that previously ill-posed or computationally intractable problems eventually do become soluble in a mathematically optimal fashion. But beyond the newly traced optimal frontier will still remain other problems that demand heuristic solutions and that, characteristically, will often be areas of intense interest to law. As a prescriptive matter, therefore, the heuristics research is of importance to legal scholars because it compels a certain degree of realism to their theoretical work, both by demonstrating ways in which individual decision making can be highly ecologically rational despite using heuristics that are distinct from analytical optimization procedures, and, more fundamentally, by identifying certain circumstances in which the benchmark of an analytically derived optimum is unlikely to provide achievable or even cognizable prescriptive advice. In addition, as a descriptive matter, heuristics research is of importance to legal scholars because it provides a detailed window into the black box of individual decision making, offering cognitive process models for particularized decision tasks that are capable of replication, analysis, and comparison across other domains. For these reasons, we believe that much exciting work lies ahead at the intersection of heuristics and the law.

REFERENCES

Ackerman, B.A., and R.B. Stewart. 1985. Reforming environmental law. *Stanford Law Rev.* **37**:1333–1365.

Aharonov, D. 1998. Quantum computation. In: Annual Reviews of Computational Physics VI, ed. D. Stauffer, pp. 259–346. Singapore: World Scientific.

Ayton, P., and I. Fischer. 2004. The hot-hand fallacy and the gambler's fallacy: Two faces of subjective randonmness? *Mem. Cogn.* **32**:1369–1378.

Bell, D. 1976. The Cultural Contradictions of Capitalism. New York: Basic.

Benz, M., and A. Stutzer. 2002. Do workers enjoy procedural utility? Working Paper Series. Zurich: Institute for Empirical Research in Economics, Univ. of Zurich.

Cain, D., G. Loewenstein, and D. Moore. 2003. Coming clean and playing dirtier: The shortcomings of disclosure as a solution to conflicts of interest. http://www.conflict ofinterest.info/papers/Cain.pdf

Camerer, C., and G. Loewenstein. 2004. Behavioral economics: Past, present, future. In: Advances in Behavioral Economics, ed. C. Camerer, G. Loewenstein, and M. Rabin, pp. 3–51. Princeton, NJ: Princeton Univ. Press and New York: Russell Sage.

Conway v. O'Brien, 111 F.2d 611, 612 (2d Cir. 1940).

Cosmides, L., and J. Tooby. 2004. Knowing thyself: The evolutionary psychology of moral reasoning and moral sentiments. *Bus. Ethics Qtly., Ruffin Ser.* **4**:91–127.

Dhami, M.K. 2002. Do bail information schemes really affect bail decisions? *Howard J.* **41**:245–262.

Dhami, M.K., and P. Ayton. 2001. Bailing and jailing the fast and frugal way. *J. Behav. Dec. Mak.* **14**:141–168.

Epstein, R.A. 1995. Simple Rules for a Complex World. Cambridge, MA: Harvard Univ. Press.

Frank, R.H. 1999. Luxury Fever: Why Money Fails to Satisfy in an Era of Excess. New York: Free Press.

Frederick, S. 2002. Automated choice heuristics. In: Heuristics and Biases: The Psychology of Intuitive Judgment, ed. T. Gilovich, D. Griffin, and D. Kahneman, pp. 548–558. Cambridge: Cambridge Univ. Press.

Frey, B.S., and M. Benz. 2002. Being independent is a great thing: Subjective evaluations of self-employment and hierarchy. Working Paper Series. Zurich: Institute for

Empirical Research in Economics, Univ. of Zurich. http://www.iew.unizh.ch/wp/in-dex.en.php?action=query&id=135

Frey, B.S., and R. Eichenberger. 1994. Economic incentives transform psychological anomalies. *J. Econ. Behav. Org.* **23**:215–234.

Frey, B.S., and A. Stutzer. 2002a. Beyond outcomes: Measuring procedural utility. Berkeley Olin Program in Law and Economics, Working Paper 63. Berkeley: Univ. of California.

Frey, B.S., and A. Stutzer. 2002b. Happiness and Economics: How the Economy and In-stitutions Affect Human Well-being. Princeton, NJ: Princeton Univ. Press.

Gigerenzer, G. 1991. How to make cognitive illusions disappear: Beyond heuristics and biases. *Eur. Rev. Soc. Psychol.* **2**:83–115.

Gigerenzer, G. 1996. On narrow norms and vague heuristics: A reply to Kahneman and Tversky. *Psychol. Rev.* **103**:592–596.

Gigerenzer, G. 2002. Calculated Risks: How to Know When Numbers Deceive You. New York: Simon and Schuster. (U.K. edition: Reckoning with Risk, Penguin)

Gigerenzer, G. 2004. Fast and frugal heuristics: The tools of bounded rationality. In: Handbook of Judgment and Decision Making, ed. D. Koehler and N. Harvey, pp. 62–88. Oxford: Blackwell.

Gigerenzer, G., and T. Regier. 1996. How do we tell an association from a rule? Comment on Sloman (1996). *Psychol. Bull.* **119**:23–26.

Gigerenzer, G., P.M. Todd, and the ABC Research Group. 1999. Simple Heuristics That Make Us Smart. Oxford: Oxford Univ. Press.

Gilovich, T., and D. Griffin. 2002. Introduction—heuristics and biases: Then and now. In: Heuristics and Biases: The Psychology of Intuitive Judgment, ed. T. Gilovich, D. Griffin, and D. Kahneman, pp. 1–18. Cambridge: Cambridge Univ. Press.

Gilovich, T., R. Vallone, and A. Tversky. 1985. The hot hand in basketball: On the misperception of random sequences. *Cog. Psychol.* **17**:295–314.

Glimcher, P.W. 2003. Decisions, Uncertainty, and the Brain: The Science of Neuro-economics. Cambridge, MA: Bradford Books/MIT Press.

Gratz v. Bollinger, 539 U.S. 244 (2003).

Guthrie, C. 2003. Prospect theory, risk preference, and the law. *Northwestern Univ. Law Rev.* **97**:1115–1163.

Hanson, J.D., and D.A. Kysar. 1999a. Taking behavioralism seriously: The problem of market manipulation. *New York Univ. Law Rev.* **74**:630–749.

Hanson, J.D., and D.A. Kysar. 1999b. Taking behavioralism seriously: Some evidence of market manipulation. *Harvard Law Rev.* **112**:1420–1572.

Hanson, J.D., and K. Logue. 1993. Rescuing the revolution: The revived case for enter-prise liability. *Michigan Law Rev.* **91**:683–797.

Hastie, R., and W.K. Viscusi. 1998. What juries can't do well: The jury's performance as a risk manager. *Arizona Law Rev.* **40**:901–921.

Heinzerling, L. 1995. Selling pollution, forcing democracy. *Stanford Env. Law J.* **14**:300–344.

Hirsch, F. 1976. Social Limits to Growth. Cambridge, MA: Harvard Univ. Press.

Kahneman, D., and S. Frederick. 2002. Representativeness revisited: Attribute substitu-tion in intuitive judgment. In: Heuristics and Biases: The Psychology of Intuitive Judgment, ed. T. Gilovich, D. Griffin, and D. Kahneman, pp. 49–81. Cambridge: Cambridge Univ. Press.

Kahneman, D., and A. Tversky. 1974. Judgment under uncertainty: Heuristics and bi-ases. *Science* **185**:1124–1130.

Kahneman, D., and A. Tversky. 1982. Postscript: On the study of statistical intuitions. In: Judgment under Uncertainty: Heuristics and Biases, ed. D. Kahneman, P. Slovic, and A. Tversky, pp. 493–508. Cambridge: Cambridge Univ. Press.

Kahneman, D., and A. Tversky. 1996. On the reality of cognitive illusions. *Psychol. Rev.* **103**:582–591.

Kaplow, L., and S. Shavell. 2001. Fairness versus welfare. *Harvard Law Rev.* **114**:961–1388.

Korobkin, R., and T. Ulen. 2000. Law and behavioral science: Removing the rationality assumption from law and economics. *Calif. Law Rev.* **88**:1051–1144.

Kysar, D. 2003. Law, environment, and vision. *Northwestern Univ. Law Rev.* **97**:675–729.

Landes, W.M., and R.A. Posner. 1987. The Economic Structure of Tort Law. Cambridge, MA: Harvard Univ. Press.

Langevoort, D. 1996. Selling hope, selling risk: Some lessons for law from behavioral economics about stockbrokers and sophisticated customers. *Calif. Law Rev.* **84**:627–701.

Langevoort, D. 1997. Organized illusions: A behavioral theory of why corporations mislead stock market investors (and cause other social harms). *Univ. of Pennsylvania Law Rev.* **146**:101–172.

Langevoort, D. 1998. Behavioral theories of judgment and decision making in legal scholarship: A literature review. *Vanderbilt Law Rev.* **51**:1499–1540.

Latin, H.A. 1994. "Good" warnings, bad products, and cognitive limitations. *UCLA Law Rev.* **41**:1193–1295.

Lind, E.A., and T.R. Tyler. 1988. The Social Psychology of Procedural Justice. New York: Plenum.

McGarity, T.O. 1991. The internal structure of EPA rulemaking. *Law Contemp. Probs.* **54**:57–111.

McGarity, T.O. 1998. A cost-benefit state. *Admin. Law Rev.* **50**:7–79.

Moisan v. Loftus, 178 F.2d 148, 149. (2d Cir 1949).

Nozick, R. 1974. Anarchy, State and Utopia. New York: Basic.

Nussbaum, M.C. 2000. Women and Human Development: The Capabilities Approach. Cambridge: Cambridge Univ. Press.

Peters, P.G., Jr. 2000. The quiet demise of deference to custom: Malpractice law at the millennium. *Washington and Lee Law Rev.* **57**:163–205.

Pitofsky, R. 1977. Beyond Nader: Consumer protection and the regulation of advertising. *Harvard Law Rev.* **90**:661–701.

Posner, R.A. 1972. Economic Analysis of Law. Boston: Little Brown.

Rachlinski, J. 2003. The uncertain psychological case for paternalism. *Northwestern Univ. Law Rev.* **97**:1165–1225.

Ramsay, I. 1996. Advertising, Culture and the Law. London: Sweet and Maxwell.

Redelmeier, D.A., and D. Kahneman. 1996. Patients' memories of painful medical treatments: Real-time and retrospective evaluations of two minimally invasive procedures. *Pain* **116**:3–8.

Sagoff, M. 1988. The Economy of the Earth. Cambridge: Cambridge Univ. Press.

Schwartz, A., and L.L. Wilde. 1983. Imperfect information in markets for contract terms: The examples of warranties and security interests. *Virginia Law Rev.* **69**:1387–1484.

Sharp, D. 2002. Twentieth Century Architecture: A Visual History. London: Lund Humphries.

Sloman, S.A. 1996. The empirical case for two systems of reasoning. *Psychol. Bull.* **119**:3–22.

Stanford, J.L., Z. Feng, A.S. Hamilton et al. 2000. Urinary and sexual function after radical prostatectomy for clinically localized prostate cancer: The prostate cancer outcomes study. *J. Am. Med. Assn.* **283**:354–360.

Stewart, R.B. 1987. Crisis in tort law? The institutional perspective. *Univ. of Chicago Law Rev.* **54**:184–199.

Summers, R.S. 1974. Evaluating and improving legal processes: A plea for "process values." *Cornell Law Rev.* **60**:1–52.

Sunstein, C.R. 1991. Democratizing America through law. *Suffolk Univ. Law Rev.* **25**:949.

Sunstein, C.R., D. Schkade, and D. Kahneman. 2000. Do people want optimal deterrence? *J. Legal Stud.* **29**:237–250.

Tetlock, P.E. 2002. Intuitive politicians, theologians, and prosecutors: Exploring the empirical implications of deviant functionalist metaphors. In: Heuristics and Biases: The Psychology of Intuitive Judgment, ed. T. Gilovich, D. Griffin, and D. Kahneman, pp. 582–599. Cambridge: Cambridge Univ. Press.

Tetlock, P.E., O. Kristel, B. Elson, M. Green, and J. Lerner. 2000. The psychology of the unthinkable: Taboo trade-offs, forbidden base rates, and heretical counterfactuals. *J. Pers. Psychol.* **78**:853–870.

Tetlock, P., and B. Mellers. 2002. The great rationality debate. *Psychol. Sci.* **13**:94–99.

Thibaut, J.W., and L. Walker. 1975. Procedural Justice: A Psychological Analysis. Hillsdale, NJ: Erlbaum.

Tordoff, M.G. 2002. Obesity by choice: The powerful influence of nutrient availability on nutrient uptake. *Am. J. Physiol. Reg. Integr. Comp. Physiol.* **282**:1536–1539.

United States v. Carroll Towing Co., 159 F.2d 169, 173 (2d Cir 1947).

Viscusi, W.K. 1991. Reforming Products Liability. Cambridge, MA: Harvard Univ. Press.

Viscusi, W.K. 2000. Corporate risk analysis: A reckless act? *Stanford Law Rev.* **52**:547–596.

Viscusi, W.K. 2001. The challenge of punitive damages mathematics. *J. Legal Stud.* **30**:313–350.

Will, G. 1990. Suddenly: The American Idea Abroad and at Home 1986–1990. New York: Free Press.

7

The Optimal Complexity of Legal Rules

Richard A. Epstein

The University of Chicago Law School, Chicago, IL 60637, and
The Hoover Institution, Stanford, CA 94305, U.S.A.

ABSTRACT

Legal systems must deal not only with the cognitive limitations of ordinary individuals, but must also seek to curb the excesses of individual self-interest, without conferring excessive powers on state individuals whose motives and cognitive powers are themselves not above suspicion. Much modern law sees administrative expertise as the solution to these problems. But in fact the traditional and simpler rules of thumb that dominated natural law thinking often do a better job in overcoming these cognitive and motivational weaknesses in resolving private disputes. Three types of rules that help achieve this result are rules of absolute priority, rules that judge conduct by outcomes not inputs, and rules that use simple proration formulas to allocate benefits and burdens. Matters are more complex in dealing with government actions, where the optimal strategy typically involves the fragmentation of government power, and the limitation of public discretion.

COGNITION AND MOTIVATION

There is both an evident disjunction and a strong relationship between the disciplines of psychology and law. Psychology seeks to isolate the mainsprings of human behavior. Thus, it requires a detailed understanding of both the emotions, positive and negative, that influence behavior and the peculiar sensory and intellectual processes that allow people to make sense of the external world in conducting their day-to-day affairs. Often the cognitive and emotional sides of human beings work in tandem: sometimes people work better under pressure when their emotions lead to a heightened responsiveness to danger. The law for its part is concerned with the external rules, backed by the force of the sovereign, that guide and limit human behavior (Hart 1961). The linkage between these two disciplines, therefore, runs as follows. It is only possible to select legal rules (alone and in combination with social sanctions) to advance any social goal by understanding the (range of) responses that people will display toward the announcement and enforcement of these rules.

In its largest sense, my task on this occasion is to give a modern elaboration of one central problem in classical social theory: determine what is the nature of man (writ large) in order to decide what set of legal rules will bring out the best in actual human beings, by some measure of social welfare. That massive inquiry, evidently, must be broken down into smaller tasks to have any hope of success. In this context, the particular assignment is to ask what is the optimal level of complexity of legal rules to achieve that social end. In one sense, this task would be far easier if the only problem was how each individual chooses the best course of action for himself. But individual interests often clash in a world of scarcity, so that a legal system must do more than "correct" the imperfect powers of cognition and calculation to which all individuals are prey. It must also work on the motivational dimension to constrain those antisocial behaviors in which the gains to one person or group come at the expense of another, where typically we are on balance confident that the losses in question are greater than the gains observed.

If the only task of a legal system were to help individuals make accurate decisions, the task of formulating the optimal legal rules would be massively simplified. But legal rules must also constrain the set of permissible ends in addition to solidifying any means/ends connections. This dual concern often leads to a conscious effort to make certain collective decision processes *more* procedurally complex, and then in the next breath to limit the discretion of those who make the decision by adopting simple rules that set clear boundaries for human behavior (Epstein 1995, 2003).

One possible mode to achieve these two ends is to engage in complex efforts to maximize some conception of social utility, which for these purposes we can take as well-defined. That approach in the social sphere mirrors individual efforts of utility maximization in the private sphere. On this point, I agree heartily with the position taken by Gigerenzer, Todd, and the ABC Research Group that it is by and large a pipe dream to assume that any formal, or closed-form, solution will provide guidance at either the individual or the social sphere (Gigerenzer et al. 1999). Instead, decision rules in individual cases proceed indirectly, by resort to rules of thumb, whereby people make first crude, and then more subtle refinements of the basic position. One or two key elements are isolated from the welter of factors in each situation, and decisions are made with reference to them, often to the exclusion of other factors that would bear on the overall decision under some idealized model. The more grounded and concrete the context, the less likely that individuals will fall prey in their daily lives to the endless array of cognitive biases that have been identified in the path-breaking work of Daniel Kahneman and Amos Tversky (Tversky and Kahneman 1974).

The exact same process can take place in the design of legal rules to govern the social sphere. The designer of any social system could seek to design an ideal set of institutions that leads to the maximization of social utility in all future states of the world, or he could concentrate on a few key variables in the equation, and leave the rest for another day. I have no doubt that this oversimplified procedure works better than the more self-conscious efforts to achieve efficiency or social utility (Posner 2003). In law we often proceed, albeit in unsystematic fashion, by the method of presumptions, where first one side, and then the other, states a *reason* why liability should be imposed or blocked, and the full picture only comes after each side runs out of additional things that it wishes to say on its behalf (Epstein 1973). To give but one simple version of this, a system that seeks to minimize the use of force will often do better in promoting overall social utility by indirection than one that simply tries to maximize social utility head on. Once that first task is delineated, social institutions can be designed that help achieve it, after which it becomes possible to look for incremental improvements. The first cut might be "don't hit anyone else." The second cut might then provide "except in self-defense." This difference in attitude is reflected in the design of both public and private law. Let us look to how the structure emerges, starting with the design of public institutions, and then turning to the private law.

PROPERTY, CONTRACT, AND THE STATE

The Governance Challenge

The starting point for this analysis is the standard account that posits that, for good evolutionary reasons, individuals have certain well-behaved utility functions in which more counts for better, when judged by subjective standards. In general, there is enough in common between individuals because of their human origin that the things—broadly conceived, to cover not only such essentials as food, clothing, and shelter, but various forms of sociability—that tend to work for the benefit of one individual are the things that tend to work for the benefit of another. That is why they are called "goods" in the first place. To be sure, this proposition is subject to qualification for certain kinds of spillovers: what one person regards as music, his neighbor regards as noise. But those goods that are partible, like the CD that generates the sounds, will have positive value to both, one in use, and the other in sale.

Confining our attention to these separable objects, even if what counts as a good is more or less uniform across people, the intensity of their preferences will differ for various goods. That differential level of desire allows for possible gains from (voluntary) trade, which in turn will take place with greater ease if a system of clear property rights reduces transaction costs in order to facilitate exchange and cooperation (Coase 1960). Those desirable market institutions, however, are not self-sustaining because the property rights on which they rest cannot be created by contract. No set of feasible voluntary transactions will allow any "owner" to bind the rest of the world to forebear from the interference with his person or property. Some positive legal norm must impose "keep off" signs to set the social framework in which two- (or multiple-) party voluntary transactions take place. That in turn requires the imposition of some system of taxation to fund the creation of public goods, such that each person is ideally benefited by an amount greater than the tax imposed to achieve that social investment. Markets operate best in that intermediate zone of human behavior, between the initial collective decisions to create property rights in individuals or in external things, and the creation of state institutions, operated by real persons, whose job it is to define and enforce the rights in question.

This brief description of social relations points to a government with strong coercive powers that operates only within well-defined spheres to achieve its primary objectives—the maintenance of the order and infrastructure that make voluntary transactions possible. These transactions should not be understood exclusively in a narrow economic sense, although commercial transactions are surely critical: voluntary organizations with educational, charitable, or political objectives also fall within the class of protected activities. This vision of the world owes a good deal to the writings of Thomas Hobbes (1651); John Locke (1690); David Hume (1739); Adam Smith (1776); James Madison (1788), one of the founders of the American Constitution; and in more modern times, Friedrich Hayek (1960). What is the optimal complexity of law within this sort of framework? That answer depends in part on what we think to be the greatest obstacles toward the achievement of a stable political order. Here the modern preoccupation with behavioral economics and cognitive limitations tends to find the weak link in human behavior in the ability to integrate information and to calculate the odds of future events. Expected utility calculations are a mirage for all concerned (Kahneman et al. 1982).

The Administrative State

One possible implication of this view is that voluntary exchanges frequently founder because ordinary individuals are not intelligent or rational enough to be able to calculate the odds, and cannot be trusted to make key decisions without relying on state-supplied information or abiding by state protective rules. If cognition and calculation are the chief problems with which any government must cope, there is a natural tendency to accept the delegation of core, critical decisions to government officials whose greater *expertise* allows them to make these decisions with fewer errors than naïve individuals. The rise of the administrative state has many causes. Much environmental regulation stems from the observation, for example, that private rights of action cannot control a pervasive set of nuisance-like externalities.

For these purposes, however, in the United States and Western Europe, the administrative state owes much to the widespread perception that incompetence, not self-interest (let alone corruption), is the largest obstacle to sound government (Stewart 1975). The upshot is a set of discretionary laws that delegate extensive responsibility to particular administrative agencies whose job is to announce and implement rules to advance the "public interest, convenience and necessity" (Coase 1959; Hazlett 1990). The administrative agency typically propounds directives that rely on multi-factored tests, without specific weights, for making allocative decisions. Thus, the Federal Communications Commission assigns and renews broadcast licenses not by bid, but by asking each applicant to explain in detail how it will best serve the local community in accordance with loose criteria (local ownership, technical experience, public service broadcasting, diversity representation, and the like) (Coase 1959). The simpler view (which is itself no easy task)— that the government should define and auction off permanent property rights in the spectrum to the highest bidder —is treated as a genteel anachronism beloved only by sentimental market economists. In the well-known phrase of Justice Felix Frankfurter, the purpose of the state (here in the context of broadcast licenses) is to determine not only the rules of the road but also the composition of the traffic. No one who has looked closely at this result thinks that it has succeeded in creating the ideal mix. Similar critiques can be made of modern labor and much of zoning law, which follow the same administrative program. It is difficult to confine any administrative program to the control of externalities and the neutralization of informational asymmetries. Frequently, the delegation of key decisions to administrative boards props up state cartels and monopolies, often with deleterious economic effects.

The Classical Synthesis

This common account of the government role gets it exactly backward. The initial structural decisions of the founders of the American Constitution—pardon the parochialism—contained a far shrewder judgment about the strengths and weaknesses of the human condition than this modern fascination with the rise of the administrative state. That view accepted the necessity of conferring discretion on someone to make decisions about the future, but differed from the modern view by treating concentrated and discretionary state power as one of chief dangers to social order. Quite simply, the classical thinkers had little doubt that ordinary individuals could make decisions that advanced their own self-interest even in complex social situations. What concerned them was the willingness of ordinary people to put themselves, their families, and their close friends first, so that they would be largely indifferent to the welfare of outsiders. The great challenge of political governance was to make political structures resistant to the dangers of self-interest, while leaving them sufficient power to be able to respond both to the life and death crises that faced a nation and to the mundane business of public administration. Taking their cue from James Madison's sage observation that "enlightened statesmen may not always be at the helm" (Madison 1788), they had to worry about "who guards the guardians?" and to create institutions that could withstand abuse in bad times just as they promote effective governance in good times.

In this setting, the grand objective is *not* to minimize the level of complexity in government structure. A chief feature of the American Constitution (many of whose elements have been copied elsewhere with mixed success) is the fragmentation of power that consciously reduces short-term efficiency in order to counteract the corrupt motivations of political actors. Four major techniques were used to fragment power (Currie 1985). First, the separation of powers between the different branches of government—legislative, executive, and judicial—meant that no individual or coterie controlled all functions of government. Second, the separation of powers ushered in a system of checks and balances, which includes presidential vetoes and congressional overrides, judicial review of legislation, and impeachment of executive and judicial officers. Third, the American Constitution is laced with elaborate electoral rules designed to slow down the election of public officials. Originally, the Electoral College was organized as a *deliberative* body that limited the influence of the electorate in choosing its President; and senators were chosen by state legislatures, not direct elections, until the passage of the Seventeenth Amendment in 1913. The more indirect the process, the harder it is for any one cabal to seize the reins of power. Finally, the system of federalism, with enumerated powers in the Congress and reserved powers in the states, was in its inception designed to divide power among rival and coordinate sovereigns, so that no single group could hold all the keys to the kingdom. The creation of independent agencies that blend legislative, executive, and judicial functions was not part of the original plan. Rather, it was only read into our Constitution during the transformative period of the New Deal when the basic fears of government power gave way to the perception that expertise trumped self-interest in maintaining the overall system.

THE PRIVATE LAW

Any resistance to the concentration of power in government hands requires limited discretion in public officials coupled with a broader scope of action for private decision makers. Here, of course, it would not do to reduce the size of the state to zero because then nothing could be done to restrain the worst excesses of ordinary people, save by transient private alliances that would fall under their own weight. A good substantive law, therefore, seeks to create a clear framework for private decisions that in turn reduces the calculations that private actors need to make. No legal rule can eliminate the natural uncertainty attributable to floods or external aggression. But it can control against much human-made uncertainty that comes from an indefinite system of private rights and duties. In many ways, the classical private law rules of both common and civil law countries (more the former, as it turns out) did a powerful job in achieving the optimal set of legal rules, from which more modern rules have, as a rough generalization, tended to stray.

Salient Characteristics of Sound Legal Rules

This short paper cannot outline in systematic fashion the full set of rules that is needed to take individuals out of the state of nature and into the modern state. Suffice it to say for these purposes that these rules include governance for the acquisition, transfer, and protection of property, including (as it were) property in one's own labor. They must also provide for ways for state officials to obtain the needed resources to operate this system. Let me address three types of approaches that offer some simple and effective solutions to these challenges: rules that establish clear temporal priority; rules that judge behavior by outputs, not inputs; and rules that prorate the benefits and costs of various joint and collective decisions. Since these rules operate in part as beneficial heuristics, it is important to indicate the settings in which they break down as well as those in which they function well.

Temporal Priority

One fundamental concern for any legal system is to match specific persons with specific resources: my house, your field. The traditional common and civil law approach to this question follows the maxim "prior in time is higher in right." Several observations are pertinent about this approach.

First, this rule works as an ordinal and not a cardinal measure. In any race to obtain a given resource, the only question is who gets there first. The margin of the victory is utterly immaterial to the outcome. These rules are similar to those which have been well honed in athletic competitions. The gold medal goes to the competitor who finishes first; the margin of victory is utterly immaterial. The source of the analogy is potent. Private organizations have the right incentives to find optimal rules because they internalize the gains and losses of their collective decisions. When a legal system uses similar rules to adjudicate claims among strangers, the presumption is that they are on the right track. Independent argument supports the same result. The reason for this tough all-or-nothing rule lies in its ability to avoid the incredible complexity of the alternative approach. Once the margin of victory counts, two additional tasks have to be accomplished. Someone has to give a precise measure of the margin of victory, which may be possible in a race, but is not possible in an unstructured encounter where many people are seeking the same resource. In addition, someone has to develop an appropriate sharing rule that indicates what margin of victory entitles the winner to what fraction of the whole. Any such scale is arbitrary, and no single scale will be suitable for all different arenas.

Second, this rule is robust across multiple individuals because the rule is explicitly comparative. It says that *higher* in time is *prior* in right. It does not say that *first* in time is *highest* in right. That difference is critical whenever more than two individuals are in competition for any particular resource. Thus, with respect to the acquisition of land or other property, it sometimes happens, especially in turbulent times, that *A* owns property which is taken from him by *B*, which in turn is taken from *B* by *C*. If the only rule were that first in time were higher in right, the legal system could not deal with any conflicts between *B* and *C*, or any subsequent possessor. But the strict ordinality of this rule is complemented by the principle of *relative* title. If *A* is out of the picture, then *B* will prevail over *C*. If *B* is out of the picture, then *A* will prevail over *C*. Further extensions and permutations are possible so that the rule is robust over a broad range of cases. It bears little demonstration that if any system of apportionment founders in setting fractions in conflicts between two persons, then it surely founders when three or more people are in competition for the same resource.

Third, this system of priority is of great importance not just for the acquisition of property rights in un-owned objects. It is also useful in setting the priorities among various creditors of a single debtor (Baird et al. 2001). Thus, suppose that *A* owns property worth $1,000, and *B*, *C*, and *D* take out successive mortgages on the property for $500, $300, and $100. If the asset retains its value, each of these individuals can collect their debt in full no matter what the sharing rule with respect to the proceeds from the sale of the asset. But if the asset in question falls in value to under $900, the value of the collateral is less than the outstanding value of the debts, and some *priority* rule has to be established. Here again the absolute priority rule is universally adopted among secured creditors, such that *B* gets his $500 before *C* gets his $300, and *C* gets his $300 before *D* gets his $100. The hard rule is made clear in advance, so that individuals can adjust the level of interest charged to take into account the relative riskiness of their loans. In addition, the clarity of the priority rule makes it easier to determine the price at which these loans can be sold or pooled, an exit option for the original lender which increases the willingness to extend credit in the first instance.

Fourth, the absolute priority rule is capable of reinforcement by sensible legislative interventions. One serious question with the sequential creation of property interests is how to establish these priorities. The universal answer is the creation of a single state system of recordation for claims, by which claimants can give a simple description of their claim and the plot of land to which it attaches. All other individuals are charged with notice of what is recorded in the system, much the way in which students are charged with knowing any assignment that is posted on the bulletin board. This system means that the prior-in-time rule no longer applies to the acquisition of property, but to its recordation. Some individuals might argue that this means that the state has taken property from those who prevail under the ordinary private law rule but lose under the statutory scheme. The answer is that even if they lost the property *ex post*, they gained full compensation for that loss *ex ante* from the improved security of transactions for all players, regardless of when they arrived at the scene. And any danger of monopoly power is offset by a rule of open and universal access to the public registry, which allows private intermediaries to gather and reconfigure the information in ways that facilitate the creation of a competitive market.

Fifth, the system of priority can be applied to various forms of intellectual property that cannot be reduced to ordinary possession, such as patents, copyrights, trade names, and trademarks (Landes and Posner 2003). Sometimes, the rule of prior-in-time-is-higher-in-right leads to some momentous patent races in which one inventor (e.g., Alexander Graham Bell and the telephone) wins out over a rival (Elisha Gray) by a hair and keeps the full set of patent rights. The European system follows this rule rigorously, but the American law of patents does not, and allows for the displacement of the first to file if the second inventor can show that he had the basic conception first and diligently struggled to bring it to market. The adoption of this complex American rule just invites trouble. The ostensible rationale of the rule is to allow small inventors a fair shot against their more well-heeled rivals. The actual effect is to introduce a gratuitous measure of uncertainty that often allows large inventors (or the corporations for whom they work) to use this set of neutral rules against the smaller inventors whom the rule was intended to protect. This additional twist has the exact opposite effect of the recordation rules, for its added complexity increases uncertainty to the *ex ante* disadvantage of everyone.

Sixth, this system of strict temporal priorities sometimes breaks down. Here the critical condition is this: the ordinal rule works well when the cardinal gaps tend to be large. If the question is the slow expansion of the frontier, settlers will come at large intervals. Each will tend to limit the amount of land that he claims to defensible borders, so the system will tend to fill in naturally, as it were. But in some cases, the parties do race, as with the Oklahoma "Sooners." In this case, the U.S. set the ground rules such that all homesteaders gathered at the border, which they were allowed to cross only at 12:01 A.M. on the appointed day. The net effect was that many claimants jumped the line "sooner" than they should have, creating mass chaos. The same situation could apply today if one sought to occupy the broadcast spectrum by a first possession rule, which in fact had some brief success in the early days of radio in the 1920s in the U.S. before it was overturned by statutory rule (Hazlett 1990). But today any unallocated portion of the spectrum could be occupied in milliseconds under a first-in-time rule. So the system has to shift. One response is the comparative hearing that requires each applicant to inflate its virtue. A better choice is to sell off predetermined frequencies by auction, which people could then use as they choose. Here the system will favor those with the highest use value, which the bid alone is sufficient to communicate, without the release of valuable trade secrets, and without the risk of government favoritism in making allocations. Once acquired, the frequencies could then be freely alienated after acquisition, and their use patterns could change with new technology, just as land that once was used for farming becomes with urbanization the site of a factory. Likewise, it is difficult to use a priority rule for general creditors who do not record, or for riparians who come to the river at different times. Here the legal system tends to shift to a second simple procedure, that of proration, regardless of time, which is of course after priority and auctions, the third simple rule.

Judge Outputs, Not Inputs

A second guideline is to determine liability based on outputs, not inputs. Once again, sports provide a useful analogy. Whether a ball is in-bounds or out-of-bounds depends on where it lands, not on how well it has been hit. Whether a goal or touchdown is scored likewise depends on whether the ball has crossed the line, not on whether the offensive player has used reasonable efforts to score. Luck, therefore, has a place in all competitions, even if it does not always even out in the end.

Torts. This approach carries over to disputes over bodily injury and property damage (Epstein 1999). The body of law that polices disputes between strangers (who meet randomly) and neighbors (who stand in fixed permanent relationship to each other) is triggered in the first instance by *entry* into the protected space of another person. A defendant could hit the plaintiff or walk onto his land. The defendant could damage the property of another by throwing rocks or emitting fumes across the boundary line. In highway accidents, a defendant could enter an intersection in violation of the rules of the road. In all cases, the illicit boundary crossing is necessary to establish the basic case of liability. The dilemma is whether the law should also look to the inputs generated by the defendant, chiefly the level of care taken to avoid the initial invasion of the plaintiff's space. For example, a court could ask whether drivers tried to comply with the rules of the road, or were impaired by epilepsy or drowsiness from behaving correctly. In all these contexts, the best and simplest response is a "strict liability" approach, which keys the success of the plaintiff's case to the consequences of the defendant's action. The intentions of the defendant and the level of care taken to avoid the harm are no more relevant than in athletic competitions, at least in the absence of malice or flagrant fouls. What one has done, not what was intended or might have happened, should be all that matters.

Here is why it is best to ignore the varied elements of moral responsibility. First, the strict liability system is much cheaper to operate than one that seeks to investigate levels of care. Any decision on liability versus no liability necessarily raises an on/off question, unlike the measure of damages for harm caused, which varies continuously with the extent of the loss. As a matter of decision theory, any on/off determination is best linked to an on/off switch, rather than to some continuous variable, such as care level. Any variables on care level (e.g., what do particular precautions cost, how effective are they likely to be) are difficult to estimate after the fact because they involve a heavy reliance on unobservable choices with indefinite costs and benefits. Hindsight bias is an obvious problem given the tendency of fact finders to overweigh the events that did occur relative to the ones that did not. Using a rule that makes public decisions more reliable allows private parties to make their own private judgments as to whether certain precautions are worth taking or not. There is, moreover, no reason to think that this strict rule of liability has inferior incentive effects to those rules that ask fact finders to calculate the optimal level of care, notwithstanding all the risks of hindsight bias. Even if both rules were perfectly administered, the defendants would take exactly the same level of care, eschewing all but cost-justified precautions.

Second, the strict liability rule works in all cases, regardless of the causal mechanism. There has been a regrettable tendency in the law to adopt different standards of liability in different kinds of cases. Thus at one time, it was thought that a strict liability rule should apply to particulate damage, such as that caused by throwing debris on the land of another, but a negligence rule should apply to damages caused by concussion, without debris. Today, it is common to apply the rule of strict liability solely to activities that are denominated "ultra-hazardous or abnormally dangerous" (e.g., fumigation, oil drilling, blasting) but not to ordinary automobile accidents. A similar distinction applies a strict liability rule to damages caused by dangerous, but not tame, animals. However, in none of these settings is it explained why the *ex ante* difference in probability (which is relevant to the question of whether injunctive relief should be supplied) should matter once the harm has come to pass. All distinctions are costly to police. These refinements thus violate one basic principle of simplicity that holds: only introduce a distinction between related cases where it is likely to offer some system-wide improvement on private incentives to take care, which is not at issue here.

It is important to note some limitations to the rule. The first is that the definitions of causation have to be kept narrow. This system will not work if causation is defined to go much beyond the use of force and the creation of traps to cover, for example, the sale of tobacco or fatty foods, whose generic properties are well known to consumers. Lest strict liability be criticized for these complications, note that any negligence rule will also be every bit as sprawling without strong steps to limit the scope of causation.

The second limitation (as with the prior-in-time rule) depends on the frequency and distribution of boundary crossing events. Between neighbors, the harms in question often involve high-frequency, low-level interactions. In these cases, the so-called live-and-let-live rule adopts an automatic set-off mechanism whereby neither party can sue the other for any harms comprehended by the rule (voices, kitchen smells, background noises) on the grounds that both parties—a classic Pareto improvement—gain more with their additional freedom of action than they suffer by their loss of seclusion. These low-level interference rules also apply to spectrum interference, under the same rationale of mutual benefit from state-imposed deviation of the no-boundary-crossing rule.

Second, the noninvasion rule is always subject to variation by a private land use plan, often designed and imposed by a single developer, which alters (usually increases, say by esthetic requirements) the burdens imposed on individual landowners. The subdivision program helps to correct any initial mistakes in the resolution of boundary disputes generated by the off-the-rack rules supplied by the legal system. However, the variations found in these alternative rules, and the private governance structure needed to enforce them, make it impossible to incorporate them as background government norms. The system can also have governance procedures that build in flexibility for changed circumstances, and are less prey to the factional intrigue that often infects zoning decisions.

Third, the strict liability rule need not apply to injuries that arise in consensual settings, such as the liability of a physician to a patient, the landlord to a tenant, or the employer to an employee. But frequently some other on/off switch is available. Thus, for example, the occupier of premises could be liable in the event that the premise hazard was latent, but not patent. Therefore, slip-and-fall cases generally come out for the plaintiff if a spilt liquid is the same color as the tile floor; and, more likely, the other way if it is not. The source of the distinction is that the first case involves a *trap* while the second warns the customer or tenant of the danger. In addition, the huge expansion in product liability cases comes from the rule that obvious defects expose defendants to liability even when the injured party has the option to withdraw, say, from the use of machine tools. Once the open-and-obvious rule is set aside, the only backstop is the same kind of elaborate cost-benefit analysis used in negligence cases involving strangers, and subject to the same sorts of objections on cost and reliability.

Fourth, in some areas, like medical malpractice, the default norm cannot turn on physical invasion, which is what surgeons are supposed to do. A distinction between latent and patent defects also does not matter with unconscious patients. Instead, (if no contract is applicable) the correct approach usually involves an appeal to medical *custom*, which sets as bright of a line rule as is possible under the circumstances. Here multiple customs may compete with each other, and customs may change over time, but in general the physician whose care level conforms to any customary standard is able to beat back liability that would otherwise be imposed under some generalized cost-benefit standard. No matter what rules are involved, these medical cases are always more difficult to solve than routine accident cases. Generally, courts have been reluctant to second-guess medical judgments, even in light of the possible fear that the doctors will set the standards in their own favor (which does not appear to be the case, given competitive forces and technological advances). It is no accident that the rejection of customary standards in product liability design defect cases has fueled much of the expansion in product liability litigation.

Contract.   A similar analysis could apply to the analysis of contractual liability. Here the overarching principle is that the parties themselves should set the terms of their engagement, so that one central function of the law is to supply a set of *default* terms that will economize on transaction costs when certain unwanted contingencies occur (Epstein 1984). Usually, when parties enter into contracts they adopt simple rules to determine the outcome of their disputes. One implication of this position is that the performance of contractual duties is generally strict, so that parties cannot argue that they should be excused from liability so long as they used reasonable efforts to discharge their obligations. Yet owing to the variety of situations, the clear rule sometimes confers an unqualified option to withdraw from an arrangement, for either or both sides. For example, the typical employment contract calls for a contract at will, where either side can terminate for good reason, bad reason, or no reason at all, subject only to accrued obligations, such as past wages or commissions or liability for work-related injuries. This rule means that two persons do not have to continue in business when they no longer trust each other. It also means that no court has to decide whether the withdrawal from the agreement was done "for cause," another multi-factored inquiry that increases administrative expense and erodes predictability. Under these agreements, the persistent threat that each side has to pull out offers an implicit, but effective, threat against the advantage-taking of the other side to the arrangement. Thus, these arrangements often prove durable for years even though they can be terminated in the twinkling of an eye.

Under this competitive arrangement, employers are not likely to fire employees without cause no matter what the legal requirements. Any decision to remove workers will be observed by other workers who will leave voluntarily on their own terms if they think that an employer is capricious. In any case, employers have to incur substantial costs to recruit and train new workers, who themselves might not work out. The entire at-will arrangement is as durable as it is simple even though it makes no reference to the optimization of overall firm or social utility. And where it does not suit the situation, the parties can under the principle of freedom of contract craft terms that better suit their situations. Yet even here, simple rules often work well: fixed terms of service, and severance pay of a stipulated amount are common examples.

One of the great mistakes of modern regulatory law is to attack the contract at will on a variety of grounds. Many common-law courts believe that they can decide which dismissals are "unjust" and which are not, and thus plunge the area into uncertainty and induce a civil-service-like inefficiency when disruptive workers cannot be displaced. Often workers are given statutory protection along similar lines. Sometimes employers are placed under a duty to bargain with unions that are chosen to represent all workers, often including those who oppose their representation. In many cases, antidiscrimination laws introduce shadowy requirements of motive or disparate impact in ways that limit the ability to hire and fire (but never to refuse or quit). These laws have generated a vast amount of litigation, which has done little, if anything, to improve the overall situation even for workers in the protected class, in part because of the hidden traps in using shaky statistical evidence to prove discrimination (Heckman 1998). The net effect in all cases is to slow down the mobility of labor, and thus to undercut the most effective self-help remedy of workers and firms alike, which is to look elsewhere when things are bad.

Proration

The last of the simple rules that influence many areas of law is the requirement of proration of costs and benefits among individuals in similar situations. Here the basic rule has its origins in the law of partnership, whose fundamental default provisions run as follows. First, unless otherwise specified, each partner owns the same fractional share of the business, both for benefits and losses. Second, in the event that benefits (or burdens) are allocated explicitly on a non-pro rata basis, then burdens (or benefits) are allocated by that same share, unless otherwise agreed. The virtues of this simple rule are manifold. First, it helps with morale inside the business by its obvious appeal to a sense of fairness. Second, it reduces the incentives to manipulate various outcomes. Thus, if an outside offer comes to the firm, as a first approximation, any partner will accept it if his expected benefits are greater than his expected costs. So long as all partners are prorated in their interests, this self-interested calculation will lead to outcomes that similarly benefit other members of the firm as well. Of course, this simple rule has to be qualified when the efforts of individual partners vary by activity and task, which is one reason why personal service partnerships tend to remain small in light of monitoring problems. The basic principle of proration gains, however, new life with the creation of various kinds of investment vehicles, where the shareholders of the firm contribute only cash, and not labor, so that it is far easier to prorate the profits over the firm in accordance with investments. The elimination of the uncertainty over the division of spoils increases the alienability of shares (which again increases the willingness to invest) and reduces the level of tension on whether to declare dividends or retain earnings within the firm. But in this situation, the separation of ownership from management creates problems of trust that are not dissimilar to those found in government agencies. It is, therefore, no accident that the devices one sees in a constitutional setting are found in large voluntary organizations as well, most notably, some effort to separate the executive functions from the overall governance functions of the board of directors. But these parallels are not precise because the exit option (sell shares) is far more potent with corporations than with politics, where greater efforts must be made to secure voice and protection for individual citizens.

The success of this pro rata rule in joint ventures carries over to other areas that are only weakly consensual. Previously, I noted that the absolute priority rule applied to cases of *secured* debt. But the priority rule for general creditors is that they share in the assets of the debtor to the extent of their indebtedness (Baird et al. 2001). Unsecured debt is extended and modified in countless different ways. The absence of any clear record of priorities makes it foolhardy to seek to decide which creditor takes priority over the others. The key issue in these cases is often to preserve the "going concern" value of the business, so that bankruptcy codes typically contain provisions that prevent a hard-pressed debtor from paying off one creditor in preference to others in ways that would result in the destruction of the overall business.

A similar use of proration devices also applies to water rights in riparian systems, in contrast with the absolute priority rule in connection with land. Riparian rights are those which permit an adjacent landowner ("the riparian") to divert some water from a flowing stream for domestic or farming use associated with its own parcel. The amount of water that can be taken from the stream must often be limited less it be milked dry. It is typically difficult to determine which landowner came to the river's edge first; and it is unwise to encourage the rapid occupation of land by using that as the badge to create rights in water. Therefore, each riparian is treated as a general creditor, entitled to a pro rata share (measured by the amount of his interest) in the water in question. That rule will not apply in prior appropriation states where the prior-in-time rule tends to apply, precisely because in-stream uses are of little or no value. In the riparian context, however, the pro rata rule sets the framework that allows for the allocation of a common resource among multiple holders who have no independent connection. No system of voluntary negotiation could reach this result given the transactional obstacles.

The durability of these proration rules is evident as well in their key role in constitutional adjudication. Quite frequently, the government imposes comprehensive regulations over the use of land or the ability to speak. One question is whether these regulations constitute a taking of private property, or an infringement of freedom of speech (Epstein 1985). One test of the legitimacy of these regulations is the question of whether they subject individuals to prorated forms liability. It is, for example, no accident that the defenders of classical liberalism (of which I count myself as one) are drawn in general to systems of proportionate taxation, often on the explicit ground that citizens should be treated the same, as partners involved in common ventures (Smith 1776; Hayek 1960). This view of the world rejects the more extreme libertarian views that equate taxation to either theft or forced labor (Nozick 1974). It also has the twin virtues of allowing the state to reach whatever revenue targets it deems appropriate, while reducing the political pressures that each faction has to impose disproportionate liability on other groups while nabbing, if possible, a disproportionate share of the gains for itself. That test will run into difficulty where there is a strong social pressure for redistribution of wealth. However, it remains, at least in the U.S., a strong constraint with respect to taxes in specialized areas, such as the press, which receive higher scrutiny, where, for example, progressive taxation on newspaper revenue has been struck down as a limitation on freedom of speech.

The same argument applies in many other areas as well. The limitations on new construction that are imposed by a zoning law are far more likely to represent sound social policy if all the affected landowners are benefited and bound in equal proportions. At times, the U.S. Supreme Court has treated the disproportionate impact test as the sign of unjust confiscation from one group to another.

But in its willingness to allow states to transfer wealth across parties, it adopts a "pragmatic" approach that involves the same multi-factored method that wreaks such havoc in other areas. The effort to invite scientific precision turns out to be an open invitation to factional politics.

CONCLUSION

This quick Cook's tour of the logical structure of legal rules has been done in order to make this general observation: There is a sharp parallel between the logic of individual decision making and the logic of collective action. In both cases, there is a desire to achieve some global objective of utility maximization, but the formal tools of analysis to achieve that end break down in both areas. In ordinary life, people tend to resort to convenient heuristics and rules of thumb to make decisions that produce sound results in most cases, even if shipwrecks in others. In the law, the earlier writers uniformly adhered to some "natural law" rules that embodied these presumptions in simple rules that do a better job of achieving utilitarian ends than the self-conscious modern utilitarian methods. In modern times, we often use simple rules but usually we have a less intuitive and more conscious justification for their application. The strong instantaneous sense of right and wrong that allows people to work effectively in ordinary social interactions (Haidt 2001) does not explain the process of getting optimal protocols for private behavior or optimal governance structures for corporations or nations. Here it takes an enormous amount of empirical work to determine *which* simple protocol makes sense for taking care of battlefield wounds or emergency room chest pains. It also takes equal imagination to get the right incentives on all parties' budgetary or zoning processes. That many of the simple heuristics survive in these novel contexts may be testimony to their intuitive efficiency in ordinary personal interaction. But as law moves (sometimes wisely, often not) to ever more complex structures, it will have to rely ever more on conscious deliberation and reflection.

ACKNOWLEDGMENT

I should like to thank Christoph Engel of the Dahlem project for his searching questions that would take volumes to answer fully, and to Eric Murphy, University of Chicago Law School, Class of 2005, and Stefanie Diaz of the Hoover Institution for their excellent research assistance.

REFERENCES

Baird, D., T. Jackson, and B. Adler. 2001. Cases, Problems, and Materials on Bankruptcy. 3d ed. New York: Foundation Press.
Coase, R. 1959. The Federal Communications Commission. *J. Law Econ.* **2**:1–40.

Coase, R. 1960. The problem of social cost. *J. Law Econ.* **3**:1–44.

Currie, D. 1985. The Constitution in the Supreme Court: The First Hundred Years, 1789–1888. Chicago: Univ. of Chicago Press.

Epstein, R. 1973. Pleadings and presumptions. *Univ. of Chicago Law Rev.* **40**:556–582.

Epstein, R. 1984. In defense of the contract at will. *Univ. of Chicago Law Rev.* **51**:947–982.

Epstein, R. 1985. Takings: Private Property and the Power of Eminent Domain. Cambridge, MA: Harvard Univ. Press.

Epstein, R. 1995. Simple Rules for a Complex World. Cambridge, MA: Harvard Univ. Press.

Epstein, R. 1999. Torts. New York: Aspen.

Epstein, R. 2003. Skepticism and Freedom: A Modern Case for Classical Liberalism. Chicago: Univ. of Chicago Press.

Gigerenzer, G., P. Todd, and the ABC Research Group. 1999. Simple Heuristics That Make Us Smart. New York: Oxford Univ. Press.

Haidt, J. 2001. The emotional dog and its rational tail: A social intuitionist approach to moral judgments. *Psychol. Rev.* **108**:814–834.

Hart, H. 1961. The Concept of Law. Oxford: Clarendon.

Hayek, F. 1960. The Constitution of Liberty. Chicago: Univ. of Chicago Press (p. 314).

Hazlett, T. 1990. The Rationality of U.S. Regulation of the Broadcast Spectrum. *J. Law Econ.* **33**:133–175.

Heckman, J. 1998. Detecting discrimination. *J. Econ. Persp.* **12**:101–116.

Hobbes, T. 1651/1962. Leviathan, ed. M. Oakeshott. New York: Collier.

Hume, D. 1739/1888. A Treatise of Human Nature, ed. L.A. Selby-Bigge. Oxford: Clarendon.

Kahneman, D., P. Slovic, and A. Tversky, eds. 1982. Judgment under Uncertainty: Heuristics and Biases. New York: Cambridge Univ. Press.

Landes, W., and R. Posner. 2003. The Economic Structure of Intellectual Property Law. Cambridge, MA: Belknap.

Locke, J. 1690/1980. Second Treatise of Government, ed. C.B. Macpherson. Indianapolis: Hackett.

Madison, J., A. Hamilton, and J. Jay. 1788/1961. The Federalist Papers. New York: New American Library.

Nozick, R. 1974. Anarchy, State, and Utopia. New York: Basic.

Posner, R. 2003. Economic Analysis of Law. 6th ed. New York: Aspen.

Smith, A. 1776/1937. The Wealth of Nations. New York: Modern Library (p. 777).

Stewart, R. 1975. The reformation of American administrative law. *Harvard Law Rev.* **88**:1669–1813.

Tversky, A., and D. Kahneman. 1974. Judgment under uncertainty: Heuristics and biases. *Science* **185**:1124–1131.

8

Bottom-up versus Top-down Lawmaking

Jeffrey J. Rachlinski

Cornell Law School, Ithaca, NY 14853–4901, U.S.A.

ABSTRACT

Legal systems make law in one of two ways: by abstracting general principles from the decisions made in individual cases, that is to say, though the adjudicative process (from the bottom up); or by declaring general principles through a centralized authority that are to be applied in individual cases, that is to say, through the legislative process (from the top down). Each system presents the underlying legal issue from a different cognitive perspective, highlighting and hiding different aspects of a legal problem. The single-case perspective of adjudication seems, in many ways, cognitively inferior to the broad perspectives that legislatures can incorporate into their decision-making processes. The adjudicative approach, however, has advantages that are less obvious. Notably, the adjudicative process is more likely to facilitate that adoption of simple, elegant rules for decision making. The assessment of which approach is superior is therefore indeterminate. Each has its strengths and weaknesses that make it more or less appropriate for different contexts.

INTRODUCTION

Despite the wide variety of legal systems and cultures, law apparently can be made in one of only two different ways: through case-by-case adjudication by courts or through adoption of general principles by a legislative process. Adjudication requires that courts declare general principles of law through the process of deciding the outcome of individual disputes. General principles of law can then be inferred from the outcome of cases and discussions of how the legal authority (usually a judge) reached these outcomes. Adjudication thus involves building law from the ground up. Legislation requires an abstract declaration of rules by some authoritative entity, such as a legislature, regulatory agency, president, monarch, or dictator. The outcome of individual disputes is then determined by the application of these general principles. Legislation thus involves making law from the top down. These two approaches produce different cognitive structures for the kinds of social problems law addresses. In turn, they each produce different resolutions.

In theory, either adjudication or legislation would settle upon identical solutions to legal problems. For example, if the appropriate standard for liability for manufacturing defects is strict liability, then presumably a legislature could adopt such a rule just as easily as a series of court decisions. Similarly, if it is appropriate for a drug to include a warning against driving after ingesting the drug, then this requirement can be implemented either through the adoption of a regulation mandating the inclusion of the warning or through a liability rule for manufacturers of the drug who fail to include the warning. Legislative efforts intended to implement reasonable regulations should, in principle, mimic adjudicative efforts to the same end.

Numerous differences between the two systems exist, however. Judges are typically less politically accountable than legislators, thereby ensuring that adjudicative systems respond less to public pressure and political influence than legislative systems. Adjudication also typically requires courts to wait until a particular case presents itself before they may declare law, and hence evolve more slowly than legislative systems. Adjudication is also apt to operate in a decentralized fashion by including multiple levels of peers who function independently. Decision makers in an adjudicatory system will also typically deliberate privately with a small group, if they deliberate at all; legislation, by contrast is usually public, and involves broad participation and negotiation among the regulators. Finally, governments typically allocate more limited authority to adjudicative bodies than to legislatures.

Given these differences, it is perhaps not surprising that the two systems produce different results. For example, in the United States, where the common-law process dominates, a breach of a sales contract is not enforceable with specific performance unless the good is unique (such as real property), whereas in Germany, specific performance is available. In the U.S., manufacturers are strictly liable for injuries caused by manufacturing defects, whereas in most civil-law countries, they are not. Differences between a legislative system and an adjudicative system exist even within a country. No common-law process would have produced numeric damage caps on awards for pain and suffering or punitive damage awards, as many state legislatures in the U.S. have imposed. Similarly, although common-law courts in the U.S. developed causes of action for defective products and for fraud, consumer-protection laws completely banning the sale of defective products and the array of detailed protections against consumer fraud arise largely from statutes. Statutory regulation of the workplace and the environment also differ markedly from the approaches that common-law courts have taken.

Any of the numerous differences between the legislative process and the common-law process could have produced different answers to the same legal problems. The greater influence of the political process on legislatures surely has much to do with the differences, as does the limitations on the remedies that the courts may adopt. The question for this chapter, however, is whether the two approaches produce different decision-making styles that facilitate different solutions to social dilemmas. Determining the appropriate remedy for a breach of contract or the appropriate standard of liability for a manufacturer might depend on whether the issue arises in the context of a single dispute or as an issue on a legislative agenda. In cognitive terms, the representational structure of the problem differs depending upon whether courts or legislatures confront the issue. Each approach highlights some aspects of the underlying issue and makes others less salient.

The question of cognitive influence is significant because different legal regimes consciously choose between the two lawmaking processes. Notably, common-law countries have developed much of their law—notably the law governing torts, contracts, and property—through the process of adjudication, whereas countries in the civil-law tradition have made much of their law through the legislative process. Within common-law countries, modern trends favor codification of and intervention into the common law by the legislature, thereby replacing the adjudication process with the legislative process. This evolution is reflected in the supplanting of common-law rules with regulations as well as in efforts to constrain the influence of adjudicators—as in the widespread adoption of narrow guidelines to constrain judicial discretion in the sentencing of convicted criminal defendants. The choice of appropriate lawmaking function ideally reflects an effort to adopt the system best suited to the underlying problem. The differences between the two systems that arise from the nature of judicial independence and limited authority of the judiciary are well known to policy makers. Less well understood is the influence of cognitive perspective on the lawmaking process.

COGNITIVE STRUCTURE AND SOCIAL DECISIONS

Cognitive psychologists have long understood that decision-making problems embody different cognitive features that can make solutions easy or difficult to resolve. For example, Gigerenzer has noted that Bayesian problems associated with detecting low-probability events can be made much easier by simply rearranging the information provided (Gigerenzer 2002). Likewise, Cosmides and Tooby (1992) have noted that the apparent difficulty of problems, such as the Wason card-selection task, are often avoided when the context of the problem is changed from abstract to familiar, real-world situations. As to problems for which there are no correct solutions, a problem's structure can be said to alter choice. For example, describing a choice as involving gains leads decision makers to make less risky choices than when the same choice is described as involving losses (Kahneman and Tversky 1984).

The adjudicative perspective facilitates different answers to legal questions than the legislative perspective. The case-by-case approach might thwart attention to general systemic variables, highlighting instead the personalities and unique features of the parties. A legislative approach might do the opposite: hiding important individual variations while highlighting general, systematic variables. For certain kinds of problems, the adjudicative approach of building law from the ground up might thwart the goals of the legal system. For others, the top-down approach might be more troublesome. In other cases, it might simply be the case that each leads to different answers which cannot be said to be inferior or superior from a normative perspective.

The notion of a better approach, from a normative perspective, can be troubling for a legal analysis. The appropriate legal rule depends heavily on an agreement as to what the goal of the legal rules should be. Although some argue that economic efficiency is the paramount goal of a legal system, this approach has attracted few adherents. Most scholars believe that any legal system embraces multiple goals, and almost certainly include advancing society's notions of justice and fairness, however defined, along with efficiency. Comparing the merits of the adjudicative approach to lawmaking with a legislative, however, does not necessarily require resolving such concerns. One or the other system might be better at identifying legal rules that further the goals of the legal system, whatever those goals might be.

A FIRST CUT: THE INFERIORITY OF ADJUDICATION

As a preliminary analysis, the adjudicative approach to making legal rules seems inferior to the legislative approach. Resolving social issues one case at a time poses many practical problems. Courts lack the resources and abilities to inform themselves of the issues that confront them, which legislatures have. Even if courts manage to obtain adequate jurisdiction over important social issues as well as access to the same kinds of information that legislatures have available, the psychological perspective courts necessarily adopt might lead to inferior decision making. The court will see the quirks and oddities of the individual parties, whereas the legislature can put their claims into context. Aspects of an individual case that create or invoke sympathy might lead courts to adopt rules that no legislature would adopt. Oddities about individual cases rather than sensible global choices might drive law made by adjudication.

Consider the examples that arise from the influence of counterfactual thinking on judgment. Suppose an airplane crashes in the wilds of the Yukon, 100 miles from the nearest settlement. The cause of the crash is such that the families of those people killed in the crash are entitled to compensation. The pilot initially survives the crash, but succumbs to the bitter Arctic conditions as he struggles toward the settlement. Should his compensation depend upon whether he traverses only one mile from the plane before perishing or whether he traverses 99 miles only to succumb at the edge of the settlement? One would think not, and presumably no legislature would embrace such a rule. His life is worth no less in either case, and anyone responsible for the crash is no more or less culpable for the loss based on how close he came to surviving. Yet, when people are asked to assess the appropriate degree of compensation in such a crash, the pilot's progress influences the award (Miller and McFarland 1987). Subjects who read that the pilot walked 99 miles expressed a willingness to award more than subjects who read that the pilot walked only 1 mile. Miller and McFarland explain that it is easier to imagine that the pilot could have survived when he made it 99 miles and hence his death seems more regrettable. Although adjudicative bodies, which handle these cases one at a time, might be influenced by such factors, legislatures, which see only the aggregate situation divorced of the details, would not.

In addition, individual cases likely invoke the kinds of emotional responses that can be misleading. Consider the difference between a trial involving the potential liability of an airline for failing to install safety equipment and a regulatory hearing involving whether an airline should be required to install the very same safety device. Both the trial and the regulatory effort would include testimony on the relative costs and benefits of the safety device. The trial, however, would also include extensive individual testimony about the personal loss suffered by the family of the victim. The emotional content of the testimony would have multiple influences on the court. First, emotional testimony is more vivid than the pallid statistics, which would make it more memorable and influential. Second, emotional testimony can trigger reliance on an "affect heuristic" (Slovic et al. 2003); not only would courts want to find for the plaintiff, they would feel it appropriate to do so. Judges and juries are more apt to sympathize with the blameless survivors of an accident, and this sympathy can lead the court to find a way to find for the plaintiff.

Legislatures certainly cannot be said to be occupied by people devoid of sympathy. The legislative approach, however, generally includes less testimony by individuals. Legislation also involves two other features that minimize the likely impact of emotional content on decision making. First, it is prospective. Courts act retrospectively and will thus always have injured victims or aggrieved parties before them. Legislatures and regulatory bodies make rules to govern future conduct and hence, even though a decision to refrain from adopting a mandatory safety precaution is apt to result in some death or injury that could have been prevented, the legislature acts without knowing exactly who the victim is. Second, legislatures can see trade-offs that courts cannot. A legislature will act with the full knowledge that imposing a safety precaution of some sort makes an activity more expensive, and perhaps creates more social risk, not less (Sunstein 1996). For example, imposing new safety precautions on air travel might induce some number of people to drive rather than fly, possibly increasing, rather than decreasing, the overall number of transportation-related fatalities. Legislatures will face such trade-offs directly, whereas courts will see these trade-offs as only distantly related to the case before them.

Assessing legal problems one case at a time can also distort a sense of scale and proportion. In one study of such distortions, Sunstein et al. (2002) asked subjects to assign punitive damage awards to cases involving an egregious example of fraud, a significant physical injury arising from egregious conduct in products liability, or both. The subjects who evaluated the fraud case alone assigned higher damage awards than subjects who evaluated the products liability case alone. When evaluated together, however, the products liability case drew higher awards than the fraud case. The authors explain that the fraud case was a rather outrageous instance of fraud relative to the subjects' expectations about fraud, and thus the contrast with expectations produced a high award. The personal injury seemed like a more common sort of personal injury and did not produce such a contrast. When the subjects evaluated the two cases together, however, they were reminded that reckless conduct that inflicts physical injuries is more outrageous than reckless conduct that inflicts only financial injuries. Contrast effects such as this are far more likely to influence courts, which process only one case at a time, than legislatures, which are able to make broader comparisons.

Careful statistical reasoning is also apt to be more troublesome in an individual case than in the aggregate. As much of Gigerenzer's work demonstrates, frequentist presentation of statistical evidence can dramatically improve the inference process (Gigerenzer 2002). Inference problems such as the conjunctive fallacy, base rate neglect, and overconfidence do not seem as prevalent when the underlying decision is presented as one of a category of decisions (Kahneman and Lovallo 1993). Single cases, however, are apt to trigger a subjective format and hide the commonalities a case might have with a broader category. A case-by-case approach will seem to present a unique problem, whereas a legislative approach clearly requires a decision that should apply to an aggregation of cases. Indeed, scholars have noticed that at times, courts seem to make serious errors in the statistical inference process. For example, the legal doctrine known as *res ipsa loquitur* has historically incorporated a logical fallacy akin to base rate neglect (Kaye 1979). Courts also demonstrably rely on outcome evidence that could not have been known beforehand when assessing the liability of trustees for imprudent distribution of a trust's assets (Rachlinski 2000). In these instances, courts have cemented logical fallacies arising from a narrow, subjective perspective into broad legal principles.

An adjudicative process, with its emphasis on individual litigants is also more focused on attributing responsibility to individuals, rather than to situational determinants of behavior. Although there is little research directly on point, classic studies of attribution theory support this conclusion. For example, the tendency for individual actors to attribute their behavior to the product of the situation in which they find themselves, while the observers of the same behavior attribute the actor's behavior to the actor's personality, suggests the importance of perceptual salience in identifying the determinants of behavior (Nisbett et al. 1973). Psychologists believe that this "actor–observer" effect results from the salience of the situation to the actor relative to the salience of the actor to the observer. The courtroom places the individual front and center, thereby highlighting their behavior.

The adjudicative emphasis on the individual responsibility would arguably be erroneous. Social psychologists have long argued that people, at least in Western cultures, tend to attribute behavior excessively to stable traits, while ignoring aspects of a situation that can induce behavior (Ross 1976). The ordinary social interactions of everyday life seem to focus our attention onto the personality of those whom we encounter, less so than the situations which often actually determine their behavior. According to Ross, we are too quick to assume that an ordinary misstep is the result of clumsiness, rather than a wet floor; that a dour expression indicates an unfriendly demeanor, rather than a passing mood; and that the wrong answer to a trick question indicates low intelligence (Ross 1976). The error arguably induces courts to attribute too much blame to individuals and not enough to social forces (Ross and Shestowsky 2003).

Legislative approaches, in contrast, highlight social forces. They direct decision makers' attention to economic factors, social trends, and statistical approaches to regulate human activity. A casual perusal of the development of almost every area of law in the U.S. supports the conclusion that courts attend to the characteristics of individual actors whereas legislatures regulate social settings. Tort law, for example, would not allow a plaintiff to recover from a manufacturer of alcohol, firearms, or cigarettes merely because that manufacturer put these products on the market. The manufacturer has to be blameworthy in some fashion, by selling unsafe versions of such products. In contrast, legislatures throughout the U.S. regulate the sale of these goods in exacting detail. Property law will not allow me to recover from my neighbor for driving a sport utility vehicle that contributes greatly to air pollution unless the neighbor's use of that vehicle is so extreme as to construe a direct threat to my ability to use my own property. Environmental law, in contrast, regulates the use of automobiles extensively. Contract law would allow a used-car salesman to sell me a badly dysfunctional car "as is," so long as no fraud was involved. State and federal laws on the sale of automobiles, however, mandate warranties and provide consumers with a far greater array of rights than might be included in many sales contracts.

In all of these cases, legislatures adopt such measures out of a belief that the broader context in which these encounters occurs justifies such intervention. For torts, an individual court is reluctant to regulate the economy that produces guns, alcohol, or cigarettes. They take the society that produces such products as given and try to regulate only the interaction between individuals harmed by the products and the manufacturers. Legislatures have no such qualms, however, and are deeply interested in managing the economy and the products that enter into it. Likewise, courts only regulate property disputes when the harm caused between neighbors requires some resolution. Both state and national legislatures, however, treat environmental concerns on a societal level. Numerous environmental statutes regulate almost every aspect of industrial product and many statutes assign responsibility for cleanup without regard to individual fault. Likewise, with the exception of the doctrine of unreasonability, common law largely treats contracts as a matter of shared promises between autonomous individuals, legislatures attend to concerns that people enter into agreements that are one sided, due to psychological, social, and economic pressures. To address such concerns, legislatures adopt consumer-protection laws. Rather than hold parties responsible for the agreements they enter into, such laws blame social and economic context for unfortunate promises, and preclude people from making such agreements.

Thus, on the whole, legislatures seem to have a perspective that is better suited to managing social and economic interactions. Courts are apt to be persuaded by misleading signals (e.g., individual cases' emotional content); they are often unable to see how the resolution of the disputes before them fit into a broader scale of right and wrong; and they tend to focus excessively on individual conduct rather than social forces. Small wonder then, that no country today relies entirely, or even mostly, on the common-law process for developing law.

A SECOND LOOK: THE SUPERIORITY OF THE ADJUDICATIVE APPROACH

Many psychologists have argued that the human inference process in individual choice is quite reliable. The mental shortcuts that people use can be surprisingly effective in achieving desired results, even though most people navigate their lives by making one decision at a time.

Courts might not be so naïve as to adopt a myopic focus on individuals that leads them to neglect broader forces that produce the disputes they adjudicate. Over time, courts may become aware of the shortcomings of focusing on individuals and develop the means to incorporate broader horizons into their decision-making processes. In the U.S., for example, in the past half century, courts have witnessed a surge in testimony by expert witnesses that inject a wider focus into the process. Experts ranging from epidemiologists to economists regularly add social and scientific research into the trial process in a way that adds to the horizons of the adjudicative process. Furthermore, courts might adopt rules of evidence and procedure that facilitate sensible inferences and deter harmful ones. For example, the evidentiary prohibitions on character evidence might be a means of responding to the common tendency to attribute behavior too quickly to stable traits (Korobkin and Ulen 2000). Reducing testimony about an individual's personality presumably reduces the extent to which a judge or jury might make unwarranted inferences about criminal proclivities.

Courts are not a monolithic entity, and this gives them an advantage over legislatures. The common-law process is a process of trial and error. One court's pronouncement of a legal rule might be contradicted by the conclusions of a coequal court. Even identifying the present state of the law by sifting through common-law opinions is no easy task for lawyers or law professors. In many cases, only a few good decisions are needed to develop a sensible legal rule. Even if many courts adopt a misguided approach to an issue—so long as lawyers, professors, and subsequent courts have the means of identifying the sensible decisions of their predecessors—the misguided rulings will lose influence. Legislature action, in contrast, is essentially final, until the legislature revisits the issue. A legislative decision compels no fine sifting through the published experiences of parallel bodies that have encountered and resolved the same problem.

The repeated experimentation inherent in an adjudicative process might actually avoid pitfalls of judgment that plague legislatures. The repeated experience with a problem, in particular, might undo the influence of framing effects on decisions. A legislature approaches any social problem from a single, natural frame created by the status quo. Inasmuch as any solution to social problems involves a trade-off of some interests against others, the legislative approach necessarily favors the status quo.

Approaching the same social problems from a case-by-case perspective, however, can undo the framing problem that legislatures face. Courts will confront cases that present a shifting array of default conditions. Although the underlying rule might represent the same status quo that the legislature faced, the parties who approach the court might come from many different positions. Property disputes, in particular, have no persistent, natural status quo. A cement factory that begins operations which disrupt a neighboring residential community is apt to be treated as an interloper when the homeowners sue to enjoin its operations. The court might treat the status quo as a quiet neighborhood with no cement factory and judge it to be a nuisance. However, when the cement factory has been a longtime neighbor and a rise in new residential housing has simply made its operations intolerable to a greater number of people, then the residents are the interlopers. In such a case, the factory might be deemed not to be a nuisance. Likewise, contract dispute can arise in front of the court either as part of an effort by a promisee to enforce a promise or a promisor to avoid a requirement of fulfilling a promise. Although some types of disputes will consistently involve an injured party seeking recovery from an injurer, even here, the courts might face efforts to enjoin a party's actions so as to prevent future injuries. Courts will see disputes from different frames.

The various default conditions that courts face will have two beneficial effects with respect to framing. First, the differences in frame might lead individual courts to adopt different legal rules. As case law accumulates, the courts might select from these rules the most sensible, without regard to frame. Second, the courts might notice that the status quo is having an undesirable effect on the rules that they are adopting. In turn, this might lead courts to be able to step outside of the frame and see the kinds of disputes that they face from a broader perspective than the default presents. One way to avoid the effects of framing is to try to re-cast the dispute so as to see it from multiple perspectives. The process of lawmaking by adjudication, in effect, does just that.

Courts might also be more appropriately modest in the reforms that they adopt than legislatures. Courts know they only see one dispute and that their remedial authority is limited. Hence, they are apt to adopt simple, straightforward solutions to problems. Legislatures, by contrast, can adopt any solution they please, no matter how complex. Although this greater authority creates opportunities for resolving social problems that individual courts lack, it might induce legislatures to engage in excess tailoring of their solutions. That is to say, legislatures might adopt a solution so closely tied to the details of the problem as they see it, that the solution will fail to address the underlying social problem.

The concept of excess tailoring in problems of judgment arises directly from work in psychology and statistics (Gigerenzer et al. 1999). In some circumstances, simple decision rules predict future results better than the results of a multiple regression analysis. The reason for this is that the multiple regression "overfits" the data. It is so carefully tailored to the unique pattern of results that the regression model fails to uncover more stable tendencies. Hence, the simple rule can work better than the attempt by multiple regression to cover every wrinkle in the data. Courts, aware of the limitations of their approach, have little choice but to adopt simple, explicable resolutions. Their authority is limited to simple solutions and their legitimacy depends upon their ability to explain their decisions in simple terms. Legislatures, in contrast, are unlikely to resist the lure of complex solutions. Legislative solutions to social issues can be excessively tailored to the problem they are meant to address, and create regulation that serves little useful function.

Numerous examples of excessive tailoring by legislatures can be identified. In the late 1970s, the U.S. Congress became interested in the problem of abandoned hazardous waste disposal facilities, largely due to reports in the news media of a single incident that occurred in Niagara Falls, New York, in a neighborhood called Love Canal. Love Canal was a working-class neighborhood that had been constructed on an abandoned canal project into which a chemical company had dumped thousands of barrels of hazardous waste. By the late 1970s, barrels of this abandoned waste had begun to leak, and waste escaped into the backyards and basements of the residents. The U.S. Environmental Protection Agency (EPA) ultimately recommended that pregnant women and young children abandon their homes. Common-law litigation by the homeowners against the chemical company seemed an unsatisfactory means of redressing the situation, and Congress ultimately adopted a statute, known as CERCLA (Comprehensive Environmental Response, Compensation, and Liability Act) to address the problem of abandoned hazardous waste facilities. CERCLA required the

EPA to begin cleanup of hazardous waste facilities and enabled the EPA to recover for the cost of cleanup from anyone who deposited the waste and any present or past landowner of the site. The standard of liability was strict; those involved in the sites could not defend themselves by arguing that they took reasonable steps to avoid harming people.

Although hailed by many environmentalists as a laudable advance in the law, others criticized the statute for its excessive costs and the adverse incentives it creates to purchase and develop land that might be contaminated by prior disposal. These problems would not be so troublesome were it not for the concern that the statute does not, in fact, address a serious social problem. Many, including the EPA, have argued that abandoned hazardous waste disposal facilities are a limited social problem. Most stood little chance of containimating residential areas and could have been remediated with a limited government program. CERCLA is well-suited to solving problems like that at Love Canal—where a large number of residential homeowners unwittingly purchased land from a single solvent chemical company that could be easily identified. However, when applied to almost any other aspect of the problem of what to do about abandoned hazardous waste disposal facilities, CERCLA is a nightmare. Many companies are insolvent or cannot be found. The strict liability provisions create inordinate and disproportionate liability for many defendants, which led to decades of litigation at many sites. CERCLA's cleanup standards are also excessive for many areas (albeit sensible for a residential community). In short, CERCLA is an example of an excessively tailored statute.

Attributing the passage of CERCLA to cognitive dysfunction is not new. Many scholars have called CERCLA anecdote-driven legislation (Kuran and Sunstein 1999). What is usually meant by this, however, is that an underlying story was so vivid that it creates a social availability of the problem, leading the public to overestimate the extent of the harm. Whatever role cognitive availability plays in the passage of statutes like CERCLA, availability only explains the passage of some remedial measure. Abandoned hazardous waste disposal facilities might really be an unaddressed social problem, and a powerful anecdote like Love Canal might be just what is needed to fix the public's attention on it. Congress had been mulling over legislation to address hazardous waste disposal facilitates for many years before Love Canal became a major news story. The real problem was not that Congress passed legislation dealing with abandoned hazardous waste disposal facilities, but that it passed legislation that was tailored precisely to the situation at Love Canal. Similar stories can be told for other environmental statutes, workplace safety regulations, and the regulation of the securities markets.

The problem of excessively tailored statutes is stunningly similar to the problems that regression analysis can create. The observations that a statistician feeds into a regression analysis invariably incorporate some measurement error. This measurement error limits the ability of the regression model to predict future observations (i.e., its "reliability"). As statisticians note, the accuracy of the observations necessarily limits the reliability of the model. The regression equation, however, is itself blind to this concern. The analysis will produce a unique equation that best fits the data, measurement error and all. Statistical analysis accounts for this error by providing for an assessment of the predictive utility of the model (its R-squared).

The legislative process, however, contains no analogy to the R-squared, no complex test for how well the model fits the real solution. Even assuming the legislature has the relevant information about the story, the story might not be a good one upon which to found a major legislative initiative. The story that comes to the attention of the legislature might be idiosyncratic. It might not be a good reflection of the underlying social problem it represents. Indeed, the very fact that a story rises to the attention of the national media almost ensures that it has unique properties. Legislatures identify a problem, adopt a solution to cover the problem, and then move on. The reliability of the anecdote upon which the legislature found its solution is only rarely part of what the legislature considers.

One might suppose that courts face similar problems. After all, they inherently deal with stories. The stories courts review might be inaccurate, and might not be representative of the broader category of cases they represent. Courts, however, will inevitably revisit an issue as new cases arise. Their initial resolution of disputes is also apt to be modest, inasmuch as courts often refuse to address issues outside of those in the case before them. Legislatures adopt an omnibus solution to a social problem based largely on a single anecdote; courts necessarily revisit the same problem frequently.

Repeated encounters with the same issues also facilitate the remarkable human ability to categorize. The human brain seems quite adept at identifying patterns. Experts on artificial intelligence have as yet been unable to simulate the human power to identify structure and patterns. Today, machines that can make calculations millions of times more rapidly than the human brain still cannot recognize speech or handwriting with anything remotely like the accuracy that every human possesses. Chess-playing computers still cannot match the ability of chess grand masters, whose skills arise largely from their ability to identify complex patterns in the pieces. Indeed, psychologists argue that people tend to see patterns where none exist (Gilovich 1991). Superstition and myth arise largely from the beliefs in nonexistent patterns and relationships.

In the development of the common law, judges have relied heavily on pattern-recognition abilities. The process of common-law evolution consists largely of determining whether a new case is similar to older ones or whether a new category or exception needs to be carved out. Consider products liability law as an example. Products can, and have, injured people in an almost infinite variety of ways. However, the courts in the U.S. have distilled this infinite variation into three categories: manufacturing defects, design defects, and failure to warn. Every injury a product can cause fits relatively neatly into one of these three categories. The courts have also developed a body of rules governing the allocation of responsibility for injuries attributable to each of these three categories.

Not only is the common-law process remarkable at creating categories, it has amazing potential to identify similarities in seemingly disparate cases. Consider the analogies courts have found to the quirky *Summers v. Tice* (1948) case in the U.S. The case arose from a hunting accident: Three men went out hunting, proceeding through a field in a line. The center man got ahead, and when a group of birds took flight before him, both of his comrades negligently fired at his position. One of the two comrades hit him with his shot. Owing to the similarity of their firearms and situations, the court could not determine which of the two struck him. Usually, proof of causation lies with the plaintiff. This would have meant victory for both defendants, even though one of them negligently caused the injury. The *Summers* court, however, shifted the burden to the defendants. Decades later, a court reviewing the liability of a pharmaceutical manufacturer, *Sindell v. Abbott Laboratories*, (1980) found great value in analogizing to *Summers*. In *Sindell*, the court had determined that all manufacturers of a pharmaceutical were negligent in their marketing of the drug, but that the plaintiff could not identify from which manufacturer she had purchased the drug. The ability to find an analogous case with reasoning to reply upon facilitated the courts analysis of the *Sindell* case. The common-law process managed to highlight the similarities to such disparate events as a hunting accident and modern pharmaceutical marketing. There are certainly differences between the situations, but the *Sindell* court did not have to start its reasoning from scratch.

Finally, although sympathy is often cited as an impediment to process of dispassionate reasoning necessary for adjudication, it is not entirely clear that emotions are so misleading. In everyday life, of course, emotions provide a useful guide as to how to interpret and react (Frank 1989). Should this be less so in the adjudicative process? Emotional responses to various types of criminal acts or to types of plaintiffs probably have guided the development of the common law. However, this is not necessarily problematic. Judicial sympathies might well develop sensible, rather than foolish rules. A legislative process that hides the emotional aspects of a social decision might be missing an important cue.

AN INDETERMINATE ANALYSIS

Although courts are often maligned as myopic, half-witted policy makers, their single-case approach has virtues. The legislative approach avoids many of the pitfalls of the single-minded focus of the courts on resolving only the dispute before them. At the same time, courts might well be developing sensible heuristics for solving social dilemmas that legislatures might miss. Courts and legislatures alike are capable of creating misguided laws. The question, from the perspective of cognitive psychology, is what features of an underlying situation are best suited toward resolving each type of problem.

For many legal scholars the answer to which is the better approach has rested largely on complexity. Scholars have argued that many areas of law are simply too complicated for common-law courts to address. Environmental law, in particular, is thought to involve too much science and too much detail for common-law courts. Conversely, some have argued that the courts are best at implementing rules that require deeply contextual balancing. For example, implementing a negligence rule, which requires balancing costs against benefits to assess reasonableness of conduct in many different situations, is best done in the courts. Legislatures, after all, cannot easily envision all of the circumstances in which the balance they identify is to be struck. Thus, the conclusion here is that courts are best at balancing in a nuanced, contextual fashion while legislatures are best at addressing complexity.

The cognitive analysis above, however, suggests exactly the opposite: that courts will be best at developing adaptive rules for complex environments while legislatures will do best at balancing. For the reasons stated above, the courts have been able to develop simple rules that manage complex environments (Epstein 1995). The cognitive structure of the common-law process likely facilitates the process of identifying sensible rules. In particular, the necessarily modest approach of courts creates multiple opportunities to evolve slowly rules that avoid many of the pitfalls likely to ensnare legislatures that try to regulate the same issue. In contrast, courts face many cognitive obstacles to implementing sensible cost-benefit analysis. Courts are apt to see the probabilities associated with the balance in a subjective format that can impede sensible assessment of the risks and uncertainties.

REFERENCES

Cosmides, L., and J. Tooby. 1992. Cognitive adaptations for social exchange. In: The Adapted Mind: Evolutionary Psychology and the Generation of Culture, ed. J.H. Barkow, L. Cosmides, and J. Tooby, pp. 163–228. New York: Oxford Univ. Press.

Epstein, R.A. 1995. Simple Rules for a Complex World. Cambridge, MA: Harvard Univ. Press.

Frank, R.H. 1989. Passions within Reason. New York: Norton.

Gigerenzer, G. 2002. Calculated Risks: How to Know When Numbers Deceive You. New York: Simon and Schuster. (U.K. edition: Reckoning with Risk, Penguin)

Gigerenzer, G., P. Todd, and the ABC Research Group. 1999. Simple Heuristics That Make Us Smart. Oxford: Oxford Univ. Press.

Gilovich, T. 1991. How We Know What Isn't So: The Fallibility of Human Reasoning in Everyday Life. New York: Free Press.

Kahneman, D., and D. Lovallo. 1993. Timid choices and bold forecasts: A cognitive perspective on risk taking. *Manag. Sci.* **39**:17–31.

Kahneman, D., and A. Tversky. 1984. Choices, values, and frames. *Am. Psychol.* **39**:341–350.

Kaye, D. 1979. Probability theory meets *res ipsa loquitur. Michigan Law Rev.* **77**: 1456–1484.

Korobkin, R.B., and T.S. Ulen. 2000. Law and behavioral science: Removing the rationality assumption from law and economics. *Calif. Law Rev.* **88**:1051–1144.

Kuran, T., and C.R. Sunstein. 1999. Availability cascades and risk regulation. *Stanford Law Rev.* **51**:683–768.

Miller, D.T., and C. McFarland. 1987. Counterfactual thinking and victim compensation: A test of norm theory. *Pers. Soc. Psychol. Bull.* **12**:513–519.

Nisbett, R.E., C. Caputo, P. Legant, and J. Maracek. 1973. Behavior as seen by the actor and as seen by the observer. *J. Pers. Soc. Psychol.* **27**:154–164.

Rachlinski, J.J. 2000. Heuristics and biases in the courts: Ignorance or adaptation? *Oregon Law Rev.* **79**:61–102.

Ross, L. 1976. The intuitive psychologist and his shortcomings: Distortions in the attribution process. In: Advances in Experimental Social Psychology, ed. L. Berkowitz, pp. 174–221. New York: Academic.

Ross, L., and D. Shestowsky. 2003. Contemporary psychology's challenges to legal theory and practice. *Northwestern Univ. Law Rev.* **97**:1081–1114.

Sindell v. Abbott Laboratories, 26 Cal. 3d 588, 607 P.2d 924 (1980).

Slovic, P., M. Finucane, E. Peters, and D.G. MacGregor. 2003. The affect heuristic. In: Heuristics and Biases: The Psychology of Intuitive Judgment, ed. T. Gilovich, D. Griffin, and D. Kahneman, pp. 397–420. Cambridge: Cambridge Univ. Press.

Summers v. Tice, 33 Cal. 2d 80, 199 P.2d 1 (1948).

Sunstein, C.R. 1996. Health-health tradeoffs. *Univ. of Chicago Law Rev.* **63**:1533–1571.

Sunstein, C.R., D. Kahneman, D. Schkade, and I. Ritov. 2002. Predictably incoherent judgments. *Stanford Law Rev.* **53**:1153–1216.

9

Evolutionary Psychology, Moral Heuristics, and the Law

Leda Cosmides and John Tooby

Center for Evolutionary Psychology, University of California,
Santa Barbara, CA 93106, U.S.A.

ABSTRACT

The modern world, with its vast nation states peopled with millions of strangers, has little
in common with the social world in which humans evolved—a world of tiny bands peopled with a few dozen friends, relatives, and competitors. To negotiate that intimate social world, evolution equipped our minds with moral heuristics: decision rules that
generate intuitions about fairness and justice, punitiveness and approval, right and
wrong. Each was designed by natural selection to operate in a different type of ancestral
social situation, and each is triggered by cues that, in an ancestral past, indicated that type
of situation was occurring. Political debate in the present is often a struggle over how to
characterize events in terms of these ancestral situation-types, because alternative fram-
ings trigger different evolved moral heuristics.

Once triggered, a moral heuristic produces intuitions about what course of action
would be virtuous or immoral, as well as intuitions about the likely consequences of taking that course of action. These intuitions motivate lawmakers and citizens to enact laws
promoting or even mandating certain courses of action. But the mismatch between the
ancestral world and current conditions is so great that laws that seem virtuous to our
hunter–gatherer minds often have unanticipated social consequences that are disastrous,
and laws that seem morally dubious can be engines of social welfare. We illustrate with
examples drawn from the evolutionary psychology of cooperation and sharing.

HUMAN NATURE AND THE LAW

The political scientist Edward Banfield once asked the undergraduates in a sem-
inar for their gut answer to a question: Are people "basically good" or "basically
bad"? After a show of hands, he claimed that your answer predicts what kind of
laws and institutions you favor: liberals answer "basically good" whereas conservatives answer "basically bad." Banfield's speculations about the source of
political belief may be unusual but the way he framed his probe question is not:
Many people think it is sensible to ask whether human nature is inherently

"good" or "bad," and believe the answer has implications for the law. A central theme of this chapter is that this way of framing the question is incoherent: it is a value judgment, devoid of any claims about how the mind works. To be useful to citizens and lawmakers, a claim about human nature needs to be a claim about how the mind actually works: about the design of programs that process information, allowing us to learn, reason, feel, judge, and react. Human nature is not inherently good or bad: it is, "inherently," a collection of programs, which execute their functions. The real question is: Which programs reliably develop in the human mind, and how do they process information? Evolutionary psychology seeks to answer this question. Accurate answers, when they are eventually arrived at, will have implications for lawmaking. We will extrapolate (provisionally and perhaps wrongly) from the field in its infancy. Some of its implications are strange, and may invite modifications in how legislation is created and conceptualized.

Heuristics and Evolutionary Psychology

The topic of this Dahlem Workshop was heuristics and the law, so before proceeding let us quickly consider the relationship between the study of heuristics and evolutionary psychology.

A heuristic is a fast and frugal decision rule, a mental program that produces a judgment quickly based on limited information (see Gigerenzer, this volume). Most research on heuristics has focused on decision rules for making judgments that depend on some understanding of probability, risk, or quantity: Given that you tested positive for a disease, how likely is it that you have it? Given what you know about cities, which of a pair is likely to be more populous? However, fast and frugal decision rules exist for making social and moral judgments as well. Indeed, a growing body of evidence supports the view that the human mind was tailored by natural selection to develop certain social and moral heuristics: decision rules that quickly produce social and moral judgments, based on limited information. We will consider some of these social and moral heuristics below, with attention to how they may be shaping the way debates about social policy and the law are framed.

WHAT IS EVOLUTIONARY PSYCHOLOGY?

In the final pages of the *Origin of Species*, after Darwin had presented the theory of evolution by natural selection, he wrote, "In the distant future I see open fields for far more important researches. Psychology will be based on a new foundation, that of the necessary acquirement of each mental power and capacity by gradation" (Darwin 1859, p. 488). More than a century later, a number of scientists began to work out exactly how Darwin's fundamental insights could be used as a foundation on which to build a more systematic approach to psychology (for review, see Tooby and Cosmides 1992; see also Symons 1979; Cosmides and Tooby 1987; Daly and Wilson 1988; Buss 1989; Pinker 1997; Gigerenzer 2000). We were motivated by new developments from a series of different fields:

Advance #1   The cognitive revolution provided, for the first time in human history, a precise language for describing mental mechanisms, as programs that process information.

Advance #2   Advances in paleoanthropology, hunter–gatherer studies, and primatology provided data about the adaptive problems our ancestors had to solve to survive and reproduce and the environments in which they did so.

Advance #3   Research in animal behavior, linguistics, and neuropsychology showed that the mind is not a blank slate, passively recording the world. Organisms come "factory-equipped" with knowledge about the world, which allows them to learn some relationships easily, and others only with great effort, if at all. Skinner's hypothesis—that learning is a simple process governed by reward and punishment—was simply wrong (Skinner 1976).

Advance #4   Evolutionary game theory revolutionized evolutionary biology, placing it on a more rigorous, formal foundation of replicator dynamics. This clarified how natural selection works, what counts as an *adaptive* function, and what the criteria are for calling a trait an *adaptation*.

We thought that these new developments could be interlaced into a unified research framework, with precise connections linking it to the social sciences, medicine, and the humanities. We called this framework *evolutionary psychology*. The goal of research in evolutionary psychology is to discover, understand, and map in detail the design of the human mind/brain, as well as to explore the implications of these new discoveries for other fields. The long-term goal of the field is to map "human nature"—that is, the species-typical information-processing architecture of the human brain—together with the developmental programs that build it.

Like other cognitive scientists, when evolutionary psychologists refer to "the mind," they mean the set of information-processing devices, embodied in neural tissue, that are responsible for all conscious and nonconscious mental activity, and that generate all behavior. Like other psychologists, evolutionary psychologists test hypotheses about the design of these information-processing devices—these programs—using laboratory methods from all branches of psychology, especially cognitive, developmental, and social psychology, as well as methods drawn from experimental economics, neuroscience, genetics, and cross-cultural field work.

Evolutionary psychologists go beyond traditional approaches in the study of the mind, however, by actively applying an insight that other researchers overlook: The programs comprising the human mind were designed by natural selection. These programs were not selected to solve the total array of logically possible computational problems. Instead, they were selected on the basis of how well they solved the adaptive problems faced by our hunter–gatherer ancestors (e.g., finding a mate, cooperating with others, hunting, gathering, protecting children, avoiding predators). Natural selection tends to produce programs that solve problems like these reliably, quickly, and efficiently. Knowing this allows one to approach the study of the mind like an engineer. Evolutionary psychologists commonly begin with a good specification of an adaptive information-processing problem; they then perform a task analysis of that problem. This allows researchers to see what properties a program would need to have in order to solve that problem well. This approach allows evolutionary psychologists to generate testable hypotheses about the structure of the programs that comprise the mind, rather than simply casting about randomly, using blind empiricism.

From this point of view, there are precise causal connections that link the four developments above into a coherent framework for thinking about human nature and human society (Tooby and Cosmides 1992). These connections (C-1 through C-6) are as follows:

C-1   Each organ in the body evolved to serve a function: the intestines digest, the heart pumps blood, the liver detoxifies poisons. The brain is also an organ, and its evolved function is to extract information from the environment and use that information to generate behavior and regulate physiology. From this perspective, the brain is a computer, a physical system that was designed to process information (*Advance #1*). Its programs were designed not by an engineer, but by natural selection, a causal process that retains and discards design features on the basis of how well they solved problems that affect reproduction (*Advance #4*).

The fact that the brain processes information is not an accidental side effect of some metabolic process; the brain was designed by natural selection *to be* a computer. Therefore, if you want to describe its operation in a way that captures its evolved function, you need to think of it as composed of programs that process information. The question then becomes: What programs are to be found in the human brain? What are the reliably developing, species-typical programs that, taken together, comprise the human mind?

C-2   Individual behavior is generated by this evolved computer, in response to information that it extracts from the internal and external environment (including the social environment) (*Advance #1*). To understand an individual's behavior, therefore, you need to know both the information that the person registered *and* the structure of the programs that generated his or her behavior.

C-3   The programs that comprise the human brain were sculpted over evolutionary time by the ancestral environments and selection pressures experienced by the hunter–gatherers from whom we are descended (*Advances #2* and *#4*). Each evolved program exists because it produced behavior that promoted the survival and reproduction of our ancestors better than alternative programs that arose during human evolutionary history. Evolutionary psychologists emphasize hunter–gatherer life because the evolutionary process is slow—it takes thousands of years to build a program of any complexity (Tooby and Cosmides 1990). The industrial revolution—even the agricultural revolution—are brief moments in evolutionary time, too short to have selected for complex new cognitive programs.

C-4   Although the behavior our evolved programs generate would, on average, have been adaptive (reproduction-promoting) in ancestral environments, there is no guarantee that it will be so now. Modern environments differ importantly from ancestral ones, particularly when it comes to social behavior. We no longer live in small, face-to-face societies, in semi-nomadic bands of 25–100 men, women, and children, many of whom were close relatives. Yet our cognitive programs were designed for that social world.

C-5   Perhaps most importantly, the brain must be comprised of many different programs, each specialized for solving a different adaptive problem our ancestors faced. That is, the mind cannot be a blank slate (*Advance #3*).

   In fact, the same is true of any computationally powerful, multi-tasking computer. Consider the computer in your office. So many people analyze data and write prose that most computers come factory-equipped with a spreadsheet and a text-editor. These are two separate programs, each with different computational properties. This is because number-crunching and writing prose are very different problems: the design features that make a program good at data analysis are not well-suited to writing and editing articles, and vice versa. To accomplish both tasks well, the computer utilizes two programs, each well-designed for a specific task. The more functionally specialized programs it has, the more intelligent your computer is: the more things it can do. The same is true for people.

   Our hunter–gatherer ancestors were, in effect, on a camping trip that lasted a lifetime, and they had to solve many different kinds of problems well to survive and reproduce under those conditions. Design features that make a program good at choosing nutritious foods, for example, will be ill-suited for finding a fertile mate. Different problems require different evolved solutions.

   This can be most clearly seen by using results from replicator dynamics (*Advance #4*) and data about ancestral environments (*Advance #2*) to

define adaptive problems, and then carefully dissecting the computational requirements of any program capable of solving those problems.
Thus, for example, programs designed for logical reasoning would be
poorly designed to detect cheaters in social exchange, and vice versa
(Cosmides and Tooby 2005). As we will discuss, it appears that we have
programs that are functionally specialized for reasoning about reciprocity and exchange.

C-6   To understand human culture and social organization, one needs to understand these evolved programs. The mind is not like a tape recorder,
passively recording the world but imparting no content of its own.
Evolved programs—many of them content-specialized—organize our
experiences, generate our inferences, inject certain recurrent concepts
and motivations into our mental life, give us our passions, and provide
cross-culturally universal interpretive frameworks that allow us to understand the actions and intentions of others. They invite us to think certain content-inflected thoughts; they make certain ideas, feelings, and
reactions seem persuasive, interesting, and memorable. Consequently,
they play a key role in determining which ideas and customs will easily
spread from mind to mind, and which will not—that is, they play a crucial
role in shaping human culture and in stabilizing certain social forms.

Instincts—when the word is used at all—are often contrasted with reasoning
and decision making. But the reasoning programs and decision rules that evolutionary psychologists have been discovering are (a) complexly specialized for
solving an adaptive problem; (b) they reliably develop in all normal human beings; (c) they develop without any conscious effort and in the absence of formal
instruction; (d) they are often applied without any awareness of their underlying
logic, and (e) they are distinct from more general abilities to process information
or behave intelligently. In other words, they have the key characteristics that
used to be encompassed by the concept *instinct* (Pinker 1994). In fact, one can
think of these specialized circuits as *cognitive instincts*. They make certain kinds
of inferences and decisions just as easy, effortless, and "natural" to us as humans, as echolocating is for a dolphin or swimming is for a penguin.

Consider this example from the work of Simon Baron-Cohen (1995), using
what is known as the Charlie task. A child is shown a schematic face ("Charlie")
surrounded by four different kinds of candy. Charlie's eyes are pointed, for example, toward the Milky Way bar. The child is then asked, "Which candy does
Charlie want?" Like you and I, a normal four-year-old will say that Charlie
wants the Milky Way (i.e., the object of Charlie's gaze). In contrast, children
with autism fail the Charlie task, producing random responses. However—and
this is important—when asked which candy Charlie is looking at, children with
autism answer correctly. That is, children with this developmental disorder can
compute eye direction correctly, *but they cannot use that information to infer
what someone wants*.

We know, spontaneously and with no mental effort, that Charlie *wants* the candy he is *looking at*. This is so obvious to us that it hardly seems to require an inference at all. It is just common sense. However, this "common sense" is caused: it is produced by cognitive mechanisms. To infer a mental state (*wanting*) from information about eye direction requires a computation. There is a little inference circuit—a reasoning instinct—that produces this inference. When the circuit that does this computation is broken or fails to develop, the inference cannot be made. Those with autism fail the Charlie task because they lack this reasoning instinct.

As a species, we have been blind to the existence of these instincts—not because we lack them, but precisely because they work so well. Because they process information so effortlessly and automatically, their operation disappears unnoticed into the background. These instincts structure our thoughts so powerfully that it can be difficult to imagine how things could be otherwise. As a result, we take "normal" inferences and behavior for granted: We do not realize that "common sense" thought and behavior needs to be explained at all.

But it does. The joint application of an evolutionary and cognitive framework to studying the human mind is still new, but it is already becoming clear that all normal human minds reliably develop a standard collection of reasoning, emotional, and motivational programs. The social and moral intuitions these programs generate penetrate our subjective awareness, but not the intricate computational structure of the machinery that produces them. For example, people have the strong intuition that brother–sister incest is morally wrong. Moreover, it turns out that the *degree* of moral wrongness they feel is calibrated by variables that would have predicted who was a genetic relative under ancestral conditions (such as how long one co-resided during childhood with an opposite sex older sibling; Lieberman et al. 2003, 2006a, b). But people are unaware of the computations that produce this moral intuition, resulting in what Haidt (2001) calls "moral dumbfounding": When all the reasons they give for their opposition to incest (lack of consent, genetic defects in children) have been neutralized (assume both parties consent; they used foolproof contraception), people still cling to their strong intuition that sibling incest is morally wrong, finally asserting that they "just know" it is (Haidt 2001).

The structure of the programs that generate our social and moral intuitions can no more be seen by the naked "I"—by introspection alone—than the structure of a subatomic particle can be seen by the naked eye. But their structure can be revealed through careful experimentation. Research is showing that there are a multiplicity of such programs, each individually tailored to the demands of particular evolutionary functions—inbreeding avoidance, risk-sensitive foraging, reciprocal cooperation, collective action, and so on—and many equipped with what philosophers would once have called "innate ideas" (Tooby et al. 2005). A number of functionally distinct computational systems produce a variety of specific moral intuitions, each appropriate to a particular domain of human life. These make some conceptions of fairness, justice, right, and morality easier to attend to, remember, contemplate, and accede to than others (Boyer 2001; Fiske 1991; Haidt 2001; Cosmides and Tooby 1992, 1994, 2004). There are many more of these systems than anyone had suspected, and they respond far more sensitively to the particulars of human life than anyone had imagined.

To know which moral intuitions will be triggered in lawmakers,[1] judges, jurors, lawyers, scholars, and voters, one needs to understand these particulars. Which situational cues activate a given program? What inferences, emotions, and motivations will that program produce? Is the program designed to trigger responses that are contingent on the behavior of others? Most importantly, will the intuition about right and wrong it generates in the minds of lawmakers and citizens lead them to propose a policy that will have the consequences they are hoping for? In many cases, we suggest, the answer will be "no." Because so many laws and legal institutions in developed nations deal with social welfare, redistribution, property rights, fraud, and retribution, we will illustrate these points briefly using examples from the literature on the evolution of adaptations that motivate cooperation and sharing. In each case, we will give examples of how these cognitive adaptations—these moral heuristics—are activated by situational cues, and how they are invoked in the process of lawmaking.

DECISION RULES GOVERNING SHARING

Karl Marx thought that extant hunter–gatherers (and by extension, our ancestors) lived in a state of primitive communism, where all labor was accomplished through collective action and sharing was governed by the decision rule, "from each according to his ability to each according to his need." He thought the overthrow of capitalism would bring forth an economically advanced society with similar properties: abolish private property and all labor will once again be accomplished through collective action and, because the mind reflects the material conditions of existence, the hunter–gatherer communal sharing rule will emerge once again and dominate social life. Based on Marx's theory, twentieth-century laws governing property, the organization and compensation of labor, the regulation of manufacturing and trade, and the legitimacy of consent and dissent were changed across the planet, especially in China, the former Soviet Union, Cambodia, Cuba, North Korea, Vietnam, and Eastern Europe. These changes had a profound impact on the lives of the citizens of these nations, although not the utopian ones Marx had envisioned. In this light, it is reasonable to ask whether Marx's view of hunter–gatherer labor and sharing rules was correct. If

---

[1]   Henceforth, we will use the term "lawmakers" to refer to everyone involved in making the law, including legislators, policy analysts, lobbyists, advocacy groups, etc., in keeping with usage at the workshop.

not, what social and moral heuristics regarding cooperation did the selection pressures endemic to hunter–gatherer life build?

Hunter–Gatherer Sharing

Hunter–gatherers share many of the resources they acquire, and it appears our ancestors have been provisioning one another with food for at least 2 million years (Isaac 1978; Marshall 1976; Shostak 1981; Gurven 2004). The hunting of large animals is often organized as a collective action, and meat—whether caught by an individual or a cooperating group—is often shared at the band-wide level (Cashdan 1989; Kaplan and Hill 1985; Kaplan et al. 1990; Lee and DeVore 1968). These meat transfers are not characterized by direct reciprocation in any obvious way, although that remains one explanatory theory for the existence of such sharing. Although there are complex and dynamic rules governing the sharing process, an argument could be made that the outcome achieved for meat may be closest to that predicted by Marx's sharing rule.

Meat notwithstanding, hunter–gatherer life is not an orgy of indiscriminate sharing, nor is all labor accomplished through collective action. Aside from meat, very little is shared at the band-wide level. Plant foods are usually gathered by individuals, who share them primarily with other members of their nuclear family (Kaplan and Hill 1985; Kaplan et al. 1990; Marshall 1976). When sharing outside the family occurs, the neediest in the community are not the first or most likely targets (although need plays a role). Conditional sharing—reciprocation—is common. Within a community, each family partners with a small number of other families, and resource sharing is characterized by informal, implicit reciprocation with delay (Gurven et al. 2000; Gurven 2004). When an individual fails to reciprocate (or reciprocates with too little), this is a source of anger, discussion, and enormous tension (Marshall 1976; Shostak 1981). Access to foraging territories is governed by explicit, formal reciprocation, as are gift exchanges with specific individuals in distant bands who are cultivated as allies for future times of need (Wiessner 1982). Reciprocation in the form of explicit, simultaneous trade also occurs, often as economic interactions with individuals in neighboring bands (Marshall 1976; McBrearty and Brooks 2000).

That sharing among hunter–gatherers is more various, more relationship-specific, and more nuanced than Marx thought is not surprising from an evolutionary perspective. Over the past forty years, evolutionary analyses have repeatedly shown that selection would not favor indiscriminate sharing, nor would it favor a one-situation-fits-all decision rule for sharing. Different kinds of sharing rules carry selective advantages in different situations, and there is evidence that the human mind indeed contains several different programs that regulate sharing. Each produces different moral intuitions about when to provide help and to whom, and each is activated by different situational cues. Thus, based on limited information, different decision rules for sharing are activated:

different moral heuristics. Our first example involves the different sharing rules activated for meat versus gathered foods.

Luck and Effort as Cues Triggering Alternative Decision Rules

Why are meat and gathered food shared in such different patterns? It turns out that the real variable triggering different sharing rules is not meat versus plants per se, but whether variance in acquisition of the resource is high and due mostly to luck, or low and due mostly to effort.

Among hunter–gatherers, there is daily variation in an individual's foraging success, as well as variation between individuals in a band. Broadly speaking, the variance is caused by differences in effort expended, foraging skills, and pure luck—random factors outside the individual's control. The contribution of luck versus effort differs, however, depending on the resource, with important implications for the evolution of sharing rules (Cashdan 1989; Cosmides and Tooby 1992; Fiske 1991; Gurven 2004; Kaplan and Hill 1985; Kaplan et al. 1990; Kameda et al. 2003; Sugiyama 2004; Sugiyama and Scalise Sugiyama 2003). For some resources, including many gathered foods, variance in foraging success is low, and what variance exists is due more to differences in effort than luck or skill.[2] When everyone reliably has access to the same goods, there is little benefit to sharing widely, but there are real potential costs. The smaller the role played by chance, the more differences between individuals in amount of food foraged will reflect differences in effort or skill. When this is true, band-wide food sharing would simply redistribute food from those who expend more effort or are more skilled to those who expend less effort or are less skilled. Sharing under these circumstances offers few, if any, fitness payoffs for those who have acquired more food. Without chance creating reversals of fortune, there is little reason to expect that the future will be different from the present and, therefore, little reason to expect that those with less food now will be in a better position to reciprocate in the future. Under these circumstances, selection will favor adaptations that cause potential recipients to welcome sharing, but potential donors to be reluctant to share. Decision rules producing reluctance to share should be triggered, then, by the perception that a potential recipient's bad outcome resulted from his or her lack of effort.[3]

For other resources, such as meat and honey, luck is a major contributor to variance in foraging success. Among the Aché of Paraguay, for example,

---

[2] It is unclear whether skill in gathering differs greatly between people, and practice (effort) may contribute to skill.

[3] Because selection to avoid unnecessary and unrewarding effort is a pervasive selection pressure, one also expects a human psychology that attenuates effort whenever individual or family welfare does not decrease as a result. The tendency to direct effort to conditions where it leads to increases in personal and family welfare entails that humans generally should manifest some (nuanced) tendency to become free riders when circumstances permit. That means those expending effort are always at risk of exploitation by those who are free riding.

hunters making a good faith effort come back empty-handed four out of ten times (Kaplan and Hill 1985; Kaplan et al. 1990; see also Cashdan 1989). Moreover, hunting success and failure is largely uncorrelated across individuals: today you may have something and I nothing, tomorrow the reverse may be true. Under these conditions, an individual is better off redistributing food from periods of feast to periods of famine. There are two ways of doing this: through food storage or through pooling resources with others. Decay and the energetic costs of transport for semi-nomadic people mean food storage is not an option for many hunter–gatherers, but pooling resources is: If two people average their returns, variance decreases—each buys fewer days of privation at the price of fewer periods of superabundance. By adding more individuals to the risk-pooling group, variance may continue to decrease. Through a system of band-limited generalized reciprocity, food can be stored in the form of social obligations. When hunter–gatherers face frequent and random reversals of fortune, selection can favor decision rules that generate a positive desire to relieve the suffering of community members in need. These should be triggered by the perception that the suffering is caused by bad luck, rather than lack of effort (Kaplan and Hill 1985, Kaplan et al. 1990; Kameda et al. 2003). The bad luck could be caused by the vagaries of the hunt (animals, unlike plants, try to escape), by the random distribution of the resource (as with honey), or by illness and injury, a major cause of downtime among foraging people (Sugiyama 2004).

Thus sharing rules are not a function of a monolithic "culture": foragers within the same cultural group employ different sharing rules for high and low variance resources (Kaplan and Hill 1985). If this were caused by the contingent activation of alternative, domain-specific programs, then we should expect to see the same pattern in people living in industrialized cultures. Recent experiments in Japan and the United States show this is the case (Kameda et al. 2002). Like foragers, Japanese and American students were more likely to share money with others—and to demand shares from others—when it was obtained through a high variance, luck-driven process than by a low-variance process, even when effort expended was held constant. Was the effect of windfalls on intuitions about sharing caused by the students' explicit ideologies about sharing and distribution of resources? No: although ideology had some effect on the students' general willingness to share and demand resources, the effects of windfalls on sharing were found even when Kameda et al. (2002) statistically controlled for their subjects' individual attitudes toward distributive rules.

These findings suggest that different, incommensurate sharing programs— different evolved moral heuristics—are activated by the perception that bad outcomes are caused by bad luck versus lack of effort. These programs should have a grammar of their own, an internal structure. Consider, for example, the following two sentences:

1. If he is the victim of an unlucky tragedy, then we should pitch in to help him out.

2. If he spends his time loafing and living off of others, then he does not deserve our help.

The inferences they express seem perfectly natural; there seems to be nothing to explain. They may not always be applicable, but they are perfectly intelligible. But consider the following:

*3. If he is the victim of an unlucky tragedy, then he does not deserve our help.[4]
*4. If he spends his time loafing and living off of others, then we should pitch in to help him out.

Sentences (*3) and (*4) sound eccentric in a way that (1) and (2) do not. Yet they involve no *logical* contradictions. The inferences they embody seem to violate a grammar of social reasoning, in much the same way that "Alice might slowly" violates the grammar of English but "Alice might run" does not (Cosmides 1985; Cosmides and Tooby 1989, 1992, 1994). Indeed, "He spends his time loafing and living off others, so we should pitch in to help him out" (*4) sounds so strange that George Bernard Shaw used it as a point of humor in Pygmalion. Eliza Doolittle's eponymously named father argues that he should get *more* charitable help than the deserving poor, precisely because he is a lazy, drunken womanizer. After all, he has the same needs for clothing, food, and shelter as the deserving poor, but he requires far more to cover his liquor and other vices. For this argument, which violates the social grammar underlying (1) and (2), Doolittle received a grant for being a moral philosopher of great originality. No one, in fiction or in real life, would be considered original for advocating (1) or (2).

If this picture is close to correct, then the mind contains reasoning and motivational mechanisms that can reliably generate the moral intuitions expressed by (1) and (2), without also generating those expressed by (*3) and (*4). The grammar structuring these moral intuitions was selected for because of the fitness effects it had ancestrally. However, if this grammar is a reliably developing feature of the human mind—if it is part of our evolved psychology—it should continue to shape our moral intuitions about sharing and redistribution now, in policy makers, lawmakers, and the citizens they must convince. Debates about the content of the law should continue to reflect the intuitions expressed by (1) and (2)—and they do.

Consider, for example, the political and moral debate concerning increases in government help for the homeless in the U.S. Those with opposing postures frame their positions in ways that exploit the structure of this evolved psychology. A persistent theme among those who favor increases (i.e., who wish to motivate more sharing) is the idea that "there but for fortune go you or I." That is, they emphasize the random, variance-driven dimensions of the situation. The

---

4   We marked sentences with an * to denote them as "ungrammatical" to our mind's moral grammar of cooperation in the same way that linguists routinely star sentences that are ungrammatical.

potential recipient of aid is viewed as worthy because he or she is the unlucky victim of circumstances, such as unemployment, discrimination, or mental illness. On the other hand, those who oppose an increase in sharing with the homeless emphasize the putatively chosen or self-caused dimensions of the situation. Potential recipients are viewed as unworthy of aid because they "brought it on themselves." They are portrayed as able-bodied but lazy, or as having debilitated themselves by choosing to use alcohol and narcotics. The counterresponse from those who want to motivate more sharing is to portray alcohol and drug use not as a choice, but as an illness, and so on.

Lawmakers and citizens do not argue about the underlying logic of the decision rules expressed by (1) or (2). They argue about whether discrete classes of individuals meet the input conditions specified in the antecedent clause of (1) and (2)—in this case, about whether this bad outcome, homelessness, was caused by bad luck or by lack of effort. They do not argue about which sharing pattern is then entailed. They do not need to: the implication for sharing is embedded in the grammar of the evolved moral heuristics.

The Law and Social Welfare

Many laws are advocated on the basis that they promote general social welfare (Sen 1989; Epstein 1995). Moral intuitions expressed by the decision rules in (1) and (2) were not, however, selected for because they promoted or maximized general social welfare within a hunter–gatherer band. These decision rules were selected for because they promoted their own reproduction, by promoting the reproduction of the individuals whose minds were equipped with them and therefore shared in accordance with them. That is how natural selection works. Our minds are not equipped with moral intuitions designed to promote general social welfare, even in the contexts for which they evolved.[5] When they have this effect—and sometimes they do, as we discuss below—it is a side effect of their design, a fortuitous accident emerging when minds designed for a vanished world interact in a modern context.

Moral heuristics, like other decision rules, were designed to operate well in particular environments; they cannot be expected to produce the same effects outside these conditions. There is no such thing as an omniscient, omnipotent algorithm, one that can calculate the best course of action in any imaginable environment (Cosmides and Tooby 1987; Gigerenzer and Selten 2001; Tooby and Cosmides 1992). Decision rules are *mechanisms*, programs with a causal structure. They were designed to produce fitness-promoting outcomes in the environments that selected for their structure. In the case of the moral heuristics

---

[5]   It is possible that some moral intuitions were selected to direct small group-level coordination to mutually beneficial outcomes (but such group-restricted coordination is hardly *general* social welfare). Regardless of whether that happened, it is a certainty that small group coordination is only one of many selection pressures shaping the human repertoire of evolved moral heuristics.

described by (1) and (2), that environment was a band of roughly 25–50 cooperating people; many of them were relatives, who could be closely monitored for free riding because of the close proximity of their living conditions. Donors would be intimately familiar with the characters and need levels of potential recipients.

What happens when these moral intuitions operate outside the environment for which they were designed, in a modern nation of strangers, numbering in the millions? One goal of law is to create "rules of the game" (North 1990) to promote the general social welfare. Will the rules embedded in heuristics like (1) and (2) be good candidate rules of the game? Does the easy activation of these particular moral intuitions lead lawmakers and citizens to overlook better solutions, ones more likely to have a consensually desired outcome in the modern world?

When millions of relatively anonymous people interact in a modern market, the results can be counterintuitive and surprising. For example, rent control is often advocated as a way of giving homes to the homeless and of preventing the working poor from becoming homeless. Rent control makes sense to a hunter–gatherer mind: If housing is more expensive than a poor person can afford, then use the law to make it less expensive. *If he is the victim of bad luck, we should pitch in and help him out.*[6] Those who have the unequally distributed resource—landlords—should share it with those in need. Punish landlords who violate this sharing rule (see below on punishment in collective action).[7] Use the force of the state to punish landlords who charge "too much."

Yet does rent control have the effect of *actually* helping the homeless? Using a large sample of cities in the U.S., Tucker (1990) analyzed what factors predict rates of homelessness. Surprisingly, unemployment and poverty rates did not predict rates of homelessness, but rent control and mean temperature did—indeed, they were major and significant predictors. Cities with rent control had significantly *higher* homeless rates than cities without it. It turns out rent control has a range of unanticipated secondary effects. In particular, it deters construction of rental units and motivates the owners of existing housing to avoid placing or keeping units on the rental market. The supply of rental units consequently shrinks or stagnates, resulting in fewer places for poor people to live and skyrocketing prices in unregulated or informal sectors of the housing market. Voting for rent control may make citizens feel good about themselves (even when they are not directly benefitting themselves), as it is a way of acting on the moral intuition expressed by (1). However, by doing so, they appear to be condemning

---

[6]   Many cities first adopted rent control during World War II. This is interesting for two reasons: (a) war creates many victims of unlucky tragedy; (b) warfare is one of the few contexts that activates coalitional cooperation with norms of communal sharing among hunter–gatherers (see next section).

[7]   Secondarily, of course, landlords are a minority. So the impulse is typically: force others—landlords—to share with those in need (as well as those not in need, renters voting in their self-interest).

the actual victims of bad luck to a brutal life on the streets. Providing housing vouchers (for example) from general tax revenues would allow the homeless to obtain housing without these negative effects on the rental supply.

COLLECTIVE ACTION, FREE RIDERS, AND PUNISHMENT

Marx's theory appeals to some of our evolved moral heuristics (as well as to our hunger for a small-scale world of affectionate communal sharing). He advocated a world in which most labor is organized as a collective action, where people cooperate as a group to produce goods that are then communally shared. Game theorists, economists, political scientists, anthropologists, evolutionary biologists, and psychologists have been studying the psychology and dynamics of this form of collective action, and some of the results are surprising. The dark harvest of nation states centrally organized around collective action has principled explanations rooted directly in an evolved psychology of cooperation and punishment (Tooby et al. 2006).

Coalitional cooperation (as opposed to a two-person exchange) exists when three or more individuals coordinate their behavior with one another to achieve a common goal, and then share the resulting benefits. Among hunter–gatherers, coalitional cooperation among nonkin most commonly occurs in two contexts: cooperative hunting and intergroup aggression (small-scale warfare). Most other labor is pursued in other ways.

Whether the common goal is to produce resources (as in cooperative hunting) or to seize them from others (as in intergroup aggression), achieving that goal requires a sophisticated form of cooperation. Individuals within the group must coalesce into a coalition, i.e., a cooperative unit whose members act together to attain a goal. This form of collective action often produces public goods but—as economists, evolutionary biologists, and game theorists have recognized—the payoff dynamics inherent in collective action create the incentive to free ride, rendering coalitional cooperation unstable and difficult to sustain (Olson 1965; Henrich and Boyd 2001; Price et al. 2002).

Kin selection mitigates some of these problems, and information-processing mechanisms that enable coordinated action and cooperation among multiple genetically related individuals have evolved a number of times (e.g., the social hymenoptera (bees, ants); Hamilton 1964). However, coalitional cooperation among unrelated individuals is zoologically rare, with humans and chimpanzees as the only uncontroversial examples (Wilson and Wrangham 2003; Wrangham and Peterson 1996). Unlike most other species, humans readily form multi-person cooperative alliances that change dynamically, rapidly dissolving, shifting, and re-forming as new tasks, issues, and conflicts arise. What is the evolved psychology that makes this possible?

Free Riding, Punishment, and Collective Action

When faced with the decision to participate in a collective action, there are two choices: free ride or participate. Ever since Mancur Olson's trenchant analysis, economists have understood that free riding generates a higher payoff than cooperation: participants and free riders get the same benefit—a successful outcome—but free riders do not incur the cost of participation (Olson 1965). This incentive to free ride results in a paradoxical outcome: participation unravels and the project fails, even though each individual would have been better off if the project's goal had been successfully achieved.

Evolutionary biologists find cooperation in collective actions puzzling for a different, but related, reason. In evolutionary biology, the different payoffs to alternative choices are relevant only if they cause differential reproduction of alternative designs (alternative programs) that cause those choices. The fact that collective action is rare in the animal kingdom means that most organisms *lack* programs that cause participation: free riding, therefore, is the default choice. If payoffs to collective action translate into reproductive advantages, then how could designs causing participation have gained a toe-hold in a universe dominated by non-participants? Those who participated in a successful collective action would have experienced an increase in their fitness, but free riders would have benefited even more (by getting the benefits of the achieved goal without suffering the costs of participation). The currency is differential reproduction of participant versus free-riding designs; this means that individuals equipped with programs that caused free riding would have out-reproduced those equipped with programs that caused participation. Consequently, free-rider designs would have been selected for, and any participation designs that arose in a population would have been selected out. If so, then why do we see individual human beings routinely and willingly participating in collective actions? How did participant designs outcompete free-rider designs? How is the free-rider problem solved?

Recent models of the evolution of collective action have focused on the role of punishment in solving the free-rider problem (Boyd et al. 2003; Gintis 2000; Boyd and Richerson 1992; Henrich and Boyd 2001; Kameda et al. 2003; Panchanathan and Boyd 2004). These models show that willingness to contribute to a public good can be evolutionarily stable as long as free riders are punished, along with those who refuse to punish free riders. These analyses propose that humans have evolved moral heuristics that produce the intuition that free riders should be punished.

There is evidence supporting this prediction. Recent research from evolutionary psychology and experimental economics indicates that individuals who contribute to public goods feel punitive toward free riders. Research in experimental economics using public goods games has shown not only that contributors do punish free riders, but they are willing to *pay* out of pocket to do so

(Dawes et al. 1986; Fehr and Gachter 2000a; Masclet et al. 2003; Ostrom et al. 1992; Sato 1987; Yamagishi 1992). In sharp contrast to predictions of rational choice theory, people incur personal costs to punish free riders even in one-shot games; that is, even when it appears that they are unlikely to have future interactions with the individual they punished and, therefore, are unlikely to recoup their losses in the form of increased cooperation from that person in the future (for review, see Gintis 2000). Decision rules designed to maximize personal payoffs in response to modern situations would *not* produce this outcome, but decision rules designed for a small social world of repeated interactions would.[8]

Psychological studies support the view that one's own willingness to contribute to a collective action triggers punitive sentiments toward free riders[9] (Price et al. 2002; Price 2003, 2005). The more one contributes, the more punitive one feels toward those who do not. This occurs not only in undergraduate populations (Price et al. 2002), but in Shuar hunter–horticulturalists engaged in sugar cane cultivation in the Ecuadorian Amazon (Price 2003, 2005). Analysis of individual decision making in experimental economics games converges on the same pattern: punishment is more severe as a function of how much less the free rider has contributed than the punisher, and how far below the group average the free rider's contribution falls (Masclet et al. 2003).[10]

Research on contributions to public goods in experimental economics shows that people continuously monitor the state of play, adjusting their behavior accordingly (Brewer and Kramer 1986; Fehr and Gachter 2000a, b; Kurzban et al. 2001; Masclet et al. 2003). If the game allows punishment, higher contributors inflict punishment on undercontributors right away (which has the secondary consequence of allowing levels of cooperation to spiral up toward the welfare-maximizing optimum of 100% contribution to the common pool; Fehr and Gachter 2000a; Masclet et al. 2003; for analysis, see Price et al. 2002). When there is no opportunity to punish, high contributors ratchet back their own contribution to something like the group average. As this monitoring and adjustment process iterates, contributions gradually diminish to rational choice theory expectations (Kurzban et al. 2001). However, this iterative ratcheting back does not reflect the emergence, through learning, of rational choice: when a new collective action begins, the very same people start out contributing to the common pool at relatively high levels (about 60% of their endowment; rational choice theory predicts 0%).

In other words, people have a taste for punishing free riders, and collective actions are more likely to succeed when they exercise this taste. The desire to

[8] Not only do hunter–gatherers typically experience repeated interactions, but the possibility always remains that they will interact with a given individual in the future—they cannot be sure a situation is one-shot until one of them is dead.

[9] The level of punitive sentiment toward free riders is predicted by subjects' willingness to contribute, even when their self-interest in achieving the group goal is controlled for statistically.

[10] Sometimes very low contributors punish very high contributors as well, perhaps to discourage high contributors from inflicting punishment on them (Masclet et al. 2003).

punish free riders does not result from a strategic rational analysis, with backward induction, of the current and future payoffs of alternative decisions. If it did, people would not pay to punish in one-shot games, and their level of punitive sentiment would be independently predicted by how much they think they will benefit from the collective action succeeding (it is not; see Price et al. 2002). Instead, the decision rule is more like a moral heuristic that is activated by participating in a collective action, which uses limited information to judge how much punishment is deserved. The inputs are (a) one's own level of contribution, (b) the average contribution level in the group, and (c) the contribution level of each individual in the group. More punitive sentiment is felt toward those who contribute less than the self as well as those who contribute less than the group average.

Lawmakers Are Members of the Species Too

Every year, idealistic young Americans vie for internships and jobs with public advocacy groups in Washington, D.C., yearning to work for the public good. Nevertheless, many volunteers (and even paid workers) are lost to "burnout": a catastrophic drop in morale triggered by the accumulating perception that only you and a few others are making substantial contributions, while most people free ride. This realization is frequently accompanied by bitterness and anger (punitive sentiment?) toward non-participants, who are disparaged as indifferent, selfish, ignorant, or malign. The punitive moral heuristic described above implies that the very experience of working hard for a collective good should trigger negative sentiments toward those who do not: Contribution entitles you to punish noncontributors. The loss of interest in making further contributions is also expected: these are private groups that lack the ability to punish free riders, a circumstance that triggers the strategy of iterative ratcheting back.

Less obviously, the moral heuristic that generates punitive sentiment in proportion to one's own contributions to a collective action might color the legal solutions favored by those who work hard for advocacy groups (or collectivist governments). Consider the implications of the work showing that, although willingness to participate in a collective action triggers punitive sentiments toward free riders, it does not trigger a desire to reward fellow participants (Price et al. 2002; Price 2003, 2005).

Producing cleaner air is a classic public good. In an effort to reduce air pollution, one could advocate a pro-reward policy (e.g., tax incentives for businesses that contribute to the goal by reducing their pollution) or a punitive policy (e.g., fines levied on businesses that do not reduce their pollution). Which is more effective is an empirical matter, and the goal of clean air is best served by choosing the most effective policy. (N.B.: the authors have no opinion about which works best). Still, the very act of participating in a collective action triggers punitive sentiments toward free riders (businesses that do not reduce their pollution), not pro-reward sentiments toward contributors (businesses that do reduce their pollution) (see Price et al. 2002). Indeed, the more energetically one works for an environmental advocacy group, the more punitive one should feel toward businesses who do not curtail their pollution and toward fellow citizens who do not contribute to the group's work. Once this moral sentiment is activated, policies that impose sanctions and laws that mandate contributions toward the goal (through taxes and state agencies) may seem more reasonable and just. Indeed, individuals who, before joining an environmental advocacy group, had favored pro-reward policies might be expected to undergo a change of heart after joining. Once they are actively participating, they can be expected to experience an ethical tug in the direction of punitive sanctions and enforced contributions, and away from policies that reward businesses for curtailing pollution.

More broadly, different subsets of the population have different values and envision or embark on different collective projects. From the point of view of an individual involved in one project, others with diverging projects (and different views and values) appear to be free riders with respect to one's favored enterprises. Because government monopolizes the means of unilateral punishment, struggles over the reins of power can be expected, even by the initially well-intentioned. Their sacrifices for their governing enterprise will intensify the activation of their moral heuristics so that dissenters and those who (to their vision) undercontribute will seem to deserve punishment. Indeed, to the extent that members of any government department imagine themselves to be involved in projects for the collective good, they can be expected to accumulate punitive sentiment toward the public at large. As the nineteenth-century novelist Liu E comments, "everyone knows that corrupt mandarins are evil, but few know that irreproachable mandarins are worse; [they] delude themselves that because they turn down bribes, they have the right to impose any decision they wish. Their clear consciences...can lead them to massacre the innocent" (quoted in Leys 1979, p. 137).

Working with Human Nature

Are there ways of harnessing these moral sentiments in the service of reducing negative externalities such as pollution? Clean air is a public good, but the individuals charged with enforcing pollution standards are government bureaucrats at agencies like the Environmental Protection Agency (EPA). Imagine a slightly different system: "pollution courts," where companies that had contributed to the public good by demonstrably reducing their own pollution levels had standing to both present evidence of pollution by their free-riding competitors and request the imposition of fines. Might this give companies an incentive (a) to prove they deserve standing (by lowering their own pollution levels) and (b) to investigate cases of pollution, thereby reducing the EPA's burden? Could this system wipe out the profit advantage the free-riding polluter has over companies that voluntarily curtail their pollution?

Another possibility is to develop market-based solutions, which operate by creating incentives to reduce pollution while allocating productive resources efficiently. For example, in cap and trade schemes, legislatures put a cap on the total amount of gas emissions permitted, and a market is created in which rights to emit a certain quantity of these gases can be bought and sold (for an informative discussion of market-based methods for improving the environment, see *The Economist*, April 23, 2005). But market-based solutions do not punish free riders directly, and they are rarely advocated by environmental groups. Is this because they are ineffective? Or is it because they do not satisfy the punitive sentiments lawmakers and citizens feel toward free-riding polluters?

Becoming aware of our moral heuristics is as important as careful economic policy analysis. To solve problems, we need to know our own minds: it is the only way to distinguish between policies that are appealing because they make us feel virtuous and policies that are unappealing but actually work.

Punitive Heuristics and the Organization of Production

Marx argued for a system in which most labor is organized as a collective action on a grand scale, but most collective action events among hunter–gatherers involve a small group (3–7) of well-acquainted individuals who live together and can respond to individual differences in performance sensitively and dynamically. Interestingly, psychological experiments suggest that in the absence of punishment, contributions to public goods start to fall as group size starts to exceed eight individuals (Brewer and Kramer 1986). Will an evolved psychology of collective action designed for working groups of a few well-known, easily monitored individuals scale up to factories and farms with thousands or societies of millions? Can collective action work well on all scales of social organization? How does Marx's vision of each individual working to the best of his ability, and giving the fruits of his labor to others according to their need, square with the existence of free riders? Will collective actions on a grand scale elicit free riding on a grand scale? Under these conditions, will heuristics motivating punishment of free riders be activated in those committed to making the system of collective cooperation work, creating a punitive social climate? What outcomes should we expect when the law prohibits private action and mandates collective action?

Communitarian methods of organizing production have a strong ethical pull for many people, including ourselves. Equal division of profits can seem fair (under the assumption that everyone is contributing equally) or at least humane (under the assumption that everyone who is capable of contributing is doing so). The fairness of these compensation schemes is predicated on the assumption that no one free rides. Their efficacy is predicated on the assumption that if free riding does occur, contributors will continue to work at the same level—there will be no iterative ratchet effect. Are these reasonable assumptions?

Lawmakers and citizens need to consider whether certain methods of compensation invite free riding and dwindling participation, given the kind of minds we have.

Price (2003, 2005) conducted detailed studies of punitive sentiments toward free riders among a group of Shuar men living in the Ecuadorian Amazon. These men had decided to cultivate sugar cane, and they had organized their labor as a collective action. The labor consisted primarily of using machetes to clear the fields for cultivation. Everyone who participated was guaranteed an equal share of the proceeds from selling the crop, and there were consensually agreed upon fines for not showing up to clear the fields. Price found out how large each man felt the fine for free riding should be, and discovered that the size of the fine was predicted by how much each man actually contributed to this collective action project.

Interestingly, the Shuar collective action in sugar cane cultivation ultimately failed. The fines had no bite: instead of being levied after each work episode (each episode in which participation occurred and could be monitored), the fines were to be deducted from each individual's profit once the crop was harvested and sold. The iterative ratchet effect ensued. Over time, participation in the cultivation effort dwindled to the point where the project failed and there were no proceeds to share. It is worth noting that everyday life among the Shuar involves norms promoting generosity and sharing at levels rarely seen in large scale industrial societies.

Farms, factories, restaurants—all involve multi-individual cooperation and hence collective action. The question is: Should these projects be organized as public goods (everyone benefits equally, regardless of their level of participation), or should payoffs be organized such that effort is rewarded and free riding is punished? One of many natural experiments was provided by agricultural policy in the former Soviet Union. The state nationalized farmland and forced farmers to organize their labor as a collective action. But they allowed 3% of the land on collective farms to be held privately, so local farming families could grow food for their own consumption and privately sell any excess. The results were striking. Estimates at the time were that this 3% of land produced 45% to 75% of all the vegetables, meat, milk, eggs, and potatoes consumed in the Soviet Union (Sakoff 1962). The quality of land on the collectively held plots was the same; their low productivity was due to the iterative ratchet effect. People shifted their efforts away from the collective to the private plots. Without these private plots, it is likely that the people of the Soviet Union would have starved. In China, when all peasant land was collectivized into mass communes of roughly 25,000 people apiece, the result was the largest famine in human history. Population statistics indicate that at least 30 million people starved to death during 1958–1962, and cannibalism was widespread (Becker 1997). Presumably this was not the intention of the lawmakers. The operation of our evolved psychology creates large scale dynamics in mass societies. We need to pay careful attention to these dynamics scientifically, rather than being deluded by the outputs of our moral heuristics—heuristics that evolved when the social world was radically smaller.

A great deal is still unknown about the motivational systems deployed in collective actions. But so far, the evidence suggests that the human mind has motivational systems that:

1. lower one's level of contribution when this does not adversely affect the welfare of oneself, one's family, or one's small circle of cooperators (note 3);
2. lower the amount of effort one expends on a collective action as a function of whether others are free riding; and
3. increase punitive sentiments toward undercontributors by contributors (which, presumably, includes those in leadership and coercive military social roles).

Sufficiently large collective actions decouple reward from effort, initiating a process of declining effort by some, which stimulates matching withdrawal by others. This free riding and the dwindling participation it engenders intensify punitive sentiments toward undercontributors, culminating in social systems organized around coercion and punishment (where rulers can deploy it) or culminating in dissolution (where they cannot). Indeed, the rapid and universal recourse by a diversity of communist regimes to extreme (and sometimes genocidal) punitiveness as a regular tool of state policy may have been driven, at least in some measure, by the operation of these moral heuristics.

Collective action and commensal sharing—constitutive of our closest family relationships—beckon to us as the ideal form of human social organization: everyone participates, everyone benefits, no one is left behind. Acting on this appetite, without solving the problematic outputs of our moral heuristics, will mean the future of collectivist nation states will be like the past.

PRIVATE EXCHANGE AS A FAST AND FRUGAL HEURISTIC?

The human cognitive architecture contains a neurocognitive system that is well engineered for reasoning about dyadic social exchange: cooperation for mutual benefit between two social agents (Cosmides 1989; Cosmides and Tooby 1989, 1992, 2005; Fiddick et al. 2000; Gigerenzer and Hug 1992; Stone et al. 2002; Sugiyama et al. 2002). By well-engineered, we mean there is a precise fit between (a) the design features of the inference and decision rules that comprise this system and (b) engineering specifications derived from models of the evolution of reciprocation developed by evolutionary game theorists and behavioral ecologists (Cosmides and Tooby 1992, 2005). The neurocognitive system regulating social exchange includes a functionally and neurally isolable subroutine for detecting cheaters (individuals who accept benefits but do not reciprocate them). To detect cheaters, this moral heuristic samples very limited information, attending only to those who have failed to provide a benefit (to see if they accepted one) and those who accepted a benefit (to see if they failed to provide one).

The inference procedures and decision rules involved were designed to regulate private exchange and reciprocal sharing, not to motivate helping at a grander societal level. Yet since Adam Smith, economists have known that under certain conditions (e.g., many interactants, minimal externalities, consensual interactions) freely conducted trade does systematically promote general social welfare. Adam Smith himself was exact on this point: He argued that private exchange promotes the wealth of nations, even when traders intend to pursue private gain rather than social goods. In apparent defiance of common sense, societies dominated by central economic planning (rationally designed to produce increases in general welfare) end up producing far lower levels of welfare than societies in which the private exchanges (not aimed at producing general welfare) substantially replace government decision making.

It is worth considering whether this is because private trade itself embodies fast and frugal heuristics that produce high levels of social welfare in the modern world. When coercion and fraud are disallowed so that interactions between people are based on their mutual consent, two individuals agree to an exchange only when each expects a net benefit from the interaction.[11] Each voluntary exchange that is undertaken with correct foreknowledge of its consequences would therefore increase the welfare of the interactants themselves, or they would not choose it.[12]

In such a system, each individual can operate with very limited information about values and preferences—you need to compute your own, situation-specific preferences and trade-offs, and do not need to know very much about others: You can simply listen to their proposals, and select those that in your evaluation will improve your welfare the most. Significantly, the human mind was intensely selected to evolve mechanisms to evaluate its own welfare, and so is equipped by natural selection to compute and represent its own array of preferences in exquisite and often unarticulable detail. The array of n-dimensional rankings that inhabits our motivational systems is too rich to be communicated to others or represented by them, which is one reason why displacing value-guided decision making to remote institutions systematically damages social welfare. Under a system of private exchange, this richness need not be communicated or understood by anyone else—its power is harnessed effectively by a simple choice rule built into the human mind: pick the alternative with the

---

[11] Because the law forbids coercion and fraud, exchanges involving the infliction of coercion or fraud on others are disallowed.

[12] Perfect foreknowledge of consequences is unnecessary for the argument to work. All that is needed is that these estimates of benefit net to an on average benefit summed over interactions.

highest payoff.[13] The prices others set for what they are willing to exchange
constitutes a fast and frugal heuristic for discovering others' exchange preferences, even when they are strangers. The emergence of money (a culturally accepted medium of exchange) makes the operation of this heuristic even faster
and simpler: price can be communicated by a unidimensional quantity. If someone cheats you, there is a fast and frugal way to punish the cheater and protect
yourself in the future: trade with others instead.[14] (Indeed, this option is more
easily exercised in large modern societies with many alternative trading partners
and low costs of information than it was in small ancestral ones with few.) The
parties themselves are generally the most motivated, the most attentive, and the
best situated to discover defects or insufficient value in the exchange outcome.
They are the individuals most motivated to alter their subsequent choices advan-
tageously. Because the transaction is private, you do not need to get prior permission from an unmotivated and remote government representative to improve
your welfare through trade, or to change to a different supplier (De Soto 1989).
(For government actors to systematically improve upon self-regulation by participants, welfare-promoting government actors would need to be motivated by
the welfare of the participants—a public choice problem—know the values of
the participants as well as the participants do themselves—requiring unbounded
rationality—and otherwise have access to huge arrays of information that is
generally inaccessible to them.)

Recursively, formalized dyadic exchange interactions can network individuals into n-person units (partnerships, corporations, nonprofit organizations, etc.)
that can then be substituted back into dyadic interactions as one of the two parties (Tooby et al. 2006). Rich complexities internal to the organization need not
be understood or represented by external parties who interact with it; they can
cognitively reduce it to a single agent on the other side of a two-party exchange.
That is, voluntary exchange directly scales up to include increasing numbers of
interactants, so long as it is structured at each interaction as a system in which
each party can choose without coercion the best alternative it is offered by any
other party. Each dyadic interaction pumps up average welfare among the

---

[13] Obviously the cognitively impaired can be exploited, and exploitation can also occur whenever
outcomes cannot be evaluated over the short run.
[14] A legal system committed to enforcing contracts can also provide redress and restitution, of
course. Our point is that there is a clean way of avoiding future exploitation, even without the
courts. Interestingly, this method—avoid interacting with the cheater in the future—is not available when labor is organized as a collective action. Avoiding a free rider means abandoning the
entire group effort, not just a single individual. It may be the fact that collective action ties people
together that selects for punitive sentiments toward free riders in those contexts. Interestingly,
punishment of free riders increases their subsequent contributions to public goods games, but it
does not do so in situations involving dyadic exchange (McCabe et al. 1998). The most common
response to cheating in exchange may be simply to cooperate with someone else, rather than to
inflict costly punishment. If so, then the motivational system of cheaters may be to be particularly responsive to the possibility of exclusion and ostracism, rather than punishment.

interactants, and since everyone is linked through these distributed dyadic interactions, the increase in welfare is distributed (although not always equally) throughout the network. The system uses limited information about values that is only available locally (what do I want, what am I willing to do) and simple heuristics (choose the alternative that is better for me/us) to progressively move to ever-increasing levels of social welfare. There are no problems of unbounded rationality: Unlike a command and control economy, the government does not need to set prices by figuring out how much each individual in the society values each resource and act (Hayek 1972). The law in combination with distributed choice becomes, in effect, a system for distilling out increasingly well-ordered benefit–benefit transactions, which no set of planners could have foreseen or implemented.

Of course, people are only free to seek out benefit–benefit interactions[15] when the rules of the game—the law—prevent coercion through sanctioning those who seek to gain a benefit by forcing others to incur costs (for a detailed legal analysis, see Epstein 1995). This is why government coercion is so commonly welfare destroying across the globe. The voluntariness of exchange creates a built-in fail-safe floor in the damage it can do: Others typically cannot make you worse off through exchange. Under voluntary consent, the worst others can do is refuse your offers, leaving you with the same welfare level you had before. In contrast, the passage and coerced compliance with laws by lawmakers has no such fail-safe floor enforced heuristically by distributed choice. That is, there are no limits to how much worse off the individual or the collective can be made under coercion, and often no way to know in advance what the costs will be. The inevitable failure to represent all of the consequences in all the varied and unimagined circumstances where a law will be applied eliminates any necessary relationship between the lawmakers' intentions and actual outcomes. By prohibiting a given category of interactions, the law throws away local or rapidly changing information about variation in values in a way voluntary consent expressing itself in changing prices does not.

In short, voluntary exchange systematically propels net aggregated social welfare upward in a hill-climbing process to the extent that the opportunity to engage in it is distributed through the population. The system is driven by consent-driven feedback to sort for ever-increasing benefit–benefit interactions among sets of individuals, so that modern market interactions far transcend what any boundedly rational entity (such as a government) could have planned or discovered. In contrast, the process of decree even by elected representatives has no such richly sensitive feedback element to tailor law to individual circumstances.

---

15 See De Soto (1989) for a sobering analysis of how the transaction costs of multiple permits impairs trade and creates poverty.

In *Simple Rules for a Complex World*, Richard Epstein (1995) provides a detailed exposition of the kinds of laws—simple and few—needed for dyadic cooperation to become a fast and frugal engine of social welfare. It is not perfect: as with any system, negative externalities can occur even when force is disallowed, and there need to be legal mechanisms for minimizing them. Moreover, it requires political and legal institutions that limit the extent to which the coercive force of the state can be used by lawmakers, businesses, and coalitions of citizens to favor special interests, using compulsion to take what they cannot gain consent for through persuasion or trade. Even with these problems, when compared to the performance of command and control economies, freer economies—ones where the rule of law more closely approximates Epstein's system—have a far better empirical track record in providing the most goods for the greatest number. Berlin, the site of this Dahlem Workshop, provides a particularly clear natural experiment. The striking differences between East and West Berlin before the fall of the Wall were visible for all to see. Logically speaking, large-scale collectivization during the twentieth century *could* have liberated human productive energies, but empirically, it did not. Whether one is speaking about Ujamaa villages in Tanzania, the impact of block committees in Cuba, intentional communities like New Harmony in the U.S., famine-stricken North Korea versus South Korea, or Taiwan and Hong Kong versus Maoist China, the negative effects of channeling human productive energies through collective action are large, systematic, and remarkably consistent.

In this light, we find the following observation interesting: When considering how to improve social welfare as a whole, removing restrictions on private trade is rarely considered by anyone without an economic education (e.g., the 1947 price decontrols that ended widespread hunger in West Germany were widely opposed[16]). Such proposals seem counterintuitive, retrograde, and even sinister. Is this because it is an ineffective method, or because the neurocognitive system activated by opportunities to trade produces intuitions about private gain rather than public good? We intuitively recognize how we might benefit from others sacrificing for the common good; but our minds are not designed to recognize how we benefit in aggregate from others' private exchanges.

---

[16] It is common knowledge that in 1947, the elimination of price controls, combined with tax rate reductions and currency reform led to a dramatic turnaround in German economic performance—the so-called German Economic Miracle (Lutz 1949; Heller 1949; Hirshleifer 1987; Mendershausen 1949; Wallich 1955). Prior to these reforms, price controls on food had kept hunger widespread. Yet with decontrol, "[t]he spirit of the country changed overnight. The gray, hungry, dead-looking figures wandering about the streets in their everlasting search for food came to life," as Yale economist Henry Wallich observed (Wallich 1955). American New Deal advisors of the occupation forces, as well as German politicians, generally opposed the deregulation that saved so many lives (Wallich 1955; Heller 1949). American opposition was fortunate, in that it allowed Ludwig Ehrhardt to present the reforms politically as a form of nationalist opposition to foreign authority—the exploitation of another fast and frugal moral heuristic, ethnocentrism, to save lives.

CONCLUSIONS

In an article on psychology and the law, Richard Korobkin explains that the law has two broad functions, one intrinsic and the other instrumental. The intrinsic function is fulfilled "when law codifies *some social conception of right, justice, or morality*." The instrumental function is fulfilled "when law is used to shape the behavior of those governed in a way that creates a society that is closer in practice to *some social conception of right, justice, or morality* than it would otherwise be" (Korobkin 2001, pp. 319–320; italics added).

There is a tension between these two functions. Our minds are equipped with moral heuristics that were designed for a small world of relatives, friends, and neighbors, not for cities and nation states of thousands or millions of anonymous people. Laws that satisfy our moral intuitions—our conceptions of right, justice, and morality—satisfy the law's intrinsic function through codifying some of our intuitions about justice. But because our moral heuristics are now operating outside the envelope of environments for which they were designed, laws that satisfy the moral intuitions they generate may regularly fail to produce the outcomes we desire and anticipate; that is, laws that satisfy the law's intrinsic function may fail to satisfy its instrumental function.

Even worse, moral heuristics may cause us to overlook policies that do satisfy the law's instrumental function. These mental programs so powerfully structure our inferences that certain policies may seem self-evidently correct and others patently exploitive. But modern conditions often produce outcomes that seem paradoxical to our evolved programs: self-interested motives can be the engines that reliably produce humane outcomes, and what seem like good intentions can make a hell on earth.

Many legal ethicists are consequentialists. If you are a consequentialist, however, then real consequences should matter to you. To determine what the consequences of a new law will be, we cannot rely solely on rational choice theory because it is not an accurate description of human nature. Nor can we rely on the intentions or intuitions of lawmakers and citizens: As members of the species, our intuitions about a policy's likely consequences are often readouts of moral heuristics designed to operate in a social world of a few score individuals, not a nation of millions.

How, then, can policy makers predict the likely consequences of new laws? Economic analysis and agent-based modeling provide methods for inferring how the choices of many individual decision makers aggregate into patterns at the societal level. To be an improvement over rational choice theory and moral intuitions, however, these analytic methods must be grounded in accurate scientific knowledge about the design of the human mind. To do this, we need to know the evolved decision rules to be found in the human mind, including its rich collection of social and moral heuristics.

Leaving aside the instrumental, what can evolutionary psychology tell us about the intrinsic function of the law? When considering the law's intrinsic function, it is worth reflecting on where our conceptions of right, justice, and morality come from. Some of these conceptions spring from evolved moral heuristics. But these did not evolve because they produced objective justice (whatever that may be), even when operating in the ancestral environments that selected for their design. They evolved only because they advanced the fitness of their own genetic basis under ancestral conditions. These bizarre events of ancestral DNA editing are a strange foundation on which to confidently erect moral principles or modern legal systems.

REFERENCES

Baron-Cohen, S. 1995. Mindblindness: An Essay on Autism and Theory of Mind. Cambridge, MA: MIT Press.

Becker, J. 1997. Hungry Ghosts: Mao's Secret Famine. New York: Free Press.

Boyd, R., H. Gintis, S. Bowles, and P. Richerson. 2003. The evolution of altruistic punishment. *Proc. Natl. Acad. Sci.* **100**:3531–3535.

Boyd, R., and P.J. Richerson. 1992. Punishment allows the evolution of cooperation (or anything else) in sizable groups. *Ethol. Sociobiol.* **13**:171–195.

Boyer, P. 2001. Religion Explained: The Evolutionary Roots of Religious Thought. New York: Basic.

Brewer, M., and R. Kramer. 1986. Choice behavior in social dilemmas: Effects of social identity, group size, and decision framing. *J. Pers. Soc. Psychol.* **50**:543–549.

Buss, D.M. 1989. Sex differences in human mate preferences: Evolutionary hypotheses tested in 37 cultures. *Behav. Brain Sci.* **12**:1–49.

Cashdan, E. 1989. Hunters and gatherers: Economic behavior in bands. In: Economic Anthropology, ed. S. Plattner, pp. 21–48. Palo Alto, CA: Stanford Univ. Press.

Cosmides, L. 1985. Deduction or Darwinian Algorithms? An Explanation of the "Elusive" Content Effect on the Wason Selection Task. Ph.D. diss., Harvard Univ. *Univ. Microfilms #86–02206.*

Cosmides, L. 1989. The logic of social exchange: Has natural selection shaped how humans reason? Studies with the Wason selection task. *Cognition* **31**:187–276.

Cosmides, L., and J. Tooby. 1987. From evolution to behavior: Evolutionary psychology as the missing link. In: The Latest on the Best: Essays on Evolution and Optimality, ed. J. Dupre, pp. 277–306. Cambridge, MA: MIT Press.

Cosmides, L., and J. Tooby. 1989. Evolutionary psychology and the generation of culture, Part II. Case study: A computational theory of social exchange. *Ethol. Sociobiol.* **10**:51–97.

Cosmides, L., and J. Tooby. 1992. Cognitive adaptations for social exchange. In: The Adapted Mind: Evolutionary Psychology and the Generation of Culture, ed. J.H. Barkow, L. Cosmides, and J. Tooby, pp. 163–228. New York: Oxford Univ. Press.

Cosmides, L., and J. Tooby. 1994. Beyond intuition and instinct blindness: The case for an evolutionarily rigorous cognitive science. *Cognition* **50**:41–77.

Cosmides, L., and J. Tooby. 2004. Knowing thyself: The evolutionary psychology of moral reasoning and moral sentiments. In: Business, Science, and Ethics, ed. R.E. Freeman and P. Werhane, pp. 93–128. The Ruffin Series in Business Ethics, vol. 4. Charlottesville, VA: Society for Business Ethics.

Cosmides, L., and J. Tooby. 2005. Neurocognitive adaptations designed for social exchange. In: Handbook of Evolutionary Psychology, ed. D.M. Buss, pp. 584–627. New York: Wiley.

Daly, M., and M. Wilson. 1988. Homicide. New York: Aldine.

Darwin, C. 1859. On the Origin of Species by Means of Natural Selection London: Murray.

Dawes, R.M., J.M. Orbell, and J.C. Van de Kragt. 1986. Organizing groups for collective action. *Am. Pol. Sci. Rev.* **80**:1171–1185.

De Soto, H. 1989. The Other Path: The Invisible Revolution in the Third World. New York: Harper Collins.

Epstein, R. 1995. Simple Rules for a Complex World. Cambridge, MA: Harvard Univ. Press.

Fehr, E., and S. Gächter. 2000a. Cooperation and punishment in public goods experiments. *Am. Econ. Rev.* **90**:980–994.

Fehr, E., and S. Gächter. 2000b. Fairness and retaliation: The economics of reciprocity. *J. Econ. Persp.* **14**:159–181.

Fiddick, L., L. Cosmides, and J. Tooby. 2000. No interpretation without representation: The role of domain-specific representations and inferences in the Wason selection task. *Cognition* **77**:1–79.

Fiske, A. 1991. Structures of Social Life: The Four Elementary Forms of Human Relations. New York: Free Press.

Gigerenzer, G. 2000. Adaptive Thinking: Rationality in the Real World. New York: Oxford Univ. Press.

Gigerenzer, G., and K. Hug. 1992. Domain-specific reasoning: Social contracts, cheating and perspective change. *Cognition* **42**:127–171.

Gigerenzer, G., and R. Selten, eds. 2001. Bounded Rationality: The Adaptive Toolbox. Dahlem Workshop Report 84. Cambridge, MA: MIT Press.

Gintis, H. 2000. Strong reciprocity and human sociality. *J. Theor. Biol.* **206**:169–179.

Gurven, M. 2004. To give and to give not: The behavioral ecology of human food transfers. *Behav. Brain Sci.* **27**:543–583.

Gurven, M., W. Allen-Arave, K. Hill, and A.M. Hurtado. 2000. It's a wonderful life: Signaling generosity among the Ache of Paraguay. *Evol. Hum. Behav.* **21**:263–282.

Haidt, J. 2001. The emotional dog and its rational tail: A social intuitionist approach to moral judgment. *Psychol. Rev.* **108**:814–834.

Hamilton, W.D. 1964. The genetical evolution of social behaviour. *J. Theor. Biol.* **7**:1–52.

Hayek, F.A. 1972. Individualism and Economic Order. Chicago: Regnery.

Heller, W.W. 1949. Tax and monetary reform in occupied Germany. *Natl. Tax J.* **2**:215–231.

Henrich, J., and R. Boyd. 2001. Why people punish defectors: Weak conformist transmission can stabilize costly enforcement of norms in cooperative dilemmas. *J. Theor. Biol.* **208**:79–89.

Hirshleifer, J.W. 1987. Economic Behavior in Adversity. Chicago: Univ. of Chicago Press.

Isaac, G. 1978. The food-sharing behavior of protohuman hominids. *Sci. Am.* **238**: 90–108.

Kameda, T., M. Takezawa, and R. Hastie. 2003. The logic of social sharing: An evolutionary game analysis of adaptive norm development. *Pers. Soc. Psychol. Rev.* **7**:2–19.

Kameda, T., M. Takezawa, R.S. Tindale, and C. Smith. 2002. Social sharing and risk reduction: Exploring a computational algorithm for the psychology of windfall gains. *Evol. Hum. Behav.* **23**:11–33.

Kaplan, H., and K. Hill. 1985. Food sharing among Ache foragers: Tests of explanatory hypotheses. *Curr. Anthro.* **26**:223–246.

Kaplan, H., K. Hill, and A.M. Hurtado. 1990. Risk, foraging and food sharing among the Ache. In: Risk and Uncertainty in Tribal and Peasant Economies, ed. E. Cashdan, pp. 107–143. Boulder, CO: Westview Press.

Korobkin, R.B. 2001. A multi-disciplinary approach to legal scholarship: Economics, behavioral economics, and evolutionary psychology. *Jurimetrics* **51**:319–336.

Kurzban, R., K. McCabe, V. Smith, and B.J. Wilson. 2001. Incremental commitment and reciprocity in a real time public goods game. *Pers. Soc. Psychol. Bull.* **27**:1662–1673.

Lee, R.B., and I. DeVore, eds. 1968. Man the Hunter. Chicago: Aldine.

Leys, S. 1979. Broken Images. London: Allison and Busby.

Lieberman, D., J. Tooby, and L. Cosmides. 2003. Does morality have a biological basis? An empirical test of the factors governing moral sentiments relating to incest. *Proc. Roy. Soc. Lond. B* **270**:819–826.

Lieberman, D., J. Tooby, and L. Cosmides. 2006. The architecture of kin detection in humans, in press.

Lieberman, D., J. Tooby, and L. Cosmides. 2006. The evolution of human incest avoidance mechanisms: An evolutionary psychological approach. In: Evolution and the Moral Emotions: Appreciating Edward Westermarck, ed. A. Wolf and J.P. Takala. Palo Alto, CA: Stanford Univ. Press, in press.

Lutz, F.A. 1949. The German currency reform and the revival of the German economy. *Economica* **16**:122–142.

Marshall, L. 1976. Sharing, talking, and giving: Relief of social tensions among the !Kung. In: Kalahari Hunter–Gatherers: Studies of the !Kung San and Their Neighbors, ed. R.B. Lee and I. DeVore, pp. 350–371. Cambridge, MA: Harvard Univ. Press.

Masclet, D., C. Noussair, S. Tucker, and M.-C. Villeval. 2003. Monetary and non-monetary punishment in the voluntary contributions mechanism. *Am. Econ. Rev.* **93**:366–380.

McBrearty, S., and A. Brooks. 2000. The revolution that wasn't: A new interpretation of the origin of modern behavior. *J. Hum. Evol.* **39**:453–563.

McCabe, K.A., S.J. Rassenti, and V.L. Smith. 1998. Reciprocity, trust, and payoff privacy in extensive form bargaining. *Games Econ. Behav.* **24**:10–24.

Mendershausen, H. 1949. Prices, money and the distribution of goods in postwar Germany. *Am. Econ. Rev.* **39**:646–672.

North, D. 1990. Institutions, Institutional Change and Economic Performance. New York: Cambridge Univ. Press.

Olson, M. 1965. Logic of Collective Action: Public Goods and the Theory of Groups. Cambridge, MA: Harvard Univ. Press.

Ostrom, E., J. Walker, and R. Gardner. 1992. Covenants with and without a sword: Self-governance is possible. *Am. Pol. Sci. Rev.* **86**:404–417.

Panchanathan, K., and R. Boyd. 2004. Indirect reciprocity can stabilize cooperation without the second-order free rider problem. *Nature* **432**:499–502.

Pinker, S. 1994. The Language Instinct. New York: Harper Collins.

Pinker, S. 1997. How the Mind Works. New York: Norton.

Price, M.E. 2003. Pro-community altruism and social status in a Shuar village. *Hum. Nat.* **14**:191–208.

Price, M.E. 2005. Punitive sentiment among the Shuar and in industrialized societies: Cross-cultural similarities. *Evol. Hum. Behav.* **26**:279–287.

Price, M.E., L. Cosmides, and J. Tooby. 2002. Punitive sentiment as an anti-free rider psychological device. *Evol. Hum. Behav.* **23**:203–231.

Sakoff, A. 1962. The private sector in Soviet agriculture. *Mthly. Bull. Agr. Econ.* **11**:9.

Sato, K. 1987. Distribution of the cost of maintaining common resources. *J. Exp. Soc. Psychol.* **23**:19–31.

Sen, A. 1989. On Ethics and Economics. Oxford: Blackwell.

Shostak, M. 1981. Nisa: The Life and Words of a !Kung Woman. Cambridge, MA: Harvard Univ. Press.

Skinner, B.F. 1976. Walden Two. New York: Prentice Hall.

Stone, V., L. Cosmides, J. Tooby, N. Kroll, and R. Knight. 2002. Selective impairment of reasoning about social exchange in a patient with bilateral limbic system damage. *Proc. Natl. Acad. Sci.* **99**:11,531–11,536.

Sugiyama, L. 2004. Illness, injury, and disability among Shiwiar forager-horticulturalists: Implications of health-risk buffering for the evolution of human life history. *Am. J. Phys. Anthro.* **123**:371–389.

Sugiyama, L., and M. Scalise Sugiyama. 2003. Social roles, prestige, and health risk: Social niche specialization as a risk-buffering strategy. *Hum. Nat.* **14**:165–190.

Sugiyama, L., J. Tooby, and L. Cosmides. 2002. Cross-cultural evidence of cognitive adaptations for social exchange among the Shiwiar of Ecuadorian Amazonia. *Proc. Natl. Acad. Sci.* **99**:11,537–11,542.

Symons, D. 1979. The Evolution of Human Sexuality. New York: Oxford Univ. Press.

Tooby, J., and L. Cosmides. 1990. On the universality of human nature and the uniqueness of the individual: The role of genetics and adaptation. *J. Personal.* **58**:17–67.

Tooby, J., and L. Cosmides. 1992. The psychological foundations of culture. In: The Adapted Mind: Evolutionary Psychology and the Generation of Culture, ed. J. Barkow, L. Cosmides, and J. Tooby, pp. 19–136. New York: Oxford Univ. Press.

Tooby, J., L. Cosmides, and H.C. Barrett. 2005. Resolving the debate on innate ideas: Learnability constraints and the evolved interpenetration of motivational and conceptual functions. In: The Innate Mind: Structure and Content, ed. P. Carruthers, S. Laurence, and S. Stich, pp. 305–337. New York: Oxford Univ. Press.

Tooby, J., L. Cosmides, and M.E. Price. 2006. Cognitive adaptations for n-person exchange: The evolutionary roots of organizational behavior. *Manag. Dec. Econ.* **27**, in press.

Tucker, W. 1990. The Excluded Americans: Homelessness and Housing Policies. Washington, D.C.: Regnery Gateway.

Wallich, H.C. 1955. Mainsprings of the German Revival. New Haven, CT: Yale Univ. Press.

Wiessner, P. 1982. Risk, reciprocity and social influences on !Kung San economics. In: Politics and History in Band Societies, ed. E. Leacock and R. Lee, pp 61–84. Cambridge: Cambridge Univ. Press.

Wilson, M.L., and R.W. Wrangham. 2003. Intergroup relations in chimpanzees. *Ann. Rev. Anthro.* **32**:363–392.

Wrangham, R., and D. Peterson. 1996. Demonic Males: Apes and the Origins of Human Violence. Boston: Houghton Mifflin.

Yamagishi, T. 1992. Group size and the provision of a sanctioning system in a social dilemma. In: Social Dilemmas: Theoretical Issues and Research Findings, ed. W. Liebrand, D. Messick, and H. Wilke, pp. 267–287. Oxford: Pergamon.

10

The Evolutionary and Cultural Origins of Heuristics That Influence Lawmaking

Wolfgang Fikentscher

Chair, Commission for Studies in Cultural Anthropology, Bavarian Academy of Sciences, Philosophical–Historical Class, Munich, Germany

ABSTRACT

Heuristics may play different roles when applied to different anthropological modes of thought. Against the background of human genetic universality, cultural mind-sets influence the way in which humans conclude. The Western, Greek-thinking-influenced, cultural mode of thought is suitable for logical conclusions (including evaluations) that use generalizations and specifications, subsumptions of factual specifities under generalizations, and projections from generalized consequences onto specific situations. Legal conclusions usually operate in this manner, thus being able to make use of rules that stand for normative regularity. For the same reason, heuristic shortcut conclusions in law usually do not provide for the desired predictability of results and repeatability and control of the mental process in which the results were reached. However, heuristics may serve as tools for widening perspectives, adding new points of view, and furnishing associations which lie out of reach of the closed circle of subsumption and projection. There are examples in the history of law that, on the one hand, show the failure of heuristics in law and, on the other, prove these liberating effects.

Non-Western cultural modes of thought may be, in their own specific way and thus differently, characterized by ways of concluding which are a-logic (in the Greek sense). For example, they may work with associative, serial, topical, metaphorical, or still other ways of coming to a conclusion. Thus, at first sight, they may look similar to heuristics. However, to call them animist, East and South Asian, Hinayana Buddhist, Mahayana Buddhist, Hindu, Islamic, etc., *heuristics* would amount to an ethnocentric judgment. *How* this non-Western learning, knowing, and deciding operates on the basis of the relevant mode of thought, raises questions not addressed in this chapter.

MEANINGS AND KINDS OF HEURISTICS

Classical Meaning of Heuristics

Heuristics is a method of finding new knowledge. In philosophical terms, and broadly speaking, it belongs to epistemology—the philosophical manner of getting to know something. Heuristics in this sense do not deal with the material substance of that something, but rather in the way one approaches the object.

In a more narrow sense, heuristics is not just any method for finding new knowledge; it envisages the search for certain contents. Accordingly, heuristics remain a method of epistemology but focus on distinct contents still to be discovered. In an even narrower sense, when knowing certain new contents is the goal, heuristics attempt to enhance consciousness of information about the envisaged contents.

In the context of this Dahlem Workshop, I interpret that heuristics are meant in the third sense, because our object of study concerns the gathering of data and their conscious use to find law. In other words, the task is to learn how law can be drawn, or derived, from the environment. Having identified as the *genus proximum* (the closest possible generalization) of heuristics a goal-oriented, data-use conscious mental method of discovery, we need to identify the *differentia specifica* (the distinguishing specifications). From other goal-oriented, data-conscious epistemological methods, heuristics are distinguishable by their nonlogical, nonsystematic nature. Heuristics are the "art of finding" (in contrast to systematics as the "art of proving") scientific truths as well as—when we follow Immanuel Kant—moral or aesthetic propositions (Winkler and Prins 1951). Hence, *heuristics*, itself a Greek word, is the opposite of what is called Greek logic (Bochenski 1968, 1971). Greek logic, as a manner of proof, works with generalizations from found data (induction or reduction) and specifications that pin down a certain result by distinguishing it from other results (deduction). Thus, Greek logic draws conclusions in a systematic (i.e., perspective and triangular) tri-polar way by fixing one point in relation to at least two others. By contrast, heuristics designate the problem-solving procedure that involves a hypothetical answer to a problem at the outset of inquiry for purposes of giving guidance or direction to the inquiry itself. This consists of (a) developing a concept of what one expects to discover, (b) using that concept to guide seeking, selecting, and assigning meaning to facts in a straightforward manner, and (c) continually developing new, more adequate conceptions as the discovery and interpretation of facts proceed (from point to point without looking right and left for comparison). There is no end to the heuristic process.[1]

Hence, heuristics may open the way to later logic and systematic evaluation, which would appear to make all knowledge open to doubt. Therefore, the classical meaning of heuristics takes its essence from the distinction between logical and systematic thinking, on one hand, and nonlogical, nonsystematic thinking on the other—the latter being called heuristics. In brief, heuristics are a

---

[1] See definition in *Encyclopaedia Britannica*, 15th ed., *Micropaedia*, Chicago, 1943–1973, "Art: Heuristics"; see also "Art: Thought Processes, Series and Types of," *Encyclopaedia Britannica*, vol. 18; and Newell and Simon (1961) who, disregarding Kant's synthetic reasoning, describe heuristics as creative human thinking about the ways to knowledge most likely to lead to success of inquiry.

shortcut conclusion that avoids the elements of generalization (induction) and specification (deduction) of classical logic. It is an intuitive, "hunch-based" conclusion, a good guess that can point to experience, reiteration, regularity, normalcy, etc.

Fast and Frugal Heuristics and Their Borrowing from System and Logic

Gigerenzer and Todd (1999) provide a survey on how the heuristics that are used for the ABC (adaptive behavior and cognition) research program relate to earlier notions of heuristics. Starting from the Greek meaning of "serving to find out or to discover," they discuss the English use of the term during the early 1800s up until 1970. Early on, *heuristics* referred to a useful, indispensable cognitive process or processes for solving problems that cannot be handled by logic and probability theories. After 1970, according to Gigerenzer and Todd, a second meaning emerged in the fields of psychology and decision theory according to which heuristics receive a pejorative meaning as cognitive processes misapplied to situations where logic and probability theories should be applied instead. For a third interpretation, Gigerenzer and Todd refer to a remark by Albert Einstein, who viewed a heuristic as an approach to a problem that is necessarily incomplete.

These three meanings can each be termed the auxiliary, the pejorative, and the modesty approach. Gigerenzer and Todd (1999) proceed by mentioning a fourth: heuristics as an approximation for a rule of thumb to guide research. Within the boundaries of the ABC Research Group activities, the term *heuristic* is used in a positive sense, emphasizing its beneficial role in guiding search and suitability for creating computational models. Heuristics are thus presented as an alternative to logical and systematic reasoning, as a shortcut that facilitates, under the appropriate circumstances, cognition.

For their own purposes, the ABC Research Group use heuristics with a particular interest in confronting cognitive tools with environmental circumstances. Three elements characterize fast and frugal heuristics: (a) they are an alternative to logic and system, having been described as the essence of heuristics in the classical sense (e.g., Winkler and Prins 1951), (b) they are accessible for work with computers, and (c) they enable a close link to the environment of the object to be searched. The latter element, closeness to reality, modifies heuristics at the expense of the first. The reason for this is that fast and frugal heuristics occupy certain parts of logic and systematic thinking so that the borderline to logic and system becomes blurred. The following examples demonstrate this:

1. Ecological and economic behavior is alleged to be predictable by observation. "... [Robinson] Crusoe kept track of the rainy and dry days in each

month, and subsequently sewed seed only when rainfall was highest" (Hertwig et al. 1999, p. 209). A similar rational behavior is reported during belug hunting by Inujjuamiut Eskimos, who weigh the expected hunting success against hunting efforts. Country lore has it that when it rains on June 27, rainy weather will persist for seven more weeks. In Germany, this day is called the day of the Seven Sleepers, in recollection of seven Christian martyrs who survived their execution sleeping (see McCulloh 1979). Meteorologists say that at the end of June, the weather will indeed settle on either a sunny or rainy summer. Much of country lore rests on centuries-old observations so that these heuristic cues refer to physical systematics that use the tools of generalizations and specifications (predictions on the basis of inductions and deductions, and therefore in systematic form) of Greek logic.

2.   Categorizing is one of the main steps of logical induction. As observed by Berretty et al. (1999), the method by which small rodents categorize birds as a pigeon or a bird of prey, according to their shape, does not amount to a heuristic undertaking but is rather a quite logical operation.

3.   A third aspect relates to the concept of "ecological rationality." In his comments on the book's back cover (Gigerenzer et al. 1999), Reinhard Selten stresses that "This book ... illustrates that the surprising efficiency of fast and simple procedures is due to their fit with the structure of the environment in which they are used. The emphasis on this 'ecological reality' is an advance in a promising and already new direction of research." Similar to the rationality of country lore based on observation, ecological rationality draws logical and systematic inductions and deductions into fast and frugal heuristics.

In all of these examples, systematics and logical inductions and deductions color the effects of heuristic cognition. These and other more logical and systematic limitations of heuristic cognition do not, however, deprive heuristics of their cognitive merits, rather they enhance the cognitive success of heuristics. In chaos theory, it is said that the most frugal "areas" of chaos are those that border linear mathematics. Similarly, the most frugal heuristic seems to approach logic, system, and probability. Still, there is no mix. Heuristics remain heuristics even if they make use of their proximity to logic. Logical reasoning may help heuristics to understand an inherent systematic order of an environment to be searched. But without logical operations of induction and deduction, this understanding "by immediate access" remains heuristic. Thus, fast and frugal heuristics are not "soft system" or "logic light." The difference between Greek logic and heuristics should and will be maintained as we examine the connections between law and heuristics. Otherwise, law could not be assigned to either logical or heuristic cognitive procedure. Let us keep in mind, however, that the heuristics of the ABC Research Group borrow extensively from Greek logic.

The Role of Information and Information Deficits

Before turning to law, one possible mistake concerning information and its role for decision making should be eliminated. Both Greek logic and heuristics work with either complete or incomplete information. Therefore, from a methodological perspective, limited information is no argument against rational judgment. Limited information can very well be handled in rational, systematic methodology. An example is the rules of taking evidence in many, including legal, procedures. Any decision maker, lawyers included, has to define the amount of truth needed to make judgments. A good deal of the rationality of judgments stems from the fact that certain rules of evidence have been established. The rational procedures of induction and deduction—the gist of rational conclusions—work to discover new insights. If somebody views an animal flying, the logical inductive conclusion by an observer who knows birds is that the animal is a bird. The conclusion, however, is a logical inductive step if the observer sees this bird and its shape for the first time: It might belong to a hitherto unknown species. The lack of information about this still unknown species is filled by a logical induction.[2]

Limited information is the lawyer's fate. Were it true that limited information would prevent logical systematic decision making, law would be limited to guesses and could not be conceived as a science at all. However, a person who knows better, decides better because the upper and lower hermeneutical point of return can be precisely defined, so that knowing more narrows the range of possible solutions. When in the course of generalization the upper hermeneutical point of return is reached, further generalizations and less information make no sense for deciding a case; when the lower hermeneutical point of return is approached, further specialization and refinement of information also makes no sense for deciding a case. Thus, when the lower hermeneutical point of return is being approached, more knowledge and more information do not help in finding a better solution (Fikentscher 1977).[3]

Plato, the cofounder of idealist rational thinking, and Socrates, as well as Socrates' teacher, Parmenides, all worked with limited information about ideas which were taken for facts. Limited information is absolutely no reason to turn to heuristics and away from logical conclusion. The theories of judgment and partial knowledge are two separate issues.[4]

---

[2] The conclusion is, of course, falsifiable and may therefore be wrong. The flying animal could be a bat or a flying fish. In this case, the *genus proximum* and the *differentia specifica* were misapplied, leading to a logical mistake.

[3] "Knowing more" for engaging in refinements necessary for obtaining the decision-appropriate rule (Anglo-American legal term: "distinguishing") is a task of knowledge, whereas "knowing more" as a requirement for fixing the frame between the upper and the lower hermeneutical point of return itself is a meta-task.

[4] For example, Plato, Phaidon 85c, d; quoted in Eigler (1990).

In the context of social norms, the information issue leads to two different kinds of heuristics. First, there are heuristics that play a role within the framework of making (or implementing) social norms (e.g., legal, moral, behavioral, religious rules) by de-complexifying them. They achieve this by making the normative requirements more general. Such simplification heuristics reduce complexity on the side of the requirements of such norms and, through this, make norm application more transparent. They may also de-complexify the side of the sanctions of such norms: Any norm consists of a set of requirements under which a set of facts is subsumed, and a sanction from which a change of real facts is to be derived. De-complexifying the requirements is more interesting in the present context. De-complexifying the sanctions is effectuated, for example, in the form of sentencing or bail setting guidelines. However, these instruments are used to interpret broadly formulated legal rules, not heuristics. In law, the de-complexifying task is part of what is called the concretion of a norm for the preparation of its application. Concretion is indispensable for both Continental code law and Anglo-American case law (Cardozo 1921).[5]

Second, there are heuristics that do not influence the making (or the implementation) of norms (rules) but rather establish the communicable shortcut, described above, from a set of facts to the change of facts. Here, the simplifying task of heuristics does not consist of de-complexifying the requirements of a norm but in avoiding subsumption under, and deducing the changed facts from, a social norm altogether. Since these heuristics dispose of an issue without normative guidance, they may be called dispositive heuristics. The main difference between the two kinds of heuristics is the use or nonuse of social norms in finding the solution to a social problem.

To illustrate, three practical examples for de-complexifying heuristics are enumerated:

1.   In recent years, the European Court of Justice and the E.U. Court of First Instance refused, in a series of cases, to sustain antitrust complaints

---

5   Frequently, subsumption implies the interpretation of normative requirements before the bits and pieces of the facts can be subsumed under them (this is by no means an interpretation of facts; the latter is necessary when facts are incompletely presented to the decider). The mutual disregard of the essence of rule-thinking—subsumption plus "desumption" (= projection of the abstract consequence of the rule's requirements onto concrete, real life)—makes the debate between Sloman (1996) and Gigerenzer and Regier (1996) inconclusive as far as law or any other normative social science is concerned. Sloman, on one hand, and Gigerenzer and Regier, on the other, discuss dichotomies such as analysis versus heuristics, arguments versus suggestion, or rule versus association. However, the issue of social norm application is not so much the search for the properly defined norm (in anthropology: for the proper forum), important as this may be, but the way for facts to be changed to the normative requirements, from those requirements to the normative sanctions *in abstracto*, and from there to the *in concreto* changed facts. Neither analysis nor heuristics, neither argument nor suggestion, neither rule nor association can escape from the need to follow this way. Otherwise, a mental tracking or ought-indicated change of facts would not be possible.

against monopolistic behavior and other restraints of competition, raised by the E.U. Commission, on grounds of "lack of economic evidence." In some interest groups, this caused a call for "economizing E.U. antitrust." However, to other observers and antitrust experts, the demands for more "economic evidence" in E.U. antitrust seem excessive, consumer-hostile, influenced by industrial lobbyists, or merely aping U.S. economic analysis of law antitrust policies. At any rate, it is obvious that industry and bar favor complicated requirements. Max Weber called this phenomenon *Herrschaftswissen* (dominance knowledge).

2. It has been alleged that the "Basel-II" requirements (a cartelized international banking standard for a bank's liquidity reserves) have been made so complex that only specialists are able to apply and control them. If these allegations are true, this would amount to an advantage for banks at the expense of transparency and monetary security for bank customers.

3. The German public health care system is purported to be overcomplicated to such an extent that its efficiency and financing are affected. Recently, proposals were made to "de-complexify" its normative requirements (for details, see Schottdorf et al. 2004).

De-complexifying and Dispositive Heuristics as Alternatives to Conclusions

Moving beyond the information issue to express the same conception of de-complexifying versus dispositive heuristics, in terms of theories of conclusion, a distinction can be made to characterize de-complexifying and dispositive heuristics as follows. Heuristics, as simplified manners of concluding, work in either of two possible ways.

Intralogical Heuristics

Intralogical heuristics function as "de-complexifying heuristics." In law, the logical way of concluding distinguishes between a rule and its implementation (= application). Every rule consists of two parts (similar to a mathematical equation): a set of requirements (in law: presuppositions) that describes in an abstract form a part of the real world (= environment), and a life-and-environment changing abstract consequence that is attached to this description (in law: legal consequence). The rule is applied (= implemented, materialized) by subsuming bits and pieces of the real world under the requirements of the rule and then projecting the abstract consequence of that rule back onto the concrete, real object.

To illustrate, a rule may state, "I passed my exam (= requirements), so now it is time to look for a job (= consequence)." A subset of rules is social norms (e.g., "when your mother has a birthday, you should write her a letter"). A subcategory of social norms is legal norms, technically called either (broad) principles or (envisaging a case to be decided) rules. For example, a legal principle is that a contract should be performed. An example of a legal rule is that agreements in restraint of competition (= requirements) are prohibited (= consequence). In law, there is no sharp dividing line between principle and rule, but rather a transition by imperceptible degrees.

German competition law does not provide for the possibility that agreements in restraint of competition be prohibited. Instead, it distinguishes between horizontal agreements in restraint of competition, such as a cartel where all participants are agents on one economic level (e.g., producers), and vertical agreements in restraint of competition where the participants belong to different economic levels: a producer binds a dealer to sell only the producer's products and not the merchandise manufactured by a competitor. In its present form, German competition law prohibits horizontal agreements in restraint of competition but permits—under a complicated system of abuse control—vertical agreements in restraint of competition. European law (Art. 81 E.C. Treaty), however, does not distinguish between horizontal and vertical agreements in restraint of competition. Consequently, Ordinance (EG) No. 1/2003 of Dec. 16, 2002, which contains a number of far-reaching changes of European antitrust law, does not distinguish between horizontal and vertical agreements. It does oblige, however, member states to adapt their antitrust law to the European model. In Germany, Ordinance (EG) No. 2/2003 went into effect on May 1, 2004. Now the German legislator is bound to transform the ordinance into German antitrust law and abolish the different treatment of horizontals and verticals. Indeed, the distinction between horizontal and vertical restrictive agreements, as well as the intricate abuse control system regarding the latter, seems too complicated and not justified by the intended purposes of a modern antitrust law. In addition to being bound by European legislation, it may be a good heuristic for the German parliament to abolish the overrefined distinction between horizontals and verticals and replace it with the simpler rule of straightforward prohibition. Following the European model, the draft adaptation law to the German law against Restraints of Competition stipulates that all agreements in restraints of competition are prohibited. In the draft, the abuse control system is being transformed into a system of group exemptions from the prohibition (again in conformity with European law).[6]

Thus, heuristics serve to simplify the scope of normative requirements in the law by broadening it. They counteract unnecessary overrefinements. The respective yardstick is the legal–political purpose of the law of concern.

---

[6] In the meantime, the 7th amendment of the German Law against Restraints of Competition from June 16/17, 2004 (Federal Gazette 2004 I 1954), went into force. Its Section I no longer distinguishes between horizontal and vertical agreements in restraints of competition (for comment, see W. Fikentscher, Wettbewerb oder Markt oder beides? Gewerblicher Rechtsschutz und Urheberrecht, Internationaler Teil 2004/9 (Festschrift Rudolf Krasser), 727–731.

Extralogical Heuristics

Extralogical heuristics may be called "dispositive heuristics" because they more or less effectively dispose of an issue by a conclusion. They operate in a manner that is parallel to a logical procedure, but outside of logical reasoning. There is no rule consisting of requirements and consequences to be followed. Thus, there are no rule requirements to be subsumed under nor an abstract rule consequence to be projected onto concrete, real life.

Extralogical heuristics conclude works by estimating similarities to reach a desired goal. Compared to rule application, on average, less information will be needed. Cogent reasoning does not have to rendered. Dispositive heuristics work fast and frugally; however, they risk failure for lack of precision: the more precision, the less scope. When one looks for examples in the social sciences, it appears that dispositive heuristics are less numerous than de-complexifying heuristics. At least those heuristics are dispositive that do not make inroads into logical conclusions (see discussion above). In terms of lawmaking (Haidt et al., this volume), the following story may serve as an example.

In 1953, the Federal Republic of Germany needed a new set of marital property rules. Until then, the rights and duties of marriage partners were treated differently. The Constitution of 1949, however, established equal treatment of women and men, and gave the federal government time until 1953 to adapt the marital property laws to the constitutional requirement. The legislature, however, was too preoccupied with other matters to meet the 1953 deadline. Judge-made law helped out, but could not cover all necessary technicalities. Under time pressure, the legislature decided to introduce the Scandinavian marital property system (separate property with a balancing of gains when marriage ends). Apart from some general statements, no extensive research in historical and comparative marital property law was undertaken, nor were broad sociographic factors investigated. It was sufficient that the role of Scandinavian married women appeared about as modern as what the parliament thought acceptable for postwar Germany. On this preponderantly heuristic basis, the new law concerning marital property was passed in 1957. In view of the brevity of preparation and the many radical changes involved, the adaptation has worked out surprisingly well to this day. Most legal transplants seem to work along similar lines (*Lübecker Stadtrecht*, reception of Roman law in Germany, of Swiss law in Turkey, etc.).

Thus, dispositive heuristics replace evaluative subsumption and project abstract rule consequence onto real life through estimations, associative hints, and impressions of similarity of situations in view of envisaged results. The procedure works parallel to logical reasoning, without the latter's precision, is broader in scope, and, in particular, is open to new insights, associations, comparisons, and visions.

THE NATURE OF THE LEGAL CONCLUSION AND HEURISTICS

The Nature of the Judgment in Law

The lawyers among you will forgive me as I try to present legal thinking in a nutshell. The aim is to provide a basis upon which we can answer the question of whether law is logical or an object of heuristics.[7] In the following description of legal reasoning, I have confined discussion to Western legal culture. As we speak about it here, heuristics, because of its inherent juxtaposition to Greek logic (see above), is of necessity a product of Western thinking, in general and in law. In non-Western cultures, one has to talk about "heuristics" in different, culture-specific senses, and we will see that it is better and less ethnocentric to avoid the term altogether.

Let us for the moment forget about the rest of the world and concentrate on traditional and modern legal thinking, as applied on the European continent and in the common-law legal systems, most notably Great Britain and the United States. Scandinavian countries apply a mix of code and judge-made law. In thinking law, German practice and theory follow the "expert's opinion style" (*Gutachtenstil*) or, synonymously, the "opinion method" (*Gutachtenmethode*), of which there are two types: the nonlitigious opinion style (*Stil des unstreitigen Gutachtens*) and the litigious opinion style (*Stil des streitigen Gutachtens*).

The difference between these two methods of legal reasoning is taught to law students at the very beginning of their studies. It forms the basis upon which hypothetical and real cases are discussed, and is repeated again and again during the course of their study of law.

Law professors tell their students right from the beginning that it is the purpose of their *university* studies to learn how to write a *nonlitigious* opinion. By contrast, it is the aim of their work as *law clerks* (or interns) to learn the *litigious* opinion. The litigious opinion is (a) what the German judge puts on a scrap of paper before rendering a judgment; (b) what a German private attorney jots down before writing a brief or, as state attorney when filing an indictment in a criminal court; or (c) what the legal advisor to a county administration drafts before the county director is briefed on a zoning ordinance or some other administrative issue.

Let us take a brief look at the *nonlitigious* opinion; in other words, let us play students and professor in the first week of the first term at law school.

---

[7]   The title of this chapter preempts an answer to this question in favor of heuristics. However, the title was assigned to me. The following lines will qualify that preemption (C. Engel suggested reformulating the title of my chapter; it has correctly been remarked that the chapter—with its philosophical and culture-comparative orientation—is difficult to reconcile with the workshop's collective discussions). The text in this section is revised from: Fikentscher, W., What are law schools for? A Paper presented at the International Bar Association 26th Biennial Conference, Berlin, Oct. 20–25, 1996, IBA, 271 Regent Street, London W1R 7PA, England.

> *A* is missing her car keys and finds them in the pocket of *B*'s jacket.
> *B* refuses to return them. *A* says: "I want to have my keys back."

Students learn how to find the appropriate rule of the Civil Code, Section 985, which states that the owner of a property has a legal claim against the possessor. Next, the student is taught to select circumstantial pieces from the story that was told as the "case" and try to fit these to the various requirements of the legal norm. Thereafter a decision must be reached as to whether the circumstances fit the requirements of the norm.

Section 985 of the Civil Code stipulates three requirements: ownership, possession, and a chattel or real estate. The student must decide whether each of these requirements correspond to any of the bits and pieces of the story. It was told that *A* was the owner of the keys; furthermore, *B* has the physical power over the car keys and is therefore possessor (under Section 854, Civil Code where possession is defined by further requirements such as the obtainment of physical power, etc.); also, the keys are movable property under Section 90 of the Civil Code.

In this way, students learn to bring the requirements of the various sections of the code into a logical sequence. In Section 985, possession is a requirement in addition to ownership; however, in Section 854, possession is a legal conclusion from other requirements. After having worked out the logical genealogy of the appropriate rules, and after having fitted all requirements of the law to the circumstances of the case, the conclusion to be drawn is that *A* has a claim against *B* to return the keys. If only one of all the requirements is missing, the opinion has to be stopped at this very point of the deduction, and a negative statement as to claim has to be made. It would be a great mistake to go on further examining requirements.

The fitting together of legal requirements and factual circumstances of the case is called *subsumption* (derived from "to subsume or to arrange under"). Subsumption is a logical conclusion of the "modus-barbara-II" type: (a) all ...; (b) *X* is a sample of all these ...; (c) therefore, *X* is treated ....

The nonlitigious opinion begins with a question: Could *X* have a claim against *Y* for ..., based on...? The subsumption then follows requirement by requirement as prescribed by the rules of the law. Third, an answer follows—*X* has a claim or *X* has no claim—and the case is decided.

This example shows the subsumption of a simple case under a simple norm when drafting a nonlitigious opinion. In the course of study at a German law school, later semesters introduce more complicated rules from the various fields of law (code law or customary law). However, the basic premises are taught and trained in the first week of the first term. A very bright student could go home after the first week in class and call himself a lawyer, because everything else—the substance of the law—can be found in print, being refined by judicial interpretation and analyses as judge-made law, all of which are accessible in various indexes. Teaching practice shows that it takes at least two to three years to acquire firm knowledge of the legal rules and their application, by subsumption, to nonlitigious cases.

University education in law focuses on the nonlitigious opinion because classrooms are not courtrooms. There are no living parties, no witnesses, no legal counsels making their arguments. Therefore, *after* law school, the German law student works as an intern or clerk for two years in one of the various types of courts, the bar, the notary public, or public administration.

As a law clerk, the student learns to write litigious opinions, that is, to handle cases with varying sets of—necessarily incomplete—facts. Thus, the litigious opinion is a good example for logical–systematic thinking *about incomplete factual information*. Life-deciding judgments have to be made on the basis of uncertain information.

At the university, the facts of the case are not litigated. In normal life, however, people fight about facts more frequently than about the law. In our simple case, *B* may answer *A*: "Yes, you gave me the keys, because you sold me the car." In the German theory of the litigious opinion, this would be called an objection. Then, *A* may answer to this objection: "Listen, we negotiated a car deal, but we never agreed on the price. There was no sale." This is termed a rejoinder. *B* may go on by duplicating: "Oh yes, we agreed on a price, and I can show you the contract." Under the theory of the litigious opinion, this is called a duplica. The story may go on and on. To solve the case, the judge would have to look at the evidence, hear witnesses, look at documents, ask experts. Of course, the trial would have to be kept as short and inexpensive as possible, and hence no evidence should be examined if it has no possible consequence for the outcome of the case. But how does one deduce which evidence is essential?

When *B* made his objection that he is entitled to the car keys because *A* had sold the car to him, the German theory of the litigious opinion requires the judge to ask himself, and jot down on her or his scrap of paper, the following four questions, in this order:

1. What does the objection purport (contain)?
2. Against which of the various claims is the objection directed?
3. Which factual foundations are being asserted for this objection to appear convincing?
4. How does the objection, if true, legally affect the claim?

The judge has to filter out the rules of the law, this time looking for rules that destroy the claim (Pts. 2 and 4), and subsume the facts alleged by the defendant to see whether they fit their requirements of those rules (Pts. 2 and 3).

If a rejoinder is made by the plaintiff, the search is for legal rules invalidating the objection if the facts support the rejoinder, and the subsumption of those facts under those rules repeats itself. The same holds true for the answer to the rejoinder (= the replica), and the answer to the replica (= the duplica), and so on.

Thus *at the root of the examination of every claim, objection, rejoinder, duplica, triplica, etc., there is a nonlitigious opinion.* Here we have the link between the nonlitigious and the litigious opinion, that is, between law school and practice.

The four questions which have to be asked for objections, rejoinders, duplicas, etc., in German are called the "examination of relevance." Correct examination of relevance prevents the judge from looking at immaterial evidence.

This is the essence of the litigious opinion, of an opinion on how to solve a case that involves litigated facts; and German law clerks are trained to handle these cases in the described way. After the second state exam, in which these abilities are to be demonstrated by the candidates, all legal professions are open to what is called the "full jurist" (*Volljurist, Assessor*). Professional possibilities include judgeship, which is quite logical because the litigious opinion technique, learned during clerkship, is exactly what a judge has to do.

In practice, the judge does not tell the parties the whole litigious opinion. Instead, the judge renders a "decision," a judgment, and this decision is the litigious opinion turned upside down: The decision *begins* with the outcome, *continues* with the legal *rules* that support the claims, objections, rejoinders, duplicas, etc., and *ends* with the subsumptions. This sequence is presented claim by claim, objection by objection, rejoinder by rejoinder, duplica by duplica, etc., the whole judgment being arranged by the plaintiff's claims. By contrast, as has been said, the nonlitigious opinion *starts* with an open question (Could the plaintiff have this claim?), *continues* with the subsumption, and *ends* with a conclusion.

As stated, in German law school, the *nonlitigious* opinion underlies the examination of every claim, objection, rejoinder, duplica, etc. Therefore, education at law school, the practical work of the law clerk and, after the second state exam, in later life are closely connected. Whoever does not master the nonlitigious opinion cannot decide real cases. Without nonlitigious opinions, neither the appropriateness of any claim, nor the relevancy of objections, rejoinders, or duplicas, etc. can be determined. This is why the drafting of a nonlitigious opinion is the first thing learned. All the rest is adaptation of the nonlitigious opinion to the various tasks of the law.

For these reasons, German legal education focuses on the role of the judge. The traditional orientation of German legal education toward the role and activity of the judge does not follow from the fact that the Germans like or adore the judge more than any other person involved with the law, or that a judge may be held in higher esteem than other law persons. It is simply because *all* lawyers are unified in the use of the nonlitigious opinion as the basis for all professional activity. A German law person can anticipate how a judge will approach her or his ruling when confronted with a given case. Therefore, a German attorney can write a brief, and a German administrative official can do the work of her or his superior. It is not the persona of the judge, but the message of the nonlitigious opinion and, derived from it, the litigious opinion that puts the judge in the center of German education.[8] Any change in this legal educative style and practice affecting this feature would not ruin or diminish respect for the judge, but it would deprive the bar of being able to write a brief or plead in court effectively.

The fact that Anglo-American and Scandinavian common law are largely built on and almost exclusively taught by precedents does not make a difference. This is because a precedent does not only contain a *descriptive ratio decidendi* why a case has been decided this way, but also amounts to a *prescriptive ratio decidendi*. The latter, in theory and practice, is handled like a code provision, under which the case is to be subsumed to find its solution. Another name for the prescriptive *ratio decidendi* is rule. The distinction between principle and rule corresponds to the German distinction between *Rechtsgrundsatz* (principles) and *Norm* (rule). Code law contains principles or rules, as does the law that is being developed from cases or codes by the judges. The logical process of subsumption is the same in Continental, Anglo-American, and Scandinavian law.[9]

The logical–systematic theory of the subsumption is a field of the logic of the law, in general, and of the theory of concluding, in particular.[10] A large number of the requirements of a legal norm (in the sense of a Continental code norm and of common-law rule), probably the majority, need an evaluative interpretation for subsumption (e.g., "adequate," "timely," "due care," "contributory negligence," "due process"). Value judgments require specific interpretation. Again, the theory of legal interpretation cannot be rendered here. Suffice it to say that under normal requirements, the subsumption which asks for an evaluation poses no specific *logical* difficulties. At least on the Continent, assaying values is not unscientific (see section below on **Kant's Theory of Judgment**).

To conclude this survey, for the dominant opinion in theory and for the legal practice, both on the Continent and in common-law countries, legal reasoning is a matter of logical–systematical derivation, also when it comes to evaluations. However, repeated attempts are made by legal theorists and practitioners to question the legal logic and system and to rely on heuristics instead. Below I include a nonexhaustive list of such attempts.

Heuristic Law Finding

An early example of heuristic law finding can be found in the German lay courts from the fourteenth, fifteenth, and early sixteenth centuries (Kisch 1919; Dawson 1968; Kantorowicz 1970; Otte 1971). Then, a judgment by a German lay court did not contain reasons. Comparing this with English court decisions

---

[8] For discussion on the central role of the judge in German law, see, e.g., Markesinis (1986, 1996).

[9] For details of this parallel treatment of a Continental norm and a common-law rule, see Fikentscher (1975a, pp. 58–150, 240–272), from where it should be apparent that I am not concerned with what is sometimes called "formal logic." Formal logic is a technical term in the science of logics of much narrower scope than "logical conclusion" and should not be quoted in the present debate.

[10] For further discussion, see Fikentscher (1976, pp. 180–184; 250–267).

from the twelfth and thirteenth centuries, one notices that in the English decisions, arguments were exchanged and discussed. Decisions by these German lay courts, however, did not quote applicable law or the reasons why the applicable law should be applied or not, and what the judges brought to their ruling. Only the facts of the cases and the final holding of the judges were reported.

Under such a legal system, a comparison of decisions, the engagement of law-related arguments, and the writing of briefs were impossible. Cases cannot be said to be "the same" or distinguished in any way. The only law that the parties learn is what the judges think the legal outcome of this case should be. Thus, neither equal nor unequal treatment under the law can be discussed. In the sixteenth century, however, German legal practice became more sophisticated and tended toward the preparation of a court decision through the writing of briefs, the exchange of oral arguments, discussion of precedents, and thinking about distinctions. After the rediscovery of Roman law in Northern Italy, legal education at Northern Italian universities—at least in the later Commentators' phase—looked out for reasoning, repeatability of decisions, arguments, and distinctions. This corresponded to the achievements of classical Roman law. To German lawyers of the time, Northern Italian legal education and court practice seemed superior, and Roman law or, rather Northern Italian law, began to replace the German tradition of the lay courts.

This is not to say that the decisions of the lay courts were unjust or arbitrary. In some good heuristic manner, experienced lay judges were certainly able to find just and adequate results for most of the cases. The problem was that decisions could not be explained, reenacted, or therefore understood; they could not be prepared or supported by pleas, pleadings, briefs, or argumentation. Yet such are the concerns for the law. This is probably grounded in the perception that like cases should be decided alike and unlike cases should be decided differently for explicable and understandable reasons. In any event, the heuristic hunches of German lay judges from the late middle ages did not pass the test of time.

Almost four hundred years later, the famous Justice Oliver Wendell Holmes, Jr., raised serious doubts whether law is a matter of logic (Fikentscher 1970, 1975b). Instead of relying on the logic of the system, Holmes preferred to rely on history when deciding a case: "A page of history is worth more than a volume of logic" (J. Holmes in *New York Trust Co. v. Eisner*). Holmes denied the importance of principles and rules for the law, derogatorily calling such instructions for human behavior "general propositions." Rules for human behavior follow from values. Values are shared preferences. Inversely, shared preferences amount to what is called values. What comes first—the chicken or the egg—is thus a matter of the ontology and epistomology chosen. Holmes, a believing agnostic and relativist, was critical of values. Therefore, he had difficulties with legal rules. When the Chief Justice of the U.S. Supreme Court assigned a case to him for drafting a proposal, Holmes is reported to have been overcome by nervousness and restlessness until he "hit" upon the decision he wanted to propose to his brethren. Holmes said: "It is the merit of the common law that it decides the case first and determines the principle afterwards ... lawyers like other men, frequently see well enough how they ought to decide on a given state of facts without being very clear as to the *ratio decidendi*" (Kessler 1944, p. 52). Holmes could not rationalize how he arrived at his decisions; he just had a good feeling for what should be the law. His "method" could be called heuristic. Today, Holmes' decisions are often criticized for being too arbitrary and radical.

A German attempt at heuristic finding of the law was the so-called free law school (*Freirechtsschule*) (Wieacker 1967; Fikentscher 1976).[11] The free law school was a firework-like phenomenon in German legal history. After only a few years the—partly temperamental—attacks of its followers against the dominant legal methodology simmered down, and no lasting imprint was made. Still, the protagonists of the free law school are quoted as representing a memorable phase in German legal development, and students are told that this should not serve as a model for the implementation of law.[12] The even more short-lived French counterpart to the German free law school movement was the "*phénomène Magnaud.*"[13]

About twenty years later, in the U.S. and in Scandinavia, a theoretical program in the law developed what has become known under the key word "realism." Legal realism took hold of a number of legal minds from the late 1920s to the early 1940s. Both American and Scandinavian legal realism found considerable attention and discussion. Details cannot be repeated here; however examples are provided by Reich (1967), Casper (1967), and Fikentscher (1975b). A special branch of legal realism was the one based on legal psychology.[14] In this context a much-used term, especially in the writings of Jerome Frank, is "hunch." It was a claim of the legal realist that a judge does not decide according to a logical derivation, but follows his or her "hunch."[15] In German, the term could to some extent be translated as *Judiz*. German legal language uses *Judiz* when the speaker wants to stress the apparent ability of a law person, such as a judge, to point to a correct decision without much ado of cumbersome reasoning. *Judiz* is not just intuition, but a mix of professional knowledge, experience, legal talent, and a good "nose" for settling a particular case. Of course, in

---

[11] I would like to revoke my earlier remarks on Martin Kriele's position: Kriele cannot be called a follower of the *Freirechtsschule*.

[12] Some free law school adherents: Fuchs (1907a, b, 1912, 1929, 1965); Gnaeus Flavius [Hermann U. Kantorowicz] (1906, 1909, 1911, 1925); Riebschläger (1968); Lombardi (1967, pp. 167 f.).

[13] A French judge proposed finding the law intuitively from a feeling of justice. One of the best descriptions, including its total failure, of the *phénomène Magnaud* is given by Gény (1898/1954, vol. 2 no. 160 f.). On the free law school movement and the *phénomène Magnaud*, see also Fikentscher (1975a, pp. 383–386, 464; 1976, p. 380, with references).

[14] For details, see Fikentscher (1975b, pp. 295–298). The most important names are Oliphant, Rodell, Petrazycki, Jerome Frank, Albert Ehrenzweig, and Harold D. Lasswell.

[15] Hutcheson (1929, p. 274) seems to be the first to use this word for purposes of legal methodology.

Continental tradition, neither the *phénomène Magnaud* nor the German *Freirecht* or *Judiz* ever became an accepted manner in deciding cases, if not accompanied and supported by inductive and deductive reasoning. In the common-law system, however, "hunches," "aspects," "approaches," and "obviousness" occur more frequently in actual court cases, especially when they are formulated with wit, spirit, and brevity (Fikentscher 1975b).

In the 1960s there was a certain renaissance of the *phénomène Magnaud*, the free law school, and American and Scandinavian legal realism when Josef Esser (1956, 1970) presented, under the influence of Hans Gadamer (1972), two books that were critical of the German mainstream legal methodology. Esser's *Grundsatz und Norm* reported on Benjamin Cardozo's distinction between principle and rule, and on the concept of "hunch" used in the American legal realism; *Vorverständnis und Methodenwahl* warned against falsifications of the legal process by bias, sociological background, and the hermeneutical circle. Both were welcomed as refreshing criticisms of overestimating legal logic and system, but they did not alter the influence of both value-oriented rule thinking and obligatory subsumption, legal methods that Esser, too, did not wish to change.[16]

From the foregoing it follows that heuristics are a part of Western thinking. They form that part of Western thinking that is not in line with Greek logic, and thus barred from conclusions. It is worth mentioning that there is a type of non-Greek, medieval kind of thinking and presenting, called topics, which found a short-lived renaissance in Germany. Topics may be regarded as part of heuristics. Topical thinking moves from point to point, usually following a certain order of calling up such points; rejects (or, historically, does not know of) system, logic, and conclusion by subsumption; and is open for imagination and observation of points and objects of interest beyond the Parmenidean–Platonic–Kantian theory of judgment. Examples of topics are the alphabet and the pre-Bach suite.[17] Another example is rhymed mnemonic verses, such as the one for the Latin prepositions that govern the ablative: *a, abs, e, ex,* and *e, cum* and *sine, pro* and *prae.* The scholastic writer M. Gribaldus Mopha is credited with a distich that describes and prescribes the scholastic method of topical reasoning in theology, philosophy, and law as follows:

> Premises give, and abstracts, authorities add, and quote cases
> carefully read, and give reasons, compare, and object.[18]

Through the topical method, points are raised beyond any system and logic, and then presented in a traditional, but not inflexible, order. In our times, Theodor

---

[16] Intensive discussion on this took place in Germany and beyond its borders from 1968 to about 1975 (Fikentscher 1976, pp. 299 f., 361–453, 739–759).

[17] The alphabet is no system; it would be a system if, e.g., all vowels came first, then the consonants, the consonants being divided up in labial sounds, hissing sounds, etc. The pre-Bach suite is a conventional series of dances without a systematic structure. A Beethoven symphony is a system by virtue of its inner structure of keys and recurrent themes.

[18] In Latin: *Praemitto, scindo, summo, casumque figuro, perlego, do causas, commoto, objicio*

Viehweg (1953) discusses the possibilities of reusing the topical method in modern law, an experiment that found widespread interest but little following.[19] Topics do not work cogently enough to render a legal decision. A ruling based on topics is not accessible to appeal and *certiorari*. Topics show their heuristic merits by pointing to their basically open-minded expandability to additional points of interest.

Thus, Western legal thinking consists of reasoned judgments that are founded on logically deduced judgment and built into a system of legal rules, with an open eye for inventive heuristics including topics. What about non-Western modes of thought?

Not all of the above-mentioned historical challenges of the dominant inductive–deductive method of Continental and Anglo-American law deserve the title "heuristic." Nevertheless, they directed noticeable objections against exaggerated logicism and systematization in law. In the classroom, law students on both sides of the Atlantic are told that decisions of legal cases need to be understandably reasoned, supported by subsumptions under the applicable norm, and thus made arguable, repeatable, usable as precedents, and comprehensible by laypersons, because of the duty to treat citizens alike under the law and to equip lawyers to prepare future cases. The "hunch," the *Judiz*, the "legal long-range shot," the "blind hen," which at times may also find a legal corn, and similar heuristic shortcuts are not forbidden—so the students are told—but should be used as controls. Erwin Seidl, professor of civil law and legal history in Erlangen, used to tell us that we as young and learning lawyers should first make a guess of what we would think to be a good and just solution to the case. Second, we should "construe" the case according to the rules of the nonlitigious opinion. Third, we should ask ourselves whether the "constructive" result would fit our "first guess." If not, we should start the "construction" from scratch. Hereby, most probably, we would detect a mistake within the construction which, in many cases, would be an inadequate evaluation. In Western culture, most lawyers work this way.

Fast and frugal heuristics are, as mentioned before, heuristics modified by their opposite: analytic logic and system. Erwin Seidl's advice may be called analytic logic and system modified by a grain of their opposite: heuristics.

BRIEF REMARKS ABOUT THE ESSENCE OF SYSTEM AND LOGIC IN WESTERN LAW

Parmenides, Plato

As far as we know, Socrates' teacher, the philosopher Parmenides, was the creator of the theory of judgments, which form part of Western (Greek) logic. In

---

[19] For further discussion, see Fikentscher (1975a, pp. 38 f., 364–418 ff.; 1975b, p. 431; 1976, pp. 349 f., 356, 408, 438, and 448).

ancient Greece, the axial age did not lead to a total religion of world denial, as in Middle, South, and Far East Asia, but rather to a total religion of active participation in this world, in view of probable failure. The defense organization against probable failure was the polis: an entity that is more than the sum of its citizens (corresponding to the mathematical principle of super-additivity, or "oversum").[20] The invention of the polis brought the super-additive entity in juxtaposition to its parts, the citizen. This generated the distinction between the public and the private sphere (in Thucydides, *oikos* and *polis*; in Latin: *res publica* and *res private*) (Fikentscher 1993). The person takes on the role of the individual as a member of a super-additive unit. Simply stated, the individual is placed in front of an ideal object. Parmenides was the first, for these reasons, to confront the individual and the object, and he connected both by a third element, thinking. By thinking about an object, the individual ends up with the judgment. Parmenides distinguished the three judgments that are possible for a human being: true/untrue, good/bad, and pleasing/ugly. Upon this Socrates/Plato built an ontology and an epistemology, and demonstrated the process of making a judgment about an object by use of dialog.

Kant's Theory of Judgment

Theory of judgment—the essence of Western thinking—was refined by I. Kant. The main advantage of Kant's theory of judgment is its openness for logical judgments of evaluation. The often heard statement—law cannot be a matter of logic because law involves evaluation—is wrong under the Kantian theory of logical judgment. To include evaluations in the theory of logical judgment, Kant distinguishes analytical and synthetic judgments. Analytical judgments are deductive and do not produce new insights: "It's raining, you will get wet." Synthetic judgments open new insights: "This lecture is boring, it makes me sleepy." Then, Kant squares the distinction between analytical and synthetic judgments with the distinction between a priori and a posteriori judgments. This yields four possibilities. All four possibilities can be applied to the three Parmenidean judgments about the true, good, and the aesthetically pleasing. Out of the number of these possible judgments (in theory: twelve), one is termed, by Wolfgang Stegmüller, the fateful question of all philosophy: the synthetic judgment a priori about good and bad.

David Hume (1711–1776) remarked that no matter how many times a human act is repeated, a judgment—good or evil—about the moral quality of this act will never flow from repetition. Exclusion of the judgment about good and evil from empirical observation removes moral judgment from science and consequently qualifies the morally good as a matter of individual assessment. The

---

[20] For a detailed discussion, see Fikentscher (1995, pp. 157–188, 355–401; Fikentscher, W., Laokoon and the Anthropology of Judgment, in prep.).

exclusion places morals outside science. For Kant (1724–1804), this represented a challenge to be answered: Kant holds moral (and thus right/wrong)
judgments a priori to be possible, thus opening the road to a scientific treatment
of morals and of right and wrong. For the lawyer, this implies that law can be a
science. Thus, the term *legal science* can only be used against the historical,
however influential, background of Kantian epistemology. The limitation of the
concept of science to judgments of truth in Anglo-American culture is evidence
of a limited reception of Kant's theory of judgment and of the extensive discussion (which cannot be reported here) that followed Kant's dogma. In this sense,
and in the wake of Justice Oliver Wendell Holmes's (in so far Humean) legal
philosophy, evaluations in Anglo-American law are, essentially, guesswork. Put
negatively, they are unscientific.

Psychologically, the more profoundly Kant's theory of judgment is internalized, the less there is a need for "holding" values to be heeded without convincing reasoning. To the extent that Kant's access to scientific handling of values is
not accepted, an epistemological lacuna opens up in terms of evaluations. This
lacuna can be filled in two alternate ways: either by real guessing, including the
use of heuristic associations and hunches, or by reliance on extralegal value data
in some natural-law manner. Such natural-law references can be made to history,
sociology, psychology, politics, economy ("economic analysis of law"), biology, or any other so-called realities.

Thus, the methodological mainstream, which is present in the Anglo-American common-law system (represented, e.g., by Benjamin N. Cardozo's [1921]
Nature of the Judicial Process, which was influenced by Friedrich Karl von
Savigny and Francois Gény) is in agreement with the Continental method of
subsumption. It treats law as a matter of logical conclusion.[21]

Nonetheless, scientific treatment of evaluation remains an open problem in
Anglo-American law. Because of an only partial reception of Kant's theory of
judgment, legal evaluation (i.e., judgments about just or unjust) escapes scientific treatment within the law and must rely on an incessant series of "realisms,"
which serve as value suppliers. Justice Holmes' historical and sovereign
power-oriented realism was followed by sociological realism (Roscoe Pound),
psychological realism (Jerome Frank, Oliphant, Rodell, Petrazycki, Jerome
Frank, Albert Ehrenzweig, and Harold D. Lasswell), the great realist movement
of the late 1920s through the 1930s (Karl N. Llewellyn, Alf Ross, and others), a
Catholic natural law realism (Francis Lucey, S.J.), political realism (Critical

---

21 Cf. Cardozo (1921, 1931). Charles Sanders Peirce's pragmatism and relational logic, which
adds view-enlarging "abduction" to induction and deduction from an anti-nominalist, gnostic–realist point of view, did not influence mainstream Anglo-American rule technique as presented by Cardozo, at least not directly. There was, of course, Peirce's influence on Holmes
through the meetings of the "Metaphysical Club" in Boston (Fikentscher 1975a, p. 282, note
29); and there is an influence of Peirce on Arthur Kaufmann and his *Gleichsetzungslehre* (literally: law-and-fact-identification theory) as developed against the backdrop of relational-onto-
logical hermeneutics (Fikentscher 1976, pp. 751–753, and Arthur Kaufmann, pers. comm.).

Legal Studies), economic realism (economic analysis of law by Richard Posner and others), biological realism (sociobiology), and so on. Anglo-American law runs the risk of gathering the values that are needed to decide legal cases from fields outside the law. This is borrowed science, not heuristics (Fikentscher 2000). Unlike these realist movements in the U.S., against the background of the Kantian theory of judgments, a legal science about just and unjust is possible, and this has been the mainstream in Continental legal history since Kant.

In conclusion, Western (Greek/Judaic/Christian secularized) law follows, in its mainstream, Greek logic and systematic methodology and is characterized by inductions, deductions, and subsumption under principles and rules that are made and applied by individuals as members of super-additive units. The desire for treatment under a law that is equal for every individual participant is so strong that rules and principles are felt to be needed, so that shared preferences and thus prescriptive values become indispensable. Western law, in its mainstream, cannot solely or even partially resort to heuristics. Nevertheless, throughout legal history, legal theorists have repeatedly warned against exaggerated legal constructivism and the poverty of imagination that goes along with Parmedian, Platonic, and Kantian theories of judgment. The German saying: "*Ein Narr ist der Mensch, wenn er denkt, ein Gott, wenn er träumt*" [man is a fool when he thinks, a god when he dreams] is sometimes expressed by jurists. Usually, these admonitions are welcomed but only insofar as they do not deflect Continental and Anglo-American common law from its logical–systematical course.

Philosophically, the plea for heuristics as an acceptable epistomological tool is one aspect of the debate, which concerns the question of whether values can be handled scientifically. The scientific position holds that the answer is no. Kant would hold that the answer is yes, from the viewpoint of his categorical imperative as the core concept of the *synthetic judgment* a priori on moral issues. For non-Kantians, such as David Hume or Martin Heidegger, values and preferences remain holdings and conjectures. For them, heuristics are the beatification of guessing because they purport that guessing is, under certain conditions, an acceptable method to distinguish between good and bad.

With regard to law, it follows that the delineation between Greek logic and heuristics remains clear cut. Concessions from both sides are permissible and made. Nevertheless, heuristics remain the opposite of Greek logic.

OTHER MODES OF THOUGHT: GENERAL
AND IN LAW

Our point of departure assumes that Greek logic is a cultural specificity. It follows that the relationship between the logical–systematic theory of judgment of the mainstream, on one hand, and heuristics, on the other, is a thought-modal specificity.

To obtain a better grasp of the about 10,000 cultures ethnographers estimate to have existed or to exist on this planet, a grouping according to culture-defining modes of thought has proved useful for anthropological study. Whereas early anthropology divided all cultures into just two groups, developed and primitive (Lévy-Bruhl 1922, 1951), modern anthropology accepts a larger number of modes of thought to which the several cultures can be assigned.[22] In earlier publications (Fikentscher 1970, 1975a, b, 1976, 1995/2004), the proposal was made to distinguish at least the following cultural modes of thought:

- preaxial age (synonymously: animism in the wide sense),
- Hinduism,
- Buddhism, to be subdivided into Hinayana and Mahayana Buddhism,
- the Greek Tragic Mind which, in combination with Judaism and Christian traditions, developed into modern "secular" Western thinking,
- Islam, and
- modern totalitarians.

Preaxial Age Modes of Thought

Of all modes of thought, the preaxial age modes of thought are most difficult to assess in few words because they are defined by the absence of *total religions* or belief systems and are characterized by one or more of many *religious types*, such as totemism, deus otiosus and eternal dream beliefs, cult of the dead, ancestor worship, animatism and taboo, witchcraft, idolatry, magic, divination, animism in the narrow sense, fetishism, polydaemonism, and polytheism. These religious types can be mixed, and they usually are. For example, the Hopi in Arizona, U.S., combine totemism, ancestor worship, witchcraft, animism in the narrow sense, and magic. Their neighbors, the Navajo, combine ancestor

---

[22] A mode of thought is a mind-set that connects human data perception with mentally reflected behavior in a culture-shaping way that is predominantly covert. Religions are parts of cultures and thus thought-modally shaped, too. An older theory distinguished "primitive" and "developed" mentalities (Lévy-Bruhl). Modern anthropology distinguishes more than two modes of thought. Instead of "primitive," newer terminologies use "early," "animist," "natural," "original," or "culture-specific." Also, other names were used for mentality, e.g., thinks-ways, thought-ways, worldviews, modes of thought, frames of thought, mind-sets, mindscapes, thought patterns, etc. Presently, all these terms are in use for essentially the same concept, with a preponderance of the designation modes of thought (see literature below). Departments of anthropology offer regular classes or seminars on modes of thought A selected list of publications follows. For a more complete list, see Fikentscher (2004, p. XVII, note 20): Lévy-Bruhl 1922, 1951; Embree 1950; Lienhardt 1954; Hall 1955, 1959, 1968, 1970, 1983, 1990; Horton 1964, 1967; Horton and Finnegan 1973; Appiah 1992 (Appiah speaks highly of Horton and mentions on p. 215 three of Horton's unpublished manuscripts, among them "Thought Patterns: The Case for a Comparative Approach"); Moerman 1964, 1965; Hamburger 1965, 1967; Hallpike 1979; Holland and Quinn 1987; Quinn and Holland 1987; Fikentscher 1995/2004 (with a prefatory note to the 2d ed.); Wiredu 1996; Olson and Torrance 1996; Hinz and Patemann 2006.

worship and animism in the narrow sense. In every culture, a different mix can be expected. The preaxial age cultures were and are, as a rule, much more complex than modern postaxial age societies.

In preaxial age cultures, a Parmenidean theory of judgment does not exist; thus the philosophical and psychological consequences are not discussed. For law, the absence of the triad subject–object–thinking leads to a manner of legal deciding that depends on the religious types and their eventual mix that exists in that particular culture. For a legal decision, a totemist will rely on the attribution of tribal people to plants, lineages, extended or nuclear families characterized by a totem. If magic is used within the mind-set of a given culture, law may depend on magic causalities. Polydaemonist and polytheist cultures may use a *deus-ex-machina*, and so on.

It is impossible to repeat all of the details here. If there is any denominator for preaxial age cultures and to their ways to make, find, and implement law, it is a relationship to nature that is taken for guidance by analogy, metaphor, or other kind of comparison. For determining preaxial age legal thinking, each culture has to be examined separately.

Can all of this be called "heuristics"? A positive answer to this question would mean putting non-mainstream Western law and the law of thousands of preaxial age cultures on the same footing, a simplification that would certainly not do justice to any culture involved. To call all legal methods that do not root in Greek logic *heuristic* amounts to intolerable ethnocentrism. Conceptually, this simplification would bring nothing. For the understanding of a legal process in a given preaxial age culture, calling it *heuristic* is meaningless, because the description as "non-Greek" does not render describable contents. In this world, there are elephants and other things. It would make no sense to call all the items of this world, except for elephants, "no-elephants." Heuristics, applied to non-Western thinking, is such a no-elephant.[23]

Therefore, I propose to call "heuristics" only that part of the Western mode of thought that is not based on Greek logic starting from the Parmenidean subject–object–thinking triad, and which leads to a judgment about the object in a discursive, reasoned, and therefore repeatable, controllable, appealable manner. Concluding thinking in other cultural modes of thought should not be called "heuristics" and certainly not the thinking in preaxial age cultures.

If somebody would esteem Western thinking as being so important as to prefer lumping together all non-Western mind-sets of this world and their thinking into one category "heuristics," the result again would be wrong, because the differences in thinking, reasoning, combining causes and effects, looking for discoveries and so on are so different from one mode of thought to the other, that the term "heuristics" should in any case be divided up into "preaxial age heuristics," "Hindu heuristics," Buddhist heuristics" (again divided up into Hinayana and Mahayana), "Islam heuristics," and "modern-totalitarian heuristics" (the latter

---

23 The joke is not mine. It is Max Radin's who criticized Wesley N. Hohfeld's "no-rights."

characterized by central secular prescriptive values such as "blood and soil" or "use value").

Of course, a detailed description of thinking procedures in the other modes of thought, and their implementation to law, cannot be given here.[24] It is sufficient to give brief hints to make the point that non-Greek legal thinking is thought-modally diverse.

Hinduism

Whether Hinduism as a mode of thought is to be categorized as a preaxial belief system, based on religious types, or as a postaxial age belief system, implying a total religion or belief system, depends on the weight given to various factors of Hindu belief. When the weight is mainly attributed to the polytheism repre-sented by Brahma, Vishnu, Shiva, and the other Gods and Goddesses of the Hindu religion, the polytheist and therefore preaxial age side is taken. When weight is placed on the nonattachment philosophy of the Bhavagat-Gita or other world-critical or world-denying factors, the vision of a total religion prevails. Hinduism includes both. The original mode of thought of the Indo-European in-vaders of the Indian subcontinent around 1000 B.C.E. was similar to Greek or Germanic late animism and polytheism bordering at the "heroic society" and thus not very distinct from later developments in the West. However, since the time of the Upanishads (around 800 B.C.E.), the Karma belief of self-betterment introduced the gradual development of South and East Asian gnostic belief sys-tems. The Vedic amendments to the Hindu tradition, which were primarily taught and adhered to by the followers of Brahmanism, called for an indiffer-ence to the traditional bondings to clan, family, relatives, friends, or military loy-alty (Bhagavad-Gita), if those bonds stood in the way of personal perfection (Fikentscher 1995). A generalized de-tribalized and de-nationalized attitude to-ward good and bad was combined with a belief in reincarnation according to the merits or failures in former lives. Thinking aimed at detaching the individual's soul from the bonds to this world. For law, this meant individualization of the person and predetermination of that individual's behavior by Karma. This leaves little room for personal responsibility in front of this-worldly values. The working of Karma in a legal proceeding was described by Rebecca Redwood French (1995).[25] The judge knows that the criminal has his karma, as has his victim. At least in classical Tibetan law, punishment depends, in part, on a com-parison of the actors' and the victims' karmas.

---

[24] Fikentscher (1995) provides discussion on the implications of East and South Asian religiosity (p. 334 f.), the Greek tragic mind, Judaism and mainstream Christianity (pp. 341–400), thought-modal implications of Islam (419 f.) as well as Marxism and Nazism (452 f.). Further discussion is found in Fikentscher (1975a, b, 1976, 1977).

[25] Rebecca Redwood French (1995) studied traditional Tibetan Buddhism, a religion that has nearly identical karma concepts as classical Hinduism.

Is this heuristics? As indicated before, the proposal is to speak of Hindu (or Tibetan) law rather than of heuristics. Modern Indian law received much from Anglo-American law, as a heritage from British colonial times. Legal schooling in India looks at least comparatively to common-law influence. Throughout South and East Asia, from Western India to Timor, and from Mongolia to New Guinea, the work of Indian lawyers enjoys highest respect. Litigating parties try to retain, if possible, lawyers who have received modern Indian legal education. Experts of international business law attribute this to the grammar of Indo-European Hindi, a language that permits the expression of logical–systematical inductions, deductions, and conclusions. Agglutinating languages seem to have more difficulties in achieving this, according to this theory. According to Ludwig Wittgenstein, language makes thinking possible. Also in South and East Asian practical law work, there seems to be a demand for logic and system in law, not for heuristics. It would be worth the effort to study this issue in more detail.

Buddhism and Confucianism

Experts of East Asian law say that the main difference between Asian and European thinking is law. This statement is often heard in discussions of intercultural legal issues. The main difference seems to consist in the role of the individual in law. Westerners assign subjective rights to individuals, whereas Easterners see law as an instrument to maintain an ordered society. The Buddhist principle of nonattachment to this world favors the latter stance. A consequence is that, for the detached or semi-detached (Confucianism) modes of thought of East Asia, law is mainly understood as criminal, not civil, law. Methodologies vary but center around proper treatment of crime. On Chinese scrolls that depict court proceedings, the judge is seen talking to the two parties separately. The parties do not exchange arguments with one another. "Just" is what the parties deserve, not the result of a Platonic dialog on the ideal justice and the epistemological ways to it with the help of propositions and proof. Does this constitute heuristics? Each cultural mode of thought should be regarded separately, the strictly world-denying attitude of Hinayana Buddhism, the guidance to Nirvana through caring Bodisatvas in Mahayana Buddhism, and the ethical standards of fitting in hierarchical structures in Confucianism. The mix of Confucianism and Marxism in modern Chinese legal practice profits from the fact that the political contents of top-cadre-determined use values can easily be combined with those hierarchical structures. While Mao Tse Tung was still alive, the accuracy of Chinese naval artillery was improved by reading, during the maneuver, the "Mao Bible."

Is this heuristics? It is certainly not a Greek-logic-and-Kantian-judgment-based derivation. However, when the judge knows what is fitting and the party cadres determine the use value, this is more than negatively defined ("non-Greek") Western heuristics; it is cultural essence.

The Japanese bubble economy and, according to some critics, the still ongoing practice of handing out foul credits to business friends and social relationships can be attributed to the traditional Japanese reliance on society groupings instead of on rational criteria of credit-worthiness. Does Japanese credit law work heuristically? Or is this just the Japanese way?

Islamic Mode of Thought

Islamic thinking is guided by the exclusive reliance on God's kind and divine predetermination of worldly events. It is God's, not a human's, task to evaluate. Judgments are not up to the human mind. There is no element of critical thinking to be placed between the subject and the object (in Parmenides' sense), and hence no epistomological dialog (although the Iranian opposition is demanding it, calling its political position by the Greek-derived word "epistemologism"). To connect the subject with the object by a third instance, independent thinking, would mean to place a second God next to Allah. *Mé génoito* [God forbid]! This is why, within Islam, there is no Koran critique, only Koran recitation.

What constitutes a "problem"? The Greek word describes a situation where thinking about the subject may reach different results. Thus, the concept of problem is a derivative of Greek thinking, more precisely, of Parmenidean judging the true, the good, or the beautiful. This explains why non-Western modes of thought do not work with the concept of problem nor do they try to solve it with the aid of a Platonic dialog. Instead, non-Western thinking uses mode-of-thought specific parallels to the concepts of problem and dialog. In Islam, for example, the parallel is the search for Allah's will. Newspapers reported: When the rescue teams of the Iranian Halfmoon gazed at the rubble of the earthquake-stricken city of Bam without moving to get to work, the flown-in German rescue workers asked them why they did not get started ("we have dogs, trained to find the victims"). The Germans saw a problem, the Iranians saw God's will at work, journalists reported. If the reports are true, in the view of the Iranians there was no Parmenidean judgment to make. Their education to watch and observe Allah's judgment told them to be present and watch, in modesty and submission, instead of unruly activism of rendering judgments.

This does not mean that Islam is a world-denying mode of thought similar to Buddhism. Islam is an active belief system just as Christianity and Judaism. However, the context of motivation and the expected result, connected through Judaic-Christian thought-modal causality, cannot be expected from a Muslim's mind. According to Islamic philosophical tradition, there is no *propter hoc*, merely a *post hoc*. To retain activity, bargains have to be made. What in Greek thinking is epistemological judgment, is in Islam "bargaining for reality" (Rosen 1978, 1984). The ontology of this reality is the result of a bargain for influence. Rules drawn from values are difficult to handle because of the principle of non-evaluation by humans. A Muslim acts under the proviso *"Inshallah"* [provided, God willing]. In principle, it is impossible to deter a Muslim. The only convincing clue for God's missing blessing is failure, a judgment *a posteriori*.

Finding out true or false, right or wrong, beautiful or ugly in a mode of thought that does not work with rationally derived judgments is not easy. A lot is left to spontaneous activity; hence, to "heuristics"? Again, the term does not fit here. Bargaining reality is not the kind of finding the true, the good, or the beautiful that respects the cooperation of another person's mind, within a super-additive entity where the whole is more than the sum of the parts, and thus opening the frame for dialog.

Modern Totalitarians

Representing total belief systems (not religious types) and thus willing to give human beings an all-encompassing instruction to a good life, modern totalitarian systems work with a central value, the contents of which are defined by political dictatorship. Dictatorships are totalitarian when they take possession of the human mind by enforcing that central value as a behavioral guideline. Germany's national socialism used the central value, defined by the *Führer*, of "blood and soil" as a point of reference for acceptable behavior. For the same purpose, Marxism employs the concept of use value (as opposed to exchange value, which enables the class of capitalists to siphon off surplus value). Use values cannot be measured, they have to be "scientifically" destined by the top cadres in the metropolises. Their decisions cannot be placed under control, not even by the control of economic cost.[26] From the perspective of heuristics, the question can only be what brings the *Führer*, or the top cadres in the metropolises, to reach the correct instructions for the governed ones. To use the term heuristics in this context does not seem appropriate either.

The result of this sketch of the modes of thought in search for the evolutionary and cultural origins of heuristics is that non-Western thinking and nonuse of Greek logic *within* Western thinking should not be tarred with the same brush.

SUMMARY

Although law is a real environment in the Western, Greek-logic influenced, cultural mode of thought, law is not a suitable environment for heuristics. Assuming that heuristics lead to legal decisions of equal quality as legal decisions, based on a subsumption of the modus-barbara-II type, it would be wrong to

---

[26] For a discussion of the proposals of the Soviet reformer, Y. Liberman, see Fikentscher (1995, pp. 446–448, with references).

state—for defining the frame, and for filling that frame, between the upper and the lower hermeneutical point of return—that a person who knows more about the environment decides better.

In law, guesses, rules of thumb, and hunches may serve stimulating and controlling functions. However, the need for equal treatment under the rule of law implies a high degree of predictability and repeatability, which heuristics cannot guarantee. Non-Western cultural modes of thought are characterized by ways of concluding, which are determined by the relevant mode of thought. To call them animist, East and South Asian, Hinayana Buddhist, Mahayana Buddhist, Hindu, Islamic, etc., heuristics would be both unjustified and confusing, as this would amount to an ethnocentric expansion of nonlogic and nonsystematic Western thinking into the wealth of non-Western cultures. Whether these non-Western cultures and the modes of thought behind them —and thus *their* way of learning, knowing, and deciding—deserve cultural attention and respect, and *how* this learning, knowing, and deciding works, respectively, are questions beyond the scope of this chapter. Respect and tolerance, it seems, is owed at least to those who respect and tolerate others, outside and inside their territories.

REFERENCES

Appiah, K.A. 1992. In My Father's House: Africa in the Philosophy of Culture. New York and Oxford: Oxford Univ. Press.

Berretty, P.M., P.M. Todd, and L. Martignon. 1999. Categorization by elimination: Using few cues to choose. In: Simple Heuristics That Make Us Smart, G. Gigerenzer, P.M. Todd, and the ABC Research Group, pp. 235–254. Oxford: Oxford Univ. Press.

Bochenski, I.M. 1968. Ancient Formal Logic. Amsterdam: North Holland.

Bochenski, I.M. 1971. Die zeitgenössischen Denkmethoden. 2d ed. Munich: Franke.

Cardozo, B.N. 1921. The Nature of the Judicial Process. New Haven, CT: Yale Univ. Press.

Cardozo, B.N. 1931. Growth of the Law. New Haven, CT: Yale Univ. Press.

Casper, G. 1967. Juristischer Realismus und politische Theorie im amerikanischen Rechtsdenken. Berlin: Duncker and Humblot.

Dawson, J.P. 1968. The Oracles of the Law. Ann Arbor: Univ. of Michigan Press.

Eigler, G., ed. 1990. Platon, Werke in acht Bänden: Griechisch und Deutsch. Sonderausgabe, Dritter Band, Phaidon, Das Gastmahl, Kratylos. Darmstadt: Wissenschaftliche Buchgesellschaft.

Embree, J.F. 1950. Thailand: A loosely structured social system. *Am. Anthropol.* **52**:181–193.

Esser, J. 1956. Grundsatz und Norm in der richterlichen Fortbildung des Privatrechts. 2d ed. 1964; 3d ed. 1974.Tübingen: Mohr.

Esser, J. 1970. Vorverständnis und Methodenwahl in der Rechtsbildung. 2d ed. 1972. Frankfurt a.M.: Athenäum.

Fikentscher, W. 1970. Rechtswissenschaft und Demokratie bei Justice Oliver Wendell Holmes, Jr.: Eine rechtsvergleichende Kritik der politischen Jurisprudenz. Juristische Studiengesellschaft Karlsruhe, Schriftenreihe 96. Karlsruhe: C.F. Müller.

Fikentscher, W. 1975a. Methoden des Rechts in vergleichender Darstellung, vol. I. Tübingen: Mohr Siebeck.

Fikentscher, W. 1975b. Methoden des Rechts in vergleichender Darstellung, vol. II. Tübingen: Mohr Siebeck.

Fikentscher, W. 1976. Methoden des Rechts in vergleichender Darstellung, vol. III. Tübingen: Mohr Siebeck.

Fikentscher, W. 1977. Methoden des Rechts in vergleichender Darstellung, vol. IV. Tübingen: Mohr Siebeck.

Fikentscher, W. 1993. Oikos und Polis und die Moral der Bienen: Eine Skizze zu Gemein- und Eigennutz. In: Festschrift für Arthur Kaufmann zum 70. Geburtstag, pp. 71–80. Heidelberg: Müller.

Fikentscher, W. 1995. Modes of Thought: A Study in the Anthropology of Law and Religion. (2d ed. 2004. Tübingen: Mohr Siebeck.)

Fikentscher, W. 2000. Ein juristisches Jahrhundert. *Rechtshist. J.* **19**:560–567.

French, R.R. 1995. The Golden Yoke: The Legal Cosmology of Buddhist Tibet. Ithaca, NY: Cornell Univ. Press.

Fuchs, E. 1907a. Die Gemeinschädlichkeit der konstruktiven Jurisprudenz. Leipzig: Teutonia.

Fuchs, E. 1907b. Schreibjustiz und Richterkönigtum. Leipzig: Teutonia.

Fuchs, E. 1912. Juristischer Kulturkampf. Karlsruhe: Braun.

Fuchs, E. 1929. Was will die Freirechtsschule? Rudolstadt: Greifenverlag.

Fuchs, E. 1965. Gerechtigkeitswissenschaft, ed. A.S. Foulkes and A. Kaufmann. Karlsruhe: C.F. Müller.

Gadamer, H.-G. 1972. Wahrheit und Methode: Grundzüge einer philosophischen Hermeneutik. 3d ed. Tübingen: Mohr.

Gény, F. 1898. Méthodes d'interprétation et sources en droit privé positif. Paris, 2d ed. (reprint) Paris 1954, vol. 2 no. 160 f.

Gigerenzer, G., and T. Regier. 1996. How do we tell an association from a rule? Comment on Sloman (1996). *Psychol. Bull.* **119**:23–26.

Gigerenzer, G., and P.M. Todd. 1999. Fast and frugal heuristics: The adaptive toolbox. In: Simple Heuristics That Make Us Smart, G. Gigerenzer, P.M. Todd, and the ABC Research Group, pp. 3–34. Oxford: Oxford Univ. Press.

Gigerenzer, G., P.M. Todd, and the ABC Research Group. 1999. Simple Heuristics That Make Us Smart. Oxford: Oxford Univ. Press

Gnaeus Flavius [Kantorowicz, Hermann U.]. 1906. Der Kampf um die Rechtswissenschaft. Heidelberg: Winter.

Gnaeus Flavius [Kantorowicz, Hermann U.]. 1909. Zur Lehre vom richtigen Recht. Berlin: Rothschild.

Gnaeus Flavius [Kantorowicz, Hermann U.]. 1911. Rechtswissenschaft und Soziologie. Tübingen: Mohr (reprint: Karlsruhe 1962: C.F. Müller).

Gnaeus Flavius [Kantorowicz, Hermann U.]. 1925. Aus der Vorgeschichte der Freirechtsschule. *Rechtsgeschichtliche Studien* **2**. Mannheim.

Hall, E.T. 1955. The anthropology of manners. *Sci. Am.* **192**:84–90.

Hall, E.T. 1959. The Silent Language. Garden City, NY: Doubleday.

Hall, E.T. 1968. Proxemics. *Curr. Anthro.* **9**:83–108.

Hall, E.T. 1970. Beyond Culture. Garden City, NY: Doubleday (2d ed. 1989. New York: Anchor Books).

Hall, E.T. 1983. The Dance of Life: The Other Dimension of Time. Garden City, NY: Doubleday.

Hall, E.T. 1990. The Hidden Dimension. New York: Anchor Books.

Hallpike, C.R. 1979. Foundations of Primitive Thought. Oxford: Oxford Univ. Press.

Hamburger, L. 1965. Fragmentierte Gesellschaft: Die Struktur der Thai-Familie. *Kölner Z. Soziologie u. Sozialpsychologie* **17**:49–72.

Hamburger, L. 1967. Fragmented society. *Sociologus* 54–71.

Hertwig, R., U. Hoffrage, and L. Martignon. 1999. Quick estimation: Letting the environment do the work. In: Simple Heuristics That Make Us Smart, G. Gigerenzer, P.M. Todd, and the ABC Research Group, pp. 209–234. Oxford: Oxford Univ. Press.

Hinz, M.O., and H. Patemann. 2006. Progress and self-created modernity: Two concepts discussed. In: The Shade of New Leaves: Governance in Traditional Authority: A Southern African Perspective, ed. M.O. Hinz et al. Berlin: LIT Verlag, in press.

Holland, D., and N. Quinn, eds. 1987. Cultural Models in Language and Thought. Cambridge: Cambridge Univ. Press.

Horton, R. 1964. Ritual man in Africa. *Africa* **34(2)**:85–104.

Horton, R. 1967. African traditional religion and Western science. *Africa* **37**:50–71, 155–187.

Horton, R., and R. Finnegan, eds. 1973. Modes of Thought: Essays on Thinking in Western and Non-Western Societies. London: Faber and Faber.

Hutcheson, J.C., Jr. 1929. The judgment intuitive: The function of the "hunch" in judicial decision. *Cornell Law Qtly.* **14**:274.

Kantorowicz, H.U. 1970. Rechtshistorische Schriften, ed. H. Coing and G. Immel. Freiburger rechts- und staatswissenschaftliche Abhandlungen 30. Karlsruhe: C.F. Müller.

Kessler, F. 1944. Natural law, justice and democracy: Some reflections on three types of thinking about law and justice. *Tulane Law Rev.* **19**:32–52.

Kisch, G. 1919. Leipziger Schöffenspruch-Sammlung. Leipzig: Hirzel.

Lévy-Bruhl, H. 1922. La mentalité primitive. Paris: Alcan. [Engl. trans: 1966. Primitive Mentality. New York: Beacon.]

Lévy-Bruhl, H. 1951. Les fonctions mentales dans les sociétés inférieures. Paris: Presses univ. de France.

Lienhardt, R.G. 1954. Modes of thought. In: The Institutions of Primitive Society, ed. E.E. Evans-Pritchard et al., pp. 95–107. Oxford: Blackwell.

Lombardi, L. 1967. Saggio sul diritto giurisprudenziale. Milano: Giuffré.

Markesinis, B.S. 1986. Conceptualism, pragmatism and courage: A common lawyer looks at some judgments of the German Federal Court. *Am. J. Comp. Law* **34**: 349–367.

Markesinis, B.S. 1996. The comparatist (or a plea for broader legal education). In: Pressing Problems of the Law, ed. P.B.H. Birks, vol. 2, What Are Law Schools for?, pp. 107–118. Oxford: Oxford Univ. Press.

McCulloh, J., ed. 1979. Rabani Mauri Martyrology. In: Corpus Christianorum Continuatio Mediaevalis, vol. 44. CETEDOC Library. Turnhout: Brepols.

Moerman, M. 1964. Western Culture and the Thai Way of Life. Berkeley: Univ. of California Press.

Moerman, M. 1965. Ban Ping's Temple: The Center of a "Loosely Structured" Society. Berkeley: Univ. of California Press.

Newell, A., and H. Simon. 1961. Computer simulation of human thinking. *Science* **134**:2011–2017.

New York Trust Co. v. Eisner, 256 U.S. 345, 349.

Olson, D.R., and N. Torrance, eds. 1996. Modes of Thought: Explorations in Culture and Cognition. Cambridge: Cambridge Univ. Press.

Otte, G. 1971. Dialektik und Jurisprudenz: Untersuchungen zur Methode der Glossatoren. Frankfurt am Main: Klostermann.

Quinn, N., and D. Holland. 1987. Culture and cognition. In: Cultural Models in Language and Thought, ed. D. Holland and N. Quinn, pp. 3–40. Cambridge: Cambridge Univ. Press.

Reich, N. 1967. Sociological Jurisprudence und Legal Realism im Rechtsdenken Amerikas. Heidelberg: Winter.

Riebschläger, K. 1968. Die Freirechtsbewegung: Zur Entwicklung einer soziologischen Rechtsschule. Berlin: Duncker and Humblot.

Rosen, L. 1978. The negotiation of reality: Male–female relations in Nefrou, Morocco. In: Women in the Muslim World, ed. L. Beck and N. Keddie, pp. 561–584. Cambridge, MA: Harvard Univ. Press.

Rosen, L. 1984. Bargaining for Reality: The Construction of Social Relations in a Muslim Community. Chicago: Univ. of Chicago Press.

Schottdorf, B., F. Haft, and W. Fikentscher. 2004. Gesundheit! Berlin: ABW Verlag.

Sloman, S.A. 1996. The empirical case for two systems of reasoning. *Psychol. Bull.* **119**:3–22.

Viehweg, T. 1953. Topic und Jurisprudenz. 5th ed. 1974. Munich: Beck.

Wieacker, F. 1967. Privatrechtsgeschichte der Neuzeit unter besonderer Berücksichtigung der deutschen Entwicklung. 2d ed. Göttingen: Vandenhoeck and Ruprecht.

Winkler and Prins Encyclopaedie. 1951. "Heuristiek," vol. 10, p. 627. Amsterdam: Elsevier.

Wiredu, K. 1996. Cultural Universals and Particulars. Bloomington: Indiana Univ. Press.

Left to right: Eric Johnson, Jon Haidt, Susanne Baer, Indra Spiecker genannt Döhmann, Richard Epstein, Leda Cosmides, Jeff Rachlinski, Clara Sattler de Sousa e Brito, and Wolfgang Fikentscher

11

Group Report: What Is the Role of Heuristics in Making Law?

Jonathan Haidt, Rapporteur

Susanne Baer, Leda Cosmides, Richard A. Epstein,
Wolfgang Fikentscher, Eric J. Johnson, Jeffrey J. Rachlinski,
Clara Sattler de Sousa e Brito, and
Indra Spiecker genannt Döhmann

ABSTRACT

In making and applying law, many agents and institutions aim for some optimal solution, yet end up mired in complexity and inefficiency. Their decision-making processes may therefore be improved by the judicious use of simplifying heuristics. In this report we examine some of the ways that heuristics might be used (and should not be used) in the creation and application of laws and regulations.

We begin by distinguishing m-heuristics (mental heuristics used by a person) from l-heuristics (legal heuristics as simplified procedures encoded into law). The human mind appears to be prepared by evolution to use certain m-heuristics when making moral judgments. To the extent that l-heuristics map onto m-heuristics, they are likely to be cognitively easy and to seem legitimate to many participants. We next examine the lawmaking process and the steps at which m- and l-heuristics might be used by specific agents.

In the third section we take Roman law as a case study in which l-heuristics were widely and effectively employed. We consider the lessons of ancient Rome for modern law. In the fourth section we consider legal and moral objections to the use of heuristics, such as constitutional prohibitions on using factors such as age, sex, and race in decision making, or the need for explicit listings of reasons to allow for judicial review. In the fifth section, we examine the social and institutional factors that support or inhibit the effectiveness of heuristics. We conclude with suggestions for further research, including the question of how to explain and justify l-heuristics in ways that people will understand and accept.

INTRODUCTION

The Goddess of Justice is represented in many forms across cultures. In the West she is often modeled after *Justitia*,[1] the Roman personification of justice, shown blindfolded and carrying the scales of justice. In the main hall of the Japanese Supreme Court, the bodhisattva of mercy, *Kannon*, is depicted with her eyes open. In an image on the cover of the *Yale Journal of Law & Feminism*, Justitia takes off her blindfold, ready to comprehend the complexity of information, values, goals, and techniques that faces the law today.

The differences in these depictions reflect the key theme of our discussions: To what extent should Justitia exhaustively search, and to what extent should she purposely ignore information? This tension between the complex balancing of all information, as represented by the scales, and ignoring some information, as suggested by the blindfold, parallels the distinction between the ambition to optimize and the desire to simplify.

Suppose Justitia were to put down her scales, take off her blindfold, and pick up some recent books and articles on decision making (e.g., Gigerenzer et al. 1999). In an epiphany, Justitia realizes that there might be alternatives to the careful weighing of arguments and evidence that she had been doing for all of her eternal life. She wonders if the selective use of heuristics could provide a faster, simpler, and more reliable way to help contentious human beings approach the divine ideal of justice.

As the Goddess reads on, she thinks about all the domains over which she presides. She sees that heuristics might be helpful not only in the courtroom but in all aspects of lawmaking. In making law, the range of possibilities is often infinite, and figuring out which law or administrative policy is most likely to lead to the best outcome is fraught with difficulty. Yet the stakes can be so high that even a slight improvement in the lawmaking process could yield enormous benefits. The Goddess therefore decides to commission a report on the possibilities for the use of heuristics in lawmaking. This chapter is a very rough draft of such a report.

Our working definition is that a "heuristic" is a simple decision or action procedure that ignores some of the available information. Heuristics can be used consciously or unconsciously. In some natural settings they are created in the twinkling of an eye, but in many political or administrative settings they take the form of simple rules that are created only by lengthy processes of deliberation and research. The crucial feature of a heuristic is that it is easy to use when compared to a direct attempt to select the optimal choice using all available information. While heuristics are well described by other reports in this volume, we do think a further distinction is useful for our project. Specifically, we will

---

[1] *Justitia* was a personification, not a Goddess, and she did not wear a blindfold. In modern images, however, she is often thought of with both attributes, and we prefer to work for a Goddess than for a personification.

distinguish between *m-heuristics* and *l-heuristics*. An m-heuristic, or mental heuristic, is a simplified procedure existing as part of the cognitive processes of an individual decision maker. An l-heuristic, or legal heuristic, in contrast, is a simplified procedure that has been encoded into law or the lawmaking process.

In this chapter, we will examine some ways that heuristics are used, might be used, and should not be used in the lawmaking process. Our report grows out of a spirited discussion among a diverse group of scholars—lawyers and psychologists, German and American. We believe our differing perspectives helped us to think broadly about our topic. We begin descriptively by exploring the ways that the human mind might be structured or prepared to use heuristics in general and certain m-heuristics in particular. We next look at the lawmaking process: which are the arenas and actors entrusted with making new law, what are the steps in the process, and which of these steps seem most amenable to the use of heuristics? In the third section we examine a particular context—Roman law—in which l-heuristics appear at an early stage in Western legal history to have been quite effective in resolving private disputes between two, or very few, individuals. We next take a more normative perspective and consider when heuristics should and should not be used, especially as we move to more modern contexts. In the section on WHAT ARE NORMATIVE CONSTRAINTS ON THE USE OF HEURISTICS IN LAWMAKING?, we consider some legal, moral, and practical concerns that might limit the use of l-heuristics. Thereafter we ask about the kinds of environments in which heuristic approaches to lawmaking might flourish. In the final section we take a prescriptive stance and offer the Goddess (and the lawmaking community) some very tentative suggestions. In addressing this question we uncovered differences among ourselves as to whether the simple heuristics found in natural settings work for complex institutional arrangements. Because there are so many unanswered questions, our recommendations are posed as suggestions for potentially fruitful research.

IS THE MIND "PREPARED" FOR THE USE OF HEURISTICS?

Animals, even those with brains small enough to fit inside the head of an ant, manage to solve an extraordinary variety of adaptive problems, and every animal species other than our own manages to do so without the benefit of language, logic, or conscious verbal reasoning. Rats, for example, use a simple heuristic to help them figure out whether or not to eat a newly encountered food: try a new food if you smell it on the mouth of another rat, but not if you smell it on any other body part (Galef 1988). This heuristic operates across species. It is not an attempt by individual rats to optimize their predictive powers, for even the smell of a new food on a dead rat's mouth is taken, wrongly, as a signal of food safety. Natural selection has produced many such mechanisms in animal minds that assemble a great variety of simple if-then rules for behavior. Animal minds are not blank slates, and mounting evidence suggests that human minds are not either (Cosmides and Tooby 2004).

Human minds, however, are different from those of other animals in two major ways. First, our long childhood and large, slowly developing frontal cortex means that we have a vastly expanded ability to learn new tricks, tips, and techniques for solving adaptive problems. Second, we do indeed have language, logic, and conscious reasoning. Humans, like rats, take their cues about palatability from their peers, yet few humans would fall into the trap of copying the food choices of a suddenly dead human. These two differences make a difference in the ways that humans learn and employ heuristics.

Many recent theorists in social and cognitive psychology have proposed that people have a "dual-processing" mental architecture (Chaiken and Trope 1999; Sloman 1996; for a critique of this view, see Gigerenzer and Regier 1996). Most of what our minds do they do by using quick, automatic, heuristic-laden processing. Our visual system, for example, is able to achieve its miracles by massive use of heuristics, such as assuming that lines continue even when parts are occluded. This first cognitive system is sometimes called the automatic system, or intuitive system, or simply "system 1." But sometimes we really do think about a problem, consider counterfactual situations, entertain suppositions, weigh possibilities, and consciously decide upon a solution. This sort of thinking is slow, labored, and easily disrupted by other tasks; it is sometimes called the reasoning system, or controlled processing, or simply "system 2." Optimizing, in the unbounded rationality sense employed by many who invoke rational choice theory would deeply involve system 2 thinking. Yet there is nothing about system 2 thinking that precludes the conscious and deliberate use of heuristics. They are then colloquially referred to as rules of thumb. Empirically, people rely on them even in highly complex social settings, and often for good reason.

For our purposes, the most important point is that all people, regardless of education or intelligence level, are extremely good at using system 1 processes, whereas system 2 processes are much harder to master because they are more dependent on education, intelligence, and the opportunity to devote one's full attention to the task at hand. To the extent that laws and procedures only require people to rely on system 1 processes, they are asking people to do something that is cognitively easy. To the extent that laws and procedures require people to seek out more information and then weigh multiple outcomes (i.e., to rely on system 2 processing), they are asking people to do something that is more difficult, even if it is at times necessary.

The human mind, however, may not just be prepared to use heuristics; it may be prepared to use certain specific heuristics. There appears to be some similarity across cultures in the content of moral codes, at least at a high level of abstraction. One recent review (Haidt and Joseph 2004) suggests that these similarities result from the existence of four basic sets of intuitions involving: (a) suffering, harm, and violence; (b) reciprocity and fairness (including revenge); (c) hierarchy, duty, respect, and related intuitions about the social order and one's place in it; and (d) purity and related intuitions about chastity and piety. An intuition is an automatic evaluation that appears in consciousness, with no awareness of having gone through steps of reasoning or inference. One sees a social situation and instantly forms a judgment that something good or bad has happened. These intuitions are the foundations upon which a wide array of cultures construct their specific sets of virtues (e.g., cultures of honor build upon all four intuitions, while modern Western cultures make much less use of hierarchy and purity intuitions).

This perspective on morality has three implications for our report. First, an intuition is not by itself a heuristic, however many common moral heuristics are little more than injunctions to use one of the four sets of intuitions. For example, many of the behavioral instructions that parents give their children fall neatly into one of the four categories (e.g., "don't hit," "share and take turns," "respect your elders," and for teenage girls in many cultures "guard your purity").

Second, this perspective helps us understand many of the most daunting moral and legal quandaries, because intuitions often collide. Take, for example, the very modern issue of organ donation. Here our moral intuition to help others who are suffering conflicts with our sense of disgust. Our charitable self is frequently repulsed by the idea of bodily mutilation. Such opposing intuitions are common to many quandaries: abortion, the death penalty, cloning, or euthanasia. These quandaries are common when medical advances call old rules of human behavior into question.

Third, this perspective makes it clear that the law often serves as a constraint by imposing sanctions on behavior that is motivated, in part, by our evolutionary heritage. For example, a very large percentage of murders is committed by men who are acting on deep motivations for revenge (reciprocity), often related to feelings of tarnished honor (Fessler 2005; Nisbett and Cohen 1996).

WHERE CAN HEURISTICS PLAY A ROLE
IN LAWMAKING?

To understand the interaction between m-heuristics and l-heuristics, one needs a sense of how new law is being made, including a sense of how law is changed to be applicable to new sets of facts. In a rough way, one may distinguish two dimensions: one organizational and one procedural. In the organizational dimension, one specific arena for the generation of new law is characterized by the scope of its jurisdiction to prescribe; by those who hold lawmaking power; by (potentially) others who have access to the arena, ranging from a simple right to be heard to veto power; by the sources of law that may originate in the arena.

In the procedural dimension, the most common form to stylize facts is the so-called policy cycle. It starts with setting an issue on the agenda. In problem definition, the issue is given definite shape. Hereafter, one of usually many potential solutions is selected and enacted. It next must be implemented. Eventually, to close the cycle, the new rule is evaluated. If it does not perform to satisfaction, the cycle starts anew. Take ordinary legislation as an illustration. In most states, in this arena, the jurisdiction to prescribe is almost unlimited. Decision making is with Parliament, which often is organized in more than one chamber. Government has formal access, often together with further organs of the state. Indirectly, all actors have access if they possess veto power. The standard output of this lawmaking process is a statute. Competing or complementing arenas include the courts (for judge-made law), administrative agencies, up through civil society (for customary law, or as a more or less accepted actor in parliamentary proceedings).

The resulting taxonomy helps avoid overgeneralization in the search for l-heuristics. It does not make sense to ask whether "the lawmaking process" or "the production of judge-made law" rely on heuristics. One may, however, investigate whether lawyers use heuristics when they select a case, write a brief, argue in court in front of a judge or in front of a jury. Likewise, one may ask whether politicians use heuristics when they set an agenda for new statutes, seek support in their political party for this agenda, argue in a parliamentary committee, draft a clause, seek expert support, talk to the media, or cast their vote on a bill.

Second, the taxonomy facilitates the understanding of how m-heuristics and l-heuristics interact. Consider, for instance, how the lawmaking process reacts to an exogenous shock. Suppose that a horrible automobile accident occurs in which a father and his two children burn to death. Further imagine that by coincidence, the accident was filmed in detail by a news camera crew. The news media repeatedly broadcast the vivid scene of the accident. Subsequent investigations reveal that although that model of automobile has a good safety record overall, it has suffered such fires before and that the fires could have been averted with an expensive design change. Investigations also reveal that the father negligently ran a red light, causing the accident. How will the legal system respond to an event with multiple causes, some individual and some structural?

First, one must ask how citizens will react. The ghastly scenes might invoke a range of anger toward the automobile manufacturer and desire to compensate the victims. The human mind—well suited to both outrage and empathy for such scenes—may be primed for such reactions. These reactions might well lead to behavior, such as writing to a member of the legislature or voting in a particular way, that builds on these system 1 reactions. Less accessible will be a system 2 analysis of whether the regulatory system is sensibly designed to maximize social utility. Suppose that the auto safety system at the time relies mostly on the tort system and consumer demand for auto safety, rather than regulation. In effect, what one will observe is a mismatch between the m-heuristics of the population in how to analyze this tragedy (which may well involve absolutist thinking, such as "safety at any price") and l-heuristics that the system has embraced (buyers should be careful as to what cars to drive, but can recover in tort for hidden defects which make the vehicle fail in ordinary use).

Public-interest organizations that promote automobile safety might well seize the opportunity to replay and reinforce these scenes as often as possible. Their efforts might be met by automobile manufacturers who introduce statistics about auto safety and the undesirability of embracing a complex regulatory solution to the perceived problem. Yet their efforts must overcome a mismatch between the cost-benefit approach these endorse and the intuitive sense of outrage and sympathy that most people will bring to the problem. The automakers might attempt, in turn, to focus attention on the negligent driver to refocus the outrage away from them. Generally, public interest groups will have the upper hand at this early stage of the policy cycle.

The reaction in the populace might then have altered the environment in which legislators operate. Public-spirited legislators, themselves relying on the natural grammar of outrage and sympathy, might come to believe that existing law offers insufficient protection to drivers and their families. Alternatively (and more cynically), legislators might simply worry that the failure to respond to the public outcry will risk the wrath of the voters. The legislators' own beliefs about the legal system might also interact with their concerns about voter wrath. They might worry that another accident at a critical moment in the electoral process might cost them their jobs, and therefore openly support stiffer regulatory measures.

The interaction between m-heuristics and l-heuristics might then recur in the courts. The accident is apt to influence the outcome of the inevitable lawsuit that the mother of the children would bring against the automobile manufacturer. Claims that the car's accident rate is statistically better than that of similar vehicles might prove unconvincing to a jury faced with a grieving mother and wife. These claims would not resonate well with the grammar of outrage and sympathy that humans seem well equipped to receive. Second, the manufacturer of this model of car might face strict liability for all future accidents of a similar sort—the car now having a reputation as dangerous. Third, the accident might lead the court to think about bending any rules that preclude damages to these identifiable victims. For example, the court might rethink rules that bar recovery for negligent plaintiffs.

The result in any case could be (and indeed in many jurisdictions is) the swift adoption of a regulatory regime, or a change in an existing regime in the rules that govern the definition of product defect, the proof of causation, and the role of plaintiff's misconduct. It may also consist of a vague clause in auto safety law (*Stand der Technik* or the best available technology) or of a new mandate to a regulatory agency ("automobiles must include all practicable safety precautions"). The agency will, in turn, begin to develop this standard into a set of workable, concrete standards to govern the automobile industry. Whether the agency staff is also influenced by the same grammar of outrage and sympathy is less clear. Their mandate requires them to hear expert evidence or even to commission systematic studies that could lead to a more dispassionate stance. Indeed, the agency might deliberately arrange its functions so as to minimize reliance on system 1 thinking. Accountability of the agency to other bodies (courts through judicial review, the legislature through the budgetary process) might also influence their preparedness to rely on l-heuristics.

Searching for general principles concerning the interaction between the human mind and the lawmaking process is thus perilous. One can see from the automobile example a nearly chaotic interaction between an exogenous event and the multilevel institutional response that it triggers. This interaction would not necessarily produce a predictable change in the underlying law. Several institutions (public-interest groups, the courts, administrative agencies) mediate the public reaction.

Nevertheless, one general principle that seems continuously at work is the power of *narrative* to move public opinion, incite a change in the judicial system, and foster legislative reform. Stories organize information in a way that is manageable to the human mind. They contain a limited number of keys and trigger a disregard of additional facts, yet they leave the impression that the whole problem is known and understood. At the same time, traditional legal theory resists their use on the ground that their disregard of facts often amounts to stereotyping and biased decisions.

The emphasis on context also suggests that the sketched taxonomy would even have to be further extended. How is arbitration or mediation different from or similar to adjudication in courts? Do they merit separate categories? What about other forms of private dispute resolution and lawmaking? Does education (being a lawyer, being a psychologist, …), cultural background (coming from the United States, from Germany…), gender, political affiliation, or belief in certain theories of justice impact on the use of heuristics and other modes of decision making? All of these questions await further research.

THE SPECIAL CASE OF JUDGE-MADE LAW IN THE COMMON-LAW TRADITION

The above scenario shows the creation of law through the interaction of multiple legal systems. In earlier systems of law, the administrative state often took a back seat to judge-made law, found in both the Roman and English law systems (see Epstein 1995). Because it worked on a more limited canvas, judge-made law is usefully treated as a special category where heuristics could have a greater explanatory power. In these older systems, disputes tended to be dyadic, in sharp contrast to modern complex, multi-party litigation and complex administrative procedures. It seems appropriate to contrast the above discussion with an account of how heuristics operated in the relatively simple environments that might prove more congenial to simple rules of thumb. This exercise should not be merely considered a historical detour; much of the manner of thinking that arose in these simpler environments survives today.

Classical legal systems, it can be argued, depended heavily on systems of classification to break down and organize legal experience. Categories of organization in the Roman and early English systems seem to map surprisingly well onto the four sets of moral intuitions discussed above. Thus intuitions or concerns about harm and suffering seem related to the system of delictual rules (an early cross between torts, private civil wrongs, and criminal law) and which may be a universal part of every legal system. The interests that these rules protected were largely the bodily integrity of the person and the physical inviolability of land and other forms of physical property. The second great category of legal obligations is that of contract or exchange, which matches up with intuitions related to reciprocity. The concept of exchange was so important that the general practice in both Roman and English systems is to deny the enforcement of gift promises while offering fairly extensive protection to exchange relationships, such as contracts of sale or hire. These regimes, it should be noted, do not involve a full commitment to a modern conception of freedom of contract, for it seems that many of the subsidiary terms of the agreement (e.g., on the allocation of risk of loss) were not easily waivable by the parties. Within that constraint, however, these arrangements were only rarely under the kind of legislative solutions (e.g., minimum wages, maximum prices) that abound in modern legal systems. These two bodies of law survive pretty much into their modern form today. There was also a complex law of persons, which deals with the position of slaves, children, and women, which seems to have engaged intuitions about hierarchy and status, most of which have given way in recent times. Finally, there were elaborate prohibitions, usually as part of the public law that regulated various sexual and religious practices. These regulations may have built upon moral intuitions about purity, disgust, and piety, which again are increasingly called into question today.

The ancient common-law courts largely lacked explicit notions of social utility maximization and might thus provide a marvelous arena in which to assess the interplay between m-heuristics and l-heuristics. Ancient systems might have thus focused more on how to resolve or prevent violent disputes that posed a direct threat to social order. Here are some of the kinds of heuristics that seemed to be at play in the system. First, the liability under the rules was not triggered unless there was some manifest form of physical injury, such as *os fractum* (a broken bone). With resources stretched thin, there was little desire to get involved with mental distress or various forms of soft-tissue injury of the sort that could not be diagnosed reliably in any event under the primitive technology of the time. The purpose of the rule, as it came to be explained by some later authors, was that it cut out of the legal system those cases that were difficult to observe and for which it was difficult to control fraud and abuse.

For those harms which passed the initial barrier, the next question was to set the rules for liability. Here again, theories of causation did not rest on abstract conceptions of "necessary" or "sufficient" conditions. The initial rule of liability was *corpore corpori* (by the body to the body) where the immediate physical connection tended to remove most doubts as to the origin and the deadliness of the harm in question. As with all subsequent systems, ultimately the rules of causation were not limited to these push/pull relationships but had to cover various cases of indirect harms, for which again early legal systems maintained tight legal connections. The Roman system did not develop a formal conception of "proximate causation," but it did stress the importance of the distinction between latent and patent defects. If the defendant dug a hole and covered it up with dirt and leaves, then he was liable to the party who, not seeing the peril, stepped into it. If, however, the hole were open to plain view, then the risk of loss remained on the plaintiff. In effect the older system used the latent/patent distinction as a proxy for asymmetrical information and imposed liability on a defendant only when he had created a peril (of which he had to know) of which the plaintiff was ignorant. The common-law rules reached this same result by holding that liability went with the last wrongdoer, so as once again to shorten the causal chains in question. Rules developed without reference to tests of utility often worked in practice to achieve just that end.

Some of these principles, having developed in a context in which they worked well, remain in force, despite a rise in the complexity associated with the modern state. Today, for example, the ancient rules governing latent and patent defects continue to rely on single factors to determine liability. These rules cut out a great deal of information that people might in practice think to be relevant to an overall decision as to who was at fault. Modern legal systems, starting in the late nineteenth century and gaining force from the middle of the twentieth century, have tended to change one half of the rule: the liability for the latent defect remains unchallenged but the rule of nonliability for patent defects has undergone a radical challenge. The newer approach holds that the obvious nature of the condition is relevant to the question of whether the defect is actionable but adopts instead a comprehensive cost-benefit analysis, often involving multiple factors to guide a jury in its deliberation as to whether this obvious defect should create liability. The use of this regime applies not only to holes in streets but also to dangerous equipment, such as saws and machine tools for which either an employer or a manufacturer could be held liable. The choice between these two regimes is a choice between a fast and frugal heuristic and a comprehensive social optimization rule. The former looks at one key fact on which liability turns, whereas the latter allows both sides to explain why some safety guard might have prevented the loss in question without causing undue inefficiency in the operation.

All these modern crosscurrents do not resolve the normative question of whether l-heuristics such as this should dominate across the full range of modern litigation. There are surely modern forms of liability under various environmental protection statutes that may not be amenable to these same techniques. Nonetheless, a simple l-heuristic that maps well onto prevailing m-heuristics might well remain useful. Take, for example, the notion that the common law of environmental regulation consisted of a simple rule of "live-and-let-live"; that is, you cannot sue your neighbor for annoying odors or smells and she cannot sue you for the same. One could argue that the rule makes sense from the point of view of a preindustrial society in which most people had the capacity to reciprocate in kind against such annoyances. The rule translates the m-heuristics associated with reciprocity into an easy-to-apply l-heuristic. We still possess many of the same m-heuristics, even now when they are sometimes ill-suited to the modern environment in which ordinary homeowners may find themselves living next to enormous factories. Reciprocity no longer accurately describes these interactions between neighbors so that the law must then adapt to the scale of the new technologies, even as it retains a sensible intuitive set of l-heuristics.

By the same token, it hardly follows that simple l-heuristics should be dismissed out of hand by courts who recognize that times have changed. After all, simple l-heuristics may have matched well with m-heuristics in a way that has many benefits for society at large. For example, the rule from the traditional nuisance law could operate as the clean-up target for environmental law, so that the huge costs of eliminating the last traces of pollution would be effectively eliminated. In addition, the environmental law could follow the common-law approach of strict liability that applies in ordinary nuisance cases so as to avoid complex determinations about the level of precautions taken by key actors: instead they proceed by looking solely at the harm caused.

This approach to liability cannot, of course, handle some kinds of environmental decisions. The issue of whether to purchase a public park or to clean up rivers and lakes from natural sources of pollution or pollution that arises from the combined activities of many small businesses does not appear to be subject to a simple heuristic, but rather invites a longer cost-benefit analysis where the emphasis is on efforts to see that the same number of dollars in two different sites reduces the expected harm from pollution by like amounts. These issues, however, draw us into a discussion of the administrative state and its approach to various social harms.

There is nothing that says that the simple heuristics which work well on a small canvas will operate as well on a large one, and some reason to believe that more overtly utilitarian calculations will have to guide the overall inquiry. Still, in addressing those issues of system-design, there may be a place for using these heuristics in setting up a clear and efficient enforcement mechanism that intermediates between the grand social plan as well as the individual target of regulation. Those issues shift the inquiry from judicial to legislative and administrative lawmaking to which we now turn.

WHAT ARE NORMATIVE CONSTRAINTS ON THE USE OF HEURISTICS IN LAWMAKING?

Even if it could be proven that in a certain context simple heuristics led to better outcomes than more complex deliberative procedures, there are a number of restrictions or constraints upon their use. Such constraints may arise out of fundamental legal values, they might stem from environmental factors, or they might be dependent upon particular psychological structures. Legal constraints may find their basis in legal theory, in constitutional or even international restrictions, or in statutory law or precedents. There are potential legal constraints on all levels of decision making, although there are fewer for members of civil society than for actors in the judicial, administrative/executive, and legislative arenas. The constraints also differ between the continental and the case law systems. The following illustrates the dimensions.

Constitutional Constraints

A number of constraints can be identified which are, in most Western legal systems, derived from constitutional laws, but may also be found in trans- or international legal systems. Constitutional constraints affect all levels of legal decision making, either directly or indirectly. For example, *accountability* is one fundamental way of legitimizing legal decisions which can be hostile to the use of heuristics. Holding the decision maker responsible for her decision follows from the regulative idea of a reasoned, deliberative decision-making process in which the decision maker evaluates alternatives. The regulative idea is violated if heuristics are employed.

If this, however, becomes publicly known, the decision maker is easily exposed to public scrutiny. This may be more difficult if deliberative processes bring many aspects of a complex problem to light and thus may help hide the decision maker behind a veil of complexity. A fast and frugal decision may in this case create more accountability.

Other constitutional limitations on the use of heuristics include the *constitutional right of equal treatment, rights of due process, retroactivity, separation of powers, limits on standing, or the right to judicial review of administrative acts*.

Statutory or Precedent Law Limitations

Statutes or precedents may, like constitutions, make the use of heuristics doubtful in law-setting processes. Such laws find their application on several occasions of the official law-setting process, and even within agenda-setting as often establishing a social norm. One example, found in both the continental and American legal traditions, is the *Anti-Age-* and *Anti-Gender-Discrimination* laws that specify constitutional provisions.[2] Such rules create presumption against the use of such factors as race, gender, and, at least in the U.S. and in current E.U. law, against age in decisions. To the extent that heuristics rely on stereotypes about race, gender, or age, their use is plainly at variance with these statutory rules. However, heuristics with different cues may be a fast and frugal protective device against illegal discrimination.

Another good example of ordinary law-building barriers to the use of heuristics lies in procedural checks and balances (even if their violation does not entitle the defendant to appeal the case). In the German system, the rule of law principle (*Rechtsstaatsprinzip*) gives this constraint on the application of heuristics constitutional backing. Another example can be found in the practice of some independent agencies in the U.S., which provide for internal review of their administrative decisions before the case can be taken to court. As a review process can only function if a decision carries reasons, the existence of control procedures sends out messages to the primary decision makers to not employ heuristics for the actual decision making unless these can later be defended by rational arguments of the system 2 variety. Whether this eventually is beneficial is a different matter. As was stated in our brief review of relevant psychology, reasoning is often motivated and twisted to reach desired ends. Cost-benefit analyses can be tweaked to reach conclusions desired for other reasons, legitimate or illegitimate.

Other statutory-anchored constraints on the use of heuristics include *rules of evidence* in an adversarial litigation regime of law that require the possibility of counter-evidence. Courts and administrative bodies alike are also bound by a rule that requires *hearing evidence from all interested parties*. The use of heuristics can potentially violate these duties, as heuristics cut off most discussion and argumentation before the final decision.

Legal and Political Theory

Legal and political theory raise additional concerns about the application of heuristics. *Public concern* over an issue and *public acceptance* can both be a legitimizing force for a legal decision, yet these may be unacceptably neglected when a heuristic shortens the decision-making process in ways that preclude broadscale political "buy-in." These considerations may predominantly affect the legal actors in the law-setting process, but may also influence private actors when making their law-setting decisions whether to go to trial, or whether to make an effort in the agenda-setting process. Nevertheless, heuristics can also further public attention and acceptance in one of two ways: they can focus

---

2 Here we find a difference on the constitutional level, because the German constitution is very explicit on gender (in Art. 3) while the U.S. constitution (in the 14th Amendment, passed in the aftermath to the American Civil War) refers neither to race nor gender, but was historically applied first and more strongly to race than gender, at least insofar as public acts were concerned.

attention on a salient aspect of the problem or they can point the way to a common understanding of a complex problem.

General Concerns

Other general concerns that may counsel those making new law not to use heuristics include the amount of *potential harm* involved or the potential effects on general *trust in law*. Also, the stronger and more focused the *interest* of interested parties is, the less likely heuristics are applied. Another factor might be that heuristics use "cut-offs instead of trade-offs": They do not allow for a *balancing of interests* or an evaluation of different, *competing goals*. Heuristics, when used as a justification, do not respect the laws of *reason and logic* so fundamental for legal self-understanding. These many constraints—be they legally, psychologically, or morally motivated—deserve further consideration.

WHAT ENVIRONMENTS SUPPORT THE
USE OF HEURISTICS?

Because environments matter, institutions matter. Institutional analysis and institutional design is the subject of many fields, from political science to organizational behavior. Most of this work embraces a rational choice perspective and it might be that the analysis of institutions is most sensibly accomplished through this lens. Some recent work, however, develops the role of heuristics in institutional settings (Langevoort, this volume). Herbert Simon, of course, was himself deeply interested in the study of institutions and found the concept of bounded rationality a tremendously valuable tool to study institutions (Simon 1947). Institutional design influences the interaction of m-heuristics and l-heuristics. Some designs might even foster optimization strategies sensibly.

Determining whether the concept of heuristics provides helpful insights into institutions first requires a definition. In economics, institutions are broadly defined. In legal theory, institutions may be entities of actors and/or resources. We suggest that legal institutions can be helpfully defined as an arrangement of rules, routines, habits, and allocations of resources within which rules are generated as well as applied. Note that, for our purposes, the definition does not include the legal rules themselves. This definition highlights two areas of inquiry for the role of heuristics in legal institutions: (a) institutions operate as mediators between law and individual behavior; (b) legal institutions themselves can be and are adjusted in ways that affect individuals' thought processes.

First, the perspective on heuristics advanced in this chapter suggests that institutions mediate the interplay between law and behavior. Lawmakers can produce complex statutes that necessitate professional intermediation simply to explain the law to the regulatory targets. These are intermediaries of all kinds, both

public and private, who translate legal rules so those who need them (not necessarily those to whom they are addressed, because the legislator may privilege
one group to the detriment of another) can understand them. U.S. Government
agencies often issue short explanations of the complex rulings that they propose
on such matters as conflict of interest regulation for their employees.[3] Independent organizations such as the American Law Institute help convert messy or
complicated areas of law into digestible concepts through their use of the Re-
statements of Law (which might be thought of as an example of the creation of
l-heuristics). Note, however, that other organizations might better serve their
own interests by making law more complicated and difficult to understand.

Second, much of law is explicitly about the design of lawmaking institutions.
Many constitutional systems deliberately separate different governmental functions. Although a primary reason is to prevent the tyranny that might accompany
the aggregation of power, this separation surely changes how people in the different branches of government think about the problems that they face
(Rachlinski and Farina 2002). As can be seen in the discussion on common-law
courts, the interplay between m-heuristics and l-heuristics operates in a certain
way in the courts. This interplay might be completely different in a legislative
committee, or a decision-making body within an administrative state. If lawmaking requires the interplay between different organizations, this likely influences how people within those institutions think. For example, accountability
might encourage transparency. Administrative agencies that have to explain
their decisions to reviewing courts or legislatures might give brief and clear reasons for any decisions and never use a chart (or always use one), or use clear
legal language (instead of the many languages the E.U. uses).

Division of labor is an important feature of the lawmaking processes. For
example, in governments, different branches have to work together to produce
government drafts. In parliaments, different committees have to somehow work
together to prepare for a plenary decision on passing the statute. Compared to
this, the broader division of powers between legislative, administrative, and
judicial branches has a different effect, because this design is not necessarily
governed by a need to reach consensus, but by the need to check and balance. In
addition, different majority rules will change modes of decision making. It
would be interesting to look at what kind of majority rule should be based on
which heuristic to work well. (It may not be so clear what it means to "work
well," since efficiency may be at odds with other considerations, as we discussed above.)

Another feature of institutional design in the legislative process is the position of political parties, as well as the role of government versus parliament, of
citizens, NGOs, lobby groups, and of experts. For example, in the choice of

---

[3] For an example, see National Institutes of Health, Summary of NIH Specific Provisions in In-
terim Final Rule—Prohibited Outside Activities. http://www.nih.gov/about/ethics/020105COI
summary.pdf

experts, the heuristic used may be party affiliation or tendency to agree with party politics on broad issues ("he/she fits in," "hired guns"), rather than a decision based on an assessment of academic quality. The same can be observed in judicial proceedings: names may have to be published or not, academic records may be checked and made public or not, some other actor may have a say in the choice of experts or not, expert opinions may be excluded or limited to a very specific question or not, and some additional heuristics rules may govern the presence of experts, for example diversity in jury selection, or gender parity in German committee law (*Bundesgremienbesetzungsgesetz*, which requires government agencies to send male and female experts to certain committees).

PRESCRIPTIONS FOR RESEARCH

At this point we reveal the obvious: we are at a beginning, not an end. Like so many who have commissioned reports before, the Goddess of Justice is left with a rather long list of additional research that is needed. In this closing section we describe some questions and strategies that we think are particularly interesting.

Where to Look?

We suggest that the common law and judge-made law is likely to be a more fruitful venue for the study of both l- and m-heuristics. First, most of the literature on the efficacy and problems of heuristics is limited to the study of individuals. Understanding the m-heuristics used by judges is easier, given that the larger-scale units of administrative and legislative law involve complex sets of actors. Prior studies of heuristic use in small groups and of decision making in juries (Hastie and Wittenbrink, this volume; Pennington and Hastie 1990) suggest that these levels of analysis might also be most amenable to research efforts. One example of this research may be the use of moral intuitions in judicial decision making. Similarly, while the common law is by no means simple, we think an understanding of where l-heuristics have emerged and their efficacy is very important. For example, simplified procedures such as a statutes of limitations are l-heuristics, in contrast to, say, a rule that said that the amount won in a civil suit would be discounted over time. We suspect that this l-heuristic produces reductions of complexity and uncertainty in ways that more than justify the reduction in accuracy.

For What Do We Look?

Simplicity, however, comes at a potential cost. By definition, heuristics ignore some potentially relevant information. The magic of heuristics is performed by exploiting the environment (e.g., the nature of redundancy in information). This suggests two limits. The first is that dynamic environments, subject to rapid changes in the nature of information, may be particularly dangerous places for the use of heuristics. As observed by Payne et al. (1993), an adaptive decision maker must have a repertoire of heuristics and knowledge of when to use them. Single rule use may, indeed, be maladaptive. The second occurs when the environment is controlled by a potentially hostile opponent. If an opponent knows the heuristic in use, he might alter the environment so that this heuristic will do badly. For example, the effort savings of the Take The Best heuristic could be exploited by an environment in which the weights attached to variables are equal. Similarly if the opponent is playing a heuristic strategy, the assumption of complete and mutual rationality can in fact lead to outcomes that are *inferior* to one generated by an algorithm that provided the best response to the heuristic. This raises the important question of how complex is the repertoire of legal decision strategies, and how they might adapt to competitive, and adversarial environments.

These observations are particularly relevant given our distinction between l- and m-heuristics. Unlike m-heuristics that can be selected by the decision maker as environments change, l-heuristics are typically applied consistently because they are part of the law or legal procedure. While heuristics have the advantage of increasing transparency, they also have the disadvantage of potentially being exploited and resulting in unintended consequences.

What Wins? Complexifying versus Bounded Rationality

In contrast to our appeal to simplicity, we suspect that complexifying is a common response to attempts to introduce heuristics. While heuristics may increase transparency, that may not be in the interest of all parties involved. Complexifying procedures are often used to reduce transparency. Many parties with vested interests do not support transparency, and would benefit from the abandonment of l-heuristics.

How to Communicate?

Our perspective suggests that heuristics that fit with our basic moral intuitions are more likely to be adopted and respected. The new field of *cultural epidemiology* (e.g., Boyer 2001; Sperber and Hirschfeld 2004) looks at how ideas and innovations spread through a culture. Just as the spread of a pathogen depends on the physiological and behavioral properties of its host, the spread of an idea depends on the *cognitive* properties of the (host) minds it inhabits. If the (enculturated) human mind is prepared to care about (some subset of) harm, fairness, hierarchy, and purity, then l-heuristics that mesh with those minds will feel good, right, and just. They will be easily understood and readily transmitted. They will be infectious, inhabiting many minds in the population in a stable way.

In contrast, l-heuristics that violate intuitive ethics will feel strange and are more likely to generate resistance and resentment.

An important research area is therefore the use of heuristics for communication. Much as people have thought of brand recognition as a simplified way of making product choices, or of political parties as simplified ways of choosing candidates, we suspect that the simple names given complex laws and regulations may in fact be named in a way to tap moral intuitions. Casual observations are abundant: Legislative acts in the U.S. are often named so as to push people's intuitive ethical buttons. For example, how could any American oppose "The Patriot Act," which reduces civil liberties to combat terrorism? Or how could anyone be so coldhearted as to oppose "Megan's Law," named after a young female victim of a released sex offender, which specifies a complex set of procedures for notifying residents of the presence in their neighborhoods of former sex offenders. A model for such research might be Heath et al.'s (2001) studies of folk beliefs and urban legends.

CONCLUSION

We have suggested that, in general, when l-heuristics match up with m-heuristics, a variety of benefits are likely. However not all such matches will be beneficial. After all, minds designed for the small-group living conditions of hunter–gatherers are now operating in advanced market economies and nation states. Policies that seem just and reasonable to such minds may have disastrous consequences because our minds are not equipped to compute the emergent properties of interactions among millions of people over long periods of time. Determining whether any of our proposed research would generate worthwhile interventions requires understanding complex social welfare consequences. Clearly this requires scientific research, mathematical analysis, and debate; that is, a great deal of system 2 reasoning by a population of specialists. These specialists may, in the end, produce policies that rely on heuristics, but they need to think about unintended consequences and other factors which emerge when heuristics are applied in a domain as dynamic and adversarial as the making of the law. There are reasons to be cautious in using heuristics in lawmaking, but there are reasons to be optimistic as well. We recommend that the Goddess should keep reading, and stay tuned for further findings in the coming years.

REFERENCES

Boyer, P. 2001. Religion Explained: The Human Instincts That Fashion Gods, Spirits, and Ancestors. London: Heinemann.
Chaiken, S., and Y. Trope, eds. 1999. Dual Process Theories in Social Psychology. New York: Guilford.

Cosmides, L., and J. Tooby. 2004. Knowing thyself: The evolutionary psychology of moral reasoning and moral sentiments. In: Business, Science, and Ethics, ed. R.E. Freeman and P. Werhane, pp. 93–128. The Ruffins Series in Business Ethics, vol. 4. Charlottesville, VA: Society for Business Ethics.

Epstein, R. 1995. Simple Rules for a Complex World. Cambridge, MA: Harvard Univ. Press.

Fessler, D. 2005. Violent response to transgression as an example of the intersection of evolved psychology and culture. In: Missing the Revolution: Darwinism for Social Scientists, ed. J.H. Barkow, pp. 101–117. Oxford: Oxford Univ. Press.

Galef, B.G., Jr. 1988. Imitation in animals: History, definition, and interpretation of data from the psychological laboratory. In: Social Learning: Psychological and Biological Perspectives, ed. T.R. Zentall and B.G. Galef, Jr., pp. 3–28. Hillsdale, NJ: Erlbaum.

Gigerenzer, G., and T. Regier. 1996. How do we tell an association from a rule? Comment on Sloman (1996). *Psychol. Bull.* **119**:23–26.

Gigerenzer, G., P.M. Todd, and the ABC Research Group. 1999. Simple Heuristics That Make Us Smart. Oxford: Oxford Univ. Press.

Haidt, J., and C. Joseph. 2004. Intuitive ethics: How innately prepared intuitions generate culturally variable virtues. *Daedalus* **133**:55–66.

Heath, C., C. Bell, and E. Sternberg. 2001. Emotional selection in memes: The case of urban legends. *J. Pers. Soc. Psychol.* **81**:1028–1041.

Nisbett, R.E., and D. Cohen. 1996. Culture of Honor: The Psychology of Violence in the South. Boulder, CO: Westview Press.

Payne, J.W., J.R. Bettman, and E.J. Johnson. 1993. The Adaptive Decision Maker. New York: Cambridge Univ. Press.

Pennington, N., and R. Hastie. 1990. Practical implications of psychological research on juror and jury decision making. *Pers. Soc. Psychol. Bull.* **16**:90–105.

Rachlinski, J.J., and C.R. Farina. 2002. Cognitive psychology and optimal governmental design. *Cornell Law Rev.* **87**:549–615.

Simon, H. 1947. Administrative Behavior. New York: Macmillan.

Sloman, S.A. 1996. The empirical case for two systems of reasoning. *Psychol. Bull.* **119**:3–22.

Sperber, D., and L.A. Hirschfeld. 2004. The cognitive foundations of cultural stability and diversity. *Trends Cog. Sci.* **8**:40–46.

12

Heuristics for Applying Laws to Facts

Reid Hastie and Bernd Wittenbrink

Center for Decision Research, University of Chicago,
Chicago, IL 60637, U.S.A.

ABSTRACT

The most successful framework to interpret juror decision making in the American petit jury is the "story model" for explanation-based decision making. But, what role do fast and frugal heuristics and other inference processes play within that general framework? This chapter provides a review of past proposals for heuristic reasoning in jurors' decisions and concludes that it is usually embedded in a larger explanation-based process. However, there is some behavioral evidence that prejudice-based judgments play a heuristic role that may sometimes replace explanation-based reasoning.

INTRODUCTION

Over the past 25 years, a model for legal decision making has emerged that is generally accepted as providing the best overview of the American lay juror's decision process. This model describes the juror's decision as an active, constructive comprehension process in which evidence is selected, organized, elaborated, and interpreted during the course of the trial to create a summary mental model, in the juror's head, of what happened in the events under dispute. This theoretical framework is called the "story model" because in most cases, jurors rely heavily on a summary of the trial evidence in the form of a narrative story. The story model seems intuitively correct to professionals who try legal cases for a living (e.g., Amsterdam and Bruner 2000; Moore 1989). In addition, competitive scientific tests favor the descriptive validity of the story model over competing hypotheses (Hastie 1993; Pennington and Hastie 1992; cf. Schum and Martin 1982). Furthermore, the small stock of behavioral research on the trial judge's decision process also points toward the centrality of narrative, story evidence summaries in the trial judge's cognitive processes (e.g., Wagenaar et al. 1993).

In this chapter we consider the role of an alternative interpretation of juror's decisions: the hypothesis that decisions are primarily based on fast and frugal, heuristic judgment processes. Our conclusion will be that, with few exceptions, simple inferences, personal prejudices, and fast and frugal cognitive heuristics play their parts as components of the overarching quest for a summary explanation (story) of the evidence. Therefore, to understand the role of fast and frugal legal judgments, we must first understand the overarching task within which they occur.

First, we review the story model framework for jurors' decision processes. Then we consider the possible roles of component inference processes, including fast and frugal, heuristic judgments in that larger decision process. Finally, we entertain the possibility that some legal decisions are based solely on one simple, fast and frugal judgment heuristic.

THE PARTY LINE: THE STORY MODEL FOR JUROR DECISION MAKING

Most juror and judge decisions in criminal and civil trials can be described by a general model of *explanation-based judgment* (Hastie 1999, 2001; Hastie and Pennington 1994, 1996; Pennington and Hastie 1981, 1986, 1988, 1991, 1992, 1993; for similar views see also Bennett and Feldman 1981 and Wagenaar et al. 1993). The explanation-based approach to decision making proposes that decision makers reason about evidence in order to construct a summary in the form of a mental model of important, decision-relevant events and the causal relations between them. Then, this intermediate representation, rather than the original "raw" evidence, is the basis of the final decision. Interposition of this causal representation facilitates evidence comprehension, directs additional inferences, and is the primary determinant of the confidence assigned to the decision. Other researchers have proposed comprehension-based interpretations of simple decisions (e.g., Simon and Holyoak 2002; Kintsch 1998; Trabasso and Bartolone 2003), and some have shown how simple causal models underlie well-known judgment errors (e.g., base rate neglect: Sloman et al. 2003; framing effects: Jou et al. 1996; the conjunction fallacy: Kintsch 1998; the planning fallacy: Buehler et al. 2002). The explanation-based approach to decision processes parallels studies of the role of explanations in categorization behavior (Ahn et al. 1995; Keil and Wilson 2000; Murphy and Medin 1985; Rehder and Hastie 2001), category learning (e.g., Schank et al. 1986), planning (Wilensky 1983), and learning by generalization from examples (e.g., Lewis 1988).

The American lay juror's decision task is a prototype of the tasks to which explanation-based models apply: First, a massive "database" of evidence is encountered at trial, frequently requiring several days to present. Second, the evidence comes in a scrambled order in which several witnesses and exhibits convey pieces of a historical puzzle in a jumbled temporal sequence. Third, the evidence is piecemeal and there are many gaps in its depiction of the historical events that are the focus of reconstruction: event descriptions are incomplete, usually some critical events were not observed by the available witnesses, and information about personal reactions and motivations is not presented (usually because of the rules of evidence in American courts). Finally, subparts of the evidence (e.g., individual propositions or episodes) are interdependent in their probative implications for the verdict (Anderson and Twining 1991; Wigmore 1937). The meaning of one statement cannot be assessed in isolation because it depends on the meanings of related statements.

The juror's decision process in a criminal trial can be broken down into three component processes corresponding to those shown in Figure 12.1:

1. Construction of an explanation, in the form of a narrative story, which accounts for the evidence.
2. Learning the choice set of decision alternatives by comprehending the verdict categories presented in instructions on the law.
3. Reaching a decision by classifying the story into the best-fitting verdict category.

The major variations on this model in American trials apply to the verdict categories. In civil trials, the instructions often convey information about how to infer causality, responsibility, and motivations from the evidence (in practice, from the evidence-based story) and thus the choice set is often not structured as a set of categorical attributes, as it is in criminal cases. Also, in contrast to jurors, judges usually already know the relevant verdict categories before they hear the evidence (from which they also construct narrative summaries), and they usually appear to infer the verdict based on analogies to prior cases, rather than from black-letter law. In addition to descriptions of processing stages, the central claim of the model is that the story the juror constructs *causes* the decision. The explanation-based theory also includes four certainty principles—coverage, coherence, uniqueness, and goodness-of-fit—that govern which story will be accepted, which decision will be selected, and the confidence with which the selected decision will be made.

More generally, according to the explanation-based framework, the type of causal model constructed to explain the evidence will depend on the decision domain. Different domain-specific causal rules and knowledge structures will underlie an internist's causal model of a patient's medical condition (Patel and Groen 1991), an engineer's mental model of an electrical circuit (de Kleer and Brown 1983), an epidemiologist's model of the effect of radon contamination on health (Bostrom et al. 1992), a manager's image of factors affecting his profits (Hogarth et al. 1980), an economist's cognitive maps of economic events (Sevon 1984), or a diplomat's causal map of the political forces in the Middle East (Axelrod 1976; for additional examples, see Klein et al. 1993). In short, there is a great deal of empirical, behavioral evidence that explanation-based reasoning plays a role in many fundamental judgments and decisions (Hastie and Pennington 1995, 2000).

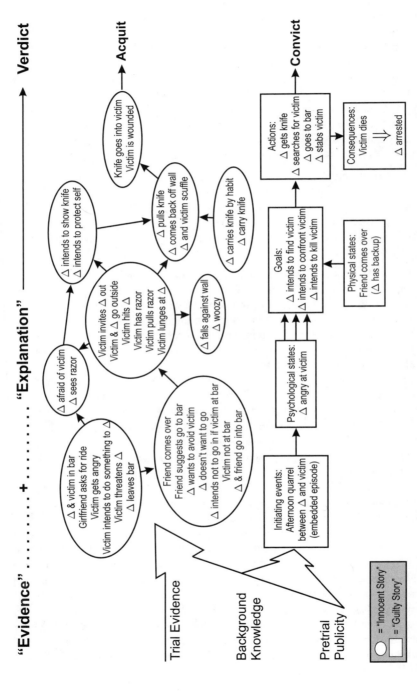

Figure 12.1 Story model of the juror's decision process. Δ = defendant. Figure courtesy of BerlinScienceWorks.

THE JUROR'S DECISION TASK

To illustrate the explanation-based decision process, we use illustrations from one of the simulated trials that we have used in our research, *Commonwealth of Massachusetts v. Johnson*. In this trial, the defendant Frank Johnson was charged with first-degree murder. The undisputed background events include the following: the defendant Johnson, and the victim, Alan Caldwell, had a quarrel early on the day of Caldwell's death. On that morning, Caldwell threatened Johnson with a razor. Later in the evening, they were again at the same bar. They went outside together, got into a fight, and Johnson stabbed Caldwell, resulting in Caldwell's death. The events under dispute include whether or not Caldwell pulled a razor in the evening fight, whether Johnson actively stabbed Caldwell or merely held his knife out to protect himself, how they got outside together, whether or not Johnson intentionally went home and got his knife after the morning altercation, and whether Johnson went back to the bar to find Caldwell or went to the bar because it was his habit.

Constructing an Explanation

Our empirical research has focused on the claim that the juror's explanation of legal evidence takes the form of a "story" in which causal and intentional relations among events are prominent. We have shown that, under the conditions that hold in a typical criminal jury trial, jurors spontaneously construct story structures (and not other plausible structures); jurors who choose different verdicts construct different stories; and the story summary constructed by an individual juror is a *cause* of that juror's decision. According to the theory, the story is constructed from three types of knowledge: (a) case-specific information acquired during the trial (e.g., statements made by witnesses about past events relevant to the decision); (b) knowledge about events similar in content to those that are the topic of dispute (e.g., knowledge about a similar crime in the juror's community); and (c) generic expectations about what makes a complete story (e.g., knowledge that human actions are usually motivated by goals). This constructive mental activity results in one or more *interpretations* of the evidence in the form of narrative stories. One of these interpretations (stories) will be accepted by the juror as the best explanation of the evidence. The story that is accepted is the one that provides the greatest coverage of the evidence and is the most coherent, as determined by the individual juror.

Stories involve human action sequences connected by relationships of physical causality and intentional causality between events. In its loosest form, a story could be described as a "causal chain" of events in which events are connected by causal relationships of necessity and sufficiency (Charniak 1991; Trabasso and van den Broek 1985). However, psychological research on discourse comprehension suggests that story causal chains have schematic structure, both when considering the discourse itself and when considering the reader's "mental models" of the discourse. Stories appear to be organized into units called *episodes* (Mandler 1984; Rumelhart 1977; Schank 1975; Stein and Glenn 1979). Episodes fulfill particular roles and are connected by certain types of causal relationships to form stories. And, within episodes *initiating events* cause characters to have psychological *responses* and to form *goals* that motivate subsequent *actions* which cause certain *consequences* and accompanying *states*. An example of an episode in the Johnson case is the following sequence: Johnson and Caldwell are in Gleason's bar. Caldwell's girlfriend, Sandra Lee, goes up to Johnson and asks him for a ride to the dog track the next day (initiating events). Caldwell becomes angry (internal response), pulls his razor, and threatens Johnson (actions, note that a goal is missing and must be inferred by the observer), and Johnson backs off (consequence).

Stories also have a schematic structure that reflects within-episode structure. In their analysis of legal decisions, Amsterdam and Bruner (2000, pp. 113–114) provide an "austere definition" of a narrative that closely resembles the interpretation just provided:

> A narrative can purport to be either a fiction or a real account of events; it does not have to specify which. It needs a cast of human-like characters, beings capable of willing their own actions, forming intentions, holding beliefs, having feelings. It also needs a plot with a beginning, a middle, and an end, in which particular characters are involved in particular events. The unfolding of the plot requires (implicitly or explicitly):
>
> 1. An initial steady state grounded in the legitimate ordinariness of things.
> 2. This state gets disrupted by Trouble consisting of circumstances attributable to human agency or susceptible to change by human intervention.
> 3. This, in turn, evokes efforts at redress or transformation, which succeed or fail.
> 4. The old steady state is restored or a new (transformed) steady state is created.
> 5. The story concludes by drawing the then-and-there of the tale that has been told into the here-and-now of the telling through some coda (e.g., Aesop's characteristic moral of the story).

Stories may have further structure by virtue of the fact that each component of an episode may be an episode itself. For example, the entire episode above (characterized as Caldwell threatens Johnson) is the *initiating event* in one version of the Johnson story. In this version, the morning "threat" episode causes Johnson to be angry, to want to pay Caldwell back. Thus, a story is a hierarchy of embedded episodes. The highest-level episode characterizes the most important features of "what happened." Components of the highest-level episode are elaborated in terms of more detailed event sequences in which causal and intentional relations among subordinate story events are represented.

The structure of stories, according to our theory, plays an important role in the juror's comprehension and decision-making processes. The story constructed by the juror will consist of some subset of the events and causal relationships referred to in the presentation of evidence, *and* additional events and causal relationships inferred by the juror. Some of these inferences may be suggested by the attorneys and some may be constructed solely by the juror. Whatever their source, the inferences serve to fill out the episode structure of the story. Furthermore, expectations about the kinds of information necessary to make a story, tell the juror when important pieces of the explanation structure are missing and when inferences must be made.

Knowledge about the structure of stories allows the juror to form an opinion concerning the completeness of the evidence—the extent to which a story has all its parts. Second, the structure of episodes in a story corresponds to the structure of our knowledge about human action sequences in the world. That is, story construction is a general comprehension strategy for understanding human action (Schank and Abelson 1977, 1995). Thus, the juror can easily compare the structure that is being imposed on the evidence to already encoded prior knowledge. Finally, the hierarchical episode and causal structure of the story provides an "automatic" index of the importance of different pieces of evidence (Trabasso and Sperry 1985). In the example above, the details of the embedded "threat" episode are subordinate in importance to the details of the top-level episode that reveal what Johnson did in order to pay Caldwell back. This indexing of importance is something that emerges from the *structure* of the story.

Learning the Choice Set (Verdicts)

The decision maker's second major task is to learn or to create a set of potential solutions or action alternatives that constitute the choice set. In criminal trials the legal information for this processing stage is given to jurors at the end of the trial in the judge's instructions about the verdict alternatives available to the juror. These instructions provide only a sketchy outline of the decision categories, and jurors may also have prior ideas concerning the meaning of the verdict alternatives. The verdict definition information in the judge's instructions is usually abstract and often couched in unfamiliar language: a crime is named and then abstract features are presented that define the crime. Features typically describe requirements of identity, mental state, circumstances, and actions that constitute the crime (Kaplan 1978).

Again, constructive inference processes are rampant and it is common for prior conceptions of the verdicts (e.g., from news media and fictional accounts of trials) to intrude into the verdict representations (for additional empirical results on verdict representation, see Smith 1991). But, many gaps and errors remain in the jurors' operative conceptualizations of the law (cf. Elwork et al. 1987; Hastie et al. 1983).

Matching the Story to the Verdicts

The final stage in the global decision process involves matching summary evidence representation to the decision alternatives to find the best match. It is even possible that many definitions of legally significant actions are organized in a format that matches narrative structures (i.e., the definitions of many crimes in terms of identity, mental state, circumstances, and actions may anticipate the most common organization imposed on the evidence). Because verdict categories are unfamiliar concepts, the classification of a story into an appropriate verdict category is likely to be a deliberate inferential process. For example, a juror may have to decide whether a circumstance in the story such as "pinned against a wall" constitutes a good match to a required circumstance, "unable to escape," for a verdict of not guilty by reason of self-defense. In this example, these inferences would depend on knowledge from the trial evidence, from the judge's instructions, and from the juror's background knowledge about human motivations (Was the defendant "trying" to escape?), mental processes (Was the person incapacitated?), and the physical world (Was it physically possible for the person to escape?).

The story classification stage also involves the application of the judge's procedural instructions on the presumption of innocence and the standard of proof. That is, if not all of the verdict attributes for a given verdict category are satisfied "beyond a reasonable doubt," by events in the accepted story, then the juror should presume innocence and return a default verdict of not guilty.

Confidence in Decisions

More than one story may be constructed by the juror. However, one story will usually be accepted as the "best" story. And the juror will have a level of confidence in that "best" story that may be high or low. The principles that determine acceptability of a story, and the resulting level of confidence in the story, we call *certainty principles*. According to our explanation-based theory, two certainty principles govern acceptance: *coverage* and *coherence*. An additional certainty principle—*uniqueness*—contributes to confidence. A story's *coverage* of the evidence refers to the extent to which the story incorporates and accounts for evidence presented at trial. The greater the story's coverage, the more acceptable the story as an explanation of the evidence, and the greater confidence the juror will have in the story as an explanation, if accepted. An explanation that leaves a lot of evidence unaccounted for will have a lower level of acceptability as the correct explanation. Poor coverage should lower the confidence in a story and consequently lower confidence in the ultimate decision.

A story's *coherence* also enters into its acceptability, and level of confidence in a decision based on that story. Coherence itself can be decomposed into three components: *consistency, plausibility*, and *completeness*. A story is *consistent* to the extent that it does not contain internal contradictions either with evidence believed to be true or with other parts of the explanation. A story is *plausible* to the extent that it corresponds to the decision maker's knowledge about what typically happens in the world and does not contradict that knowledge. A story is complete when the expected structure of the story "has all of its parts" (according to the rules of the episodic structure and discussion above). Missing information or lack of plausible inferences about one or more major components of the story will decrease confidence in the explanation. Thus, the coherence of the explanation reflects the consistency of the explanation with itself and with world knowledge, and the extent to which parts of the explanation can be inferred or assembled. These three ingredients of coherence (consistency, plausibility, and completeness) may be fulfilled to a greater or lesser degree and the values of the three components will combine to yield the overall level of coherence of a story. Combination of these ingredients, however, is not strictly additive. For example, completeness interacts with plausibility. If a story is plausible, then completeness increases confidence. However, if a story is implausible, completeness does not increase confidence (it might be thought that completeness of an implausible story would actually decrease confidence but this is not the case).

Finally, if more than one story is judged to be coherent, then the stories will lack *uniqueness*, which contributes to confidence in a story and in a decision. If there are multiple coherent explanations for the evidence, belief in any one of them over the others will be lessened (Einhorn and Hogarth 1986; Van Wallendael 1989). If there is one coherent story, this story will be accepted as the explanation of the evidence and will be instrumental in reaching a decision. (McKenzie et al. [2002] have demonstrated the comparative nature of juror decisions by showing that a weak affirmative case can actually reduce belief more than no case at all, when confronted by a strong opposing case.)

THE ROLE OF REASONING AND HEURISTIC JUDGMENTS WITHIN EXPLANATION-BASED DECISIONS

The juror's global decision process is best described as an active, constructive comprehension process in which evidence is organized, elaborated, and interpreted during the course of the trial to create a summary mental model of what happened in the events under dispute. Some story elements are accepted as true directly on the basis of their appearance as evidence from one or more credible sources (or occasionally because they are asserted by a persuasive attorney); they are reasonably well established as fact. For example, an evidence item, "Caldwell was in Gleason's Bar," is direct testimony, is not a matter of dispute, and it appears in all jurors' individual stories. Where in the story an event will appear, depends on its causal relationships to other events.

Many pieces of the story, however, are produced as a result of inferences and judgments. This is the role that Pennington and Hastie assign to fast and frugal heuristics and other reasoning processes, and this is the view of the comprehension process held by many cognitive psychologists today. To illustrate, a listener hears a simple narrative: "Billy went to Johnny's birthday party. When all the children were there, Johnny opened his presents. Later, they sang 'Happy Birthday' and Johnny blew out the candles." Many listeners will infer spontaneously, and most will agree when asked, that there was a cake at the birthday party. Yet, no cake is mentioned in the sentences above. The cake is inferred because we share knowledge about birthday party traditions and about the physical world (the candles had to be on something). Another illustration comes with the comprehension of the sentence, "The policeman held up his hand and stopped the car." Most of us understand this sentence in the cultural context of the policeman's authority, shared signals, a driver watching the policeman while controlling the car, etc. Indeed, this is a sentence that would be puzzling to a person from a different culture.

Probably the most common inferences are best described as *modus ponens* or condition–action rule applications (Smith et al. 1992). Pennington and Hastie (1993) documented many of these logic-like inferences that jurors mention when they report on their decision processes. For example, a typical deduction from world knowledge in the "Johnson case" consists of the following premise (P1–P2) and conclusion (C) structure:

P1. A person who is violent causes other people to be afraid (from world knowledge).
P2. *Caldwell was violent (from evidence).*
C.   Johnson was afraid of Caldwell (inferential conclusion).

In this example, the juror matches features of Caldwell from undisputed evidence (P2) and a previous inferential conclusion (P3) to world knowledge about the consequences of being confronted with such a person (P1) to infer that Johnson was afraid (C). More impressive are the many inference forms that illustrate more complex logical inference rules, like *modus tollens* (which are rarely observed in laboratory studies of deductive reasoning).

P1. If Johnson was afraid of Caldwell he would never go back to the scene of the fight (from world knowledge).
P2. *Johnson did go back to the scene of the fight (from evidence).*
C.   Johnson was not afraid (inferential conclusion).

Pennington and Hastie (1993) used a taxonomy to describe inference procedures based on a system proposed by Allan Collins and his colleagues (Collins and Michalski 1989). The Collins' system is an elaboration of traditional logical inference rule systems (see Rips [1983, 1994] for a comprehensive theory of inference processes). Pennington and Hastie proposed that inference rules are the primary tools for the construction, interpretation, and application of an explanatory mental model to perform an overarching decision task (cf., this proposal may be a partial resolution of the dispute between Johnson-Laird and Byrne 1991, versus Rips 1986, 1989).

What additional kinds of judgment capacities do we want to add to the elementary inference capacities Pennington and Hastie have proposed? Saks and Kidd (1980) were among the first to present legal examples of heuristic reasoning (based on Tversky and Kahneman's [1974] collection of heuristics for judgment under uncertainty). They suggested that reasoning by representativeness (similarity) diverted jurors' attention from statistical evidence as they relied on person stereotypes to judge dangerousness and other traits and mental states of witnesses, victims, and defendants. They noted that reasoning based on availability might explain why graphic evidence has greater impact than pallid conceptual or statistical evidence on jurors' decisions (e.g., the apparently large impact of case-based expert vignettes versus scientific evidence in attributions of legal liability to companies manufacturing breast implants). They also noted that some rules of evidence seem to underestimate the probative value of statistical evidence (see also Koehler 2001; Wells 1992).

Rachlinski (2004) provides more examples of heuristic processes in legal judgments. For example, he suggests that the fundamental attribution error (which is often attributed to reliance on an anchor-and-adjust judgment procedure; Jones 1979) affects the evaluation of confession evidence, judgments of a defendant's mental state, and more generally responsibility for injury and damage. He cites additional examples of demonstrations that ad damnum requests and caps on damage awards can act as anchors and "attract" juror award judgments. Rachlinski cites examples of poor reasoning with probabilistic evidence and suggests that mathematically important base rates are frequently neglected (e.g., in assessing DNA evidence; expert predictions of violence; and inferences of causality based on indirect evidence that injury does not occur when reasonable care is provided, absent evidence of different probabilities of injury with versus without reasonable care). He documents examples of the effects of the context of alternative verdicts in the jurors' or judges' choice set on verdict choices. When more severe alternatives were available (e.g., first degree murder), more serious verdicts were chosen (e.g., Kelman et al. 1996; Koch and Devine 1999). Rachlinski (and Saks and Kidd, above) cite hindsight as a common problem for jurors asked to assess the causal and moral responsibility of defendants for plaintiffs' injuries. Finally, Rachlinski cites several studies demonstrating effects of conceptual categories on damage award magnitudes, especially the confusion of judgments of magnitude of fault and magnitude of injury (Anderson and MacCoun 1999; Poser et al. 2003; Darley and Huff 1990; Greene et al. 1999, 2001; Robbenholt 2002).

Gigerenzer (this volume) and Hertwig (this volume) suggest several fast and frugal heuristic procedures that may underlie legal judgments. Lindsey et al.

(2003) found that law students and legal professionals were confused by DNA match evidence presented in a probability format, but that erroneous conclusions were reduced when a frequency format was adopted. However, no specific fast and frugal judgment process is proposed, rather the focus is on amelioration of the errors with better evidence formats. Both Gigerenzer and Hertwig cite Dhami and Ayton's (2001) study of British magistrate's bail-setting judgments. In these decisions, magistrates relied on one or two cues from the cases, with the heaviest reliance on the prosecutor's recommendation (for a similar result, see Ebbesen and Konecni 1975), similar to the Take The Best judgment strategy proposed by Gigerenzer (2004). And, both interpret this finding as an illustration of a social "buck-passing;" Dhami and Ayton called it the "matching heuristic." Goldman (2002) also proposes that fast and frugal inferences may underlie many evidence-based legal decisions. He speculates that a Take The Best heuristic may describe jurors' judgments of eyewitness reliability, criminal confessions, police testimony, and expert testimony.

These reviews provide an interesting collection of possible heuristic judgment processes in legal tasks. However, it is important to notice that there is empirical evidence for only a few *heuristic processes*. As Rachlinski notes there are many examples of "anchor effects" in legal judgments, especially damage award assessments. Dhami and Ayton make an empirical case for their fast and frugal "matching heuristic." But, those seem to be the only judgment heuristics that have been empirically identified in legal judgments. Several of other judgment phenomena, that have been shown to occur, are not individual heuristics, but rather behavioral patterns. Thus, we cannot count demonstrations of verdict context effects, statistical reasoning errors, and hindsight effects as evidence for the operation of specific cognitive heuristics. This is not to deny that a heuristic interpretation is appropriate, just that none has been identified by behavioral research. In fact, the best interpretation we know for hindsight effects is that they are the result of the multitude of coherence-creating inferences made in a global explanation-based process (Hawkins and Hastie 1990). Finally, Marder (1997) summarized post-trial interviews and found that jurors sometimes claimed that a single witness or one important item of evidence was solely responsible for their verdicts. These remarks are consistent with a Take The Best reasoning process, but are only suggestive without more systematic behavioral evidence.

One reaction to the claim that jurors (and magistrates) rely on heuristic judgments is to say that there is no conflict between these heuristic judgments and the story model. Pennington and Hastie proposed that many inferences and assessments of uncertainty and confidence occurred *in the course of* constructing and evaluating evidence summaries like stories. For example, when set membership relationships are involved in inductive, deductive, abductive, or analogical inference processes, "representativeness" or the typicality of instances or subsets provides one cue to the certainty of conclusions (also, Cherniak 1984; Osherson et al. 1990). Similarly, heuristic errors in reasoning about statistical evidence or anchor effects on damage awards can all be seen as occurring within the larger explanation-based process.

What would be useful would be to see more specific proposals for the role of heuristic reasoning processes. As we just noted, one proposal would be that heuristic processes are among the many processes used in the construction of a causal account, usually a story, of the evidence relevant to the legal decision. Under this interpretation there might be decisive inferences. For example, we might conclude that the decisive inference in a case was the heuristic, similarity-based evaluation of a the credibility of a witness or the choice of a company's annual revenue as an anchor from which to infer damages or reliance on the single "best" cue in assessing responsibility. However, heuristic judgment processes would not have exclusive claim to this role of "decisive inference." The application of a logic-like inference rule could also be decisive. For example, in the Johnson case, the most frequently identified decisive inference underlying First Degree Murder verdicts was a *modus tollens* form: If Johnson was just going out to watch the baseball game, then he would not have carried his 12-inch knife. He was carrying his 12-inch knife; therefore, he was not just going out to watch the baseball game. (Jurors inferred Johnson must have had a special purpose when he went back to the bar and confronted Caldwell. They then went on to make additional commonsense inferences to reach the conclusion that he was carrying the knife in pursuit of the goal of getting revenge on Caldwell for humiliating him earlier in the day.) We would not, however, say that the entire decision process was due to only this inference, any more than we would attribute the victory in a chess match to only one move.

THE POSSIBILITY OF SOLELY HEURISTIC LEGAL DECISIONS

A more radical proposal is that sometimes heuristic judgments are the sole cause of a decision. Perhaps verdicts are determined by a unitary, simple inference process. Perhaps at some point in the evaluation of the evidence, the decision maker makes a verdict decision by relying on one simple fast and frugal heuristic process. The most common example of such a process in legal decisions would be a prejudice-based decision. Maybe, in some cases, jurors (and judges) ignore the evidence and make a judgment based almost solely on the defendant's (or other party's) social category membership. For example, as the trial starts, a white juror observes an African American defendant and experiences a strong negative emotion-laden reaction. On the basis of prejudice against African Americans, the juror concludes that the defendant is guilty. At this point the decision process is essentially complete. (The juror's conclusion is probably not absolutely irrevocable. If sufficient exonerating evidence were presented, for example, the proverbial alibi from a convent of nuns, the decision maker would change the outcome. However, absent strong counterevidence, the decision process would be a fast and frugal, one-step process.)[1]

Legal authorities have been concerned about the role of prejudice for a long time and many procedures and instructions are designed to mitigate the potential effects of prejudice against parties at trial. Let's take a closer look at the nature of implicit prejudice. For present purposes we will focus on the universal problem of the potential for race-based prejudices in legal judgments, but there are many other social prejudices that might serve as the basis for a unitary heuristic judgment (gender, age, gang membership, profession, corporate identity, etc.).

Psychology regards prejudice as a negative attitude toward a social group; a negative evaluation of the members of a group which stems from negative feelings and beliefs associated with the group. Psychologists often assume these feelings and beliefs are unwarranted by facts of everyday experience, and to be rigid, stable, and resistant to counter-belief evidence. Prejudiced attitudes can influence a person's judgments and behavior toward members of the group and thus lead to discrimination. Much like legal conceptions of discrimination, this influence of prejudice on behavior has traditionally been thought to result from a person's deliberate consideration of his or her attitudes. However, in light of recent research on the role of awareness and intentional control in cognitive processing, this perspective has shifted or, at least, become significantly more differentiated. Psychological research on implicit prejudice has been accelerated by the invention of procedures to assess implicit, automatic influences of prejudiced attitudes (see Fazio 2001). The two most widely used measures are the so-called Bona Fide Pipeline procedure and the Implicit Associations Test.

Here is one perspective on the nature of implicit prejudice. (The present conceptualization borrows from many current formulations, but it should be attributed to the authors only; cf., N.H. Anderson 1996; Fazio 1990; Greenwald et al.

---

[1]   Under this interpretation, as noted above, stories that are constructed concomitantly with or after the essential decision process could be an epiphenomenon. Pennington and Hastie's demonstrations that manipulating story structure has an impact on the decision would need to be discounted, perhaps by arguing that they are not generalizable. For example, a critic could argue that Pennington and Hastie put *mock* jurors on their best behavior, and, when people know they are being observed, they were likely to rely on stories to make their decisions. However, story-based decisions are not the norm outside of experiments. Similar arguments would be made against Wagenaar et al.'s (1993) conclusions about trial judges. After all, their analysis is based almost exclusively on the contents of judges' justifications of their decisions, written after the decisions were made.

Gigerenzer (this volume) makes an interesting observation, vis-à-vis the extensive reliance on think-aloud self-reports by story model researchers. He notes that magistrates in Dhami and Ayton's (2001) studies of bail setting lacked insight into their own policies (i.e., there was a substantial discrepancy between their implicit judgment policies, as captured by the frugal "matching heuristic," and their explicit rankings of cue importance) and appeared to review a lot of information about the cases which had no impact on their decisions. The implication is that story model researchers may be fooling themselves by relying too heavily on verbal reports of the decision processes.

2002; Tourangeau and Rasinski 1988; Wheeler and Petty 2001; Wilson et al. 2000; and others.)

1. Our experiences deposit knowledge, opinions, and evaluations of social groups in our minds (we will refer to all of this mental material as "information").

2. This information can be described as residing in an extensive associative network in long-term memory. But, at any moment, a sample of the larger corpus of information relevant to our current goals and circumstances is actively available in working memory.

3. Upon encountering a group member, some information stored in memory is activated. This activation is automatic. It requires no intentional consideration of one's memory contents. Its effects may remain outside of the person's conscious awareness. If a summary evaluation of the group has already been consolidated in a person's memory, then this will be activated (e.g., members of group X—"I don't like them"). Other information may be spontaneously activated in addition to this evaluation (e.g., members of group X—"dangerous"). Under conditions where cognitive processing is limited, the evaluative implications of these automatically retrieved associations will be the primary determinants of the person's response (e.g., if a person is engaged in a demanding cognitive task at the same time as a judgment or action is required, the influence of automatically activated, perhaps unconscious information, will be amplified).

    When there is opportunity and motivation to do so, a deliberation stage can also occur. During this stage an intentional, controlled memory search is undertaken to retrieve associations that might be relevant to the group. These retrieved associations may then affect a subsequent response (e.g., members of group X—"face a lot of obstacles;" some members of group X—"are exemplary"). During the deliberation phase, social normative and strategic information may also be retrieved, and these may affect the response (e.g., "group membership should not bias my judgment").

    What information is activated from memory varies to a significant degree from context to context. For example, people's thoughts relevant to African Americans are different if they have just finished watching a news report of Rodney King's arrest for wife beating versus a report on the peace process in the Middle East from Secretary of State Colin Powell versus a report on author Toni Morrison's receipt of the Nobel Prize for Literature versus an interview with tennis star Serena Williams. Both implicit *and* explicit influences can vary as a result of such contextual factors.

4. Finally, the information is integrated into a single judgment or overt behavior. This stage can be further influenced by social goals of being

strategic in presenting oneself in particular ways to others ("Don't act like a bigot"). Thus a person's overt behavior and judgments may reflect explicit influences of his or her attitudes (through deliberate retrieval of information from memory) as well as implicit influences through spontaneous, unmonitored memory activation. Many social judgments and behaviors involve a combination of both types of influences.

In summary, the fast, automatic, affect-laden implicit prejudice response is a good candidate for a fast and frugal heuristic, and one that could plausibly serve as a unique, unitary basis for a legal decision. In fact, similar responses have already been dubbed the "affect heuristic" (e.g., Slovic et al. 2002). There is good reason to believe that there may be an evolutionarily selected, genetically conveyed habit to make quick ingroup/outgroup evaluative judgments and to act on them (e.g., Cosmides et al. 2003; Hargreaves-Heap and Varoufakis 2002).

What would a model of the affect heuristic (or the "prejudice heuristic") look like? The structure of such a model would be analogous to the structure of the recognition heuristic proposed by Goldstein and Gigerenzer (2002). The notion is that whenever a new person is encountered, a primitive memory retrieval process produces an evaluative response (probably in parallel with and perhaps even a bit faster than the automatic recognition, "I've seen him before" response). The automatic evaluative response is based on the positive–negative valence of past experiences with the person, similar persons, and persons from the same social categories (Zajonc 1984; see Zola-Morgan et al. [1991] for a neural analysis of the emotional response system). Just as the recognition response is used to make judgments, when more valid cues are unavailable, the affect response is used to make judgments of evaluatively toned criteria such as guilt–innocence, good-employee–poor-employee, etc.

Another precedent for a fast, emotion-laden judgment heuristic comes from research supporting the "social intuitionist model" for moral judgments (Haidt 2001). Some of Haidt's examples of moral judgments are very close to legally relevant judgments ("Is incest immoral?"). The central claim of his social-intuitionist model is that moral judgment is caused by quick moral intuitions and is followed (when needed) by slow, *ex post facto* moral reasoning. He does not claim that all moral judgments are exclusively intuitive, but he does argue that most are.

Haidt's primary evidence for intuitionist moral judgments come from examples of "moral dumbfounding" cases in which people have strong (usually negative) moral evaluations, but are unable to provide articulate reasons for these evaluations. "I just know incest is bad, but I can't tell you exactly what's wrong with it." Of course, in a legal trial, with an emphasis on fact-finding, and with parties presenting their strongest competing cases, decision makers are unlikely to appear to be "dumbfounded." They will have plenty of readily available arguments for whatever conclusion they endorse. However, this does not mean that a fast and frugal intuitionist process is not the true source of their decision. Decision makers may even be fooling themselves with *post hoc* confabulations to explain their verdicts to themselves (and to others).

What do we know from behavioral research about the role of implicit prejudices in legal decisions? The most substantial research we have is a series of experiments by Sommers and Ellsworth (2000, 2001) in which white college students judged cases with white or black defendants. Their conclusion was surprising, but consistent with our brief sketch of a theory of implicit prejudice (above). When race issues were blatant in the to-be-judged case (e.g., in the critical incident in the case, a person refers to the defendant's race), there was no evidence for anti-black, race-based prejudice in the verdict or punishment judgments. However, when the defendant was black, but race was *not* salient in the incident, there were differential judgments, with black defendants receiving more punitive treatment.

These findings are consistent with a dual-process system: a quick automatic "affect heuristic" judgment that can be corrected or overridden by a secondary, deliberative, controlled process. However, like all juror decision-making studies of which we are aware, these studies do not find strong evidence for a simple, dominant decision process, like a unitary heuristic judgment. In fact, the judgment is most likely to be a mixture of intuitive and deliberate processes. For example, within a story construction process, the implicit prejudicial responses may bias inferences attributing responsibility to one party or another, or bias the interpretation of an action based on an incomplete verbal description by a witness (cf. Wittenbrink et al. 1997).

Still, we are open to the possibility of legal decisions that are dominated by unitary fast and frugal heuristic processes. However, we think it is important to lay some theoretical groundwork before making strong claims. In what kind of overarching decision process do the heuristics operate? What does it mean to claim that a simple, unitary heuristic is the sole (or dominant) cause of a decision? We have nominated our favorite candidate for such a process: fast and frugal prejudice. Still, even here we are unsure of the causal status of such a process. Is it reasonable to assign it a unique, dominant causal role? Or is it best described as a biasing factor within an essentially deliberative decision process? At present we believe that there is scant behavioral evidence for the occurrence of dominant fast and frugal decision processes. What kind of empirical test could provide persuasive support for the causally distinctive role of a fast and frugal heuristic judgment process?

Finally, in contrast to many examples (e.g., Haidt's evidence for intuitive moral judgments), American legal decisions occur within a context in which procedures are in place, specifically designed to make the decision process deliberative and controlled. For example, jurors are repeatedly admonished not to rely on intuitive judgment habits or to use cues such as the defendant's race. They are prevented from hearing relevant (perhaps "best cue") evidence such as information about a defendant's record of past crimes. They are given careful instructions on presumptions and standards of proof. They are even given instructions on some inferences they should and should not draw. And, finally, they are instructed to consider alternative views on the verdict and group decision rules (e.g., super-majority and unanimity requirements) force them to pay special heed to unpopular views. All of these conditions are aimed to reduce legal decision makers' reliance on solely heuristic judgment habits. But, of course, none of these measures are guaranteed to prevent fast and frugal decisions.

REFERENCES

Ahn, W.-K., C.W. Kalish, D.L. Medin, and S.A. Gelman. 1995. The role of covariation versus mechanism information in causal attribution. *Cognition* **54**:299–352.

Amsterdam, A.G., and J.S. Bruner. 2000. Minding the Law. Cambridge, MA: Harvard Univ. Press.

Anderson, M.C., and R.J. MacCoun. 1999. Goal conflict in juror assessments of compensatory and punitive damages. *Law Hum. Behav.* **23**:313–330.

Anderson, N.H. 1996. A Functional Theory of Cognition. Hillsdale, NJ: Erlbaum.

Anderson, T.J., and W. Twining. 1991. Analysis of Evidence. Boston: Little Brown.

Axelrod, R., ed. 1976. Structure of Decision: The Cognitive Maps of Political Elites. Princeton, NJ: Princeton Univ. Press.

Bennett, W.L., and M.S. Feldman. 1981. Reconstructing Reality in the Courtroom: Justice and Judgment in American Culture. New Brunswick, NJ: Rutgers Univ. Press.

Bostrom, A., B. Fischhoff, and G. Morgan. 1992. Characterizing mental models of hazardous processes: A methodology and an application to radon. *J. Soc. Iss.* **48**:85–100.

Buehler, R., D. Griffin, and M. Ross. 2002. Inside the planning fallacy: The causes and consequences of optimistic time predictions. In: Heuristics and Biases: The Psychology of Intuitive Judgment, ed. T. Gilovich, D. Griffin, and D. Kahneman, pp. 250–270. New York: Cambridge Univ. Press.

Charniak, E. 1991. Bayesian networks without tears. *AI Mag.* **12**:50–63.

Cherniak, C. 1984. Prototypicality and deductive reasoning. *J. Verb. Learn. Behav.* **23**:625–642.

Collins, A., and R. Michalski. 1989. The logic of plausible reasoning: A core theory. *Cog. Sci.* **13**:1–49.

Cosmides, L., J. Tooby, and R. Kurzban. 2003. Perceptions of race. *Trends Cog. Sci.* **7**:173–179.

Darley, J.M., and C. Huff. 1990. Heightened damage assessment as a result of the intentionality of the damage-causing act. *Brit. J. Soc. Psychol.* **29**:181–188.

DeKleer, J., and J.S. Brown. 1983. Assumptions and ambiguities in mechanistic mental models. In: Mental Models, ed. D. Gentner and A.L. Stevens, pp. 155–190. Hillsdale, NJ: Erlbaum.

Dhami, M.K., and P. Ayton. 2001. Bailing and jailing the fast and frugal way. *J. Behav. Dec. Mak.* **14**:141–168.

Ebbesen, E.B., and V.J. Konecni. 1975. Decision making and information integration in the courts: The setting of bail. *J. Pers. Soc. Psychol.* **32**:805–821.

Einhorn, H.J., and R.M. Hogarth. 1986. Judging probable cause. *Psychol. Bull.* **99**:3–19.

Elwork, A., J.J. Alfini, and B.D. Sales. 1987. Toward understandable jury instructions. In: In the Jury Box: Controversies in the Courtroom, ed. L.S. Wrightsman, S.M. Kassin, and C.E. Willis, pp. 161–179. Thousand Oaks, CA: Sage.

Fazio, R.H. 1990. Multiple processes by which attitudes guide behavior: The Mode Model as an integrative framework. *Adv. Exp. Soc. Psychol.* **23**:75–109.

Fazio, R.H. 2001. On the automatic activation of associated evaluations: An overview. *Cog. Emot.* **15**:115–141.

Gigerenzer, G. 2004. Striking a blow for sanity in theories of rationality. In: Models of a Man: Essays in Memory of Herbert A. Simon, ed. M. Augier and J.G. March, pp. 389–409. Cambridge, MA: MIT Press.

Goldman, A. 2002. Quasi-objective Bayesianism and legal evidence. *Jurimetrics* **42**: 108–129.

Goldstein, D.G., and G. Gigerenzer. 2002. Models of ecological rationality: The recognition heuristic. *Psychol. Rev.* **109**:75–90.

Greene, E., D. Coon, and G. Bornstein. 2001. The effects of limiting punitive damage awards. *Law Hum. Behav.* **25**:215–232.

Greene, E., M. Johns, and J. Bowman. 1999. The effects of injury severity on jury negligence decisions. *Law Hum. Behav.* **23**:675–693.

Greenwald, A.G., M.R. Banaji, L.A. Rudman et al. 2002. A unified theory of implicit attitudes, stereotypes, self-esteem, and self-concept. *Psychol. Rev.* **109**:3–25.

Haidt, J. 2001. The emotional dog and its rational tail: A social intuitionist approach to moral judgment. *Psychol. Rev.* **108**:814–834.

Hargreaves-Heap, S., and Y. Varoufakis. 2002. Some experimental evidence on the evolution of discrimination, co-operation, and perceptions of fairness. *Econ. J.* **112**:679–703.

Hastie, R., ed. 1993. Inside the Juror. New York: Cambridge Univ. Press.

Hastie, R. 1999. The role of "stories" in civil jury judgments. *Michigan J. Law Reform* **32**:1–13.

Hastie, R. 2001. Emotions in jurors' decisions. *Brooklyn Law Rev.* **66**:991–1009.

Hastie, R., and N. Pennington. 1994. Review of the book *Anchored Narratives: The Psychology of Criminal Evidence*. *J. Behav. Dec. Mak.* **7**:293–296.

Hastie, R., and N. Pennington. 1995. The big picture: Is it a story? In: Knowledge and Memory: The Real Story, ed. R.S. Wyer, Jr. and J.K. Srull, pp. 133–138. Hillsdale, NJ: Erlbaum.

Hastie, R., and N. Pennington. 1996. The O.J. Simpson stories: Behavioral scientists look at *The People v. O.J. Simpson* trial. *Univ.of Colorado Law Rev.* **67**:957–976.

Hastie, R., and N. Pennington. 2000. Explanation-based decision making. In: Judgment and Decision Making: An Interdisciplinary Reader, ed. T. Connolly, H.R. Arkes, and K.R. Hammond, 2d ed., pp. 212–228. New York: Cambridge Univ. Press.

Hastie, R., S.D. Penrod, and N. Pennington. 1983. Inside the Jury. Cambridge, MA: Harvard Univ. Press.

Hawkins, S.A., and R. Hastie. 1990. Hindsight: Biased judgments of past events after the outcomes are known. *Psychol. Bull.* **107**:311–327.

Hogarth, R.M., C. Michaud, and J.L. Mery. 1980. Decision behavior in an urban development: A methodological approach and substantive considerations. *Acta Psychologica* **45**:95–117.

Johnson-Laird, P.N., and R.M.J. Byrne. 1991. Deduction. Hillsdale, NJ: Erlbaum.

Jones, E.E. 1979. The rocky road from acts to dispositions. *Am. Psychol.* **34**:107–117.

Jou, J., J. Shanteau, and R.J. Harris. 1996. An information processing view of framing effects: The role of causal schemas in decision making. *Mem. Cogn.* **24**:1–15.

Kaplan, J. 1978. Criminal Justice: Introductory Cases and Materials. 2d ed. Mineola, NY: Foundation Press.

Keil, F.C., and R.A. Wilson. 2000. Explanation and Cognition. Cambridge, MA: MIT Press.

Kelman, M., Y. Rottenstreich, and A. Tversky. 1996. Context-dependence in legal decision making. *J. Legal Stud.* **25**:287–318.

Kintsch, W. 1998. Comprehension: A Paradigm for Cognition. New York: Cambridge Univ. Press.

Klein, G.A., J. Orasanu, R. Calderwood, and C.E. Zsambok, eds. 1993. Decision Making in Action: Models and Methods. Norwood, NJ: Ablex.

Koch, C.M., and D.J. Devine. 1999. Effects of reasonable doubt definition and inclusion of a lesser charge on jury verdicts. *Law Hum. Behav.* **23**:653–674.

Koehler, J.J. 2001. When are people persuaded by DNA match statistics? [References]. *Law Hum. Behav.* **25**:493–513.

Lewis, C.H. 1988. Why and how to learn why: Analysis-based generalization of procedures. *Cog. Sci.* **12**:211–256.

Lindsey, S., R. Hertwig, and G. Gigerenzer. 2003. Communicating statistical DNA evidence. *Jurimetrics* **43**:147–163.

Mandler, J.M. 1984. Stories, Scripts and Scenes: Aspects of Schema Theory. Hillsdale, NJ: Erlbaum.

Marder, N.S. 1997. Deliberations and disclosures: A study of post-verdict interviews with jurors. *Iowa Law Rev.* **82**:465–546.

McKenzie, C.R.M., S.M. Lee, and K.K. Chen. 2002. When negative evidence increases confidence: Change in belief after hearing two sides of a dispute. *J. Behav. Dec. Mak.* **15**:1–18.

Moore, A.J. 1989. Trial by schema: Cognitive filters in the courtroom. *UCLA Law Rev.* **37**:273–341.

Murphy, G.L., and D.L. Medin. 1985. The role of theories in conceptual coherence. *Psychol. Rev.* **92**:289–316.

Osherson, D.N., E.E. Smith, O. Wilkie, A. Lopez, and E. Shafir. 1990. Category-based induction. *Psychol. Rev.* **97**:185–200.

Patel, V.L., and G.J. Groen. 1991. The general and specific nature of medical expertise: A critical look. In: Toward a General Theory of Expertise: Prospects and Limits, ed. K.A. Ericsson and J. Smith, pp. 93–125. New York: Cambridge Univ. Press.

Pennington, N., and R. Hastie. 1981. Juror decision-making models: The generalization gap. *Psychol. Bull.* **89**:246–287.

Pennington, N., and R. Hastie. 1986. Evidence evaluation in complex decision making. *J. Pers. Soc. Psychol.* **51**:242–258.

Pennington, N., and R. Hastie. 1988. Explanation-based decision making: Effects of memory structure on judgment. *J. Exp. Psychol.: Learn. Mem. Cog.* **14**:521–533.

Pennington, N., and R. Hastie. 1991. A cognitive theory of juror decision making: The story model. *Cardozo Law Rev.* **13**:519–557.

Pennington, N., and R. Hastie. 1992. Explaining the evidence: Tests of the story model for juror decision making. *J. Pers. Soc. Psychol.* **62**:189–206.

Pennington, N., and R. Hastie. 1993. Reasoning in explanation-based decision making. *Cognition* **49**:123–163.

Poser, S., B.H. Bornstein, and E.K. McGorty. 2003. Measuring damages for lost enjoyment of life: The view from the bench and the jury box. *Law Hum. Behav.* **27**:53–68.

Rachlinski, J.J. 2004. Heuristics, biases, and governance. In: Blackwell Handbook of Judgment and Decision Making, ed. D.J. Koehler and N. Harvey, pp. 567–603. New York: Blackwell.

Rehder, B., and R. Hastie. 2001. Causal knowledge and categories: The effects of underlying causal beliefs on categorization, induction, and similarity. *J. Exp. Psychol. Gen.* **130**:323–360.

Rips, L.J. 1983. Cognitive processes in propositional reasoning. *Psychol. Rev.* **90**:38–71.

Rips, L.J. 1986. Mental muddles. In: The Representation of Knowledge and Belief, ed. M. Brand and R.M. Harnish, pp. 128–141. Tucson: Univ. of Arizona Press.

Rips, L.J. 1989. The psychology of knights and knaves. *Cognition* **31**:85–116.

Rips, L.J. 1994. The Psychology of Proof: Deductive Reasoning in Human Thinking. Cambridge, MA: MIT Press.

Robbenholt, J.K. 2002. Punitive damages decision making: The decisions of citizens and trial court judges. *Law Hum. Behav.* **26**:315–341.

Rumelhart, D.E. 1977. Understanding and summarizing brief stories. In: Basic Processes in Reading: Perception and Comprehension, ed. D. LaBerge and S.J. Samuels, pp. 265–303. Hillsdale, NJ: Erlbaum.

Saks, M.J., and R.F. Kidd. 1980. Human information processing and adjudication: Trial by heuristics. *Law Soc. Rev.* **15**:123–160.

Schank, R.C. 1975. The structure of episodes in memory. In: Representation and Understanding: Studies in Cognitive Science, ed. D.G. Bobrow and A. Collins, pp. 237–272. New York: Academic.

Schank, R.C., and R.P. Abelson. 1977. Scripts, Plans, Goals, and Understanding. Hillsdale, NJ: Erlbaum.

Schank, R.C., and R.P. Abelson. 1995. Knowledge and memory: The real story. In: Knowledge and Memory: The Real Story, ed. R.S. Wyer, Jr., pp. 1–86. Hillsdale, NJ: Erlbaum.

Schank, R.C., G.C. Collins, and L.E. Hunter. 1986. Transcending inductive category formation in learning. *Behav. Brain Sci.* **9**:639–686.

Schum, D.A., and A.W. Martin. 1982. Formal and empirical research on cascaded inference in jurisprudence. *Law Soc. Rev.* **17**:105–151.

Sevon, G. 1984. Cognitive maps of past and future economic events. *Acta Psychologica* **56**:71–79.

Simon, D., and K.J. Holyoak. 2002. Structural dynamics of cognition: From consistency theories to constraint satisfaction. *Pers. Soc. Psychol. Rev.* **6**:283–294.

Sloman, S.A., D. Over, L. Slovak, and J.M. Stibel. 2003. Frequency illusions and other fallacies. *Org. Behav. Hum. Dec. Proc.* **91**:296–309.

Slovic, P., M. Finucane, E. Peters, and D.G. MacGregor. 2002. The affect heuristic. In: Heuristics and Biases: The Psychology of Intuitive Judgment, ed. T. Gilovich, D. Griffin, and D. Kahneman, pp. 397–420. New York: Cambridge Univ. Press.

Smith, E.E., C. Langston, and R.E. Nisbett. 1992. The case for rules in reasoning. *Cog. Sci.* **16**:99–112.

Smith, V.L. 1991. Prototypes in the courtroom: Lay representations of legal concepts. *J. Pers. Soc. Psychol.* **61**:857–872.

Sommers, S.R., and P.C. Ellsworth. 2000. Race in the courtroom: Perceptions of guilt and dispositional attributions. *Pers. Soc. Psychol. Bull.* **26**:1367–1379.

Sommers, S.R., and P.C. Ellsworth. 2001. White juror bias: An investigation of prejudice against Black defendants in the American courtroom. *Psychol. Publ. Pol. Law* 7:201–229.

Stein, N.L., and C.G. Glenn. 1979. An analysis of story comprehension in elementary school children. In: New Directions in Discourse Processing, ed. R.O. Freedle, vol. 2, pp. 83–107. Norwood, NJ: Ablex.

Tourangeau, R., and K.A. Rasinski. 1988. Cognitive processes underlying context effects in attitude measurement. *Psychol. Bull.* 103:299–314.

Trabasso, T., and J. Bartolone. 2003. Story understanding and counterfactual reasoning. *J. Exp. Psychol.: Learn. Mem. Cog.* 29:904–923.

Trabasso, T., and L.L. Sperry. 1985. Causal relatedness and importance of story events. *J. Mem. Lang.* 24:595–611.

Trabasso, T., and P. van den Broek. 1985. Causal thinking and the representation of narrative events. *J. Mem. Lang.* 24:612–630.

Tversky, A., and D. Kahneman. 1974. Judgment under uncertainty: Heuristics and biases. *Science* 185:1124–1131.

Van Wallendael, L.R. 1989. The quest for limits on noncomplementarity in opinion revision. *Org. Behav. Hum. Dec. Proc.* 43:385–405.

Wagenaar, W.A., P.J.J. van Koppen, and H.F.M. Crombag. 1993. Anchored Narratives: The Psychology of Criminal Evidence. London: Harvester Wheatsheaf.

Wells, G.L. 1992. Naked statistical evidence of liability: Is subjective probability enough? *J. Pers. Soc. Psychol.* 62:739–752.

Wheeler, S.C., and R.E. Petty. 2001. The effects of stereotype activation on behavior: A review of possible mechanisms. *Psychol. Bull.* 127:797–826.

Wigmore, J.H. 1937. The Science of Judicial Proof, as Given by Logic, Psychology, and General Experience, and Illustrated in Judicial Trials. 3d ed. Boston: Little Brown.

Wilensky, R. 1983. Planning and Understanding: A Computational Approach to Human Reasoning. Reading, MA: Addison-Wesley.

Wilson, T.D., S. Lindsey, and T.Y. Schooler. 2000. A model of dual attitudes. *Psychol. Rev.* 107:101–126.

Wittenbrink, B., P.L. Gist, and J.L. Hilton. 1997. Structural properties of stereotypic knowledge and their influences on the construal of social situations. *J. Pers. Soc. Psychol.* 72:526–543.

Zajonc, R.B. 1984. On the primacy of affect. *Am. Psychol.* 39:117–124.

Zola-Morgan, S., L.R. Squire, P. Avarez-Royo, and R.P. Clower. 1991. Independence of memory functions and emotional behavior: Separate contributions of the hippocampal formation and the amygdala. *Hippocampus* 1:207–220.

13

Heuristics in Procedural Law

Gerhard Wagner

Institute of Civil Procedure, Rheinische Friedrich-Wilhelms
University, 53113 Bonn, Germany

ABSTRACT

Courts lack access to the "objective truth." Therefore, they have to reconstruct the facts of the case from the pieces of information put in evidence by the parties. This task is anything but easy. The law has always taken account of these problems and developed its rules and requirements with an eye toward the informational constraints a decision maker inevitably faces when presented with contested questions of fact. More often than not, the law takes an "indirect" approach toward the facts which are really relevant, relying on circumstances which are easy to verify rather than on complex requirements saturated with subjectivity.

This chapter explores some techniques of fact-finding in civil practice, drawing on examples mainly taken from the German legal system. The subject matter areas covered include contract law, family law, medical malpractice, and the law of evidence in general. As it turns out, even with respect to a single factual requirement, courts work with relatively complex and multi-layered sets of specific decision rules rather than with one single "fast and frugal" heuristic. Whether this practice may still qualify as employing heuristics depends on which concept of heuristics is used and remains a matter for debate.

THE IMPOSSIBILITY OF OPTIMIZATION

Only a relatively small fraction of transactions and disputes ends up in a court of law. In the overwhelming majority of cases, legal obligations are discharged voluntarily. In this relatively small fraction, but absolutely high number of cases that do end up in court, the success of the claim is contingent on a set of legal requirements which in turn refer to certain factual situations. To enter into a decision and dispose of the dispute one way or another, the judge or judges involved have to make up their minds as to whether the requisite facts have been established or not. Obviously, this is a task that is anything but easy to perform. In the familiar case of a tort suit growing out of a motor accident, the judge will not have been present at the sight of the accident when it occurred and thus will not have observed what happened. Even if he knew what "happened," uncertainties might remain. Under the motor accident example, the decision maker may be unable to conclude whether the defendant could have stopped his car before hitting the plaintiff's vehicle or whether under the particular circumstances there was no such chance. To settle these issues, the court needs to know, for example, the braking distance of the defendant's car as well as the speed of the vehicle at the time the defendant was able to depict the plaintiff.

Given that the judges themselves do not observe the relevant facts, it is inevitable for them to rely on "second-hand" accounts of reality. The court may hear witnesses (i.e., people who happened to have observed the historical situation relevant to the resolution of the case) and it may employ experts who give advice in the evaluation of the facts or investigate them with the help of their expertise. Even in very simple cases, these tasks—if taken seriously—are extremely difficult to perform. It is part of the human condition that the "truth" is hard to establish: witnesses may not be available, they may fall prey to their particular interests and perspectives, they may have forgotten what happened but be unable to be honest about that, they may have told the story so many times to friends and relatives that it is impossible for them to find a way back to the original version. There is a traditional proverb in German that states that there is a vast difference between having an entitlement to something and being able to enforce that entitlement in court. In addition, most practitioners confirm the view that the outcome of the overwhelming number of disputes depends on the resolution of the factual issues—not of the legal ones. All too often, to win or to lose is not a matter of the substantive law but of the success or failure to prove the relevant facts.

These difficulties are serious but still nothing to bemoan. It is a hallmark of modern legal systems that the decision maker is a neutral and disinterested person who has never been in touch with the dispute or its factual foundation before it ends up in his court. In this sense, ignorance of the facts is by no means regrettable but something that qualifies a person to serve as a decision maker.

THE STANDARD OF PROOF

For the outcome of practical cases, the importance of the law of evidence—or rather, the process and rules of fact gathering —can hardly be underestimated. Given the uncertainties and complexities involved in any attempt to establish the "truth," even the idea of optimization—in the sense of the attempt to maximize the fit between the findings of the court and reality, or rather history—seems misplaced or even absurd. In most cases it is simply impossible for a court to really "establish" the "truth" in any meaningful sense, and in most disputes trying to achieve this goal would entail prohibitive costs. Instead of working toward an illusion, the law and practice of procedure and evidence follow a pragmatic model, aiming at a situation where it may reasonably be determined which pieces of information brought before the court are reliable enough to support a decision in one direction or the other.

A simple illustration is the standard of proof applied to civil cases in both the United States and in Germany. In the U.S., standard of proof differs in criminal and in civil cases. Conviction of the offender requires that the court be certain beyond a reasonable doubt that the person accused committed a crime, whereas in civil trials it is sufficient for the plaintiff to succeed if his case appears to be true by the preponderance of the evidence. Thus, the court that hears the civil case may forego efforts at illuminating remaining doubts concerning the factual basis of its decision. It may, instead, content itself with the view that if the truth is unattainable, it is sufficient to take for real those representations that are probably true in the sense of the "more likely than not" test. In contrast, German law does not distinguish between criminal and civil trials but requires certainty beyond a reasonable doubt for both types of trial. However, the application of this standard does not refute the thesis developed here that courts, in their everyday practice, do not aim to establish the truth in an ambitious sense of the term. For one, the beyond-any-reasonable-doubt-standard embodied in Sect. 286 of the German Code of Civil Procedure (ZPO [*Zivilprozeßordnung*]) allows for a broad spectrum of judge-made exceptions, which enables a court to decide hard cases without constant recourse to *non-liquet* decisions. Second, the standard is understood to be subjective— the relevant test is not whether the objective likelihood of the plaintiff's or defendant's case to be true is approaching 1, but only the perception of the individual judge (*Entscheidungen des Bundesgerichtshofs in Zivilsachen* [BGHZ] 53, 245, 255f.; Zöller/Greger 2004, §286 no. 13). If the court "feels" convinced, the facts are thought to have been established "beyond reasonable doubt" (Gottwald 1979; *Alternativkommentar ZPO*/Rüßmann 1987, §286 no. 14 f.). It is this subjective element that allows German courts to operate in much the same way as their American counterparts, even though they may be slightly more reluctant to allow claims (and defenses) than an American court. In concrete cases involving scientific uncertainties that are impossible to clarify (e.g., as is typical in medical malpractice actions), the Federal Supreme Court (BGH) has repeatedly warned the lower courts that they should not exaggerate the standard of proof but operate pragmatically (*Bundesgerichtshof* [BGH] *Versicherungsrecht* [VersR] 1994, 52, 53; Müller 1997; Giesen 1982). It is obvious, then, that even under German law of civil procedure, the "objective truth" is not what the courts are aiming at when evidence is gathered and evaluated.

The question remains as to why German law adheres to a subjective reading of the standard of proof rather than an objective one. The crucial point is, again, the impossibility to come up with a coherent and workable framework for an objective evaluation of the evidence or even for a "calculation" of evidentiary weight. To start, probability theory in its technical sense is of little help to decision makers because they have to deal with unique events, whereas probability refers to the distribution of outcomes over a series of identical trials (Koch and Rüßmann 1982). Thus, there is simply no "probability" that X murdered Y. This truism applies even when "hard" statistical data are available. The grotesque failure of the court in the case of *People v. Collins* (1968) is a good demonstration of the pitfalls inherent in a naïve application of probability theory to the area of judicial decision making.

What might help instead are likelihood calculations, which would allow a decision maker to reason backward and ask how probable a given outcome is, assuming either the presence or the absence of a particular event (cause). Applying Bayesian reasoning, it might be possible to identify formally causes and link them to outcomes (cf. Koch and Rüßmann 1982). Although likelihood calculations seem attractive in theory, they are difficult or even dangerous to operate in practice. This is because repeated likelihood calculations are subject to serious flaws. It is impossible to take circumstantial evidence from various contexts and simply multiply the likelihoods without knowing the correlations between the different pieces of evidence (Koch and Rüßmann 1982). Repeated multiplication of likelihoods is permissible only if the several pieces of circumstantial evidence are perfectly independent from another. Thus, in the area of paternity suits, likelihood calculations are only used after a complex survey of biological data has shown the defendant to be a possible father of the child. The reason for the complexity of the official guidelines to be followed by experts taking the stand in paternity suits[1] has to do with the multitude of biological properties of the would-be father, mother, and child that together determine the likelihood of paternity, and that all of these biological properties of the several individuals are correlated to some degree. In this case, guidelines recommend a multistage procedure that strives to eliminate more than 90% of the male population as possible fathers by way of exclusionary criteria, which are relatively easy to establish and apply. Only after this work has been done can the expert work with priors of equal magnitude to establish that the defendant did or did not father the child. The example of paternity suits may well be generalized, as it is by no means unusual that there is at least some measure of correlation between the different pieces of evidence. In such a situation, to pretend it were otherwise and to start calculating would be deceptive and could lead to incorrect results. Rather than trying to calculate what cannot be calculated, judges follow their intuitions. In other words, they apply a subjective standard of proof.

The same reasoning also explains why German law of civil procedure has been purged from rules of evidence. As Sect. 286, §2, ZPO emphatically provides, the court is not bound by rules of evidence unless the law holds otherwise, which it does only rarely. The underlying belief is that rules of evidence cause more harm than they do good, as reality is much too complex to allow for strict rules to govern the process of decision making. A pertinent example is the ancient rule that the conviction of an offender accused of having committed a

---

[1] *Richtlinien für die Erstattung von Abstammungsgutachten: Novellierung* (1996), *Zeitschrift für das gesamte Familienrecht* (1997); see also Hummel (1981); Koch and Rüßmann (1982); Wagner (2003).

serious crime requires either his admission of guilt or the testimony of two eye-witnesses (Schmoeckel 2000). This heuristic is fast and frugal indeed, but this advantage comes at the price of a high error rate. As every practitioner in the field of criminal law knows, the admissions entered into by suspects do not necessarily correspond to the truth (Schmoeckel 2000). Second, the heuristic creates incentives for a murderer to simply keep his mouth shut, which in turn was the starting point for the infliction of torture (Schmoeckel 2000).

EVIDENCE LAW AS A SYSTEM OF HEURISTICS

In the present context, one needs to ask whether the obvious moderations of evidence law, as exemplified by the preponderance of the evidence standard, count as heuristics. If heuristics are defined as simple (frugal) rules that allow for fast decision making, the answer must be a straightforward "no." The evidentiary standard applied in civil litigation is neither environment specific nor does it enable the court to draw conclusions quickly from a simple set of circumstances. What it does is to create a legal framework in which heuristics may operate. Since the aim of a civil trial is not to establish the objective truth, the court is able to apply heuristics as context-specific parameters to allow decisions to be made on the basis of incomplete information and under serious time constraints. The purpose of the subjective standard of proof is to provide leeway for heuristics to operate.

A pervasive feature of procedural law lies in the fact that it is impossible to maximize the effort when investigating the relevant circumstances. It is neither possible for a court to establish the "objective truth" nor even desirable to try hard, as any attempt to do so would consume time and resources in a disproportionate amount to the value of the dispute. Therefore, procedural law is replete with rules and institutions to enable the court to enter into a decision without having investigated the case to the fullest extent possible. Pertinent examples include general rules of evidence in the style of *"res ipsa loquitur"* (see discussion below under the section, *Res Ipsa Loquitur*), specific institutions tailored to a particular class of cases (e.g., the presumption that in medical malpractice a failure to disclose on the part of the doctor triggers a presumption that the patient would have refused the treatment had he known the risk; see below section on **Presumptions and the Burden of Proof**), and the murky area of the judge's *forum internum*, where the decision maker decides whether a party carried the burden of proof or not. If such rules and institutions may count as heuristics, procedural law would be a bonanza for the present subject.

Such a perception may turn out to be misguided, as not every simplification in the process of decision making that procedural law allows must necessarily be categorized as a heuristic in the technical sense of the term. Important as this admonition may be, it does not seem advisable to explore it at this point of the inquiry in more detail. Instead of doing this and thereby closing the door to a more thorough investigation of the workings of procedural law, it appears to be promising to begin with analyses of particular rules and institutions and ask only subsequently whether one or the other may count as a heuristic in the technical sense of the term or not.

Another caveat should be noted: The boundary between substantive and procedural law is not clear-cut but rather murky and disputed. What in some legal systems counts as a rule of substantive law may be regarded in others as a procedural matter. Furthermore, it is received wisdom that institutions of substantive and procedural law, respectively, may be used as functional equivalents for one and the same legislative purpose. It would thus be artificial to limit the inquiry to rules of procedural nature only. Every rule or institution that helps a court make decisions in spite of the difficulties and imperfections of establishing real-life events must be analyzed for its heuristic power.

SURVEY OF EXAMPLES

Formal Requirements in Contract Law

In the general population, it is common knowledge that "a verbal contract is not worth the paper it is written on," as Samuel Goldwyn once put it (cf. Beale, Bishop et al. 2002, p. 139). However, contrary to popular wisdom, modern law begins with the reverse principle of nonformalism: exceptions aside, even a verbal contract is binding upon the parties.

The principle of consensualism, understood to mean that a promise need not be put in writing or satisfy other formal requirements in order for it to be binding, rests on complex normative foundations which will not be explored in this chapter. It should not go unnoticed, though, that the abstention from the imposition of formal requirements with respect to contract formation has serious consequences not only for the parties but also for the courts. These effects are easy to depict by going through the various reasons advanced for the many exceptions to the principle of consensualism. Among those justificatory objectives, the evidentiary function of formal requirements is well accepted. If the binding force of promises is limited to those put in writing, it is much easier for a court to identify the existence and contents of those promises it is called upon to enforce.

At this point of the inquiry, the first question to ask is whether formal requirements may properly be characterized as heuristics. The answer should be in the affirmative, although it will readily be granted that the heuristic function is not the only one to be guarded by the principle of formality. In a world where every contract must be put into writing in order to be enforceable by law, it is relatively easy for a court to identify those agreements with which it must concern itself. Unless the plaintiff, or another party seeking to enforce rights allegedly growing out of the contract, is in a position to produce the relevant document, no action has transpired and the courts are free to devote their efforts to other cases.

Given that formal requirements are heuristics, what is the "environmental circumstance" that a heuristic is designed to approximate? Quite obviously, it is not only the fact that in reality a contract has been consummated but also, and more importantly, that the parties actually meant what they "said" (i.e., that they acted with the relevant intention to be bound). It is this second requirement for a contract to be perfected and for a contractual obligation to arise that is apt to cause major problems for the courts. It is anything but easy for a plaintiff to establish that the other party actually made the disputed promise, and it is equally difficult when testing facts to make the relevant decision. In the absence of any documentary evidence, the court and parties have no choice but to hear a number of witnesses or even to rely solely on the testimony of the parties themselves. In this situation, the insistence on formal requirements works as a "fast" and "frugal" decision rule: If the plaintiff can produce a document evidencing the disputed transaction, then the court will decide in his favor; if he fails to supply documentary evidence, it will decide in defendant's favor. Thus, the existence of a written document serves as proxy for the fact that the defendant actually made the promise upon which the plaintiff is suing; in other words, the parties actually entered into a contract.

After having celebrated the virtues of formal requirements, let us now turn to the flipside of the issue. A rule that states that promises are enforceable only if they have been put in writing is surely "fast" und "frugal," but these properties also point to its limits. Not every promise that has been put into writing must therefore be valid. Also, the parties may have had good reason *not* to draw up a document, or such a document might have gotten lost or destroyed through no fault of the plaintiff. There is a whole set of legal doctrines (e.g., about mistake, fraud, duress, unconscionability, contracts of adhesion) that address situations in which there is a contract that appears to be valid *prima facie* but may, upon closer inspection, turn out to be defective. These doctrines cannot be explained here in detail. However, it seems worthwhile to acknowledge that they are complex legal institutions whose factual bases are difficult to establish in the context of a legal dispute. Provided that the party interested in overturning its promise succeeds in proving mistake, fraud or the like, the heuristic "contracts which have been put into writing are valid" is pushed aside.

To illustrate this point, imagine that the law would insist on written form across the board. In such a legal environment, a grocery store would have to draw up contracts and hand them out for signature by its customers before a food could be purchased. Costs of such an exercise clearly outweigh the benefits in terms of legal certainty and ease of decision making. Accordingly, no legal system dares to disturb transactions of everyday life, where the attendant obligations have been discharged by both parties. With respect to executory promises, German law is relatively generous as it limits the ambit of formal requirements to contracts which either involve land or are of gratuitous nature only. Even here, defects in formality of a contract may be solved by way of performance (cf.

Sect. 311b, §1, cl. 2, German Civil Code [BGB, *Bürgerliches Gesetzbuch*] [sale of land]; Sect. 518, §2, BGB [gratuitous promises]). With respect to chattels and services, oral agreements are enforced irrespective of the value involved. Likewise, the legal systems under common law require written form for executory promises involving the sale of land and a number of other cases. In addition, §2-201 of the Uniform Commercial Code (UCC) requires written form for the enforcement of promises for the sale of goods priced at $500 or more.

The most interesting solution for the workings of heuristics in the law is found in the French legal system. Article 1341, §1, Code Civil is not a regulation about form but about proof with the help of witnesses (cf. Beale, Hartkamp et al. 2002). It stipulates evidence other than in a written form is not admissible if the value of the subject matter of the disputed contract exceeds a certain amount; currently this has been set at 800 Euros. This restriction on the admissibility of oral evidence, however, becomes invalid when the party interested in enforcing the contract is successful in providing *some* written evidence to suggest that an agreement was perfected, the so-called "*commencement de preuve par écrit,*" as defined in Art. 1347, §1, Code Civil. Translated into the language of heuristics, the two articles of the French Code may be described as an interplay between two fast and frugal rules. The court starts with the assumption that an alleged agreement, which the parties did not care to reduce to writing, was either never entered into or never intended to be seriously binding. This fast and frugal rule of decision, however, fails once some written evidence is produced to suggest that the parties in fact concluded an oral contract. In short, the simple rule that every serious engagement will be put into writing is supplemented by another simple rule opening up the whole spectrum of means of evidence, once there is a little piece of documentary evidence. In 1975, the French Parliament added another exception, holding that the absence of a party summoned by a court to be heard on the subject of contract formation counts as "*commencement de preuve par écrit*" (Art. 1347, §3, Code Civil). The underlying heuristic is obviously based on the notion that a party trying to avoid being questioned by a court has something to hide, which, in turn, allows the conclusion that the allegations of the other side with respect to the existence of a valid promise are in fact true (Couchez et al. 1998, no. 883; Vincent and Guinchard 1999, no. 1078).

Family Law: The Failure of a Marriage

Under German family law, parties may successfully file for divorce if the marriage has failed (Sect. 1565, §1 BGB). The legal system no longer insists on the inseparability of the spouses. However, it does maintain a normative interest that prevents the husband and wife terminating their marriage prematurely, without due consideration of the consequences and without exploring ways and means to save their relationship. As plausible as these concerns may be, how can a court possibly investigate whether an application for divorce is filed prematurely or not? If the court tries to base its decision on the "true facts" of the case, it would have to interrogate the parties thoroughly about the state of their relationship as well as consult their children, neighbors, relatives, colleagues, and the like to ascertain whether the account given by the parties is valid. Such an investigation would not only entail high costs, it would also be anything other but agreeable. Under the previous principle of fault, each party had an incentive to dig up dirt on the other.

How does the law react to these problems? Does it adopt simple heuristics? When the court hears a petition for divorce, it is not forced to investigate the personal relationship between the parties. Instead, a set of presumptions and definitions are used that allows a decision to be made about the failure of the marriage without thorough investigation. The information needed by the court is twofold:

1. Has the divorce petition been filed by both parties, as it is in the cases of consensual divorce, or by only one side, that is, against the will of the other spouse?
2. For what length of time have the parties been living separately?

The combination of these two factors yields the following decision rules:

1. If the parties seek divorce jointly, the only guard against premature dissolution of their relationship is a waiting period of one year, during which the spouses must not have been living together (Sect. 1566, §1, BGB). To reduce even further the amount of investigative efforts, the courts have developed the doctrine that the spouses may live separately even within their common house or apartment, and have added the rule that it is enough for the divorce petition to be successful if the waiting period is completed during the legal proceedings (Palandt/Brudermüller 2004, Sect. 1565 no. 13, Sect. 1566 no. 1, Sect. 1567 no. 3). Thus, the actual rule is: Provided that both parties file for divorce and allege that they have been living separately for at least one year, the court will follow suit and grant an immediate divorce.
2. In cases where only one of the parties seeks divorce and the other side wants to continue the marriage, the relevant time of separation is three years (Sect. 1566, §2, BGB). Since, by definition, the spouses are in conflict, the party interested in divorce will often be forced to prove that the three-year time of separation has in fact lapsed. In this regard, the court may have to evaluate the evidence. However, once the lapse of the three years has been proven, there is no point arguing whether the marriage has actually failed as the presumption of failure is irrefutable.
3. Section 1565, §2, BGB serves as a rule of last resort in the exceptional case that neither the one-year nor the three-year delay has lapsed. In such a situation, the court may divorce the spouses only if continuation of the marriage would impose a severe hardship upon the spouse petitioning for instant divorce. It is only under these restrictive conditions that the court

is forced to investigate the reasons for the failure of the particular marriage. In practice, petitions under Sect. 1565, §2, BGB are extremely rare. Thus, the court will usually divorce the parties without inquiry into the circumstances and development of their relationship.

4.   The reverse rule to Sect. 1565, §2, BGB is found in Sect. 1568, BGB, which requires the court to deny the divorce petition even when the three-year delay stipulated for cases of nonconsensual divorce has lapsed. Again, the threshold is severe hardship albeit now on the part of the spouse who wants to continue the relationship, e.g. in the interest of common children.

The decision tree depicted in Figure 13.1 explains the process of decision making in divorce cases.

In sum, the legal regime governing divorce may be analyzed as a rather complicated system which relates simple heuristics to complex exception clauses. The great majority of cases are disposed of on the basis of simple presumptions of failure of marriage predicated upon the lapse of a one-year waiting period in the case of consensual divorce or a three-year waiting period in cases of

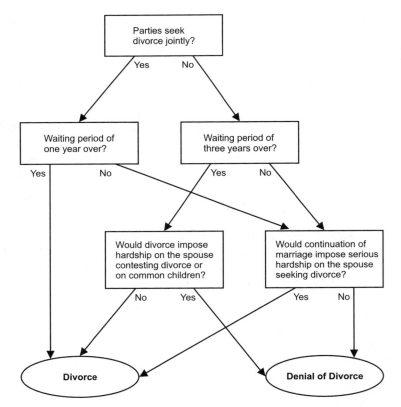

Figure 13.1   Decision tree depicting the process of decision making in divorce cases.

nonconsensual divorce. These simple presumptions are qualified by exception clauses that require a thorough investigation of the facts, but which only apply to cases of severe hardship.

The Law of Evidence

Destruction and Detention of Evidence

Under German law of civil procedure, the obligation upon the parties to disclose documents in their respective possession is very narrowly defined (for a detailed account, see Wagner 2001). However, narrow as it may be, the law must address the issue of how to deal with cases where a party, who has been ordered to produce a document that is under its control, fails to do so. A common-law court would sanction the recalcitrant party by imposing fines for contempt. Such sanctions are, however, unavailable to a civil law court.

On the European continent, a court confronted with a case of detention or destruction of evidence would instead apply a fast and frugal heuristic, treating the allegations of the other side about the contents of the document as true. This is precisely what Sect. 427, ZPO states with respect to the failure to produce a document; however, the principle has been generalized and transferred to other cases where a party withholds or even destroys evidence relevant to the case before the court. Again, the heuristic is not an absolute one in the sense that it is strictly binding upon the decision maker. The language of Sect. 427, ZPO makes it clear that the court "may" treat the allegations of the party interested in the production of the document as true, but it may also hold otherwise. The court will do so if it finds the allegations of the other side about the contents of the document highly unlikely to be true.

Distinction between Parties and Witnesses

Unlike most other legal systems, German civil law still follows the ancient rule that parties to the dispute may not be heard as witnesses: *nemo testis in propria causa* (nobody may be a witness in his own cause). Of course, each party is entitled to participate in the proceedings and to be present at the hearings. The statements the party makes at a hearing remain mere allegations, though; they do not count as testimony and thus are not admissible as means of evidence. If the other side disputes these allegations, the party making them cannot rely on its own testimony to prove them. It must produce documentary evidence or testimony of a third party—a witness in the technical sense of the term—in order to prevail.

The distinction between parties and witnesses for purposes of the law of evidence rests on complex historic foundations. In particular, the ancient concept of a decisory oath played an important role as it was available in German civil procedure until the 1930s. For such a system, the distinction between parties and witnesses is inevitable, as the contested and sworn allegations of a party may only be treated as true under certain restrictive conditions, which guard against fraudulent behavior. Under the old law, these conditions were spelled out in the complicated rules governing decisory oaths.

When German lawmakers abolished the decisory oath, they put party interrogation in its stead. In spite of this conceptual change, restrictive conditions remain intact. Even today, a party must not solely rely on its own testimony to prove the contested facts underlying its claim or defence. Pursuant to Sect. 445, 448, ZPO, a party may be interrogated as a means of evidence either upon the application of the *other* party (Sect. 445, ZPO) or in a situation of "*commencement de prevue*," i.e., where the court already has some evidence suggesting that the account of the party interested in its interrogation is in fact true (Sect. 448, ZPO).

What is the rationale behind the distinction between parties and witnesses, and what is the basis for the restrictive requirements set up for the interrogation of a party?

Despite the historical pitfalls and accidents which certainly play a role, the answer is that parties are thought to be less reliable as a means of evidence than other people. It is common knowledge that someone having a strong interest in the outcome of a case is less trustworthy as a source of information than a disinterested third party. For one, the incentive to lie is much stronger for a party than for a witness, as the latter usually has nothing to gain from giving false testimony. Second, even bona fide testimony of a party is unreliable, as someone involved in a dispute is more likely to be deceived by his own interests and perspective than a neutral observer. During the time when English law still followed these assumptions, and thus drew a distinction between parties and witnesses, Jeremy Bentham (1827/1962, p. 394) challenged them, arguing that an absolute rule against the testimony of a party is untenable:

> Between two opposite propositions, both of them absurd in theory, because both of them notoriously false in fact, the choice is not an easy one. But if a choice were unavoidable, the absurdity would be less gross to say "No man who is exposed to the action of interest will speak false" than to say, "No man who is exposed to the action of interest will speak true." Of a man's, of every man's, being subject to the action of diverse mendacity-restraining motives, you may be always sure: of his being subjected to the action of any mendacity-promoting motives, you cannot be sure. But suppose you were sure. Does it follow, because there is a motive of some sort prompting a man to lie, that for that reason he will lie? That there is danger in such a case is not to be disputed: but does the danger approach to certainty? This will not be contended. If it did, instead of shutting the door against some witnesses, you ought not to open it to any.

The "two opposite propositions," which Bentham denounces as "notoriously false," may be analyzed as heuristics. It then turns out that they may very well be "false" in the sense that they may be wrong in particular cases. Every fast and frugal decision rule may be disparaged for a failure to get it right in each and every case that is conceivable. The crucial question is not whether the two propositions are true or false but whether their predictive powers are equally strong, or whether one proposition clearly outplays the other in terms of predictive accuracy. The answer is straightforward: The assumption that a party to a dispute is lying or unconsciously not testifying truthfully is much more plausible than the reverse assumption that it is speaking true. Thus, the distinction between parties and witnesses and the discrimination of the former by the law of evidence may be justified as a valuable heuristic tool.

This optimistic perspective of the party/witness distinction is premature in important respects. Bentham certainly exaggerated when he insinuated that the probabilities of a party speaking the truth or lying were equal. However, he had a point in arguing that it might go too far to suppose that parties are always lying, or that they do so in the overwhelming number of cases. The crucial question then becomes whether the proposition that a party to a dispute is not testifying truthfully is born out by reality in so many cases that the adoption of a heuristic against party testimony results in more good than bad. Only if answered in the affirmative can the discrimination of party testimony as a means of evidence be justified. Phrased this way, the critique of Bentham looks much more attractive. Upon closer inspection, there appears to be a whole range of reasons that might motivate a party to testify truthfully, even if doing so hurts its own case. It may be that the party has a reputation to lose, that it is fearful of being prosecuted for perjury, or that it may be difficult to come up with a fictitious story sufficiently consistent for surviving interrogation and the like.

On the other hand, every litigator with some practical experience knows that the accounts given by third-party witnesses are anything but trustworthy. One source of unreliability stems from the fact that witnesses may very well have an interest in the outcome of the case. In this regard, the most suspect witnesses are the spouses or loved ones of the drivers of motor vehicles who have been a passenger or observing the disputed accident from within the vehicle. Another class of witnesses well known for their unreliability is employees of corporations testifying on behalf of their employers. It is very difficult to maintain that these types of witnesses are any more reliable than the party itself (i.e., the driver of the car or the employer, the latter acting through its executive officer). Thus, the European Court of Human Rights has held it to be a violation of the principle of fair trial enshrined in Art. 6 of the European Convention on Human Rights that the former Dutch Code of civil procedure discriminated against the testimony of a party in a similar fashion as German law does today.[2] Interestingly, the case before this court was one where an individual had sued a bank for breach of pre-contractual duties, such that the plaintiff was barred from testimony as a party but the bank was allowed to call in its employees to testify. In such a situation, the

---

[2] *Europäischer Gerichtshof für Menschenrechte* (EGMR), 27.10.1993 (*Dombo Beheer B.V. ./. Niederlande,*) *Zeitschrift für Europäisches Privatrecht* (ZEuP) 1996, 484.

rationale of the distinction between party and witness breaks down so that the heuristic should be abandoned.

The analysis for the party/witness distinction in the law of civil procedure yields interesting insights for the theory of heuristics. The beneficial properties of a decision rule are obviously contingent on its probabilistic accuracy. It will readily be granted that the call for optimization, in the sense of minimization of errors, goes too far as it ignores the real-world constraints of day-to-day decision making in terms of time and costs of gathering, processing, and analyzing information and of drawing inferences from the established facts. Conversely, it would be equally wrong to ignore the costs of heuristics, that is, of fast and frugal rules of decision making. The workings of heuristics are beneficial only if the benefits outweigh the costs (i.e., if decision making upon a more thorough analysis of each particular case yields benefits in terms of accuracy that are not worth the attendant costs). Even if the answer is in the affirmative, one would still have to think of other heuristics whose balance of benefits and costs is even better than the one of the heuristic under consideration.

Res Ipsa Loquitur

The doctrine of *res ipsa loquitur* (the thing speaks for itself) is a recurring feature of modern systems of procedural law. In Germany, the relevant concept is that of *Anscheinsbeweis*. With the help of this mechanism, the court may draw a conclusion from the ordinary course of events to the facts of the particular case in the area of causation and fault (i.e., negligence). Once the plaintiff has succeeded in establishing either causation or fault, the other requirement for a damage claim is then presumed to have been established as well. Some examples may help to illustrate this point: Provided that a plaintiff has convinced the court that the defendant has contravened some statutory or judicial rule of conduct, the requirement that this breach be the cause of the injury may be established with the help of *res ipsa loquitur*. Under this concept, it is sufficient for the plaintiff to show that the harm suffered is the typical result of the negligence under the complaint. Motor accidents are a common field of application: If it can be proven that a defendant exceeded the speed limit, further requirements that the accident could have been avoided are not needed. Likewise, it may be established via *res ipsa loquitur* that someone who carelessly started and maintained an open fire close to barns and farmhouses is in fact responsible for the roof of one of these buildings catching fire (BGH VersR 1975, 379). Patients carrying the HIV/AIDS virus were allowed to sue the hospital that had administered a blood transfusion, provided that the plaintiff did not belong to a risk group (e.g., male homosexuals or drug addicts) and that it was established that the hospital had failed to screen its blood donors with appropriate care. Under these conditions, the crucial fact that the blood used for the transfusion was contaminated and that this contamination caused the infection with the HIV/AIDS virus could be established with the help of the *res ipsa loquitur* (BGHZ 114, 284, 290f.).

The HIV/AIDS example provides valuable insights into the workings of the doctrine of *res ipsa loquitur*. First, it is evident that the heuristic employed here is the commonsense assumption that if negligent behavior ordinarily causes a particular type of injury, then it is highly likely that it did just that in the case at hand. However, the heuristic does not define the conditions under which it is "highly likely." As the HIV/AIDS example illustrates, the answer may involve complex factual propositions. It would be dead wrong to suppose that there is a high degree of likelihood that an HIV/AIDS patient contracted the disease while undergoing a blood transfusion in a hospital. Quite the contrary, statistics reveal that most HIV/AIDS patients have contracted the virus either during sexual intercourse or through the use of a contaminated needle for the infusion of drugs. This does not hold, however, for a person who is not a male homosexual and who has never used hard drugs yet still suffers from an HIV/AIDS infection. In such cases, the blood transfusion usually appears to be the only source of the infection conceivable; however, this feature alone would not be sufficient to allow a plaintiff's damage claim. The further fact that must be established is that the hospital administering the transfusion did not screen its blood donors or other suppliers with appropriate care. If the plaintiff succeeds on this point, he or she will prevail. Framed in the language of heuristics, the lesson from the HIV/AIDS example is that courts work with a series of stopping rules. The hierarchy of decision rules is thus:

1. Does the plaintiff belong to a high-risk group (i.e., is the plaintiff a male homosexual or a user of hard drugs)? If so, the claim is dismissed.
2. Did the hospital fail to screen its blood donors with appropriate care? If the hospital behaved diligently, the claim is dismissed. If negligence is established, the burden of proof shifts to the hospital by way of *res ipsa loquitur*.

The doctrine of *res ipsa loquitur* does not stop here, though. The defendant may exonerate himself upon proof that the negligent behavior on his part did not cause the harm in question. However, matters are even more complicated. Just as the doctrine of *res ipsa loquitur* allows the plaintiff to hold the defendant liable if it only appears likely that the defendant's negligence was the cause of the injury, it also allows the defendant to escape liability upon showing that another cause may have intervened (i.e., to establish that in this particular case the ordinary course of events might have been disturbed by an intervening factor). For example, the hospital may negate the *res ipsa loquitur* established by the patient by adducing evidence that the patient contracted the disease from another source. Once it is established, for instance, that the spouse of the victim also carried the HIV/AIDS virus, the *res ipsa loquitur* gives way and the burden of proof of causation shifts again to the plaintiff. The crucial point here is that the hospital is not held to establish beyond reasonable doubt that another source caused the disease, but merely to convince the court that the case at hand is special in the sense that it is impossible to base a decision upon the ordinary course of events. If the defendant succeeds, the plaintiff retains the option if establishing causation on the facts of his/her particular case (i.e., to prove beyond doubt that the blood transfusion in the hospital caused the infection). Thus, the hierarchy of decision rules must be supplemented by two more rules:

1. The hospital may exonerate itself upon proof that the case is extraordinary in the sense that it appears not to be unlikely that the patient contracted the virus from some other source (e.g., from his/her spouse).
2. The patient then retains the right to prove causation on the particular facts, for example, by proving that the virus carried by the spouse is of a different variety than the one from which he/she is infected.

The decision tree depicted in Figure 13.2 visualizes the decision-making process. After having gone through the different stages of the workings of the *res ipsa loquitur*, it is abundantly clear that it provides anything other than *one* simple decision rule. This does not mean, however, that there is nothing to learn for the theory of heuristics. The lesson taught through this example is that the courts work with "systems" of heuristics (i.e., a hierarchy of decision rules with one premised upon the other). Such a strategy enables courts to dispose of simple cases easily but also to take the inquiry further if the facts require closer attention and more effort.

Medical Malpractice I: The Causal Link between Mistreatment and Harm

In medical malpractice, a familiar problem is this: The plaintiff succeeds in establishing that the doctor made some mistake (i.e., discharged his professional duties in a negligent way). Further, there is no doubt that the patient suffered harm because the disease has not been cured or because he suffers from side-effects from the treatment. What is unknown, however, is whether the doctor's negligence caused the harm in question or whether the true cause of the harm is the result of the overall condition of the patient or simply bad luck. The underlying problem is that doctors usually render their services in favor of people who suffer from disease anyway; their duty is to *improve* a patient's condition. However, the health of every human being is unique, and the success rate of any but the most simple and basic kinds of medical treatments is smaller than 1. Thus, in most cases it is simply impossible to know whether the doctor's malpractice caused the harm. There are exceptions, however, as in a case when tissues or scissors are left behind in the patient's abdomen at the finish of an operation, or when a patient is operated on his left leg instead on the right. In the majority of the litigated cases, however, matters are not as simple as that. How could a court possibly react to the difficulties in establishing a causal link—or the absence of a causal link—between the doctor's negligence and the patient's harm?

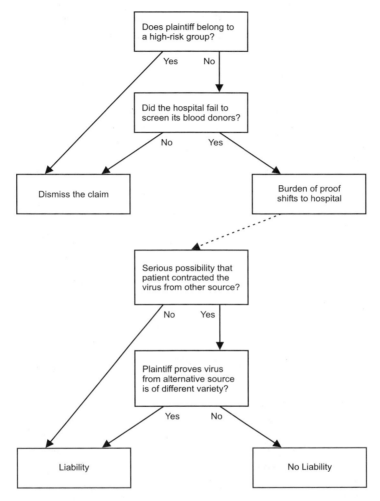

Figure 13.2 Decision-making process for proof of causation after contraction of the HIV/AIDS virus.

One response may be to reverse the burden of proof. Then it would be up to the doctor to prove that his negligence did not cause the health problems under which the patient suffers. Yet how could a doctor possibly do that? If it were possible to distinguish between those cases where the harm is the consequence of negligence on the part of the doctor and others, where it is due to the patient's overall physical condition or the workings of destiny, the problem would not have surfaced in the first place. Reversal of the burden of proof is an appropriate answer if—and only if—access of the parties to the relevant information is asymmetric, with the party initially carrying that burden posited on the short end. In medical malpractice suits, the situation is different, since in most cases it is equally impossible both for the doctor and for the patient to establish the "true cause" of the harm.

The reverse solution (i.e., that matters are left to themselves) must also be ruled out. It would be the end of medical malpractice suits if the burden of proof were solely with the patient. In all but the simple cases referred to above, the doctor could escape liability by exploiting the patient's inability to establish that it was the doctor's negligence, and not his overall condition or destiny, that made him sick or left him in the poorer state than before the treatment started.

German courts have developed a simple tool to escape both the Scylla of no liability and the Charybdis of excessive liability. The doctrine of "gross mistake" (*grober Behandlungsfehler*) works to the detriment of the doctor, as it shifts the burden of proof to the doctor, who must establish that the treatment administered did not cause the harm complained of—a proof that is impossible to furnish. For this move, it is not sufficient that the victim proves mere negligence; rather, the victim must prove that the mistake was serious. A recurring motive in the pertinent decisions of the Federal Supreme Court maintains that the failure on the part of the doctor must be "inexplicable," that is, so serious that there is simply no excuse or explanation available.[3] Examples of this are found in cases where the physician has ignored the teachings of standard textbooks of medical science or failed to react to clear results of diagnostic measures (*Oberlandesgericht* [OLG] Celle VersR 2002, 854, 855). This doctrine of gross mistake has come to dominate lawsuits for medical malpractice to the extent that the claims are not based on a failure to inform the patient about the attendant risks of a particular medical treatment.

The crucial question here is whether the doctrine of gross mistake may pass as a heuristic. The answer is "yes" if the state of affairs without this rule serves as a benchmark. Then the doctrine indicates a way out of the classic calamity of medical malpractice litigation that it is impossible to know the course of events had the doctor discharged his professional duties diligently. On the other hand, one must acknowledge that the doctrine of gross mistake is anything but fast and frugal. It involves a complex issue of law, that is, whether the failure on the part of the doctor amounts to a "gross mistake." It bears mentioning that the courts have been sensitive to the complexity of the doctrine and thus have refined the rule, stripping it of some of its complexity. To see this it is crucial to bear in mind that the concept of "gross negligence," as understood under German law, requires the court to find that the defendant behaved egregiously, not only by an objective standard, but also under a subjective yardstick that takes the particular capabilities and other idiosyncrasies of the defendant into account. It needs no further explanation that such an inquiry is complex and difficult, and that its

---

3   BGHZ 138, 1, 6 = *Neue Juristische Wochenschrift* (NJW) 1998, 1780, 1781; BGH NJW 1993, 2376, 2377; 1995, 778; 1996, 1589; 1996, 2428; 1997, 798; 1998, 814, 815; 1998, 1782, 1783; 1999, 862f.; VersR 2001, 1030; 2001, 1115; 2001, 1116, 1117.

outcome will be hard to foresee. Matters are different with "gross mistake" in medical malpractice law. The relevant test is not whether the defendant doctor as an individual behaved egregiously, but whether his behavior may be deemed grossly negligent from a purely objective point of view. To put the matter bluntly, the court will not inquire into the life, character, and skills of the defendant but simply consult a standard medical textbook: If the defendant did not follow its teachings, he will lose his case on the basis of "gross mistake." Thus, said doctrine may very well pass a heuristic.

Medical Malpractice II: Causation and Lack of Informed Consent

A doctor is not only obligated to treat a patient diligently but also to solicit his consent to the treatment administered (i.e., not to treat him at all without prior consent). "Consent" is itself a complex legal concept, as it requires more than a mere nod before the operation starts. For consent to be a defense against liability, it must be valid, and it is only deemed such if the patient knew what he consented to. As a result, the doctor must inform the patient about the risks and expected benefits involved in the proposed operation or other medical treatment, and he must also disclose the nature and attendant risks and benefits of alternative strategies of medical care. The doctor must draw up a balance sheet of the prospective improvements and risks of the several treatments available to cure a particular illness.

How do these rules of substantive law play out in litigation? The familiar setting is that the patient complains of a harm suffered subsequently to medical surgery, a kind of harm he was allegedly not informed about at the time he gave his consent to the operation. The burden of proof with respect to the timing and scope of disclosure is upon the doctor as he is in charge of the medical files where the relevant documents should have been stored away.[4] If the file is lost, the plaintiff's allegations are taken as true, based on the frugal heuristic that the doctor might have a good reason not to find the file.[5] Under these principles, failure to disclose is not difficult to establish before a court of law.

A popular defense on the part of doctors sued for failure to disclose is again lack of causation. The argument is that the patient would have consented to the surgery anyway, even if he had been properly informed about all the risks involved. If this defense were permissible, most lawsuits premised on lack of consent would end right here. The patient would be hard pressed to prove beyond doubt that he would have withheld his consent, even though his physical condition needed treatment. Again, it would also go too far not to allow the defense at all and to always hold doctors liable in lack-of-consent cases. The difficult issue is how to strike the right balance.

---

[4]   BGH NJW 1980, 633; 1981, 2002, 2003; 1984, 1807, 1808; 1985, 1399; 1992, 741, 742; OLG München VersR 1988, 525; OLG Düsseldorf VersR 1990, 852, 853; Müller G. 1997, 3049, 3051; Musielak 1983, 609, 615.

[5]   Cf. BGHZ 138, 1, 4f. = NJW 1998, 1780, 1781; BGH NJW 1996, 780f.; cf. also Groß (2000).

Once more, the solution drawn up by the German courts is a rather complicated set of heuristics. To begin, the doctor may very well defend himself by alleging that the patient would have given his consent to the surgery anyway—even if he had been properly informed. However, the patient may challenge this defense not only by proving that he would have withheld consent upon proper information—which would amount to a *probatio diabolica*—but also by showing that he would have found himself in a serious conflict of mind had he known about the true risks involved in the operation. If the victim wins on this point, it is then for the doctor to prove that he would have given his consent anyway. In this regard, the courts apply a strict standard, allowing the doctor to escape liability only in the exceptional cases of urgent and lifesaving surgery.

Presumptions and the Burden of Proof

Substantive law is replete with provisions stipulating that certain facts, or even the legal concept based upon such facts, shall be presumed without additional proof. A simple example is the presumption that possessions are owned by an individual who exerts control over the items (Sect. 1006, BGB). A similar presumption applies to the ownership of land; however the facts triggering the presumption are different. In the case of land, possession is irrelevant as all that counts is the public land registry. The person listed in such registry as the owner of the land is supposed to be the legal owner, until convincing evidence to the contrary is before the court (Sect. 891, BGB). Lawmakers did not roll the dice when they settled on these rules. These presumptions allow the court to generalize the most familiar fact patterns as long as these are not challenged by a party interested in overturning the presumption. Since usually the person listed in the public registry as the owner of the land will also be the legal owner, the fast and frugal rule of Sect. 891, BGB makes life very easy for the decision maker.

The virtues of presumptions are particularly obvious where they have not been inaugurated by lawmakers but instead developed incrementally by the courts. Here, an interesting example is provided by the law of products liability: failure to warn against the risks involved in the use of a product constitutes liability. Given that the court finds that the producer of a dangerous product failed to warn against the risks inherent in its use, the claimant would still be required to prove that he would have observed the warnings had they been supplied. At this point, the courts have developed a presumption that the victim would have observed the warnings and recommendations of the producer.[6] Likewise, if a doctor fails to warn the patient against driving within two weeks after surgery

---

[6] BGHZ 116, 60, 73 = NJW 1992, 560, 562f.—Kindertee-I; referring to BGH *Juristenzeitung* (JZ) 1989, 249, 261 w. note v. Bar, although this decision does not deal with any such factual presumption (*tatsächlicher Vermutung*); precisely so OLG Hamm *Neue Zeitschrift für Vermögensrecht* (NZV) 1993, 310, 311; OLG Frankfurt/Main NJW-*Rechtsprechungsreport* (RR) 1999, 27, 29f.

and the patient suffers an injury in a motor accident, ordinary rules of procedure would require the patient to prove that he would have followed the doctor's advice had it been given to him in time. Again, the courts have developed a presumption to the effect that it is to be assumed that the patient would have taken the warnings and recommendations of the doctor seriously and behaved accordingly.[7]

CONCLUSION

The issues outlined in this chapter were whether the countless principles, rules, and niceties of evidence law which aid decision makers, who know nothing about the factual background of the case before they are called to dispose of it, may actually count as heuristics. From the various examples surveyed, the answer seems to depend on the concept of heuristics itself. If defined narrowly, as a fast and frugal decision rule, most rules of evidence are too complicated to pass the test. The usual scenario is that a whole hierarchy of decision rules is brought to bear on one and the same issue, with the court and parties proceeding from one step to the next. On the other hand, it has also become apparent that each decision rule may very well qualify as a heuristic. The crucial point is that courts work with *sets of heuristics* rather than with one simple decision rule. These hierarchies of heuristics are applied to single issues, not to the case at large. Thus, the overall decision of the court, allowing or dismissing the claim, is based on a multiple application of different sets of heuristics to the disputed factual issues. As it turns out, then, disputes are much too complicated to be resolved by a single fast and frugal decision rule, but they are subject to the same constraints in human decision making that apply to any other social setting.

REFERENCES

Alternativkommentar zur Zivilprozeßordnung. 1987. Wassermann, R., ed. Luchterhand: Neuwied.

Beale, H.G., W.D. Bishop, and M.P. Furmston. 2002. Contract: Cases and Materials. London: Butterworth.

Beale, H.G., A. Hartkamp, H. Kötz, and D. Tallon. 2002. Cases, Materials and Text on Contract Law. Oxford: Hart.

Bentham, J. 1962. Rationale of Judicial Evidence, 1827. In: The Works of Jeremy Bentham, ed. J. Bowring, vol. VII, book IX, part III, chap. III. Edinburgh: Tait.

Couchez, G., J.-P. Langlade, and D. Lebeau. 1998. Procédure Civile. Paris: Dalloz.

Dombo Beheer B.V. ./. Niederlande. EGMR 27.10.1993; ZEuP 1996, 484.

Giesen, D. 1982. Arzthaftungsrecht im Umbruch (III): Beweisrechtsprobleme in der Rechtsprechung seit 1974. *Juristenzeitung* **37**:448–459.

---

[7] BGHZ 89, 95, 103 = NJW 1984, 659; BGH NJW 1989, 2320, 2321; Staudinger/Hager 1999, §823 BGB §I 53.

Gottwald, P. 1979. Schadenszurechnung und Schadensschätzung. Munich: Beck.

Groß, W. 2000. Beweiserleichterungen für den Patienten bei Unterlassung medizinisch gebotener Befunderhebung. In: Festschrift für Karlmann Geiß zum 65. Geburtstag, ed. H.E. Brandner, H. Hagen, and R. Stürner, pp. 429–435. Cologne: Heymann.

Hummel, K. 1981. Das Blutgruppengutachten: Seine Bedeutung vor Gericht. *Neue Jurist. Wochenschr.* **34**:605–610.

Koch, H.-J., and H. Rüßmann. 1982. Juristische Begründungslehre: Eine Einführung in die Grundprobleme der Rechtswissenschaft. Munich: Beck.

Müller, G. 1997. Beweislast und Beweisführung im Arzthaftungsprozeß. *Neue Jurist. Wochenschr.* **50**:3049–3056.

Musielak, H.-J. 1983. Die Beweislast. *Juristische Schulung* **23**:609–617.

Palandt, O. 2004. Bürgerliches Gesetzbuch. 63d ed. Munich: Beck.

People v. Collins, 438 P.2d 33 (Cal. 1968).

Richtlinien für die Erstattung von Abstammungsgutachten—Novellierung 1996. 1997. *Z. ges. Familienrecht* **44**:344.

Schmoeckel, M. 2000. Humanität und Staatsraison: Die Abschaffung der Folter in Europa und die Entwicklung des gemeinen Strafprozeß- und Beweisrechts seit dem hohen Mittelalter. Cologne: Böhlau.

Staudinger, J. von. 1999. Kommentar zum Bürgerlichen Gesetzbuch: Zweites Buch, Recht der Schuldverhältnisse, §§823–825. 13th ed. Berlin: Sellier-de Gruyter.

Vincent, J., and S. Guinchard. 1999. Procédure Civile. 25th ed. Paris: Dalloz-Sirey.

Wagner, G. 2001. Europäisches Beweisrecht: Prozessrechtsharmonisierung durch Schiedsgerichte. *Z. Eur. Privatrecht* **9**:441–547.

Wagner, G. 2003. Enforcing contracts: Should courts seek the truth? *J. Instit. Theor. Econ.* **159**:70–75.

Zöller, R. 2004. Zivilprozessordnung. 24th ed. Cologne: O. Schmidt.

14

Train Our Jurors

Jonathan J. Koehler

McCombs School of Business, The University of Texas,
Austin, TX 78712–0212, U.S.A.

ABSTRACT

Lay jurors are often legally and logically unprepared for trial. In response, it is recommended that jurors receive training in how to make better legal decisions. This chapter
suggests that jurors should receive comprehensive training in critical legal doctrines and
in how to reason with legal evidence. Jurors who cannot be trained to achieve minimal
levels of competence (in the law or in basic reasoning) should be excused from jury service. Suggestions are given as to how policy makers and researchers who are interested in
jury reform may wish to proceed.

INTRODUCTION

One of the central goals of a legal trial is the discovery of truth.[1] We want juries
to determine what "really" happened and to provide accurate verdicts. However,
verdict accuracy is not the only goal of a trial. Various process, policy, and individual rights concerns are important as well. Consequently, the search for truth
proceeds within the confines of a strict set of procedures and rules, and the verdicts that juries render should reflect a balance of accuracy and policy concerns.
This balancing act is most apparent, perhaps, in criminal cases where jurors are
explicitly told to presume that the defendant is innocent and to return a guilty
verdict only if the prosecution has overcome that presumption by meeting a very
high standard of proof ("beyond a reasonable doubt"). Thus, when juries acquit
defendants in cases where the evidence is more consistent with guilt than innocence, we remind ourselves that the elevated standard of proof serves an important policy goal, even if it sometimes hinders the production of accurate verdicts.

Research in psychology with mock jurors, as well as anecdotal observation
of actual jurors, suggests that jury verdicts may also reflect systematic biases
that arise from the mental shortcuts—some of which may qualify as

---

[1] According to the United States Supreme Court, "the basic purpose of a trial is the determination
of truth" (*Tehan v. United States ex rel. Shott* 1966, p. 416).

heuristics[2]—that jurors use when trying to apply the relevant rules of law and logic to a target case. Although some mental shortcuts that jurors use may have all of the desirable properties that accompany good heuristics (e.g., they save time, make the task manageable, positively correlate with outcomes given by normative rules in particular environments), I suggest that the shortcuts that untrained jurors use are often infused with a good deal of ignorance, misunderstanding, confusion, and illogic. Jurors misunderstand rules of law, legal presumptions, and applicable standards of proof. They rely on information that they are told not to use, ignore crucial evidentiary points, and make inappropriate inferences. Sometimes jurors falsely "recognize" elements of cases that are consistent with their preferred stories of what actually occurred, even when these elements were not present as evidence (Pennington and Hastie 1988). Other times jurors concoct theories "from left field" (Caplow 2002, p. 799).

In the sections below, I suggest that lay jurors are often legally and logically unprepared for trial.[3] There are many ways the law might respond to this problem. One way is to change the offending legal rules. For example, if jurors have trouble remembering evidence during deliberations, consideration might be given to allowing jurors to use various decision aids (e.g., personal notes, pretrial conversations with fellow jurors). A second approach to the problem is to change the task environment in ways that compliment the heuristics that people are likely to employ when thinking about legal evidence. This solution should be appealing to psychologists who have demonstrated that decision performance can be improved by varying the task environment. A third way is to acknowledge the inherent value in the first two solutions, but to suggest that there may be value in training jurors to make better legal decisions. This third approach is my focal point in this chapter. I propose that jurors receive comprehensive training in critical legal doctrines (e.g., standards of proof) and in how to reason with evidence (e.g., how to assess evidentiary relevance).[4] The training in any particular case should be based on the parameters of the target case in conjunction with empirical research on misunderstandings jurors may have and ways to resolve those misunderstandings. In addition, I add my voice to those who have called for rule modifications that make jurors more active members of the trial process to improve the quality of their judgments. Finally, I anticipate criticisms of my plans and offer specific suggestions for how policy makers and researchers interested in jury reform may wish to proceed.

---

[2]   As other chapters in this volume indicate, there is no single, agreed-upon definition of what a heuristic is and is not. Having said this, I assume here that heuristics are shortcuts (or rules of thumb) for decision making that are associated with a mental process.

[3]   Although I assume a criminal context throughout, the general points apply to civil trials as well.

[4]   In suggesting that jurors are logically unprepared for trial, I am only tangentially concerned with the usual array of cognitive shortcomings (e.g., hindsight, overconfidence, and insufficient adjustment from anchors). My point is less psychological, though psychology may help provide solutions. My claim is that, absent training, jurors may not have the skills they need to achieve minimal levels of competence as legal decision makers.

LEGAL IMPAIRMENTS

We exclude mentally impaired people from jury service and no one questions the wisdom of this. We exclude them because they cannot understand the law and they cannot reason well enough to make an informed legal decision. I suggest that there is another, larger group of prospective jurors who are *legally* impaired. These people have such a poor grasp of legal doctrine and/or have such inadequate reasoning skills that they should not be permitted to be on juries in their current state. As I note later in this section, some key legal doctrines are so hard to comprehend that mild legal impairment may be unavoidable.

Everyone agrees that jurors take their task seriously. They generally try to make judgments based on the evidence and the applicable rules of law.[5] This impression receives some support from jurors' post-verdict comments about their deliberations. According to Marder (1997), jurors most frequently comment on the relationship between their verdicts and the evidence, and between their verdicts and the applicable laws. This is the good news. The bad news is that jurors frequently misunderstand the law. To the extent this occurs, the judgments rendered by juries may be erroneous and our jury system loses credibility. As Pizzi (1996, p. 1035) notes, "no matter how well the evidence rules are crafted, or how well the investigatory procedures are designed, if the fact finders cannot be trusted, the system will be weak."

Misunderstanding Instructions

Currently, in the United States, jurors typically receive information about the law through a set of verbal instructions delivered by the trial judge. These instructions, which are usually presented at the close of trial, cover procedural rules of the trial (e.g., do not talk about the case, the verdict must be unanimous), the requirements of proof (e.g., the presumption of innocence, the applicable standard of proof), and the applicable substantive law (e.g., definitions of the crimes charged, elements that must be proved). Jurors widely report that these instructions are helpful and understandable.

Research with both mock jurors and actual jurors, however, suggests that something is deeply amiss in the world of jury instructions. Studies reveal that jurors do not understand jury instruction terminology and cannot remember, recognize, or paraphrase the instructions after they have heard them. In one study of actual jurors, only 3% of jurors said they were confused about their instructions, but these jurors could not answer 30% of questions that were central to the legal judgments they had just made (Saxton 1998). Similarly, Ellsworth (1989) showed that jurors missed 35% of important true–false legal questions

---

[5] At the same time, jurors often resolve disagreements by splitting differences. This tactic enables jurors to go home more quickly, an extra-legal goal that frequently emerges during difficult deliberations.

shortly after hearing judicial instructions. Smith (1991) reported that instructed jurors were not able to apply the law to the instant case better than uninstructed jurors. Sometimes, jurors' understanding of certain key legal concepts actually *diminished* following judicial instruction (Ellsworth 1989).[6]

Misunderstanding Key Legal Concepts

Confusion about the presumption of innocence and the standard of proof ("beyond a reasonable doubt") are of special concern. Only one in five jurors can paraphrase the presumption of innocence (Lieberman and Sales 1997), and half of the jurors mistakenly believe that defendants must provide evidence of their innocence. Forty percent of jurors believe that the charge itself constitutes evidence of guilt, whereas 20% believe that the charge constitutes "strong" evidence of guilt. Though a Bayesian might find such beliefs to be reasonable, they are inconsistent with the presumption of innocence.[7]

The standard of proof is also widely misunderstood. Nearly seven in ten people who received jury instructions in actual cases erroneously believed that one must be "100% certain" before voting to convict in a criminal case (Saxton 1998). One in ten of these jurors agreed with this statement: "In a criminal trial, all that the state has to do is to convince the jury that it is more likely than not (i.e., that there's a better than 50–50 chance) that the defendant committed the crime that the defendant is accused of" (Saxton 1998). At this 10% rate, the chances are nearly 3 in 4 that at least one juror in a group of 12 will enter the jury room believing that a 51% chance of guilt suffices for conviction. Jurors are also confused about what exactly it is that the prosecution must prove beyond a reasonable doubt. Reifman et al. (1992) as well as Ellsworth and Reifman (2000)

---

[6] An anonymous legal reviewer dismissed all of the experiments cited in this chapter that indicate that people have trouble with legal rules and reasoning because the experiments do not document erroneous verdicts. The reviewer wrote that, without such documentation, "there is literally no evidence" of a problem. On the one hand, this criticism need not be taken seriously. If there is a connection between ability to engage in elementary reasoning operations and the ability to produce accurate verdicts, then evidence that people fail to understand judicial instructions or fail to understand relations among items of evidence certainly constitutes evidence of a problem, even in the absence of proof of verdict error in a particular case. On the other hand, I am sympathetic to the idea that social scientists should be sensitive about the inferential limits of laboratory data. I also think that social scientists who wish to affect policy should conduct studies that lawyers and legal policy makers are most likely to find persuasive. To this end, see the discussion in the section on **Research Reform** below.

[7] In unpublished written comments on this chapter, Rick Lempert wrote, "I don't share Koehler's concern with confusion about the presumption of innocence and standard of proof. For me, the most meaningful operational definition of overcoming the presumption of innocence through proof beyond a reasonable doubt is the fact that 12 jurors will concur on guilt." In response, I suggest that the agreement 12 jurors achieve as an operational matter is orthogonal to the confidence we should have that those jurors interpreted the proof standard appropriately. To suggest otherwise confounds the descriptive (what jurors do) with the prescriptive/normative (what jurors should do).

report that many jurors mistakenly believe that the prosecution must prove motive, opportunity, and other individual elements of their theory of the case beyond a reasonable doubt.

Post-verdict interviews with actual jurors indicate shocking degrees of naiveté about the trial process and standards. In one interview, jurors revealed that a secret ballot for jury foreman yielded 18 ballots from the 12 voting jurors. Apparently, two of the twelve jurors mistakenly believed that they were voting for "four men" rather than a single foreman. In another case, jurors indicated that they relied heavily on impermissible evidence to find against a defendant. An appellate court brushed aside this complaint on grounds that it "ignores the jury's thorough analysis of the totality of the evidence during their deliberations" (*United States v. Taubman* 2002). In general, Appellate courts are reluctant to correct jury error, even when jurors profess confusion. In *State v. Ronquillo and Sarausad II* (1998), two jurors said they convicted a defendant of second-degree murder because they mistakenly believed they were obliged to do so once they had convicted his codefendant of first-degree murder. The appellate court upheld the conviction.

Standard of Proof in State of Texas v. Baker Steven Lucas (1994): Ten years ago I watched the televised murder case of Texas businessman Steven Lucas on Court television. Lucas was accused of murdering his mother by throwing her over a staircase. The jury convicted Lucas of murder on the second day of deliberations. In a post-verdict interview with the jury, one juror revealed that he was one of four who supported acquittal on the first day of deliberations. However, when he awoke the following morning, he switched his vote because he realized that there was "a preponderance of evidence" against the defendant. Following weeks of testimony from numerous witnesses, at least one juror apparently switched his vote from not guilty to guilty based on a misunderstanding of the criminal standard of proof. The fact that no juror corrected him during the interview hints that this improper standard may have been used by others as well.

The Beyond-a-Reasonable-Doubt Instruction

I would not be surprised if the problem that arose in the Lucas case is widespread. However, at least part of the problem may be endemic to the reasonable doubt standard or to inadequate descriptions of the standard. Consider a typical "reasonable doubt" instruction:

> A reasonable doubt is an honest and reasonable uncertainty in your minds about the guilt of the defendant after you have given full and impartial consideration to all of the evidence. A reasonable doubt may arise from the evidence itself or from a lack of evidence. It is a doubt that a reasonable person hearing the same evidence would have (*State of New Jersey v. Medina* 1996).

How helpful is this instruction? Does it clarify the proof standard for one who has never been asked to apply it? How exactly does the circular explanation that a reasonable doubt is "a doubt that a reasonable person … would have" clarify the standard? A separate question, and one that resides at the heart of the matter, is whether jurors who hear this explanation will make better legal decisions than those who do not.

In fairness, the instruction above, which was crafted by the New Jersey Supreme Court from various other recommended jury charges, continues as follows:

> Proof beyond a reasonable doubt is proof, for example, that leaves you firmly convinced of the defendant's guilt. In this world, we know very few things with absolute certainty. In criminal cases the law does not require proof that overcomes every possible doubt. If, based on your consideration of the evidence, you are firmly convinced that the defendant is guilty of the crime charged, you must find him guilty. If, on the other hand, you are not firmly convinced of defendant's guilt, you must give defendant the benefit of the doubt and find him not guilty (*State of New Jersey v. Medina* 1996).

Note that the Court's attempt to define the beyond-a-reasonable-doubt standard, actually produces a new standard, namely a "firmly convinced" standard. That is, a case against a defendant is proved "beyond a reasonable doubt" if it leaves jurors "firmly convinced that the defendant is guilty." It is hardly clear that a state of "firm conviction" is identical to a state in which reasonable doubt is absent. The latter standard appears to be weaker than the former. Jurors may be firmly convinced about the truth of many propositions about which they cannot say that they have no reasonable doubt. If so, then the "firmly convinced" language may induce juries to convict in cases where they would otherwise acquit.

Jurors in the recent high profile Martha Stewart trial heard another popular instruction on reasonable doubt:

> [Reasonable doubt] is a doubt based on reason and common sense and arising from the evidence or lack of evidence. It is a doubt that a reasonable person would have after carefully weighing all of the evidence. It is a doubt that would cause a reasonable person to hesitate to act in a matter of importance in his or her personal life. Proof beyond a reasonable doubt must, therefore, be proof of such a convincing character that a reasonable person would not hesitate to rely and act upon it in the most important of his or her own affairs (Blodget 2004).

As before, this definition includes the circular logic in which reasonable doubt is defined as "doubt that a reasonable person would have." In addition, this definition explains that such doubt would cause a reasonable person to "hesitate" before taking an action. However, it is not clear to me that whether somebody would or would not "hesitate" before taking action is an adequate proxy for whether that person does or does not have reasonable doubt. A thoughtful person is likely to "hesitate" before making *any* momentous decision, yet surely such hesitation provides an insufficient basis on which to infer reasonable doubt.

In light of the difficulty clarifying the meaning of beyond a reasonable doubt, perhaps it is best to leave the standard undefined. Alternatively, we should replace this standard with one that jurors can understand. The "firmly convinced" language from the New Jersey instruction is one possibility. Whereas few laymen have occasion to ponder whether they believe something "beyond a reasonable doubt," most people probably have thought about the degree to which they are *convinced* of a proposition. Thought should also be given to which among many possible adverbs—if any—should precede the word "convinced" (e.g., strongly, completely, etc.).[8]

What about quantifying the burden of proof? The notion that the beyond-a-reasonable doubt standard should be associated with a subjective probability threshold (e.g., 90% or 95%) has been proposed and debated from time to time. The clarity that such a standard provides is part of its appeal. However, quantifying the burden of proof raises numerous policy problems (Tribe 1971) and is unlikely to generate much political support.

LOGICAL IMPAIRMENTS

Just as jurors must understand legal rules, standards, and policies to perform their duties effectively, they also need to be able to think appropriately about these rules, standards, and policies. Judges often instruct jurors to use "reason and common sense" to draw conclusions from the evidence that they have heard (Devitt 1992). Presumably, then, if a juror possessed neither sufficient reason nor sufficient common sense, he/she would or could not abide by this legal requirement and should be excused from jury service. I doubt that there exist agreed-upon standards of common sense. If not, then it would be hard to say whether a juror met a minimal threshold for this requirement.

However, there are various rules associated with proper reasoning. Some of these rules appear in normative theories of logic and probability.[9] For example, if all members of set A have characteristic B, and element C does not have characteristic B, then C cannot be a member of set A. This is an elementary rule of logic, and failure to abide by it constitutes poor reasoning. We also know that if two events are independent and the probability of each event is 0.60, then the probability that both events occur is given by the product of their individual probabilities, $0.60 \times 0.60 = 0.36$. This is an elementary rule of probability and failure to abide by it likewise constitutes poor reasoning.

The credibility of our legal system rests, in part, on the ability of jurors to reason properly with evidence. Of course, this does not mean that all jurors must

---

[8]   The French actually do use such a standard. According to Newman (1993), the French Code of Criminal Procedure instructs panels that consist of three judges and nine lay jurors a single question: "Are you thoroughly convinced?"

[9]   Although ability to reason encompasses more than the ability to follow the rules of logic and probability, the present discussion of shortcomings in reasoning focuses on statistical shortcomings largely because there is much empirical work in this area.

reach the same conclusions. After all, jurors may disagree about whether C is, in fact, a member of set A, or whether the unconditional probability of an event really is 0.60. However, jurors should not be free to reason according to their own unique brands of logic to obtain a desired result.

This is not to say that a qualified juror would never violate a logical rule. After all, Kahneman and Tversky (see, e.g., Kahneman et al. 1982) taught us that nearly everyone can be seduced into violating some normative principle on occasion. However, prospective jurors who broadly fail to understand and accept the rules of logic and probability theory when applied to everyday matters have questionable reasoning skills. Because evidence presented at trial is increasingly complex and statistical in character (Feinberg 1989), the system should impose minimal standards to ensure that our legal fact finders are up to the task.

Problems Understanding the Random Match Probability

One hundred years ago, probabilities were dismissed by most courts as "speculative" evidence. As one appellate court noted, "Quantitative probability ... is only the greater chance. It is not proof, nor even probative evidence of the proposition to be proved" (*Day v. Boston and Maine R.R.* 1902, p. 774). Today, probabilities are widely admitted as evidence and form the backbone of scientific testimony in many cases. Juries routinely hear testimony that includes Z values, p values, regression coefficients, and a host of other statistics and probabilities that they are expected to understand using "reason and common sense."

Consider a murder case in which DNA evidence recovered from a crime scene reportedly matches the DNA of the defendant. The strength of this match is generally identified via a random match probability (RMP). The RMP identifies the theoretical probability that a randomly selected person from the general population would match these samples. Though the suspect population or the potential source population are more appropriate sample spaces from which to construct an RMP, the RMP can inform jurors who have some question about whether the match may be the result of coincidence. As the RMP becomes smaller, coincidence becomes an increasingly unlikely explanation for the reported match.

However, there is substantial evidence that people are easily confused and misled by small probabilities such as RMPs. When DNA statistics are presented in conditional probability form (e.g., P(Reported Match | Suspect is Not the Source)), jurors commonly invert the conditional probability (Koehler 1996). Though one would hope that the lengthy testimony that DNA experts ordinarily provide at trial help jurors understand the meaning of the probabilities and statistics they hear, I remain skeptical.

Several years ago, Stuart O'Brien interviewed four jurors shortly after they convicted a defendant of murder in a case that included extensive DNA testimony (reported in Koehler 2001). O'Brien asked the jurors questions about the meaning of DNA statistics and found that the jurors understood little or nothing about them despite exposure to extensive adversarial discussion of these numbers at trial. O'Brien provided the jurors with a written murder scenario in which DNA evidence recovered from clothing worn by a suspect matched the DNA profile of the victim. The RMP was 1 in 100. One of the jurors indicated that this probability meant that there was a 99% chance that the victim is the source of the evidence. This is a logical error. The source probability (i.e., the probability that a particular person is or is not the source of material recovered from a crime scene) cannot be computed as one minus the RMP (see Koehler 1993a).

The statistical error committed by the other three jurors was worse. They concluded that the 1 in 100 RMP indicated that there was only a 1% chance that the blood belonged to the victim. By equating the profile frequency with the source probability, these veteran jurors revealed that they have no idea what the RMP mean. If the profile frequency actually did equal the source probability, then a rare blood match (e.g., 1 in 1,000,000) would be *less* probative than a common blood match (e.g., 4 in 5)! Apparently, then, jury service on a case that includes testimony about DNA evidence provides insufficient reason to believe that jurors will understand how to reason with that evidence.

TRAINING JURORS

There is good reason to believe that jurors are confused about the law and have difficulty reasoning with evidence (statistical evidence in particular). One drastic solution is to replace jurors with judges. Presumably judges have a much better understanding of the law as well as better reasoning skills. In England, jury trials have practically been eliminated in favor of three-judge panels. However, this solution is likely to be quite unpopular in the United States where the public is broadly suspicious of elite decision-making authorities. A second solution is to employ blue-ribbon juries, particularly in cases that include complex or technical evidence. These juries could include people who are familiar with the specific, technical issues of the instant case. Such juries are sometimes used in complex civil cases in areas such as intellectual property, medical malpractice, products liability, and toxic tort injuries (Kondo 2002). Though specialized juries have some appeal and I would support their expansion, it is unrealistic to imagine that blue-ribbon juries could broadly replace layperson juries.

Thus I propose that we train layperson juries to improve their ability to make effective legal decisions. An effective legal decision is one that helps achieve the various process, policy, and accuracy goals of our legal system. Jurors and juries can only make judgments that help achieve these goals if they understand what the goals are and have a few basic cognitive tools at their disposal.

Regarding the process and policy goals, jurors should receive training in the trial process, the goals of a trial, and the standards that should be applied during deliberations. This training should seek to correct widely held misconceptions about legal goals and policies that could affect jurors' judgments. As noted earlier, the training should be based on empirical research that identifies both the shortcomings in legal reasoning and ways to overcome those shortcomings. Following training, jurors should be required to agree to uphold legal and logical principles, and demonstrate (through testing) that they understand much of what they have been taught.

Regarding accuracy, jurors must understand basic rules of logic and inference. They must be able to distinguish between weak and strong items of evidence for different hypotheses, and they must have some sense of how to combine multiple items of evidence. Therefore, jurors should probably receive basic training in how to think generally, and how to reason with legal evidence in particular. The content of the jurors' training should be determined by theory-driven empirical research that identifies (a) shortcomings in intuitive reasoning, and (b) lesson content that demonstrably improves the judgments and decisions people reach. As before, jurors should demonstrate that they understand much of what they have been taught, and agree to reason according to those principles.

Training Jurors in the Law

Although trial judges currently instruct jurors prior to sending them off to deliberate, there is broad agreement that these instructions are inadequate. As Ellsworth and Reifman (2000) note, jurors are "poor at remembering, understanding, and applying the relevant laws." Assuming that this is not a hopeless state of affairs, I recommend that the current practice of providing jurors with a short, canned set of verbal instructions immediately prior to deliberations be replaced by a comprehensive pretrial training program. As noted throughout, the style and substance of the program should be an on-going process rooted in empirical research and feedback. Some training modules would likely be common across all criminal trials (e.g., instruction on presumptions and burdens of proof), whereas other modules would be tailored to reflect the issues in the focal case.

The program could include a series of short, videotaped instructional segments delivered to jurors over the course of several hours. The trial judge, guided by relevant statutes, would select the segments and materials for individual juries. The taped segments should convey a wealth of essential information in a way that maintains a high level of juror interest and participation. For example, jurors could answer key questions as the training proceeds, or request reviews of particular topics.

The tapes should take pains to rebut commonly held misconceptions. This is important because research shows that jurors rely on their preexisting beliefs about legal constructs, even when the judge's instructions are clear (Diamond and Casper 1992). Jurors should also receive supplementary materials that they may rely on during deliberations. Minimal comprehension standards should be identified, and jurors who fail to meet those standards should either be retrained or excused from the jury panel for cause.

Reducing the Influence of Attorney Spin

A comprehensive jury training program can reduce sources of systematic and random error across trials and juries. For example, jurors who learn about legal doctrines from training sessions may be less likely to rely on adversarial attorneys' descriptions of those doctrines. This is a good thing, because attorneys commonly spin legal requirements in ways that can adversely affect jurors' understanding of those principles.

Consider, once again, the "beyond a reasonable doubt" standard of proof. This is a heavy burden of proof that defense attorneys often try to make even heavier through linguistic sleight of hand. Some defense attorneys implore juries not to convict if they have *any* doubt that is reasonable. By introducing and emphasizing the word "any," defense attorneys subtly convey a stronger standard of proof. With the assistance of a strategic pause between the phrases "any doubt" and "that is reasonable," defense attorneys may even be able to get convince jurors to require proof "beyond *any* doubt" for conviction.

Similarly, some defense attorneys refer to the standard of proof as "beyond *all* reasonable doubt." By inserting the word "all," attorneys—and some Supreme Court Justices (see e.g., Justice Blackmun's dissent in *Victor v. Nebraska* 1994, p. 1254)—may create a higher threshold for a guilty verdict than the actual standard requires. For now, the significance of this linguistic distortion remains an unexplored empirical question.

A more insidious distortion occurs when defense attorneys imply that jurors must apply the "beyond a reasonable doubt" standard to each contested fact at trial. This strategy was used, perhaps successfully, in the criminal O. J. Simpson case (Bugliosi 1996). I contend that a thoroughly trained jury would have a firmer grasp of the standard of proof and therefore be less vulnerable to attorneys' linguistic machinations.

Training Jurors to Reason

Jurors should be able to employ elementary rules of logic and inference to make sense of the evidence and arguments that come before them. Toward this end, jurors should receive training in how to think logically about evidence. Studies by Richard Nisbett and colleagues in the 1980s and 1990s indicate that people can be trained to reason in relatively short order (e.g., Fong and Nisbett 1991; Nisbett et al. 1987). According to this research "even brief formal training in inferential rules may enhance their use for reasoning about everyday life events" (Nisbett et al. 1987, p. 625). For example, less than 30 minutes of abstract instruction on samples, populations, parameters, and sample size variation, produced significant and lasting improvements in people's understanding of the law of large numbers. Importantly, this training session improved statistical reasoning "for problems that people rarely think of in terms of probability" (p. 628).

Research by Gerd Gigerenzer and colleagues offers even more reason for optimism. Whereas Nisbett and colleagues can improve performance in less than 30 minutes using rule-based techniques, Gigerenzer and colleagues can turn laymen into full-blown Bayesians "in less than two hours" using a different technique (Sedlmeier and Gigerenzer 2001). These researchers obtained substantial improvements in statistical reasoning ability by teaching people how to construct frequency representations. Apparently, people can reason quite well with information that is presented simply and in ways that clarify the underlying sample space. Hoffrage et al. (2000) demonstrated the significance of this idea for legal decision making. They showed that when powerful DNA statistics were presented as natural frequencies (which clarify the sample space), law students and future judges treated the evidence as much more compelling proof of guilt than they did when the evidence was presented as probabilities.

This research hints that jurors who are exposed to carefully constructed training modules[10] may improve their ability to reason about legal matters, both when the evidence is explicitly probabilistic and otherwise.[11] Though definitive studies have yet to be conducted, the training might include instruction on the rules of conjunctive and disjunctive probability, base rates, likelihood ratios, sample spaces, and different ways to represent information. I stop short of recommending that jurors receive training in Bayes's theorem.

Conjunction

The issue of conjunction often arises in cases involving scientific evidence. For example, jurors who hear DNA testimony are commonly told that the RMP is based on a multiplication process in which the probabilities of a random match at each of several DNA loci are multiplied together to form an aggregate RMP. Thus, if there is a 0.10 chance of a random match at locus A, and a 0.05 chance of a random match at locus B, then there is a $(0.10)(0.05) = 0.005$ chance that a random person would match at both loci. This use of the "product rule" is justified because empirical study shows that the characteristics at each locus are roughly independent of the characteristics at all other loci. (See National Research Council [1996, p. 122] for a "conservative" computation method that takes account of possible dependencies.) Because DNA samples are typically tested at multiple loci, aggregate RMPs are often quite small.

Laypeople are often suspicious of the product rule in any context. For many, it is not intuitively clear why the individual probabilities are multiplied together

---

[10] Modules should take into account the limits of teaching reasoning; e.g., training in abstract rules of logic is ineffective unless concrete examples are also provided (Nisbett et al. 1987).

[11] If future studies demonstrate that particular statistical formats facilitate more accurate verdicts, the courts might consider requiring witnesses to present statistical evidence in those formats.

rather than, say, added. A brief hands-on training session could be helpful here.[12] Implications of the conjunctive rule should also be taught. For example, jurors should know that the joint probability of a pair of events (e.g., "he planned the murder" and "he committed the murder") cannot be greater than either of the relevant unconditional probabilities (e.g., "he committed the murder").

Disjunction

Consider the juror who wishes to identify the probability that a reported DNA match between a crime scene sample and a defendant is due to either laboratory error or coincidence. If A = the chance of an incriminating error, and B = the chance that the defendant matches the crime scene sample by coincidence then, by the disjunctive rule of probability, $P(A \text{ or } B) = P(A) + P(B) - P(A \text{ and } B)$. When the probability of event A is several orders of magnitude higher than the probability of event B (as it is here), then a reasonable approximation of the disjunctive probability is, simply, $P(A)$ (Koehler et al. 1995).

Suppose a juror believes that the chance of an incriminating laboratory error is 1 in 1,000, and the chance of a coincidental match is 1 in 1,000,000,000. This juror should believe that the chance that either of these events occurred is about 1 in 1,000. Untrained jurors are unlikely to intuit this implication of the disjunctive rule. Instead, they are likely to average the two small probabilities and, in doing so, arrive at estimates that increase the chance that they will return guilty verdicts against the defendant (Koehler et al. 1995; Lempert 1991a).

Base Rates

Jurors are also likely to be unsure about the significance of background probabilities, or base rates. It is well known that people often attach relatively little weight to base rates in many probabilistic judgment tasks. Although greater base rate usage may improve verdict accuracy (Koehler and Shaviro 1990; Koehler 1993b), explicit use of base rates will often be outweighed by various legal policy goals (e.g., perceptions of fairness). Sometimes higher courts vehemently oppose the introduction of base rates at trial, but other times they uphold verdicts based on base rates alone (Koehler 2002). This is a messy area of law and it is not clear what sort of training jurors should receive in base rate usage. Though accuracy may suffer, jurors should probably be cautioned against relying on base rates related to sex, race, ethnicity, etc. during deliberations.

Relevance, Probativity, and Likelihood Ratios

Federal Rule of Evidence 401 (FRE 401) defines relevant evidence as "evidence having any tendency to make the existence of any fact that is of consequence to the determination of the action more probable or less probable than it would be

---

[12] The session should also teach jurors that the product rule does not hold for dependent events.

without the evidence." This definition is consistent with a likelihood ratio (LR) test of relevance in which LRs that deviate from unity are relevant because they change one's prior probabilities. Although LRs are closely associated with Bayesian reasoning, a likelihood-based approach to relevance or probative value "can be embraced without a commitment to Bayesian reasoning" (Kaye 1995, p. 678). That is, one may test whether evidence E makes hypothesis H more or less probable by determining whether the LR, $P(E|H)/P(E|-H)$, is greater than or less than 1. If this ratio is significantly greater than 1, then E is relevant and it makes H more probable (i.e., $P(H|E) > P(H)$). If the LR is significantly less than 1, then E is also relevant and it makes H less probable (i.e., $P(H|E) < P(H)$). Small LRs (e.g., 1/0.001) and large LRs (e.g., 1000/1) are more probative than LRs that are closer to 1 (e.g., 1/3 and 3/1).

Laymen often fail to seek the information that they need about evidence E to determine whether the E is relevant. People intuitively understand that $P(E|H)$ helps determine whether E supports H, but they fail to realize that $P(E|-H)$ is also required (Doherty et al. 1979). Even trial judges, who are responsible for admitting relevant evidence and excluding irrelevant evidence, use inappropriate shortcuts for assessing relevance. For example, in cases involving allegations of child sexual abuse, some judges admit symptom evidence if the symptoms are "common" among abused children, even when those symptoms are equally common among non-abused children (Lyon and Koehler 1996). Other times, judges exclude proffered symptoms because the symptoms appear in some children who have not been abused. These results suggest that laymen and judges alike do not think about evidence against the backdrop of different hypotheses.

If judges sometimes subscribe to illogical methods for determining evidentiary relevance, there is even more reason to train jurors to make such judgments as well. Even if jurors find it difficult to quantify the available evidence, some training in the ideas that underlie LRs may help dislodge misconceptions about how to assess evidentiary relevance and strength.

Selective Evidence

The problem of identifying the relevance and strength of evidence is complicated by the fact that the evidence that jurors hear at trial is not a representative sample of the available evidence. Instead, it is a selective sampling of facts that are biased to suit the interests of the litigants. Some evidence exists that jurors are only sensitive to selection biases in the production of evidence when the sample space within which evidentiary "matches" are found is made explicit. Koehler and Thompson (unpublished) showed that jurors who were aware of the number of leads that police investigated (i.e., the number of chances that the police had to find a "match" against the defendant) used this information to discount the strength of incriminating "matches" that were found. But when jurors were unaware of the number of leads police investigated, they treated incriminating matches as very strong proof of guilt.

Can jurors be trained to consider the significance of the search process that produced seemingly incriminating evidence? If so, can jurors be trained to assign appropriate weights to evidence found using different search techniques? Though we do not yet have the answers, the research cited earlier on the beneficial effects of natural frequency presentations indicates that it should be possible to sensitize people to this sample space issue.

What about Bayes?

Though jurors should receive some training in the principles that lurk behind likelihood ratios, it may not be a good idea to train jurors to use Bayes's theorem. Bayes's theorem provides a mathematical technique for combining one's prior beliefs with one's assessment of the strength of new evidence. Though Bayes could be a valuable aid to legal decision making, the disadvantages of trying to produce Bayesian jurors probably outweighs the advantages.

First, introduction of Bayes could create a misperception that final judgments about guilt or innocence reside in the cold mechanical inner workings of a mysterious formula rather than in the warm, compassionate hands of thoughtful, fair-minded humans. Second, jurors may have trouble translating the relevant evidence into a workable Bayesian form. This concern is most worrisome in complex cases. Likewise, jurors may become confused about input values. Identifying the correct values for priors and LRs can be quite tricky and even counterintuitive. Furthermore, jurors may confuse $P(A|B)$ with $P(B|A)$ and with $P(AandB)$. They may also confuse LRs with posteriors (Koehler 1996). Such errors could wreak havoc with the outcome of a Bayesian analysis. Of course, jurors may become confused by evidence even without trying to use Bayes. But Bayes may give jurors who misuse it an unjustified confidence in the accuracy of their conclusions. Ultimately, whether Bayes helps or hinders jurors is an empirical question.

CRITICISM

Resistance to a comprehensive jury training program is likely to be broad and stiff. The proposal will likely be attacked as unrealistic, unnecessary, unconstitutional, expensive, and time-consuming. I consider these criticisms briefly below.

Unrealistic?

Any proposal to change the current system is likely to encounter resistance from those who have the most to lose through change. Consider attorneys and trial judges. They have little or no incentive to support calls for reform in general and instructional reform in particular. Currently, attorneys can take advantage of naïve jurors by presenting information to them at trial in ways that improve their odds for a favorable outcome. Attorneys may also propose special instructions that a trial judge may or may not approve. Trial judges are likely to resist a new training system, as they will be responsible for implementing the training.

Unnecessary?

Some will oppose jury reform on grounds that we ought not tinker with the system of justice that has served us well so many years. But this conservative argument is vacuous unless and until a metric for "served us well" is identified. Furthermore, rules and procedures related to the trial system are in a constant state of flux—including the much revered standard of proof (Morano 1975). The relevant question is not whether a proposed reform is "necessary," but whether it will enhance the quality of justice relative to the status quo. A related criticism is that there are different systems of reasoning, no one of which is demonstrably superior. By this reasoning, then, it will not be helpful to train jurors to reason, and it may even be harmful. I disagree with this version of intellectual relativism, but agree that the value of a juror training program turns largely on its demonstrable benefits.

Unconstitutional?

My proposal requires that prospective jurors demonstrate some proficiency with legal standards, logic, and probability before serving on a jury. It may be hard to convince legislators that it's a good idea—or even constitutional—to exempt the group of untrainables from jury duty. However, I note that other groups of prospective jurors are exempt from jury duty under current laws. In my county, people are ineligible for jury duty if they are (a) not qualified to vote (e.g., convicted felons, non-U.S. citizens, less than 18 years of age), (b) not proficient in English, or (c) "not of sound mind and good moral character."[13] I suggest that the "sound mind" requirement—which is sometimes described as the absence of a serious physical or mental disability—should exclude those who cannot or will not abide by the most basic rules of law and reason. Because the rules of law require the ability to reason properly with evidence and arguments, those who cannot do so should not be entrusted to make legal decisions.

As a practical matter, the minimum proficiency standard should be relatively minimal so as not to produce an elite, unrepresentative decision-making body.

---

[13] In addition, people are excused from jury in many jurisdictions if they (a) are a high school or college student, (b) have primary responsibility for children or others who cannot take care of themselves, (c) are employed by the legislative branch of government, (d) are at least 70 years old, or (e) suffer from particular medical conditions.

However, even if the proportion of people who fail to meet minimum proficiency standards following training is very low, the proficiency requirement may slightly increase jury representation of some racial or ethnic groups over others. To guard against this possibility, rules might be established that preserve representation among racial and/or ethnic groups. For example, excluded jurors might be replaced by jurors from the same racial or ethnic group.

Expensive?

Implementation of a comprehensive jury training system will certainly be costly. Research will need to be conducted, personnel will need to be hired, and training modules will need to be written and produced. Video equipment, tapes, and other training materials will need to be purchased. Courtrooms will need to be equipped with the space and machinery to carry out the automated portions of the training. The training process will also add time to the jury process, particularly during the initial phase in periods. The additional time spent in training also increases the time and monetary costs on jurors, many of whom already feel stretched to the limit by the burdens that jury service entails.

However, the costs associated with reform should not doom these ideas any more than the costs associated with current trial procedures should doom the use of lay juries. The costs of reform should be traded off against the expected benefits, which could be enormous in terms of increasing the defensibility of jury verdicts, and increasing trust in a jury system that has come under fire in recent years. Moreover, if done well, the extra time that jurors spend training for their task may actually improve the jury service experience enough to offset the additional economic burden of attending training sessions.[14]

NEXT STEPS

Jury reform projects have been conducted in California, Arizona, Washington, D.C., and Colorado (Anderson 2002). These projects evaluated state jury systems and made recommendations for improvement.[15] The recommendations made by these projects are not binding on the courts, though they carry considerable influence with state Supreme Courts which have responsibility for setting

---

[14] Non-psychologists may find it hard to believe that one's experience may be improved through imposition of greater costs without any obvious offsetting benefit. However, such an outcome is predicted by a variety of well-documented psychological theories including cognitive dissonance (Festinger 1957) and self-perception theories (Bem 1967). For example, jurors who receive training may be more likely to view their service as part of an important and worthwhile activity.

[15] Reforms that I find most appealing are those that help create a more active role for the juror in the trial process. These include allowing jurors to take notes, submit questions (following screening by the trial judge), and engage in predeliberation discussions with fellow jurors. See Diamond et al. (2003) for evidence of the benefits of increasing juror participation in the trial.

trial standards. With this in mind, I recommend the formation of a *national* authority to investigate ways to improve decisions made by juries. I also recommend that social scientists who are interested in jury reform consider ways to produce data that policy makers—rather than other jury researchers—will find persuasive.

A National Research Council Panel on Jury Decision Making

Though trials standards vary by state, I recommend the appointment of a National Research Council (NRC) panel to investigate the jury decision-making process. This panel should place special emphasis on how to reduce confusion and error in legal judgments.

The NRC is the research arm of the National Academy of Sciences, a nonprofit society of distinguished scholars that advises the U.S. government on scientific and technical matters. The recommendations made by NRC panels often influence policy, including legal policy. For example, most of the key recommendations from an NRC report on how DNA evidence should be presented in courts were adopted throughout the U.S. (National Research Council 1996).

Membership on the proposed NRC panel should include leading judges, legal researchers, psychologists, decision theorists, statisticians, educators, philosophers, and others. The panel should be encouraged to identify procedures and policies that are likely to improve the quality of legal decisions and, perhaps, to improve public confidence in jury trials. The panel should base its recommendations on compelling empirical evidence rather than on legal traditions. This is not to say that the panel should ignore legal norms. Panel recommendations must conform to existing law, but they need not conform to legal traditions.

Research Reform

A large body of research on jury decision making—much of it published in *Law and Human Behavior*—hints that jurors would make better judgments if various changes were implemented. However, this research, like most jury research, has had stunningly little impact on legal policy. One explanation is that jury researchers do not design their studies with the reactions of the courts and other legal policy makers in mind. Below, I offer two recommendations to increase the impact of jury research on legal policy.

Increase Realism

Jury research generally is conducted with college student subjects who read portions of fictitious trial transcripts or listen to recreations of videotaped evidence. Live witnesses are uncommon, as are objections and other intrusions that enter into real trials. The presentation of the trial is compressed, deliberations of small groups are abbreviated, and real consequences are virtually nonexistent. Interestingly, research indicates that the results of jury studies do not depend much on how realistic the stimulus materials are or on the composition of the subject pool (Bornstein 1999). This is good news for those who wish to continue to develop scientific theory using traditional jury research methods.

But judges and other legal policy makers are unlikely to be persuaded by psychologists' assurances that highly artificial mock studies provide a sufficient basis for drawing inferences about the behavior of actual jurors. *Free v. Peters* (1993) provides a case in point. Defendant Free argued that the instructions jurors received before sentencing him to death were confusing and misleading. In support, Free produced a study by Hans Zeisel that showed that mock jurors who heard the Free instructions misinterpreted much of what they were told. Sometimes the mock jurors thought that the instructions actually conveyed the very opposite points that they were intended to convey. Writing for the 7th Circuit Appellate Court, Judge Richard Posner dismissed Zeisel's study in its entirety because there was a "lack of comparability between the test setting and the setting of the sentencing hearing," and because the study did not include "a control group consisting of persons administered a test containing what Zeisel (or Free's lawyers) would consider adequately clear instructions" (p. 705). Though a social scientist is unlikely to be persuaded by Posner's critique, the more important point is that Posner and others who have power to change the legal system are unlikely to be persuaded by social scientists' protestations.

If jury researchers wish to advance scientific theory, then traditional laboratory studies are fine. But if they seek to have an impact on trial policy, they must give judges, policy makers, and advisory groups (e.g., a diverse National Research Council panel) evidence that an alternative approach yields better results than an existing approach under realistic conditions (cf. Lempert 1991b).

Focus on Accurate Decision Making

Jury researchers generally try to identify factors that do and do not influence jurors. Sometimes consideration is given to whether these factors *should* exert an influence, or whether the degree of influence is reasonable. However, little consideration is given to the bottom line, namely, did the jurors produce an accurate verdict? One obvious reason for this shortcoming is that verdict accuracy is usually unknown. As Shari Diamond (2003, p. 150) writes, "To assess how the jury operates as a decision maker, we cannot compare the jury's verdict with some gold standard of truth because no such dependable standard exists." However, I submit that jury research can and should be designed in settings where such a gold standard of truth *does* exist. When this is done, researchers will be able to identify at least some conditions under which proposed reforms do and do not enhance verdict accuracy. I suspect that policy makers would be more interested in such data.

Jurors' judgments are rarely compared against a truth criterion that the legal community would find convincing. On the few occasions when normative comparisons are made, jurors' probability judgments are contrasted with those given by a stylized Bayesian model (Smith et al. 1996). Although such studies provide *some* basis for assessing the accuracy of jurors' judgments, real jurors do not provide explicit probability judgments. Consequently, policy makers may remain unpersuaded by probability judgment studies, even when normative standards exist.

Occasionally, jury researchers use expert judgment as a proxy for truth. Smith (1991) used the consensus judgments of four Stanford Law School professors as a benchmark for truth in a study on the efficacy of pretrial instructions. This technique has merit though, again, the results of these studies may not persuade policy makers. Whereas law professors know more about legal standards and evidentiary probativity than novice jurors, a sizable leap of faith is required to conclude that the experts' verdicts are a reliable proxy for truth.

A paradigm that policy makers may find more persuasive is one in which juries provide verdicts in cases where truths are known or knowable (to people other than the participants and jurors). For example, detailed credible confessions by defendants and others sometimes arise after a trial has ended. If the contents of these trials have been preserved (e.g., on videotape or in transcripts), mock juries could be provided with the evidence and asked to render verdicts under various conditions.

Alternatively, experimenters might consider staging crimes. In this manner, ground truths would exist (i.e., the identity of a perpetrator) and mock juries could hear testimony from actual witnesses to the staged crime. Perhaps trace evidence could also be introduced in such studies. Conducting these types of studies will be more complex and time-consuming than usual. But the time spent may be worthwhile for researchers interested in trial reform.

CONCLUSION

We Americans confidently proclaim our jury system to be "the best in the world," though most of us know nothing about other systems and very little about our own. The bravado inherent in this proclamation could be dismissed with a wink if there was good reason to believe that our legal decision makers make judgments based on the applicable law and evidence. But, in reality, the available evidence indicates that many of our prospective jurors harbor misconceptions about the law and logic that may interfere with their ability to make accurate and effective legal decisions. In response, steps should be taken to improve jurors' capabilities.[16]

---

[16] I do not mean to imply that all of the ills in the jury system can be pinned on the untrained juror.

Calls for jury reform are not new, and the reforms I favor are certainly not a panacea. However, my suggestion to provide broad training to jurors in the law and in basic reasoning is more ambitious than most pleas for reform. I envision a comprehensive, empirically based, standardized set of training modules that not only teaches jurors what they need to know to make effective legal decisions, but that also disabuses jurors of misconceptions and, in some cases, heuristic approaches that hinder their performance. Implementation of such a program will be challenging, and will encounter resistance from those who are loath to criticize the status quo, the juror, or the heuristics that people instinctively apply to complex problems. However, a justice system that cares deeply about the production of accurate verdicts should not ignore shortcomings of the untrained legal decision maker.

REFERENCES

Anderson, D.A. 2002. Let jurors talk: Authorizing pre-deliberation discussion of the evidence during trial. *Military Law Rev.* **174**:92–124.

Bem, D. 1967. Self-perception: An alternative interpretation of cognitive dissonance phenomena. *Psychol. Rev.* **74**:183–200.

Blodget, H. 2004. Preliminary verdict of this jury of one. *Slate*, March 3.

Bornstein, B.H. 1999. The ecological validity of jury simulations: Is the jury still out? *Law Hum. Behav.* **23**:75–91.

Bugliosi, V. 1996. Outrage: The Five Reasons Why O.J. Simpson Got Away with Murder. New York: Bantam.

Caplow, S. 2002. The impossible dream comes true: A criminal law professor becomes juror #7. *Brooklyn Law Rev.* **67**:785–825.

Day v. Boston and Maine R.R., 96 Me. 207, 52 A. 771 (1902).

Devitt, E.J. 1992. Federal Jury Practice and Instructions: Civil and Criminal §12.05. 4th ed. St. Paul, MN: West Publ.

Diamond, S.S. 2003. Truth, justice and the jury. *Harvard J. Law Publ. Pol.* **26**:143–155.

Diamond, S.S., and J.D. Casper. 1992. Blindfolding the jury to verdict consequences: Damages, experts, and the civil jury. *Law Soc. Rev.* **26**:513–563.

Diamond, S.S., N. Vidmar, M. Rose, L. Ellis, and B. Murphy. 2003. Juror discussions during civil trials: Studying an Arizona innovation. *Arizona Law Rev.* **45**:1–81.

Doherty, M.E., C.R. Mynatt, R.D. Tweney, and M.D. Schiavo. 1979. Pseudodiagnosticity. *Acta Psychologica* **43**:11–21.

Ellsworth, P.C. 1989. Are twelve heads better than one? *Law Contemp. Probs.* **52**: 205–224.

Ellsworth, P.C., and A. Reifman. 2000. Juror comprehension and public policy. *Psychol. Publ. Pol. Law* **6**:788–821.

Feinberg, S.E., ed. 1989. The Evolving Role of Statistical Assessments as Evidence in the Courts. New York: Springer.

Festinger, L. 1957. A Theory of Cognitive Dissonance. Palo Alto, CA: Stanford Univ. Press.

Fong, G.T., and R.E. Nisbett. 1991. Immediate and delayed transfer of training effects in statistical reasoning. *J. Exp. Psychol.: Gen.* **120**:34–45.

Free v. Peters, 12 F.3d 700 (1993).

Hoffrage, U., S. Lindsey, R. Hertwig, and G. Gigerenzer. 2000. Communicating statistical information. *Science* **290**:2261–2262.

Kahneman, D., P. Slovic, and A. Tversky, eds. 1982. Judgment under Uncertainty: Heuristic and Biases. Cambridge: Cambridge Univ. Press.

Kaye, D.H. 1995. The relevance of "matching" DNA: Is the window half open or half shut? *J. Crim. Law Criminol.* **85**:676–695.

Koehler, J.J. 1993a. Error and exaggeration in the presentation of DNA evidence. *Jurimetrics* **34**:21–39.

Koehler, J.J. 1993b. The normative status of base rates at trial. In: Individual and Group Decision Making, ed. N.J. Castellan, pp. 137–149. Hillsdale, NJ: Erlbaum.

Koehler, J.J. 1996. On conveying the probative value of DNA evidence: Frequencies, likelihood ratios and error rates. *Univ. of Colorado Law Rev.* **67**:859–886.

Koehler, J.J. 2001. The psychology of numbers in the courtroom: How to make DNA match statistics seem impressive or insufficient. *S. Calif. Law Rev.* **74**:1275–1306.

Koehler, J.J. 2002. When do courts think base rate statistics are relevant? *Jurimetrics* **42**:373–402.

Koehler, J.J., A. Chia, and J.S. Lindsey. 1995. The random match probability (RMP) in DNA evidence: Irrelevant and prejudicial? *Jurimetrics* **35**:201–219.

Koehler, J.J., and D.N. Shaviro. 1990. Veridical verdicts: Increasing verdict accuracy through the use of overtly probabilistic evidence and methods. *Cornell Law Rev.* **75**:247–279.

Kondo, L.L. 2002. Untangling the tangled web: Federal court reform through specialization for Internet law and other high technology cases. *UCLA J. Law Technol.* **2002**:1–150.

Lempert, R. 1991a. Some caveats concerning DNA as criminal identification evidence: With thanks to the Reverend Bayes. *Cardozo Law Rev.* **13**:303–341.

Lempert, R.O. 1991b. Why do jury research? In: Inside the Juror, ed. R. Hastie, pp. 242–254. Cambridge: Cambridge Univ. Press.

Lieberman, J.D., and B.D. Sales. 1997. What social science teaches us about the jury instruction process. *Psychol. Publ. Pol. Law* **3**:589–644.

Lyon, T.D., and J.J. Koehler. 1996. The relevance ratio: Evaluating the probative value of expert testimony in child sexual abuse cases. *Cornell Law Rev.* **82**:43–78.

Marder, N.S. 1997. Deliberations and disclosures: A study of post-verdict interviews of jurors. *Iowa Law Rev.* **82**:465–546.

Morano, A.A. 1975. A reexamination of the development of the reasonable doubt rule. *Boston Univ. Law Rev.* **55**:507–528.

National Research Council. 1996. Committee on DNA Forensic Science: An Update, The Evaluation of Forensic DNA Evidence. Washington, D.C.: Natl. Acad. Press.

Newman, J.O. 1993. Beyond "reasonable doubt." *New York Univ. Law Rev.* **68**:970–999.

Nisbett, R.E., G.T. Fong, D.R. Lehman, and P.W. Cheng. 1987. Teaching reasoning. *Science* **238**:625–631.

Pennington, N., and R. Hastie. 1988. Explanation-based decision making: Effects of memory structure on judgment. *J. Exp. Psychol.: Learn. Mem. Cog.* **14**:521–533.

Pizzi, W.T. 1996. Discovering who we are: An English perspective on the Simpson trial. *Univ. of Colorado Law Rev.* **67**:1027–1036.

Reifman, A., S.M. Gusick, and P.C. Ellsworth. 1992. Real jurors' understanding of the law in real cases. *Law Hum. Behav.* **16**:539–554.

Saxton, B. 1998. How well do jurors understand jury instructions? A field test using real juries and real trials in Wyoming. *Land Water Law Rev.* **33**:59–189.

Sedlmeier, P., and G. Gigerenzer. 2001. Teaching Bayesian reasoning in less than two hours. *J. Exp. Psychol.: Gen.* **130**:380–400.

Smith, B.C., S.D. Penrod, A.L. Otto, and R.C. Park. 1996. Jurors' use of probabilistic Evidence. *Law Hum. Behav.* **20**:49–82.

Smith, V.L. 1991. Impact of pretrial instruction on jurors' information processing and decision making. *J. Appl. Psychol.* **76**:220–228.

State of New Jersey v. Medina, 147 NY 43; A 2d 1242 (1996).

State v. Ronquillo and Sarausad II, 89 Wash. App. 1037, (Wash. App. Div. 1, 1998).

State of Texas v. Baker Steven Lucas III, 203 Judicial District, Dallas County, TX, Trial # F94-79501-(8-29-1994).

Tehan v. United States ex rel Shott, 382 U.S. 406, 86 S. Ct. 459 (1966).

Tribe, L.H. 1971. Trial by mathematics: Precision and ritual in the legal process. *Harvard Law Rev.* **84**:1329–1393.

United States v. Taubman, No. 01 CR 429(GBD) (S.D.N.Y.), 2002-1 Trade Cases P 73,645 (4–11–2002), WL 548733.

Victor v. Nebraska, 511 U.S. 1, 1101, 114 S. Ct. 1239 (1994).

15

Rules of Evidence as Heuristics—Heuristics as Rules of Evidence

Joachim Schulz

Law School, University of Osnabrück, 49069 Osnabrück, Germany

ABSTRACT

It is not always appropriate to use the word *heuristics* to refer to every simplification of the production of evidence. Certainly, there are some rules of evidence that seem to apply heuristics. However, the main idea of heuristics contradicts the aim of evidence law. The declaration of facts purports to be true or at least nearer to the truth than the opposite. It does not aim to achieve the best decision. Evidence law is not part of a decision theory. By contrast, the legislator, whoever he/she may be, undoubtedly uses heuristics while making the law.

THE AREA OF HEURISTICS IN GENERAL AND IN LAW

Possible Meanings of Heuristics in General

The term *heuristics* can be used to convey the most divergent concepts and procedures. The only common ground is that one refers to rules of discovery. The Greek term *heuristiké techné* (ευριστικη τεχνη) is the source of today's usage. In Latin, the term is *ars inveniendi*. The first part of the term, *heuristiké* or *inveniendi*, means "discovery" or "inquiry." *Ars* or *techné* clarifies that heuristics are not a science in a narrow sense, but rather an art or a skill. Whichever skill one is referring to determines the usage of the term *heuristics*.

Heuristics as a Means of Creativity

The person who practices the art of discovery understands that there are possible points of view and commonplaces (Greek *topoi*, Latin *loci communes*) with which to tackle a new problem. These serve as an engine of creativity and may be expressed as questions (to the person himself). The pattern is: "Did you consider that ..." or "Did you think about ...." Thus, the commonplaces do not answer a question or solve a problem, not even approximately or in a practical useful way. They simply spur on the search for answers and solutions.

Cicero's *Topica* is a treasure trove of such points of view. Cicero states, for example, that the lawyer should ask for similarities or distinctions in the case.[1] The investigator should direct his attention to what happened before (*ante rem*), during (*cum re*), or after (*post rem*) the event.[2] These general points of view can then be individualized for special situations. Under the keyword "*post rem*," one should search for "...pallor, a blush, trembling, and any other signs of agitation and a guilty conscience; and besides, an extinguished fire, a bloody sword, and other things which can arouse suspicions about a crime."[3]

These catalogs can easily be updated or extended to various fields. Advertisers, for instance, may wonder whether it is possible to alienate a popular nursery rhyme or attract attention by breaking a taboo. They may also consider whether to take advantage of a widespread prejudice by exposing it or twisting it. Humanities scholars may wonder which ancient authorities should be brought down and which ones should re-emerge on the scene. There are more books than you can count about what a lawyer should consider before taking over a mandate, before cross-examining a witness, or before filing an appeal. These books, however, are not limited to the presentation and commentary on checklists; they make proposals on how to succeed or at least to ameliorate the chance to succeed.

Heuristics as a Method of Finding a Practically Sufficient, Useful, or Optimal Solution to a Problem

The previous statement leads us to a different meaning or aspect of heuristics: they are no longer a way of getting ideas, but rather a method of optimizing actions relative to the given information and—perhaps—(background) knowledge of regularities and statistic relations. Anticipating my remarks on evidence law, I want to stress my understanding of the main idea of Gigerenzer et al. (1999): The aim of heuristics is not to get to know something or to have a better understanding of reality. The goal is to find an action that allows you to achieve your objectives. From this point of view, heuristics are merely a means of improving behavior. Decisions should be made more rational. But the rationality of decisions is not the rationality of philosophy or science that is interested in the very essence of things or in very causal connections. It is rather the rationality of improving action. The better action (i.e., better with regard to the aim and environment of the behavior [cf. Gigerenzer, this volume]) is the more rational one.

Taking this idea of heuristics to the extreme, there is not necessarily a relationship between decision-making rules and the rules of nature. For example, a

---

[1] Topica XI, 46: "*est eiusdem dissimile et simile invenire*"
[2] Topica XI, 50: "*quid aut sit aut evenerit aut futurum sit*"
[3] Topica XI, 52

person does not need to know much more about the "deadly amanita" than its name to avoid eating it. Normally, there is a connection between the world of heuristics and the "real world," but the links do not necessarily correspond. In the world of heuristics, it is not important per se for observations to represent a cause or a symptom of a disease. The only important thing is to know how to cure the disease best, taking into account the lack of time and means.

There are other possible conceptions of heuristics, of course, that connect better to the real world. They work with approximations and verisimilitudes. The latter word describes the crucial point better than "probability" or "likelihood." The Latin words *veri similis* mean "what seems to be true," which includes the near truth as well as deceptive appearance. The difference between these two aspects is not important as long as you are sufficiently guided through the world. To a certain degree this can be achieved by behaving according to tradition or general approval.

Heuristics as a Practically Sufficient Justification for a Future Behavior

Heuristics may serve to justify the rules or ways of decision making. Thus, it is necessary to determine the type of rules to be supported, but not necessarily the ways to search for them. To apply heuristics, it is not even necessary to know how to support the rules. For example, the name and appearance of the deadly amanita do not offer an explanation as to how and why the consumption of the mushroom might be lethal. Nevertheless, the decision-making rules one applies can relate to the exterior form of the item, although it is certain that the form does not cause the fungus poisoning at all. This example may seem a little distorted, but it illustrates the basic scheme.

Summary

To analyze the role of heuristics in evidence law, I suggest that *heuristics are a means to prepare actions or decisions by enabling individuals (a) to find ideas, when logical inferences are lacking; (b) to know how to solve problems without knowing why it works; and (c) to justify actions or decisions when there is no proof.* These three aspects are interdependent. However, for the present purpose, it is not necessary to analyze the relationships between them.

The Possible Area of Heuristics in Evidence Law

The world of law is the empirical world. Since Parmenides, it has been acknowledged that in this empirical world a theoretically sufficient proof is impossible. Consequently, as mentioned above, one could completely assign evidence law to the area governed by heuristics. It is, of course, of no use to form concepts in this manner. If all evidence were heuristic, useful distinctions would be impossible. Therefore, for the purpose of this chapter, it is not helpful to use the term *heuristics* when there is an inevitable lack of evidence. The theoretical deficiencies will even appear in the roughly simplified model of proof that the law requires. The judge, the jury, or whoever has to decide on the facts must draw an inference from present- to past-time events that fulfills the propositions in support or denial of a claim. Such an inference, however, cannot be valid, even under the best possible conditions, for three cogent reasons:

1.   No one can prove that the events happening at court (= presented evidence) are complete with regard to the inferences to be drawn.
2.   No general empirical law can be proven to be valid. What can be demonstrated is that general empirical laws are necessary to infer one single event from another.
3.   No one can prove that his/her inferences are faultless (Schulz 1992).

Thus, there are limitations to any practical proof of past facts. If these are the sole deficiencies, then one can be sure to have reached the best possible understanding. An older generation of scholars referred to this as "moral certainty,"[4] in contrast to "mathematical certainty."

If these three objections are the only ones that can be raised to a declaration of fact, then doubt is not reasonable because one demands more than anybody can give in any situation. Doubt is thus purely theoretical and not worthy of notice by the court. If there is no reasonable doubt, conclusive evidence is provided. Conversely, doubt is reasonable if it can be demonstrated that the deficiencies of the case are located within the boundaries previously mentioned; that is, if a gap in the evidence can be definitely identified, or if it can be shown that there is no general empirical law or that the presumed empirical law does not exist or that the inferences are defective. In accordance with procedural rules, a corresponding conjecture may sometimes be sufficient. In any case, it is just now at this point that one can enter the possible area of heuristics.

THE MAIN PROBLEM AREAS OF EVIDENCE LAW

There are innumerable uncertainties that could be the gateway to heuristics. Some are more important than others because they are as frequent as they are difficult to analyze: the proof of causation, of the inner workings of a person, and of the amount of damage.

The Problem of Causation

Causation in the Simplified World of Law

The problem of causation is one of the most discussed issues in philosophy, science, and law. The questions and even the answers to seemingly identical

---

[4]   In the social sciences, this moral certainty is thought to be sufficient as well.

questions are, however, quite different in each because they are asked in different world systems, or rather communications systems, which have different tasks to perform. In law, or more precisely in evidence law, the problem of causation is restricted to a small field. Its world consists of the near past. Therefore, the regularities of concern do not have to be eternal laws of nature. A lawyer is usually content with a limited period of validity: roughly ten or fifty years. Whether the sun stood still three hundred or three thousand years ago is of no interest. (For further discussion and examples on simplifying the world, see Schulz 1992.)

Because it is sufficient to demonstrate regularities, it is not necessary to take into account the reasons or deeper meanings of the observed sequences of events. When a sales clerk hands over a knife to a customer who has asked for one, the request has caused the act. Judges and lawyers are not at all interested in what happened in the brain of the sales clerk, let alone the biological or psychological processes. Objections can be raised, of course. One could claim, for example, that the giving of the knife was possibly caused by a television team that arranged with the shopkeeper to award every customer a knife, regardless of the actual customer's requests. If, however, there is no well-founded suspicion that events actually transpired in this way, the objection will fail. The fact that alternative causal connections, which are only possible in theory, will not be taken into account is not the consequence of heuristics. It is simply the result of following the rule, which stipulates that purely theoretical or general doubts do not count at all. Here we have the simplified world of later reconstruction.

Somehow, evidence law makes the world more complicated. In most cases, causation is a special relationship between two events that really occurred; the first usually pertains to a certain human behavior. Physicists may say that the crashing to the floor and the shattering of a glass jar were caused by gravity as well as the material properties of the glass. From a legal point of view, however, one would ask for the person who threw the glass away and whether the act of throwing caused the fragments of glass. Accordingly, one looks for an individual sequence of events. As we will soon see, this complication is somewhat lessened by several simplifying techniques.

A Simple Model of Causation in Law

Causation is a relation between particular events. The examination of this relation on the level of phenomena consists of a chronological order (Table 15.1, level 1). Event$_n$ follows event$_1$; that is, event$_n$ is *post hoc* (= after that). On a second level, sequences are analyzed and some *post hocs* are converted into *propter hocs* (= due to that). After this conversion, the first event is called "cause," the last event "effect," and the relation is called "causation."

In the present context, I cannot even begin to point out the differences between the concepts of causation in various disciplines (e.g., in medicine and

Table 15.1 The three levels of ascribing responsibility.

Level 3	Evaluated cause	Evaluated connection	Evaluated effect
Level 2	Cause	*Propter hoc*	Effect
Level 1	Event$_1$	*Post hoc*	Event$_n$

law). Even if one addresses the seemingly identical question of whether a particular medicine has caused congenital deformities (cf. the Contergan case in Kaufmann 1971), the variances in response are numerous and carry serious implications. What is important, though, to emphasize is that the law usually regulates the commonsense world and thus should be closely correlated to the commonsense concept of causation. Accordingly, most of the time it is sufficient to draw lines of *post hoc*s and to make a distinction between causes and symptoms in an almost graphic way. Sometimes, of course, you need the help of experts to draw these lines. They are, however, nevertheless the lines of the law.

On a third level, the three elements of the second level are evaluated by law. This is because causal relations in this environment are not sought. Instead, a "physical connection between the defendant's negligence and the plaintiff's damage" is desired. This wording, which I discovered in a journal for medical experts, is clearly erroneous because negligence as a result of evaluation cannot physically cause anything. But the wording shows what is expected: a normatively evaluated connection between normatively evaluated events.

The But–for Clause: A Classic Example of Heuristics in Evidence Law

Courts predominantly use the but–for clause (the *condicio-sine-qua-non* formula) to analyze causation. This clause, or formula, has been highly criticized by jurisprudence scholars.[5] The complete version of the clause usually goes as follows: cause is every condition that you cannot eliminate mentally without the effect being eliminated as well.

There are two objections to the clause. The first one states that it only addresses level two (see Table 15.1), with the consequence that Adam and Eve would have caused all human acts ever since[6] or that the victim would have caused the damage as well as the tort feasor. In other words, according to this opinion the scope of the formula should be reduced to the questions legally relevant. Restricting the empirical question in such a manner does not suggest that heuristics or particular rules of evidence be applied. It is but a normative selection and therefore does not belong here.

The second objection contends that the clause is not a means of discovery, as it purports to be. The formula could only be used if the empirical connections

---

[5]   For a report on the current opinions, comparing the situation in Germany and England see Leonard (2001), especially pages 45 ff. and 110 ff.

[6]   The exclusion of events that are "too remote" is not a matter of causation, but of evaluation.

between the events are already known and the distinction between *post hoc* and *propter hoc* has already been made. In other words, the formula does not bring about the transition from level 1 to level 2. This objection is correct. With merely mental operations one cannot even distinguish empirical from logical conditions let alone causal from temporal relations. Nevertheless, the use of the formula can be justified. The first element of the definition (i.e., "cause is every condition," with an emphasis put on "every") indicates that there is no key difference between the cause and the condition of an effect, and between important and unimportant conditions.[7] The reason for leveling the differences is not the difficulty to draw a sufficiently clear line between the concepts, but the necessity to enable the law to make a person responsible for a damage, even if he or she had only set an unimportant condition to it. Whether the person will in fact be held responsible is decided on level 3.

The second part of the formula is a kind of instruction on how to analyze the sequences of events. According to the main stream of modern philosophy of science, the questions of causation and explanation are identical. One is only entitled to convert the *post hoc* into a *propter hoc*, if e_1 (the presumptive cause) is part of an explanation of e_n (the presumptive effect). Only then is event e_1 a part of the explanation of e_n, if you can predict e_n—using a set of all-propositions, with e_1 being given (Hempel-Oppenheim scheme) (Hempel 1965).

Acting this way the law gets fewer answers than necessary and possible. On the other hand, the Hempel-Oppenheim scheme yields more answers than the law needs. Let us say, for instance, that a man fires a revolver and another man falls down bleeding and dies a second later. Applying the Hempel-Oppenheim scheme, the shot is only then the cause of the death if you can predict the death in the instant of the shooting. To do so, you have to know the exact position of the revolver as well as in what way and how strongly the hand was trembling. You have to know the direction of the wind as well as its force, etc. This information will not be available at court, and even in an experiment simulating the situation, it would take serious efforts to get them. Nevertheless, it is clear that the shot caused the death, if nobody else with a firearm was near. For more examples and details, also relating to mental causation cf. Schulz (1987).

The but–for clause shows which path to choose. Reversing the word prediction one could call this process retrodiction, but this wording is not quite appropriate because we do not want to find out the well-known event e_1, but the yet unknown relation between events. One must start with the effect (i.e., the death of the man) and ask whether it is practically possible that he did not die of the bullet wound. Next one asks whether it is practically possible that the bullet wound is the result of another gun's shot, and so on. All events, facts, and behaviors that are found on the this constructed line are causes of the effect. One can

---

[7] Cf. *Holling v. Yorkshire Traction Company Ltd*, 2 All E.R. 662, 664 (1948): "Speaking for myself I have never been able to understand the distinctions which have been drawn in many of the reported cases between a *causa causans* and *a causa sine qua non*."

literally draw that line on a paper. Erasing one of the events breaks the line drawn from event e_n to event e_1, and precisely this is what is meant by the word "eliminating" in the *condicio-sine-qua-non* formula.

This rough image could be refined, if it is theoretically or practically needed. One has to know what a bullet wound looks like, of course. Sometimes knowledge of the difference between a rifle bullet wound and a revolver bullet wound is important. The more the questions are refined, the more expertise is necessary. There are no obstacles to overcome to meet these requirements, at least not in principle.

This example shows that the Hempel-Oppenheim scheme refuses to give an answer where it is possible.[8] On the other hand, having successfully applied this scheme, one has an additional explanation of the events. At court, however, nobody aims to get an explanation; ascertainment of causation is sufficient in almost every case.

Mutatis mutandis the same can be said of all opinions that make the assertion of a causal connection dependent on an *ex post* prediction or which are not content with a mere ascertainment of causality. Since such opinions are based on a scientific or philosophical approach, they miss the practical needs as well as the practical possibilities.

This simple comparison is not quite appropriate. Scientific methods increase knowledge, if successful. In contrast, applying the but–for clause creates no information. It is the only known method to make the best out of the given information accepted by the law. Being only a method, the but–for clause sometimes comes up against its limits. Applied, nevertheless, the results would be clearly wrong. The respective cases are well known; they occur extremely seldom and are discussed in nearly every textbook with completely identical solutions.[9]

Considering these characteristics, the but–for clause fulfils all elements of the definition given above, which would actually entitle us to talk of heuristics. Whether it is useful to do so will be discussed later.

Analyzing Rules of Evidence

Types

Roughly speaking, there are two types of rules of evidence. As indicated by its name, exclusionary rules of evidence exclude evidence from being considered by the court. In many continental countries, almost all exclusionary rules have

---

[8]   This result is not hard to explain. Applying the Hempel-Oppenheim scheme to past events you do not use information you already have, namely that the (presumed) effect has happened. You predict an event as if it has not already happened yet.

[9]   This is absolutely true for the traditional patterns. Recently a new constellation has emerged: does a single voter cause a wrong group decision and in consequence the damage to the victim even if this vote was not necessary to gain the majority. For the current status of the controversy cf. Puppe (2004).

nothing to do with the search for the truth. They were established to protect the interests of the state, the interests and rights of third parties, as well as the rights of the accused. In common law, the situation is quite different. Rules like the fruit of the poisonous tree doctrine are rather new in the common-law system and, I guess, still in the minority. The main purpose of the majority of exclusionary rules is to prevent the court, particularly the jury, from being influenced by weak, irrational, and exciting evidence.

Though exclusionary rules simplify the judgment in both versions, they bear no relation to heuristics, because in every reasonable legal system exclusionary rules are not applied by the ones who make the decision. It is not really appropriate to hear the bad evidence first and thereafter to exclude it.[10] We should keep in mind that splitting the competences and responsibilities might be an equivalent to heuristics in law.

The second category of rules of evidence include *prima facie* evidence, rebuttable presumptions, including some which are rebuttable in theory but have not been rebutted yet, and presumptions that are not rebuttable even in theory.

Apart from the latter, all *prima facie* rules have one thing in common: they shift the burden of proof. I will not discuss the different conditions under which *prima facie* rules are applicable nor under which conditions they differ from one another or the legal consequences in detail. Instead, let us focus on the concept of the shifting itself.

Shifting the Burden of Proof as a Sort of Heuristics

The common basis of the shifting is that demand for full evidence would be an unreasonable hardship. This may arise from different circumstances. The evidence offered at court, for example, increases the probability of an event or a sequence of events so much, that there is no reasonable doubt except when produced by the evidence offered by the other side. Another example may serve the case that the crucial data necessary for offering evidence could only be known to the other party. Burden of proof is sometimes even shifted, when the latter has no probable chance of a successful counter-evidence.

The first two examples show that shifting the burden of proof could be a concept equivalent to applying heuristics. In the first example, demanding full evidence would be a waste of time. One party would be forced to produce full evidence, although it would be most unlikely that the results would be better, more exact, or more relevant in any respect. The possible profit is out of all proportion to the certain costs and expenses. Building this idea alone, one could assume that

---

10 I admit that in Germany all (and in the common-law countries most) cases are treated in this "unreasonable way." Is it, however, reasonable to believe that the decision maker can eliminate the information from his memory? Even if this could be done, these rules bear no resemblance to heuristics.

these kind of rules of evidence are heuristics, or the result of heuristics. An argument against this is that the other party is allowed to destroy the first appearance (the *prima facie*) or to produce counter-evidence. Providing this opportunity, the law shows its interest in finding the truth. It only simplifies the way to it and fairly distributes the costs of producing evidence among the parties, in the hopes that opposing interests of the parties will expose the proper result.

The situation is quite similar when you take a look at the second example. The principle of a fair distribution of costs and expenses is supplemented by the other principle, that is, that nobody should be obliged to produce evidence when it is theoretically or practically impossible. The shifting of the burden of proof does not at all put an end to the producing of evidence. Driven by the threat of losing the case, the other party shall rather support the finding of the truth by producing its own evidence.

Sometimes, however, the burden of proof is shifted although one realizes that neither the one party nor the other has sufficient evidence. Therefore, the reason for shifting the burden can neither be the divergent ability to produce evidence, nor a fair distribution of the burden of proof under a procedural point of view. Values or rules of the substantial law influence the formal law in a way such that one side, usually the plaintiff, is favored.

This first glance at evidence law has not painted a complete picture. To obtain this, a closer inspection of the relation between evidence law and substantial law, at least a very brief one, is necessary.

The Relation between Evidence Law and Substantial Law

Many rules address traffic accidents. One rule presumes that the person rear-ending a car is responsible for the damage. Analyzing this rule, we see that it does not follow level 1 or level 2 of Table 15.1. It does not include an inference from the cause to the effect, but from the cause to the damage, thus crossing the boundaries between the levels. However, even this description is not precise enough, because by applying the but–for clause, or any other purely empirical consideration, it is clear that both cars have caused the accident. The evaluated cause, namely the fact that the car driving behind was "too close" to the car in front, establishes the presumption. Still, we must go another step further. Strictly speaking, it is not the presumption that holds the driver of the car in back responsible for the damage, but the rules of substantial law. They forbid a driver to drive up "too closely" to the car in front. The question is, what constitutes "too close." The answer is simple: the point at which a driver is so close to another car that a rear-end collision is unavoidable if the front car stops suddenly. At first glance, all of these arguments take on a circular appearance and do not explain the presumption, particularly not why it is needed. This objection is unnecessary considering that the driver of the car in front might have violated the law as well, for example, if he brakes too suddenly without good reason. That is why the driver rear-ending the front car has to be allowed to produce corresponding proof. If successful, the damage will be divided according to the respective negligence.

What initially looked like a pure conversion of probabilities in rules of evidence eventually turned out to be an almost pure rule of substantial law. Because it is easier to look ahead you have to pay attention to the traffic in front of you. Only under special circumstances do you have to watch the traffic behind you as well. The relation to probabilities is confined to the point that the latter situation occurs much more seldom than first one. Relations to heuristics cannot be found.

The next case shows an even more complicated relation between substantial and formal law.

A patient suffering from a sharp pain in his head could not be helped by the numerous physicians who treated him over the years. He eventually thought that all his teeth had to be extracted to put an end to his headaches. His dentist, however, assured him, that the teeth were not even a possible cause of his pains and therefore refused to extract them. The dentist continued refusing to perform the procedure the next time he was consulted. When , however, he was asked again some weeks later, he finally let himself be persuaded and extracted all of the teeth, after having once more pointed out the absurdity of this action. As expected, the pains did not disappear. The dentist was convicted of having committed a grievous bodily harm, because he had not informed the patient effectively enough that it would be of no use to extract the teeth. It is not the decision itself but the grounds upon which the judgment was made that are surprising: The court did not want to establish, as a rule of substantial law, that the right of self-determination ends where the results are absolutely unreasonable. Instead, a rule of evidence was set up: An absolutely unreasonable decision of a patient proves that the explanation was not sufficient, intense, or clear enough. This proof is only rebuttable in theory. It is not clear how it can be refuted, the inference from the unreasonable decision to the ineffective information being virtually tautological. Even if we agree on the court's decision in its outcome or in its grounds of judgment, we understand that there is a closer connection between material law and evidence law than between evidence law and heuristics. The next example supports this conclusion.

There is no experience to indicate that the probability of negligence increases if a surgeon does not record his steps taken during an operation. Nevertheless, the burden of proof does shift from the patient, who usually has to prove that the surgeon has made a mistake, to the surgeon, who would now have to prove that he did not make one, which, of course, would be impossible in almost every case. This rule is certainly the result of the general tendency to favor the patients instead of the physicians. However, it is—or more precisely it was (since the substantial law has changed)—the substitute for a missing rule in substantial law, which obliges the surgeon to record everything that happens during the operation in great detail.

These two examples have in common that the rule of evidence is a rule of substantial law in disguise. There are, however, also differences. In the second case,
the rule was established to compel physicians indirectly to record what has happened, but not to omit the option of future treatment. In the first case, however,
the issue is not better information for the patient, but rather the omission of unreasonable treatments. In the second case, the rule addresses the possibilities of
future proofs ("You are obliged to create pieces of evidence"). In contrast, the
first rule will not serve a future procedural purpose, but protects the patient's
health. From this point of view, there is no relation to heuristics except when you
content yourself with the fact that the rules try to achieve their goal indirectly.

Providing evidence of parenthood serves as a final example. Soon to become
obsolete because of the increasing application of DNA tests, German law still
recognizes the rule that a married man, who had at least one sexual contact with
his wife within a certain period of time, is the father of a child. That result is only
rebuttable, if evidently impossible. Thus paternity cannot be rebutted even by
proving that the mother slept with many other men, because this does not exclude the husband from being the father. These rules, and the similar rules in
many other jurisdictions, do not reflect any probabilities.[11] The objective is
rather to make the child legitimate as far as possible. Having in mind the
above-mentioned features of heuristics, it is not quite clear how we should classify these rules. They do not sufficiently achieve the aim, if it consists of finding
out the real father. However, they do meet the goal in every respect, if the aim is
to make as many children legitimate as possible. It is the word "make" that
points out the preferable classification. Because of the rules, you cannot miss the
second target in case the husband is the possible father. The possible father "is"
the real father. This is the wording of a legal fiction, not of a presumption. So the
concept of heuristics is inappropriate.

Generally, legal consequences do not depend on mental events or the individual capacities of a person. In criminal law, however, the penalty is almost always
in relation to the inner side of the offence. Because it is difficult to prove these
events almost every known jurisdiction has established rules for a circumstantial evidence of the intention, the so-called presumptions of intent. Nowadays,
the explicit versions of these have nearly completely disappeared in Europe, the
last of them owing to the European Convention of Human Rights. How they
have been "camouflaged" under the concept of free evaluation of evidence, and
to what extent, can unfortunately not be examined here. However, it seems certain that according to the legislators' opinion, courts too often deny that the accused acted intentionally. Thus, the legislator has invented a substitute: eliminating actually necessary elements from the concept of the offence, if the
remaining elements usually or at least often coincide with those having been

---

[11] The general and overwhelming probability that a child born during a marriage is the husband's
child is not decisive. What matters are the cases which go to court because the paternity is
doubtful.

crossed out of the text of the statute. Take fraud as an example: the deed is nearly always committed to enrich oneself or somebody else. Nevertheless, the corresponding intention is sometimes difficult to prove. Eliminating these elements from the statute will have the effect that the accused, having committed the fraud with the intention of enrichment, can be convicted regardless of possible difficulties in proving this intention. The change of substantial law works like establishing an unrebuttable presumption. This strategy has the advantage of not violating the presumption of innocence explicitly. On the other hand, the few persons convicted—though not having intended their enrichment—cannot complain about being treated unjustly because they have undoubtedly violated the law. Considering this, the legislator has successfully used heuristics. He has achieved his aim that nobody at court needs to reflect upon probabilities and not even upon the structure of the intention of enrichment.

The most intricate problem of the inner side, that of free will, can only be sketched. At court, the philosophical or religious question is of no importance. Even if you concede that there is something like a free will, the problem remains as to how it can be detected in the concrete case, something that possibly does not exist at all. Accordingly, it is of no use to assure that the doctrine of the free will is a necessary fiction in social life.[12] Therefore, or in spite of this, most jurisdictions refer to free will explicitly or implicitly. In criminal law, for example, they ask the question whether the accused had the possibility to choose another action than committing the crime.

One solution to the problem could involve the idea of heuristics. We cannot ascertain the truth and not even probabilities. There has to be a decision for or against awarding damages or for or against punishment. That is why we could apply heuristics and establish the rule that the accused has to be acquitted when he suffered from certain mental diseases while committing the crime. As we have presupposed, the rule is not established because we know that the free will of the insane is more restricted than that of quite normal persons. Rather, we take the mental deviation as such as a pure criterion of decision making. Choosing this way is only rational because the public accepts the acquittal of a person considered[13] insane. That is the strong point of the argument. It is, however, the weak point as well. The reason for public acceptance is not the decision rule, but the assumption that the mentally ill person is truly not responsible for his deed.

Thus, we have to ask whether we should use the term *heuristics* where the decision has no reference to the truth, to the essence of things or to probabilities, but at least a reference to a corresponding public prejudice.

---

[12] Cf. Kohlrausch (1910, p. 26). The original wording is "eine staatsnotwendige Fiktion" (a fiction that is necessary for the state/the government). Kohlrausch did not write anything about the resulting problems of evidence, neither in this publication nor in his numerous explanations of the German penal code.

[13] Which mental states are considered insane or therefore exclude legal responsibility depends to a high degree on culture.

IS RENDERING A JUDGMENT A DECISION?

Ultimately, these details point to a more general question. Heuristics, as outlined above, are part of a theory of decision making, the latter being understood as a theory about how to act in the most rational way. This means that the rules apply to the information directly and not in a two-step manner: the first step answering the question of facts, and the second taking the appropriate consequences as if the facts were true or probable. Heuristics do not aim to ascertain facts; however, the law does, at least in all proceedings where evidence law plays an important part. The two-step method is just chosen to prevent legal consequences from having an effect on the question of guilt. This is obvious with regard to a jury trial. The verdict must not be influenced by the possible punishment. It must not depend on the question whether there is a death penalty or a fine to be expected. Certainly, criminology teaches that the reality is somewhat different. So much the worse.

Analyzing the other codes of procedure allows us to come to the same solution. Most judgments include a declaration of the facts or are declaratory in themselves under certain conditions.

HOW TO CONTROL THE DECLARATION OF FACTS

The next general question is how to control the declaration of the facts. The rationality of heuristics, as presented by Gigerenzer et al. (1999), can be directly or indirectly controlled through empirical inquiries.

However, whether the findings of the verdict are correct is usually impossible to prove empirically from outside the court. The verdict "makes the facts come true"—nearly always in social reality and according to some opinions in theory as well. What can be ascertained, however, is whether the verdict satisfies the parties and the public. The one who has lost the case is not "mentally"satisfied, of course. He has to content himself with the verdict if he cannot raise any objections that are accepted in public or if his objections are not at least supported by his friends and relatives. Therefore, the rules of evidence have to correspond with the conclusions drawn in the world of the "man on the bus from Clapham," as far as everyday life is concerned. This proposition sounds more simple and more populistic than it actually is. One has to distinguish between the general rules and the outcome of a particular trial, the latter not needing to be in accordance with every person's opinion In addition, rules have to be considered to be correct or at least not refuted by reputable experts as far as special knowledge is concerned. In short, rules have to be embedded in the social consensus (Luhmann 1975).

If law claims to have found the true culprit—which it does not always do—this goal will be achieved when the culprit, who claims to be innocent, is considered to be a grouser almost everywhere. If he is truly guilty, nobody will usually know, possibly not even the convict himself. The wording of these sentences refers to criminal procedures. Its idea, in fact, can be transferred to all proceedings where evidence law plays an important part.

REFERENCES

Cicero, M.T. 1976. Cicero in Twenty-eight Volumes, vol. II, transl. H.M. Hubbell. The Loeb Classical Library. London: Heinemann.

Gigerenzer, G., P.M. Todd, and the ABC Research Group. 1999. Simple Heuristics That Make Us Smart. New York: Oxford Univ. Press.

Hempel, C.G. 1965. Aspects of Scientific Explanation and Other Essays in the Philosophy of Science. New York: Free Press.

Holling v. Yorkshire Traction Company Ltd, All E.R. 662, 664 (1948).

Kaufmann, A. 1971. Tatbestandsmäßigkeit und Verursachung im Contergan-Verfahren. *Juristenzeitung* **18**:569–576.

Kohlrausch, E. 1910. Sollen und Können als Grundlagen der strafrechtlichen Zurechnung. In: Festgabe für Güterbock, ed. Juristische Fakultät Königsberg, pp. 1–34. Berlin: Vahlen.

Leonard, B.K. 2001. Kausalität und die Struktur des Verschuldensdelikts. Osnabrück: Universitätsverlag Rasch.

Luhmann, N. 1975. Legitimation durch Verfahren. Neuwied: Luchterhand.

Puppe, I. 2004. Wider die fahrlässige Mittäterschaft. *Goldtammer's Arch. Strafrecht* **3**:129–146.

Schulz, J. 1987. Gesetzmäßige Bedingung und kausale Erklärung. In: Festschrift für Karl Lackner, ed. W. Küper, pp. 39–51. Berlin: de Gruyter.

Schulz, J. 1992. Sachverhaltsfeststellung und Beweistheorie. Cologne: Heymanns.

Left to right: Jay Koehler, Reid Hastie, Callia Piperides, Joachim Schulz, Mandeep Dhami, Rick Lempert, Gerhard Wagner, Ron Allen, and Axel Flessner

16

Group Report: What Is the Role of Heuristics in Litigation?

Callia Piperides, Rapporteur

Ronald J. Allen, Mandeep K. Dhami, Axel Flessner,
Reid Hastie, Jonathan J. Koehler, Richard Lempert,
Joachim Schulz, and Gerhard Wagner

ABSTRACT

This chapter examines the role of heuristics in the Anglo-American and Continental litigation systems by considering two broad areas: heuristics that appear in legal rules and procedures, as well as heuristics used by various legal actors (e.g., judges, juries, lawyers).

It begins with theoretical accounts of heuristics in psychology and law. Next, it explores the role that heuristics play in the litigation process from the selection and construction of cases to the appellate process. Although procedural rules are in place to ensure that legal decision processes are deliberative, the complexities and uncertainties inherent in legal judgments promote the use of simplifying heuristic strategies. Accordingly, numerous possible instances of heuristics are identified both in legal rules and in the judgment processes of legal actors. The prescriptive utility of heuristics is considered with reference to competing legal ideals. If legal decision makers are to come closer to legal ideals, then the law must strive for perfection through complexity. If legal ideals take account of psychological reality, then the law should design an environment that recognizes human constraints and thereby facilitates heuristic decision strategies that are adaptive.

Considerably more scientific work is needed to specify the conditions under which various heuristics are used in the legal domain and under which conditions these heuristics are used successfully to achieve legal objectives.

INTRODUCTION

Virtually every human interaction can result in litigation from the most intimate interaction of family members to war. Moreover, these issues will arise in different legal, social, and cultural settings. That this bubbling mass of complexity could be usefully reduced to any single methodology, or approach, whether of rational choice theory or the heuristic approach, struck us as too implausible to deserve extended discussion. The pertinent question seemed to be what it is people actually *do* rather than whether they only optimize or only employ heuristics.

Some optimizing tools are employed occasionally, such as expected utility calculations in damages, and the law can be viewed as attempting to minimize a loss function described as the total cost of social disputes (combining damages and transaction costs). However, no one claims that optimization can describe the litigation process in its entirety. If one accepts the very narrow concept of "optimization" that has been advanced as procedures used to make a system as effective or functional as possible, then it does not capture much of interest in the litigation process. There are, by contrast, innumerable intellectual tools and strategies that are employed throughout litigation that we believe would be interesting to examine from the perspective of heuristics.

We considered heuristics from the perspective of Gigerenzer, Todd, and the ABC Research Group (1999), who identified "fast and frugal heuristics" that are adaptive and thus useful. We distinguished these from the view of heuristics proposed by Kahneman and Tversky (1974), who predominately identified the biases that may result from use of heuristic strategies. We further identified specific heuristics that may not strictly fit in either of these two approaches, but which nonetheless fit the concept of a psychological judgment heuristic.

Within the litigation process, heuristics might arise in quite different ways. They may be relevant to the decision making of legal actors. Here, researchers may try to predict whether cognitive strategies can best be described by heuristics or by more complex models. Heuristics may also be relevant to the construction of litigation systems. A legislator may attempt to optimize some function by including a role for heuristics within the operation of the system. For example, the use of heuristics might permit the minimization of a loss function. A further interesting aspect of heuristics is their capacity to be exploited by actors within the legal system.

Litigation is embedded in more general governance mechanisms and serves their purposes. Perhaps its most significant attribute is to provide incentives for behavior, including incentives to cooperate. As it becomes increasingly clear that those incentives are not accomplishing their purpose, a complicated procedural structure is set in motion, beginning with the selection of cases for litigation. The cases selected must be prepared for trial on both the legal and factual fronts. Some of those cases will then proceed to trial, which itself is an overwhelmingly complex process (taking into account the inferential tasks), and following trial may be an appeal.

We noted five dichotomies that were likely to be pertinent to all of our discussions:

1. Common versus civil law procedural contexts.
2. Criminal versus civil law cases.

3. Individual (single jurors or judges) versus collective (juries, multiple member courts) decision making.
4. Expert versus lay judgment.
5. The law in the books versus the law in action.

We have organized our discussion over the chronology of litigation, which allowed us to raise the above issues as appropriate to the debate. We first grappled with the concept of a judgment "heuristic" as defined in psychology and discussed its application in the legal domain. We then looked for instances of heuristic use at the different stages of litigation, from the selection of cases to the appellate process. We found heuristics in the form of rules of evidence and procedural law. In addition, we examined heuristics used by legal participants, such as lawyers, judges, and juries. We then considered the prescriptive utility of heuristics for both the legal decision makers and for the development of legal rules. Finally, we reconsidered our conceptualization of the term *heuristics* in light of what we had learned throughout our discussions.

THE CONCEPT OF A JUDGMENT HEURISTIC

Theoretical Background

One goal at this workshop was to explore the analogy between a heuristic information processing procedure as used by psychologists to describe cognitive processes and similar procedures, rules, methods used by actors in legal settings. Thus, we begin with a theoretical discourse of the concept of "heuristic" as it has been under construction by psychologists studying judgment and decision making.

The concept of a "heuristic" had a long history of usages in philosophy, education, mathematics, and computer science before its introduction into psychology (see Schulz, this volume, for a discussion of some of its roots). Its seminal use in the twentieth century was delineated by George Polya (1957) in his book, *How to Solve It*—an attempt to instruct mathematics students on the informal methods that are useful in solving mathematical derivation and proof problems. From Polya, it entered the field of computer science where it referred to a useful, computationally efficient method of solving problems that has a high probability of quickly reaching an effective solution, but with no guarantee of finding the optimal or best solution.

More than thirty years ago, Daniel Kahneman and Amos Tversky (1974) promoted the concept of *heuristic* in the field of judgment and decision making. They proposed that judgments under uncertainty could be understood as resulting from relatively simple mental processes that were adaptive in many situations but which were prone to distinctive systematic errors (biases) in some. For example, it is usually adaptive to estimate frequencies and probabilities by relying on the ease with which relevant instances of the to-be-judged events can be retrieved from memory (called "the availability heuristic"). When estimating the number of German participants at a conference, a quick attempt to retrieve the names of attendees from memory gives an approximate estimate of the total. However, reliance solely on memory will introduce systematic biases in the judgment; perhaps a tendency to underestimate true totals because of limits on retrieval, or a bias to overestimate the relative numbers of attendees from an especially memorable category.

More generally, we might define the Kahneman and Tversky judgment heuristic as a shortcut mental strategy to solve a judgment problem. We can describe this strategy as an information processing procedure composed of elementary cognitive capacities such as memory retrieval, similarity evaluation, or adjustment from a salient value. Some of the important contributions of the Kahneman and Tversky research program included the following ideas:

1. People rely on shortcut judgment strategies.
2. These strategies are often composed of more elementary cognitive abilities.
3. Judgment often involves substitution of inferences based on one "dimension" (e.g., ease of retrieval, similarity) for another (e.g., frequency, probability).
4. A novel and outrageously popular research method that was based on the identification of the underlying judgment process from its *signature biases* or errors.
5. The research strategy compared human performance to an explicit rational standard of logical coherence (Did the judgments conform to the rules of probability theory?) or accuracy (Did the judgments match the "answer" calculated from Bayes's theorem? Did the factual answer correspond to the true answer assessed in the external world?).

Subsequent research and reviews led to the concept of a metaphorical "cognitive toolbox" containing judgment and choice heuristics such as "availability," "representativeness," "anchor-and-adjust," "affect-based evaluation," and an "elimination-by-aspects" choice strategy.

At approximately the same time, a second research program was developing a similar analysis of choice strategies. First John Payne and then his colleagues James Bettman and Eric Johnson constructed what is now known as the "Adaptive Decision Maker" theoretical framework (1993). Their program was also based on the metaphor of a cognitive information processing system with a toolbox of useful strategies and heuristics that could be optionally selected to solve judgment and choice problems encountered in everyday life. Heavily influenced by the methods and theories of Herbert Simon (who is probably responsible for introducing the term *heuristic* to modern psychology), these theorists proposed a set of 11 choice heuristics and defined them as formal computational algorithms. Their heuristic tools aimed to solve evaluation and choice problems and included procedures such as a "weighted adding heuristic" (an MAUT calculator), a "satisficing evaluator," and various noncompensatory rules similar to elimination-by-aspects. The distinctive contributions of the Adaptive Decision Maker theorists included (a) the precise specification of a new collection of choice heuristics as computable procedures, and (b) a systematic analysis of the question of what determines the selection of a particular heuristic (from the set of 11). Here they introduced the notion that heuristic strategy selection is a rational choice based on an adaptive consideration of the potential costs and benefits of using one heuristic or another. Moreover, they used systematic computer simulations to test the performance of each heuristic. Further contributions included (c) the use of several criteria to assess the efficiency, rationality, and robustness of each heuristic across a range of hypothetical choice problems, and (d) a systematic program of behavioral research using process-tracing methods.

The most recent program of research on heuristics in judgment and choice is that of Gerd Gigerenzer and his colleagues in the Adaptive Behavior and Cognition Group (ABC) (Gigerenzer et al.1999). Like their predecessors, the ABC Group begins with the theoretical metaphor of the human as a problem solver with a toolbox of heuristic judgment and choice procedures. They have enlarged the set to include new heuristics, notably social heuristics such as "pass the buck," "imitation," and "majority rule." The distinctive contributions of the ABC Group include precise definitions of the information processing procedures underlying the heuristics; a focus on the optional inclusion and exclusion of problem-relevant information in heuristic processing; extensive tests of the performance of each heuristic in simulations based on representative samples of naturally occurring judgment and choice environments; and the use of optimal statistical models and measures of accuracy to assess the relative success of each heuristic. Perhaps most importantly, the ABC Group has also developed the concept of "ecological rationality" to emphasize the importance of evaluating the performance of hypothesized heuristics in simulations of environments in which they naturally developed and in which they are used.

A guiding precept of ecological rationality is that heuristics will usually be adaptive or appropriate to the environments in which they are used. We rely here on the same diagram as in Kysar et al. (this volume) to discuss the general paradigm for research and theory. Imagine three naturally occurring choice environments (X, Y, Z) and three choice heuristics (A, B, C). Combined they produce a space of nine heuristic–environment pairings, and each heuristic could be tested in each type of environment. Now, imagine that some pairings are more congenial, that each heuristic is especially successful in some, but not in all of the environments. For simplicity, suppose that A–X, B–Y, and C–Z are the adaptive pairings, dubbed "ecologically rational" ("ER" in Figure 16.1), and suppose that the other pairings are less successful, i.e., the "wrong," maladaptive, heuristic is used in the environment.

One of the most original contributions of the ABC research program is to evaluate the performance of heuristics across a range of representative environments, thus, yielding a more complete theory of the "organism–environment system" as endorsed by Herbert Simon (1955), Egon Brunswik (1952), and others. The guiding precept in the ABC research, namely, to identify the situations in which a given heuristic will be ecologically rational, is exemplified by the diagonal of the heuristics × environments space in Figure 16.1.[1]

We also discussed the issue of whether rational choice theory (RCT) can ever be applied to analyze a legal decision situation in a useful manner. We have to consider Gigerenzer's (and others') point that the environment is important. If we apply RCT to an idealized textbook problem (e.g., "Which gamble has the best rate of profits?"), then RCT provides the best possible analysis. Now, if we move into a real-world situation, where we can be assured that the RCT model captures most of the essential characteristics of the environment (e.g., a gambling casino), then again, RCT is the most useful model. However, let us move to a complex and ill-defined situation: two lawyers arguing over a case settlement. We are now less confident in our reliance on the RCT model. Unfortunately, it now becomes a matter of faith, or at least uncertain belief that RCT is a useful guide to behavior. The important insight here is that the usefulness of RCT—just like any heuristic analysis—depends on the situation.

To date, research by the ABC Group on "adaptive rationality" has focused on the ecologically rational conditions. Most of the results from the ABC Group seem to represent congenial heuristic–environment combinations, whereas earlier research, especially by Kahneman and Tversky inspired researchers, focused on the laws of logic and probability rather than natural environments, namely, conditions where there is a mismatch between heuristics and logical principles and where systematic discrepancies abound. Consideration of heuristic performance in a *full range of environments* is enormously important, especially when we want to speculate about performance in new environments. For example, when we want to entertain the possibility that our understanding of cognitive heuristics gained from laboratory research can provide some insights into behavior in a new setting such as legal contexts. Note that the difference between the ABC perspective and the Kahneman-Tversky view is *not* that people are mostly rational or mostly irrational. The normative difference is in the very definition of rational: the ABC rationality is ecological (see Figure 16.1); the Kahneman-Tversky rationality, by contrast, is mostly logical.

---

[1] One other behavioral research program has been concerned with the heuristics × environment system. Kenneth Hammond (1996) has characterized judgment processes as lying along a "cognitive continuum" ranging from intuitive to analytic and environments as "inducing" processing of particular types along that continuum. For instance, a computer screen displaying tables of numbers induces analytic judgment; a radar screen induces intuitive judgment. However, the goal of his research has been to identify the tendency of certain environments to *induce* certain types of cognitive processing, not to evaluate the adaptive success of one mode or processing across several environments.

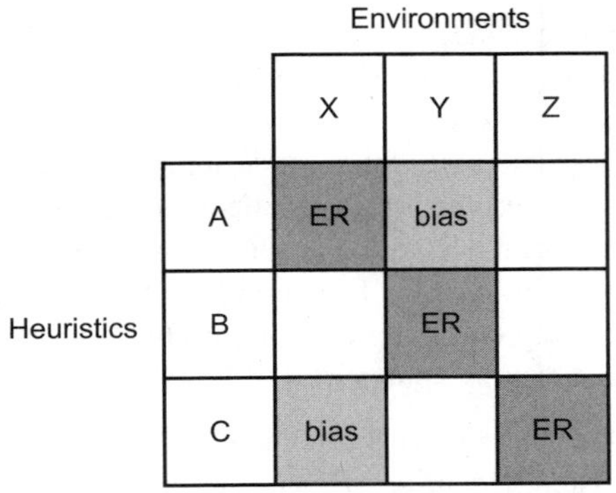

Environments

	X	Y	Z
A	ER	bias	
B		ER	
C	bias		ER

(left label: Heuristics)

Figure 16.1 A hypothetical space of choice heuristics (A, B, C) and decision environments (X, Y, Z). "ER," ecologically rational, refers to combinations of an individual heuristic used in a specific environment that are especially successful (i.e., the adaptive heuristic was used in the environment).

On closer examination of Figure 16.1, we identify some current goals for research. What is the full set of cognitive heuristics (What are the "rows" in the table?), and how are they to be organized: along an intuitive-analytic cognitive continuum, according to the natural underlying cognitive capacities (memory, similarity, evaluation), or according to cognitive computational complexity (e.g., ignorance-based heuristics, one-reason heuristics, multiple-reason heuristics)? What is the range of naturally occurring judgment and decision environments ("columns" in the table), and how should we organize that set: problems (situations) with various statistical (cue-criterion) structures, problems with good and poor feedback, or problems in which competition and principal-agent contingencies create strategic complexities? Finally, what are the adaptive relationships in fact: Do people usually rely on heuristics that are adaptive, that is, that are relatively successful in each environment? Are some heuristics generally more successful?

Heuristics in the Legal Domain

Our discussion of heuristics in legal institutions and behavior began with the proposition that heuristics abound in court because they abound in human reasoning. However, it became clear that we had different notions of what qualified as a "heuristic," both in psychology and in the legal domain. We thus needed to examine possible definitions of this term from the outset, and, if no consensus could be reached on a conceptual definition, we needed to, at least, collect a set of instructive exemplars of heuristic judgment processes.

Even within psychology, there is no perfect consensus on the definition of a "judgment heuristic." There is no litmus test that can be applied to determine if a cognitive judgment strategy definitely is or is not a heuristic. Nevertheless, there does seem to be some consensus on the types of strategies that count as heuristics, some convergence on prototypical heuristics, and conceptual progress toward a larger set of well-defined heuristics.

Decisions in the legal domain can be made at three levels: the individual (i.e., by single judges, jurors, or lawyers), the collective (i.e., by a panel of judges or the jury), and the institutional level (i.e., by legislative bodies in the construction of litigation systems or law firms). Depending on the circumstances, the decisions made might employ heuristics or rational-choice strategies. Heuristics in this framework might display some of the following criteria:

- They are mental (cognitive) shortcuts whereby a variable (or set of variables) that is easier to identify, measure, or manipulate is taken to represent a variable (or set of variables) that is harder to identify, measure, or manipulate to facilitate the process of making some kind of evaluation.
- They are rule-like and simple; still, not every rule that simplifies the law is necessarily a heuristic.
- They describe the process of encoding data and discarding information.
- They are context specific.
- Although, some heuristics are "fast and frugal"[2] (see Gigerenzer et al. 1999), some of us thought that not all heuristics are necessarily fast and/or frugal.
- Although some of us thought that sometimes heuristics might not be conscious or that they can be intuitive, others required that they be a deliberate choice.

In litigation, it seems we can look for two applications of the psychologists' concept of heuristics:

1. Can we identify specific heuristic judgment processes of actors involved in litigation? Could we study the behavior of attorneys negotiating the terms of a settlement and identify conscious or unconscious strategies that would qualify as behavioral heuristics? Can we describe the decision-making strategies of judges and juries? For instance, Dhami and Ayton (2001) carried out a behavioral analysis of magistrates setting bail in an effort to discover the heuristics upon which they rely. Can we then draw any conclusions about how well adapted a legal decision maker is to the task environment? Could we compare the heuristic analysis to a parallel analysis based on a RCT framework?

---

2 Simple or fast and frugal heuristics are defined by Gigerenzer and his colleagues as simple process models based on structural relationships between cues and judgment. The process includes information search, stop, and decision making and can be conscious or unconscious. Most heuristics do not search all relevant cues, do not integrate but substitute cues in noncompensatory way, and often base decisions on one cue. To date, a number of heuristics have been identified for different types of decision-making tasks (e.g., Take The Best for two-alternative choice tasks and matching heuristic for binary classification tasks).

2. Alternatively, at a different level of analysis, can we identify heuristic judgment procedures, analogous to the cognitive heuristics studied in the laboratory, in explicit procedures, official rules, and informal rules of thumb in litigation? For example, if we looked at an attorney's or a law firm's explicit rules of thumb for valuing a settlement offer, would we see a procedure analogous to a psychological heuristic? If we look at the explicit instructions to magistrates prescribing the legally appropriate procedure for bail setting, would we find the essence of a heuristic procedure?

Below we examine these issues at the various stages of the litigation process. During our discussions we identified numerous examples, which we thought would be interesting and useful to explore. However, our catalog is not based on systematic research, though there is research that supports some of the examples. Considerably more work is needed to identify those heuristics and other shortcuts and to specify the conditions under which, and the mechanisms by which, they operate.

THE LITIGATION PROCESS

During the litigation process, lawyers employ strategic behavior in selecting and constructing cases. At preliminary proceedings, judges decide whether cases merit a full trial. Eventually, judges and juries must reach a decision based on the facts presented and the applicable law. Moreover, the whole process must operate within the constraints of evidence and procedural rules. This is obviously a potentially fertile field for the investigation of heuristics. While not every simplified rule of prudence should be called a heuristic, there are many shortcuts for finding, presenting, and deliberating that do qualify as such.

The litigation process can be usefully, if roughly, divided into five components. First, lawyers and potential parties to an action select cases for litigation. By far, most disputes do not result in litigation; they are either ignored and their costs absorbed, or they are resolved through negotiations. There are many reasons for this, and perhaps they can be characterized in economic terms as individuals making cost-benefit calculations or in heuristic terms: It may be better to accept the costs or enter into negotiations rather than sue. Once an individual makes a decision to litigate, legal counsel will be approached to represent a party. Counsel must make similar decisions about whether to pursue the case.

Second, after a case is selected for litigation, the case must be prepared, which we refer to as "constructed for litigation." This involves two quite different processes. The lawyer must first research the law and determine its implications for the dispute. Then, he or she must investigate the case factually. In either situation, the lawyer may attempt to optimize or may rely on simple heuristics.

Third, after case construction has begun, preliminary legal proceedings will soon begin, as well. These vary over differing procedural settings. There is some uniformity, however. To our knowledge, all systems allow preliminary assessments of the legal sufficiency of the claims, and they allow constrained review of factual allegations. In all systems, an evidentiary presentation can occur in which testimony is taken and documentary evidence received.

Fourth, at some point, the evidentiary process closes, and the judge or jury make a decision on the facts and law.

Finally, another commonality of Western legal systems is an appellate process that allows some review of fact-finding and considerable review of legal determinations.

Case Selection

At the first stage of the litigation process, lawyers and potential parties to an action must select cases for trial. If they were to take rational choice analysis as a norm, the potential parties to a lawsuit would rationally assess the costs and benefits of a trial, assess the probabilities of the various potential outcomes, and then combine these assessments using a normative expectation model (e.g., expected value). The potential parties would also compute the consequences of out-of-court settlements and compare these outcomes to the trial estimates above. This approach implies that cases which actually go to trial are those in which both parties believe that they are likely to obtain a better outcome by going to trial than they would obtain by settling the case (Priest and Klein 1984).

However, the way that people think about the costs, benefits, and risks of litigation may be influenced by a variety of factors, some of which are not part of the economic rational choice model. Consequently, legal disputants may not always make value-maximizing choices. Some of the barriers to economically rational choices include optimism, recency, anchoring, availability, framing, overweighting of low probability events, etc. All of these factors have been shown to affect judgment in psychological studies (e.g., see Babcock and Loewenstein 1997; Hogarth and Einhorn 1992; Kahneman and Frederick 2002), and they may also distort disputants' judgments about their chances of winning at trial and receiving particular outcomes. If true, then case selection may lead to sub-optimal decisions. That is, some disputants may go to trial when they should settle, and others may settle when they would be better off (on average) by taking their chances in the courtroom.

One could argue, however, that the opposite may also be true: A party may rely on one or more traditionally nonrational considerations when deciding whether to go to trial and may benefit by doing so. For example, a plaintiff might choose to go to trial if he or she attaches great weight to the outcome of a recent, vaguely similar, high-profile case in which another plaintiff prevailed. The plaintiff might decide to go forward with his or her case even though the odds of prevailing in such cases have strongly favored the defendant in the past. If the jurors also perceive a similarity between the plaintiff's case and the recent high-profile case, then they may see more merit in the plaintiff's claim than they otherwise would have. The point is that if legal actors are subject to some of the same influences and biases as legal decision makers, a heuristic approach to case selection may prove to be more beneficial to the legal actors than a more traditional economic approach.

Sometimes, reliance on heuristics in case selection will clearly lead to imperfect decisions. For example, when a potential litigant elects to go to trial with one or more cases selected from among a *set* of potential cases, fact finders can be mislead. Although a plaintiff or prosecutor may be involved with just a single case at a time, he or she may have considered and investigated many other possible cases before deciding to proceed with a particular case. In such situations, the fact finder may not be aware of the breadth of the sample space from which the cases (or cases) are selected for litigation. This is a serious problem, because failure to appreciate the size of the sample space of possible cases may cause fact finders to judge the strength of the plaintiff's case to be significantly stronger than it actually is. The following example illustrates the point.

Suppose that the U.S. Attorney General (a) is concerned about the possibility of sex discrimination in promotion decisions among companies in the United States; (b) reviews the ten most recent promotions made in each of 1,000 companies in which a single male candidate competed against a single, equally qualified, female candidate; (c) finds that exactly one company, XYZ, failed to promote a single woman in its last ten promotion cases; (d) brings charges against XYZ for sex discrimination. Fact finders who are told that the XYZ company failed to promote a single woman among its last ten cases in which the female candidate was just as qualified as the male candidate are very likely to view this fact as powerful evidence of unequal treatment of the sexes. In fact, a statistical analysis indicates that such an outcome is likely to be found in about one time in 1000 by chance alone.[3] A fact finder who is not told that this particular case was selected for litigation from among a set of 1000 potential cases would likely conclude that the XYZ company's pattern of promoting men over women could not be explained by chance alone. Having reached this conclusion, the fact finder may very well conclude that the XYZ company is guilty of sex discrimination as charged. However, a fact finder who is made aware of the broader sample space would or should recognize that the pattern observed for the XYZ company is precisely the pattern that would occur every now and then *by chance alone* in a large sample space such as one that includes 1000 companies. In other words, the pattern observed in the XYZ company is perfectly consistent with the claim

---

[3]   The probability that this event would occur by chance alone is: $\binom{10}{0}(0.5)^0 (0.5)^{10} = 0.00098$.

that the pattern occurred by chance alone once the fact finder understands that this company was singled out from a very large sample space.[4]

However, will a fact finder receive this information? Probably not. The rules of evidence do not compel the plaintiff to reveal all of the other companies that were part of its investigation. Will a fact finder consider the possibility that the case before them was selected from a larger sample space, and that the strength of the case against the defendant is therefore weaker than it may at first appear? Probably not. Preliminary research on this topic indicates that people do not think much about sample space matters, unless such information is made explicit (J.J. Koehler, pers. comm.).

Case Construction

In the second stage of litigation, after case selection, the lawyer's task is to construct a case, that is, to put together a case with a view to a possible presentation in court. The lawyer must research the law and investigate the facts of the case. The supporting facts, means of proof, and legal arguments must be presented to the court in written or oral form as persuasively as possible. These deliberations are a form of strategic behavior that may rely on ready-made shortcuts or heuristics instead of more complicated and perfected judgment methods.

Lawyers in Germany often rely on shortcuts or heuristics that exist in the form of "cook books." The books contain recipes or tactical guidelines offering advice and techniques to assist in the search of evidence or in the construction of arguments. These and similar techniques are the result of many years of experience and may also be found in the unstated working habits of lawyers. The various techniques are devised to avoid overwhelming material, unreliable witnesses, unnecessary facts, evidence, and legal arguments. As to the facts, the choice may lie in stating them in full complexity or reducing the story to make it more palatable for the decision maker. As to the means of proof, a decision may have to be made whether to call many supportive witnesses or only the ones whose testimony promises to be unshakeable even under cross-examination. As to the legal arguments, the claim may be based on a number of them, but it may be easier, more straightforward, and more persuasive to bring forward only the strongest or the least complicated ones. Deals and settlements are a special case. They are in themselves a shortcut to resolving the conflict, but there may also be heuristic techniques for arriving at these shortcuts.

Heuristics in the form of tactical guidelines, techniques, and practices do not constitute unprofessional behavior, even though a more thorough treatment of

---

[4] From a Bayesian perspective, matters of sample space inform a fact finder's prior probability estimates, i.e., the chance that the defendant behaved as charged prior to the introduction of specific evidence. The probability that specific evidence (e.g., ten male promotions in succession) would arise by chance informs the fact finder's likelihood estimate, namely, the chance that the ten successive male promotions would occur if, in fact, the company did not behave as charged.

the case would have been possible. The aim of the shortcuts is to support or to replace the creativity of the lawyer, rather than to produce ready-made results that can be chosen and used mechanically. Heuristics are only a mental catalog of items, and it is up to the lawyers to choose the most appropriate.[5]

Preliminary Proceedings

At the third stage of litigation, after case construction has begun, a preliminary hearing is held. Can we identify heuristic procedures, similar to the cognitive heuristics used by legal actors, in explicit procedures?

Most systems of civil procedure are designed to allow the court to throw out a case at the earliest possible stage of the proceedings. Although this objective is common to both the civil law and the common-law approaches, there are important differences in the way the two systems address it. In German procedure, the plaintiff is not required to choose a particular "form of action" or other category in order to state a claim, but instead, is supposed to adduce facts upon which to found the claim. Thus, an attorney representing the plaintiff must ask what the relevant legal rules are upon which the claim might be based in order to allege facts corresponding to the elements the pertinent legal standards require. For the defendant, the task is a mirror image of the plaintiff's efforts. Of course, the defendant may dispute all or part of the facts that the plaintiff relied on. In addition, he or she will have to think of defenses that can defeat the plaintiff's claim even though it might be valid. With respect to these defenses, the defendant carries the burden of proof. Consequently, the defendant must consult the law, identify possible defenses, and then allege the specific facts required by the respective legal rules.

Once both parties have stated their claim and defense, respectively, the court applies a three-stage investigation to the pleadings brought before it. As a first cut, the court will assume that all of the facts relied on by the plaintiff are true and then ask whether the law supports his claim. If it does not, that is, if the claim founders on the legal issues alone, it will be dismissed outright. The crucial point here is that the court will not enter into any evidentiary proceedings or order any measures of discovery or disclosure. It will also disregard all of the information supplied—or rather alleged—by the defendant. In this sense, the court could be viewed as applying a heuristic tool.

If at the first stage it is established that the plaintiff successfully made a claim, the court will then turn to the defendant's case for the second cut. The same procedure applied to the statement of the claim will now be applied to the statement of defense. The judge will assume that all of the facts alleged by the defendant are true and then ask the question whether they have the capacity to defeat the

---

5 In the heuristics terminology, the lawyer has an "adaptive toolbox" of legal heuristics from which to select a suitable heuristic for her purposes, just as ordinary minds pick a heuristic. This process, however, is often done unconsciously.

claim. If, for example, the defendant failed to dispute those facts that form the legal foundation of the plaintiff's claim, the claim will be allowed to go through. Unless the defendant alleges that the time stipulated in a statute of limitations has run out, the court concludes that it has not. For example, the court may presume that the claim only matured at a later point in time, and thus, will "dismiss" the defendant's defense. Again, the dismissal means the plaintiff's claim is allowed to go through.

Finally, it is only if both of the cuts just described have not led to a final resolution of the case that the court opens evidentiary proceedings. Even then, the work done at the two previous stages is not worthless. The investigations at stage one and two have established as a by-product which facts are relevant for the resolution of the dispute, both with respect to the claim and the defense. Therefore, the court will only attend to those pieces of evidence that might support a party's allegations relevant to the claim and the defense. All other evidence is deemed irrelevant and is thus discarded.

The crucial question here is whether the process may be analyzed as the application of a heuristic. It seems that it can be. The court works its way through a fast and frugal decision tree (Gigerenzer, this volume) with two binary cues (see Figure 16.2):

First cue: If the plaintiff's claim fails to allege facts that are supported by the law ⇒ throw the case out. Otherwise proceed.

Second cue: If the defendant fails to dispute the facts relevant to the plaintiff's claim and fails to state a defense ⇒ allow the claim. Otherwise, enter into the evidentiary proceeding.

It seems that the American civil procedure system lacks heuristics like the ones just described. Under the rules of civil procedure, both federal and state, the plaintiff must do no more than state his or her claim in broad terms, without being specific either with respect to the law or to the facts. The factual background of the case will then be assembled through the process of discovery. For this reason, the so-called "dismissal for failure to state a claim upon which relief can be granted" is a toothless instrument. Every lawyer, supposedly, is capable of choosing such broad terms to describe the factual background of the claim on which relief can be granted that a motion to dismiss brought by defendant is bound to fail. Thus, the dismissal for failure to state a claim upon which relief can be granted does not serve the end of making final decisions without the need to investigate the case. The motion for summary judgment is not apt to fill the void either. The standard for allowing this motion is not in the form of a fast and frugal heuristic but relates to the burden of proof which is set at a very high (or low) mark. If it seems highly unlikely that the plaintiff will prevail at trial, his claim may be dismissed by way of summary judgment. To arrive at such a conclusion the court must look at all the facts and at all of the evidence, and it must not limit its attention to only a part of the information brought to its attention.

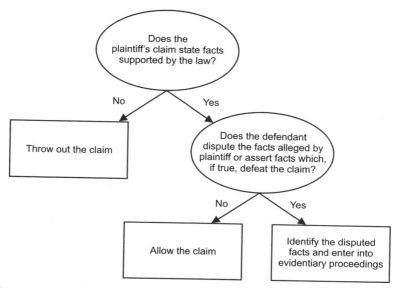

Figure 16.2 Fast and frugal tree of the preliminary proceedings in German courts. These simple trees allow a decision after each question or cue (ellipses) and have $n + 1$ exits (boxes), whereas a complete tree with n binary cues has 2^n exits. Compare the fast and frugal trees in Figures 2.1 and 2.3 (Gigerenzer, this volume).

Evidence and Procedural Rules

Once the judge at the preliminary proceedings allows the plaintiff's claim, the evidentiary presentations begin in which testimony is taken and documentary evidence is received. Similar to the German procedural shortcuts in preliminary hearings, we may be able to find examples of heuristics embedded in explicit legal rules (cf. Schulz; Wagner, both this volume).

The law of evidence is replete with rules that allow the court to ignore information, or rather sources of information. In American law, exclusionary rules are a standard means of limiting the evidence and thus the informational basis of the court. The rationale of most of these rules is that evidence thought to be unreliable is excluded. Pertinent examples are the exclusion of hearsay evidence, and the exclusion of evidence acquired by unlawful means under the "fruit of the poisonous tree" doctrine. Although the latter rule excludes information, it is not intended to be a shortcut. It aims at protecting the rights of the defendant or a witness and not at simplifying the decision process (Schulz, this volume). However, the hearsay rule may assist in expediting the evidentiary process and simplifying the decision task by substituting an easy-to-make judgment ("Is a statement hearsay?") for a harder-to-make judgment ("Is the statement reliable?").

It would be incorrect, however, to conclude that a court observing an exclusionary rule is therefore applying heuristic reasoning. In most cases, the overall decision-making task of the court will remain a complex one even after the exclusion of some pieces of evidence. On the other hand, it seems possible to regard the exclusionary rule itself as based upon a simple heuristic. To see this, one has to imagine a legal world without the exclusionary principle. In such a world, a court would have to grapple with hearsay evidence and would have to attach a particular evidentiary weight to it. In most cases, the evidentiary weight of hearsay evidence will be set at a very low level, just because it is unreliable. Fixing an exact weight to the evidence will allow little progress in the resolution of the dispute but will instead consume scarce resources. In such a situation, it may be preferable to ignore the evidence altogether, without engaging in a case-by-case analysis. Framed in the language of heuristics, the court applies a simple cue in evaluating the evidence: If the evidence is hearsay $\Rightarrow$ ignore it; otherwise $\Rightarrow$ consider it.

This heuristic is one that Anglo-American legal systems have been unable to live with, as it would exclude considerable probative evidence if regularly applied. Thus, a large set of legal rules exist that identify exceptions to the basic hearsay rule. They appear to mimic similarly the logic of fast and frugal heuristics, as they focus on easy-to-identify appearances as signs of hearsay reliability or necessity for their admission. Nevertheless, the purportedly simplifying heuristics embedded in hearsay analysis can create a system that is sufficiently complex and prone to error that the rule has never developed a foothold on the Continent as it has in the U.S. In fact, in Germany, rules of evidence have generally been weeded out of the law during the last 200 years in favor of an open and subjective standard, where judges weigh evidence at their discretion (Wagner, this volume). This, however, did not banish this class of heuristics from the courtroom. It simply removed them from the formal rules and leaves them to operate as an element of judicial evaluation.

In both Anglo-American and Continental systems, heuristics also exist in the form of presumptions. Presumptions, like exclusionary rules, have heuristics at their core. For instance, one might take the fact that a man was married to a woman, about the time she became pregnant, as an easy-to-measure indicator that the husband was the father of the child, and one will usually be correct in this judgment. Rather than require a fact finder to make this inference, some jurisdictions embody the relationship in a conclusive presumption. This means that the fact finder need only determine whether there was a marriage at the appropriate time, there is no need to look for a family resemblance, order blood tests, or even make the mental leap from fact of marriage to fact of fatherhood. Other presumptions, including the fatherhood presumption in many jurisdictions, are flexible and allow the fact finder to arrive at a different conclusion if the circumstantial evidence points in another direction. Presumptions abound in American law, but rather than replace rules of evidence, most presumptions are considered rules of evidence, and the U.S. Federal Rules of Evidence have an article dealing specifically with presumptions that provides default rules of application when the consequences of presumptions are not specifically spelled out in law.[6]

No American jurisdiction has abolished rules of evidence in ordinary trials, perhaps, because the American justice system is predicated on the jury model: a body composed of laypeople with no professional knowledge or experience in the task of weighing evidence at trials. With respect to the exclusion of hearsay, the U.S. common-law courts long ago said (albeit with many exceptions) "This statement is hearsay, one should be suspicious of it" and then went on to say, in effect, "because we don't trust the fact finder to be sufficiently suspicious we shall exclude the evidence." Conversely, in Germany, the fact finder, who is an experienced and legally trained professional judge, is officially trusted to be competent in weighing unreliable evidence appropriately whatever his or her actual skill. Indeed, to this day no one has shown empirically that systems with hearsay rules are more or less accurate in their judgments than systems of free proof.

Legal Rules as Nonheuristics

What is a heuristic depends, of course, on how one defines the concept. Most members of our group felt that legal shortcuts, like those discussed above, were properly likened to "psychological heuristics," because they were built on similar logic to psychological heuristics and worked to the same end. They are judgment heuristics that have been frozen into the legal system as rules of law to simplify the decision maker's task. However, a minority argued that these rules of law are not heuristic shortcuts, even though they may have cognitive origins, because no mental process occurs. Rather they structure the legal environment so that mental judgment is not needed. (We see no need to resolve the definitional issue here, but think it important to air it.)

These rules of law allow the legal actor to "hide the ball." Some of these we call "legal fictions." For example, statutory rape laws in most American jurisdictions assume that a female under a certain age cannot consent to sex. This seems to be based on a heuristic-type simplification, whereby age is taken as a fast and frugal indicator of an inability to consent. Yet, in many jurisdictions, the statutory rape age is set too high for age to be a plausible indicator of a true inability to know what one is agreeing to. Rather, from a moral or paternalistic perspective, the law believes girls below a certain age should not be having sex, regardless of whether they consent. Consequently, it penalizes men who have intercourse with minors; even if it was reasonable for the man to assume the woman was of an age where she could have consented, and any observer outside of a court of law would have assumed consent was freely and intelligently given. Similarly, the law considers the signature on a form contract as a cue of a

---

6   Judge trials' and most administrative trials' rules of evidence are, with a few exceptions such as privileges, greatly relaxed or even abolished as rules.

knowing and valid consent to the contract's terms, the same as the signature on any contract. However, this too the law knows to be a fiction. Rather, our economic system requires us to bind people to form contracts whether or not they would have freely consented to what the contract provides.

These rules serve as shortcuts because they are embodied in the law and do not require the fact finder to engage in any mental effort to make the connection between factual indicator and the supposed factual conclusion. The existence of the supposed factual connection is in fact irrelevant to the law's purposes. Thus, the statutory rape law could just as well say, "any sexual intercourse with a woman below the age of 16 years is rape" without bothering to presume that women under age sixteen are incapable of appreciating what they are allowing when they consent to sex. Similarly, the law of contracts might state, "If you sign your name to a form contract you are bound by its terms whether or not you read them or would have agreed to those terms had you read them." The law has no need to posit a relationship between the signature and consent.

In conclusion, we see that legal systems in general, and evidentiary rules in particular, are replete with shortcuts aimed at increasing the efficiency of case processing and legal decision making while promoting, or at least not diminishing, accuracy and justice. Whether the heuristics employed by the legal system and its other shortcuts work to promote justice and efficiency is, however, an empirical question. Although we know something about some areas, such as the mistakes that can occur if eyewitness confidence is taken as the prime sign of accuracy (see DePaulo et al. 1997), empirical answers to these questions are, by and large, hard to come by. This is especially true if justice rather than speed or cost is the outcome we are most interested in. Usually, nobody knows how to assess the correctness of a judgment as there is rarely any outcome feedback. Even where there is feedback, as with recent "DNA acquittals" of the wrongfully convicted, it is usually impossible to say whether heuristic reasoning or heuristics built into legal rules were crucial to the unjust outcome. Although there are strong partisans of the Anglo-American and Continental legal systems on both sides of the Atlantic, no one has yet demonstrated empirically that one system yields more just and accurate results than the other, or that heuristic-like evidentiary rules, such as the hearsay rule, are better or worse than German-type "free proof" in getting at the truth.

Legal Decision Makers

At some point during litigation, the evidentiary process closes, and the judge and jury are required to make a decision on the law and facts. In this context, we might apply psychological models to an analysis of the decision makers' behavior and aim to predict their strategy use. Can heuristics, rather than complex strategies, better predict the behavior of legal decision makers?

Judges

Let us start with an example of fast and frugal heuristics in English magistrates' bail decision making. The Magistrates' Court lies at the heart of the English criminal justice system as it deals with the majority of all criminal cases. The vast majority of magistrates are trained (but not necessarily legally qualified) lay people who perform judicial duties on a part-time, unpaid basis. They usually make decisions as a bench of two or three. A small minority are stipendiary magistrates who are legally qualified, experienced, and perform judicial duties on a full-time, paid basis. They usually make decisions alone. All magistrates can pass sentences concerning summary offenses, which are mostly minor (e.g., shoplifting, motoring matters, drunkenness) carrying a certain maximum penalty. They will refer very serious (indictable) offenses, such as murder, to the Crown Court for trial by judge and jury. Other offenses that are triable either way, such as aggravated bodily harm, may be tried in either court by the request of the defendant or magistrates.

Whenever a case is adjourned for trial, sentence or appeal, magistrates must make a decision as to bail (release) the defendant or remand him or her in custody until the next hearing of the case in court. This decision is guided by the law (i.e., U.K. Bail Act of 1976 with its subsequent revisions), which states that most defendants have a right to bail, although bail can be denied (thus defendants can be remanded in custody) if there are "substantial grounds" for believing that a defendant may abscond, offend, or obstruct justice. Magistrates are required to assess the risks of these events occurring by having "regard to" certain case factors (e.g., seriousness of offense, strength of defendant's community ties) as well as any others that "appear to be relevant."

However, in practice, magistrates' bail decision making may also be influenced by other features of the task. These include the order of information presentation, the availability and quality of information, opportunities to learn from the task, and time pressure. There are no statutory rules of procedure governing bail proceedings in Magistrates' Courts. There is often a lack of information available when making bail decisions. When information is available, magistrates do not know how useful different information is in predicting whether a defendant if bailed unconditionally will abscond, offend, or interfere with witnesses. There is no formal procedure for providing magistrates with outcome feedback. Finally, despite the lack of time limits for making decisions on a case, magistrates may implicitly feel that they are working under time pressure due to the high daily caseload.

Research has recently compared the bail law in books with the bail law in action. Experimental and observational studies demonstrated that individual magistrates' bail decisions and those of benches of magistrates were better predicted by a fast and frugal tree called the "matching heuristic" (Dhami 2003; Dhami and Ayton 2001). This heuristic searches through a subset of the available information and bases decisions on one cue alone (e.g., on the defendant's prior convictions) in a noncompensatory way, rather than using more complex strategies that weight and integrate all of the available information in a compensatory way (see Figure 2.3 in Gigerenzer, this volume). Different magistrates used different cues, and sometimes, based their decisions on "extra-legal" factors (e.g., the defendant's gender) or "legal" factors such as the prosecution or police requests (although these were not related to any legally relevant variables). Indeed, the simple heuristic described the decision-making behavior of both lay and stipendiary magistrates and those with more or less experience on the bench. · Other evidence for the use of such simple heuristics comes from records of the duration of bail hearings that reveal they last only a few minutes. Therefore, while the law on bail requires magistrates to consider several cues, they do not do this but rather rely on heuristic thinking.

Fast and Fragile Heuristics?

Although heuristic decision making may carry positive benefits, such as speed, economy, and reasonable accuracy (see Gigerenzer at al. 1999), trial judges' use of heuristics may sometimes result in systematically biased rulings. Consider evidentiary admissibility judgments. Trial judges must decide whether to admit or exclude evidence proffered by one side or the other. A key part of this admissibility decision turns on the judge's belief about the probative value of the evidence. In the U.S., evidence that is not probative of any material fact is excluded. Probative evidence is generally admitted unless its probative value is substantially outweighed by the danger of unfair prejudice, confusion of the issues, misleading the jury, considerations of undue delay, waste of time, or needless presentation of cumulative evidence (Federal Rule of Evidence 403). Although trial judges generally have experience making judgments of probative value, the heuristics they use may lead them to admit irrelevant evidence while excluding relevant evidence.

Consider a child abuse case in which the prosecutor wishes to introduce evidence that the alleged victim had nightmares to bolster his claim that abuse occurred. How might a U.S. judge go about determining whether nightmares are probative of abuse? The guiding rule in U.S. courts is that evidence is probative of a material fact if that evidence makes the existence of the fact more or less probable than it would be without the evidence (Federal Rule of Evidence 401). As a practical matter, judges are likely to fall back on a simple heuristic when trying to implement this legal standard. In child abuse cases, it appears that some judges use a simplifying rule we will identify as the "frequency heuristic." According to this heuristic, evidence (such as nightmares) is probative of a condition (such as abuse) if the evidence occurs frequently when the condition is known to be present. Thus, judges who use the frequency heuristic would likely conclude that nightmares are probative of abuse because it is known that abused children frequently have nightmares.

Despite its intuitive appeal and use in child abuse cases (e.g., *Commonwealth v. Dunkle* 1992), the frequency heuristic can lead judges astray. The reason is that this heuristic ignores the frequency with which the evidence occurs when the condition is absent. In our example, it ignores the frequency with which nightmares occur among nonabused children. As it happens, studies indicate that nightmares are equally common in abused and nonabused children (Hibbard and Hartman 1992). To the extent that these studies are persuasive for the instant case, nightmares are not probative of abuse, and should not be admissible. Likewise, even uncommon symptoms of abuse may be highly probative if they are still more uncommon among nonabused children. Gonorrhea has been observed in less than 5% of sexually abused children. Yet, because gonorrhea is virtually nonexistent among children who have not had sexual contact, the presence of gonorrhea in an allegedly abused child provides strong evidence that abuse has occurred (Lyon and Koehler 1996). In short, judges who use a frequency heuristic to assess probative value will sometimes make demonstrably poor admissibility decisions. However, we do not know how common such errors are, nor do we know the costs they impose on the goals of the litigation process.

Juries

Koehler (this volume) offers a pessimistic perspective about juror reasoning and decision processes. He postulates that the heuristics juries use when reaching verdicts often reflect ignorance, misunderstanding, confusion, and poor logic. He provides evidence from studies with mock jury research and from interviews and surveys with actual jurors that people commonly misunderstand rules of law, legal presumptions, and applicable standards of proof. Jurors sometimes ignore relevant evidence, and rely on irrelevant information, even when they are explicitly told not to use it. They also make inappropriate inferences by incorporating elements of cases that are consistent with their preferred stories of what occurred, even when the evidence did not include these elements. Whether these problems spring from cognitive deficits or normal psychological tendencies of decision makers who must make sense of a surfeit of complex, conflicting, and/or emotionally laden information, jurors are likely to invoke heuristics as decision aids. Below, we identify various heuristics that juries might use but can only speculate on whether or not they result in sound verdicts.

Hastie and Wittenbrink (this volume) suggest that juries employ fast and frugal cognitive heuristics to explain the evidence that they hear. Jurors weave key elements of the evidence into stories to help them make sense of the facts presented, and make inferences to fill in the details of the story. The process wherein jurors construct stories can be viewed as a heuristic. Further, research by Pennington and Hastie (1991) has shown that causal structures that facilitate story construction increase the plausibility of the claims made by the party offering the story. Jurors may use ease of story construction as a cue to the likelihood that events unfolded as the story suggests.

In complex cases, story construction may be neither fast nor frugal. However, some of the fast and frugal heuristics identified by Gigerenzer and the ABC Group (1999) no doubt play a role in jury decisions. For example, "Take The Best" may be employed when fact finders are deciding between conflicting testimony or conflicting evidence. (Take the Best goes through successive cues and bases a decision on the first cue that points in one direction, unless the cues are exhausted and the process stops.) Thus a jury confronted by opposing experts, one of whom has impressive credentials (e.g., Ph.D. from a prestigious university) while the other has weak credentials (e.g., bachelor's degree from a local college), may simply take the word of the person who has the better credentials rather than try to evaluate the quality of the scientific arguments each expert offers. Similarly, a police officer's testimony may be credited over a defendant's testimony, because the police officer is seen as an "authority" figure and thus as a better (more neutral) witness. In circumstances like these, the Take The Best heuristic may do as well as—or better than—other ways of deciding between conflicting testimony.

Difficulties arise because lawyers, knowing that jurors will rely on heuristic reasoning, strive to acquire witnesses who give the appearance of expertise and neutrality, regardless of the merits of their position. When the reliability of opposing witnesses is crafted and manipulated by lawyers, as is often the case with opposing scientific experts, the ecological rationality of the cues, and thereby of Take The Best, may decrease. This is a perfect example of a case in which a multi-agent competitive environment makes it difficult to determine if heuristic reasoning is adaptive. If there were no lawyers involved, it is plausible that the most memorable, most central evidence would be the most reliable and probative. However, lawyers manipulate evidence to make the most useful facts and inferences for their side of the case also the most memorable, most emotion-provoking, etc. (see the discussion on affect-based decisions and availability below). Now, heuristic cues and strategies are no longer correlated with the actual validity and jurors reasoning in a fast and frugal manner may be confused or misled by their normal judgment habits.

For heuristic reasoning to be successful cues must be thought to be relevant and reliable in the sense that they allow one to draw accurate conclusions concerning the underlying fact, for example, the guilt of the defendant. In addition, cues must be readily available. A heuristic is of little use if the cues it depends on are elusive or ambiguous. In these circumstances, the legal task can be made even more difficult. Yet, easy-to-come-by cues are particularly likely to be poor indicators of underlying facts because if they are common and accessible, they are likely to be associated with a wide variety of behavior. For example, eyewitness confidence seems to be used by most jurors as an indicator of eyewitness reliability, yet a body of research finds only a slight relationship, if any, between eyewitness confidence and eyewitness accuracy (e.g., DePaulo et al. 1997).

The heuristics that Kahneman and Tversky (1974) proposed may also play a role in legal decision making. For instance, "representativeness" (i.e., a strategy for making judgments based on the extent to which current stimuli resemble other stimuli or categories) may be a heuristic that jurors use and that lawyers try to manipulate (see Kysar et al., this volume). Hastie and Wittenbrink (this volume) conjecture that in some cases, jurors' (and judges') decisions turn largely on the defendant's (or other party's) social category membership, that is, they are based more on prejudice than on a fair evaluation of the evidence. A criminal defense lawyer may be aware of such prejudices and for this reason may advise his or her client, who is say a large unemployed black male, to accept a plea bargain that would be rejected if the client did not so closely fit (or represent) a likely juror stereotype of a violent criminal. As considerable research suggests, prejudice-based decisions tend to influence jury decisions when the evidence is close and does not strongly suggest a verdict.

Hastie and Wittenbrink's discussion of the role of prejudice in juror decisions is closely related to affect-based judgments; many would say that prejudice-based judgments are a specific example of the notion of an "affect heuristic." Finucane et al. (2000) describe the affect heuristic as characterized by reliance on feelings (with or without consciousness), such as a specific quality of goodness or badness, which influence decisions. In the legal domain, the feeling that fact finders have toward a witness or party may affect their judgment, even when they cannot point to specific evidence supporting that judgment. Moreover, affect might motivate a fact finder to assemble and attend to facts in ways that support a particular verdict, irrespective of the strength of other evidence. The affect heuristic may also make information more available. For instance, vivid evidence may be more influential with legal fact finders than evidence that is pallid. Whereas a vivid, bloody photograph of a murder victim may be less valuable for determining whether the defendant committed a crime than a pallid statistical analysis of fibers recovered from the crime scene, the bloody photograph may actually persuade jurors that the defendant deserves to be convicted. The vivid photograph, unlike the pallid statistical analysis, is likely to arouse strong emotions and in this way stand out for jurors and be more available to them during deliberations.

A further example is the "anchoring and adjustment heuristic." According to Kahneman and Tversky (1974), when people estimate an unknown quality (e.g., this year's murder rate), they anchor on convenient initial values (e.g., last year's murder rate), and then adjust this estimate—usually insufficiently—to take other considerations into account. In the legal domain, the anchoring and adjustment heuristic may be responsible for the finding that large damage requests tend to elicit larger jury awards than smaller requests. Even if the large request seems excessive, the request acts as an anchor that encourages jurors to return rather large awards (see Hastie et al. 1999; Chapman and Bornstein 1996).

Our final example is what might be called the "association heuristic." One concludes a fact exists not from proof of the fact, but from an association that suggests the fact's existence. For example, suppose the Pope testified as a character witness for a defendant. Putting aside the nonheuristic inferences that can be made from good character to innocence, a fact finder might conclude that the Pope would never testify for someone who is guilty. So, the very fact that the Pope was willing to be a character witness suggests, without thinking more deeply about the testimony, that the defendant must be innocent. Lawyers understand that jurors respond to association, and they may attempt to exploit this heuristic.

The adaptive value of the heuristics described here in the trial environment is relatively unexplored terrain. It may be that system characteristics are at least as responsible as human failings in leading jurors astray. In particular, in most cases one side has no interest in having a jury get at the truth. It is not surprising that decision makers can be misled by skillful attempts to do so. But even in situations where adversaries have little say, such as jury instructions in American courts, the system may, both procedurally (e.g., instructions delivered orally with no note-taking allowed) and substantively (e.g., instructions using convoluted legal language), work to complexify rather than simplify the jury's task.

Expert Witnesses and Credibility Assessments

In American law, findings of fact such as credibility judgments are the exclusive domain either of the jury or, in bench trials, of the judges. However, in Germany and other civil law countries, psychologists acting as expert witnesses are routinely called in by courts to testify about the credibility of written testimonies. It is interesting to see whether experts, similar to lay jurors, use simple heuristic strategies or whether they make more complicated judgments.

Expert psychologists use a method known as "Statement Validity Assessment" (SVA, also referred to as "content analysis") to assess the semantic content of written testimonies. In Germany, SVA is an influential piece of evidence, which can affect the outcome of the case if no other incriminating or exonerating evidence is available (Steller and Köhnken 1989). SVA is also used in the U.S. as a "lie detection" tool to assist with police investigations. Consistency analysis is one essential component of the three-stage process of SVA. It involves a comparison of witness testimonies made at successive interviews with an eye to contextual features such as consistencies, inconsistencies, omissions, and additions. Although lawyers, police officers, and laypeople, use the consistency between repeated statements as an indicator of the credibility and reliability of a testimony, research in this area is scarce (see Granhag and Strömwall 2001).

Recently, a study took a closer look at consistency in the context of expert witnesses' decision making and their use of consistency cues in SVA analyses. The expert psychologists studied analyzed the consistency of repeated narratives and made judgments about the credibility (veracity) of the narratives (Piperides 2002). The narratives were based on true experiences and false statements, which were repeated after a one-year interval. The analysis showed that a simple model with only one significant discriminating cue—inconsistencies present in the core events of narratives—best described *both* positive and negative credibility judgments. It appears then that experts, similar to laypeople acting as jurors, use heuristics rather than more complex strategies in legal decision making. In the simulated environment, unlike in real-life settings, expert performance could be measured against an external criterion (i.e., the actual veracity of the statements made). Experts' overall accuracy rate in classifying narratives was only 66%. More specifically, true statements were classified well, but false statements were strongly underestimated. However, as mentioned above, consistency analysis is only one part of the analyses required by SVA. Further steps are needed to gather all the information necessary before making final credibility evaluations. Perhaps, expert performance improves when all the necessary credibility cues are available. Further, it could be that when a decision task consists of separate decision components, some hybrid decision-making strategy is used: Perhaps, information that is gathered in a fast and frugal heuristic manner in each separate stage of the decision-making task is subsequently integrated in an optimal way to reach the final decision.

In conclusion, there are many reasons why legal decision makers might behave in a fast and frugal way: First, they have to make complicated decisions within task constraints, such as vague laws, limited information, time pressure, lack of outcome feedback. Second, as humans, they are also constrained by their own cognitive limitations, and consequently, may have problems computing weights and integrating information or organizing complex inferences. Finally, social factors might come into play, such as passing the buck or social loafing (i.e., if individuals in groups perceive that they will not be evaluated by others, they may experience diminished responsibility regarding a decision task). Assuming that decision makers, in fact, do use simple decision strategies, one may ask whether they *should* do so. In other words, what is the prescriptive utility of heuristics in the legal system? We address this issue later in this chapter.

Appeal Process

However, let us first look at the final stage of litigation. After the judge or jury has reached a decision, an appellate process may ensue. Litigation in civil law countries might be conceptualized as an ongoing trial with highly integrated parts, in which appellate judges provide close supervision of inferior judges on questions of law and fact, all the way up the chain. Common-law appellate processes, by contrast, might be better characterized as a series of judgments at different steps in the process as to the appropriateness of the proceedings below them. However, much of the following considerations apply equally or at least to a somewhat lesser degree to appellate review in civil law countries as well.

Common-law countries make a sharp distinction between questions of law and questions of fact. This is especially true in the U.S. because of the presence of jurors. Fact-finding by jurors is insulated from careful appellate scrutiny, and even fact-finding by first instance judges is more difficult to reverse than is their law determinations. Thus, in the U.S., a series of rules referred to as "standards of review" have developed that simplify decision making, although it is not clear whether these should be thought of as heuristics. Fact-finding by jurors is reviewed under the "clearly erroneous" standard, which means that it must be accepted, unless no reasonable person could have reached the result the jury did. Since a jury verdict must be unanimous in federal litigation (and have the consent of at least two-thirds of the jurors in state litigation), the probability that there would be so many irrational people together in the same room is quite low, and thus, there are very few reversals of fact-finding by jurors. Fact-finding by judges sitting without juries is reviewed under a "deferential" standard. What this is supposed to mean is that the trial court must have been unreasonable, although it need not be the case that no reasonable person could have decided as the trial judge did. Courts in the civil law world follow a similar approach when they are called to review the decision of their professional colleagues made at a lower level. In German law, the boilerplate formulation of the standard of review is that the lower court must have observed the presumptions and rules of evidence, such as *res ipsa loquitur*, applicable to the case at hand and that its reasoning must not be in conflict with the received laws of nature and common logic. The primary explanation for these rules is that each stage in the appellate process is less well situated than its predecessor to find the facts accurately; the appellate judges, for example, do not observe the witnesses. The secondary explanation is that different parts of the process do different things. Trials find what happened, trial judges and first appeal judges straighten out the law, and the highest courts are more concerned with policy.

These standards continue throughout the appellate level, and indeed, a new one is added at the Supreme Court level. The Supreme Court often says (but occasionally deviates from) that it will not reconsider a fact passed on by two lower courts. Still, as a case proceeds up the appellate chain, the facts become stylized and often bear only a tangential relationship to the richness of the factual matrix at trial. Questions of law are handled quite differently. The general rule followed by courts of civil law jurisdictions is that questions of law will be reviewed in full, as it is the primary function of the appellate courts to guarantee the equal application of the law and to promote the development of the law. Most appeals in the U.S. focus on jury instructions, as they embody the law that is supposedly applicable to the case. The comprehensibility of jury instructions often arises in psychological research, but it should be noted that jury instructions play at least one other important role in addition to informing the jury. They are the means by which hierarchical relationships between courts are maintained. Jurors do not decide questions of law; they find the facts and apply the law to them. However, one cannot analytically separate questions of law from questions of fact. As a result, we find a series of rules and guidelines that allocate decisional authority. As to what are determined to be questions of law, appellate judges are just as well, and perhaps better, situated to decide these than inferior judges, and thus no deference to prior decision making is provided. The standard of review on appeal is thus said to be "de novo"—or starting anew.

In terms of the usefulness of heuristics, if anything referred to above is one, a few implications are clear. First, these rules attempt to simplify decision making and to delineate institutional roles. Second, there are perverse effects that might arise. If a judge thinks a factual mistake was made, but cannot reverse given the standard of review, he or she may stretch the law to find a legal error so that the case can be sent back for a new trial, or whatever. Other potentially heuristic-like aids to decision making exist that can be summarized in the "duty to preserve error." To appeal an issue, the parties must first ensure that it was appropriately raised at trial, and second, that claims of error were appropriately made. As the appellate process unfolds, a party that wishes to appeal to the next level must again be sure to preserve the issue by articulating and briefing it for the court. Failure to do any of these things, at any level, will typically result in the party having "waived" or "forfeited" the issue. This can plainly be thought of as a simplifying heuristic.

The appellate process involves a rich set of interactions between individual and collective decision making. In one sense, a single trial judge can "review" the decision of a jury by considering whether to direct a verdict, or enter a judgment as a matter of law, or order a new trial. Appellate courts are always multi-member bodies, reviewing the findings of law of the trial judge, and operate on a majority vote—a decision rule that may be viewed as a heuristic, if indeed it simplifies or shortcuts deliberations. Civil and common-law countries differ in one important respect that maps onto this variable as well. Published dissents are allowed and are frequent in common-law countries, whereas they are virtually nonexistent in Europe. In the civil law world, the number of judges hearing a case is a function of the stakes of the dispute, on the one hand, and the position of the court within the chain of appeals on the other. The further one moves up the chain, the more judges participate in decision making; and, the higher the stakes of a dispute, the more judges will take care of it even at the level of first instance.

PRESCRIPTIVE UTILITY

When making legal decisions, decision makers must consider the ramifications of their decisions for both the individual defendant and for society. They must work within the relevant legal guidelines, the constraints of their task, and within their own cognitive capacities. Furthermore, legal decision making must serve legal goals or ideals. Thus, any comprehensive understanding of the role of heuristics in litigation needs to take these factors into account when considering their usefulness and when offering prescriptive advice. First, however, it is necessary to understand what the legal ideal practice is, namely what the "normative" model for legal decision makers is.

Legal Ideals

Various theoretical frameworks have been developed to help describe, explain, and evaluate the manner in which legal decisions are generally made, and how the criminal justice system operates (see e.g., King 1981; Packer 1968). Packer's (1968) due process and crime control models make a statement regarding the function of the criminal justice system and the goals and roles of the agencies operating within the system. Both models represent ideal types, or, in Packer's (1968) terms, "normative" models that lie on two opposite ends of a continuum.

The crime control model minimizes the adversarial aspect of the judicial process. It is recognized that there are only limited resources available for dealing with crime. Thus, there is an emphasis upon efficiency, speed, and finality. Packer (1968) described the system operating as a crime control model like an "assembly-line conveyor belt" where individuals are screened at each stage (p. 159). By contrast, the due process model places the adversarial aspect at the centre of the justice process. An "obstacle course" is placed along the process, and there is "an insistence on formal, adjudicative, adversary fact-finding processes, in which the factual case against the accused is publicly heard by an impartial tribunal and is evaluated only after the accused has had full opportunity to discredit the case against him" (Packer 1968, pp. 163–164). The due process model "resembles a factory that has to devote a substantial part of its input to quality control," and so, the manner in which cases are dealt with is deemed more important than the quantity of cases dealt with (Packer 1968, p. 165).

Therefore, it is evident that legal decision making is not necessarily related to discovering the truth or making the "correct" decision. For instance, a trial does not establish whether the defendant is innocent of the offense he or she has been charged with, but whether the evidence is sufficient, beyond reasonable doubt, to establish guilt. Legal decision-making tasks are probabilistic. For example, the question of whether or not a defendant would offend if released on bail cannot be perfectly predicted by the information available (e.g., the seriousness of the offense the defendant is charged with). There are two types of error that could result: Type-I error (e.g., conviction of a truly innocent defendant) and Type-II error (e.g., acquittal of a truly guilty defendant). The inverse relationship between the two types of errors means, for example, that minimizing the probability of making a Type-I error maximizes the probability of making a Type-II error. Packer (1968) pointed out that the crime control model prioritizes the conviction of the guilty, at the risk of also convicting the innocent, while the due process model prioritizes the acquittal of the innocent at the expense of also acquitting the guilty. King (1981) thus notes that the social function of the crime control model is to deal out punishment, and by contrast, the due process model functions to serve justice.

In reality, most legal systems are currently based on both due process and crime control principles, although most legal policy makers and practitioners would assert that they aspire to the latter (e.g., see Galligan 1987). Indeed, common notions of justice are synonymous with due process.

Should Legal Decision Makers Use Heuristics?

In this volume, Arkes and Shaffer argue that judges should be given cognitive aids, and Koehler proposes that jurors should be given training. In so doing, these authors implicitly assume that legal decision makers should not be using simple heuristics. Yet, can heuristic strategies work well in the litigation environment and, if so, should they be used? Clearly, any prescriptive advice must be made in relation to the ideal practice that we aspire to and must acknowledge the external environmental constraints and internal cognitive constraints faced by legal decision makers (see Gigerenzer, this volume).

For our purposes, a legal decision maker emphasizing crime control would search and weigh only certain factors compatible with evidence of guilt, and would not integrate evidence of innocence. This reflects a noncompensatory, fast and frugal strategy. By contrast, a decision maker observing due process would search all relevant information, weight and integrate it appropriately to make a balanced decision. He or she would have to consider all the factors legal guidelines lay down. This behavior reflects a compensatory, slower strategy. Thus, if we aspire to the ideal of due process rather than just crime control, legal decision makers using simple heuristics are not serving justice, as we presently know it.

However, cognitive psychological theory and research indicates that as humans, individual legal decision makers have limited cognitive abilities, such as limited memory, attention, and processing capacity. These limitations are magnified in legal environments where legal decision makers often have to interpret complex laws, understand a lot of conflicting evidence, and work under time pressure. Consequently, it is reasonable to assume that under these conditions, they will rely on simple heuristics to make decisions rather than perform complicated calculations. Moreover, social psychological theory and research demonstrates that as social beings, groups of legal decision makers, such as benches of magistrates and jurors, are likely to engage in "loafing" and "groupthink," and so it is reasonable to assume that they will not rely on complex decision strategies. As Dhami (pers. comm.) noted, these considerations lead us to conclude that psychological reality may not meet legal idealism.

To date, Gigerenzer and his colleagues have measured the value of simple heuristics in terms of their accuracy, speed, and frugality (Gigerenzer et al. 1999). And, they have mainly focused on overall accuracy. In fact, although fast and frugal heuristics have been initially shown to be accurate in computer simulations or in the lab, there is now evidence demonstrating that people in real-world environments can be accurate using these heuristics. Examples include heuristics in coronary care unit allocation (Green and Mehr 1997), in sports (Gigerenzer 2004; Johnson and Raab 2003), investment (Borges et al. 1999), and social learning (Boyd and Richerson 2001). Of course, since a heuristic is not good or bad per se, but only relative to the environment in which it is applied, heuristic decisions can also go wrong (see Harries and Dhami 2000). The same dependency holds for each strategy, including complex regression models. A full analysis of the decision maker in his or her environment is required. In many domains, including the legal domain, overall accuracy is not as important as reducing either a type I or type II error (Hammond 1996). Furthermore, people may have other goals such as accountability to consider (Tetlock 1985). Different models may achieve these goals with different levels of success.

Research first needs to address which types of decision strategies best meet different goals, before any conclusions can be drawn about the prescriptive utility of heuristics. For now, any policy implications of findings that psychological reality confronts legal idealism will depend on which side of the fence one sits. On the one hand, if we want legal decision makers to come closer to legal ideals, then perhaps we can train them and aid them. Perhaps we can train judges and jurors to abandon maladaptive heuristics in favor of an approach that is more likely to yield appropriate decisions. Koehler (this volume), for example, suggests that jurors receive comprehensive training in critical legal doctrines and in how to reason with legal evidence. On the other hand, if we want legal ideals to come closer to psychological reality, then we could attempt to adapt the legal task to human constraints and even make our legal ideals more psychologically plausible. This could entail teaching heuristic decision making in law schools.

Should Heuristics Be Used in the Development of Legal Rules?

"There are two ways to react to a world that is becoming more complex: to strive for perfection by designing ever more complex legal rules that govern every aspect of human behavior, or to stop this growth and strive for a few simple and robust legal rules...." (Todd and Gigerenzer 2000, p. 776). By striving for simplicity in law, we might be able to adapt the legal task to human constraints and thereby, perhaps, improve judges' and jurors' decision making.

One aim would be to structure the legal environment so that the legal decision task becomes cognitively simpler. The law frequently attempts to simplify the decision-maker's task—and this motive is often explicit—by establishing bright-line rules, even though it knows this will lead some cases to be misclassified. It excludes irrelevant evidence, which in theory should have no implications for the decision, because if fact finders do not need to sort the relevant from the irrelevant their task is simpler and less costly to accomplish. It establishes statutes of limitations, which means that fact finders do not have to resolve cases where the most probative evidence may well have disappeared or had its signal dulled by the passage of time. When this is not a danger, rules may change and limitation periods may be extended to be tried whenever the accused is identified. (For example, recently in the U.S., there have been "John Doe" indictments in rape cases about to be extinguished where the defendant is identified from a DNA sample.) Finally, as we have mentioned, some principles that decision makers have used as heuristics are embedded in rules so that they no longer have to think about the issue. For example, hearsay is excluded in Anglo-American jurisdictions rather than simply taken as a sign of unreliability.

A further aim might be to structure the legal environment to get the decision maker to use heuristics that promote legal values. More importantly, the aim might be to get the decision maker to not use heuristics that violate legal values. For example, as we have seen in discussing juries, representativeness is a heuristic that lawyers use to manipulate jurors' decision making. Thus, in criminal cases, they will instruct clients to get a shave and haircut, dress neatly, etc. so they do not look like a stereotype of a criminal. The prosecutors, on the other hand, will often find ways to call a jury's attention to discrepancies between the way a defendant looks on the stand and the way he or she ordinarily dresses or is groomed. By prohibiting facts that distract from charge-specific evidence, such as "character evidence," courts attempt to counteract the representativeness heuristic (see Korobkin, this volume).

Fikentscher (pers. comm.) refers to heuristics that play a role within the framework of making or implementing social norms (such as legal, moral, behavioral, religious rules) by simplifying them. "Simplifying heuristics" reduce the content complexity of such norms thereby making norm application more transparent. They may also simplify the sanction side of such norms: Every norm consists of a set of requirements under which a set of facts is subsumed, and a sanction that results in a change of the facts. Simplifying the requirements is more interesting in the present context. In law, the simplifying task is part of what is called "the concretion of a norm for the preparation of its application." Concretion is indispensable for both Continental code law and for Anglo-American case law (Cardozo 1921). The following is an example of the prescriptive utility of simplifying heuristics: In recent years, the European Court of Justice and the E.U. Court of First Instance, in a series of cases, refused to sustain antitrust complaints against monopolistic behavior and other restraints of competition, raised by the E.U. Commission, on grounds of "lack of economic evidence." In some camps, this caused a call for "economizing E.U. antitrust." However, to other observers and antitrust experts, the demand for more "economic evidence" in E.U. antitrust is excessive, consumer-hostile, industry lobby-influenced, and aping the U.S. economic analysis of antitrust law policies. It is obvious that the industry and the legal profession favor complicated requirements. Max Weber called this phenomenon *Herrschaftswissen* (dominance knowledge).

In searching for perfection in complexity, we are not recognizing the psychological reality of the decision maker. Would we expect a physically handicapped person to be productive and effective in an environment that has not been accommodated to his or her special needs? By using heuristics for the development of legal rules, we are modifying the environment to accommodate the decision-makers' limitations. In addition, by understanding the heuristics humans draw on, we can design the legal system so that legal decision makers who apply familiar heuristics in reasoning will be led to better rather than worse decisions.

HEURISTICS IN LITIGATION: WHAT HAVE WE LEARNED SO FAR?

In the spirit of the adaptive heuristics identified by Gigerenzer and the ABC Group, we hoped to find legal heuristics that were fast and frugal, that performed well, and that furthered the law's objectives. However, our task proved to be too ambitious. Perhaps, we did not succeed in "shooting the game," but we did find the area where it lives and these are the borders:

- Heuristics are mental shortcuts that simplify and speed up decision making at the different stages of litigation, and they can be found at various stages of the litigation process.
- Some parts of the litigation process are clearly not heuristic and here elaborate fact-finding and complex deliberations seem to be more appropriate.
- We will have shot the game if we can show that legal heuristics not only result in speedy and economical justice, but also, that these heuristics serve legal ideas at least as well as more complex and costly economic rules.

Though we may not have succeeded in this last goal, we have pointed to instances of heuristic use throughout the litigation process. We identified heuristics in the formal rules of law and heuristics used by the legal participants from case selection through the appeals process. We have thus delineated the perimeters of an interesting and potentially useful field of research.

Pertinent questions will include not only whether heuristics are used, but also what the role of heuristics is in balancing the competing goals of justice, namely, to protect the individual's right to liberty and to protect the public's right to safety. On the one hand, if heuristic decision making leads to violations of principles such as fairness, lawfulness, and consistency, then we need to reconsider and restructure the role of the decision makers. The aim would be to reduce reliance on naturally occurring heuristics by devising appropriate cognitive aids (see Arkes and Shaffer, this volume), by targeting heuristic manipulations through legal instructions, and by offering relevant educational training. On the other hand, if heuristic decision making furthers the law's objectives, then we want to facilitate heuristics that lead to "good" (i.e., accurate and fair) decisions and discourage those that do not. The aim would be to restructure the legal environment so that the heuristics used are adaptive.

Indeed, research must specify the conditions under which heuristics can be adaptive in the legal environment. A heuristic will allow one to draw "accurate" conclusions only if it uses relevant, unambiguous, and valid cues that are good indicators of the underlying legal fact. Whether heuristics work well or poorly does not simply depend on the heuristic. It also depends on the relationship of the heuristic to the decision environment. Where there is a good fit between heuristic and environment, "rational" results are likely. Thus, when considering heuristic performance, we need to study a wide range of environments, especially when we want to speculate about performance in the relatively unexplored legal environment. For example, although we have seen heuristics perform well in simulations that deal with problems with good feedback, it is less clear that heuristics will perform well in real-world environments where good feedback is typically absent. However, the same limitation holds for complex strategies.

In most cases, the overall decision-making task of the court will remain a complex one even if some of the decision processes are simplified. If we insist on perfection, we can ignore human reality and try to complexify the decision process even further. Yet if legal judgments and choices were not made unless and until they were demonstrably optimal, the system would be brought to a standstill. In the end, it seems clear that heuristics play a central role in the production of legal rules and decisions. We anticipate that future research will shed light on this role.

ACKNOWLEDGMENTS

We are very grateful to Julia Lupp and her colleagues for their impeccable organization of the workshop that facilitated the smooth running of our discussions. In particular, we wish to thank Carla MacDougall, Caroline Rued-Engel, and the editorial team for their invaluable assistance.

REFERENCES

Babcock, L., and G. Loewenstein. 1997. Explaining bargaining impasse: The role of self-serving biases. *J. Econ. Persp.* **11**:109–126.

Borges, B., D.G. Goldstein, A. Ortman, and G. Gigerenzer. 1999. Can ignorance beat the stock market? In: Simple Heuristics That Make Us Smart, by G. Gigerenzer, P.M. Todd, and the ABC Research Group, pp. 59–72. New York: Oxford Univ. Press.

Boyd, R., and P.J. Richerson. 2001. Norms and bounded rationality. In: Bounded Rationality: The Adaptive Toolbox, ed. G. Gigerenzer and R. Selten, pp. 281–296. Dahlem Workshop Report 84. Cambridge, MA: MIT Press.

Brunswik, E. 1952. Conceptual Framework of Psychology. Chicago: Univ. of Chicago Press.

Cardozo, B.N. 1921. The Nature of the Judicial Process. New Haven, CT: Yale Univ. Press.

Chapman, G.B., and B. Bornstein. 1996. The more you ask for, the more you get: Anchoring in personal injury verdicts. *Appl. Cog. Psychol.* **10**:519, 525–528, 532– 533.

Commonwealth v. Dunkle, 602 A.2d 830, 835 n. 16 (Pa. 1992).

DePaulo, B.M., K. Charlton, H. Cooper, J.J. Lindsay, and L. Muhlenbrock. 1997. The accuracy–confidence correlation in the detection of deception. *Pers. Soc. Psychol. Rev.* **1**:346–357.

Dhami, M.K. 2003. Psychological models of professional decision-making. *Psychol. Sci.* **14**:175–180.

Dhami, M.K., and P. Ayton. 2001. Bailing and jailing the fast and frugal way. *J. Behav. Dec. Mak.* **14**:141–168.

Finucane, M.L., A. Alhakami, P. Slovic, and S.M. Johnson. 2000. The affect heuristic in judgments of risks and benefits. *J. Behav. Dec. Mak.* **13**:1–17.

Galligan, D.J. 1987. Regulating pre-trial decisions. In: Criminal Law and Justice, ed. I.H. Dennis, pp. 177–202. New York: Sweet and Maxwell.

Gigerenzer, G. 2004. Striking a blow for sanity in theories of rationality. In: Models of a Man: Essays in Memory of Herbert A. Simon, ed. M. Augier and J.G. March, pp. 389–409. Cambridge, MA: MIT Press.

Gigerenzer, G., P.M. Todd, and the ABC Research Group. 1999. Simple Heuristics That Make Us Smart. New York: Oxford Univ. Press.

Granhag, P.A., and L.A. Strömwall. 2001. Deception detection based on repeated interrogations. *Leg. Criminol. Psychol.* **6**:85–101.

Green, L.A., and D.R. Mehr. 1997. What alters physicians' decisions to admit to the coronary care unit? *J. Fam. Practice* **45**:219–226.

Hammond, K.R. 1996. Human Judgment and Social Policy: Irreducible Uncertainty, Inevitable Error, Unavailable Injustice. New York: Oxford Univ. Press.

Harries, C., and M.K. Dhami. 2000. On the descriptive validity and prescriptive utility of fast and frugal models. *Behav. Brain Sci.* **23**:753–754.

Hastie, R., D.A. Schkade, and J.W. Payne. 1999. Juror judgments in civil cases: Effects of plaintiff's requests and plaintiff's identity on punitive damage awards. *Law Hum. Behav.* **23**:445, 462–463.

Hibbard, R.A., and G.L. Hartman. 1992. Behavioral problems in alleged sexual abuse victims. *Child Abuse Negl.* **16**:755–762.

Hogarth, R.M., and H.J. Einhorn. 1992. Order effects in belief updating: The belief-adjustment model. *Cog. Psychol.* **24**:1–55.

Johnson, J.G., and M. Raab. 2003. Take the first: Option generation and resulting choices. *Org. Behav. Hum. Dec. Proc.* **91**:215–229.

Kahneman, D.J., and S. Frederick. 2002. Representativeness revisited: Attribution substitution in intuitive judgment. In: Heuristics and Biases, ed. T. Gilovich, D. Griffin, and D. Kahneman, pp. 49–81. New York: Cambridge Univ. Press.

Kahneman, D., and A. Tversky. 1974. Judgment under uncertainty: Heuristics and biases. *Science* **185**:1124–1131.

King, M. 1981. The Framework of Criminal Justice. London: Croom Helm.

Lyon, T.D., and J.J. Koehler. 1996. The relevance ratio: Evaluating the probative value of expert testimony in child sexual abuse cases. *Cornell Law Rev.* **82**:43–78.

Packer, H.L. 1968. The Limits of the Criminal Sanction. Palo Alto: Stanford Univ. Press.

Payne, J.W., J.R. Bettman, and E.J. Johnson. 1993. The Adaptive Decision Maker. New York: Cambridge Univ. Press.

Pennington, N., and R. Hastie. 1991. A cognitive theory of juror decision making: The story model. *Cardozo Law Rev.* **13**:519–557.

Piperides, C. 2002. Expert Witness Use of Consistency Cues: Judging the Veracity of Adult Testimonies. Master's thesis (Diplomarbeit), Dept. of Psychology, Freie Universität Berlin, Berlin, Germany.

Polya, G. 1957. How to Solve It. 2d ed. Princeton, NJ: Princeton Univ. Press.

Priest, G.L., and B. Klein. 1984. The selection of disputes for litigation. *J. Legal Stud.* **13**:1–55.

Simon, H.A. 1955. A behavioral model of rational choice. *Qtly. J. Econ.* **69**:99–118.

Steller, M., and G. Köhnken. 1989. Criteria-based statement analysis. In: Psychological Methods in Criminal Investigation and Evidence, ed. D.C. Raskin, pp. 217–245. New York: Springer.

Tetlock, P.E. 1985. Accountability: The neglected social context of judgment and choice. In: Research in Organizational Behavior, ed. B. Staw and L. Cummings, vol. 7, pp. 297–332. Greenwich, CT: JAI Press.

Todd, P.M., and G. Gigerenzer. 2000. Précis of simple heuristics that make us smart. *Behav. Brain Sci.* **23**:727–780.

17

Adapt or Optimize?

The Psychology and Economics of Rules of Evidence

Robert Cooter

Law School, University of California at Berkeley,
Berkeley, CA 94720–7200, U.S.A.

ABSTRACT

In civil disputes, the plaintiff must prove his case by the preponderance of the evidence. To reach this standard, the plaintiff accumulates evidence by combining facts. In this chapter, two models of this process are compared. First, decision makers can adapt their behavior for improved results, as assumed in some psychological models. Adaptive models predict that court practice will allow the plaintiff to combine facts according to relatively simple rules. Second, decision makers can optimize their behavior for best results, as assumed in most economic models. Optimization models predict that court practice will require the plaintiff to combine facts in ways that conform to the laws of probability theory.

Predictions from these two models contradict each other when simple, adaptive rules violate the laws of probability theory. It is shown that actual practice in a California court allows the plaintiff to combine facts according to relatively simple rules that sometimes violate the laws of probability theory. Adaptation is, consequently, a better descriptive theory than optimization. Procedures that violate the laws of probability theory, however, are vulnerable to criticism. Given that trials proceed with deliberate speed under expert guidance, suboptimal adaptations are irrational. Optimization, consequently, is a better normative theory than adaptation.

INTRODUCTION

Decision makers can adapt their behavior for improved results, as assumed in some psychological models of behavior. Adaptation relies on adjusting relatively simple rules, called "heuristics," that are effective in most circumstances. Alternatively, decision makers can optimize their behavior for best results, as assumed in most economic models of behavior. Optimization often requires deliberation and calculation. I distinguish between these two models of behavior and apply them to civil litigation.

In civil litigation, the plaintiff must prove his case by the preponderance of the evidence. To reach this standard, the plaintiff accumulates evidence by combining facts. Combining facts sometimes requires combining probabilities. To be rational, the combination of probabilities should obey the laws of probability theory as developed by statisticians. Courts that combine probabilities in ways that violate these laws are irrational, which results in bad decisions. Optimization models predict that court practice will require the plaintiff to combine facts according to rules that do not violate the laws of probability theory. In contrast, adaptive models predict that court practice will allow the plaintiff to combine facts according to rules that violate the laws of probability theory in some circumstances.

I will show that actual practice in a California court allows the plaintiff to combine facts according to relatively simple rules that sometimes violate the laws of probability theory. Adaptation is, consequently, a better descriptive theory of court behavior than optimization. This conclusion is unsurprising since most members of courts lack the technical training required to apply the laws of probability theory directly to cases. Rules of evidence, whose use requires knowledge of probability theory, are inappropriate for courts. These arguments respond to a puzzle recently posed by Saul Levmore (2001): Why does the law avoid the issue of conjunctive probability?[1]

However, courts may seek the advice of statistical experts when making judgments or creating rules. Heuristics that violate the laws of probability theory, however, are vulnerable to sharp criticism—they are irrational. Unlike the optimum, heuristics are approximations that sometimes fail to give the best result and thus can cause injustice. Courts should use experts to help develop rules that lead courts to behave consistently with probability theory. Optimization, thus, is a better normative theory of the court's aspiration than adaptation.

DELIBERATE AND CALCULATED VERSUS FAST AND FRUGAL

To contrast optimization and adaptation, let us begin with an example: To get to the top of a mountain, a climber can deliberate and calculate the best path for the ascent. I call the best path "optimal" and the process of calculating it "optimization." Alternatively, the climber can follow a simple rule that does not require calculating the best path. For example, the climber can follow the rule, "Always go up from where you stand in the direction with the steepest angle that you can climb." I call this rule a "heuristic" and the process of applying it "adaptation."

A good heuristic yields the optimal result in most circumstances. For example, following the steepest feasible contour line gets the climber to the top of any mountain with a single peak. This is also the way that some computer programs

---

[1] Levmore's solution to the puzzle (Levmore 2001) focuses on aggregating the judgments of different jurors. I focus on the psychology of a single decision maker.

search for the maximum of a concave function. Sometimes, however, optimization and adaptation lead to different results. To illustrate, following the steepest feasible contour line will not necessarily get the climber to the top of a mountain with two peaks.

Although the heuristic sometime errs, it has potentially offsetting advantages. To illustrate with the preceding example, assume that you enter a competitive race to climb to the top of an unfamiliar, uncharted mountain. If time and circumstances permit, you should study the mountain with a telescope before the race starts and calculate the best route for the ascent. Time and circumstances, however, may not permit these calculations. Perhaps the race starts before anyone has time to calculate, or perhaps the peak is shrouded in fog that your telescope cannot penetrate. In these circumstances, you may increase your probability of winning by making your best guess concerning the path to take and acting immediately.

In general, an adaptive heuristic may perform better than optimization in three circumstances. First, if time is scarce, then adaptation is often quicker than optimization. Second, if information is scarce, then adaptation may be feasible and optimization may be infeasible. Gigerenzer and Todd (1999) emphasize that quick decisions require a rule that is "fast" in the sense that its application takes little time, and scarce information demands a decision rule that is "frugal" in the sense that it uses only the "best" information and ignores the rest. This can increase its predictive accuracy over complete optimization methods. Third, if decision makers are likely to make large calculation errors, then correctly applying a simple heuristic may yield better results than solving incorrectly a complex optimization problem. Conversely, when time and information are plentiful, and errors can be corrected before they cause harm, optimization yields better results than adaptation.

LEGAL OBLIGATION FOR DELIBERATE AND TIMELY DECISIONS

I have explained that optimization and adaptation are best under different circumstances. When time and information are plentiful, careful calculations usually get closer to the best result with fewer mistakes. In view of this fact, law sometimes imposes a duty to collect the relevant facts and deliberate before taking actions that affect others. Professionals often have a fiduciary duty or a duty of "due diligence" to prepare themselves carefully before making a decision.[2] To illustrate, assume that the board of directors of a public corporation must make an important decision. If the board collects the facts and deliberates with care, the "business judgment rule" shields the board from liability for making a

---

[2] In the context of corporations and securities, "due diligence" refers to a prospective buyer's investigation of a target company, a piece of property, or a newly issued security, especially before recommending a security for purchase. More generally, the phrase refers to reasonable care in discharging a legal obligation. See *Black's Law Dictionary*.

bad decision. If, however, the board fails to collect the facts and makes a hasty decision, it may breach its fiduciary duty to stockholders.[3] Breach of fiduciary duty makes the board members liable to stockholders for losses resulting from a bad decision.

Conversely, when circumstances require a quick decision, law sometimes imposes a duty for timely action. To illustrate, the board of directors of a company has a duty to review large payments that the company makes to its officers. If the chief executive pays a large sum of the company's money to one of its officers and the board of directors fails to conduct a timely review, the board members may be liable for "sustained inattention."[4] The wrong consists in failing to take timely action, not in taking the wrong action.

A CASE OF ALLEGED MEDICAL MALPRACTICE

To contrast adaptation and optimization, especially as applied to the rules of evidence in civil trials, let us consider a case of alleged medical malpractice. The case was tried in 2003 in the Superior Court of Alameda County, State of California. The account that follows is based on observations during the two weeks that I spent as a juror in the case,[5] and on my subsequent research concerning rules that I observed the court applying.

The Facts

A man went to the hospital for a hernia operation. Before the operation, the anesthesiologist gave the patient a medical examination. Having passed the exam, the anesthesiologist put the patient to "sleep." In an ordinary case, the anesthesiologist would keep the patient "sleeping" until the surgeon repaired the hernia, the patient would wake up, and the patient would leave the hospital and go home the same evening. In this particular case, however, the patient had trouble breathing early in the operation, stopped breathing, suffered cardiac arrest, and died. An autopsy revealed that the victim's heart muscles were excessively thick and scarred, which was indicative of a condition commonly called a "heavy heart." This condition makes a person susceptible to a heart attack. Until the autopsy after his death, no one knew, however, that the patient had a heavy heart.

---

[3] The two leading cases that hold that directors are liable for insufficient preparation are *Smith v. Van Gorkom* (1985) and *Cede v. Technicolor, Inc.* (1993). The former case was settled by the directors after the Delaware Supreme Court decision. The latter case was remanded, and the trial court found that no injury had resulted.

[4] The business judgment rule requires that a judgment—a decision—be made. A new and important leading lower-court case holding that inattention (as opposed to bad preparation to make a decision) gives rise to liability is the *Walt Disney Company Derivative Litigation* (2003).

[5] According to applicable rules of procedure, the attorneys on each side can challenge candidates for the jury and remove a certain number of them without giving any reason for doing so. Consequently, law professors are often removed from juries by one of the attorneys. Unlike the past, neither attorney challenged me in the case, so I was seated on the jury.

The strain of the operation, which is unproblematic for a normal heart, caused cardiac arrest in this patient.

When the patient died, his descendants sued the anesthesiologist. Before the operation, the anesthesiologist was responsible for examining the patient and deciding whether or not to proceed. During the operation, the anesthesiologist also administered the drugs that put the patient to sleep and maintained the patient's breathing and other vital functions while the patient was asleep. The plaintiff made two accusations of wrongdoing by the anesthesiologist. First, the plaintiff alleged that the anesthesiologist had not conducted adequate tests before the operation to determine if the patient had a condition such as a heavy heart. In brief, the plaintiff alleged negligence in the pre-operation screening. Second, the plaintiff alleged that when the patient began to have trouble breathing during the operation, the anesthesiologist responded too slowly and incorrectly. In brief, the plaintiff alleged negligence in the operating procedure.

In this chapter, I will not consider the legal standard of care. Instead, I pose the following question: In weighing the evidence, did the legal procedure require the jury to combine facts consistently with adaptation or optimization? Reducing the evidence to probabilities sharpens the contrast because combining facts consistently with the laws of probability theory is necessary for optimization and unnecessary for adaptation. Consequently, in some circumstances, the laws of probability theory are consistent with optimization and inconsistent with adaptation. To illustrate my argument, I consider the special case where uncertainty can be represented by probabilities.

Pre-operation Screening

For pre-operation screening, the anesthesiologist followed this simple rule:

> Check the patient's age and blood pressure, and ask the patient if he had any history of heart problems. If the patient meets the cutoff for age and blood pressure, if he reports no history of heart problems, and if there are no other obvious medical problems, then proceed with the operation without further tests. Otherwise conduct further tests.

The plaintiff alleged, in effect, that the actual rule, which is based on three factors (age, blood pressure, and previous history), was too simple for the circumstances. Specifically, the plaintiff was grossly overweight. (He weighed more than 400 pounds.) A better rule, according to the plaintiff, would include a fourth factor, specifically the patient's weight. According to the plaintiff, further tests should be performed before anesthetizing a grossly overweight patient. The defendant, however, denied that further tests are required before anesthetizing an obese patient. According to the defendant, the screening criteria did not need changing, partly because there is no relationship between obesity and a heavy heart. If additional tests had been done in response to the patient's obesity, the defendant asserted, the results would not have revealed the heavy heart or otherwise reversed the decision to operate on this patient.[6] The jury had to decide whether the anesthesiologist's pre-operation screening was negligent or non-negligent.

After the patient passed the pre-operation screening, the anesthesiologist proceeded to put the patient to "sleep." The second alleged wrongdoing concerned the anesthesiologist's response when the sleeping patient began to have trouble breathing. When the patient struggled to breathe, the anesthesiologist had to decide when to intervene, and, in addition, the anesthesiologist had to choose between two possible interventions. The plaintiff alleged that the anesthesiologist delayed too long in deciding to intervene and then chose the wrong intervention.

Combining Facts

Thus far I have discussed the facts about the two alleged acts of negligence. Now let us turn to the rules of evidence the court used to weigh the facts. The plaintiff had to prove that the preponderance of the evidence favors the conclusion that the victim's death was caused by the defendant's negligence. I will focus on the legal rules for combining evidence to construct such a proof.

In discussing the facts, I described two points in time where the the defendant's negligence might have caused the victim's death. If pre-operation screening had detected the heavy heart, the operation would never have occurred and the patient would not have died. Negligence could have occurred in the pre-operating screen. Once the operation began, if the anesthesiologist had responded more quickly to the emergency and chosen a different intervention, the patient's life might have been saved. Negligence could have occurred in the operating procedure.

The plaintiff argued for negligence at both points in time. How should the court apply the standard of proof—the preponderance of the evidence—to the two points in time? The simplest approach is to apply the standard of proof independently to the acts. By this approach the court decides whether the preponderance of the evidence about the pre-operation screening indicates negligence. Entirely independently, the court decides whether the preponderance of the evidence about the operation indicates negligence. An affirmative answer to either inquiry implies liability, whereas a negative answer to both inquiries implies no liability.

To implement independent decisions, the judge might instruct the jury as follows:

---

[6] Technically, the defendant denied negligence and causation. According to the defendant, pre-operation screening was not negligent and, if it were negligent, it did not cause the patient's death.

If the preponderance of the evidence indicates that the defendant was negligent in conducting the pre-operation screening and his negligence caused the patient's death, then you should find him liable for the resulting loss and end your deliberations. Otherwise, you should consider the operating procedure. If you find that the preponderance of the evidence indicates that the defendant was negligent in the operating procedure and his negligence caused the patient's death, then you should find him liable for the resulting loss. Otherwise you should find him not liable and end your deliberations.

The independent, sequential decision making prescribed by these instructions is simple and usually produces a good result. Cognitive psychologists who favor adaptive heuristics sometimes commend independent, sequential decision making (Gigerenzer 2004). The alternative, which I will now describe, is more complicated and more strictly correct. Instead of applying the legal standard of proof independently at the two points in time, the evidence could be combined into an overall judgment. Combining evidence into an overall judgment allows for the possibility that evidence about negligence at one point in time affects the believability of evidence about negligence at another point in time.

To illustrate, assume that plaintiff alleges that defendant was drunk. If defendant was drunk, then he is likely to have behaved negligently in screening and operating. Consequently, if the court concluded that screening was not negligent, it is less likely that he was in fact drunk, and hence it is less likely that he operated negligently. In general, if plaintiff alleges that negligence was caused by some factor that operated at both critical points in time, then strength of evidence at one point in time affects the strength of evidence at the other point in time.

To implement combining evidence in an overall judgment, the judge might instruct the jury as follows:

If you find that the preponderance of the evidence indicates that the defendant's negligence in the pre-operation screening or the operation caused the patient's death, then you should find him liable for the resulting loss. To find liability, it is sufficient that the preponderance of the evidence indicates that defendant's negligence caused the patient's death one way or the other. If you find that the preponderance of the evidence indicates that the defendant was not negligent in the pre-operation screening and the operating procedure, then you should find him not liable and end your deliberations.

Combining evidence into an overall judgment might cause the court to conclude that the preponderance of the evidence favors the conclusion that the defendant was negligent in screening or the operation, even though applying the standard independently reaches the opposite conclusion.[7] The next section demonstrates this fact by using probabilities.

---

[7] Others have discussed the difference between deciding a case as a whole or decomposing it into its component issues and deciding them seriatim. The fact that the two approaches yield different results when courts consist of panels of several judges is called "paradox of decision" (see Kornhauser and Sager 1993, 2004; List and Pettit 2005).

Probabilistic Representation

When applying the legal standard of proof in a civil case, courts do not normally reduce evidence to probabilities. Probabilities suggest a precision that is usually absent and often unattainable in the court's reasoning about evidence. However, modeling the facts of this case in terms of probabilities clarifies my argument by increasing its precision. For this reason, I will represent the problem of proof in terms of probabilities. The reader should bear in mind that I do not think that jurors in this case actually reasoned in terms of precise probabilities or should have done so. In assigning probabilities, I will depart from my practice so far of presenting the facts in the actual case as accurately as possible.

Figure 17.1 depicts the court's problem as a decision tree. For now, focus on its branches, not the probabilities. The first branch indicates that the anesthesiologist may have been negligent or non-negligent in the pre-operation screening. If the preponderance of the evidence indicates that he was negligent in the pre-operation screening, and non-negligent behavior would have prevented patient's death, then the jury should find the defendant liable. If, however, the preponderance of the evidence indicates that he was non-negligent in pre-operation screening, then the jury must go on to the next branch in the decision tree and consider the operating procedure. In the second branch of the tree, the anesthesiologist may have been negligent or non-negligent in the operation. If the preponderance of the evidence indicates that he was negligent in the operation, and non-negligent behavior would have prevented patient's death, then the jury can find the defendant liable. If, however, preponderance of the evidence indicates that the anesthesiologist was not negligent in screening or operating, then the jury should find the defendant not liable.

Assume that the "preponderance of the evidence" means that the event is more probable than not. "Preponderance of the evidence" will be interpreted as a probability of 0.5 or greater. According to Figure 17.1, the evidence indicates

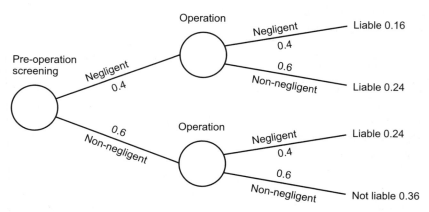

Figure 17.1   Uncertainty as probability.

that the probability is 0.4 that negligence in pre-operation screening caused the patient's death. Consequently, the plaintiff has not proved negligence in the pre-operation screening by the preponderance of the evidence.

Proceeding to the jury's next decision, if the preponderance of the evidence indicates that the anesthesiologist was negligent in the operating procedure, and non-negligent behavior would have prevented patient's death, then the jury can find the defendant liable. According to Figure 17.1, the evidence indicates that the probability is 0.4 that negligence in the operating procedure caused the patient's death. Consequently, the plaintiff has not proved negligence in the operating procedure by the preponderance of the evidence.

I have shown that independent and sequential application of the standard of the preponderance of the evidence leads to the conclusion that the anesthesiologist was not negligent. What about combining probabilities to reach an overall judgment? If the probabilities on each branch of the tree are independent,[8] the laws of probability theory prescribe a simple rule to combine them: the multiplication rule. Applying this rule to Figure 17.1, the probability that the anesthesiologist was not negligent in the pre-operation screening and also not negligent in the operating procedure is 0.36. Equivalently, the probability that the anesthesiologist was negligent in the pre-operation screening or in the operating procedure is 0.64. Thus the preponderance of the evidence indicates that the defendant's negligence caused the patient's death one way or the other.

The decision tree clarifies the fact that independent and sequential application of the preponderance of the evidence standard sometimes yields the wrong result. Specifically, the result is wrong when the preponderance of the evidence indicates that defendant's negligence caused the patient's death one way or the other, but does not indicate which way it was caused. To reach this conclusion, I have made some simplifying assumptions in my decision tree.[9] A full consideration of the complexities, however, would not change my conclusions.

When evidence can be represented as probabilities, independent and sequential application of the preponderance of the evidence standard violates the laws of probability theory. Independent and sequential application of the preponderance of the evidence standard is a heuristic that is easy to understand, and it works most but not all, of the time. Combining the facts to reach an overall judgment is more correct and more complicated.

---

8 The theory of negligence presented by the plaintiff in this case is consistent with the assumption of independent probabilities. The plaintiff did not present any argument that linked negligence in the two acts. For example, the plaintiff did not argue that the anesthesiologist suffered from a temporary cause of inattention (e.g., a hangover), or a permanent cause of bad judgment (e.g., bad training). From the plaintiff's argument, it seems that the alleged negligence was the result of a lapse in judgment by a generally sound physician.

9 If the probabilities on each branch of the tree are dependent, the laws of probability theory prescribe a more complex way to combine them than the multiplication rule. Also, note that I do not discuss whether or not the probabilities in the tree should be understood as subjective uncertainty or objective frequencies.

Judge's Instruction to the Jury

How did the judge instruct the jury in this case? The judge read the jury a form that was intended to explain what we were supposed to decide and then he gave the form to the jury foreman (me). The form was not entirely clear about whether we were to make sequential and independent decisions about the evidence, or whether we were to reach an overall judgment. Trying to parse the ambiguity, my best interpretation of the form favored sequential and independent weighing of the evidence. The jury in this case decided that the plaintiff had not carried the burden of proof, so our decision was "no liability." If the jury had received clear instructions to reach an overall judgment, the case would have been a closer call and the decision might have gone differently.

In my opinion, part of the reason why we did not receive clear instructions on this point concerned the plaintiff's attorney. At the beginning and end of the trial, the plaintiff's attorney gave his summary of what we were to decide. He should have explained to us on both occasions that we were to determine whether it was more likely than not that the defendant's negligence in the pre-operation screening or the operation caused the patient's death. He should have added that we should find the defendant liable if the evidence indicates that defendant's negligence caused the patient's death one way or the other, even if we are unsure which was the cause. The defendant's attorney would no doubt have challenged the plaintiff's attorney on this point. The exchange between attorneys would have forced the judge to focus on whether the jury was to make sequential, independent decisions, or combine information to reach an overall judgment.

Since the best interpretation of the jury instructions favors independent and sequential decision making, I conclude that adaptation is a good descriptive model for how this court required the jury to apply the standard of the preponderance of evidence. However, the fact that the court did not ask the jury to reach an overall judgment is a serious criticism in this case. In general, optimization provides a powerful normative theory for critiquing the evidentiary procedures.

DECOMPOSITION

A complicated event like this operation consists of many acts by the defendant. Each of the defendant's acts is potentially negligent. In general, the plaintiff gains an advantage in arguing the case by decomposing the event into many small acts provided that negligence in any one of them is sufficient for liability. The preceding account of the operation decomposed it into two acts of alleged negligence: pre-operation screening and performance of the operation. Consider the consequences of identifying a third act by the anesthesiologist and alleging negligence in its performance. Assume contrary to fact that the anesthesiologist examined the patient several weeks before the operation to determine whether or not an operation should be scheduled. After this examination, the anesthesiologist scheduled the operation. The plaintiff might argue that the defendant was negligent because he scheduled the operation instead of ordering further tests.

This additional allegation of negligence may help the plaintiff to satisfy the standard of proof required for liability. If the court evaluates the claim of negligent scheduling independently from the other claims, then the plaintiff's case is helped if there is a positive probability that the court will find that the probability of negligent scheduling exceeds 0.5. Otherwise, this additional allegation does not strengthen the plaintiff's case. The situation is somewhat different if the court applies the standard of proof to the overall evidence. Even a small possibility of negligent scheduling would normally increase certainty that negligence caused the death in one way or another. In probabilistic terms, if the probability of negligent scheduling is positive, then, under the usual conditions,[10] the overall probability that the defendant's negligence caused the victim's death in one way or another must increase.

As shown, decomposing the event into acts that are individually *sufficient* for liability helps the plaintiff's case. However, the defendant gains an advantage by decomposing the event into many small acts that are jointly *necessary* for liability. The anesthesiologist might want to decompose the tests that he performed on the patient into a sequence of small tests, all of which would have to be "positive" in order for the anesthesiologist to conclude that the patient might have a heavy heart. If the likelihood is small that every one of these tests would be positive, then the failure to order further tests did not cause the patient's harm. Decomposition is thus a tool for the plaintiff or the defendant, depending on how it is applied.

CONCLUSION

Applying the legal standard of proof independently to the elements of a case is relatively simple. It is also consistent with adaptive heuristics. In the case of alleged malpractice described above, that is what the jury thought the judge instructed it to do. Reducing evidence to probabilities, which juries do not ordinarily do, reveals a problem with this approach: Independent consideration of evidence is inconsistent with the laws of probability theory. In a case such as this, the plaintiff could reasonably object to being disadvantaged by the court interpreting the rules of evidence to contradict probability theory. To be consistent with probability theory, the court should ask whether the preponderance of evidence favors the conclusion that defendant's negligence caused the victim's harm in one way or another. Although adaptation is a better descriptive theory in this case, optimization is a better normative theory.

---

[10] As before, this argument requires independent probabilities or particular forms of dependent probabilities. The proposition is untrue under some unusual forms of dependent probabilities.

ACKNOWLEDGMENT

For comments and suggestions, I would like to thank the faculty at the Tel Aviv Law School, especially Ariel Porat and Omri Yadlin, David Sklansky, Mel Eisenberg, and participants from the Dahlem Workshop, in particular Ron Allen and Rick Lempert.

REFERENCES

Cede v. Technicolor, Inc., 634 A.2d 345 (Del. 1993).

Gigerenzer, G. 2004. Fast and frugal heuristics: The tools of bounded rationality. In: Blackwell Handbook of Judgment and Decision Making, ed. D. Koehler and N. Harvey, pp. 62–88. Oxford: Blackwell.

Gigerenzer, G., and P.M. Todd. 1999. Fast and frugal heuristics: The adaptive toolbox. In: Simple Heuristics That Make Us Smart, G. Gigerenzer, P.M. Todd, and the ABC Research Group, pp. 3–34. New York: Oxford Univ. Press.

Kornhauser, L.A., and L.G. Sager. 1993. The one and the many: Adjudication in collegial courts. *Calif. Law Rev.* **81**:1–51.

Kornhauser, L.A., and L.G. Sager. 2004. The many as one: Integrity and group choice in paradoxical cases. *Philos. Pub. Aff.* **32**:249–276.

Levmore, S. 2001. Conjunction and aggregation. *Michigan Law Rev.* **99(4)**:723–576.

List, C., and P. Pettit. 2005. On the many as one: A reply to Kornhauser and Sager. *Philos. Pub. Aff.* **33**:377–390.

Smith v. Van Gorkom, 488 A.2d 858 (Del. 1985).

Walt Disney Company Derivative Litigation, 825 A.2d 275 (Del. Chancery 2003).

18

Do Legal Rules Rule Behavior?

Ralph Hertwig

Department of Psychology, University of Basel, 4055 Basel, Switzerland

ABSTRACT

Economic analyses of law share an implicit or explicit belief in unbounded rationality. Here two boundedly rational psychological principles are discussed that together provide an alternative explanation for why most people behave in accordance with legal rules most of the time. These principles are the capacity for social learning and the impact of environmental cues and constraints. The ability to observe others' behavior and its consequences helps people conform to behavioral norms without memorizing the legal canon or Miss Manners's rules of etiquette. Environmental and institutional constraints help winnow down the set of actions available to people, and environmental cues suggest which of the available actions are desirable. If people who aspire to live by legal rules, standards, and institutions are to have a chance of doing so, lawmakers must recognize the psychological realities of boundedly rational decision making.

INTRODUCTION

Do racially segregated neighborhoods in big cities prove the existence of entrenched racism? In his book *Micromotives and Macrobehavior*, Thomas Schelling (1978) concluded no. Using a checkerboard to represent a city, he randomly distributed equal numbers of two kinds of "agents"—pennies and dimes—on the board while leaving some cells vacant. Schelling assumed that the agents were not highly prejudiced: Each was content to live in an integrated, "penny-and-dime" neighborhood as long as at least three of the eight adjacent agents were like itself. Thus, agents moved to a randomly selected vacant place only when half or more of their neighbors were unlike themselves. Updating the agents' locations on the basis of this simple rule, Schelling found that the originally integrated neighborhoods became highly segregated within just a few rounds. Schelling's simulations thus elegantly demonstrated that even people who prefer fairly integrated neighborhoods might wind up living in segregated ones. More generally, Schelling's (1978) analysis suggests that macrobehavior—that is, behavior at the aggregate level—does not necessarily equal the sum of individual micromotives. Even seemingly straightforward inferences about micromotives made on the basis of macrobehavior may be wrong.

This insight inspired the current chapter. Just as inferences from macro-behavior to micromotives can be deceptive, so can inferences from macro-motives to microbehavior. In the present context, the macromotives are legal rules, and the microbehavior is the actions of individual people. The question is: Do legal rules rule individual behavior, and if so, how? I suggest that the answer offered in classical economic analyses of legally relevant behavior—namely, that laws shape behavior by setting costs and benefits that individuals consider when choosing the optimal course of action—is probably wrong under most cir-cumstances. The problem is that the classical approach makes assumptions about people's knowledge and reasoning power that do not hold in most real-world contexts, as I will discuss shortly. But if the causal arrow does not go from law to behavior, why do most people nevertheless conform to legal norms and regulations most of the time? My thesis is that legally relevant behavior is governed by psychological rather than legal principles. Chief among them are *social learning* and *environmental constraints*.

Before I turn to these psychological principles, I use a recent change in Ger-man tax legislation to illustrate how the impact of law on individual behavior has been explained in economic analyses.

TO COMPLY OR NOT TO COMPLY WITH THE LAW: A DECISION REQUIRING UNBOUNDED RATIONALITY

Germany's dismal economic performance, high unemployment rate, and sky-rocketing budget deficits have left state coffers empty (*The Economist*, Feb. 19, 2004). It was therefore no surprise when the Minister of Finance offered am-nesty to German citizens who, wishing to evade the capital gains tax hikes of the early 1990s, shifted their assets to tax havens such as Switzerland, Liechten-stein, and Luxembourg. Swiss banks alone are said to be holding many billion Swiss Francs of private German investment. Until now, the dilemma faced by repentant tax sinners was that there was no legal way to bring the money back to Germany without paying penalties of up to 60% of its worth. The new tax am-nesty, which went into effect in January 2004, exempts from penalties all unde-clared tax on income received after Dec. 31, 1992, and before Jan. 1, 2003. Un-der the new scheme, investors face a tax rate of 25% or 35%, depending on the assets' worth, on assets repatriated by the end of 2004—a deal the government argues is attractive compared with the 48% tax rate that otherwise would have applied. How will the new law affect the behavior of tax evaders?

In an economic analysis, the individual is believed to act rationally on the ba-sis of the costs and benefits associated with legal and illegal choices. Thus, the tax sinner is assumed to compute his subjective expected utility of accepting the amnesty deal and of choosing alternative courses of action (e.g., keeping his money abroad). If the expected utility of accepting the deal exceeds that of the alternatives, he will repatriate the money; otherwise, he will select the alternative with the highest expected utility. More generally, this view stipulates that legal rules put implicit or explicit prices on different behaviors, and people adjust their behavior to those prices in much the same way as they adjust to relative prices in economic markets (see Ulen 2000).

One of the most prominent examples of an economic analysis of legal and illegal behavior is that of Gary Becker (1968; for a critique, see Wilson and Abrahamse 1992). In his paper "Crime and punishment: An economic approach," Becker (1968, p.170) argued, "A useful theory of criminal behavior can dispense with special theories of anomie, psychological inadequacies, or inheritance of special traits and simply extend the economist's usual analysis of choice." In other words, criminals, like everyone else, are rational utility maximizers. They decide whether to comply with the law by comparing the expected costs and benefits of committing a crime and of obeying the law, respectively. The expected costs of a crime are calculated by multiplying the subjective probabilities of the crime's being detected and of the perpetrator's being apprehended and convicted by the negative utility of any monetary sanction and any nonmonetary losses he might suffer (e.g., reputational damage, jail time). The expected benefits of the crime are calculated by multiplying the subjective probability of getting away with it by the value of the monetary and nonmonetary utility it would bring (e.g., being known in one's community as someone to be reckoned with). The maximizer will then choose whichever option promises the higher subjective expected utility. In this view, there is a direct route, henceforth called the *rational choice pathway*, between the law and the individual mind: The law divides the world into legal and illicit actions and defines some of the consequences of these actions (e.g., in terms of "legal costs and benefits"; Kornhauser 2001); the individual responds by applying the expected utility calculus.

Will German citizens who stashed their fortunes abroad decide whether to cut a deal with the German revenue service by using the excepted utility calculus? Although we do not know (because people rarely discuss their Swiss bank accounts with researchers), we can gain some insight into tax sinners' decision making by examining the publicly available advice of their lawyers. Not long after the amnesty was announced, tax lawyers began to offer advice on how to respond to the amnesty. In the on-line journal *manager-magazin.de*, for instance, Busse and Fischer-Zernin (2004) published a "Guide for Tax Sinners" outlining the kinds of information that a rational utility maximizer would require: (a) how much money in taxes one would have to pay if one returned the money, (b) what alternative courses of action are available, (c) how high the risk of being detected is, (d) what kind of legal sanctions a tax evader who is caught faces, and so on. But when they got to the heart of the matter (Should one strike a deal with the government or not?), Busse and Fischer-Zernin seemed to abandon the rational choice approach. Instead of instructing readers to feed all the listed information into the expected utility calculus, they appealed to intuition: "We have presented the crucial rational decision parameters; yet in the end much is a question of your gut feeling."

Of course, Busse and Fischer-Zernin's (2004) apparent reluctance to counsel expected utility maximization when it comes to obeying tax laws cannot be taken to reflect the psychological plausibility or implausibility of the rational choice pathway. The more interesting lesson from this episode is that treading the rational choice pathway from the law to an individual's decision about whether to follow the law is bewilderingly difficult. Imagine a tax sinner who aims to choose whether to take advantage of the amnesty on the basis of a subjective expected utility analysis. Although Busse and Fischer-Zernin have given her a head start, much work that cannot be delegated remains to be done. To compute subjective expected utility for accepting the government's deal, she would have to list all the possible consequences of doing so (e.g., having more resources legally available for consumption or investment, being subject to additional taxation in the future), attach a quantitative probability and subjective utility to each one, multiply each utility by its associated probability, and add up all these products to estimate the subjective expected utility of accepting the deal. She would have to go through the same procedure to estimate the subjective expected utility of not accepting the deal, which encompasses all alternative courses of action. Finally, she would have to compare the subjective expected utilities and choose the alternative with the higher one.

Completing all these steps requires knowing the law in detail, identifying the different courses of action, and gathering reliable information about the actions' consequences and the consequences' probabilities and utilities. Even assuming that the possible consequences of a course of action are finite and knowable, a person might have to invest days, weeks, or perhaps months and years of effort into this analysis, leaving her little time for activities other than managing her taxes. Just learning the relevant tax laws is a daunting task. One prominent commentary on the German income tax code, for example, consists of 2,262 pages (Kirchhof 2002), and the American tax code is estimated to include more than 50,000 pages (*The Economist*, Sept. 23, 2004). To suppose that a person can respond to all or some of the laws that make up the social and economic order of a community by applying the maximization calculus is tantamount to assuming that humans have unlimited cognitive abilities, knowledge, and time. This vision of *unbounded rationality* paints humans in God's omniscient image (Gigerenzer et al. 1999).

ECONOMIC ANALYSIS OF LAW: AS-IF MODELS AND CONSTRAINED OPTIMIZATION

One may fault the above depiction of economic analyses of law for outlining a view that perhaps was common early in the evolution of the field but that very few contemporary law and economics scholars would endorse. Today, many would interpret the economic models in an "as-if" sense. Others would agree that cognitive resources, time, and money are limited and would assert that economic models explicitly take such limits into account. Let us consider each of these views in detail.

Unboundedly Rational in an As-if Sense

When proponents of an economic analysis of law acknowledge that their models assume unrealistic mental abilities, they often argue that this is merely an as-if assumption. On this interpretation, economic analyses of criminal acts, for example, do not describe underlying reasoning processes but rather behavioral outcomes on the aggregate level. In that case, the fact that the processes on the level of the individual actor are psychologically implausible is beside the point. But do contemporary proponents of an economic analysis of law hew to this as-if interpretation? Let us consider, for example, Robert Cooter and Thomas Ulen's (2004) best-selling textbook *Law and Economics*, now in its fourth edition, which offers students an introduction to the economic analysis of law. How do these authors portray economic models of law?

In an analysis of embezzlement, Cooter and Ulen (2004) describe how someone might go about deciding whether to commit this crime. Specifically, they "assume an informed criminal, who knows the costs, benefits, and probabilities associated with the crime" (p. 462). The "rational embezzler calculates an expected value for the crime, which equals the gain minus the punishment multiplied by the probability of being caught and convicted" (pp. 456–457). Thus, in their view, "the economic model may be understood as an account of the *deliberations* of a rational, amoral person when deciding in advance whether to commit a crime" (p. 463, emphasis added).

These excerpts from Cooter and Ulen's (2004) influential textbook suggest that at least two contemporary proponents of an economic analysis of law do not consider their models of, for instance, rational crime to be mute on the subject of psychological processes. It is therefore reasonable to ask to what extent their analysis includes deliberative steps that rest on unrealistic assumptions about the human mind.

Constrained Optimization

Many contemporary economic models explicitly aim to take bounded rationality into account by, for instance, assuming limited rather than unlimited search for information. Limited search requires a stopping rule, that is, a way to decide when to stop looking for more information. Often put under the rubric of "optimization under constraints," one class of economic models assumes that the stopping rule *optimizes* search with respect to the constraints of time, computation, money, and other resources being spent. In this view, the mind should

calculate the marginal benefits and the marginal costs of searching for further information and stop search as soon as the costs outweigh the benefits (e.g.,
Sargent 1993; Stigler 1961). Although the rule "stop search when costs outweigh benefits" sounds plausible at first glance, optimization under constraints
can demand even more knowledge and computation than classic models of unbounded rationality. This is because they assume that the decision maker takes
into account not only cost-benefit calculations but also opportunity costs and
second-order costs for making those calculations (Conlisk 1996; see also
Gigerenzer et al. 1999).

To summarize the argument up to this point, the rational choice pathway from
legal rules to the human mind suggested by economic analyses of law rests on
assumptions that are unworkable under most circumstances. Moreover, this argument cannot be simply dismissed by claiming that contemporary economic
analyses of law represent as-if models or constrained optimization models.
How, then, do macromotives affect microbehavior? My thesis is that they generally do not. Specifically, there is no direct causal pathway from legal rules to individual behavior, and legal norms are often unknown to those subject to them.[1]
Why do most people nevertheless act in accordance with legal rules most of the
time?

Perhaps the most radical answer is that the causal arrow from legal rules to
behavior actually points in the opposite direction. In other words, social practices may be a source rather than a product of the law. In that case, laws are not
created but rather deduced through observation of evolved social norms (Parisi
2000). Because custom is only one source of law, however, it can provide only a
partial explanation for people's adherence to legal norms that they do not know.
In what follows, I discuss two other mechanisms that could help account for this
phenomenon. I focus on these mechanisms not to suggest that they alone can explain law-abiding behavior but to highlight contributors that I believe to be particularly relevant (for others see, e.g., Ellickson 1991).

HOW BOUNDEDLY RATIONAL PEOPLE FOLLOW
LEGAL RULES: SOCIAL LEARNING

Last year I moved to Basel, an experience that has taught me that Switzerland is
indeed a special case. The oldest continuous democracy in the world, it has a
widely envied political system; it remains fiercely independent; it has four official languages; and it is home to so many ethnic and religious groups that, in a recent survey of the country, *The Economist* (Feb. 12, 2004) wondered how it has

---

[1] After writing this chapter, I discovered that Robert Ellickson, a fellow participant at this Dahlem
Workshop, has put forth a similar view. He pointed me to his excellent book *Order without Law:
How Neighbors Settle Disputes* (1991), where readers can find a thought-provoking explanation for how order can emerge in the absence of legal knowledge as well as a summary of empirical studies that document the paucity of legal knowledge among laypeople (pp. 144–145).

managed to stick together for so long. Switzerland is also special when it comes to the informal laws that govern its social life. For instance, when you greet someone you know fairly well, you are expected to kiss the person lightly on the cheek three times in this order: right, left, right; importantly, however, men usually shake hands with one another instead. When you clink glasses with someone, it is important to look the person in the eye as you make a toast. During a meal, you should keep your hands above the table rather than in your lap. At work, the afternoon coffee break is a ritual observed by nearly everyone regardless of how busy they are. Although my German upbringing exposed me to variants of some of these rules, my lack of familiarity with their nuances has brought me into a few awkward situations.

When in Rome ... For the most part, however, I have been able to avoid making gaffes in my country of residence. Why? I propose that the capacity for social learning helps people to act in accordance with both legal and social rules without necessarily having explicit knowledge of them. Very generally put, social learning occurs when a person or an animal learns a behavioral pattern or acquires a preference as a result of observing or interacting with conspecifics (see Laland 2001). In humans, perhaps the best-known mechanism of social learning is what I will call the *imitation heuristic*, the purposeful copying of others' behavior. Indeed, imitation is the mechanism by which I learned how to greet people at a Swiss party. After observing a colleague who shook hands and either greeted by name or introduced himself to everyone present, I followed suit. Judging from my reception, this was the right thing to do.

Imitation can help one behave in accord with other social rules as well—for instance, to decide whether and how to queue in a store (e.g., if one sees other customers take a number, elbow others out of the way, or stands in line, one can simply do the same) and whether and for whom to hold the door. Copying other people can also help one avoid violating legal rules of which one is uncertain or ignorant. Take traffic laws, which vary greatly from place to place. Unless there is a sign to the contrary, making a right turn on a red light is legal in Los Angeles; it is illegal in New York. In deciding whether to turn right on red, make a U-turn, or drive on the left or the right side of the road, intentionally copying others' behavior is generally an efficient strategy for staying on the right side of the law. Similarly, imitation can help one determine the legal boundaries on drinking alcohol (e.g., whether one is permitted to drink in public), smoking cigarettes or marijuana (the latter is legal in the Netherlands and illegal almost everywhere else in Europe), and waste disposal (e.g., when and where to put out one's trash).

Social imitation is not a surefire way to stay on the right side of the law; that is, it will not *invariably* produce behavior consistent with legal rules. For example, a driver cannot necessarily infer that car traffic flow always falls within the legal speed limit, and smoking marijuana may be illegal even if most of one's peers do it. The claim here is simply that, by watching and copying others' behavior, an observer can learn to act in accordance with the practices in his social environment. When these social practices are in step with legal rules, as they generally are, the observer will behave consistently with the law (for more on the link between social learning and legal rules, see Engel 2004). By the same argument, however, when social practices and legal rules diverge from one another, observing and copying others' behavior will result in rule violations.[2]

The Bounded Rationality of the Imitation Heuristic

As Laland (2001) pointed out, social learning—of which imitation is an example—allows individuals to learn about their environment without engaging in potentially hazardous learning trials or wasting a large amount of time and energy on exploration, information search, and deliberation (see also Henrich and McElreath 2003). The imitation heuristic is particularly versatile in that it can be more nuanced than an unconditional "do-what-others-do" strategy. Studies of social learning in species as diverse as rats, pigeons, and guppies, for instance, suggest that these animals sometimes adopt a "do-what-the-majority-of-others-do" strategy (Laland et al. 1996). In such contexts, the probability that an individual learns a behavior from others depends on the number of other individuals exhibiting the behavior. Moreover, humans and animals can learn from the outcomes of others' actions (*inadvertent social information*, Danchin et al. 2004). For example, bats that fail to locate food alone seem to use a "do-what-the-most-successful-individuals-do" strategy, following bats that have previously found food to feeding sites (Wilkinson 1992).

To conclude, imitation is not a monolithic strategy. Probably depending on situational cues and opportunities, the behavior copied may be that exhibited by the majority, by the most successful individuals, or by the nearest individual; and whether a behavior is copied or avoided can also depend on feedback regarding its consequences, when such is available. The crucial point is that using any variant of the imitation heuristic (or even simpler forms of social learning; see Noble and Todd 2002) can speed up decision making by reducing the need for direct experience and information gathering. The imitation heuristic is a prime example of a *boundedly rational* decision strategy (Simon 1990; Gigerenzer et al. 1999).

Did Adam Maximize His Utility?

Under the present view, there is no causal pathway from legal rules to individual behavior. Instead, macrobehavior that appears to be regulated by macromotives is actually driven by other means, such as the use of simple heuristics by individuals whose knowledge of social rules and legal standards is nil or only tacit. One

---

2   Of course, there are myriad other reasons why people violate legal rules, but social learning mechanisms can help explain when and why people do so.

may fault this argument for skirting the problem of how the individuals whose behavior is copied learned to behave. Presumably, they too imitated others, but somebody must have shown a given behavior for the first time. Could it be that the rational choice model is descriptively appropriate for the first human actors, Adam and Eve?

Although one may doubt the soundness of Adam's decision to eat the forbidden fruit, he may have indeed performed the kind of rational calculations posited by classical economic theory and concluded that, given his utility function, eating the fruit had a higher expected utility than refraining from doing so.[3] Alternatively, there may have been a single noncompensatory reason for his decision; for instance, he may simply have been hungry or wished to impress Eve with his sangfroid. There are many routes by which an individual might arrive at a behavior that for whatever reason becomes an example for others, among them trial and error, coordination between agents, application of a boundedly rational heuristic, and deduction from first principles. There is no need to assume that Adam's choice was based on expected utility calculations. Even when a threatened punishment such as prison time or banishment from the Garden of Eden influences a decision maker (Eide 2000), his behavior can be explained not only by rational utility maximization but also by simple, boundedly rational choice heuristics (e.g., the priorty heuristic; Brandstätter et al. 2006).

HOW BOUNDEDLY RATIONAL PEOPLE FOLLOW LEGAL RULES: ENVIRONMENTAL CUES AND CONSTRAINTS

Many textbooks and articles on human decision making begin with the premise that people constantly make decisions. In the classic theory of utility maximization, this premise is typically interpreted to mean that people are constantly deliberating about the costs and benefits of possible actions (see Camerer et al. 2005). Several reasons make this fiction intuitive to researchers. As Camerer et al. (2005) suggested, as self-observers we may have a bias to interpret our own behavior as the outcome of a deliberate decision process because the neural activity that is associated with other processes (such as automatic ones) is inaccessible to consciousness. In addition, we students of human decision making may fall prey to the correspondence bias or fundamental attribution error—a phenomenon that we see in our subjects—which is the tendency to draw strong inferences about a person's disposition from his behavior even when his behavior is highly constrained by situational factors (Ross and Nisbett 1991). Efforts to understand legally relevant choices mostly or exclusively in terms of careful

---

[3] Going back even further, one may ask why Eve ever suggested eating the fruit and whether she did so on the basis of the expected utility calculus.

deliberation recall the correspondence bias in that they overlook the potential of the environment to make decisions for us or at least to winnow down the set of decision options.

As Norman (1988) observed, the environment puts myriad physical, semantic, cultural, and logical constraints on what we can do and how we can do it. Focusing on everyday things such as doors, water faucets, and light switches, he argued that well-designed objects exploit those constraints, making objects easy to understand and operate by restricting the set of possible actions. To understand the role of constraints better, consider the task of building a toy alien using nine pieces found in an *Überraschungsei* ("surprise egg") (Figure 18.1, top). Theoretically, there are 9—or more than 350,000—orders in which the 9 pieces could be assembled, only a few of which would result in success. Chances are, however, that even without instructions, you could put the pieces together correctly in a couple of minutes (Figure 18.1, bottom). How is this possible?

The role of each part of the alien, like each part of many other objects, is unambiguously determined by a set of constraints. Physical properties constrain the ways in which an object can be moved, placed in relation to other objects, put together, and so on. For instance, the alien's arms have sockets, indicating that something needs to be inserted into them. Semantic and cultural constraints further narrow the set of possible actions. For instance, knowing what an arm is, one can infer that the arms connect with the torso at the sockets. And knowing that most tools are manipulated by hand, one would guess that the stick belongs in the alien's grip.

The alien example (inspired by Norman 1988) illustrates that environmental constraints can aid decision making even in novel situations by limiting what can be done and by making desired actions obvious. Environmental constraints guide people's behavior not only in the assembly of children's toys and the operation of water faucets. I argue that they also signal what behavior is legal and desired. As in the case of social learning, environmental cues and constraints can influence behavior without there being a causal pathway from legal norms to the human mind. They can shape behavior directly. Consider laws against taking things owned by other people. Even if one did not know about property laws, there are environmental constraints on what can be taken. For instance, fences, walls, barbed wire, and locked doors all restrict one's access to other people's things and also provide cues regarding desired behavior.

Take traffic behavior as another example. The physical environment confronts the driver with curbs, speed bumps, median strips, guardrails, barricades, trees, houses, pedestrians, and other vehicles. All of these objects limit what the driver can do. Moreover, crosswalks, traffic lights, street signs, and traffic circles serve to signal what the driver may do. Finally, the physical environment of the car itself can be designed to prevent behavior that conflicts with legal rules. In some new car models, for instance, the engine can be started only after the seat belts have been fastened.

Figure 18.1 A nine-piece toy alien from an *Überraschungsei* (surprise egg) before (top) and after (bottom) construction.

In other domains, it is often institutional constraints that narrow the range of possible behaviors. For example, evading income taxes is not only illegal; it is difficult. For instance, for the large majority of workers in the United States and Germany, federal income taxes are deducted from gross wages before paychecks are even cut. Although a worker may try to reduce his tax burden by omitting or misrepresenting his other income or the number of his dependents, he will have to pay at least some income tax simply by dint of being on a payroll.

To conclude, explaining the behavioral effects of a legal norm in economic terms perpetuates the idea that people are round-the-clock decision makers. This fiction ignores that some and perhaps much of the work of making decisions is done not in the mind but in and through the external environment. Natural as well as artificial environmental constraints help restrict the set of actions to those that are lawful, and environmental cues signal actions that are desirable. Although some environmental constraints and cues are direct expressions of legal norms (e.g., speed bumps), many others are not. Of course, environmental constraints and cues are not the only reason why people generally adhere to the law, but any analysis of why people follow rules of which they have no explicit knowledge needs to take account of the structure of the environment.

LEGAL STANDARDS: HOW AN UNREALISTIC VIEW
OF THE HUMAN MIND MAKES ADHERENCE
TO LEGAL STANDARDS LESS LIKELY

The rational choice framework assumes that legal rules are known to those who are subject to them (Kornhauser 2001). Although I have argued that this assumption often does not hold, it holds in at least some contexts, for instance, in the courtroom.[4] Turning from the effects of legal standards on individuals to their effects on behavior within legal institutions such as the courtroom, I devote this final section to the argument that here, too, understanding actual behavior requires making realistic assumptions about how people make decisions.

When the Representation of Uncertainty Determines the Degree of Doubt

The "beyond-a-reasonable-doubt" standard has been a pillar of the Anglo-American criminal justice system for more than 200 years (Shapiro 1991). In the United States, judges explicitly instruct jurors to vote for criminal conviction only if they believe the defendant to be guilty beyond a reasonable doubt. Determining whether this criterion is met can be a daunting task. But advances in forensic methods over the last decade, especially DNA analysis, which has revolutionized criminal investigation, can make the task more manageable. Scheck et al. (2000, p. xv) went so far as to suggest "DNA testing is to justice what the telescope is for the stars: not a lesson in biochemistry, nor a display of the wonders of magnifying optical glass, but a way to see things as they really are. It is a revelation machine."

Indeed, DNA fingerprinting was initially received as a nearly foolproof means of identifying a criminal who left biological traces at the crime scene. There is no doubt that DNA analysis has enormous potential not only for identifying criminals but also for preventing false convictions (Scheck et al. 2000). But the value of DNA fingerprinting, like that of all diagnostic tools, depends on people's ability to interpret the results. The benefits of even the most valuable diagnostic tool can be offset by a lack of understanding of the uncertainties associated with the data gathered with it (Gigerenzer 2002; Hertwig and Hoffrage 2002). In an economic analysis of the behavioral effects of legal standards, people's ability to understand and process information about uncertainties does not warrant attention because the theory of expected utility maximization

---

[4]   In fact, some legal scholars at the Dahlem Workshop thought this assumption much too optimistic. Referring to the situation in the courtroom, one legal scholar argued: "There is reason to believe that much law is not known to lawyers, or to judges, even there. For example, new legislation, which introduces significant conceptual change in a legal system may be unknown, or known and not applied although applicable. In a study on sexual harassment law, we found that many judges hardly know new law in certain areas."

presupposes that people reason in accord with laws of probability and statistics such as Bayes's rule. As Cooter and Ulen (2004, p. 433) put it: "An economically rational decision maker begins with some prior beliefs and updates them in light of new evidence by conforming to certain rules of inference." Ignoring, however, how people actually reason about uncertainty can interfere with due process.

Although a criminal suspect is unlikely to share a DNA profile with a piece of incriminating evidence by coincidence, how unlikely that coincidence is depends on the frequency of a specific combination of genetic features in a specific reference population. *Random match probability* is the frequency with which that genetic combination, or profile, occurs in a reference population such as American males or residents of a particular city. This statistic, which is typically provided to judges and jurors in the courtroom, may be fairly interpreted as the chance that someone selected at random would have the profile in question. In the courtroom, however, the random match probability seems to be widely misunderstood by judges, jurors, and even DNA experts. One misinterpretation is to take the low frequency of a DNA profile in a given population to be the likelihood that the defendant is innocent (for this and similar examples, see Koehler 1993).

Confusion about the meaning of DNA evidence suggests that judges, jurors, and sometimes even DNA experts do not spontaneously understand uncertainties that are expressed in terms of conditional probabilities. Adopting a more realistic conception of the human mind can facilitate the development of ways to communicate evidence such that people are able to interpret the results of forensic scientific analyses correctly. For most of the time over which the human mind evolved, information about uncertainties was experienced in the form of natural frequencies, that is, event counts that are not normalized with respect to base rates; mathematical probability representations, of which the random match probability is an example, were not devised until the seventeenth century (Gigerenzer et al. 1989). Gigerenzer and Hoffrage (1995) argued that, although natural frequencies and probabilities are mathematically equivalent, representation matters because Bayesian updating is simpler with natural frequencies relative to conditional probabilities.

To investigate whether natural frequencies foster insight into the uncertainties associated with DNA evidence, Lindsey et al. (2003; Hoffrage et al. 2000) asked 127 advanced law students and 27 legal professionals to evaluate two criminal case files. The files were nearly identical to those in two real cases in Germany, one a rape and the other a murder. In both cases, a match was reported between the DNA of the defendant and a DNA trace found on the victim. Aside from the DNA match, there was little reason to suspect that the defendant was the perpetrator. Lindsey et al. (2003) focused on the following questions: Do lawyers understand the uncertainties involved in DNA fingerprinting better when they are represented in terms of natural frequencies than conditional

Table 18.1   Text for the conditional probability version and the natural frequency version of one of the two tasks involving forensic DNA evidence used by Lindsey et al. (2003).

Conditional Probabilities

In a country the size of Germany there are as many as 10 million men who fit the description of the perpetrator. The probability of a randomly selected person having a DNA profile that matches the trace recovered from the crime scene is .0001%. If someone has this DNA profile it is practically certain that this kind of DNA analysis would show a match. The probability that someone who does not have this DNA profile would match in this type of DNA analysis is .003%. In this case, the DNA profile of the sample from the defendant matches the DNA profile of the trace recovered from the crime scene.

Natural Frequencies

In a country the size of Germany, there are as many as 10 million men who fit the description of the perpetrator. Approximately 10 of these men would have a DNA profile that matches the trace recovered from the crime scene. If someone has this DNA profile it is practically certain that this kind of DNA analysis would show a match. Of the some 9,999,990 people who do not have this DNA profile, approximately 100 would be shown to match in this type of DNA analysis. In this case, the DNA profile of the sample from the defendant matches the DNA profile of the trace recovered from the crime scene.

---

probabilities, and does the type of representation affect their judgments regarding the defendant's guilt?

Half the law students and the legal professionals received the uncertainty information in conditional probabilities; the other half received it in natural frequencies. Table 18.1 summarizes the relevant passages from the file for one of the two cases. Participants were asked to estimate two probabilities: (a) the probability that the reported match is true, that is, that the defendant actually has the same DNA profile as the forensic trace (true match probability); and (b) the probability that the defendant is the source of the trace (the source probability).

When the information was presented in probabilities, the students and the professionals alike were hopelessly bad at computing the requested probabilities. For example, as Figure 18.2 shows, only about 1% of the students and 10% of the professionals determined the true match probability correctly. When the information was presented in natural frequencies, these percentages increased to about 40% and 74%, respectively. Why did the representation make such a big difference?

To estimate the true match probability, one must take false positives—that is, "untrue" matches between the defendant's DNA and the forensic trace—into account. False positives can occur because current DNA technology is not perfect and because of human error (e.g., contamination of the sample in the laboratory). Bayes's rule is required to combine the false positive rate with the base rate of the DNA profile in the relevant population:

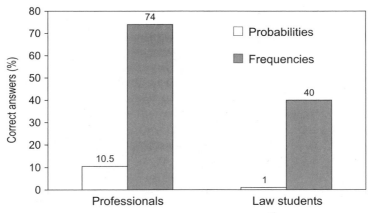

Figure 18.2 How a natural frequency representation improves probabilistic reasoning in law students and legal professionals. Percentages of correct Bayesian inferences in the probability and natural frequency representations are taken from Lindsey et al. (2003).

$$p(\text{profile}|\text{match}) = \frac{p(\text{profile})\,p(\text{match}|\text{profile})}{p(\text{profile})\,p(\text{match}|\text{profile}) + p(\neg\text{profile})\,p(\neg\text{match}|\text{profile})}.$$

Inserting the statistical information displayed in Table 18.1 into Bayes's rule results in a true match probability of 0.09:

$$p(\text{profile}|\text{match}) = \frac{(0.00001)(1.0)}{(0.00001)(1.0) + (0.99999)(0.0001)} = 0.09.$$

The relatively complex probability computations above can be drastically simplified by representing the information in natural frequencies. To compute the probability of a person having a particular DNA profile given a match using natural frequencies, one needs merely to know the number of people who actually have the profile out of all the people who match the profile. The natural frequency computations amount to solving the following equation:

$$p(\text{profile}|\text{match}) = \frac{\text{match \& profile}}{\text{match \& profile} + \text{match \& } \neg\text{profile}} = \frac{10}{10 + 100} = 0.09.$$

Natural frequencies facilitate Bayesian computations by obviating the need to take base rates into account directly. With frequencies, one recognizes immediately that there are 10 men in the population with the same DNA profile as the defendant and another 100 men for whom a match will be reported although

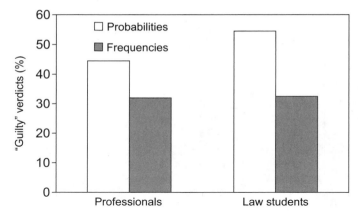

Figure 18.3 How the representation of information about uncertainties influences verdicts made by law students and legal professionals. Percentages of guilty verdicts as a function of representation are taken from Lindsey et al. (2003).

there is no true match. In other words, it is easy to see that, out of 110 men for whom a match is reported, only 10—or 9%—actually have the DNA profile.

The final decision in a criminal trial is about the defendant's guilt or innocence, and it is cast in yes-no terms. Did the representation of the DNA evidence affect the verdicts of the law students and the legal scholars in Lindsey et al.'s (2003) study? Yes. As Figure 18.3 shows, more students and more professionals judged the defendant to be guilty when the evidence was presented in terms of probabilities—that is, when the large majority of them had performed the wrong calculation—than when it was expressed in natural frequencies. In both groups, the proportion of guilty verdicts increased substantially when the DNA evidence was couched in terms of conditional probabilities.

To conclude, the representation of DNA evidence can mean the difference between freedom and imprisonment or even life and death. With conditional probabilities, essentially none of the law students or legal professionals in Lindsey et al.'s (2003) study estimated the true match probabilities in accord with Bayes's theorem, but they were much more likely than with natural frequencies to conclude that the DNA evidence proved the defendant's guilt beyond a reasonable doubt. This result by no means implies that the lawyers to whom the DNA evidence was presented in probabilities did not evaluate the evidence conscientiously. In fact, the authentic nature of the case files was so motivating that they spent an average of more than an hour and a half reading and deliberating about the two cases. To blame their poor estimates of the true match probability on negligence would be to miss the key point: How uncertain evidence and legal standards such as "beyond a reasonable doubt" combine in the minds of jurors and judges can be understood only if one takes account of psychological knowledge, for instance, about how information representation influences reasoning.

Heuristics Evoked by Law

In the DNA example, confusing representations of uncertain evidence produced an apparently inflated sense of certainty regarding the guilt of the defendant. In the next and final example, I will show how a law can require people to do things that exceed their cognitive abilities, thus evoking the (implicit) use of heuristics that, in turn, appear to violate the principles of due process. One of the most common decisions that must be made in the legal system is whether to release a person on unconditional bail, release the person on conditional bail, or keep the person in custody (the first decision is nonpunitive, whereas the latter two are punitive). In the English system, bailing decisions are made by magistrates, nearly all of whom belong to the local community and have no formal legal training. According to the Bail Act of 1976 and revisions thereof, when making a bail decision magistrates should pay attention to the nature and seriousness of the offense; the defendant's character, community ties, and bail record; the strength of the prosecution's case; the likely sentence in the event of conviction; and any other factor that appears to be relevant (see Dhami and Ayton 2001). The law gives no guidance, however, on how much attention magistrates should pay to each factor or how they should integrate the pieces of information into the final decision; nor does the law offer feedback on the appropriateness of past decisions.

Left to their own devices but exhorted to consider all the available evidence, how do magistrates actually make their bail decisions? Based on an analysis of several hundred bail decisions made by magistrates in two London courts, Dhami (2003) found that a simple decision tree accounted for about 95% of all bail decisions. The decision tree in the first court was as follows. If the prosecution requests a punitive decision, then concur. If the prosecution does not request a punitive decision or no information regarding its request is available, go to the next branch: If a previous court has already imposed conditions on bail or remand in custody, then follow suit. If not or no information is available, then make the same bail decision as the police. Dhami (2003) captured the second court's bail decisions using a decision tree identical to the first one with the exception of one branch. The trees accounted for 96% of the first court's decisions and 95% of the second court's decisions.

In this case, the decision makers knew the relevant law and the legal standard involved, and yet they seem to have implemented a "pass-the-buck" policy. That is, they appear to have copied others' behavior, basing their decisions on those previously made by the prosecution, past benches, or the police. Although this approach deviates from the ideal of due process, it is impossible to find out how accurate the decision tree is. Judging from the good performance of other "fast and frugal" decision-making heuristics, however, it may not result in less accurate judgments than due process (see Gigerenzer, this volume).

Dhami's (2003) analysis of bail decisions points to another possible pathway from legal rules and standards to individual behavior. To the extent that a legal norm requires people to do things that are beyond their limited processing abilities, people may respond by evolving "approximate methods" to handle the task (Simon 1990, p. 6). In other words, laws that rest on ideals that real people cannot live up to, might influence people's behavior through their use of simple heuristics that could have developed for the express purpose of implementing the law or could have been co-opted from other contexts. What these heuristics are and whether they lead to the kind of behavior that the law aims to promote are two exciting questions that a psychological analysis of the law's behavioral effects can address.

MACROMOTIVES AND MICROBEHAVIOR

In this chapter, I questioned economic analyses of the behavioral effects of legal rules, which often assume that the rule is known to those who are subject to it and that individuals respond to the rule as if they maximized their utility (e.g., Cooter and Ulen 2004; see also Cooter, this volume). I argued that any analysis of the pathway from macromotives to microbehavior is doomed to fail unless it rests on a psychologically plausible conception of individual actors. Specifically, I speculated that people have no explicit knowledge of most of the laws that make up the political and social systems of which they are a part. Yet most people behave in accordance with the law most of the time. Various psychological principles help explain this puzzle. The ones I discussed are the capacity for social learning and environmental cues and constraints. Specifically, the ability to observe others' behavior and the consequences thereof allows people to conform to behavioral norms without memorizing the legal canon or Miss Manners's rules of etiquette. Natural and artificial constraints in the environment help winnow down the set of actions available to the individual, and environmental cues suggest what actions are desirable. Using the interpretation of DNA evidence and bail decisions as examples, I demonstrated that not even within legal institutions such as the courtroom can one presuppose that the law governs people's behavior as it was intended to. If lawmakers aim to design legal rules, standards, and institutions such that people who aspire to live by them have a chance of doing so, the psychological realities of boundedly rational human decision making must be appreciated.

ACKNOWLEDGMENT

I thank Christoph Engel and Gerd Gigerenzer for inviting me to ponder what was a new topic for me. Writing this chapter was great fun, and I hope at least some readers have as much fun reading it. I am also grateful to all the anonymous reviewers of the chapter and to the participants in the Dahlem Workshop for offering many valuable reactions and suggestions and to Valerie Chase for editing the manuscript and for challenging my thoughts on the impact of legal rules on behavior.

REFERENCES

Becker, G.S. 1968. Crime and punishment: An economic approach. *J. Pol. Econ.* **76**:169–217.

Brandstätter, E., G. Gigerenzer, and R. Hertwig. 2006. The priority heuristic: Making choices without trade-offs. *Psychol. Rev.*, in press.

Busse, A., and J. Fischer-Zernin. 2004. Amnestie: Ein Leitfaden für Steuersünder. *Manager-Magazin.de.* http://www.manager-magazin.de/geld/geldanlage/0,2828, 286672,00.html

Camerer, C., G. Loewenstein, and D. Prelec. 2005. Neuroeconomics: How neuroscience can inform economics. *J. Econ. Lit.* **43**:9–64.

Conlisk, J. 1996. Why bounded rationality? *J. Econ. Lit.* **34**:669–700.

Cooter, R., and T. Ulen. 2004. Law and Economics. 4th ed. Boston: Addison-Wesley.

Danchin, É., L.-A. Giraldeau, T.J. Valone, and R.H. Wagner. 2004. Public information: From nosy neighbors to cultural evolution. *Science* **305**:487–491.

Dhami, M.K. 2003. Psychological models of professional decision making. *Psychol. Sci.* **14**:175–180.

Dhami, M.K., and P. Ayton. 2001. Bailing and jailing the fast and frugal way. *J. Behav. Dec. Mak.* **14**:141–168.

The Economist. 2004. George Bush's tax agenda. Sept. 23, p. 96.

The Economist. 2004. Germany's struggling economy. Feb. 19, p. 13.

The Economist. 2004. A special case. Feb. 12.

Eide, E. 2000. Economics of criminal behavior. In: Encyclopedia of Law and Economics, ed. B. Bouckaert and G. De Geest, vol. 5, pp. 345–389. Cheltenham: Edward Elgar.

Ellickson, R.C. 1991. Order without Law: How Neighbors Settle Disputes. Cambridge, MA: Harvard Univ. Press.

Engel, C. 2004. Learning the law. Preprints of the Max Planck Institute for Research on Collective Goods Bonn 2004/5. http://www.mpp-rdg.mpg.de/pdf_dat/2004_5 online.pdf

Gigerenzer, G. 2002. Calculated Risks: How to Know When Numbers Deceive You. New York: Simon and Schuster. (U.K. edition: Reckoning with Risk, Penguin)

Gigerenzer, G., and U. Hoffrage. 1995. How to improve Bayesian reasoning without instruction: Frequency formats. *Psychol. Rev.* **102**:684–704.

Gigerenzer, G., Z. Swijtink, T. Porter et al. 1989. The Empire of Chance: How Probability Changed Science and Everyday Life. Cambridge: Cambridge Univ. Press.

Gigerenzer, G., P.M. Todd, and the ABC Research Group. 1999. Simple Heuristics That Make Us Smart. New York: Oxford Univ. Press.

Henrich, J., and R. McElreath. 2003. The evolution of cultural evolution. *Evol. Anthro.* **12**:123–135.

Hertwig, R., and U. Hoffrage. 2002. Technology needs psychology: How natural frequencies foster insight in medical and legal experts. In: Etc: Frequency Processing and Cognition, ed. P. Sedlmeier and T. Betsch, pp. 285–302. New York: Oxford Univ. Press.

Hoffrage, U., S. Lindsey, R. Hertwig, and G. Gigerenzer. 2000. Medicine: Communicating statistical information. *Science* **290**:2261–2262.

Kirchhof, P. 2002. EStG KompaktKommentar: Einkommensteuergesetz. Heidelberg: Müller.

Koehler, J.J. 1993. Error and exaggeration in the presentation of DNA evidence. *Jurimetrics* **34**:21–39.

Kornhauser, L. 2001. Legal philosophy: Economic analysis of law. In: The Stanford Encyclopedia of Philosophy, ed. E.N. Zalta. Winter edition. http://plato.stanford.edu/entries/legal-econanalysis/

Laland, K. 2001. Imitation, social learning, and preparedness as mechanisms of bounded rationality. In: Bounded Rationality: The Adaptive Toolbox, ed. G. Gigerenzer and R. Selten, pp. 233–247. Dahlem Workshop Report 84. Cambridge, MA: MIT Press.

Laland, K.N., P.J. Richerson, and R. Boyd. 1996. Developing a theory of animal social learning. In: Social Learning in Animals: The Roots of Culture, ed. C.M. Heyes and B.G. Galef, Jr., pp. 129–154. New York: Academic.

Lindsey, S., R. Hertwig, and G. Gigerenzer. 2003. Communicating statistical DNA evidence. *Jurimetrics* **43**:147–163.

Noble, J., and P.M. Todd. 2002. Imitation or something simpler? Modelling simple mechanisms for social information processing. In: Imitation in Animals and Artifacts, ed. K. Dautenhahn and C.L. Nehaniv, pp. 423–439. Cambridge, MA: MIT Press.

Norman, D.A. 1988. The Psychology of Everyday Things. New York: Basic.

Parisi, F. 2000. Spontaneous emergence of law: Customary law. In: Encyclopedia of Law and Economics, ed. B. Bouckaert and G. De Geest, vol. 5, pp. 603–630. Cheltenham: Edward Elgar.

Ross, L., and R.E. Nisbett. 1991. The Person and the Situation: Perspectives of Social Psychology. New York: McGraw-Hill.

Sargent, T.J. 1993. Bounded Rationality in Macroeconomics. Oxford: Oxford Univ. Press.

Scheck, B., P. Neufeld, and J. Dwyer. 2000. Actual Innocence: Five Days to Execution, and Other Dispatches from the Wrongly Convicted. New York: Doubleday.

Schelling, T.C. 1978. Micromotives and Macrobehavior. New York: Norton.

Shapiro, B.J. 1991. Beyond Reasonable Doubt and Probable Cause: Historical Perspectives on the Anglo-American Law of Evidence. Berkeley: Univ. of California Press.

Simon, H.A. 1990. Invariants of human behavior. *Ann. Rev. Psychol.* **41**:1–19.

Stigler, G.J. 1961. The economics of information. *J. Pol. Econ.* **69**:213–225.

Ulen, T.S. 2000. Rational choice theory in law and economics. In: Encyclopedia of Law and Economics, ed. B. Bouckaert and G. De Geest, vol. 1, pp. 790–818. Cheltenham: Edward Elgar.

Wilkinson, G. 1992. Information transfer at evening bat colonies. *Anim. Behav.* **44**:501–518.

Wilson, J.Q., and A. Abrahamse. 1992. Does crime pay? *Justice Qtly.* **9**:359–377.

19

Should We Use Decision
Aids or Gut Feelings?

Hal R. Arkes and Victoria A. Shaffer

Department of Psychology, The Ohio State University,
Columbus, OH 43210–1222, U.S.A.

ABSTRACT

A large body of research supports the conclusion that decision aids are generally superior to "gut feelings" in a large variety of judgment tasks. However, human judges are still needed to select the cues upon which the decision aids are to be based and to assign the appropriate value to each cue. We suggest that there are two areas in which the use of gut feelings may still be necessary. The first pertains to complex environments where humans have had a plethora of experience but in which all of the relevant cues have not yet been identified. The second pertains to instances in which an affective outcome is the to-be-predicted event. Although gut reactions are certainly not infallible in this domain, research by Wilson and colleagues suggests that making explicit the bases for one's affective judgments may actually result in post-decision satisfaction lower than when an overall gut reaction is used to make the judgment. We summarize research findings in the legal domain in which decision aids and procedural rules are used to improve performance in such areas as the prediction of dangerousness. In these areas, gut reactions result in less accurate performance than judgments based either upon the use of decision aids or procedural guidelines, an example of the latter being the recently developed rules used to regulate eyewitness identification. We conclude by suggesting that the general superiority of decision aids over gut reactions is due principally to the greater consistency of the former and consequentially the greater susceptibility to context effects of the latter.

SHOULD WE USE DECISION AIDS
OR GUT FEELINGS?

Meehl's 1954 book began what has come to be known as the "clinical versus actuarial controversy." The "clinical" advocates asserted that gut feelings generated more accurate predictions, classifications, or diagnoses than did regression equations and other statistical techniques. The "actuarial" advocates asserted the opposite. In this chapter we will compare gut feelings to decision aids, the latter representing a wider array of tools than actuarial techniques. For example, practice guidelines, protocols, and other aids are often employed by such professionals as physicians, who could use their gut feelings instead of relying on such aids. We intend to address the question: when should each be used? Meehl stated that people should very rarely use their head—or gut—instead of an actuarial formula. We intend to reexamine Meehl's advice in light of the research that has occurred in the last half century. We begin with two definitions and then a very brief review of the relevant literature.

For the purposes of this chapter we define "gut feelings" as unaided judgments, usually accompanied by a limited ability to articulate accurately the bases upon which the judgment is rendered. These judgments are also referred to in the literature as "clinical judgments."

"Decision-aided" judgments are ones using explicit and validated cues which are combined by an explicit rule or algorithm. These are sometimes called "actuarial" judgments or "mechanical" judgments.

A number of the most famous publications comparing gut feelings and decision-aided judgments have been of the "scorecard" variety, the most recent and extensive being that of Grove et al. (2000). One hundred thirty-six comparisons between clinical and mechanical predictions were included in their meta-analysis. Mechanical, i.e., algorithmic or statistical, procedures substantially outperformed clinical "gut feeling" predictions in 33–47% of the comparisons. Clinical predictions were substantially more accurate in 6–16% of the comparisons. On average the mechanical predictions were about 10% more accurate than the clinical ones. The superiority of the mechanical technique found in this meta-analysis is typical of the conclusions drawn by most prior researchers (e.g., Dawes et al. 1989). What was surprising was that 6–16% of the comparisons favored gut feelings, given the microscopic victory rate for such judgments in prior scorecards.

The superiority of the mechanical or actuarial method is usually attributed largely to the consistency of such techniques. A regression equation, when provided with the same value of each predictor, always generates the same predicted event. This boring regularity is to be contrasted with clinical judgment, which has far lower reliability. The same cues do not always generate the same prediction in the unaided judge, who has lapses of attention or other episodic occurrences of nonoptimal behavior. Because reliability establishes a ceiling above which validity cannot rise, the lower reliability of the unaided judge represents an extremely serious impediment to good decision making.

There have been at least two recent theoretically important developments with regard to the superiority of the actuarial model. The first has been the advent of the "fast and frugal" heuristics of Gigerenzer and his colleagues (e.g., Gigerenzer et al. 1999). One such heuristic is the "Take The Best" strategy. Persons utilizing this heuristic make a decision based upon only a single cue, hopefully the one with the highest validity. To take one of the examples from

Gigerenzer et al. (1999), suppose that the decision task was to select the German city with the larger population when given a series of pairs of German city names. One possible cue to use would be to select the member of each pair which was a national capital because this cue is highly related to population; national capitals are generally larger in population than noncapitals. Gigerenzer et al. (1999) presented shocking evidence that the Take The Best rule slightly outperformed multiple regression—the prototypic decision aid—on such a task! Note that the success of any "fast and frugal" heuristic is not necessarily a victory for "gut reactions" over decision-aided judgments, because such heuristics can be based on explicitly identified cues which are combined by an explicit algorithm (e.g., Green and Mehr 1997). Thus fast and frugal heuristics can often be accurately characterized as decision aids. However, the fast and frugal heuristic research does show that a decision aid need not contain information about all available cues in order to be highly effective.

The second development has been the research of Klein (1998) and his associates, who have promoted the field of "naturalistic decision making." Rather than documenting the shortcomings of decision makers compared to a normative model, Klein has studied the performance of experts who react competently in naturalistic settings, such as firefighters who respond to an emergency situation. These experts often rely on intuition, some of which is based on factors they do not or cannot articulate. In other words, they rely on gut feelings.

A major purpose of the current chapter is to delineate where decision aids and where gut reactions may each effectively be used. We will conclude by highlighting the use of these two strategies in legal settings.

IF THE DECISION AIDS ARE SO GOOD, SHOULD THE GUT EVER BE USED?

Despite the superior reliability of decision aids, human judges are still necessary to play key roles in the judgment process. For example, clinical judgment is essential for the creation of every actuarial model; human input is crucial not only for identifying the critical variables but also for assigning the appropriate values to each variable. Einhorn (1972) demonstrated this principle in an experiment examining the prediction of survival rates for patients with Hodgkin's disease. Physicians were given access to a biopsy slide taken on each patient's first hospital admission. Using Likert scales, the clinicians were asked to judge the relative amount of nine histological characteristics that they saw in each patient's slide. In addition, physicians were asked to give an overall judgment of the severity of the disease. These global severity judgments were used to predict survival time of the patients. A negative correlation was expected between the severity global judgment and survival time due to the fact that a higher judgment of severity is related to shorter survival times. However, none of judges' correlations differed significantly from zero; the correlations ranged from -0.13 to

0.10. Yet, the correlations significantly increased when an actuarial combination of the judge's own evaluations of the nine histological components was used to predict survival time. These correlations ranged from 0.20 to 0.26. (Because these correlations do not assess the relation between severity and survival but instead the value of the histological cues and survival, these correlations are positive.) This experiment demonstrated that the physicians' global impressions were inferior to a mechanical combination of their own histological inputs in the prediction of survival time from Hodgkin's disease. Both the actuarial and human predictions were based on the physicians' expert knowledge; however, the mechanical combination amalgamated the information in a superior manner.

Yaniv and Hogarth (1993) proposed that clinical intuition would have an advantage over statistical prediction in a complex decision environment where judges are able to exploit contextual information. They demonstrated this phenomenon in an experiment where participants were required to predict the second and fifth letters of a word that appeared in a *New York Times* article when given the first letter of the word. There were three conditions in this experiment: impoverished (only the first letter was supplied), partial (the words before and after the target word were presented), and rich (the full sentence that included the target word was supplied as well as the title of the article). The responses of the human judges were compared to the predictions of a word completion rule that was generated from a published table of base rate frequency counts for word-length and letter-position combinations. The accuracy of the human predictions varied between the conditions, whereas the base rate predictions provided by the word completion rule remained constant across conditions. In the rich conditions, human judges were able to outperform the base rates by relying on the contextual cues available to them due to their extensive knowledge of English. On the other hand, the impoverished conditions supported the use of statistical models. The limited number of cues available to a human judge favors the use of statistical models within these decision environments. However, the partial-context condition led to mixed results. Levels of accuracy were similar between the two groups with the human judges occasionally outperforming the base rates. This environment is noteworthy because it likely contains some valid cues, however, not enough to sustain a useful prediction method. (Accuracy ranged from 42–47% in the second letter and 33–39% in the fifth letter.) The authors argued that perhaps combining actuarial and clinical judgment in this type of environment would prove to be the most successful strategy. Combination rules which used the judges' predictions when their confidence exceeded 50% and the base rate when it did not were as good as or better than judges who did not have access to the base rate predictions. The accuracy of the combination models exceeded that of the base rate models in the partial and rich conditions. Similarly, Blattberg and Hoch (1990) found that they were able to obtain greater accuracy in forecasting product demands using a model that combined actuarial and clinical judgment. The combination model was more successful than either the actuarial or clinical models alone. Blattberg and Hoch argued that the flexibility of human intuition can also be beneficial when working in highly dynamic decision environments. Statistical models cannot account for unpredictable fluctuations, such as "broken-leg" cues. Meehl coined this term to denote a cue, the presence of which would defeat an actuarial prediction. Take, for example, the prediction of whether an individual would go to the movies on a particular day. The inputs to the actuarial prediction—the nature of the movie, the day of the week—all suggest that the person would attend. However, the potential movie-goer has just suffered a broken leg. The actuarial prediction would not be able to take this cue into account. But an experienced judge would potentially be able to utilize this cue, thereby demonstrating an instance in which the human judge's performance would surpass that of a decision aid. However, this conjecture relies on the judge's ability to discriminate true broken-leg cues from bogus ones, which itself may be a daunting task.

Yaniv and Hogarth (1993) argue that human judgment or intuition can be most useful in complex environments where all of the contextual cues have not been modeled or perhaps not even identified. In their experiments, human judges were able to outperform the base rates during the word completion task when provided with rich contextual information. However, the domain chosen by Yaniv and Hogarth—language—may not be a typical arena in which to compare actuarial and clinical judgments. The rules of language are opaque to its users even though people are highly fluent users of the rules. For example, what is the past pluperfect of the verb "to give"? Even though most English speakers cannot articulate the past pluperfect conjugation rules, these same speakers can still use the verb entirely appropriately. In domains such as language where performance levels greatly exceed knowledge of the bases of the good performance, "gut reactions" would have an advantage. They are quick and accurate, whereas struggling to adhere to the past pluperfect conjugation rules may be neither. We doubt that many domains have these characteristics, although we concede that language does.

Therefore, we argue that the strength of human intuition lies in its *potential* ability to identify useful contextual information and random fluctuations, or "broken-leg cues." Furthermore, in contrast to the conclusions made by Meehl and others, there may be other occasions when relying solely upon intuition or a "gut reaction" results in a more valid response. For example Wilson and Schooler (1991) demonstrated that intuitive responses, compared with those based on careful introspection, were more strongly correlated with the judgments of experts. Participants were asked to taste several jams; half of the participants were only asked to give one overall rating of each jam while the remaining participants were asked to first provide their reasons for liking and disliking each jam and then give a holistic judgment. The overall ratings of each group were compared with ratings from a panel of experts, trained consultants who rated the jams for *Consumer Reports*. The ratings of the participants in the "holistic" group or control group, who provided only one overall response, were in closer agreement with the experts ($R = 0.55$) while the correlation between the ratings of the experts and the reasons group was not significantly different from zero ($R = 0.11$). Wilson and Schooler concluded that there were situations in which a "gut reaction" was more optimal than a response that relied on introspection.

Wilson et al. (1993) also examined the effect of introspection prior to a decision on post-choice satisfaction. Participants were asked to evaluate five posters: two were reprints of paintings from popular artists (Monet and Van Gogh) and three posters had a more contemporary, humorous style. In pretests, the Monet and Van Gogh paintings received more positive ratings than the other three posters. Half of the participants were assigned to the reasons group and half to the control group. The reasons group was instructed to describe why they liked or disliked a poster prior to rating the poster, while the control group was simply asked to rate the poster. After the experiment was complete, the participants were given the option to take one of the posters home with them. Participants in the control condition liked the art posters better than the humor posters and opted to take those home, whereas those in the reasons condition liked the humor posters best and took those home. From two to three weeks after the experiment, each participant was contacted at home and was asked five questions about his/her satisfaction with the poster. Participants in the control condition were significantly more satisfied with their choice than those in the reasons condition. This experiment was the most convincing demonstration of introspection's potential to foster nonoptimal decision making.

This line of research by Wilson and colleagues provides evidence that "gut reactions" or intuitions can provide more valid responses than those based upon articulated characteristics. Note that the articulated characteristics used by the participants in the reasons group may not be valid cues in that they did not highly correlate with either the opinion of experts nor, more importantly, with the participants' reported satisfaction with the stimuli a few weeks later. Thus the reasons group may not be considered a decision-aid group due to the highly questionable validity of their articulated cues. Still, the research by Wilson and colleagues does show that in affective tasks, gut reactions may be more effective than in the prediction tasks surveyed by Grove et al. (2000). In an effort to analyze why gut reactions did relatively well in Wilson's affective tasks, Millar and Tesser (1986) argued that there are two separate components of attitudes: the cognitive component and the affective component. The cognitive component contains the attributes of an attitude object and the individual's beliefs about that object, while the affective component contains his/her feelings connected with that object. In addition, the elicitation method, or the task required of the participants, can also be characterized as either cognitive or affective. For instance, articulating the basis for a decision is a cognitive task while providing an overall measure of liking is an affective task. Furthermore, Millar and Tesser argued that in order to have a valid measure of an attitude, one must match the elicitation method (or type of task) to the component of the attitude object to be measured. For example, in the jam experiment, the authors were interested in the participants' liking of each jam, which corresponds to the affective component of their attitude about jam (Wilson and Schooler 1991). The control group was asked to provide one overall rating of their liking—an affective task; the reasons group was asked to provide reasons for their decision—a cognitive task. Thus those in the control group were asked to perform a task which corresponded to the desired attitude component of affect, whereas the task in the reasons group—a cognitive one—did not match the desired attitude component of affect. Therefore, when the liking ratings of the two groups were compared with the affective rating provided by the experts, those that provided responses that matched the chosen attitude component were in agreement with the experts, while those that provided responses through a method that did not match the chosen attitude component disagreed with the experts. Similarly, in the poster study, the participants in the reasons group again performed a cognitive task while those in the control group performed an affective task. When the participants were eventually asked about their satisfaction with their choice, which is an expression of the affective component of their attitude, those in the control group again demonstrated greater post-choice satisfaction than those in the reasons group due to the match between the task and the measured attitude component.

In summary, if we consider decision aids to be cognitive tasks and intuitive responses to be affective tasks, then we can begin to understand when gut responses may compete well with decision aids. Intuitive responses may be at their best when measuring the affective component of an attitude.

AFFECT, GUT REACTIONS, AND THE LAW

Damasio (1994) contrasts the rational, deliberative mode of decision making with what he calls the "somatic-marker" mode, in which affective gut reactions to various aspects of the situation play a major role. Damasio asserts that the latter mode should not be seen as irrational but instead as vital to making good decisions. In fact, people with prefrontal lobe damage who have negligible affective reactions to impending stimuli make terrible decisions. However, Damasio relies principally on decisions made by a person that would affect their own welfare, such as the consideration of gambles. This is similar to the Wilson et al. (1993) research in which people had to decide which type of poster they would subsequently enjoy. The decision has no gold standard other than one's future satisfaction. In law, however, decisions are typically made about the fate of other people. The judge and jury make decisions about the defendant, the parole officer makes decisions about the prisoner, and the expert makes forensic decisions about the accused. Furthermore, the law requires objectivity and rationality. Citizens must know what specific behaviors are proscribed so that those who wish to obey the law will know what objective criteria will be used to define criminal behavior. One must be able to count on rational rather than arbitrary adjudication of disputes. In such an environment, gut reactions would seem to be particularly problematic. Hilton and Simmons (2001) examined the performance of tribunals who had to decide whether to detain forensic patients in maximal security. Because so much prior research had shown that actuarial assessments of violent risk are much more accurate than unaided judgments, the authors tested whether the actuarial risk data would influence the tribunal's decisions. Sadly, the data had no influence whatsoever. However, the attractiveness of the patient did have a significant influence, as it has in many other studies pertaining to the evaluation of defendants and patients. We believe that most legal observers would agree that one's affective reaction to the attractiveness of a person should not play a role in whether a person is maintained in a maximal security facility, released to the community, etc. Although Damasio may be entirely correct that the wisdom of affective, somatic reactions may help one more accurately evaluate one's options, decisions based on affective reactions cannot surpass the accuracy of decisions based on decision aids in areas such as violence assessment. As Meehl and Dawes asserted years ago, the amalgamation of multiple sources of data is not a strength of human decision making. It is a glaring weakness.

Werner et al. (1983) asked psychologists and psychiatrists to assess the imminent dangerousness of 40 male patients admitted to an acute-care psychiatric unit. As usual, these professionals were unable to predict future dangerousness with much accuracy. A linear regression was much more accurate. Among the problems leading to the professionals' poor performance was their reliance on invalid cues. For example, the two cues weighted most heavily by the professionals were the hostility and excitement rating of the patient. These two cues probably elicited strong affective reactions in the evaluators. However, neither cue had a significant relation with subsequent dangerous behavior. Hogarth (2001) noted that illusory correlations (such as those exhibited between dangerousness and hostility and dangerousness and excitement of the patient) tend to exist in domains where theory development has outpaced theory verification.

As another example, Carroll et al. (1982) analyzed 1,035 parole decisions in Pennsylvania. Predictions of the parole board "were virtually unrelated" to post-release outcomes. However, an actuarial prediction rule was developed which surpassed the accuracy of the unaided parole board.

These examples should not be construed as advocacy solely for linear regression decision aids. A vast number of aids have been developed which do not depend on regression. For example, Gardner et al. (1996) used simple branching algorithms to classify individuals. Gardner et al. were aware of the fact that many actuarial methods, while highly accurate, are not utilized. For example, one senior health care administrator told us that a very helpful decision aid had been developed which would assist physicians in reading electrocardiograms (EKGs). The aid would print its interpretation as the EKG was being printed.

However, much to her dismay, the physicians turned off the aid when generating the EKGs! Gardner et al. did not want this to happen to the aid they were developing which would assist professionals in assessing violence risk. They hypothesized that aids which require substantial calculation are not perceived as user-friendly, and this feature may lead to their woeful lack of use. The researchers developed a branching algorithm that required professionals to ask no more than three questions. This decision aid was just as accurate in classifying potentially hostile individuals as was an aid based on much more sophisticated statistical procedures, reminiscent of the conclusion of Gigerenzer et al. (1999). However, the algorithmic aid would be substantially much easier to understand.

PROCEDURAL RULES AS DECISION AIDS

Each country has its own judicial procedures that must be followed by all parties. These may be considered as decision aids, in that their intent is to promote the best possible decisions. Like more traditional decision aids, they lay out the procedure by which the decision is to be made rather than providing any content knowledge. Procedural rules are similar to decision aids in two other respects: they often regulate which cues are to be used in the decision, and sometimes they specify the combinatorial rules which amalgamate the cues. For example, procedural rules prohibit the use of hearsay evidence, no matter how well such evidence resonates with one's gut feeling concerning the guilt or innocence of the defendant. Cues related to prior convictions are also barred from some proceedings, no matter how diagnostic such cues might be from a Bayesian perspective. With regard to combinatorial rules, legal definitions often specify how decisions should be organized. For example, for a public figure to prove that he or she has been libeled, it is necessary to show that the statement in question is (a) false, (b) defamatory, and (c) published maliciously, meaning that the person who wrote or said it had the knowledge that the statement was false, had serious doubts as to whether it was true, or had reckless disregard to whether it was true.

Of course, just because a country has decided upon a particular judicial procedure does not mean that the procedure will be effective in promoting good decisions. For example, a common judicial procedure pertains to the disregarding of evidence. Often it is necessary for a judge to rule that some evidence is inadmissible. Unfortunately, the original presentation of such evidence may have occurred when the jury was present and, following the ruling of inadmissibility, the judge must instruct the jury to ignore such evidence. Can the jurors comply with this request? Substantial research suggests that this procedure, while well meaning, is ineffective. Once jurors know some information, they find it difficult to remove from their future consideration. For example, Casper et al. (1988) presented mock jurors with a search and seizure case in which police officers improperly entered a person's apartment without a warrant and injured the resident. Some jurors read that the police found contraband in the apartment.

Despite the fact that they were told that this information should not be considered in deciding upon the damages the resident should receive for his injuries, the jurors awarded significantly less damages when the contraband was present than when it was either absent or not mentioned. Instructions to ignore the contraband were ineffective. However, Sommers and Kassin (2001) have shown that mock jurors can disregard inadmissible testimony under some circumstances but not in others.

This problem is particularly acute in cases such as malpractice in which jurors must first decide if the practitioner met the standard of care. In the course of such trials the jurors learn what the nature of the injury was to the plaintiff. Extremely negative outcomes, while lamentable, should not have a bearing on whether the professional was negligent. Very bad medical outcomes, for example, might be due to the disease rather than to the treatment. Most research has demonstrated the ineffectiveness of entreaties to decision makers to base their decision not on their knowledge of the outcome but on the behavior of the defendant in the trial or the protagonist in the story. Because the judge's instructions which are designed to eliminate the impact of inadmissible evidence have generally not been successful, alternative procedures have been advanced. For example, Arkes and Schipani (1994) suggested consideration of a bifurcated trial in cases of medical malpractice. According to this scheme, the jury would not hear anything of the outcome of the medical procedure in the first portion of the trial in which a determination of negligence would be made. Only if negligence is deemed to be present would the second portion of the bifurcated trial occur, in which damages would be determined. This procedure would shield to some extent the jurors' knowledge of the nature of the outcome during their deliberations concerning the presence of negligence.

Another procedure which has been investigated in recent years is juror note taking. For many years courts prohibited note taking by jurors, because courts were apparently fearful that assiduous note takers would unfairly take a leading role in juror discussions. Hence this prohibition was an official procedure designed to foster a fairer trial. However, recent research has shown that allowing jurors to take notes results in significant improvements in a number of areas. For example, Horowitz and ForsterLee (2001) found that compared to jurors who were not allowed to take notes, those who did were better able to distinguish among differentially worthy plaintiffs, recall more probative evidence, and reject statement foils which were not actually presented as evidence. Fortunately courts in the United States have recently begun to take a much more favorable view of jury note taking. As a result, what used to be a procedure thought to improve decision making (e.g., not taking notes) is being replaced with a decision procedure—taking notes—that actually does improve decision making.

Perhaps the most extensive group of decision aids in the U.S. justice system involves the procedures governing eyewitness identification. Wells et al. (1998) analyzed 50 cases in which DNA evidence exonerated persons who had been convicted of crimes they did not commit. In 36 of these cases, erroneous eyewitness identification had led to the conviction of these persons. Data such as these led the attorney general of the U.S. to convene a committee comprised of law enforcement officials, attorneys, and psychologists in order to develop procedures designed to improve eyewitness identification decisions. Among the most prominent recommendations of *Eyewitness Evidence: A Guide for Law Enforcement* are the following:

1. Encourage the witness to volunteer information without prompting.
2. Ask open-ended questions.
3. Caution against guessing.
4. Use only one suspect per identification procedure.
5. Select line-up foils who generally fit the witness' description of the perpetrator.
6. Before the line-up occurs, instruct the witness that the perpetrator may or not be present in the line-up.
7. Use a sequential line-up with only one possible perpetrator being presented at any one time rather than a simultaneous line-up with all possible perpetrators being presented at one time.

What was most noteworthy about these guidelines was that they were all based upon empirical research. In other words, research had demonstrated that obeying these rules resulted in higher levels of eyewitness identification accuracy than not obeying these rules. These guidelines may be considered as decision aids in that they promote better judicial decisions than would otherwise be the case. It is notable that the correlation between confidence in one's eyewitness identification and the accuracy of one's identification is only +0.29 according to meta-analyses (Wells et al. 2000). This suggests that relying on one's "gut feelings" concerning accuracy is not prudent. Relying on decision guidelines is a much wiser strategy.

SUMMARY: THREE EXAMPLES

For the first example, consider a study by Shafir (1993) in which mock jurors were asked to decide either to which of two parents they should award custody or to which of two parents they should deny custody. The parents' characteristics are listed in Table 19.1. The majority of the group of mock jurors asked to award sole custody selected parent B. However, the majority of the group of mock jurors asked to deny custody also selected parent B. It seems incoherent for the same parent to be both awarded and denied custody. Shafir points out that when one is choosing, the positive features of an option loom larger. When one is rejecting, the negative features of an option loom larger. Parent B is an enriched option, in that this person has both positive and negative features. Parent B's

Table 19.1   Characteristics of parents in a mock custody case.

Parent A	Parent B
Average income	Above-average income
Average health	Minor health problems
Average working hours	Lots of work-related travel
Reasonable rapport with the child	Very close relationship with the child
Relatively stable social life	Extremely active social life

positive features will dominate parent A's neutral features, and parent B will be selected. However, parent B's negative features will look inferior to parent A's neutral features, and parent B will also be rejected. It is understandable that people required to select or reject an option will look for reasons to do so. The problem is that each of these tasks brings to light a different set of reasons.

A problem with gut reactions is that they are subject to a number of such context effects. Question wording, the compatibility between features of the options and the features of the decision to be made, the order of the presentation, and many other factors are all possible influences on a decision maker's performance. Also, gut reactions tend to have low consistency, whereas decision aids tend to be boringly reliable.

The second example pertains to subjectivity in judgments of justice. Van den Bos (2003) asked people to assess the justice in various situations, such as the allocation of rewards among participants and the availability of opportunities for participants to voice their opinion concerning how the rewards should be divided. When there was uncertain information about the rules which would govern these matters, participants who were in a good mood rated the procedural justice to be higher than did participants who were in a bad mood. In Experiment 3, Van den Bos (2003) found that both the good and bad mood participants differed from the control group in their assessments of justice, with the bad group diverging more.

Most observers would agree that the degree of procedural justice in a situation should not depend on the mood of a person who considers that situation. People have moods; decision aids do not. If it is possible to make a decision on parole, dangerousness, or any other judicial matter using a decision aid rather than unaided judgment, it is probably wise to use the aid.

The third example is from a high-stakes medical situation in which health-care professionals must ascertain the correct dosage of an anticoagulant to use with patients in a critical-care unit (Brown and Dodeck 1997). Either too little or too much anticoagulant can have catastrophic consequences. Physicians comprised one group of decision makers. They used their gut reaction to decide upon the dosage levels of the coagulant. The second group was comprised of nurses who used an uncomplicated nomogram—a decision aid which took into account a small number of very straightforward pieces of information, such as the patient's weight, in calculating the recommended dosage of anticoagulant. Compared to the doctors who used their unaided judgment, the nurses who used the simple nomogram were able to achieve the appropriate anticoagulant dosage significantly more quickly and with significantly fewer adjustments. Of course, doctors and nurses are equally capable of weighing a patient and collecting a small number of other easily obtainable measures. What a decision aid can do better than a nurse or doctor is combine these pieces of information (Dawes et al. 1989).

If the dependent variable pertains to one's affective reaction to the selected option, decision aids may not result in the most satisfactory choice (Wilson and Schooler 1991). For example, the aid may inform you that the salad is the better choice, but you may not like it nearly as much as the chocolate parfait. If the dependent variable pertains to the selection of the perpetrator or to the accurate prediction of violence risk, the data compel the conclusion that decision aids are superior to gut reactions.

REFERENCES

Arkes, H.R., and C.A. Schipani. 1994. Medical malpractice and the business judgment rule: Differences in hindsight bias. *Oregon Law Rev.* **73**:587–638.

Blattberg, R.C., and S.J. Hoch. 1990. Database models and managerial intuition: 50% model + 50% manager. *Manag. Sci.* **36**:887–899.

Brown, G., and P. Dodeck. 1997. An evaluation of empiric vs. nomogram-based dosing of heparin in an intensive care unit. *Crit. Care Med.* **25**:1534–1538.

Carroll, J.S., R.L. Weiner, D. Coates, J. Galegher, and J.J. Alibrio. 1982. Evaluation, diagnosis, and prediction in parole decision making. *Law Soc. Rev.***17**:199–228.

Casper, J.D., K. Benedict, and J.R. Kelly. 1988. Cognitions, attitudes and decision-making in search and seizure cases. *J. Appl. Soc. Psychol.* **18**:93–113.

Damasio, A.R. 1994. Descartes' Error. New York: Avon (pp. 170–175).

Dawes, R.M., D. Faust, and P.E. Meehl. 1989. Clinical versus actuarial judgment. *Science* **243**:1668–1674.

Einhorn, H.J. 1972. Expert measurement and mechanical combination. *Org. Behav. Hum. Perf.* **7**:86–106.

Gardner, W., C.W. Lidz, E.P. Mulvey, and E.C. Shaw. 1996. A comparison of actuarial methods for identifying repetitively violent patients with mental illness. *Law Hum. Behav.* **20**:35–48.

Gigerenzer, G., P.M. Todd, and the ABC Research Group. 1999. Simple Heuristics That Make Us Smart. New York: Oxford Univ. Press (p. 86).

Green, L., and D.R. Mehr. 1997. What alters physicians' decisions to admit to the coronary care unit? *J. Fam. Pract.* **45**:219–226.

Grove, W.M., D.H. Zald, B.S. Lebow, B.E. Snitz, and C. Nelson. 2000. Clinical versus mechanical prediction: A meta-analysis. *Psychol. Assess.* **12**:19–30.

Hilton, N.Z., and J.L. Simmons. 2001. The influence of actuarial risk assessment in clinical judgments and tribunal decisions about mentally disordered offenders in maximum security. *Law Hum. Behav.* **25**:393–408.

Hogarth, R.M. 2001. Educating Intuition. Chicago: Univ. of Chicago Press.

Horowitz, I.A., and L. ForsterLee. 2001. The effects of note-taking and trial transcript access on mock jury decisions in a complex civil trial. *Law Hum. Behav.* **25**:373–392.

Klein, G. 1998. Sources of Power. Cambridge, MA: MIT Press.

Meehl, P.E. 1954. Clinical versus Statistical Prediction: A Theoretical Analysis and a Review of the Evidence. Minneapolis: Univ. of Minnesota Press.

Millar, M.G., and A. Tesser. 1986. Effects of affective and cognitive focus on the attitude-behavior relation. *J. Pers. Soc. Psychol.* **51**:270–276.

Shafir, E. 1993. Choosing versus rejecting: Why some options are both better and worse than others. *Mem. Cogn.* **21**:546–556.

Sommers, S.R., and S.M. Kassin. 2001. On the many impacts of inadmissible testimony: Selective compliance, need for cognition, and the overcorrection bias. *Pers. Soc. Psychol. Bull.* **27**:1368–1377.

Van den Bos, K. 2003. On the subjective quality of social justice: The role of affect as information in the psychology of justice judgments. *J. Pers. Soc. Psychol.* **85**:482–498.

Wells, G.L., R.S. Malpass, R.C.L. Lindsay et al. 2000. From the lab to the police station: A successful application of eyewitness research. *Am. Psychol.* **55**:581–598.

Wells, G.L., M. Small, S. Penrod et al. 1998. Eyewitness identification procedures: Recommendations for lineups and photospreads. *Law Hum. Behav.* **22**:603–647.

Werner, P.D., T.L. Rose, and J.A. Yesavage. 1983. Reliability, accuracy, and decision-making strategy in clinical predictions of imminent dangerousness. *J. Consult. Clin. Psychol.* **51**:815–825.

Wilson, T.D., D.J. Lisle, J. Schooler et al. 1993. Introspecting about reasons can reduce post-choice satisfaction. *Pers. Soc. Psychol. Bull.* **19**:331–339.

Wilson, T.D., and J. Schooler. 1991. Thinking too much: Introspection can reduce the quality of preferences and decisions. *J. Pers. Soc. Psychol.* **60**:181–192.

Yaniv, I., and R.M. Hogarth. 1993. Judgmental versus statistical prediction: Information asymmetry and combination rules. *Psychol. Sci.* **4**:58–62.

20

Law, Information, and Choice

Capitalizing on Heuristic
Habits of Thought

Chris Guthrie

Vanderbilt University Law School, Nashville, TN 37203–1181, U.S.A.

ABSTRACT

American law seeks to foster individual autonomy and choice by mandating the disclosure of information in a wide variety of settings. Whether mandatory disclosure requirements succeed in fostering choice depends on whether the intended recipients of the information are able to use that information to make wise decisions. Empirical evidence suggests that individuals often make sound decisions using limited information, so lawmakers should require limited disclosures (as heuristics-based decision theories would recommend) rather than full disclosure (as rational choice theory would recommend). By identifying the specific information to be disclosed, by requiring that the information be presented in a manner designed to attract attention and comprehension, and by imposing some limits on the amount of information disclosed, lawmakers can enhance autonomy and choice.

INTRODUCTION

"Anglo-American law starts with the premise of thoroughgoing self-determination, each man considered to be his own master" (*Scott v. Bradford* 1979). Subject to a few notable constraints, the "each man his own master" principle underlies much public and private law in America. From Congressional enactments to Administrative pronouncements to common-law cases, American law generally seeks to give expression to individual autonomy and choice.

Consistent with this foundational principle, lawmakers frequently require one party to disclose information to others to enable them to make informed choices. In some instances, lawmakers explicitly require such disclosures through enacted law; for example, "Regulation FD (Fair Disclosure)" imposes disclosure requirements on publicly traded firms. In other instances, lawmakers implicitly require the disclosure of information through the common law; for example, the doctrine of informed consent exposes medical professionals to potential malpractice liability if they fail to provide patients with sufficient information to enable them to make informed decisions about their medical care.

Whether explicit or implicit, information disclosure requirements are ubiquitous in the law. Consider, by way of illustration, the following examples:

- The Federal Rules of Civil Procedure require litigants to disclose information to one another during the pre-trial litigation process.
- Commercial law requires lenders, creditors, and others to disclose a plethora of information to consumers who seek to borrow, establish credit, enter into leases, and so forth.
- The securities laws require firms to disclose information in annual reports, proxy statements, and other filings to enable potential investors to make informed investment decisions.
- Products liability law requires those introducing potentially dangerous products into the stream of commerce to provide warnings.
- State laws require those selling residential real estate to provide disclosures about the condition of the property.
- Gaming laws require sweepstakes operators to disclose the rules of their contests, the odds of winning, and other material terms.

These and other mandatory disclosure laws enhance individual choice only if the recipients of the information are able to use it to make better decisions. But are they? Does the law facilitate better decision making by mandating the disclosure of information to consumers, patients, potential litigants, and so forth? In other words, does the law capitalize on the way individuals are likely to process information and make decisions? If so, how does it do so? If not, how could it?

Rational choice theory and heuristics-based decision theories offer different responses to these questions. Rational choice theory assumes that individuals will fully process all of the disclosed information, identify each available course of action, carefully calculate the costs and benefits of each course of action, and then select the one that maximizes their expected utility (Korobkin and Ulen 2000). For rational choice theorists, disclosure requirements remove informational deficits that might otherwise prevent the affected individuals from making rational decisions.

Heuristics-based decision theories reject the assumptions of rational choice theory. Proponents of both the "fast and frugal heuristics" program (Gigerenzer and Selten 2001; Gigerenzer et al. 1999) and the "heuristics-and-biases" program (Gilovich et al. 2002; Kahneman et al. 1982) contend that individuals use mental shortcuts or "heuristics" to make decisions on the basis of limited information. According to the fast and frugal theorists, individuals using such heuristics will often obtain outcomes comparable to those they would have obtained if they had followed the rules and procedures of rational choice theory

(Gigerenzer and Selten 2001; Gigerenzer et al. 1999). The heuristics-and-biases theorists agree that individuals will often obtain satisfactory outcomes using heuristics, but they worry that heuristics can also be maladaptive, leading to poor decisions in some circumstances (Gilovich et al. 2002; Kahneman et al. 1982). Despite this modest difference in emphasis, both heuristics-based approaches agree that individuals will generally use less information, rather than more, to make good decisions.

For lawmakers seeking to craft effective disclosure rules, these decision theories suggest different approaches. Rational choice theory suggests that lawmakers should mandate full disclosure to enable the affected individuals to make fully rational decisions. By contrast, the heuristics-based theories suggest that lawmakers should require limited information disclosure because individuals are unlikely to possess the "demonic" decision-making abilities required by rational choice theory (Gigerenzer and Todd 1999).

This chapter examines both the rational choice and heuristics-based approaches to disclosure laws. Because empirical evidence provides greater support for the latter than for the former, the chapter argues that lawmakers should heed the central lesson of the heuristics-based theories that individuals will generally make decisions on the basis of limited amounts of information. Given this, lawmakers are more likely to enhance individual autonomy and choice not by mandating full disclosure but rather by mandating limited disclosures designed to induce individuals to use heuristics adaptively.

RATIONAL CHOICE APPROACH

Rational choice theory assumes that individuals possess unlimited time, attention, and computational abilities. Armed with these capacities, individuals make decisions using a "compensatory" strategy like the "weighted adding" or "multi-attribute utility" strategy. Employing such a strategy, individuals identify and evaluate all available options, assess and weight all of the salient attributes of each option, and then select the option they evaluate most favorably. John Payne and James Bettman (2001, p. 126) provide a particularly lucid account in a chapter prepared for an earlier Dahlem Workshop:

> [The rational choice] process consists of considering one alternative at a time, examining each of the attributes for that option, determining the subjective value of the attribute values, multiplying each attribute's subjective value times its importance weight, and summing these products across all of the attributes to obtain an overall value for each option. Then the alternative with the highest value would be chosen, i.e., the decision maker maximizes over the calculated values.

This approach to decision making is generally deemed "rational" because it involves "the use of all relevant information" and the "making [of] explicit trade-offs" (Payne et al. 1993).

To illustrate the application of rational choice theory in a setting involving mandatory disclosures, consider the law governing informed consent. This body of law requires physicians to disclose sufficient information to enable patients to make informed decisions about their medical care. Failure to do so may result in the imposition of civil liability on the physician (Dobbs 2000).

Suppose, then, that a physician tells a patient with a potentially fatal form of cancer that she has three treatment options: (1) surgery; (2) chemotherapy; and (3) radiation. Suppose further that she describes each option along three dimensions: (1) long-term survival rate (the "survival-rate" dimension); (2) mortality rate during treatment (the "mortality-during-treatment" dimension); and (3) level of discomfort associated with the treatment (the "discomfort" dimension).

Following a compensatory decision strategy, our hypothetical patient will first decide how important each dimension is to her. Suppose she decides that the most important dimension to her is the mortality rate during the procedure, followed closely by the long-term survival rate, with level of discomfort a distant third. Based on this assessment, she decides that 50% of her decision should be based on the mortality-during-treatment dimension, 40% on the survival-rate dimension, and 10% on the discomfort dimension.

Having identified and weighted the salient dimensions of each option, she then assigns a subjective value to each option on each attribute. Suppose she does so on a 10-point scale, where "1" is the lowest possible score and "10" is the highest. Because the mortality rate is highest during surgery, lower during chemotherapy, and lower still during radiation, she assigns surgery a score of 6, chemotherapy a score of 7, and radiation a score of 9. Mortality rates during each of these treatments are roughly inversely correlated with the long-term survival rates, so on this dimension of her decision, she assigns a score of 10 to surgery, 8 to chemotherapy, and 2 to radiation. Finally, recovery from surgery will be painful, so she rates it a 3 on the discomfort dimension. The discomfort is likely to be great during chemotherapy, but the regimen will last only a couple of months, so she assigns it a score of 4 on the discomfort dimension. Radiation will make her tired but will not cause much pain, so she rates it an 8 on this dimension. Table 20.1 shows her subjective valuations of each option.

To calculate a weighted added value for each dimension of each treatment option, she then multiplies the importance weighting she assigned to each dimension (50% mortality during treatment, 40% survival rate, and 10%

Table 20.1   Subjective valuation.

	Surgery	**Chemotherapy**	**Radiation**
Treatment mortality	6	7	9
Long-term survival	10	8	2
Discomfort	3	4	8

discomfort) by the rating she gave to each option on each dimension. As noted in Table 20.2, surgery obtains the highest overall score (7.3 versus 7.1 and 6.1 for each of the other options). Assuming she follows this compensatory strategy to its logical end, she will elect surgery. Based on a careful assessment of each option, each salient dimension of each option, the relative importance of each dimension, and a subjective valuation of each option on each dimension, surgery is the optimal choice for her. When making simple decisions, individuals like our hypothetical patient might follow a compensatory strategy (Payne et al. 1993). When confronted with complicated decisions that require the processing of more information, individuals tend to make "non-compensatory" decisions in which they rely on limited information and do not fully weight and evaluate all options (Payne et al. 1993).

In one study, for example, Naresh Malhotra recruited 300 people to participate in a hypothetical home-purchase study. He randomly assigned participants to one of 25 groups, which varied based on the number of homes available for purchase (5, 10, 15, 20, or 25) and the number of attributes on which information was provided (5, 10, 15, 20, or 25). Malhotra asked each participant to rank-order the houses under consideration. He compared the participants' rank-ordering to their preferred alternative based on responses to a series of questions designed to assess their ideal house. He found that participants made much less accurate decisions as the number of options under consideration reached 10 or 15. Holding the number of attributes constant, 70% of the participants selected the preferred house when only five houses were under consideration. But when 10 houses were under consideration, only 48.3% of the participants selected the house that most closely approximated their true preference. And when 25 houses were under consideration, only 36.7% of participants made the "correct" choice (Malhotra 1982).

Similarly, in a real-world empirical study, Judith Hibbard and her colleagues examined how several large companies selected health care plans for their employees and families. The researchers interviewed 33 professional purchasers employed by companies in four regions of the country. Half of the purchasers admitted it was difficult for them to consider all of the attributes they should consider in selecting the plans; some admitted that they avoided making any

Table 20.2   Weighted added values.

	Surgery	**Chemotherapy**	**Radiation**
Treatment mortality (50%)	6 (3.0)	7 (3.5)	9 (4.5)
Long-term survival (40%)	10 (4.0)	8 (3.2)	2 (0.8)
Discomfort (10%)	3 (0.3)	4 (0.4)	8 (0.8)
Total	7.3	7.1	6.1

trade-offs between the available options; and 12% admitted "that they made their choices on the basis of a single dimension such as cost or geographic access." Only 20% of the purchasers appeared to use a compensatory strategy (Hibbard et al. 1997).

Suppose, then, that our hypothetical patient is overwhelmed by her treatment decision and feels incapable of evaluating all of her options along all of the relevant dimensions. If this were to happen, she might employ a non-compensatory strategy like the "lexicographic" strategy or the "elimination-by-aspects" strategy to decide on a treatment. Suppose first that she adopts a lexicographic strategy, which calls for her to select the option with the highest value on the dimension that is most important to her (Payne et al. 1993). In this instance, she would select radiation because it has the highest score (9) on the mortality-during-treatment dimension.

Now imagine that she uses an elimination-by-aspects strategy (Tversky 1972). This strategy eliminates options that fall short of a minimum cutoff value on an attribute. This elimination process is then repeated, with processing continuing until a single option remains. Assume our patient determines that her minimum acceptable score on all dimensions is 7 and that she begins her choice process with the mortality-during-treatment dimension. Comparing the three options, she would eliminate surgery because it falls below her minimum cutoff score of 7. Assuming she then considers the survival-rate dimension, she would compare the remaining two options and eliminate radiation because it falls below her minimum cutoff score of 7. By following this elimination strategy, then, she would elect to undergo chemotherapy.

For rational choice theorists, the problem with non-compensatory decision making is that "alternatives may be eliminated (or chosen) based on the value of one attribute without considering the values of other potentially compensating attributes" (Kahn and Baron 1995). This means that individuals employing non-compensatory decision strategies, like our hypothetical patient, may fail to select their preferred option, at least as measured by the logical and mathematical rules of rational choice.

HEURISTICS-BASED APPROACHES

The heuristics-based decision approaches—both the fast and frugal heuristics program and the heuristics-and-biases program—offer a different view of human decision making. Relying largely on empirical evidence, they posit that individuals use mental shortcuts to make decisions on the basis of limited information.

Fast and Frugal Heuristics Program

Proponents of the fast and frugal heuristics program reject rational choice theory on both normative and positive grounds. From a *normative* perspective, they argue that decision strategies should be assessed on the basis of their success or failure in real-world environments, not according to the logical and mathematical rules that comprise rational choice theory:

> There are no optimal strategies in many real-world environments in the first place. This does not mean, though, that there are no performance criteria in the real world. As a measure of the success of a heuristic, we compare its performance with the actual requirements of its environment, which can include making accurate decisions, in a minimal amount of time, and using a minimal amount of information. We have thus replaced the multiple coherence criteria stemming from the laws of logic and probability with multiple correspondence criteria relating to real-world decision performance (Gigerenzer and Todd 1999, p. 22).

From a *positive* perspective, they reject rational choice theory on the grounds that it paints an unrealistic picture of how individuals actually process information and make decisions. They propose, instead, a "psychologically plausible" approach to decision making:

> The goal of the program is to understand how actual humans make decisions, as opposed to heavenly beings equipped with practically unlimited time, knowledge, memory, and other infinite resources. The challenge is to base models of bounded rationality on the cognitive, emotional, social, and behavioral repertoire that a species actually has (Gigerenzer 2001, p. 38).

In short, the fast and frugal theorists claim that individuals can, do, and should use simple heuristics because these heuristics will generally produce good outcomes in a fast and frugal manner.

The fast and frugal theorists have identified several specific heuristics that individuals use in real-world environments, including the "imitation" heuristic and several "one-reason" heuristics (Gigerenzer and Goldstein 1999; Goldstein et al. 2001; Henrich et al. 2001). To illustrate each, recall our hypothetical patient who is trying to decide whether to undergo surgery, chemotherapy, or radiation to battle her potentially fatal illness. How would she decide using these fast and frugal heuristics?

Using the imitation heuristic, she would simply mimic the decision made by relevant others. In some circumstances, she might do what most others confronted with the same decision have decided to do; here, for instance, she might make the same choice made by most other patients confronted with her form of cancer. In other circumstances, she might defer to those whom she deems to have greater status than her; here, for instance, she might simply do what highly visible public figures confronted with this form of cancer have done (Goldstein et al. 2001; Henrich et al. 2001). Closely related to the imitation heuristic, she might simply defer to what her physician recommends (Degner and Sloan 1992; Gawande 2002).

Using any of the one-reason heuristics, our hypothetical patient would select a treatment option based on one salient dimension. Employing the Take the Last heuristic, for instance, she would attempt to use the same cue that enabled her to make a decision before (Gigerenzer and Goldstein 2001). Suppose, for example, that this is a recurrence of cancer. Suppose further that when she faced this illness before, she used the mortality-during-treatment cue to select radiation over the other treatments. Here, she could use that same cue to select the same treatment option again this time.

Using the Take the First heuristic—a strategy most appropriate for "repeat-player" experts—she would select the first treatment option that comes to her mind (Goldstein et al. 2001). Because the first option that occurs to her might very well be the option she selected previously, the Take the First heuristic might yield the same result as the Take the Last heuristic, but the mental processes underlying these heuristics are distinct.

Finally, using the Take the Best heuristic, she would select the option that scores the best on the dimension she deems most valid (Gigerenzer and Goldstein 1999). Researchers report evidence suggesting that those using the Take the Best heuristic perform as well as those using compensatory models in some circumstances, even though the Take the Best heuristic requires substantially less information processing (Czerlinski et al. 1999).

Heuristics-and-Biases Program

Like the fast and frugal heuristics program, the heuristics-and-biases program rejects rational choice as a *positive* model of choice, arguing, instead, that individuals often use heuristics to make decisions. Unlike the fast and frugal program, however, the heuristics-and-biases program embraces rational choice as a *normative* model of decision making. Because heuristics-and-biases theorists believe individuals *should* decide according to rational choice but observe that they often *do not*, they hold a more pessimistic view of heuristics than the fast and frugal theorists. This pessimism should not be overstated, though. The heuristics-and-biases theorists believe that heuristics generally enable individuals to make sound decisions in an expeditious manner.

Like the fast and frugal theorists, the heuristics-and-biases theorists have identified a number of specific heuristics that individuals use to make decisions. In their seminal article in *Science*, Tversky and Kahneman (1974), the founding fathers of the heuristics-and-biases program, identified three general-purpose heuristics: availability, representativeness, and anchoring. More recently, Kahneman and Frederick (2002) have argued that the three general-purpose heuristics are actually availability, representativeness, and the affect heuristic. Most researchers in this tradition use the term "heuristics and biases" more loosely to include several mental shortcuts that decision makers are likely to take.

To illustrate the use of some of the heuristics this research program has identified, recall again our hypothetical patient deciding whether to undergo surgery, chemotherapy, or radiation. Also, recall that she wants to base her decision largely on mortality rates during treatment and her long-term survival prospects. In assessing these probabilistic outcomes and making treatment decisions, she is likely to be influenced by "availability," the closely related "salience" or "vividness" heuristic, and so-called "framing effects."

Rational choice theory assumes our hypothetical patient will carefully weigh the probabilistic information provided by her physician. In some cases, of course, she will do this; often, however, she will assess her chances of living or dying based largely on some highly available instance from her own life (Tversky and Kahneman 1974). If, for example, a friend of hers recently died during chemotherapy treatments, she might overestimate the likelihood that she, too, would die during that treatment, and thus, avoid chemotherapy.

Availability might be exacerbated by the salience or vividness heuristic, which indicates that individuals are "much more influenced by vivid, concrete information than by pallid and abstract propositions of substantially greater probative and evidential value" (Nisbett and Ross 1980, p. 44). To the extent our hypothetical patient has vivid images in her mind of her friend dying during treatment, these images may weigh disproportionately on her judgment.

Finally, as she evaluates the information her physician provides, she may be influenced by the way that information is framed (Kahneman 1992). In one famous study, Barbara McNeil and her colleagues found that patients, graduate students, and even physicians making treatment decisions were affected by whether outcome data were presented in terms of mortality (likelihood of dying) or survival (likelihood of living) (McNeil et al. 1982).

Note that if our hypothetical patient were to use any of the heuristics from the fast and frugal heuristics program or the heuristics-and-biases program, she would base her treatment decision on a fraction of the information that a rational choice theorist would recommend. Indeed, in the case of the imitation heuristic, she would not even need to know about survival rates, mortality rates during treatment, and so on. All she would need to know is what relevant others have decided in the same situation. Similarly, if she were to rely heavily on the availability and salience heuristics, she would base her decision largely on a prior occurrence rather than on the detailed information provided by her physician.

USING DISCLOSURE LAWS TO ENHANCE AUTONOMY AND CHOICE

Heuristics-based theories demonstrate that individuals often make decisions using limited information. To foster autonomy and choice, lawmakers should heed the lessons of these theories. Rather than requiring full disclosure (as rational choice theory would recommend), lawmakers should require limited disclosures (as the heuristics-based theories would recommend). Namely, lawmakers should identify the specific pieces of information to be disclosed; require that this information be presented in a manner designed to attract attention and inform understanding; and impose limits on the total amount of information provided. By regulating the content, presentation, and amount of information disclosed, lawmakers are more likely to craft mandatory disclosure laws that facilitate good decisions.

Content

Individuals are likely to make decisions based on limited information, even where extensive information is provided. This suggests that lawmakers should require regulated entities to disclose the specific information that individuals are most likely to need to make sound decisions.

Consider, for example, Regulation Z or the "Truth in Lending" regulations governing closed-end credit. Section 226.18 of these regulations identifies on an item-by-item basis each piece of information to be disclosed, including the identity of the creditor, the amount financed, the annual percentage rate, the variable rate (if applicable), the payment schedule, the total of all payments, and so forth. These regulations also require disclosures to be "grouped together" and prohibit "any information not directly related to the [required] disclosures" from being identified in the same place. In short, these regulations increase the likelihood that the intended recipients will use relevant information when making borrowing decisions.

Presentation

Lawmakers should also be attentive to the manner in which information is presented. Because individuals will often base their decisions on limited information, lawmakers should require the pieces of information generally deemed most important to be presented in such a way as to make them salient and comprehensible to the recipients of the information. Among other things, lawmakers might segregate the most important information; present statistical information in a frequency format; and provide visual representations, if applicable (Gigerenzer and Edwards 2003).

Consider, again, the Truth in Lending regulations, which require disclosures to be segregated from other information and require two key terms (i.e., "finance charge" and "annual percentage rate") to be made more conspicuous than others:

> The creditor shall make the disclosures required by this subpart clearly and conspicuously in writing, in a form that the consumer may keep. The disclosures shall be grouped together, shall be segregated from everything else, and shall not contain any information not directly related to the disclosures required under Section 226.18.
> The terms "finance charge" and "annual percentage rate," when required to be disclosed under Section 226.18(d) and (e) together with a corresponding amount

or percentage rate, shall be more conspicuous than any other disclosure, except the creditor's identity under Section 226.18(a).

Additionally, the Truth in Lending regulations require lenders to provide concrete illustrations in some circumstances and include with the regulations a model disclosure form. In so doing, these regulations increase the likelihood that individuals will actually attend to, and base decisions on, the appropriate information.

Amount

Lawmakers should regulate not only the information to be disclosed but also the information *not* to be disclosed. In other words, lawmakers should impose reasonable limits on the amount of information that regulated entities can disclose to members of the public.

Limiting the amount of information disclosed can facilitate individual choice in two ways. First, research suggests that individuals are less likely to make decisions when those decisions involve multiple options and substantial information (Iyengar and Lepper 2000; Schwartz 2004). Thus, lawmakers who limit the amount of information disclosed increase the likelihood that individuals will actually make decisions by decreasing the likelihood that they will be overwhelmed by the choices confronting them. Second, individuals are likely to focus on limited information when making choices. If the information set they consult excludes less important information, they are more likely to focus on the most important information when making their decisions.

CONCLUSION

Fostering individual autonomy and choice is a central goal of the American legal system. Choice requires information, so mandatory disclosure laws are ubiquitous in the U.S. Too often, though, lawmakers require disclosure without carefully considering how to do so in a way that actually facilitates informed choice. Rational choice theory *assumes* that the law should mandate full disclosure, yet what we know about individual decision making suggests that this approach may be counterproductive. Heuristics-based decision theories *demonstrate* that individuals often make decisions on the basis of limited information. Accordingly, lawmakers are more likely to facilitate autonomy and choice not by mandating full disclosure but rather by requiring that the right information be disclosed in the right way.

This approach to mandatory disclosure laws will not address all of the challenges confronting lawmakers. Lawmakers will not always know what information to require regulated entities to disclose; regulated entities might still be able to present information in self-serving ways; and the same disclosures may target consumers with very different knowledge bases and cognitive capacities. None-theless, if implemented in a careful and impartial way, the "content, presenta-tion, and amount" approach advocated here promises to enhance autonomy and choice by capitalizing on the way real people are likely to think and decide.

REFERENCES

Czerlinski, J., G. Gigerenzer, and D. Goldstein. 1999. How good are simple heuristics? In: Simple Heuristics That Make Us Smart, G. Gigerenzer, P. Todd, and the ABC Group, pp. 97–118. Oxford: Oxford Univ. Press.

Degner, L.F., and J.A. Sloan. 1992. Decision making during serious illness: What role do patients really want to play? *J. Clin. Epidemiol.* **45**:941–950.

Dobbs, D.B. 2000. The Law of Torts. St. Paul, MN: West Group.

Gawande, A. 2002. Complications: A Surgeon's Notes on an Imperfect Science. New York: Holt.

Gigerenzer, G. 2001. The adaptive toolbox. In: Bounded Rationality: The Adaptive Tool-box, ed. G. Gigerenzer and R. Selten, pp. 37–50. Dahlem Workshop Report 84. Cam-bridge, MA: MIT Press.

Gigerenzer, G., and A. Edwards. 2003. Simple tools for understanding risks: From innumeracy to insight. *Brit. Med. J.* **327**:741–744.

Gigerenzer, G., and D.G. Goldstein. 1999. Betting on one good reason: The take the best heuristic. In: Simple Heuristics That Make Us Smart, G. Gigerenzer, P. Todd, and the ABC Research Group, pp. 75–95. Oxford: Oxford Univ. Press.

Gigerenzer, G., and R. Selten. 2001. Bounded Rationality: The Adaptive Toolbox. Dahlem Workshop Report 84. Cambridge, MA: MIT Press.

Gigerenzer, G., and P.M. Todd. 1999. Fast and frugal heuristics: The adaptive toolbox. In: Simple Heuristics That Make Us Smart, G. Gigerenzer, P. Todd, and the ABC Re-search Group, pp. 3–34. Oxford: Oxford Univ. Press.

Gigerenzer, G., P. Todd, and the ABC Research Group. 1999. Simple Heuristics That Make Us Smart. Oxford: Oxford Univ. Press.

Gilovich, T., D. Griffin, and D. Kahneman. 2002. Heuristics and Biases: The Psychology of Intuitive Judgment. Cambridge: Cambridge Univ. Press.

Goldstein, D.G., G. Gigerenzer, R.M. Hogarth et al. 2001. Group report: Why and when do simple heuristics work? In: Bounded Rationality: The Adaptive Toolbox, ed. G. Gigerenzer and R. Selten, pp. 173–190. Dahlem Workshop Report 84. Cambridge, MA: MIT Press.

Henrich, J., W. Albers, R. Boyd et al. 2001. Group report: What is the role of culture in bounded rationality? In: Bounded Rationality: The Adaptive Toolbox, ed. G. Gigerenzer and R. Selten, pp. 343–359. Dahlem Workshop Report 84. Cambridge, MA: MIT Press.

Hibbard, J.H., J.J. Jewett, M.W. Legnini, and M. Tusler. 1997. Choosing a health plan: Do large employers use the data? *Hlth. Aff.* **6**:172–180.

Iyengar, S.S., and M.R. Lepper. 2000. When choice is demotivating: Can one desire too much of a good thing? *J. Pers. Soc. Psychol.* **79**:995–1006.

Kahn, B.E., and J. Baron. 1995. An exploratory study of choice rules favored for high-stakes decisions. *J. Cons. Psychol.* **4**:305–328.

Kahneman, D. 1992. Reference points, anchors, norms, and mixed feelings. *Org. Behav. Hum. Dec. Proc.* **51**:296–312.

Kahneman, D., and S. Frederick. 2002. Representativeness revisited: Attribute substitution in intuitive judgment. In: Heuristics and Biases: The Psychology of Intuitive Judgment, ed. T. Gilovich, D. Griffin, and D. Kahneman, pp. 49–81. Cambridge: Cambridge Univ. Press.

Kahneman, D., P. Slovic, and A. Tversky. 1982. Judgment under Uncertainty: Heuristics and Biases. Cambridge: Cambridge Univ. Press.

Korobkin, R.B., and T.S. Ulen. 2000. Law and behavioral science: Removing the rationality assumption from law and economics. *Calif. Law Rev.* **88**:1051–1144.

Malhotra, N.K. 1982. Information load and consumer decision making. *J. Cons. Res.* **8**:419–430.

McNeil, B.J., S.G. Pauker, H.C. Sox, Jr., and A. Tversky. 1982. On the elicitation of preferences for alternative therapies. *New Engl. J. Med.* **306**:1259–1262.

Nisbett, R., and L. Ross. 1980. Human Inference: Strategies and Shortcomings of Social Judgment. Englewood Cliffs, NJ: Prentice-Hall.

Payne, J.W., and J.R. Bettman. 2001. Preferential choice and adaptive strategy use. In: Bounded Rationality: The Adaptive Toolbox, ed. G. Gigerenzer and R. Selten, pp. 123–145. Dahlem Workshop Report 84. Cambridge, MA: MIT Press.

Payne, J.W., J.R. Bettman, and E.J. Johnson. 1993. The Adaptive Decision Maker. Cambridge: Cambridge Univ. Press.

Schwartz, B. 2004. The Paradox of Choice: Why More Is Less. New York: Harper Collins.

Scott v. Bradford, 606 P.2d 554 (Okla. 1979).

Tversky, A. 1972. Elimination by aspects: A theory of choice. *Psychol. Rev.* **79**:281–299.

Tversky, A., and D. Kahneman. 1974. Judgment under uncertainty: Heuristics and biases. *Science* **185**:1124–1131.

Left to right: Ralph Hertwig, Chris Guthrie, Hal Arkes, Christoph Engel, Elke Weber, Martin Beckenkamp, Stephanie Kurzenhäuser, Bob Ellickson, Robert Cooter, and Dan Goldstein

21

Group Report: How Do Heuristics Mediate the Impact of Law on Behavior?

Daniel G. Goldstein, Rapporteur

Hal R. Arkes, Martin Beckenkamp, Robert Cooter,
Robert C. Ellickson, Christoph Engel, Chris Guthrie,
Ralph Hertwig, Stephanie Kurzenhäuser, and Elke U. Weber

ABSTRACT

How do people make decisions about legally relevant actions? In this group report we look at the demand side of legal information, the supply side of legal information, and how the law reaches its addressees through a range of real-world examples familiar to ordinary citizens.

The first part of the report is concerned with the issue of how people decide to act under laws. Since optimization is impossible in ordinary minds, we speculate about what other processes may be at play in determining behavior. In the second part, we look at how people learn about laws that may govern behavior. Since modern law is too massive for any individual to comprehend fully, we aim to understand how people figure out what the laws are, and when to undertake research into the law. The third part outlines, by way of examples, ways by which actual laws make their way to their addressees. We conclude by exploring policy considerations that present themselves when viewing law's impact on behavior as mediated by heuristics.

INTRODUCTION

How do people make decisions about legally relevant actions? Rational choice theory has been the dominant source of assumptions about the actions of people impacted by laws (Posner 2003; Cooter and Ulen 2004), from ordinary citizens who face a broad range of private and criminal laws, to judicial agents (such as judges, prosecutors, attorneys, or jury members) who need to follow a range of substantive and procedural laws. In the rational choice framework, legal rules are modeled as restrictions. Actors are assumed to maximize preferences they would hold in an institution-free state of nature, given the restrictions of the law. The last half-century has seen the arrival of alternative models of human information processing, which make assumptions about human judgment and decision processes that take into consideration the psychological processes underlying human cognition. In the 1950s, Herbert Simon's notion of bounded rationality suggested replacing the view of the mind as having unlimited resources with one that respects real-world constraints of limited time, knowledge, and computational might (Simon 1957). In the 1970s, Tversky and Kahneman's "heuristics-and-biases" research program strove to uncover the heuristics with which people make decisions (for a summary account, see Kahneman and Tversky 2000). In the 1980s and 1990s, Payne, Bettman, and Johnson's Adaptive Decision Maker program (1993, 1997) and Gigerenzer and colleagues' Adaptive Behavior and Cognition initiative (1999) formalized cognitive heuristics, allowing them to be simulated on computers, analyzed mathematically, and detected in process data. As a result, psychologists are now equipped to understand how cognitive heuristics will perform in various environments.

Heuristic information processing characteristically uses less information to arrive at decisions, and capitalizes on past experience and expertise within the decision domain to select wisely from among available options—the resulting decisions can be as good as or better than those obtained by more comprehensive cost-benefit calculations. This relative advantage of heuristics (equal quality at reduced effort) is achieved by their situational (content and context) specificity; that is, the success of a specific heuristic is highly contingent on multiple aspects of the decision environment, and a useful theory of heuristic processing thus needs to specify the environmental conditions or cues that should trigger specific heuristics (Payne et al. 1992; Gigerenzer et al. 1999).

In this chapter, we consider the implications of making assumptions about heuristic judgment and decision rules of people in legal contexts. We limit ourselves largely to an examination of the behavior of ordinary citizens rather than of agents of the law, since the latter topic is covered elsewhere in this volume. We further confine our analysis to what we will call "legally relevant decisions" or decisions that have the *potential* to give rise to legal rights or duties.

Many decisions are legally irrelevant. When an individual decides to get up at 7:00 rather than 8:00, or to drink coffee rather than tea, such choices are highly unlikely to have any legal implications. (In unusual circumstances, even these mundane decisions can involve legal rights. For example, if an individual is burned while drinking unreasonably hot coffee from McDonald's, she might have a quite viable tort claim against the company.)

However, a surprising number of decisions do have potential legal implications. Deciding what agreements to enter into, what precautions to take while driving, what taxes to pay, what financial arrangements to make for one's heirs, how to communicate with one's landlord, how to sort one's recyclable garbage, and so on are all examples of legally relevant decisions. In fact, some decisions may give rise to multiple legal implications. To take just one example, an individual who decides to drive above the posted speed limit faces both potential *criminal* liability (for violating the state's traffic laws) and a higher likelihood of *civil* liability (by engaging in unreasonable driving behavior, she is both more likely to cause harm to another and more likely to be held responsible for that harm).

For law to influence behavior, individuals must have some knowledge of what the law is. This invites consideration of the nature of markets for legal information. The demand side of this market consists of the individuals and associations who seek legal information. We begin with a look into the nature of this demand. How are ordinary citizens likely to act when their behavior may be subject to the law? We next explore how ordinary citizens are likely to learn about the law in those rare instances where they feel they must do so in order to know how to act. Thereafter we consider the supply side of legal information, focusing on how the state may seek to communicate law to its intended audiences. The state may seek to publicize its own rules or may delegate this task to a corporation (as in a German recycling example that we explore at some length). Important intermediaries in the supply of legal information might also include the news media, trade associations, lawyers, producers of legal software (e.g., tax preparation software), and so on. Finally, we explore two sets of policy implications: (a) how psychology can simplify the way the law is represented and (b) how psychology can induce greater compliance with the law. We conclude with some caveats.

THE DEMAND SIDE OF LEGAL INFORMATION

How Do We Decide to Act under Laws?

An individual considering taking an action may employ heuristics to locate a normative rule or rules that might govern the permissibility of that action. The task has a cognitive and a normative side. The individual must learn about the contents of the rule, and she must be willing to comply with what she has learned. Suppose, for example, that a professor is considering whether or not to make photocopies of a journal article for a class of twenty university students. In the United States, if the article is protected by copyright (as most journal articles are), in the ordinary case the applicable legal rules ordinarily require that the author obtain permission in advance from the owner of the copyright.[1] If the professor's decision objective were to call for both consulting the law and complying with the law under these circumstances, there would be little unconsented photocopying of this sort. In fact, however, such unconsented photocopying is rampant. This suggests that ordinary citizens often make legally relevant decisions without consulting the law. What, then, do they do?

---

[1]   §53 III *Urhebergesetz* [German copyright law] under certain conditions entitles teachers to make copies and to hand them out to their pupils.

Undoubtedly, citizens will behave differently depending upon the context and circumstance. Ellickson (1991) has developed a useful framework for thinking about the sources of authority individuals might consult. According to Ellickson, citizens consult five sources of authority, some of which are first-party, some second-party, and some third-party.

First, there are the first-party *personal ethics* that a person may impose on himself. Professors might decide not to photocopy because they regard unconsented photocopying as immoral and would feel guilty if they violated their own moral standards. As Cooter (1997) has forcefully argued, much of behavioral control occurs in this manner—through the enforcement upon oneself of norms internalized during childhood (see also Posner 2000).

Second, actors sometimes enter into *contracts* that govern their behavior in particular situations. These contracts provide second-party rules of conduct. More generally, such rules can result from any form of reciprocal exchange, be it legal or not (the large literature on reciprocity includes Fehr et al. 1997; Schlicht 1998). A person who breaches a reciprocal relation commonly fears that the promisee will exercise self-help to remedy that breach. Thus, in the unusual situation where the hypothetical professor had previously entered into a governing contract with the copyright owner, the professor's heuristics might direct the professor to consult that contract to find the rules governing photocopying privileges.

The remaining three sorts of rules all are third-party rules. That adjective is descriptive because these rules are created by persons other than the immediate parties to the controversy—in this instance, by persons other than the professor and the copyright owner. The *social norms*, which diffuse social forces create, are in many situations a powerful instrument of social control. A professor who had openly violated academic norms restricting photocopying of copyrighted work could expect to feel the sting of negative gossip and even ostracism by peers. In the U.S., academic norms permit the unconsented photocopying of a copyrighted journal article for a small number of students. Although the law does not, professors regard this as a permissible "fair use," in part because it greatly facilitates the free exchange of ideas. Academic norms in the U.S. do not, however, permit a professor to photocopy, for example, more than half of a book that the professor readily could have arranged for his students to buy in advance at the university bookstore.

Organizations other than governments also can create rules. The professor's university, for example, might have its own *organizational rules* governing photocopying of copyrighted work on its machines. This is another type of third-party rule.

Finally, the state through its legal system may create normative rules, that is, *laws*. While a state may aspire to make its laws paramount, in many contexts, citizens, when they turn to rules to help guide their own behavior, will look to rules other than law. When they consider photocopying, most professors apparently consider law an inferior source of rules.

What situational cues prompt an actor to look to one or another of these various sources of normative rules? An actor is highly unlikely to look to the legal system when both the stakes of a controversy are low (cf. Kirchgässner 1992) and the actor is in a continuing relationship with the party on the other side of the impending dispute. For example, in a jurisdiction without rent control, most disputes that arise between a landlord and tenant enmeshed in an ongoing relationship involve only small stakes. Landlords and tenants are likely to resolve informally hassles that arise between them, without invocation of formal legal entitlements. However, in a rent-control jurisdiction (such as Germany or New York City) stakes are higher because the tenant's loss of the apartment would be a more grievous event. In addition, when rent control is in effect, the law greatly limits landlords' power to end the tenancy and tenants in general do not want to leave. With the self-help tool of exit thus denied to both sides, landlords and tenants are less able to operate by personal contract and norms, and the law becomes more important.

By extension, a person's heuristics are most likely to direct him to apply law when stakes are great and the dispute is with someone who is socially distant. Thus, individuals immediately think of law when they are involved in serious traffic accidents, or confront the state itself over an issue such as taxation or immigration.

A Decision-tree Approach for Modeling How to Act under Laws

Consider the three classes of rules presented: (a) first-party rules (deontic rules: must, ought, etc.) stemming from the actor's ethics; (b) second-party rules of conduct dictated by contracts into which the actor has entered; and (c) third-party rules imposed on the actor by society (in terms of noninternalized social norms), nongovernmental organizations, and the legal system.

In a speculative venture, we now attempt to translate these classes of rules into a decision tree that aims to model how people decide what to do in potentially legally relevant situations. This is an admittedly immodest endeavor in that it requires making assumptions about human decision making that are extremely unlikely to be correct in detail. Yet simplistic, false models sometimes allow us to make progress toward explaining phenomena that might otherwise remain inexplicable (Albert 1978). With these qualifications in mind, let us begin the exercise with a bold speculation.

Routinized Action

Many textbooks and articles on human decision making assert that people constantly make decisions. This common wisdom is almost certainly wrong. In the vast majority of all human activities, we do not make an endless series of decisions but rather circumvent decision making altogether by resorting to routinized actions ("habits") and to rules such as "do what I have done before." In addition, the environment (e.g., other actors or constraints in the external world) makes decisions for them. Indeed, second-party rules of conduct may be seen as an instance of delegating decisions to the environment. According to this view, the problem of how to make a decision in situations in which one's behavior has potential legal ramifications is limited to a small subset of human activities. Members of this subset include the decision whether to photocopy copyrighted work for a class and the decision whether to download music from the Internet, both of which are new to the realm of human affairs. Inspired by our taxonomy of rules, our first, tentative decision tree assumes that people proceed through a maximum of four sequential steps (see Figure 21.1).

By way of concrete illustration, suppose an individual is deciding whether to download music from the Internet. If this situation has been encountered many times before, a person is likely to simply what has been done before. If this is new, however, she will initially turn to her first-party rules. A first-party rule that may come to mind in this context is the rule, "Do not steal somebody else's property." Whether this rule can provide guidance depends on whether the rule

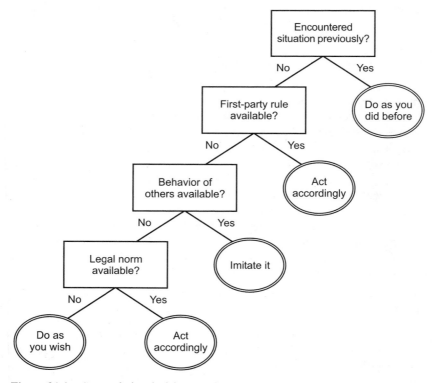

Figure 21.1   A speculative decision tree for how to act under laws.

is applicable in the current context. In other words, the first-party rule comes with auxiliary "matching rules," on the basis of which it can be inferred whether the current context is in the rule's proper domain. Such matching rules consist, for instance, of a set of subjective criteria that characterize the notion of "property." If the current context and cues it emits do not *match* these criteria (e.g., cues such as "Is it a tangible good?" "Is it in the possession of somebody?" and "Is it publicly accessible?"), it will be inferred that the simple rule is not applicable.

If the potential music downloader's first-party rule does not dictate a course of action, she moves on to the next step in the decision tree, which represents the notion that decisions can be delegated to one's social environment, that is, to other actors. At this stage, the person observes or finds out how other people behave when facing the same situation. Such social referents can include exemplary individuals (e.g., those who have dealt with the situation successfully or enjoy high prestige for other reasons), the person's social network or, more generally, "the crowd." Returning to the previous taxonomy of rules, one may even speculate that third-party rules that take the form of social norms are proxies for the crowd's behavior because they enable a person to predict it reliably and accurately without observing it. If information about others' behavior, whether inferred from social norms or observed firsthand, is available, the person reaches a decision at this stage: specifically, she copies the behavior of others. For instance, if they download music from the Web, she will too.

Only if consulting her social environment does not render a decision possible—because, for instance, the crowd is split or there are no other actors—she will move on to the fourth step in the decision tree. At this point, she will bother to find out which legal rule (legal rules being a subset of third-party rules), applies in the current context and will conform to it. If no legal rule is found, then she will do as she wishes.

This decision tree, which has the structure of a fast and frugal tree (Gigerenzer, this volume), suggests that the legal system is a last-resort decision module that is consulted only if all other modules (e.g., habits, internal norms, others' behavior) fail to render a decision. It also implies that in many contexts we may not know what the relevant legal rule is because there is no need to discover it (unless one reaches the final stage). Finally, it assumes that there is no integration across decision steps: As soon as a given step enables the person to decide, she will make the decision on that basis, ignoring considerations that would have mattered had she progressed through the later steps.

A Decision-tree Approach in the Domain of Tort Law

Here we attempt to apply this decision tree to two legally relevant decisions individuals are often called upon to make: deciding whether to take some precaution that might prevent harm against others and deciding what speed at which to drive.

The law of torts governs civil wrongs other than contracts (Keeton et al. 1984). Most tort cases involve accidents in which one party inadvertently injures another, like automobile accidents, slips-and-falls, and malpractice. For purposes of illustration, suppose that an individual is contemplating whether to take a precaution to avoid tort liability. Suppose, specifically, that an individual homeowner lives in a single-family home with a sidewalk that extends across the front of his land. Suppose further that individuals from within and outside the neighborhood occasionally walk on this sidewalk. Finally, suppose one morning that the homeowner discovers that it snowed several inches the previous night, and he must decide whether to shovel the snow off the sidewalk to decrease the likelihood that a passerby might be injured (and thereby subject him to liability under tort law). How will the homeowner decide?

A Rational Choice Approach

"Negligence" is the body of law that purportedly regulates this conduct. To determine whether a defendant is liable for harms negligently caused another, the law usually applies the so-called "reasonable person" standard rather than a fixed rule like a posted speed limit. According to this standard, an individual is liable for harms caused to another if he failed to behave as a "reasonable person would have behaved under the same or similar circumstances" (Keeton et al. 1984).

Law and economics scholars (and a famous judge named Learned Hand) have interpreted the reasonable-person standard to embody the tenets of rational choice theory. From their perspective, a prospective defendant should (and will) make an economically rational decision about whether to take a precaution to protect against some harm he might cause. If the costs of prevention exceed the benefits of prevention (which are measured by multiplying the probability of the potential harm by the magnitude of that harm), the defendant should not take the precaution, and if the harm results, he should not be held liable. If, however, the costs of prevention are lower than the benefits, the defendant should take the precaution; if he does not, and if the harm occurs, he should be held liable (Posner 1972; *United States v. Carroll Towing Company*). Law and economics scholars generally argue that this is normatively appropriate (net social benefits will exceed net social costs, leading to efficient outcomes) and descriptively accurate (because the common law tends toward efficiency).

In this example of shoveling the walk, the homeowner following the dictates of rational choice theory will (and should) make an economically rational decision about what to do, carefully balancing the costs and benefits of shoveling (or not) the snow. But how is the homeowner to value the costs and benefits? How is the homeowner to assess the likelihood that harm will befall someone if he does not shovel the snow? What harm could he reasonably anticipate would come to a pedestrian injured in the fall? These questions—and the calculations they require—seem beyond the ken of most individuals. Instead of engaging in economically rational calculation, we believe ordinary citizens employ, implicitly, a heuristic-based approach to determine how to behave. Below, we use the heuristic-based decision tree developed above to describe how an ordinary citizen might decide whether to take precautions to prevent against harm to another, like the potential harm in this hypothetical case.

A Heuristic-based Decision-tree Approach

Note that the decision tree presented here considers cues that are differently ordered than the decision tree presented in the previous section. The law covers a tremendous range of human behaviors from jaywalking to homicide; any model that would cover all domains would be too general to be useful in prediction. Our analysis is necessarily tentative and might vary for different individuals in different places under different circumstances.

At the outset, we speculate that our individual homeowner will do what he has done before if he has been confronted with this decision in the past. In other words, we believe he will simply defer to habit or routinized action. If habit does not dictate how to behave, we believe he will proceed as follows, as depicted in Figure 21.2.

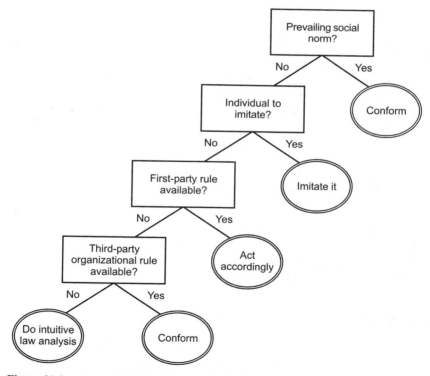

Figure 21.2   A speculative decision tree in the domain of tort law.

He will conform to the prevailing social norm and imitate the actions of other homeowners in his neighborhood. If there is no prevailing social norm—that is, if the norm is ambiguous—he will attempt to choose between norms by imitating the behavior of the homeowner located closest to him, the homeowner whom he most respects, and/or the homeowner with whom he has the closest relationship. If his attempt to choose between norms is unsuccessful, he will consult his own personal morality, that is, a first-party rule. If his moral code does not dictate a particular decision in a case like this, he will investigate and conform to applicable third-party organizational rules, like the rules governing the homeowners' association (although the apparent variety of behavior on the part of his neighbors may prevent him from complying with any rule requiring him to shovel snow). If the organizational rules do not dictate his behavior, he will conduct an informal and intuitive legal/economic analysis (i.e., he will conduct a rough cost-benefit analysis and unwittingly seek to comply with the governing law, but he will not research the law or seek the advice of a lawyer).

This analysis is incomplete, contestable, subject to individual differences, and undoubtedly affected by context. For example, how might our homeowner's decision be influenced by a spouse requesting that he shovel the sidewalk? Or how might his decision differ if those who normally walked on his sidewalk were young children or the elderly?

Despite these flaws, we believe the analysis supports three interesting propositions for the emerging "heuristics and law" dialogue. First, we believe that individuals are likely to use heuristics or decision rules when making legally relevant decisions (e.g., "conform to applicable norms"). Second, we expect that the law will be less important than many legal scholars assume, particularly for non-expert decision makers. Finally, we doubt that most decision makers will base their decisions on an elaborate, complete, and quantitative rational choice model—a topic we look at in closer detail next.

A Decision-tree Approach in the Domain of Traffic Law

Traffic laws govern the roadways, including the speed at which a citizen may drive. The law specifies speed limits for different roads (or different stretches of the same road), posts those speed limits, and authorizes police officers to enforce those laws, generally by giving them sanctioning power. How does a driver decide what speed to drive in light of these laws?

An Optimization Approach

All optimization requires the specification of an objective function to optimize. The objective function can be chosen to optimize one or several criteria. In the simplest case, suppose the driver has only one goal: minimize the cost of speeding tickets. To simplify the matter, consider the case of driving in good weather with good road conditions and posted speed limit signs. In the absence of police error, the only way to be sure to avoid being fined for speeding is to drive the speed limit or lower. Given the assumed goal function, this is an optimal strategy. Will optimization be so simple in more realistic scenarios?

Few drivers elect never to exceed the speed limit; most care about the time spent traveling as well. An optimizing strategy for two or more criteria requires the specification of a function relating them. Perhaps this joint criterion would have the form:

$$W_1 Y_1 + W_2 Y_2$$

where Y_1 is the cost of speeding tickets over the course of a year, and Y_2 is the time spent commuting in the year, and W_1 and W_2 are the relative weights of the two concerns. Is one hour saved worth \$5 in fines, or \$50 in fines? An infinite set of weights is possible. Similarly, the relationship between cost of tickets and time spent traveling may have another functional relationship:

$$W_1 Y_1 \cdot W_2 Y_2 \text{ or } W_1 Y_1^{W_2 Y_2}.$$

Assuming the simple linear relationship holds, we would now need to let our optimization procedure have access to information relating driving speed to driving time, as well as relating driving speed to expected cost of tickets. This, however, is not so simple. The expected cost of tickets depends on the likelihood of getting pulled over, which depends on visual cues indicating the presence of police, the time of day, local knowledge, and even time of month (as ticket writers have quotas). Assuming all this were known well enough to specify the driving-speed to ticket-cost relationship, an optimizing procedure could be carried out, on a computer at least.

Interestingly, this analysis reveals that where violations of the law are concerned, there is always a minimum of two criteria that need to be combined for optimization purposes: the benefit of the violation (e.g., reducing driving time) and the cost of the sanction (e.g., paying a fine).

Why stop with thinking about speed and cost of tickets? Certainly the number of tickets is also relevant. Both in the U.S. and in Germany, a license is suspended after a certain number of "points" are accumulated. The likelihood of getting in an accident matters not only to our health and our wallets, but also to our conscience. Few realistic scenarios are worse to imagine than our behavior taking an innocent life. In addition to these practical concerns, driving speed may serve ineffable criteria. We exceed the speed limit not only to save time, but to alleviate boredom, challenge ourselves, seek distraction, learn about the performance of our automobile, and other concerns that elude the modeler's grasp. If these factors cannot be functionally specified, how can they be optimized? Table 21.1 spells out considerations involved in one-, two-, and multiple-criteria optimizations.

Table 21.1 Considerations in what an optimizing approach for determining driving speed would entail in increasingly complex models.

	One-criterion optimization	Two-criteria optimization	Multiple-criteria optimization
Target(s)	Y_1: Cost of speeding tickets	Y_1: Cost of speeding tickets Y_2: Commute time	Y_1: Number of speeding tickets Y_2: Cost of speeding tickets Y_3: Commute time Y_4: Number of accidents Y_5: Cost of accidents Y_6: Likelihood of injuring another Y_7: Likelihood of injuring self Y_8: Enjoyment of driving
Cues	Speed-limit signs	• Speed-limit signs • Cues for presence of police cars and associated probabilities: time of day, likely hiding places, day of month, local knowledge • Expected cost of tickets given rate of speed	• Speed-limit signs • Cues for presence of police cars and associated probabilities: time of day, likely hiding places, day of month, local knowledge • Expected cost of tickets given rate of speed • Cues for likelihood of accident and associated probabilities • Expected cost of accidents given rate of speed • Components of driving pleasure, if definable
Optimization possible	Yes	Yes, if a function specifying the relationship between Y_1 and Y_2 is precisely specified and probabilities are known	Unlikely, as a function specifying the relationship between the variables would be difficult or impossible to isolate
Optimal strategy	Drive at or below speed limit	• Maximize objective function • Obtain a function relating driving speed to cues • Drive according to function	Unlikely

A Fast and Frugal Approach

In contrast, consider a heuristic approach to determining driving speed. Such an approach will probably not find the best speed at which to drive in order to

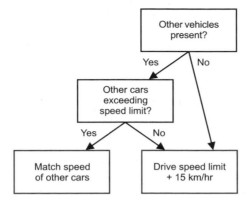

Figure 21.3   A heuristic for determining driving speed under good weather and road conditions.

minimize ticket cost or driving time. Unlike the optimizing approach, the heuristic approach can be easily carried out by the unaided mind. Additionally, it *may* find a solution that is in the neighborhood of that determined by optimizing means.

A model determined from the authors' introspection is spelled out in Figure 21.3. If there are other cars on the road, check to see if they are exceeding the speed limit. If so, match their speed; if not, drive 15 km/hr over the posted speed limit.

At first blush, we thought that a strategy that leads to no tickets would be too conservative. Interestingly, while this strategy is not overly conservative, it will probably result in no tickets. This points out another difficulty of an optimizing approach: one must accurately state one's preferences for an objective function, when doing so is hardly a natural task. Legal scholars and psychologists alike would not be surprised to find that stated preferences for functional relationships contradict what is revealed by behavior.

This heuristic is not optimal. It will not minimize a function relating driving time, exposure to ticketing, likelihood of accidents, or other variables. However, it is a rule that is easily implemented, and it may find solutions close to those determined by optimizing procedures under a variety of parameter combinations.

HOW DO WE LEARN ABOUT LAW?

Some laws constrain us, such as safety regulations and the criminal code. To avoid legal sanctions, people need to conform to these laws. Other laws enable us to accomplish our ends, such as contracts and wills. Sometimes people can conform to laws or use law for their ends without knowing much law, and sometimes people need to know a lot about laws. Modern law is so massive that most people know something about parts of it and nothing about much of it. For example, most people know something about traffic regulations and nothing about securities regulations. The previous section suggested that law is often a relatively unimportant source of guidance when we are called upon to make legally relevant decisions (for more on this conjecture, see Hertwig, this volume). Nonetheless, we do, in some circumstances, attempt to learn about the law. This part explores how we might do so, focusing on cues that indicate to us that our conduct may have legal implications.

Cues to Invoke Awareness of the Law: Social Norms

We begin by discussing the cues that alert a person to the need to learn something about law. The first cue comes from social norms. A good political and legal system raises selected social norms to the level of legal obligations. For example, the obligation to keep promises is raised to the level of legal obligations when the promise constitutes an enforceable contract. Insofar as law tracks social norms, the socialization process that teaches morality directly also teaches legality indirectly (Engel 2004). By tracking morality, law decreases the amount that people need to learn in order to know the law, and law also aligns with peoples' sense of fairness.

When law tracks morality, the fact that an action impinges on a social norm provides a cue to a person that the action also impinges on the law. For example, the fact that a businessman has a moral obligation to keep a certain promise is a cue that he might also have a legal obligation to keep it. Fairness is another cue for legality (cf. Fehr and Schmidt 2000). Similarly, the recognition that a course of action may result in social conflict, especially conflicting claims of fairness, suggests that it might cause litigation.

Social norms have an internal and an external dimension, which corresponds to internal and external cues about legality. The internal cue is conscience. When a person feels that his action contravenes morality, he is alerted to the possibility that his action might contravene legality. Guilt is a cue for illegality.

ˈIs the use of guilt a heuristic? Morality consists in simple rules that are usually stated without exceptions and without instruction on how to balance competing values. The Ten Commandments, for example, have this character. This fact is consistent with the maxim in adaptive heuristics that "less is more" (Goldstein and Gigerenzer 2002). Cognitive psychology might be used to explain why moral rules are so simple. The explanation might help to explain the advantages of designing law to track morality and improve the ability of lawmakers to design laws that track morality.

The external cues about socials norms consist in the behavior of other people. Social norms usually describe what most people do. In so far as law tracks social norms, people can usually succeed in conforming to the law by doing what others do. The maxim, "do what others require of you do" has been the subject of research by social psychologists for many years; see the work of Bandura (1986) or the work of Asch (1956) on conformity.

Besides describing what most people do, social norms usually describe what most people think that everyone ought to do. Consequently, many people will apply social sanctions such as criticism or worse against other people who violate social norms (Fehr 2000). Loss of reputation is a powerful deterrent for many people.

Size of Stakes

We have explained that social norms provide a simple guide to laws that track morality, even to very complex laws such as the law of contracts. Social norms reduce conflict by controlling the interaction of people. The state has a special responsibility to dampen conflicts and redirect them into courts for resolution. Reducing conflict provides a reason for the state to take a special interest in disputes with large stakes. Consequently, the size of the stakes in a potential dispute is a simple cue that behavior is legally relevant. For example, the "statute of frauds," which is an ancient English law with many modern variants, requires promises above a certain value to be written in order to qualify as enforceable contracts. Thus a promise to sell a house for a given price is unenforceable until embodied in writing.[2]

Potential of Harming Others

In a liberal society, social norms that get enacted into law are the ones that prevent people from harming others. This is true for crimes and accidents. The possibility of hurting someone else is thus a cue that law regulates the behavior in question. We expect to have to learn about laws regulating actions that endanger others. For example, acquiring a driver's license typically requires taking an exam that includes questions about traffic laws.

Long-term Relationships

In general, law provides a mechanism for punishing wrongdoing. Long-term relationships between people also provide a mechanism to punish wrongdoing by the other party. To illustrate, the strategy of "Tit-for-Tat" means, "repay pain with pain, and repay pleasure with pleasure." Long-term relationships provide scope for the parties to use such strategies for punishing wrongdoing. Since law and relationships are substitutes for each other, law often restricts the scope of its interference in relationships. For example, most aspects of the relationship among family members are uncontrolled by law. Consequently, people who are in long-term relationships tend not to resort to the law to resolve their disputes. To illustrate, if the husband in a traditional marriage promises to be home on time for dinner, his late arrival does not prompt his wife to sue for breach of

---

[2] The same holds in Germany, according to §311b I Civil Code (*Bürgerliches Gesetzbuch*).

contract, but he may find that she has already eaten and his food is burned. The existence of a long-term relationship is a cue that law may be practically irrelevant to behavior.

Conversely, the absence of a long-term relationship is a cue for the need to understand the law and invoke it. To illustrate, real-estate purchases typically involve high stakes and no relationship between buyer and seller. Knowing these facts, few people are so foolish as to enter a real-estate contract without receiving expert advice from a lawyer or a real-estate broker.

Verifiability

Another important cue for law is verifiability, by which we mean "provable to a tribunal." When acts are difficult to verify, laws and contracts have difficulty controlling the acts. To illustrate, laws against "date rape" are often ineffective because the parties are the only witnesses, and they provide conflicting testimony. Some acts are difficult to verify because the affected parties cannot observe them. The observable nature and verifiability of an act are cues that law may control it.

HOW DOES THE LAW REACH ITS ADDRESSEES?

We have focused on the demand for legal information, both how people make legally relevant decisions and how people receive cues indicating that they should turn to the law for guidance. Now we turn our attention to the supply of legal information. In this part, we explore how the law reaches its intended audience.

Government institutions, including schools, provide citizens with some information about the law. Indeed, the democratic ideal that law is public implies some publicizing of it. For example, important trials are widely reported in the newspaper or even televised in some jurisdictions. Perhaps the trial of O.J. Simpson increased the knowledge of legal procedure among Americans more than any other event in recent years.

Besides the state, the legal profession is another major source of professional information about the law. Lawyers in many countries still work under laws that severely limit their ability to advertise their services and otherwise inform the public about what they do. A vigorous attack on these restrictions as monopoly practices that harm the public resulted in large changes in the legal profession in some jurisdictions, including the U.S. Advertising is especially intense where restrictions have been removed and lawyers are allowed to work on contingency fees, as in the U.S. The contingency fee system directs lawyers to disseminate relatively accurate information about law to uninformed people with potentially large claims. Advertisers are very familiar with the principles of cognitive psychology, which are now put in the service of attracting business for lawyers. For example, television advertising in the U.S. promotes the simple heuristic, "If your property or person were injured in an accident, then call a lawyer."

Computer programs and the Internet have provided cheap sources of legal advice and algorithms to simplify the solution to legal problems, such as filing income tax returns.

The legal documents that lawyers produce are often directed at courts, not at citizens. For example, the warnings on pharmaceuticals are probably more effective at avoiding liability than conveying information to consumers. If these warnings used heuristics more and relied less on a comprehensive list of side effects, the law would communicate more information to the users of drugs. Laws that require effective communication, not just comprehensive and logical presentation of information, can increase information about the law.

Below we take a close look at one example of the law reaching its intended audience through an intermediary. Germany has given high priority to treating waste in an environmentally friendly way (the following builds on Lüdemann 2004). It believes in recycling, rather than disposal. The highest rank is given to recycling in kind, and with one waste fraction, plastics, this is demanding. If the goal for recycling in kind is set significantly above 50%, recycling industrial waste is not enough. The regime must be extended to waste originating in households. Household waste comes in comparatively small amounts. Traditionally, there was just one dust bin per household, or even per block. The recycling quota for plastics can only be met if households separate waste. There is indeed a rule in the waste management statutes of many German states to this effect, but it is beyond doubt that this is merely law in the books. It would even be constitutionally questionable if governmental officials poked around in citizens' dustbins. More importantly, the transaction costs would be prohibitive. The only realistic option was putting the separation of waste into people's minds.

This is indeed what has happened. More precisely, this is what government has brought about by a clever scheme. The scheme starts out from an entirely different angle. Recycling in kind is costly. Having each household pay for the cost of recycling by the unit of packaging waste is a practical impossibility. The transaction cost would be prohibitive. More importantly, it would entail a counterproductive incentive for littering. Hence the government wanted to add the price of recycling to the cost of purchasing the packaged product. However, assessing this cost poses a severe information problem. The solution is a monopoly called the *Duales System Deutschland* (DSD). It collects the money from the producers of packaged products, and it uses this money to pay for recycling. Inside the company, both the producers and the recycling industry are represented. Year by year they negotiate the recycling price separately for each waste fraction, handing the problem of information generation thus over to negotiation. The legal monopoly is, however, conditional upon outcome. It vanishes if DSD no longer meets the fairly high recycling quota.

Bringing about a sufficient degree of waste separation in the households is therefore paramount for the very existence of this monopoly and, indirectly, for all producers who sell packaged goods. DSD has responded by investing heavily into advertising. Thereby, every German knows that she is expected to separate her waste. Most households do not only have separate bins in the back-yard. They also keep separate collections in the kitchen. Actually, the rule fol-lowed by most households is a simple heuristic. If merchandise is packed in plastic, put the package into the yellow bin. The correct rule would be: if it car-ries the sign for having paid the DSD, which is a green dot, then it should go into this bin. Because not all plastics are marked with this green dot, DSD has to han-dle more than 10% of waste they would not be obliged to process. They accept this, since transmitting the more complex, correct rule might generate too much complexity and uncertainty and thereby endanger the overall recycling quota. Even most lawyers do not know that there is indeed also a legal obligation to separate. It is never enforced. Separating waste has meanwhile almost become a definitional element of the German national character. The good citizen is a per-son who correctly separates the proverbial yogurt container into the plastic frac-tion (the beaker) and the aluminum fraction (the lid). Originally, children learned this in kindergarten, and subsequently educated their parents. By now, separating has become so natural that most Germans no longer feel any obliga-tion. Behavior that was originally guilt driven, after being turned into a morality issue, has now become a mere habit, an element of the German culture, much like drinking beer or driving fast on motorways.

A second example exhibits a very different behavioral pattern. It again is taken from the German legal order. In Germany, tenants are strongly protected. Business premises notwithstanding, a landlord cannot simply give the tenant notice. Basically, he has this right only if he can prove that he himself wants to move into the flat. This typically turns the rental contract into a long-term rela-tionship. Now the price level for flats changes over time, as does the cost for building houses, and for maintaining them. A complex set of legal rules there-fore regulates under which conditions the landlord is entitled to raise the rent. This set of rules creates a natural tension between landlord and tenant. It ex-plains why many landlords, as well as many tenants, have a fairly developed knowledge of the pertinent legal rules. Quite a few do indeed read the text of the statute. Others glean this information from their peers, especially after a bad ex-perience. Still others precautionarily become members of landlords' or tenants' associations, just in case they might need legal help one day.

POLICY IMPLICATIONS

How Can Psychology Simplify the Presentation and Representation of the Law?

User-friendliness

Software is more complicated than it was 25 years ago, yet software is also eas-ier to use than it was 25 years ago. The statements seem to contradict one another, and nevertheless both are true. Software has to be functional at two levels: the internal mechanism responsible for adequate outputs depending on the inputs is one side of the coin. Modern software for word processing is so advanced that one can publish a whole book on a desktop computer. Twenty-five years ago, no manufacturer would have tried to implement such complexity within a single program. The other side of the coin is the user interface. Software has become easier to handle than it was 25 years ago when there was no mouse, no graphical icons to click on, and no menu bars. Nowadays, we have easy-to-handle software with complicated machinery behind it—at least this is how we expect that software should be.

There are several similarities between this example and the law. Law is also complex. It has to coordinate action, it has to help prevent serious conflicts, it should give orientation, and have an expressive function. Law integrates many special tasks that concern only a small subset of its addressees. Law has to be functional in its machinery. The analogy to software suggests another issue. Despite its complexity in order to achieve adequate functionality, law should be easy to handle for the addressees. It should be user-friendly. Lawmakers might sympathize with the problem of making complex laws easy to use for the addressees, but they feel that this problem is outside of their area of expertise. They need some psychological insight in order to make law user-friendly, in domains where user-friendliness is desirable.

A first idea how this goal could be achieved might be that the addressees should "intuitively" do the right things. According to this idea, the design of rules should be such that they are very easy to comprehend and to apply. This goal can be achieved by focusing on different psychological mechanisms: behavioral (stimulus-response), cognitive (analogies, framing, conversational maxims, statistical formats), social (ostracism and cheater detection). How and when these mechanisms can be applied depends on whether social norms are in congruence or at odds with the law.

Behavioral Mechanisms

Behavioral strategies try to modify the physical environment in a manner such that these modifications are stimuli for the addressees that lead to the desired responses (cf. Skinner 1938). Consumer psychology is a prominent field that mainly focuses on the usage of behavioral mechanisms (Norman 1988). The placement of goods in a supermarket is based on the assumption that most people tend to go counterclockwise in a circle around the store. Knowing that, the merchant strategically places goods where he thinks that people might spontaneously buy them within this circle. Goods that people really need in everyday life are placed elsewhere. Additional stimuli (like "special offers" with canceled old prices) augment the probability that clients will buy the product. Knowledge of how people interact with a particular environment might allow for innovations that promote adherence to the law. Certain road markings, for instance, have been designed in order to give the subjective impression of an increase in speed even when speed is held constant, and thus make people correct their own speeding behavior. Another example would be cars that can only be started after the seat belt has been fastened. The physical environment can be shaped in a fashion that it guides the addressees to the desired behavior.

Cognitive Mechanisms

Framing. One and the same situation may lead to different behavioral results depending on the frame where the situation is embedded (Kahneman and Tversky 2000). For example, framing a prisoner's dilemma game as a "community game" or a "Wall Street game" leads to completely different results (Ross and Ward 1996). So it is not the rules of the game itself (the prisoner's dilemma in this example), but the context in which they are embedded that matters. If the goal of a law is to increase organ donation rates, framing can matter. Depending on whether the default is being a donor or not being a donor, rates of organ transplantation between countries will differ significantly (Johnson and Goldstein 2003).

Similarly, lawmakers can make use of framing effects to motivate healthy behaviors. Health-relevant communications can be framed in terms of gains (highlighting the potential benefits of an option) or losses (highlighting the potential costs of an option). The relative influence of gain- or loss-framed appeals is contingent on the degree to which performing a health behavior is perceived as risky. Illness-detecting behaviors (e.g., cancer screening, HIV testing) are perceived as risky because they can inform people that they may be sick, whereas illness-preventing behaviors (e.g., sunscreen use, condom use) are not perceived to involve risk because they affirm health. Research on the effect of verbal framing has focused on positive versus negative framing and on gain versus loss framing (Tversky and Kahneman 2000). Positive and negative frames refer to whether an outcome is described, for instance, as a 97% chance of survival (positive) or a 3% chance of dying (negative). The evidence is that positive framing is more effective than negative framing to persuade people to choose risky treatment options. Similarly, risky options are chosen more often when a loss frame is used (highlighting the potential costs of an option) rather than a gain frame (highlighting the potential benefits of an option).

Analogical Reasoning. When a law is complex, and it is important that the law is understood by the addressee, then analogies might help foster understanding. Comprehending why downloading of music is an infringement of property rights could be facilitated by using an analogy of a store selling music CDs. Taking a CD without paying at the register is theft. To make analogies successful, a careful analysis of the source problem, the relevant objects, and the relations between them has to be performed (see Gentner's structure mapping theory; Gentner and Markman 1997). It must be clear that the mapping from the source problem to the target problem is unique, that is, which object of the source domain has to be mapped onto which object of the target domain. Given that such a unique mapping is possible and that it has been made transparent to the addressees, the advantage of analogies lies in the fact that the relations between the objects of the source domain are automatically (or "intuitively") mapped to the target domain, such that there is an immediate understanding of the structure of the target domain. The analogy of a theft in a CD store in comparison to the downloading of music would probably fail, because from the point of view of the addressee the theft took already place by the provider of the site where he can download the CD free of charge.

Conversational Rules. Grice (1975, 1989) described four maxims of cooperative conversation that guide most of our daily communication processes. As a default, it is assumed that listeners tacitly expect that the speaker will try to meet certain standards of communication. In particular, we assume that information that is given to us is truthful (maxim of quality), relevant to the aims of the conversation (maxim of relevance), clear (maxim of manner), and that the message we receive is as informative as is required, but not more informative than is required (maxim of quantity). If both listener and speaker follow these cooperative rules, the communication process is facilitated. The listener, for instance, does not have to filter the information he gets for relevance if he can trust that the speaker adheres to the relevance maxim.

When maxims of communication are violated, it can end in health risks and lawsuits. The U.S. Food and Drug Administration (FDA) requires pharmaceutical companies to disclose potential negative side effects of medications. To comply with their duty to warn, these companies provide an extensive list of adverse outcomes with each medication, most of which are expected to occur with an infinitesimal probability. Because the list is so long, it is therefore printed in small font size. As a result of these two factors, most consumers do not read the compendium of potential side effects. This may be an example in which more information results in a message that is less clear, less informative, and less relevant than the actual goal of the communication requires. By forcing pharmaceutical companies to list so many side effects, the FDA may actually discourage consumers from reading *any* of the list. Thus, a more effective warning might be a shorter warning. However, the portion of the list of side effects removed from the primary list should be made available to those consumers who are motivated to read about every possible adverse outcome. Note that the suggestion to shorten the primary list is motivated by recognition of the cognitive or motivational limitations of the consumer. By forsaking the requirement to provide the consumer with complete information, the FDA might instead match the information available in the environment to the information-seeking needs of the typical consumer.

An example of the U.S. Federal Trade Commission's (FTC) recognition of the cognitive limitations of the consumer occurred in the "Listerine case" (Harris and Monaco 1978). The manufacturer of Listerine mouthwash did not assert in their television commercial that "Listerine prevents colds." Of course, neither Listerine nor any other brand of mouthwash can prevent colds. However, the manufacturer of Listerine did include in the commercial a number of statements that, as a group, strongly implied this conclusion. An experiment was executed in which the text of the commercial was presented to people. These participants were then asked if the sentence "Listerine prevents colds" had been included in the commercial's text. Every participant mistakenly claimed that this statement had been included. This exemplifies the basis for the FTC action: while explicitly stating nothing that was false, the manufacturer had implied a false conclusion. Due to the fact that people often cannot distinguish what was presented from what was implied (Bransford and Franks 1971), this cognitive limitation led to the participants' faulty memory for the offending sentence. Through their administrative action, the FTC recognized this as an understandable confusion that should not be exploited.

As in the case of the truncated list of potential side effects, knowing about people's cognitive limitations should inform legal requirements for information display. More information will not necessarily foster optimal behavior. The ability to draw seductive but unwarranted inferences confers no advantage.

Statistical Formats.   Statistical information can be expressed in many different ways. For instance, the risk of a major side effect associated with a particular medical intervention can be described as happening "very rarely," or "in only 0.5% of the cases," or "in 50 out of 10,000 cases." Research on statistical thinking has shown that the choice of statistical format has a strong impact on understanding of the information (Gigerenzer and Hoffrage 1995; Hoffrage et al. 2000). In particular, it is easy to confuse people with statements on single-event probabilities (e.g., "You have a 0.5% chance of a side effect from this drug"), conditional probabilities (e.g., "If you have a positive result in this screening test, your chance of having the disease is 10%"), and relative risks (e.g., "This screening test reduces mortality by 25%"). One way to reduce the confusion is to choose alternative representations of the same information that reduce the ambiguity inherent in these statements. Conditional probabilities, for instance, can be better understood if they are represented in terms of natural frequencies (e.g., "Out of 100 people like you who have a positive result in this screening test, 10 have the disease"), because the reference classes of the statistical information is made transparent (Gigerenzer and Edwards 2003). Selecting the format of statistical information is a very simple way of shaping the information environment for the addressees of risk communication.

How Can We Generate Compliance to Laws, Once They Are Understood by Their Addressees?

The second type of problem situation encountered by the law, to which knowledge about human psychology might provide some assistance, is the question of how to get people to comply with laws that are well understood (assuming compliance is desirable). This could either be laws that are short and simple (e.g., the requirement to wear a seat belt while driving) or more complex laws in a simplified presentation format, as discussed in the previous section.

While the law has a multiplicity of social or collective distal goals and intentions (e.g., to increase societal efficiency or distributive justice), the state also pursues the more proximal goal of getting its citizens to comply with the law. Rational choice theory implies that compliance with the law will result when the sanctions or penalties for prohibited actions that are specified by the law are well known to citizens, of sufficient magnitude to outweigh the benefits of actions prohibited by the law, and credibly enforced. Noncompliance with well-understood and credibly enforced laws suggests that the specified sanctions, or monitoring, need to be increased. The picture is different if we allow for the possibility that citizens engage in actions that either comply or fail to comply with the law as the result of processes that fall short of comprehensive deliberation and analysis of pros and cons. As discussed, the ideal scenario has citizens engage in the collectively beneficial behavior specified by the law without *any* conscious deliberation, in a habitual fashion, without any conscious awareness of the possibility of alternative actions (examples: putting on one's seat belt automatically, as soon as one sits down in a motor vehicle; cleaning a plastic yogurt container after consuming its content and putting it into the designated plastics section of the waste disposal area in one's kitchen).

Especially for laws that require simple, relatively noncontingent behavior, there is a good chance that compliance behavior can be automated by following one or more of the following steps. Automation of any behavior requires its execution over a large series of trials (or instances). As discussed in the above section on psychological mechanisms, we have multiple ways at our disposal to motivate people to engage in the socially desirable behavior prescribed by the law. We can, for example, invoke the threat of fines, use social norms and people's fear of embarrassment or social ostracism, or capitalize on people's tendency to imitate the actions observed by others by flooding them with appropriate role models in movies or advertisements, to increase people's likelihood of engaging in the desired behavior (e.g., buckling up) over an extended period of time. While such behavior will initially be consciously or unconsciously calculation based or rule based (e.g., buckling up because of the fear of a fine or because admired actresses do it in the movies), the behavior will eventually become second nature, in the sense of being executed without conscious awareness, i.e., without the realization that not buckling up is an option (for an account in terms of learning theory, see Anderson 2000, Chap. 9). Such automatic acceptance of a behavior is typically accompanied by a negative emotional signal if one is prevented for some reason from executing the behavior. A defective seat belt encountered on the back seat of a taxi leaves one feeling unsafe for the duration of the ride, and one's inability to find a plastic recycling bin in the vacation rental in the U.S. leaves one feeling outraged at the lack of environmental awareness of American consumers.

It should be noted that it is easier by a large margin to establish new automatic behaviors than to change existing automatic behaviors. In terms of policy implications, this latter case can be a problem, as we discuss next.

Policy Caveat: Entrenchment of Habit

Generating a habit can be a powerful tool for bringing about compliance with the law. When law targets the behavior of individuals, this is almost the only route to effectiveness. But before turning that insight into a piece of advice for governance, policy makers should consider the likely cost of this approach. On balance, this cost may well seem prohibitive. If so, the policy maker would want to find more indirect methods, e.g., targeting an industry rather than individuals. Safety belt legislation illustrates the point. As mentioned, some countries have obliged manufacturers to design cars so that it is impossible to turn the ignition key unless all those in the car have fastened their seat belts.

The recycling example used earlier illustrates why the cost of generating a habit may indeed be high. As laid out, German policy makers indeed have been successful in turning Germans into world champions in separating plastic waste. This has been done on the assumption that recycling plastic waste in kind is good for the environment, and that Germany is rich enough to afford the cost. However, there is serious dispute whether the total environmental cost of recycling plastic waste from households does not exceed the benefit to the environment (Giegrich et al. 1999). Esteemed scientists now claim that burning this waste fraction would be preferable. Assume this became accepted wisdom. Society might then want to change back to its previous policy. The cost for doing this, however, might well be prohibitive. Not only would German society have to go through a collective process of unlearning, the waste separation habit has also been established as a highly salient symbol for attitudes toward the environment, if not a visible expression of good citizenship. This policy maker may not want to put this at risk for the small gain of treating plastic waste in an environmentally more appropriate way.

Policy Caveat: Bad Laws

It is plausible that insights gleaned from the study of heuristics can be applied to make law more effective. Making law more effective commonly enhances social welfare. But it need not. If a law is a bad one, it is not wise to make it more effective. Examples of bad laws are easy to find. In the U.S., the Prohibition Amendment departed sharply from prevailing social norms and was increasingly violated as time passed. Americans eventually concluded that Prohibition was a bad law and repealed it after a few years. Similarly, when a well-organized industry successfully lobbies for protectionist legislation, consumers suffer. Making bad laws of this sort more effective is hardly wise.

Moreover, some domains of human life are better regulated by methods of social control other than law. For example, a husband and wife have to work out which of them will cook the meals, take out the trash, and so on. These sorts of decisions generally are better controlled by contract and norm than by law. If a legislature were to be foolhardy enough to pass a law that ordered, say, wives to take out the trash, the legislature would have entered a domain it should not have touched. Analysts who applied their knowledge of heuristics to make it easier for wives to understand this law would not be enhancing social welfare.

CONCLUSION

How do people decide how to act under laws? How do laws reach their addressees? The theory of the mind as a rational optimizer leaves the answer to these questions in a black box, assuming that changes in behavior will eventually come about if the incentives are right. In this chapter we have discussed a psychologically plausible alternative: models of bounded rationality that use different cognitive and motivational processes in a sequential and contingent fashion and can be described by a simple set of rules or heuristics to navigate a complex legal environment. Understanding people as users of heuristics instead of as optimizers allows for more transparent models that can yield predictions about how laws will be transmitted and when they will be followed—predictions that should be of great concern to those who shape policy.

REFERENCES

Albert, H. 1978. Traktat über rationale Praxis. Tübingen: Mohr.

Anderson, J.R. 2000. Learning and Memory: An Integrated Approach. New York: Wiley.

Asch, S.E. 1956. Studies of independence and conformity: A minority of one against a unanimous majority. *Psychol. Mono.* **70**:1–70.

Bandura, A. 1986. Social Foundations of Thought and Action: A Social Cognitive Theory. Englewood Cliffs, NJ: Prentice Hall.

Bransford, J.D., and J.J. Franks. 1971. The abstraction of linguistic ideas. *Cog. Psychol.* **2**:331–350.

Cooter, R. 1997. Normative failure theory of law. *Cornell Law Rev.* **82**:947–979.

Cooter, R., and T. Ulen. 2004. Law and Economics. Boston: Addison-Wesley.

Ellickson, R. 1991. Order without Law. Cambridge, MA: Harvard Univ. Press.

Engel, C. 2004. Learning the law. Preprints of the Max Planck Institute for Research on Collective Goods, Bonn. http://www.mpp-rdg.mpg.de/pdf_dat/2004_5online.pdf

Fehr, E. 2000. Cooperation and punishment in public goods experiments. *Am. Econ. Rev.* **90**:980–994.

Fehr, E., S. Gächter, and G. Kirchsteiger. 1997. Reciprocity as a contract enforcement device: Experimental evidence. *Econometrica* **65**:833–860.

Fehr, E., and K.M. Schmidt. 2000. Theories of fairness and reciprocity: Evidence and economic applications. Cesifo Working Paper Ser. 403. http://Papers.Ssrn.Com/ Paper.Taf?Abstract_Id=255223

Gentner, D., and A.B. Markman. 1997. Structure mapping in analogy and similarity. *Am. Psychol.* **52**:45–56.

Giegrich, J., H. Fehrenbach, W. Orlik, and M. Schwarz. 1999. Ökologische Bilanzen in der Abfallwirtschaft: Forschungsbericht 20310606, neu:29431606, UBA-FB 99-014. UBA–Texte 10/99. Berlin: Umweltbundesamt.

Gigerenzer, G., and A. Edwards. 2003. Simple tools for understanding risks from innumeracy to insight. *Brit. Med. J.* **327**:741–744.

Gigerenzer, G., and U. Hoffrage. 1995. How to improve Bayesian reasoning without instruction: Frequency formats. *Psychol. Rev.* **102**:684–704.

Gigerenzer, G., P.M. Todd, and the ABC Research Group. 1999. Simple Heuristics That Make Us Smart. New York: Oxford Univ. Press.

Goldstein, D.G., and G. Gigerenzer. 2002. Models of ecological rationality: The recognition heuristic. *Psychol. Rev.* **109**:75–90.

Grice, H.P. 1975. Logic and conversation. In: Syntax and Semantics, ed. P. Cole and J. Morgan, vol. 3, Speech Acts, pp. 41–58. New York: Academic.

Grice, H.P. 1989. Studies in the Way of Words. Cambridge, MA: Harvard Univ. Press.

Harris, R.J., and G.E. Monaco. 1978. The psychology of pragmatic implications: Information processing between the lines. *J. Exp. Psychol: Gen.* **107**:1–22.

Hoffrage, U., S. Lindsey, R. Hertwig, and G. Gigerenzer. 2000. Communicating statistical information. *Science* **290**:2261–2262.

Johnson, E.J., and D.G. Goldstein. 2003. Do defaults save lives? *Science* **302**:1338–1339.

Kahneman, D., and A. Tversky. 2000. Choices, Values, and Frames. Cambridge: Cambridge Univ. Press and New York: Russell Sage.

Keeton, W.P., D.B. Dobbs, R.E. Keeton, and D.G. Owen, eds. 1984. Prosser and Keeton on the Law of Torts. 5th ed. St. Paul, MN: West Publ.

Kirchgässner, G. 1992. Toward a theory of low-cost-decisions. *Eur. J. Pol. Econ.* **8**:305–320.

Lüdemann, J. 2004. Edukatorisches Staatshandeln. Baden-Baden: Nomos.

Norman, D.A. 1988. The Psychology of Everyday Things. New York: Basic.

Payne, J.W., J.R. Bettman, and E.J. Johnson. 1992. Behavioral decision research: A constructive processing perspective. *Ann. Rev. Psych.* **43**:87–131.

Payne, J.W., J.R. Bettman, and E.J. Johnson. 1993. The Adaptive Decision Maker. Cambridge: Cambridge Univ. Press.

Payne, J.W., J.R. Bettman, and E.J. Johnson. 1997. The adaptive decision maker: Effort and accuracy in choice. In: Research on Judgement and Decision Making: Currents, Connections, and Controversies, ed. W.M. Goldstein and R.M. Hogarth, pp. 181–204. Cambridge: Cambridge Univ. Press.

Posner, E.A. 2000. Law and Social Norms. Cambridge, MA: Harvard Univ. Press.

Posner, R.A. 1972. A theory of negligence. *J. Legal Stud.* **1**:29–96.

Posner, R.A. 2003. Economic Analysis of Law. New York: Aspen.
Ross, L., and A. Ward. 1996. Naïve realism: Implications for social conflict and misunderstanding. In: Values and Knowledge, ed. E.S. Reed, E. Turiel, and T. Brown, pp. 103–105. Mahwah, NJ: Erlbaum.
Schlicht, E. 1998. On Custom in the Economy. Oxford: Clarendon.
Simon, H.A. 1957. Models of Man: Social and Rational. New York: Wiley.
Skinner, B.F. 1938. The Behavior of Organisms: An Experimental Analysis. New York: Appleton Century.
Tversky, A., and D. Kahneman. 2000. Rational choice and the framing of decisions. In: Choices, Values and Frames, ed. D. Kahneman and A. Tversky, pp. 209–223. Cambridge: Cambridge Univ. Press.
United States v. Carroll Towing Co., 159 F.2d 169 (2d Cir 1947).

Author Index

Name Index

Subject Index

property law 148, 165, 400
  marital 215
propter hoc event 331, 333
proration 141, 149, 154, 155
prospect theory 8, 35
public goods theory 62, 193
punishment 29, 177, 188–198
  consistency in 134
  role in free riding 190, 191
punitive damage 160, 164

random match probability 310, 311, 403
rational choice 62, 63, 393, 402
  theory 6–11, 22–45, 46, 50, 65, 77,
    105–111, 115–119, 122, 191, 201,
    344, 348, 426–435, 439, 446, 461
rationality 3, 21, 61, 62, 328, 340, 347
  (*see also* bounded rationality, ecological rationality, unbounded rationality)
  adaptive 348
  Great Rationality Debate 111
  logical 3, 8–11
reasonable doubt 283, 303, 306–309,
  313, 330, 335, 402, 406
reasonable person standard 128, 307,
  308, 446
Rechtsgrundsatz 220
reciprocity 2, 10, 19, 180–185, 442
  evolution of 197
recognition heuristic 2, 8, 21, 274
rent control 188, 443, 456
representativeness 109, 113, 121, 365,
  432
reputation 2, 3
  loss of 293, 453
res ipsa loquitur 164, 285, 294, 295, 296
retrodiction 333
rewards 177, 192, 193, 196
  in a firm 88, 92, 93
risk 49, 95, 97, 125, 127, 460
  failure to inform 300
  information 120, 126, 127
  willingness to take 93
robustness 4, 31, 38
routines 6, 31, 443, 444
  in firms 90, 95
rules of discovery 327, 328

rules of evidence 338, 351, 354, 358, 368
  exclusionary 284, 285, 334–358
rules of logic 310, 312, 315
rules of thumb 2, 12, 17, 31, 141, 142,
  156, 209, 234, 242, 247, 351

salience 20, 433
sample space 353, 354
Scandinavian legal system 215, 216,
  220–223
science of heuristics 7, 17, 19, 23, 24,
  31, 33, 41
search 32, 80
  limited 2, 395
  sequential 32, 35
second-party rules 443, 444
self-interest 46, 96, 122, 141, 145, 146,
  191, 201
sensory input 65, 68, 74
sharing rules 175, 182–185, 188
signal detection theory 10
simplicity 2, 12, 359
  architecture of 87
single-event probabilities 460
size of the stakes 453
social dilemmas 61, 75, 77, 81
  climate change 5, 62–65, 78, 79, 80
  models of behavior 75
social exchange (*see* cooperation)
social learning 105, 121–124, 372, 391,
  392, 396–400, 408
social norms 212–214, 396, 442, 445,
  448, 452, 453
social welfare 46, 51, 187, 188, 200
speed 23, 360, 362, 370, 371
standard of proof 282–285, 306, 307,
  313
Statement Validity Assessment 366, 367
status quo bias 50, 57
stopping rule 32, 33, 70, 395
story model 259, 260, 262, 266–268
  constructing 263–265, 271, 364
strict liability 126, 150–152, 160, 169,
  245, 249
suboptimal rules 47, 53
substantial law 336–339
subsumption 217, 218, 220, 226